MARITAL INTERACTION

MARITAL INTERACTION

Analysis and Modification

Edited by

KURT HAHLWEG
Max-Planck-Institute for Psychiatry

and

NEIL S. JACOBSON
University of Washington

THE GUILFORD PRESS
New York   London

© 1984 The Guilford Press
A Division of Guilford Publications, Inc.
200 Park Avenue South, New York, N.Y. 10003

Printed in the United States of America

LIBRARY OF CONGRESS CATALOGING IN PUBLICATION DATA

Main entry under title:

Marital interaction.

Based on an international conference held July, 1981
in the Federal Republic of Germany and sponsored by the
Max-Planck-Gesellschaft.
   Includes bibliographical references and indexes.
   1. Marital psychotherapy—Congresses. 2. Behavior
therapy—Congresses. I. Hahlweg, Kurt. II. Jacobson,
Neil S., 1949–   . III. Max-Planck-Gesellschaft zur
Förderung der Wissenschaften.
RC488.5.M356   1984   616.89'156   84-4565
ISBN 0-89862-637-4

Contributors

Hertha Appelt, Ph.D., Department of Sex Research, University of Hamburg, Hamburg, Federal Republic of Germany

Donald H. Baucom, Ph.D., Psychology Department, University of North Carolina at Chapel Hill, Chapel Hill, North Carolina, U.S.A.

Ian Bennun, Ph.D., Institute of Psychiatry, University of London, London, United Kingdom

Ingo Bögner, Dipl.-Psych., Institute for Psychology, Free University of Berlin, Berlin, Federal Republic of Germany

Johannes C. Brengelmann, Ph.D., M.D., Max-Planck-Institute for Psychiatry, Munich, Federal Republic of Germany

M. J. Crowe, M.Phil., D.M., MRCP, MRCPsych, Consultant Psychiatrist, Maudsley Hospital, London, United Kingdom

Richard W. Elwood, Department of Psychology, University of Washington, Seattle, Washington, U.S.A.

Paul Emmelkamp, Ph.D., Department of Clinical Psychology, Academic Hospital, Groningen, The Netherlands

Frank J. Floyd, Ph.D., Laboratory of Psychological Studies, VA Medical Center, Brockton, Massachusetts, U.S.A.

William C. Follette, Ph.D., Department of Psychology, University of Washington, Seattle, Washington, U.S.A.

Kurt Hahlweg, Ph.D., Dipl.-Psych., Max-Planck-Institute for Psychiatry, Munich, Federal Republic of Germany

Neil S. Jacobson, Ph.D., Department of Psychology, University of Washington, Seattle, Washington, U.S.A.

Karen Jamieson, M.A., Department of Psychology, University of Denver, Denver, Colorado, U.S.A.

Guljit Kohli, Dipl.-Psych., Max-Planck-Institute for Psychiatry, Munich, Federal Republic of Germany

Hans Kunert, Dipl.-Psych., Max-Planck-Institute for Psychiatry, Munich, Federal Republic of Germany

Donald MacGillavry, Department of Clinical Psychology, Academic Hospital, Groningen, The Netherlands

Howard J. Markman, Ph.D., Department of Psychology, University of Denver, Denver, Colorado, U.S.A.

Susan Kaplan Mehlman, Ph.D., Springfield Hospital Center, Sykesville, Maryland, U.S.A.

Gerda J. Methorst, Department of Psychiatry, Jelgersma-Kliniek (psychiatric hospital), State University of Leiden, Oegstgeest, The Netherlands

Lillith Reisner, Dipl.-Psych., Max-Planck-Institute for Psychiatry, Munich, Federal Republic of Germany

Clive Reuben, Dipl.-Psych., Clinical Psychologist, General Hospital, Boeblingen/ Baden-Würthenberg, Federal Republic of Germany

Dirk Revenstorf, Ph.D., Dipl.-Psych., Psychological Institute, University of Tübingen, Tübingen, Federal Republic of Germany

Cas Schaap, Ph.D., Department of Clinical Psychology, Catholic University Nijmegen, Nijmegen, The Netherlands

Ludwig Schindler, Ph.D., Dipl.-Psych., Max-Planck-Institute for Psychiatry, Munich, Federal Republic of Germany

Scott M. Stanley, M.S., Department of Psychology, University of Denver, Denver, Colorado, U.S.A.

Mieke van der Helm, Department of Clinical Psychology, Academic Hospital, Groningen, The Netherlands

Berendien van Zanten, Department of Clinical Psychology, Academic Hospital, Groningen, The Netherlands

Bernd Vogel, Dipl.-Psych., Max-Planck-Institute for Psychiatry, Munich, Federal Republic of Germany

Margrit Vollmer, Dipl.-Psych., Psychosomatic Clinic, Windach, Federal Republic of Germany

Robert L. Weiss, Ph.D., Department of Psychology, University of Oregon, Eugene, Oregon, U.S.A.

Monika Wiech, Dipl.-Psych., private practice, Freiburg/Baden-Würthenberg, Federal Republic of Germany

Hildegard Zielenbach-Coenen, Dipl.-Psych., Institute for Psychology, Free University of Berlin, Berlin, Federal Republic of Germany

Dirk Zimmer, Ph.D., Dipl.-Psych., Psychological Institute, University of Tübingen, Tübingen, Federal Republic of Germany

Preface

This volume is an outgrowth of the first international conference on behavioral marital therapy (BMT), which took place in July 1981 in the Federal Republic of Germany and was sponsored by the Max-Planck-Gesellschaft. The general aim of this symposium was to discuss the empirical status and the future development of BMT and the assessment strategies used in this area. An international panel of professionals participated.

The specific goals of the small-group symposium were to discuss the following topics:

1. Status of BMT research in Europe and the United States
2. Future development of BMT and its theoretical framework (e.g., integration of cognitive approaches)
3. Scope and implementation of prevention programs
4. Status and future development of dyadic interaction analysis
5. Feasibility of cooperative international research

In order to discuss these topics in detail the course of the conference was made flexible, allowing for presentations of 45 minutes each, followed by intensive discussion.

The conference was held at a picturesque little castle called "Schloß Ringberg," about 60 kilometers southeast of Munich, and was sponsored by the Max-Planck-Gesellschaft (MPG). The castle, which is specifically suited to have small conferences of 20 or 30 participants, is owned by the MPG.

The Max-Planck-Gesellschaft is a research organization whose 50 member institutes carry out scientific work for the benefit of the public. The activities of the Max-Planck-Institutes mainly relate to basic research in the fields of natural sciences and the humanities.

This conference was instigated by a group of psychologists (Dirk Revenstorf, Ludwig Schindler, and Kurt Hahlweg) working at the Max-Planck-Institute for Psychiatry (MPIP), located in Munich. The MPIP consists of two institutes, one for basic research and one for clinical research including a wide range of disciplines (e.g., neurochemistry, neuropharmacology, adult and child psychiatry, and psychology).

The need to investigate marital distress within a psychiatric institute is based on the growing awareness that the quality of intimate relationships can strongly influence the development of psychiatric symptoms, their treatment, and the risk of relapse. Thus, the emphasis of the Max-Planck group in Munich was on: (1) the development and validation of assessment instruments for BMT, including questionnaires and observational coding systems; (2) analysis of interpersonal communication; and (3) the development of effective means of treating marital distress especially suited for a broader treatment program with psychiatric patients.

Most of the chapters in this book represent papers that were presented at the conference. However, many of them have been altered to reflect issues raised during the informal discussions that followed each presentation. Indeed, some of the chapters (e.g., Chapter 8, by Jacobson, Follette, and Elwood) are based almost entirely on ideas generated via those discussions. There was a general feeling among the participants that the conference was a profoundly enriching experience. "Reciprocity," a central concept in behavioral models of marriage, was very much in evidence. Each contributor affected the contributions of others, and each was in turn affected by the work of others. The conference, and hence this volume, was truly an interactional phenomenon.

The present volume is divided into three parts. The contents of each are briefly described here.

Treatment Outcome Research

This section shows the value of an empirical approach within clinical psychology in general and within marital therapy more specifically.

The controlled studies by Baucom; Bögner and Zielenbach-Coenen; Crowe; Emmelkamp, van der Helm, MacGillavry, and van Zanten; and Hahlweg, Schindler, Revenstorf, and Brengelmann leave no doubt that BMT is definitely more effective than a waiting-list control condition in reducing marital distress.

These studies also show that at the present time there is little need for further comparative studies, since BMT proved to be either equivalent or only mildly superior to other treatment approaches such as communication skills training (Emmelkamp et al., Hahlweg et al.), system-theoretic therapy (Emmelkamp et al.), or insight therapy (Crowe). Crowe also provides an excellent demonstration of a manipulation check within a comparative outcome study, an analysis that demonstrates the similarities and differences among treatment conditions. Furthermore, there were few differences among treatment modalities within BMT, with a conjoint approach proving to be a slightly "safer" treatment than a conjoint group modality (Hahlweg et al.). With regard to treatment component research, Baucom did not find major differences among contracting, problem-solving/communication training, and a combination of both.

The Bögner and Zielenbach-Coenen chapter provides some interesting findings regarding the maintenance of treatment gains by altering the time structure of a standardized BMT program from the usual 1-hour weekly session to longer sessions that are faded out at the end of therapy. The chapter by Reuben, Wiech, and Zimmer shows an innovative application of BMT to a new target population (communal households). Two chapters (Baucom and Mehlman; Hahlweg *et al.*) provide interesting data with regard to the prediction of marital quality and status following BMT. In the final chapter of this section, Jacobson *et al.* discuss the "state of the art" of outcome research on BMT and point to some fundamental methodological and conceptual issues in this area.

Assessment and Analysis of Marital Interaction

In this section further developments with regard to assessment and statistical analysis of observational data are reported. Schaap presents the most complete literature, review to date on studies that employ observational methods to analyze the interaction of maritally distressed and nondistressed couples. He also presents new data on this topic, using both frequency and sequential methods of analysis.

The two chapters by Revenstorf and his colleagues are concerned with new methods to analyze and evaluate ongoing marital interaction. The authors propose the use of time series methodology to analyze dyadic interaction on a day-to-day basis. For the microanalysis of the couples' problem-solving process in a standardized laboratory situation, they developed a new method for sequential analysis. Their results show that couples treated within BMT change both their style and process of communication almost to a normal, nondistressed pattern.

Hahlweg, Reisner, Kohli, Vollmer, Schindler, and Revenstorf describe a new observational system (KPI) especially designed to assess couples' communication and problem-solving skills. Promising results on the reliability and validity of the system are presented.

Both Weiss and Markman present intriguing new data on the interrelationships among variables commonly studied by marital interaction researchers. Despite differences between their approaches, both are interested in exploring the ramifications of insiders' and outsiders' perspectives.

Clinical Extensions and Innovations

In this section new developments in the theoretical framework and the clinical practice of BMT are presented.

The first four chapters are all concerned, in one way or another, with exploring the role of cognitive factors in the conceptualization and treatment of marital distress. Jacobson's chapter focuses on the rationale for moving in a cognitive direction, the continuity between a cognitive emphasis in early exchange theory and current trends, and the potential for cognitive change in current behavioral techniques. He also suggests strategies for incorporating new cognitive techniques into behavioral treatments.

Schindler and Vollmer attempt to bridge theory, research, and practice with regard to cognitive factors in BMT. They describe the implementation of cognitive techniques, mainly self-instructional, within a BMT framework in order to enhance individuals' abilities to cope with crisis situations in their relationships. Revenstorf tries to enlarge the framework of cognitive restructuring. His hypothetical tripartite model of the escalation process consists of biological, instrumental, and respondent components that call for different intervention strategies. Weiss extends his recent work on strategic BMT to describe the clinical implications of his earlier work. This chapter provides a useful analysis of how a strategic approach can be applied at various stages of therapy to foster the kinds of cognitive changes that promote long-term relationship satisfaction.

Bennun's chapter discusses an area that is often considered taboo among family therapists: marital therapy with one partner. Going against the prevailing ideology, Bennun presents a rationale and some examples of clinical strategies that promote relationship change even in the absence of one partner.

Methorst reviews the literature on sex differences in psychiatric illnesses, which indicates that women have a greater chance than men of becoming psychiatric patients. The implications of these sex differences and the handling of couples with an "identified" patient are discussed. Appelt argues against a real distinction between sex and marital therapy, since the joint occurrence of sexual dysfunction and marital discord is very common in couples asking for professional help. She argues for an integration of behavioral, attributional, and psychodynamic formulations in order to achieve a more comprehensive understanding of the interplay between the sexual dysfunction and the type of marital relationship.

Finally, the concluding chapter by Markman, Floyd, Stanley, and Jamieson describes the detailed application of BMT to the prevention of marital discord. The chapter is both rich in clinical detail and persuasive in arguing that prevention is a much needed and insufficiently emphasized focus in BMT research.

The audience for which this volume is intended includes theorists, researchers, and clinicians who are interested in an experimental approach to studying the complex phenomena of marital interaction or treating couples with marital problems.

It is our hope that this book will stimulate both research and clinical innovation, and will foster further international collaboration.

We are very grateful to the Max-Planck-Gesellschaft, which enabled us to bring together the various colleagues from Europe and the United States and provided Schloß Ringberg, an excellent place to have stimulating conferences.

Kurt Hahlweg
Neil S. Jacobson

Contents

PART ONE

TREATMENT OUTCOME RESEARCH

1

The Munich Marital Therapy Study

KURT HAHLWEG, LUDWIG SCHINDLER, DIRK REVENSTORF,
AND JOHANNES C. BRENGELMANN

The experimental status of marital therapy has been evaluated by different reviewers. In general, two divergent points of view have been expressed:

1. Jacobson (1978a) stated that the effectiveness of only two approaches (behavioral marital therapy — BMT, and communication skills training — CT) is moderately supported by the experimental literature.

2. Gurman and Kniskern (1978) stated that marital therapy in general (i.e., irrespective of treatment format) is effective for 65% of all clients, thereby supporting the conclusion of Luborsky, Singer, and Luborsky (1975) that all forms of psychotherapy (in this case, marital therapy) are winners and that there are no losers.

Almost as divergent as their conclusions are their methods for evaluating the overall effectiveness of the treatment. Jacobson (1978a) discussed and criticized every controlled study in detail but refrained from calculating percentages of effectiveness. Gurman and Kniskern (1978) used the so-called box-score approach, which calculates the number of studies or significance tests in which one treatment was significantly better or worse than another treatment or a control group. This method has been criticized on many grounds. The most complete and recent discussion is by Rachman and Wilson (1980). Two of their major arguments are:

1. Reviewers typically combine very different treatments in calculating the box score, implying that "psychotherapy" is a uniform and homogeneous treatment. One result is that ineffective treatments gain credibility through their association with the more effective ones. Gurman and Kniskern (1978), for example, analyzed "behavioral" and "nonbehavioral" marital therapies separately. Jacobson and Weiss (1978) pointed out that "in their section on nonbehavioral marital therapy they combine studies from an incredibly miscellaneous group of approaches, conducted with widely variable degrees of

Kurt Hahlweg, Ludwig Schindler, and Johannes C. Brengelmann. Max-Planck-Institute for Psychiatry, Munich, Federal Republic of Germany.

Dirk Revenstorf. Psychology Institute, University of Tübingen, Tübingen, Federal Republic of Germany.

methodological sophistication and present grossly misleading summary statistics on an ostensibly monolithic treatment" (p. 159).

2. Reviewers include studies with unsatisfactory methods of assessing treatment outcome. Because the instruments are neither reliable nor valid, differential treatment effects are blurred.

Rachman and Wilson (1980) concluded that this type of meta-analysis will lead to the erroneous conclusion that there are no differences in effectiveness between various approaches, and that it would have been remarkable had Luborsky *et al.* (1975) uncovered reliable differences.

According to these arguments, the conclusion of Gurman and Kniskern (1978) that the "64 per cent rate of superiority to control conditions for BMT is virtually identical with the 66 per cent rate . . . of nonbehavioral couples therapy" (p. 853) is by no means a surprise.

With regard to the nonbehavioral marital therapies they concluded, furthermore, that the "studies offer reasonable evidence of the salience of nonbehavioral marital . . . therapies" (p. 845).

In order to challenge Gurman and Kniskern's egalitarian views and to show that they drew misleading conclusions due to their inappropriate clustering of studies, we reanalyzed their data. We combined the controlled "nonbehavioral" studies in a different way, establishing a CT group and a group for miscellaneous studies (MS) (see Appendix A).

Applying the box scores calculated by Gurman and Kniskern (1978, p. 847), the CT formats were superior to the control conditions in 73.3% of all comparisons (11 out of 15).

In the MS group Friedman's study (1975) was difficult to evaluate, because Gurman and Kniskern (1978) did not give exact figures ("treatment > control on most measures," p. 847). In the original study the following significant changes were reported for the marital therapy group in contrast to the minimal contact group: psychiatric global rating scale — none; psychiatric symptom rating scale — 1 out of 10 comparisons; self-report — 1 out of 15; family roles — 3 out of 19; marital relations — 4 out of 36. These results clearly do not support the notion that marital therapy was superior to the control group in most of the variables, because these results could have been achieved by chance!

We therefore rated Friedman's marital therapy condition as not superior on any of the five criterion variables reported by Gurman and Kniskern (1978, p. 847). Subsequent calculation revealed a 25% superiority rate for the MS group!

These results challenge the conclusions of Gurman and Kniskern (1978) and support Jacobson's statement (1978a) that only for BMT and CT does some empirical support exist. Furthermore, our reanalysis showed that the result of a box-score approach is to a great degree dependent on the way the studies under review are combined, and that the conclusions drawn by this method should be evaluated very carefully, particularly given the methodo-logical flaws in the published studies. In general the reanalysis indicates the need for better-controlled experiments in the field of marital therapy.

The Munich Study: Design, Assessment, and Prediction Results

Keeping in mind these points, the Munich Marital Therapy Study on com-paring different formats and modalities was planned in 1976; up to then no controlled BMT experiment and only a few CT studies had been published. However, the available evidence suggested that a comparison of BMT and CT was worth drawing, because these formats were the only treatments that had shown some effectiveness. Also awaiting experimental investigation was the question of the differential effectiveness of a conjoint versus a conjoint group modality. Couples in CT had been treated primarily in conjoint groups, whereas in BMT couples were treated conjointly. To address both of these questions, the following factorial design was employed in the study (see also Table 1.1).

In all, 85 couples were involved in the study: 17 in BMT conjoint treat-ment, 16 in BMT conjoint group, 16 in CT conjoint treatment, 19 in CT con-joint group, and 17 in a waiting-list control group (waiting period: 3 to 4 months). Couples were recruited by public announcements on the Bavarian radio station (70%) and referrals from mental health agencies (30%). The mean age of clients was 33.7 years. The couples had been married or living together for an average duration of 8 years. Of the couples, 90.3% were mar-ried and 74.5% had at least one child. Overall, the sample represented at least moderately distressed couples. After an initial interview the couples were ran-domly allocated to the treatment conditions. Subsequent statistical analysis revealed no significant differences among the groups on a variety of demo-graphic and personal characteristics.

TABLE 1.1. Design of Study

Format	Modality	
	C	CG
BMT	17	16
CT	16	19
WLCG	17	

Note. Cell frequencies represent n of couples. BMT = behavioral marital therapy; CT = communication skills train-ing; WLCG = waiting-list control group; C = conjoint (1 cou-ple, 1 therapist); CG = conjoint group (3–4 couples, 2 ther-apists).

Since detailed results of the study have been published elsewhere (Hahl-weg, Schindler, & Revenstorf, 1982b), this chapter focuses on details on the multiple assessment battery and provides some results on the question of predicting treatment success; in addition, the treatment procedures as well as the short-term and long-term results (follow-ups lasted for 1 year) are briefly summarized.

To describe both the process of therapy and the type of distress, we tried to assess as many aspects of the relationship as possible. In addition to questionnaires we relied on behavioral observations in the laboratory. Both data served the purpose of evaluating outcome in terms of pre- and postcomparisons. Observational data also provided the opportunity to analyze interaction in distressed (and nondistressed) couples on a micro level (see Revenstorf, Hahlweg, Schindler, & Vogel, Chapter 10, this volume). As another method of therapy evaluation we were interested in process analysis. For this purpose the couples had to rate several aspects of their interaction on a daily basis, using a standardized diary. Whereas observational data allowed for moment-by-moment description of couples' interaction, the diary data assessed the ongoing interaction on a continuous but macro level. By using time series analysis, several ways of extracting information are possible: analyzing the shape, the interrelation, and the predictive validity of the time series (see Revenstorf, Hahlweg, Schindler, & Kunert, Chapter 12, this volume).

Treatment

Six male therapists including the authors treated the couples in the study. Each therapist carried out both treatment formats. As one can see from the treatment descriptions, the two formats do not constitute totally different therapies, because a slightly different communication skills training is used in the BMT format as well. Furthermore, the behavioral techniques used to teach the skills are identical in both formats and included role-play procedures, modeling, and shaping. This research is best conceptualized as a "treatment component study" comparing a pure process approach (CT) with a combined process–content approach (BMT).

Both treatment formats lasted 15 sessions and consisted of three different phases: behavioral analysis and assessment (Sessions 1–4 and 15), basic skills training (Sessions 5–8), and problem solution (Sessions 9–14). In the conjoint modality each session lasted for 50 to 60 minutes. In the conjoint group modality each couple was seen individually during the assessment phase. From Session 5 through Session 14, three or four couples were treated in a group (duration of session: 2.5 to 3 hours).

COMMUNICATION SKILLS TRAINING

The standardized CT program was based on a literature review as well as our own clinical experiences. The procedures were mainly derived from Guerney's

Relationship enhancement (1977) and Berlin's *Das offene Gespräch: Paare lernen Kommunikation* (1975). In addition the couples were assigned a programmed textbook consisting of six chapters, which is a rewritten version of *Das offene Gespräch* (Berlin, 1975). The basic aim of Sessions 5–8 was to enable the clients to learn and practice the following speaker and listener skills.

Speaker Skills. The use of the following speaker skills was expected to lead to enhanced self-disclosure on the part of the speaker: (1) Use "I" messages (express your own feelings about the topic). (2) Describe specific situations (speak of specific situations in order to avoid generalizations like "always" or "never"). (3) Describe specific behaviors (speak of specific behaviors in specific situations in order to avoid labels like "lazy" or "cold"). (4) Stick to the "here and now" (discuss one problem at a time in order to avoid sidetracking).

Listener Skills. The following listener skills were encouraged: (1) Listen actively (indicate by your nonverbal behavior that you are listening to your partner). (2) Paraphrase (summarize your partner's remarks and check their accuracy). (3) Ask open-ended questions when you do not understand your partner's feelings/thoughts. (4) Give positive feedback for appropriate responses by your partner. (5) Disclose your own feelings (when hurt by a statement of your partner, respond with an "I" message).

During the didactic phase the couple role played standardized problem situations, trying to make use of these new skills. Training included the interchange of the speaker and listener roles while discussing first simple and then more complex conflicts.

In the problem solution phase of the program the clients discussed their own problems, beginning with rather simple and easily solvable problems. The following scheme of conflict discussion was used:

In Step 1 each partner had to express his/her feelings about the problem in the most direct and open way (conveying of feelings) while the other partner provided feedback, in Step 2 both partners had to describe their wishes and needs regarding the problem, in Step 3 the couple used a brainstorming procedure to generate possible solutions to the problem, and in Step 4 the couple tried to reach an agreement. Specific problem-solving skills and contract management as used in behavior marital therapy were not included in the treatment.

BEHAVIORAL MARITAL THERAPY

The BMT program was based on both a literature review and our own clinical experience. The basic procedures were derived from Liberman, Wheeler, and Sanders (1976); Stuart (1976); and Weiss, Hops, and Patterson (1973). The treatment program consisted of four different components (see Hahlweg, Schindler, & Revenstorf, 1982a).

Establishing Positive Reciprocity. To enhance both partner and self-observation of positive behaviors, a homework assignment developed by Liberman, Wheeler, and Sanders (1976) was used during the first week of treatment: "Catch your spouse doing/saying something nice and let him/her know about it." Beginning the following week, couples were asked to perform "caring days" (Stuart, 1976). In this procedure each partner had to choose one day of the week on which he/she was to emit caring behaviors independently of the actions of the spouse. Each partner had to record the planned and received caring behaviors. At the beginning of each treatment session the course of the "caring days" was reviewed.

Communication Skills Training. In the communication skills training module the previously described speaker and listener skills were taught (Sessions 6 and 7). By employing the communication skills it was hoped that partners would avoid blaming, criticizing, and sidetracking; increase their mutual understanding; and generate specific solutions to their problems. The core skills are reciprocal self-disclosure of feelings, attitudes, and thoughts either about a specific problem in the relationship or about a general point of discussion, and accepting of (not necessarily agreeing to) the speaker's utterances.

Problem-Solving Training. To help the couple solve their own problems a structured discussion scheme was developed. In Step 1 both partners conveyed their views of the conflict — disclosing their feelings, thoughts, and attitudes toward the problem — and provided mutual feedback. In Step 2 each partner described his/her needs and wishes regarding the problem. In Step 3 they had to generate specific solutions for the problem through brainstorming. In Step 4 partners practiced negotiating agreements, and an informal "good faith" contract was prepared for that purpose (O'Leary & Turkewitz, 1978).

Crisis Management. The crisis management component of treatment was introduced toward the end of therapy, in Session 11 or 12, as a step toward enhancing generalization. Using the previously taught problem-solving skills in particularly problematic situations where aversive exchanges tend to occur, the coping skills were tested under supervision of the therapist.

Following a progressive escalation process, four stages may be identified: Stage 1 represents the period before one spouse points out a specific behavior pattern in the other which is particularly disliked. Stage 2 becomes relevant when the spouse decides that the conflict issue should be addressed now. Stage 3 represents coping with an imminent quarrel. Stage 4 refers to the situation after a heated quarrel when communication between the partners has broken down and each spouse should be responsible for adopting positive interaction again.

For each of these stages, spouses are taught to use self-statements (Meichenbaum, 1977) that can help to avoid the increase of an aversive exchange and support direct communication. (For a detailed description see Schindler & Vollmer, Chapter 16, this volume.)

Measures of Treatment Outcome

Multiple outcome criteria were used to determine treatment effectiveness, including several questionnaires, laboratory observation, and ratings of the therapists by the clients (see Hahlweg *et al.*, 1982b). The questionnaires were administered before and after therapy and at the 6- and 12-month follow-up. They were completed by both partners independently of one another. The observation of laboratory interaction was conducted before and after therapy. In this chapter we describe the development of the main questionnaires and present the statistical properties of the assessment battery.

PARTNERSHIP QUESTIONNAIRE (PFB)

The 30-item PFB was developed for diagnosis and evaluation of couples in therapy (cf. Hahlweg, 1979). In the first study a pilot questionnaire including 178 items was completed by 224 distressed and nondistressed spouses. Factor analysis yielded three scales with a total of 45 items. These scales were cross-validated with a sample of 183 distressed and nondistressed partners. To improve the validity of the scales as a measure of therapeutic change, data from 60 couples treated with BMT were used. Items showing no significant change from pre to post were eliminated, leaving the following scales with 10 items each.

The first scale (Quarreling) deals with aggressive or quarreling behaviors ("He/she blames me when something goes wrong" and "When we quarrel he/she keeps taunting me"). The second scale (Tenderness) includes verbal and nonverbal behaviors indicating tenderness and intimacy ("He/she caresses me tenderly" and "He/she tells me that he/she loves me"). The third scale (Togetherness/Communication) includes items like "We talk to each other for at least half an hour every day" and "We make plans for the future together." Each item is answered according to a four-point scale based on how frequently it occurs: never or very seldom, seldom, often, very often. (For the questionnaire and the scoring key, see Appendix B.)

Table 1.2 shows the means and standard deviations for two criterion groups of distressed and nondistressed couples. Statistical analyses (*t* test) revealed highly significant differences between both groups on every scale.

As is shown in Table 1.3, each scale has a high internal consistency (average Cronbach's $\alpha = 0.87$) and a moderate 6-month test–retest reliability (average $r = 0.75$).

PROBLEM LIST (PL)

The PL was used in the behavior analysis phase of the therapy. It consists of 17 possible problem areas of marriage, for example, finances, household management, leisure time, sexuality, tenderness, and social activities (see Appendix C). The list was put together using different assessment devices, for example, Marital Happiness Scale (Azrin, Naster, & Jones, 1973), Marital

TABLE 1.2. Means and Standard Deviations for Nondistressed and Distressed Couples on the Partnership Questionnaire (PFB)

	Nondistressed[a]	Distressed[b]
Scale 1: Quarreling		
M	5.7	13.7
SD	4.5	6.5
Scale 2: Tenderness		
M	19.6	10.2
SD	5.5	6.1
Scale 3: Communication		
M	21.1	12.8
SD	4.6	4.9

[a] $n = 360$.
[b] $n = 175$.

Precounseling Inventory (Stuart & Stuart, 1973), and Potential Problem Areas (Patterson, 1976). Each problem area is rated by each partner using the following categories: 0 = No problems; 1 = Problems, but we can usually solve them; 2 = Problems we cannot find solutions for, and we often quarrel; 3 = Problems we cannot find solutions for, and we don't discuss them any more. (For the PL, see Appendix C.)

During the behavior analysis phase the problem areas rated as 1, 2, or 3 were used as a guideline to structure the interview with the partners. During the problem solution phase of the therapy the list was used to construct a hierarchy of conflict areas for each couple.

For the purpose of therapy evaluation, categories 2 and 3 are summed up yielding one "Conflict Score" for each person. The test–retest reliability of this score is .66 (6-month interval, $n = 50$).

The PL was validated in an experiment with a group of 90 clients in marital therapy and a matched control group of 100 nondistressed partners (Hahlweg, Kraemer, Schindler, & Revenstorf, 1980). The results are shown in Table 1.4.

TABLE 1.3. Internal Consistency and Retest Reliability on the Partnership Questionnaire (PFB)

	Internal consistency[a]	Retest reliability[b]
Scale 1: Quarreling	0.88	0.68
Scale 2: Tenderness	0.85	0.74
Scale 3: Communication	0.88	0.83

[a] $n = 670$.
[b] $n = 50$, 6-month interval.

TABLE 1.4. Rank, Absolute Frequency, and Percentage for Each Area Based on the Sum of Answer Categories 2 and 3, and Means and Standard Deviations of the Conflict Score for Therapy and Nondistressed Couples on the Problem List (PL)

Rank	Therapy	Frequency	Percentage	Rank	Nondistressed	Frequency	Percentage
1	Sexuality	64	74.4	1	Sexuality	15	16.3
2	Affection	62	72.9	2	Values and philosophy	13	13.8
3	Temperament	58	66.7	3	Personal habits	8	10.3
4	Leisure Time	54	62.1	4	Affection	8	8.6
5	Personal habits	36	58.1	5	Leisure time	8	8.4
6	Trust	44	53.0	6	Child care and training	6	7.6
7	Guarantee of personal freedom	43	51.2	7	Temperament	7	7.4
8	Values and philosophy	40	47.1	8	Relatives	5	5.4
9	Child care and training	35	46.1	9	Job	4	4.3
10	Jealousy	36	41.4	10	Trust	4	4.2
11.5	Friendships	34	39.5	11	Household	4	4.1
11.5	Household	34	39.5	12	Jealousy	3	3.3
13.5	Relatives	28	33.3	13	Physical attractiveness	2	2.2
13.5	Job	28	33.3	14	Guarantee of personal freedom	2	2.1
15	Extramarital affairs	26	31.7	15	Friendships	2	2.0
16	Finances	14	16.1	16	Extramarital affairs	1	1.1
17	Physical attractiveness	11	13.1	17	Finances	1	1.0
Conflict Score							
M		7.1				0.9	
SD		3.1				1.5	

For each area we computed how often the distressed or nondistressed respondents checked category 2 or 3. Within each group the areas were then rank ordered according to the relative frequency of the sum score.

As expected, distressed and nondistressed groups differed significantly in the total number of conflict areas. Distressed clients on an average checked 7.1 areas as conflict-producing, whereas nondistressed partners checked roughly 1 area. In each of the 17 areas the difference between both groups was highly significant. Obviously there is a quantitative difference between the two samples, but not a marked qualitative one: Among the two samples a very similar rank ordering of problem areas was found (Spearman's $\rho = .73$, $p = .001$). For both distressed and nondistressed partners the most conflict-producing areas were sexuality, affection, leisure time, temperament, and personal habits of the partner. In general the emotional–interpersonal problems rank at the top, whereas the instrumental problems (household, job, finances) are of minor importance for both groups.

GENERAL HAPPINESS RATING SCALE

The General Happiness Rating Scale was introduced by Terman (1938). In a pilot study (Hahlweg, 1979) the scale correlated highly ($r = .88$, $n = 224$) with the Marital Adjustment Scale (Locke & Wallace, 1959) and is therefore used as a global measure of distress. (For the rating scale, see Item 31 of the PFB, Appendix B.)

MARITAL INTERACTION CODING SYSTEM (MICS)

The MICS is a frequently used behavioral coding system with 28 verbal and nonverbal codes (Hops, Wills, Patterson, & Weiss, 1972; for a review, see Jacobson & Margolin, 1979, Chapter 4). In order to analyze the data, 21 MICS codes were collapsed into positive and negative categories (positive: approve, agree, accept responsibility, compromise, humor, positive solution, attention, laugh, assent, positive physical; negative: complain, criticize, disagree, deny responsibility, excuse, interrupt, negative solution, put down, no response, not tracking, turn off).

The behavior coded by the MICS consisted of couple interactions before and after therapy. For the first 10 minutes the couples had to solve up to four hypothetical marital problems from the Inventory of Marital Conflict (IMC) by Olson and Ryder (1970). Following this, they were asked to discuss a problem of their own for another 10 minutes. These discussions were videotaped and later coded by trained raters who were blind to the experimental conditions.

Interrater reliability was assessed by random checks and calculated by the formula Agreement/(Agreement + Disagreement) in a point-for-point fashion. The minimum criterion for acceptable reliability was .70. This figure was exceeded on virtually every check. The IMC and the MICS were successfully validated for the German cultural background (Hahlweg, Helmes, Steffen, Schindler, Revenstorf, & Kunert, 1979).

INTERCORRELATION OF CRITERION VARIABLES

One major requirement of a multiple assessment battery is relative independence of the variables, implying that the instruments are measuring different areas of marital interaction. In Table 1.5 the intercorrelation matrix of the battery is shown.

The correlations for the whole sample ($n = 170$) are presented above the diagonal in Table 1.5. The diagonal of the table shows the husband–wife correlations ($n = 85$). The mean intercorrelation between all variables is quite low ($r = .20$ for the whole sample), which indicates that the battery is assessing different areas of marital interaction, and that marital adjustment is not a unitary construct. The highest intercorrelations with the other variables were obtained for the General Happiness Rating Scale, pointing out the value of this scale as a global measure of distress. In general the results are in line with those of Margolin (1978), showing a very low correspondence between self-report measures and the observers' coding of communication skills. With regard to these results it seems necessary to include a wide range of assessment procedures in order to investigate the major aspects of a relationship.

The correlations between husband and wife on the same variable range from .24 (PFB, Tenderness) to .65 (General Happiness Rating Scale) with a mean correlation of $r = .41$, explaining roughly 16% of the variance. This

TABLE 1.5. Intercorrelations among the Criterion Variables[a]

Measure	1	2	3	4	5	6	7
1. PFB—Quarreling	.32**	.04	−.17*	.19**	−.30***	−.06	−.01
2. PFB—Tenderness		.24*	.34**	−.16*	.31***	.12*	.09
3. PFB—Communication			.41***	−.34***	.42***	.10	−.10
4. PL—Conflict Score				.32***	−.45***	−.12*	.06
5. General Happiness Rating Scale					.65***	.22*	−.11
6. MICS—positive						.35**	−.24*
7. MICS—negative							.55**

[a]Upper, off-diagonal data: correlations based on total sample ($n = 170$). Diagonal of table: husband–wife correlations ($n = 85$).

*$p \le .05$.

**$p \le .01$.

***$p \le .001$.

rather low correlation shows that even on the same instrument the partners view their interaction quite differently. This suggests a justification for departing from the convention of using the average husband–wife score when analyzing treatment effectiveness. At least one should look for differential effects applying the appropriate statistical procedures (e.g., using sex as an independent variable).

Results

Short-Term and Long-Term Outcome

Statistical analysis of the pretest scores revealed no significant differences among the five groups on any of the variables. The results concerning the pre- and postcomparisons can be summarized as follows (for details, see Hahlweg et al., 1982b):

1. Couples who received BMT, irrespective of modality, or conjoint communication training showed significant improvement when compared to the waiting-list control group on six out of seven variables. Specifically, they reduced their aggressive and quarreling behavior as assessed by the PFB scale Quarreling and decreased their negative interaction as measured by the MICS. Moreover, they showed a substantial reduction in the absolute number of conflict areas. On the positive side, they rated their relationship in general as much happier. They reported a substantial improvement of their day-to-day interaction as assessed by the PFB scale Communication, and showed more tenderness and intimacy as assessed by the PFB scale Tenderness. There was no significant change for MICS positive interactional behavior.

2. Couples in conjoint BMT were superior to couples in conjoint group BMT and conjoint CT in two out of seven comparisons (General Happiness Rating Scale and PL Conflict Score).

3. Couples who received CT in the conjoint group modality showed a clearly significant improvement on only one out of seven variables when compared to the waiting-list control group (MICS negative behavior). BMT and conjoint CT were significantly superior to the CT conjoint group in five out of seven comparisons.

4. Couples in the waiting-list control group remained unchanged over a 4-month waiting period.

The results at follow-up can be summarized as follows.

1. Eleven couples (16.2% of the treated couples) separated. Subsequent statistical comparison of modalities within each treatment format revealed no significant differences (for details, see Revenstorf, Schind-

ler, & Hahlweg, in press; Schindler, Hahlweg, & Revenstorf, 1983). Therefore follow-up analyses were performed combining the conjoint and conjoint group modalities within each treatment format.

2. BMT seems to have produced more lasting change than CT. BMT couples were significantly superior to CT couples in two out of five comparisons, reporting fewer conflict areas and less aggressive and quarreling behavior after 1 year.

3. Within-subject analyses revealed that BMT couples remained improved relative to pretest level on four out of five variables, while CT couples maintained improvement in only two out of five comparisons.

Clinical Significance

When applying sophisticated statistical analysis, one cannot help wondering about the clinical significance of the results. Practitioners in particular are more interested in a global and handy measure of the possible magnitude of the changes brought about by a particular treatment approach. Several methods of meta-analysis have been proposed. One is the box-score approach (Luborsky et al., 1975), which has been discussed.

Another method was suggested by Smith and Glass (1977) in their meta-analysis of psychotherapy outcome studies. They measured the magnitude of the effect of therapy by the following formula: $ES = (ME - MCG)/SDCG$. The "effect size" (ES) for an experiment was defined as the mean difference after therapy between the treated and controlled subjects divided by the standard deviation of the control group. Since it is standardized to the control group by means of z transformation, deviation from the control mean may be determined in terms of percentiles. "Thus, an ES of $+1$ indicates that a person at the mean of the control group would be expected to rise to the 84th percentile of the control group after treatment" (Smith & Glass, 1977, p. 753). Using the ES it is possible to compare very different dependent variables by calculating the respective effect sizes.

Table 1.6 shows the ESs for both treatment formats at the different assessment points. After therapy the average BMT couple was better off than 86% of the waiting-list control couples, while the average CT couple was better off than 76% of the control couples.

For ethical and practical reasons the control couples were not assessed at the two follow-up points (FU 1 and 2); instead, they were treated on request. Assuming that the untreated controls would not have changed over the follow-up period, one can use their means and standard deviations after therapy to calculate effect sizes for the nonseparated experimental couples at FU 1 and 2. For BMT couples the respective effect sizes were 84% and 89%; for CT couples these were 73% and 69%, showing a considerable superiority of BMT over CT up to 1 year after therapy.

TABLE 1.6. Effect Sizes (ESs) Based on Questionnaire Data for Non-separated Couples in Behavioral Marital Therapy or Communication Training[a]

	Post	FU 1[b]	FU 2[b]
BMT	1.10 (86)	1.01 (84)	1.25 (89)
CT	0.72 (76)	0.63 (73)	0.51 (69)

[a]Data in parentheses give the average percentile status in the control group for treated couples.
[b]ESs were computed using the data of nonseparated couples for FU 1 and 2. For control couples, postmeasurement data were used.

Another method of assessing clinical significance can be achieved by using the General Happiness Rating Scale as the criterion. This rating scale can be used in a normative sense: A client checking the answer categories 0, 1, or 2 (very unhappy to somewhat unhappy) can be regarded as distressed, while a client checking 3, 4, or 5 (somewhat happy to very happy) can be regarded as nondistressed. Thus a couple can be regarded as nondistressed when both partners rate their relationship at least as somewhat happy.

The percentages of nondistressed couples based on the General Happiness Rating Scale criterion for both treatment formats and the four assessment points are shown in Table 1.7. After therapy 81.3% of the BMT couples could be regarded as nondistressed, while only 60% of the CT couples rated themselves as nondistressed. This difference is significant [$\chi^2 (1) = 3.8$, $p < .05$]. At follow-up the percentages in both treatment formats dropped; at FU 1 and 2 they were 71.4% and 64.3%, respectively, for BMT, and 55.2% and 58.6%, respectively, for CT. The differences between BMT and CT were not significant at FU 1 and 2.

To summarize the results on clinical significance, in both types of meta-analyses (ES and General Happiness Rating Scale comparison), BMT was distinctly superior to CT after therapy. With the nonseparated couples, only the

TABLE 1.7. Percentage of Nondistressed Couples Based on the General Happiness Rating Scale for Different Assessment Points and Treatment Formats.[a]

	Pre	Post	FU 1	FU 2
BMT	18.2	81.3	71.4	64.3
CT	31.4	60.0	55.2	58.6
WL	29.4	17.7	—	—

[a]A couple is regarded as nondistressed when both partners rate their relationship at least as somewhat happy on the General Happiness Rating Scale.

ES analysis showed a substantial superiority at both follow-up points for BMT couples. Within the treatment formats improvement remained stable compared to the control couples, albeit on a lower level for CT than for BMT. Comparing the two treatments with respect to the percentage of clients reporting themselves to be at least somewhat happy on the General Happiness Rating Scale, the superiority of BMT is still obvious, but only at posttest. In both treatments there is a pronounced decay in the percentage of happy couples during the follow-up period. Yet BMT remains superior even at FU 2, although the superiority is less pronounced than at posttest. The most conservative estimate of a success rate for BMT-treated couples 1 year after treatment is 64.3% (CT: 58.6%), while the more optimistic ES estimation shows an 88% superiority of BMT (CT: 71%) when compared to the average untreated control couple.

Predictors of Outcome

In order to analyze predictors for successful therapy outcome, the following criteria were defined using the General Happiness Rating Scale as the criterion variable at posttest and FU 1 and 2 assessment times.

A couple was rated as successful when (1) both partners rated their relationship at least as somewhat happy at the respective assessment times, and (2) at least one partner scored one point or more higher on the rating when compared to the pretest score. All other couples were regarded as unsuccessful. Overall, six criterion groups regarding marital quality were established: (1) postsuccessful/unsuccessful (POST CRIT); (2) follow-up 1 successful/unsuccessful (FU 1 CRIT), and (3) follow-up 2 successful/unsuccessful (FU 2 CRIT). Furthermore, two additional groups regarding marital stability were established: separated during the follow-up/not separated during the follow-up period (SEPARATION).

A priori, a set of pretest predictor variables were defined and clustered in three groups:

1. Conflict: These variables were designed to assess the quality and quantity of conflict resolution (PFB Quarreling, PL Conflict Score, MICS negative behavior, frequency of quarrel, length of distress, thoughts of separation).

2. Affection/intimacy: These variables were designed to assess the emotional affection of both partners to each other (PFB Tenderness, PFB Communication, MICS positive behavior, frequency of sexual intercourse).

3. Demographic characteristics: Age, length of partnership, and number of children were included to assess the major demographic characteristics.

According to the described criteria, groups were formed and chi-square or t tests calculated, using the aforementioned predictor variables. In Table 1.8 the significant differences between the groups are shown.

Within the conflict cluster only the variable "thought of separation" yielded consistently significant differences. In this rating the clients had to indicate progress toward divorce, using one of the following categories: 1 = filed for divorce; 2 = separated; 3 = trial separation; 4 = thoughts of separation/divorce; 5 = no thoughts of separation/divorce.

MICS negative behavior was significant only for short-term prediction, and, contrary to expectation, successful couples were more negative than unsuccessful couples.

Of the demographic variables, only age showed one significant result: Couples who separated during follow-up were slightly older ($M = 35$ years, 7 months) than the nonseparating couples ($M = 33$ years, 5 months).

Within the affection/intimacy cluster, PFB Tenderness and Communication, and the frequency of sexual intercourse, were useful long-term predictors.

TABLE 1.8. Predictors of Therapy Outcome and Results of Significance Tests[a] (t test or χ^2)

| | Groups | | | |
| | POST CRIT + = 46, − = 22 | FU 1 CRIT + = 35, − = 33 | FU 2 CRIT + = 34, − = 34 | SEPA-RATION yes = 11, no = 57 |
Measure				
Conflict				
PFB—Quarreling	—	—	—	—
PL—Conflict Score	—	—	—	—
MICS—Negative behavior	*	—	—	—
Frequency of quarrel	—	—	—	—
Thoughts of separation	*	***	***	**
Length of distress	—	—	—	—
Affection				
PFB—Tenderness	—	*	**	*
PFB—Communication	—	—	*	*
MICS—Positive behavior	—	—	—	—
Frequency of sexual intercourse	—	*	**	*
Demographic characteristics				
Age	—	—	—	*
Length of marriage	—	—	—	—
Children	—	—	—	—

[a]Average husband–wife scores are used in statistical analysis (t test or χ^2).
*$p \le .05$.
**$p \le .01$.
***$p \le .001$.

Subsequent analysis of the significant differentiating variables showed some significant sex differences, which leads to the conclusion that couples have an unfavorable prognosis when they show the following pretest characteristics:

1. Both partners are thinking of separation/divorce or have been separated before.

2. The frequency of sexual intercourse is less than twice per month.

3. Both partners score low (≤ 10) on the PFB scale Tenderness.

4. The wife scores low (≤ 11) on the PFB scale Togetherness/Communication.

According to these results the quality of emotional affection is far more important than the amount and handling of conflict in predicting therapy outcome.

Discussion

The results of our study suggest strongly that both comparative and component research are necessary in order to improve the effectiveness of marital therapy. Furthermore, the findings challenge Gurman and Kniskern's (1978) provocative proposal that different treatment formats produce, on the average, identical results and indicate that in the field of marital therapy there are "winners and losers."

How do our findings compare with the rest of the literature? In terms of demographic characteristics such as age, length of marriage, and average number of children, our sample is quite comparable to the samples used in the other controlled studies (Revenstorf *et al.*, in press) investigating middle-class couples who are about 33 years old, 8 years married, and at least moderately distressed.

With regard to BMT, the results of our pre- and postcomparisons are in line with the literature showing a definite superiority of BMT to a waiting-list control group. Applying the ES method to published studies that give means and standard deviations — Baucom (1982) — $z = .70$; Boelens, Emmelkamp, MacGillavry, and Markvoort (1980) — $z = 1.4$; Jacobson (1977) — $z = 2.4$; Jacobson (1978b) — $z = 2.6$; Zimmer, Anneken, Echelmeyer, Kaluza, Klein, and Klockgeter-Kelle (1977) — $z = .63$ — yields a median ES of $z = 1.4$ (92%), as compared to our own finding of $z = 1.1$ (86%). In other words, after therapy the average BMT-treated couple is better off than about 90% of the untreated control couples. As shown in other studies, this degree of improvement is maintained by the nonseparated couples for at least 1 year.

Unfortunately, it is impossible to calculate an average effect size for the CT approach because none of the published studies provides the basis for computing an ES (i.e., means and standard deviations).

However, when comparing our results with the literature using the box-score method, the apparent failure of the CT conjoint group in producing change is the most striking outcome, because this is the commonly used communication training modality and because a constant superiority of a CT conjoint group over a control group has been reported (Collins, 1977; Ely, Guerney, & Stover, 1973; Epstein & Jackson, 1978; Pierce, 1973; Rappaport, 1976; Wieman, 1976). Most of these studies used only mildly distressed or even non-distressed couples and lacked follow-up, while in our study at least moderately distressed couples were treated.

With these couples the interaction of group members within the CT format may explain the failure. As usual with CT, specific problem-solving skills and measures to increase positive interaction were not taught, leading perhaps to a "negative modeling effect" with each couple observing other couples in the group not improving (Schindler *et al.*, 1983). On the basis of our results, CT in a conjoint group modality cannot be recommended as a treatment for moderately or severely distressed couples.

Regarding the modality of treatment, the results are different within a BMT framework. Conjoint and conjoint group treatment were equally effective, particularly with respect to long-term findings. However, as has been discussed by Revenstorf *et al.* (in press), we cannot recommend a conjoint group BMT treatment without some qualifying remarks. The major problem with a group treatment lies in the possible differential rate of improvement for the couples. If all couples improve more or less equally, group treatment works well and is very beneficial to the participants because of the range of different models of problem solving and exchange of positive behaviors. But when a couple in the group is not improving, group treatment may restrict the possible range of improvement for the rest of the group. In general, the conjoint treatment seems to be a safer approach, especially with "difficult" clients (Revenstorf *et al.*, in press).

When comparing treatment formats, BMT seems to be moderately superior to CT. These results are in contrast to those of O'Leary and Turkewitz (1981) and Wieman (1976), who did not find consistent differences in the effectiveness of CT and BMT. The major distinction between their BMT approach and the present one is in the explicit focus on increasing positive reciprocity between partners, which may stabilize alternative problem-solving behaviors acquired during therapy. However, when compared with other approaches, BMT seems to be somewhat superior in the long run (Boelens *et al.*, 1980; Crowe, 1978; Liberman, Levine, Wheeler, Sanders, & Wallace, 1976). This is consistent with the present results.

There are only a few noteworthy findings in the literature regarding the prediction of successful therapy outcome. Crowe (1978) reported that couples referred from their general practitioner did significantly better than those referred by psychiatrists, and that in the BMT group the uneducated couples did better than the educated. A weak correlation suggested that sex of the referred partner may be important: Those couples where the husband was referred did better than those where the wife was referred. Since our sample differed from Crowe's, no replication was possible. O'Leary and Turkewitz (1981) found that age and duration of marriage were negatively correlated with positive outcome, and that BMT was significantly more effective with younger couples (mean age = 29.4 years) than CT. For older couples (mean age = 41 years) CT was more effective. We could not replicate these findings because our sample is too restricted in age range.

Regarding thoughts of separation as a predictor for unsuccessful outcome, our results are in line with those of Crowe (1978). He, too, found no correlation between socioeconomic variables and outcome, thus confirming our results.

However, the finding that the emotional–affective quality of the relationship (tenderness, communication, and frequency of intercourse) predicts successful outcome needs cross-validation, especially because this result has important consequences for the clinical practice of BMT.

The treatment approach chosen allows effective improvement of manifest behaviors such as problem solving and social interaction. However, it appears less well suited to deal with internal events affecting the emotional qualities of a relationship (cf. Weiss, 1980). Future research should be directed to this point so as to supplement a behavioral treatment program with emotion-enhancing procedures.

ACKNOWLEDGMENT

This research was supported by the Deutsche Forschungsgemeinschaft (DFG-Re 402/2-6).

Appendix A: Studies Used in the Reanalysis

We were not able to obtain 6 of the 11 studies, because they are unpublished doctoral theses or conference papers. To classify these studies we used the information provided by Gurman and Kniskern (1978) or by Jacobson (1978b).

The CT group comprised the following studies:

- Cadogan, D. A. Marital group therapy in the treatment of alcoholism. *Quarterly Journal of Studies on Alcoholism,* 1973, *34,* 1187–1194.
- Cassidy, M. J. *Communication training for marital pairs.* Unpublished doctoral dissertation, University of California at Los Angeles, 1973.
- Christensen, D. J. The effects of intramarriage self-esteem and decision making on a structured marriage counseling program emphasizing supportiveness. *Dissertation Abstracts International,* 1974, *35,* 3141A.
- Hickman, M. E., & Baldwin, B. A. Use of programmed instruction to improve communication in marriage. *Family Coordinator,* 1970, *20,* 121–125.

• Matanovich, J. P. The effects of short-term group counseling upon positive perceptions of mate in marital counseling. *Dissertation Abstracts International,* 1970, *31,* 2688A.

• Pierce, R. M. Training in interpersonal communication skills with partners of deteriorating marriages. *Family Coordinator,* 1973, *22,* 223–227.

The MS group comprised the following studies:

• Friedman, A. S. Interaction of drug therapy with marital therapy in depressive patients. *Archives of General Psychiatry,* 1975, *32,* 619–637.

• Graham, J. A. The effect of the use of counselor positive responses to positive perceptions of mate in marriage counseling. *Dissertation Abstracts International,* 1968, *28,* 3504A.

• Griffin, R. W. Change in perception of marital relationship as related to marriage counseling. *Dissertation Abstracts International,* 1967, *27,* 3956A.

• Pierce, R. M. (see CT group studies; Treatment II in this study was insight-oriented)

The following studies provided no appropriate control groups and therefore were excluded from the analysis:

• Alkire, A. A., & Brunse, A. J. Impact and possible causality from video-tape feedback in marital therapy. *Journal of Consulting and Clinical Psychology,* 1974, *42,* 203–210.

• Cardillo, J. P. Effects of teaching communication roles on interpersonal perception and self-concept in disturbed marriages. *Proceedings of the 79th Annual Convention of the American Psychological Association,* 1971, *6,* 441–442.

Appendix B: Partnership Questionnaire (PFB)

Name _____

Date _____

Q	T	C	SC

In a partnership people behave in many different ways. In the following items a range of these behaviors is presented. These behaviors can be shown by either partner or by both partners together. Some of these items are of a sexual nature.

Please draw a circle around the number you choose as the answer, showing how often each of these ways of behaving has occurred in your partnership in the past. Don't spend time thinking about your answers—circle the answer that expresses your first thoughts about each item. Please answer each statement and circle only one number for each item.

	Very seldom	Seldom	Often	Very often
1. He/she keeps casting up mistakes which I've made in the past.	0	1	2	3
2. He/she caresses me during foreplay so that I get sexually excited.	0	1	2	3

	Very seldom	Seldom	Often	Very often
3. I notice that he/she finds me physically attractive.	0	1	2	3
4. When we are alone together he/she tells me that he/she feels happy.	0	1	2	3
5. Before going to sleep we kiss and cuddle each other.	0	1	2	3
6. He/she makes a row about nothing just out of spite.	0	1	2	3
7. I think that he/she tells me frankly about her thoughts and feelings.	0	1	2	3
8. When we quarrel he/she showers me with insults.	0	1	2	3
9. He/she reacts positively to my sexual approaches.	0	1	2	3
10. We make plans for the future together.	0	1	2	3
11. When he/she tells me about his/her work, he/she likes to know my opinions.	0	1	2	3
12. We make plans for the weekend together.	0	1	2	3
13. He/she caresses me gently, and I find it very pleasant.	0	1	2	3
14. He/she gives me sincere compliments on my appearance.	0	1	2	3
15. He/she discusses matters concerning his/her working life with me (if she doesn't work—"matters concerning house keeping").	0	1	2	3
16. He/she is attentive to my needs and wishes, and acts accordingly.	0	1	2	3
17. He/she criticizes me in a sarcastic way.	0	1	2	3
18. He/she expresses disapproval of my opinions.	0	1	2	3
19. When he/she has obviously treated me wrongly, he/she apologizes.	0	1	2	3
20. Usually, we talk together in the evenings for at least half an hour.	0	1	2	3
21. When we quarrel we can never end the quarrel.	0	1	2	3
22. He/she blames me when something goes wrong.	0	1	2	3
23. He/she puts his/her arms around me.	0	1	2	3
24. During a quarrel he/she shouts at me.	0	1	2	3
25. In the evenings he/she asks me how things have gone for me during the day.	0	1	2	3
26. When we quarrel he/she turns around what I say so as to mean the opposite.	0	1	2	3
27. He/she tells me about his/her sexual wishes.	0	1	2	3

(continued)

	Very seldom	Seldom	Often	Very often
28. He/she caresses me tenderly.	0	1	2	3
29. He/she tells me that he/she loves me.	0	1	2	3
30. I think that my partner limits my personal freedom.	0	1	2	3

31. At this moment, how happy do you
    think your marriage/partnership is?

Very unhappy	0
Unhappy	1
Somewhat unhappy	2
Somewhat happy	3
Happy	4
Very happy	5

Appendix C: Problem List (PL)

Name _____ Date _____

In the Problem List, you will find 17 different potential conflict areas. Please indicate if and to what extent you think that in a particular area in your partnership you do have conflicts. Use the following answer categories:

    0 = No problems
    1 = Problems, but we can usually solve them
    2 = Problems we cannot find solutions for, and we often quarrel
    3 = Problems we cannot find solutions for, and we don't discuss them any more.

1. Finances and money management	0	1	2	3
2. Job	0	1	2	3
3. Household management	0	1	2	3
4. Child care and training	0	1	2	3
5. Leisure time	0	1	2	3
6. Friendships	0	1	2	3
7. Values and philosophy	0	1	2	3
8. Temperament of partner	0	1	2	3
9. Affection of partner	0	1	2	3
10. Physical attractiveness of partner	0	1	2	3
11. Trust	0	1	2	3
12. Jealousy	0	1	2	3
13. Guarantee of personal freedom	0	1	2	3
14. Sexuality	0	1	2	3
15. Extramarital affairs	0	1	2	3
16. Personal habits of partner	0	1	2	3
17. Relatives	0	1	2	3

REFERENCES

Azrin, N. H., Naster, B. J., & Jones, R. Reciprocity counselling: A rapid learning-based procedure for marital counselling. *Behaviour Research and Therapy,* 1973, *11*, 365–382.

Baucom, D. H. A comparison of behavioral contracting and problem-solving/communications training in behavioral marital therapy: A controlled outcome investigation. *Behavior Therapy,* 1982, *13,* 162–174.

Berlin, J. *Das offene Gespräch: Paare lernen Kommunikation* (Ein programmierter Kurs). Munich: Pfeiffer, 1975.

Boelens, W., Emmelkamp, P., MacGillavry, D., & Markvoort, M. A clinical evaluation of marital treatment: Reciprocity training vs. system-theoretic counseling. *Behavior Analysis and Modification,* 1980, *4,* 85–96.

Collins, J. D. Experimental evaluation of a six-months conjugal therapy and relationship enhancement program. In B. G. Guerney (Ed.), *Relationship enhancement.* San Francisco: Jossey-Bass, 1977.

Crowe, M. J. Conjoint marital therapy: A controlled outcome study. *Psychological Medicine,* 1978, *8,* 623–636.

Ely, A. L., Guerney, B. G., & Stover, L. Efficacy of conjugal therapy. *Psychotherapy: Theory, Research, and Practice,* 1973, *10,* 201–208.

Epstein, N., & Jackson, E. An outcome of short-term communication training with married couples. *Journal of Consulting and Clinical Psychology,* 1978, *46,* 207–212.

Friedman, A. S. Interaction of drug therapy with marital therapy in depressive patients. *Archives of General Psychiatry,* 1975, *32,* 619–637.

Guerney, B. G. (Ed.). *Relationship enhancement.* San Francisco: Jossey-Bass, 1977.

Gurman, A. S., & Kniskern, D. P. Research on marital and family therapy: Progress, perspective, and prospect. In S. L. Garfield & A. E. Bergin (Eds.), *Handbook of psychotherapy and behavior change* (2nd ed.). New York: Wiley, 1978.

Hahlweg, K. Konstruktion und Validierung des Partnerschaftsfragebogens PFB. *Zeitschrift für Klinische Psychologie,* 1979, *8*(1), 17–40.

Hahlweg, K., Helmes, B., Steffen, G., Schindler, L., Revenstorf, D., & Kunert, H. Beobachtungssystem für partnerschaftliche Interaktion. *Diagnostica,* 1979, *25,* 191–207.

Hahlweg, K., Kraemer, M., Schindler, L., & Revenstorf, D. Partnerschaftsprobleme: Eine empirische Analyse. *Zeitschrift für Klinische Psychologie,* 1980, *9,* 159–169.

Hahlweg, K., Schindler, L., & Revenstorf, D. *Partnerschaftsprobleme: Diagnose und Therapie* (Handbuch für den Therapeuten). Heidelberg: Springer Verlag, 1982. (a)

Hahlweg, K., Schindler, L., & Revenstorf, D. Treatment of marital distress: Comparing formats and modalities. *Advances in Behavior Research and Therapy,* 1982, *4,* 57–74. (b)

Hops, H., Wills, T. A., Patterson, G. R., & Weiss, R. L. *Marital Interaction Coding System.* Unpublished manuscript, University of Oregon, Oregon Research Institute, 1972. (Order from ASIS/NAPS, c/o Microfiche Publications, 305 E. 46th Street, New York, NY 10017.)

Jacobson, N. S. Problem-solving and contingency contracting in the treatment of marital discord. *Journal of Consulting and Clinical Psychology,* 1977, *45,* 92–100.

Jacobson, N. S. A review of the research on the effectiveness of marital therapy. In T. J. Paolino & B. S. McCrady (Eds.), *Marriage and marital therapy: Psychoanalytic, behavioral and systems theory perspectives.* New York: Brunner/Mazel, 1978. (a)

Jacobson, N. S. Specific and non-specific factors in the effectiveness of a behavioral approach to the treatment of marital discord. *Journal of Consulting and Clinical Psychology,* 1978, *46,* 442–452. (b)

Jacobson, N. S., & Margolin, G. *Marital therapy: Strategies based on social learning and behavior exchange principles.* New York: Brunner/Mazel, 1979.

Jacobson, N. S., & Weiss, R. L. Behavioral marriage therapy: III. The contents of Gurman *et al.* may be hazardous to our health. *Family Process,* 1978, *17,* 149–163.

Liberman, R. P., Levine, J., Wheeler, E., Sanders, N., & Wallace, C. J. Marital therapy in groups: A comparative evaluation of behavioral and interactional formats. *Acta Psychiatrica Scandinavica,* 1976, *266,* 3–34. (Suppl.)

Liberman, R. P., Wheeler, E., & Sanders, N. Behavioral therapy for marital disharmony: An educational approach. *Journal of Marriage and Family Counseling,* 1976, *2,* 383–395.

Locke, H. J., & Wallace, K. M. Short-term marital adjustment and prediction tests: Their reliability and validity. *Journal of Marriage and Family Living,* 1959, *21,* 251–255.

Luborsky, L., Singer, B., & Luborsky, L. Comparative studies of psychotherapies: Is it true that everyone has won and all must have prizes? *Archives of General Psychiatry,* 1975, *32,* 995–1008.

Margolin, G. Relationships among marital assessment procedures: A correlational study. *Journal of Consulting and Clinical Psychology,* 1978, *46,* 1556–1558.

Meichenbaum, D. *Cognitive behavior modification.* New York: Plenum Press, 1977.

O'Leary, K. D., & Turkewitz, H. Marital therapy from a behavioral perspective. In T. J. Paolino & B. S. McCrady (Eds.), *Marriage and marital therapy: Psychoanalytic, behavioral, and systems theory perspectives.* New York: Brunner/Mazel, 1978.

O'Leary, K. D., & Turkewitz, H. A comparative outcome study of behavioral marital therapy and communication training. *Journal of Marital and Family Therapy,* 1981, *7,* 159–169.

Olson, D. H., & Ryder, R. G. Inventory of Marital Conflicts (IMC): An experimental interaction procedure. *Journal of Marriage and the Family,* 1970, *32,* 443–448.

Patterson, G. R. *Some procedures for assessing changes in marital interaction patterns.* Oregon Research Institute Bulletin No. 16, 1976.

Pierce, R. M. Training in interpersonal communication skills with partners of deteriorating marriages. *Family Coordinator,* 1973, *22,* 223–227.

Rachman, S. J., & Wilson, G. T. *The effects of psychological therapy* (2nd ed.). Oxford: Pergamon Press, 1980.

Rappaport, A. F. Conjugal relationship enhancement program. In D. H. L. Olson (Ed.), *Treating relationships.* Lake Mills, IA: Graphic Press, 1976.

Revenstorf, D., Schindler, L., & Hahlweg, K. *Behavioral marital therapy in conjoint and conjoint-group modality: Short and long-term effectiveness. Behavior Therapy,* in press.

Schindler, L., Hahlweg, K., & Revenstorf, D. *Partnerschaftsprobleme: Möglichkeiten zur Bewältigung* (Ein verhaltenstherapeutisches Programm für Paare). Heidelberg: Springer Verlag, 1980.

Schindler, L., Hahlweg, K., & Revenstorf, D. *Short- and long-term effectiveness of two communication training modalities with distressed couples. American Journal of Family Therapy,* 1983, *11,* 54–64.

Smith, M. L., & Glass, G. V. Meta-analysis of psychotherapy outcome studies. *American Psychologist,* 1977, *32,* 752–760.

Stuart, R. B. An operant interpersonal program for couples. In D. H. L. Olson (Ed.), *Treating relationships.* Lake Mills, IA: Graphic Press, 1976.

Stuart, R. B., & Stuart, F. *Marital Pre-Counseling Inventory.* Champaign, IL: Research Press, 1973.

Terman, L. M. *Psychological factors in marital happiness.* New York: McGraw-Hill, 1938.

Weiss, R. L. Strategic behavioral therapy: Towards a model for assessment and intervention. In J. P. Vincent (Ed.), *Advances in family intervention, assessment and theory* (Vol. 1). Greenwich, CT: JAI Press, 1980.

Weiss, R. L., Hops, H., & Patterson, G. R. A framework for conceptualizing marital conflict, a technology for altering it, some data for evaluating it. In L. A. Hamerlynck, L. C. Handy, & E. J. Mash (Eds.), *Behavior change: Methodology, concepts, and practice.* Champaign, IL: Research Press, 1973.

Wieman, R. J. *Behavioral and Rogerian group marital therapy: A comparison.* Paper presented at the convention of the Association for Advancement of Behavior Therapy, New York, 1976.

Zimmer, D., Anneken, R., Echelmeyer, L., Kaluza, K., Klein, H., & Klockgeter-Kelle, A. Beschreibung und erste empirische Überprüfung eines Kommunikationstrainings für Paare. *DGVT-Mitteilungen,* 1977, *4,* 566–577.

2

On Maintaining Change in Behavioral Marital Therapy

INGO BÖGNER AND HILDEGARD ZIELENBACH-COENEN

How to maintain change is one of the basic concerns for any approach to therapy. The technology of behavior therapy (BT) today provides a considerable number of techniques capable of establishing meaningful changes in the short run. However, we still have to face difficulties in maintaining treatment success over an extended period of time (Hall & Hall, 1980).

This maintenance problem also applies to treating marital distress. In behavioral marital therapy (BMT) only 64% of the treated couples still benefit from treatment 1 year after therapy (see Hahlweg, Schindler, Revenstorf, & Brengelmann, Chapter 1, this volume), illustrating the need for innovations in the area of maintaining change.

There are several ways of extending the durability of change. In BMT one main strategy for fostering maintenance of change is the gradual shift from therapist control to self-management during the course of therapy. The concept is that couples increase expertise and autonomy during treatment, gaining the competence to cope with their own problems during and after therapy. "The sine qua non of successful problem-solving training is the couples' ability to use the skills independently of the therapist" (Jacobson & Margolin, 1979, p. 253). Philips and Johnson (1972) suggested that clients who cooperate in designing and carrying out the treatment are more motivated to change their behavior. Similarly, Davison (1979) demonstrated that clients who were involved in their own treatment planning were more likely to maintain therapy gains over time. Marital therapy must be designed to enable the partners to become modifiers of their own behavior. And as therapy proceeds, the couples have to develop confidence that they are able to solve their problems by themselves. A related strategy to enhance the durability of change is the development of specific interventions that can be added to the basic treatment approach (Kazdin & Wilson, 1978). For BMT an example of such a specific intervention is the cognitive treatment component "crisis management," described by Schindler and Vollmer (see Chapter 16, this volume).

Ingo Bögner and Hildegard Zielenbach-Coenen. Institute for Psychology, Free University of Berlin, Berlin, Federal Republic of Germany.

Apart from this, several studies suggest that booster sessions help maintain change (see Hall & Hall, 1980). These are usually brief versions of treatment sessions designed to provide additional support but not to introduce new treatment techniques.

Another strategy to enhance stability of treatment gains is to change the therapy time schedule either at the beginning or at the end of treatment. In the beginning of therapy it seems crucial to enhance the clients' hopes and confidence (Rosenthal, 1980). This can be achieved in part by more frequent or longer therapy sessions, especially during the learning phase of the communication skills or problem-solving components. This learning phase usually lasts for two or three sessions. This would lead to more rapid tackling of the clients' major problems and would subsequently enhance positive outcome expectations.

At the end of therapy it seems reasonable to change the time schedule in the opposite direction. In order to support the couples' competence to cope with their own problems after therapy, a "fading procedure" should be employed, scheduling the last sessions to be longer and to take place less frequently. Rosenthal (1980) noted that "the conventional 1-hour weekly session may be a tactical mistake" (p. 120). As one examines the BMT packages reported in the literature, one has to recognize that the issue of changing the time schedule has hitherto been neglected. For this reason the present study was designed in part to investigate the effects of the systematic inclusion of a fading procedure. In addition, this study serves as a replication of the BMT treatment package developed by Hahlweg, Schindler, and Revenstorf (1982; for the results, see Hahlweg *et al.*, Chapter 1, this volume). However, our main hypothesis is that the described changes in the time schedule will enhance the maintenance of treatment success.

Method

Design

Two experimental groups were used in the study: behavioral marital therapy (reciprocity training, or RT) in a conjoint format without fading (RTE) and with fading (RTEF). Furthermore, a waiting-list control group (WLCG) was included.

The study was designed to investigate the following questions:

1. Is RT more effective than a nontreatment waiting-list control group?

2. Are there any differences between the two approaches RTE and RTEF?

3. Are the treatment effects stable in the long run?

Measures

The following diagnostic instruments were used for measuring change: Problem List (PL; Hahlweg, Kraemer, Schindler, & Revenstorf, 1980), Partnership Questionnaire (PFB; Hahlweg, 1979), and the General Happiness Rating Scale (Terman, 1938). The questionnaires were given before and after therapy, after 2 months, and after 8 months (for a detailed description of the questionnaires, see Hahlweg *et al.*, Chapter 1, this volume).

Selection of Subjects

Couples were recruited through the newspapers *Der Tagesspiegel* and *Berliner Morgenpost*. They were accepted for the study if they complained mainly about a distressed relationship, both partners agreed to participate, they were between 22 and 45 years old, the duration of partnership was at least 1 year, they were living together, and they belonged to the middle class.

Demographic Characteristics of the Sample

Twenty-four couples participated in the study (RTE = 6, RTEF = 6, WLCG = 12). The mean age of the clients was 34.3 years. The couples had been married or had been living together for an average duration of 8.3 years. Married couples were 58.3% of the sample, and 54.2% had at least one child. All belonged to the middle class.

The average duration of distress was 3 years; 72.9% of the clients stated that they had a quarrel two or three times a week. In 66.7% of the cases discord lasted at least for 1 day and night. Only 33.3% were satisfied with their sexual lives.

In terms of demographic and personal characteristics, the randomization process was successful. Statistical analysis revealed no significant difference among the groups on variables such as age, length of partnership, marital status, frequency of quarrels, and sexual intercourse.

Procedure

The two authors served as therapists. Both were graduate students in psychology at the time, with 2 years of therapeutic experience.

Our therapeutic rationale is the same as that described by Hahlweg, Schindler, and Revenstorf (1982; see Hahlweg *et al.*, Chapter 1, this volume). In contrast to the Hahlweg *et al.* program at the Max-Planck-Institute (MPI), each of our Sessions 4–6 combined two of their sessions and lasted 1.5 hours each. Our Session 7 condensed the MPI's Sessions 10–13 to an intensive training session of 3.5 hours, in which the couples had conflict discussions and practiced contract management by themselves using the newly acquired skills. Through this extended duration of sessions the therapists were able to see whether the couples were capable of applying the acquired skills to find problem solutions on their own.

After Session 7 the RTEF couples had a break of 2 weeks in their training and another break of 3 weeks after Session 8 (see Table 2.1). Once a week we had phone contact with the couples for the sole purpose of receiving feedback on the homework assignments. If necessary the tasks were modified according to the individual needs of each couple. The RTE couples were seen on a weekly basis.

In Session 9 a final interview was held in which the couples were asked to provide feedback regarding the therapy. The couples were asked to return the completed questionnaires in the following week.

A follow-up (FU 1) contact of 1 hour took place 2 months after the end of training. A second follow-up (FU 2) contact took place 8 months after the

TABLE 2.1. Flow Chart of the Therapeutic Procedure

Sessions			Experimental group	
MPI study[a]	Present study	Content	RTE	RTEF
1	1	Initial interview	1st week	1st week
2	2	Interview, partner A	2nd week	2nd week
3	3	Interview, partner B		
4, 5	4	Rationale of therapy Positive reciprocity	3rd week	3rd week
6, 7	5	Speaker skills Listener skills	4th week	4th week
8, 9	6	Conflict discussions	5th week	5th week
10, 11, 12	7	Conflict discussions	6th week	6th week (2-week break)
13, 14	8	Crisis management	7th week	9th week (3-week break)
15	9	Final interview	8th week	13th week
		FU 1 contact	2 months after the end of training	2 months
		FU2 contact	8 months after the end of training	8 months

[a]Hahlweg et al. (1982).

TABLE 2.2. Means and Standard Deviations on Criterion Variables at Pretest, Posttest, FU 1, and FU 2

Variables	RTE				RTEF				WLCG	
	Pre	Post	FU 1	FU 2	Pre	Post	FU 1	FU 2	Pre	Post
PFB—Quarreling										
M	15.5	9.1	11.2	11.7	19.0	9.1	9.2	6.3	18.7	22.1
SD	3.6	3.9	4.4	6.3	5.4	2.0	1.9	4.2	4.2	3.6
PFB—Tenderness										
M	12.9	16.8	16.1	14.6	9.6	17.7	17.0	18.2	10.7	9.4
SD	4.6	4.3	3.5	6.5	4.2	3.3	4.8	5.8	2.1	2.5
PFB—Communication										
M	11.9	19.8	17.3	13.9	8.4	20.3	18.2	19.6	11.9	9.3
SD	6.2	3.7	4.4	5.4	4.4	4.5	4.9	7.2	4.0	3.3
PL—Conflict Score										
M	13.0	2.8	3.8	5.4	13.3	1.2	1.6	2.0	12.3	13.0
SD	0.3	2.4	1.7	3.8	1.6	0.6	0.8	0.7	1.6	0.9
General Happiness Rating Scale										
M	1.8	3.0	3.1	2.8	1.3	3.2	3.0	3.2	1.4	1.1
SD	0.4	0.0	0.5	1.0	0.5	0.3	0.6	0.8	0.6	0.6

end of training. The questionnaires were sent back by the couples the following week.

Results

Statistical Data Analysis

The following statistical methods were used: pretreatment comparison — one-way analysis and Duncan test; Posttreatment and FU 1 and 2 comparison — analysis of variance (ANOVA), with prescores as covariates. Couples were analyzed as units using the average husband–wife score. One-way analysis revealed no significant differences among the three groups on any of the variables at the beginning of therapy.

Table 2.2 presents the results for criterion variables, and Table 2.3 provides information on the significance tests.

Partnership Questionnaire (PFB)

QUARRELING

The ANOVA revealed highly significant overall differences among the groups, F (2, 20) = 89.4, p = .000. At posttest, couples in RTE and RTEF reported significantly less quarreling behavior as compared to the beginning of therapy, while couples in WLCG remained unchanged. RTEF couples reduced the quarreling score significantly more than couples in RTE. Analy-

TABLE 2.3. Significance Tests Regarding Pre, Post, FU 1, and FU 2: Comparison on the Criterion Variables

Variables	One-way, pre[a]	ANCOVA			t test (p)[b]			
		Post	FU 1	FU 2	RTE+RTEF/WLCG	RTEF/RTE	RTE	RTEF
PFB—Quarreling								
F	1.3	89.4	2.1	2.5				
p	0.30	0.000	0.18	0.15	2: 0.000	2: 0.05	1/3: 0.07 1/4: 0.09	1/3: 0.004 1/4: 0.01
PFB—Tenderness								
F	1.5	30.6	1.5	1.1				
p	0.24	0.000	0.25	0.33	2: 0.002	2: 0.02	1/3: 0.009 1/4: 0.40	1/3: 0.02 1/4: 0.07
PFB—Communication								
F	1.3	30.1	0.2	1.7				
p	0.31	0.000	0.71	0.22	2: 0.000	2: 0.17	1/3: 0.019 1/4: 0.44	1/3: 0.04 1/4: 0.05
PL—Conflict Score								
F	1.2	197.7	8.3	3.0				
p	0.33	0.000	0.18	0.11	2: 0.00	2: 0.05	1/3: 0.000 1/4: 0.005	1/3: 0.000 1/4: 0.000
General Happiness Rating Scale								
F	1.2	61.8	0.0	0.9				
p	0.31	0.000	0.89	0.38	2: 0.000	2: 0.02	1/3: 0.007 1/4: 0.021	1/3: 0.000 1/4: 0.005

[a]Degrees of freedom for one-way analysis and ANCOVA post = 2.20; for ANCOVA FU 1 and 2, df = 1.9.

[b]t test: 2 = Post; 1/3 = Pre/FU 1; 1/4 = Pre/FU 2. df for 1/3 and 1/4 = 5; df for 2 = 2, 20.

sis of covariance was not significant at either follow-up. Intragroup analysis showed that RTEF couples remained stable while RTE couples relapsed to pretest level.

TENDERNESS

The ANOVA was highly significant, F (2, 20) = 30.6, p = .000. After therapy, clients in RTE and RTEF reported significantly more tenderness behavior as compared with the beginning of therapy, while clients in WLCG remained unchanged. RTEF couples reported significantly more tenderness behavior than the couples in RTE. The ANOVA was not significant at either follow-up. RTE and RTEF couples remained stable at FU 1, while at FU 2 they relapsed to the pretest level.

COMMUNICATION

The ANOVA was highly significant, F (2, 20) = 30.1, p = .000. After therapy, couples in RTE and RTEF reported a significant increase in feeling of togetherness and communication, while WLCG couples remained unchanged. The ANOVA was not significant at either follow-up. RTE and RTEF couples remained stable at FU 1. At FU 2 only RTEF couples remained stable, while RTE clients relapsed to the pretest level.

PROBLEM LIST (PL)

The ANOVA revealed highly significant differences among the groups, F (2, 20) = 197.7, p = .000. After therapy, couples in RTE and RTEF reported significantly fewer problem areas as compared to the beginning of therapy, while the WLCG couples remained unchanged. RTEF couples reduced the conflict score significantly more than couples in RTE. The ANOVA was not significant at either follow-up. RTE and RTEF remained stable.

GENERAL HAPPINESS RATING SCALE

The ANOVA was highly significant, F (2, 20) = 61.8, p = .000. After therapy, couples in RTE and RTEF reported a significant increase in General Happiness Rating Scale scores, while couples in WLCG remained unchanged. Couples in RTEF improved significantly more than couples in RTE. The ANOVA was not significant at either follow-up. Couples in RTE and RTEF reported stable increases in General Happiness Rating Scale scores at FU 1 and FU 2 when compared to pretest scores. While the average RTEF couples scored in the normal range ($M \geq 3.0$), the average RTE couples scored in the unhappy range ($M \leq 2.8$) at FU 2.

Discussion and Summary

Couples that received reciprocity training showed substantial improvement after therapy as compared to the waiting-list control group on every one of the criterion variables. This is in line with the results of Hahlweg, Revenstorf, and Schindler (see Hahlweg *et al.*, Chapter 1, this volume) and represents a successful replication of their findings. Regarding the two formats, RTEF was significantly superior to RTE on all variables except the PFB variable Communication at postmeasurement. However, there were no significant differences between the two formats at follow-up (FU 1 and 2). Intragroup analysis revealed that RTEF couples remained stable at both FUs when compared to prescore level on all variables except Tenderness at FU 2 (significant at 10% level). Up to FU 1, RTE remained stable, too, except for Quarreling on the PFB. At FU 2, RTE couples relapsed on the variables Quarreling, Tenderness, and Communication, remaining stable only on the PL Conflict Score and the General Happiness Rating Scale.

The nonsignificant comparisons at both FUs may be due to the relatively small number of couples in both experimental groups. Inspection of the means shows a superiority of RTEF on all variables after therapy and at both follow-ups. Additional statistical analysis using the individual scores as the unit of analysis showed that RTEF was significantly superior to RTE on all variables at all time points, giving support to the small-number hypothesis.

Relying on these results, one can conclude that the situational modifications of the therapy process did, in fact, yield better short- and long-term results. Taking the clinical impression into account, it seems that shortening the learning period and simultaneously intensifying the acquisition of new skills by prolonging the sessions did, in fact, enhance the clients' hopes and confidence. Unfortunately we did not assess these changes in a standardized way, so no data are available to support our impression that the heightened positive outcome expectations led to an increased willingness of the couples to make use of the newly learned skills in their natural environment. The fading procedure worked well, too, in enhancing the couples' competence.

The three modifications — variations of the time schedule, shortening of the learning period, and fading of external (therapist) control — seem to be worthwhile for implementation in BMT, and they should be tested in further experiments.

REFERENCES

Davison, G. Systematic desensitization as a counterconditioning process. In A. P. Goldstein & F. H. Kanfer (Eds.), *Maximizing treatment gains: Transfer enhancement in psychotherapy.* New York: Academic Press, 1979.

Hahlweg, K. Konstruktion und Validierung des Partnerschaftsfragebogens PFB. *Zeitschrift für Klinische Psychologie,* 1979, *8,* 17–40.

Hahlweg, K., Kraemer, M., Schindler, L., & Revenstorf, D. Partnerschaftsprobleme: Eine emprische Analyse. *Zeitschrift für Klinische Psychologie*, 1980, *9,* 159–169.

Hahlweg, K., Schindler, L., & Revenstorf, D. *Partnerschaftsprobleme: Diagnose und Therapie. Handbuch für den Therapeuten.* Heidelberg: Springer Verlag, 1982.

Hall, S. M., & Hall, R. G. Maintaining change. In J. M. Ferguson & C. B. Taylor (Eds.), *The comprehensive handbook of behavioral medicine* (Vol. 3). New York: SP Medical and Scientific Books, 1980.

Jacobson, N. S., & Margolin, G. *Marital therapy: Strategies based on social learning and behavior exchange principles.* New York: Brunner/Mazel, 1979.

Kazdin, A. E., & Wilson, G. T. *Evaluation of behavior therapy: Issues, evidence, and research strategies.* Cambridge, MA: Ballinger, 1978.

Philips, R., & Johnson, G. Self-administered systematic desensitization. *Behaviour Research and Therapy,* 1972, *10*, 93–96.

Rosenthal, T. L. Social cueing process. In M. Hersen, R. M. Eisler, & R. M. Miller (Eds.), *Progress in behavior modification* (Vol. 10). New York: Academic Press, 1980.

Terman, L. M. *Psychological factors in marital happiness.* New York: McGraw-Hill, 1938.

3

Marital Therapy with Clinically Distressed Couples: A Comparative Evaluation of System-Theoretic, Contingency Contracting, and Communication Skills Approaches

PAUL EMMELKAMP, MIEKE VAN DER HELM, DONALD MACGILLAVRY, AND BERENDIEN VAN ZANTEN

Behavior therapy has shown promise in treating marital problems (Jacobson, 1979), although others argue that this promise is as yet unfulfilled. For example, Gurman and Kniskern (1978) state that the superiority of social learning approaches has not been established. Many behavioral studies have to be discounted since they used nonclinical analogue demonstrations with minimally distressed couples. The generalizability of such studies is open to question.

To date, very few controlled studies have been reported that compared behavioral marital therapy with a nonbehavioral approach, using real clinical patients as subjects. Crowe (1978) compared (1) behavioral marital therapy, (2) an interpretative approach, and (3) a supportive (control) approach. The behavioral approach was found to be the most effective. However, several methodological confounds limit the conclusions that can be drawn. First, the behavioral therapy consisted of a mixture of reciprocity training and sex therapy along the lines of Masters and Johnson (1970); the package actually applied varied from couple to couple. Thus, the relative contribution of the different procedures cannot be determined. Second, most couples were treated by the author, which might have contaminated the results. In the Liberman, Levine, Wheeler, Sanders, and Wallace (1976) study, behavioral group therapy was found to be more effective than an interaction–insight-oriented group treatment on behavioral measures only. The behavioral group

Paul Emmelkamp, Mieke van der Helm, Donald MacGillavry, and Berendien van Zanten. Department of Clinical Psychology, Academic Hospital, Groningen, The Netherlands.

therapy consisted of both communication skills training and contingency contracting, thus precluding conclusions regarding each procedure on its own. One major limitation of the Liberman *et al.* (1976) study is the small number of couples used ($n = 9$); each condition contained one group only.

This chapter reports on a research program investigating the efficacy of various marital treatment programs conducted in The Netherlands. In a series of studies we evaluated the relative contribution of contingency contracting, communication skills training, and system-theoretic counseling. An important feature is that only severely distressed couples were used as subjects: All couples were referred to our department by a community mental health center for treatment of their relationship.

Study 1: Contingency Contracting versus System-Theoretic Counseling

Since the first study has already been published (Boelens, Emmelkamp, MacGillavry, & Markvoort, 1980), the main findings are only briefly summarized here. Twenty-one couples were randomly allocated to three different conditions: eight received reciprocity counseling, eight received system-theoretic counseling, and five received no treatment. Advanced clinical psychology students, who were extensively trained, served as therapists.

Assessment and Treatment

Assessment included self-report (Maudsley Marital Questionnaire — MMQ, Marital Deprivation Scale — MDS, and Main Target Problems) and direct behavioral observation (Marital Interaction Coding System — MICS). In addition , an assessor, who was blind with respect to the treatment that couples received, rated the couples on (1) affective relationship, (2) marital distress, and (3) problem-solving skill on rating scales with a range of 1 to 5.

The reciprocity counseling treatment followed the format used by Azrin, Naster, and Jones (1973) and involved contracting training. Partners established specific behavioral commitments for self and other, and compromised with each other. It is important to note that communication skills training was not part of the treatment.

The system-theoretic counseling involved a structured therapy. The goal of this treatment program was to provide partners with insight into their overt or covert power struggles, assuming this insight to lead to a change in interaction and communication patterns (details are given later). Neither contingency contracting nor communication skills training was part of this counseling procedure.

Treatment in both conditions consisted of 10 sessions, each lasting 60 minutes. Treatment was conducted twice a week for the first 2 weeks, and further sessions were held once a week. The waiting-list control group had no contact with the therapist during this period.

Assessments were conducted at pretest, posttest, and at 1- and 6-month follow-ups.

Results

The results on self-report scales are summarized in Figure 3.1. Both treatment groups improved on the MMQ, MDS, and the Main Target Problems, in contrast to couples from the waiting-list control group. The improvement was maintained 6 months after the posttest, although a relapse was found for some couples of the system-theoretic counseling group 1 month after treatment. In contrast, the patients who received contingency contracting continued to improve. The relapse of some system-theoretic-counseled couples at 1-month follow-up suggests that insight into the interaction pattern alone is insufficient. To give an impression of the clinical status, degree of improvement was defined as amount of change in Main Target Problem scores, with more than 50% change as much improved, between 25% and 50% change as moderately

FIGURE 3.1. Mean scores on self-reports (○ = reciprocity counseling; X = system-theoretic counseling; ● = waiting-list control).

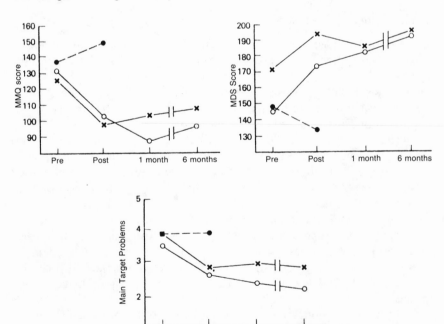

improved, and less than 25% change as no change. At 6-month follow-up one couple in the reciprocity counseling condition showed no change, four were moderately improved, and three were rated as much improved. The results for system-theoretic counseling were less positive: Two couples were divorced, two showed no change, two were moderately improved, and two were much improved.

Although the MICS revealed a significant between-group difference on positive social reinforcement between treatment conditions and controls, no significant within-group changes were found. The lack of significant improvement on this measure might be due to the fact that patients had to discuss hypothetical problems from the Inventory of Marital Conflicts (IMC; Olson & Ryder, 1970) rather than their own problems. In addition, the lack of improvement on this measure may be attributed to not having practiced communication skills during treatment.

Study 2: Contingency Contracting versus Communication Skills Training

Many of the behavioral programs reported in the literature have combined elements from contingency contracting and communication skills training. As stated by Luber (1978), "These models seem to be largely subjective, random combinations apparently based on the assumption that since each method has accumulated some independent validation they should be effective in union" (p. 86). Several authors suggest that contingency contracting should be used prior to communication training (e.g., Stuart, 1975; Weiss, Hops, & Patterson, 1973). Others, however, support the use of communication skills training as a prerequisite to the implementation of contingency contracting (e.g., Rappaport & Harrel, 1975). Some (e.g., Jacobson, 1978; and Liberman et al., 1976) have even questioned the viability of contingency contracting as a treatment strategy. Liberman et al. suggest that "contingency contracting is worth just about the paper it's printed on without the family members having adequate interpersonal communication skills" (p. 32). To date, only one study with clinically distressed couples compared communication training and behavioral exchange directly (O'Leary & Turkewitz, 1978). No significant differences between treatment conditions were found.

The present study was undertaken to investigate the relative contribution of contingency contracting and communication skills training. Since we were not only interested in the effects of each procedure on its own, but also in the interactional effects when they are joined in package treatment approaches, a cross-over design was used. This means that all couples were treated with both contingency contracting and communication training, but the order of treatment was randomly varied. Thus, after the pretest one group of couples received contingency contracting and one received communication skills training. The effect was measured (intermediate test), and then a second period of treatment followed, but now with each group being given the treatment that the other group had first received. In toto, treatment consisted of 14 sessions, seven contingency contracting and seven communication skills sessions. Assessments were repeated at posttest and at 1-month and 12-month follow-ups.

Patients

All couples were referred by a community mental health center for treatment of their marital problems. Couples were accepted for the study unless the main complaint consisted of a sexual dysfunction or one of them was psychotic or addicted to drugs. In addition, partners had to be living together for the time of treatment, though not necessarily married.

A total of 23 couples met these criteria. They were randomly assigned to treatment groups. In the course of treatment several couples dropped out for a variety of reasons: One left treatment due to a traffic accident; in another couple the man was admitted to a psychiatric hospital; one couple dropped out since they found their relationship already improved as a result of the treatment; two couples decided to live apart; and for another couple treatment did not meet their expectations. Thus 17 couples completed the project. The mean age of the participating couples was 31.4 years (range: 22–48); couples had been living together on the average for 8.7 years (range: 1.5–26). The mean number of children was 1.5 (range: 0–3). The mean occupational level was slightly above modal.

Therapists

Four advanced clinical psychology students served as therapists (two male, two female). Each couple was treated by one therapist. All therapists were versed in behavior therapy, three of them having 2 years of clinical experience in conducting behavior therapy with individual patients. Before the start of the project, therapists were extensively trained in the treatment procedures to be used. Therapists were supervised by the senior author.

Measures

SELF-REPORT MEASURES

All self-report measures were filled in by both partners, independently of each other.

Maudsley Marital Questionnaire. The MMQ is a 20-item questionnaire relating to marital, sexual, and general life adjustment. This questionnaire was based upon the Marital Adjustment Scale of Crowe (1978). All questions were rated on a 0–8 scale. Scores range from 0 to 160, high scores indicating marital dysfunction.

Marital Deprivation Scale. The MDS (Frenken, 1976) is a version, adapted for use in The Netherlands, of the Marital Evaluation Scale of Schutz (1967). The scores of three of the four subscales were added up and considered as one score. The three scales measure: (1) the Need for Inclusion Behavior, (2) the Need for Inclusion Feeling, and (3) the Need for Affection Behavior and Feelings. The score range is 27–135, high scores indicating low marital deprivation.

Main Target Problems. Both partners had to formulate three main marital problems and to score these on rating scales with a range of 1 to 5. The three scores were summed and divided by three. Scores range from 1 to 5, a high score indicating severe problems.

DIRECT BEHAVIORAL OBSERVATION

Both partners had to solve their own problems. Due to technical faults most of the videotapes could not be coded. Thus, the results on this measure could not be processed in the data analysis. All self-report measures were filled in at the pretest, intermediate test, posttest, follow-up 1, and follow-up 2.

Procedure

Upon arrival a 60-minute interview was conducted by the therapist. This interview was held to provide the therapist with information regarding the main marital problems and to delineate three target problems in the relationship, which both partners had to rate. After the interview the videotaped behavioral interaction test took place. Finally, the MDS, the MMQ, and a questionnaire concerning demographic characteristics were completed. For both the reciprocity counseling group and the communication training group, seven sessions of treatment followed, each session lasting 60 minutes. Treatment was conducted once a week. At the intermediate test the MDS and MMQ were readministered. In addition, couples had to rate their target problems. After another seven treatment sessions the posttest was held. One month after the posttest an appointment was made for a follow-up interview. Upon arrival both partners completed the Main Target Problems, MMQ and MDS. Then a conference with the therapist was held. Couples did not receive treatment between posttest and follow-up 1. Each couple was sent a packet containing two forms of the Main Target Problems, MMQ, and MDS, 1 year following the posttest. Two couples did not return the completed questionnaires; both couples no longer lived together.

Treatment

RECIPROCITY COUNSELING

Treatment followed the format used by Azrin *et al.* (1973). The first session was designed to provide the therapist with further information regarding the couple's problems and to explain the treatment rationale to the couple. At the end of the session the couple received the Reciprocity Awareness Procedure as a homework assignment. Each partner separately had to list at least 10 satisfactions he/she was currently providing to the partner and at least 10 satisfactions that the partner was providing to him/her.

In addition, the couple received the Perfect Marriage Procedure as a homework assignment: Couples were instructed to list the type of interactions that would constitute their idea of a perfect marriage for the problem areas of the Marital Happiness Scale (MHS). Finally, couples were instructed to fill out the MHS each evening, independently from each other, and then to discuss their scores. Both partners had to rate (score: 1–10) the following areas: (1) household responsibilities, (2) rearing of children, (3) social activities, (4) money, (5) communication, (6) sex, (7) work, (8) personal independence, (9) spouse independence, and (10) general marital happiness.

At the start of the second and each following session, the MHS was discussed. In the second session the listing of satisfactions (Reciprocity Awareness Procedure) was dealt with. Sessions 2 to 7 were devoted to contracting training. Partners established specific behavioral commitments for self and other and compromised with each other. As in the study by Azrin *et al.* (1973), the couple had to sign the contract, which stated that if one did not meet his/her agreements, then the other partner would discontinue doing all satisfactions for a 24-hour period. This would start the next day if satisfactions had not been obtained by that time. All problem areas of the MHS were dealt with during treatment. In order to prepare the couple for independent functioning, a fading procedure was used: In the first few areas the therapist actively assisted in the negotiating process, while in the last few sessions the couple had to compromise in their home. Their contracts were discussed with the therapist in the following sessions. Communication skills training was not part of the treatment.

COMMUNICATION SKILLS TRAINING

Treatment focused on ways to improve communication between spouses. Couples were taught skills that enabled them to talk with each other more effectively. Treatment sessions were semistandardized. Approximately half of the time was devoted to structured exercises such as listening and empathy training, spontaneous expressing of feelings, and assertiveness. One session focused on ways to improve communication between partners regarding the exchange of physical affection. The second half of each session consisted of discussing a couple's own marital conflicts (problem-solving training). Modeling, feedback, shaping, and behavior rehearsal were used throughout treatment. Patients received homework assignments.

Results

The data of the 15 patients who completed the 1-year follow-up were processed in the data analysis. For the statistical analyses, scores for husbands and wives were combined: In all analyses couples were considered as units.

The results on the self-report scales are depicted in Figures 3.2, 3.3, and 3.4. The data were analyzed using a two-way multivariate analysis of variance design. The main effect of time was significant. No significant between-group effect was found. The interaction treatment/time was also nonsignificant. Thus, both contingency contracting and communication skills training were found to be equally effective, and the order in which the treatments were given had no statistical effects.

Multivariate orthogonal polynomial trend analyses revealed an overall significant linear trend $-F(3, 11) = 14.5$, $p < .0004$ — which was also reflected in two of the univariate F ratios, MDS $-F(1, 13) = 14.4$, $p < .002$, and Target Problems $- F(1, 13) = 22.1$, $p < .0005$. For all measures a significant univariate quadratic trend was found: MMQ $-F(1, 13) = 14.2$, $p < .002$; MDS $-F(1, 13) = 19.5$, $p < .0008$; and Target Problems $-F(1, 13) = 58.7$, $p < .0001$. This means that both groups improved until the posttest; then the improvement remained relatively stable.

FIGURE 3.2. Mean scores on the Main Target Problems, Study 2.

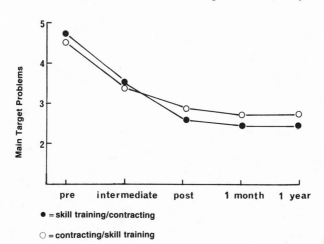

● = skill training/contracting

○ = contracting/skill training

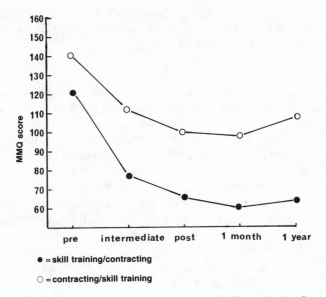

● = skill training/contracting

○ = contracting/skill training

FIGURE 3.3. Mean scores on the Maudsley Marital Questionnaire, Study 2.

FIGURE 3.4. Mean scores on the Marital Deprivation Scale, Study 2.

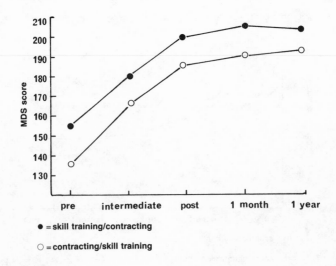

● = skill training/contracting

○ = contracting/skill training

Discussion

The effects of contingency contracting and social skills training were broadly comparable. Further, there is evidence to support neither the idea that communication skills training should precede contingency contracting nor the idea that contingency contracting should be used prior to communication training. Taken together, the present results and those of our first study demonstrate that contingency contracting on its own is a powerful therapeutic procedure for clinically distressed couples.

For ethical reasons no control group was used in the present study. In our first study, a waiting-list control group was used. Results of that study indicated that there was a trend to deterioration, and several couples dropped out during the period in which they did not receive treatment. Since the same measures were employed in the second study, there was no reason to include a no-treatment control group.

Study 3: System-Theoretic Counseling versus Communication Skills Training

In our first study we found no difference between system-theoretic counseling and contingency contracting in the short term, although some relapse was noted in the system-theoretic counseling group at follow-up. Our third study was an attempt to compare communication skills training and system-theoretic counseling, and the interaction between these treatment formats. The relapse of some of the couples after system-theoretic counseling found in the first study suggested that insight into the interaction pattern alone is insufficient, and we wondered whether communication skills training would enhance the effectiveness of the system-theoretic approach. Couples were treated in a cross-over design, with seven sessions of communication skills training and seven sessions of system-theoretic counseling. The order of the treatment was randomly varied. Assessments took place at pretest, intermediate test, post-test, and 1-month follow-up.

Patients

All couples were referred by a community mental health center for treatment of their marital problems. Couples were accepted for the study according to the same criteria as used in our previous studies. Age, duration of relationship, number of children, and occupational level were comparable to those in Study 1 and Study 2.

Therapists

Five advanced clinical psychology students who had some clinical experience served as therapists (three male, two female). Each couple was treated by one therapist. Therapists were extensively trained in the counseling procedures. The training of the communication skills program was conducted together with the therapists, who used this treatment in the second study. Therapists were supervised by a system-theoretic-oriented therapist (D.M.)

Measures and Procedure

The measures and procedure were the same as used in Study 2 (MMQ, MDS, and Main Target Problems). All self-report scales were filled in at pretest, posttest, and 1-month follow-up.

Treatment

COMMUNICATION SKILLS TRAINING
Treatment followed the format used in Study 2.

SYSTEM-THEORETIC COUNSELING
A structured relationship therapy was developed based upon system-theoretic theories (MacGillavry, 1979, 1981). The goal of this treatment format is to provide partners a reinterpretation of their overt or covert power struggles, assuming these cognitions to lead to a change in interaction and communication patterns. It is assumed that every distressed marital relationship is characterized by an ongoing power struggle over who defines the nature of this relationship. This power struggle arises when partners cannot reach agreement about their definition of the relationship in terms of equivalence or when the marital system fails to accommodate to a changed situation. Power struggles may also be the result of the wish of only one of the partners to change the relationship concerning a rearrangement of tasks, autonomous behavior, or other issues.

Typically, maritally distressed people neglect their own actions and focus only on the faults of their partners. In the system-theoretic approach, partners are instructed to think in terms of circular processes. It is explained to the couple that communication occurs at two levels: (1) report and (2) command. The command aspect of communication refers to the interpretation of the message. Throughout the therapy the command aspects of communication are clarified by the therapist as indications of power struggles and are relabeled as inadequate attempts to redefine the nature of the relationship. Spouses are urged to talk and respond to each other without addressing the therapist. Spouses are requested to communicate on the report level while exchanging feelings and opinions and while deliberating. It is explained to the couple that only if the command level of communication is omitted from their conversation will there be a real possibility to clarify power struggles and to readjust their relationship based upon the acknowledgment of each other's identity.

It is assumed that people relate to each other in a complementary, symmetrical, or parallel manner. Each interaction style can be communicated in a clear or unclear way, resulting in an overt or covert power struggle. Typically, people are unaware of the style in which messages are exchanged. Since a covert power struggle prevents one or both partners from working out the relationship problem, the first target of this treatment approach is to open up the power struggle into an overt recognition of what is going on. In the first session the treatment rationale is explained with the aid of the Interaction-Style Scheme, in which the various interaction styles and communication levels are shown. In the second and further sessions the couple's conflicts within or between sessions are analyzed and translated into the scheme. In order to accomplish this goal, two instructions are given:

1. The spouses have to monitor their conflicts and the accompanying incidents carefully in order to report them as accurately as possible in the next session. Conflicts and incidents are labeled by the therapist as characteristic for their relationship and as instructive material to be used in the session.

2. The spouses have to point out in the Interaction-Style Scheme, at first with the help of the therapist but gradually on their own, why and how, in their opinion, interaction and communication faults have occurred.

An Example. Power struggles between Mr. and Mrs. A apparently had their origin in emancipatory action of the wife, which had started some time ago. Working with the Interaction-Style Scheme, the couple learned that the needs of Mrs. A would irrevocably lead to a change in the complementary relationship in the direction of a more symmetrical (autonomous) and parallel (primarily based upon the need for deliberation) one. At the same time the couple learned that such a change in their relationship would mean an increase of autonomous behavior, on the side of the wife; and loss of control as well as a decreased ability to predict the wife's behavior, on the side of the husband.

The man was instructed (also as homework) to replace his tendency for management and coaching on several occasions without letting his wife know that he was doing this. Mrs. A was assigned to register these occasions without asking her husband or trying to question him. Mr. A was also asked to register to what extent his homework and that of his wife increased his fear of loss of control and unpredictability concerning his wife's behavior. After reporting on their assignments in the following session, the couple was instructed to talk about their feelings related to the homework assignments.

Homework. What kind of homework should be given depends on those circular processes that are typical for the couple and are displayed either during the sessions or at home, based on their reports of conflicts and incidents. Homework should aim at the promotion of new patterns of interactions so as to make the old ways of negative interaction impossible (see the preceding example). A change of relationship is attainable when negative circular processes can be stopped or replaced by positive ones, when inadequate equilibria can be broken, and when negative feedback mechanisms can be replaced by positive ones.

There are several important differences between system-theoretic counseling as used here and communication skills training. In system-theoretic counseling the interventions of the therapist are primarily directed to changing faulty interaction patterns. Although the therapist devotes attention to unproductive communication during the interview, especially power struggles, no systematic communication training is provided. In contrast to the behavioral communication skills training, coaching, behavior rehearsal, and modeling are not part of the treatment.

Further, the homework assignments used were not based on contractual agreements between the partners but were prescribed by the therapist based upon an understanding of their relationship style. Understanding of the relationship style on the part of the couple was not a prerequisite for the assignments of homework. In a number of cases paradoxical instructions were given to accomplish a change in relationship style.

Results

Figures 3.5, 3.6, and 3.7 show the results of treatment. The data were analyzed using a two-way multivariate analysis of variance design. The main effect of time was significant. No significant between-group effect was found. The interaction treatment time was also nonsignificant. Thus, both treatments resulted in comparable effects, and the sequence did not affect treatment outcome.

Multivariate orthogonal polynomial trend analysis revealed an overall significant linear trend $-F(3, 11) = 11.07$, $p < .001$ — which was also reflected in all univariate F ratios. Further, a multivariate quadratic trend was found — $F(3, 8) = 3.79$, $p < .06$. The results indicate that treatment led to improvement until the posttest. No further changes were found between posttest and follow-up.

Discussion

The most important finding of this study is that communication skills training and system-theoretic counseling are about equally effective. The present results corroborate the finding of our first study, in which no difference was

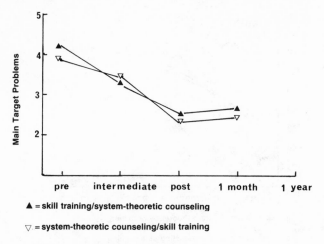

FIGURE 3.5. Mean scores on the Main Target Problems, Study 3.

FIGURE 3.6. Mean scores on the Maudsley Marital Questionnaire, Study 3.

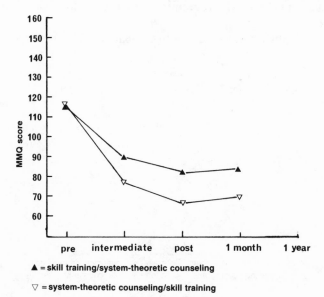

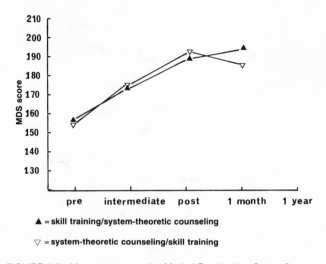

▲ = skill training/system-theoretic counseling

▽ = system-theoretic counseling/skill training

FIGURE 3.7. Mean scores on the Marital Deprivation Scale, Study 3.

found between system-theoretic counseling and another behavioral procedure: contingency contracting. The designs of the second and third study were comparable, in order to enable cross-study comparison (see Table 3.1). A statistical comparison of the data of Study 2 and Study 3 revealed no significant differences among the three treatment formats: contingency contracting, communication skills training, and system-theoretic counseling. Thus, the overall conclusion of our research program must be that all have won and all must have prizes.

A disadvantage of between-group comparisons as presented here is that

TABLE 3.1. Design of Study 2 And Study 3

	Pre	Intermediate			Post	1-month follow-up	1-year follow-up
R	T_1	X_1	T_2	X_2	T_3	T_4	T_5
R	T_1	X_2	T_2	X_1	T_3	T_4	T_5
R	T_1	X_1	T_2	X_1	T_3	T_4	
R	T_1	X_3	T_2	X_1	T_3	T_4	

Note. R = random assignment, T = test, X_1 = communication skills training, X_2 = contracting training, and X_3 = system-theoretic counseling.

it is unclear whether the same couples profit from both behavioral and system-theoretic procedures. Rather than continuing comparative studies, there is now a clear need for studies that address the issue of matching individual needs of patients to particular treatments. Who are the failures in behavioral and system-theoretic counseling? Do patients who fail with behavioral approaches also fail with system-theoretic counseling and vice versa? Are there specific patient characteristics related to success or failure with the various approaches? These seem to us important questions for further research.

ACKNOWLEDGMENTS

The authors wish to thank D. Debats, A. Kilsdonk, A. Meijer, R. Meijer, I. Plochg, and H. de Vries, who served as therapists. Particular acknowledgment goes to B. Pijl, who conducted the data analysis of Study 3 and made valuable suggestions on the statistical analysis of the data of Study 2.

REFERENCES

Azrin, N. H., Naster, B. J., & Jones, R. Reciprocity counselling: A rapid learning-based procedure for marital counselling. *Behaviour Research and Therapy*, 1973, *11*, 365–382.

Boelens, W., Emmelkamp, P., MacGillavry, D., & Markvoort, M. A clinical evaluation of marital treatment: Reciprocity counseling versus system-theoretic counseling. *Behavioural Analysis and Modification*, 1980, *4*, 85–96.

Crowe, M. J. Conjoint marital therapy: A controlled outcome study. *Psychological Medicine*, 1978, *8*, 623–636.

Frenken, J. O. C. M. *Afkeer van sexualiteit*. Deventer: Van Loghem Slaterus, 1976.

Gurman, A. S., & Kniskern, D. P. Behavioral marriage therapy: II. Empirical perspective. *Family Process*, 1978, *17*, 139–149.

Jacobson, N. S. Specific and nonspecific factors in the effectiveness of a behavioral approach to the treatment of marital discord. *Journal of Consulting and Clinical Psychology*, 1978, *46*, 442–452.

Jacobson, N. S. Behavioral treatments for marital discord. In M. Hersen, R. M. Eisler, & P. M. Miller (Eds.), *Progress in behavior modification* (Vol. 8). New York: Academic Press, 1979.

Liberman, R. P., Levine, J., Wheeler, E., Sanders, N., & Wallace, C. J. Marital therapy in groups: A comparative evaluation of behavioral and interactional formats. *Acta Psychiatrica Scandinavica*, 1976, *266*, 3–34. (Suppl.)

Luber, R. F. Teaching models in marital therapy: A review and research issues. *Behavior Modification*, 1978, *2*, 77–91.

MacGillavry, D. H. D. *Buigen, barsten of bijstellen*. Rotterdam: Donker, 1979.

MacGillavry, D. H. D. *Zolang de kruik te water gaat*. Rotterdam: Donker, 1981.

Masters, W. H., & Johson, V. *Human sexual inadequacy*. Boston: Little, Brown, 1970.

O'Leary, K. D., & Turkewitz, H. The treatment of marital disorders from a behavioral perspective. In T. J. Paolino & B. S. McCrady (Eds.), *Marriage and marital therapy: Psychoanalytic, behavioral, and systems theory perspectives*. New York: Brunner/Mazel, 1978.

Olson, D. H., & Ryder, R. G. Inventory of Marital Conflict (IMC): An experimental interaction procedure. *Journal of Marriage and the Family*, 1970, *32*, 443–448.

Rappaport, A. F., & Harrel, J. A behavioral exchange model for marital counseling. In A. S. Gurman & D. G. Rice (Eds.), *Couples in conflict*. New York: Aronson, 1975.

Schutz, W. C. *MATE, a FIRO scale: Husband's form, wife's form.* Palo Alto: University of
    California Press, 1967.
Stuart, R. B. Behavioral remedies for marital ills: A guide to the use of operant interpersonal
    techniques. In A. S. Gurman & D. G. Rice (Eds.), *Couples in conflict.* New York: Aronson,
    1975.
Weiss, R. L., Hops, H., & Patterson, G. R. A framework for conceptualizing marital conflict,
    a technology for altering it, some data for evaluating it. In L. A. Hamerlynck, L. C. Handy,
    & E. J. Mash (Eds.), *Behavior change: Methodology, concepts, and practice.* Champaign,
    IL: Research Press, 1973.

4

The Analysis of Therapist Intervention in Three Contrasted Approaches to Conjoint Marital Therapy

M. J. CROWE

Introduction

The field of content or process analysis in family and marital therapy is a fairly new one (Pinsof, 1980), and few studies of therapist activity (as opposed to family or marital interaction) have been published. The work reported here was carried out as part of a study into the efficacy of three contrasted approaches to conjoint marital therapy, which has been published elsewhere (Crowe, 1978). As part of the study, audiotape recordings of the therapy sessions were made and analyzed both as to the content of therapist interventions and to see if the sessions could be distinguished by blind raters as to which type of therapy was being carried out. This content analysis was an essential part of the study, since the only difference among treatment conditions was in the type of therapy being administered, and it was therefore necessary to check that the therapists' activity was indeed distinguishable among the different approaches.

The Outcome Study in Summary

In order to show the necessity for content analysis, an outline of the methodology of the outcome study is given here. Forty-two couples were randomly assigned to one of three types of conjoint marital therapy. One approach was behavioral or directive (D), another was group-analytic/interpretative (I), and the third (the control procedure) was a nonactive or supportive approach (S). There was no untreated control group. Fourteen couples received each approach. The couples were treated for 10 weekly 1-hour sessions of the assigned therapy. Assessment, which was by self-report and by blind assessor rating, took place before therapy, at two points during therapy, at the termination

M. J. Crowe. Consultant Psychiatrist, Maudsley Hospital, London, United Kingdom.

of therapy, and at three points during follow-up (3, 9, and 18 months after termination). The results of the outcome study are summarized in Table 4.1. Analysis was by multivariate analysis of variance, supported by t tests on the change scores, and Table 4.1 shows both the changes within treatment conditions and the differences among treatment conditions during therapy and at follow-up.

The directive treatment produced significant changes on all measures and showed significant superiority to the control procedure, both after treatment and at follow-up, in sexual and general adjustment and in target problem measures. The interpretative treatment produced significant changes on marital and target problems measures only (both after treatment and at follow-up), but it showed significant superiority to the control procedure only at 9-month follow-up on two measures (marital adjustment and global assessment of improvement). The control procedure also produced significant changes on marital and target problem measures after treatment and at some follow-up points, but it was superior to the interpretative approach on only one measure (that of neurotic symptoms at 3-month follow-up) and was never superior to the directive approach.

TABLE 4.1. Summary of Ratings on Major Adjustment Measures

Measure	Stage of treatment or follow-up					
	3 sessions	6 sessions	Posttreatment	3 months	6 months	18 months
Measures that showed significant change from pretreatment scores[a]						
Marital	– I –	D I S	D I S	D I S	D I –	D I –
Sexual	D – –	D – –	D – –	– – –	D – –	D – –
General	– – –	D – –	D – –	D – –	D – –	D – –
Target A	D I S	D I S	D I S	D I S	D I S	D I S
Target B	D I S	D I S	D I S	D I S	D I S	D I S
Measures in which there were significant differences among treatment groups[a]						
Marital	– – –	– – –	– –	– – –	D > S I > S	D > S
Sexual	D > S	D > S	D > S	– – –	D > S	D > S
General	– – –	– – –	D > I D > S	– – –	D > S	– – –
Target A	– – –	– – –	D > S	– – –	D > S	– – –
Target B	– – –	– – –	D > S	– – –	D > S	– – –
Global rating	NA	NA	– – –	– – –	I > S	– – –

Note. D = directive therapy ($n = 14$); I = interpretative therapy ($n = 14$); S = supportive therapy ($n = 14$).
[a]All significance levels $p < .05$ (t tests).

Methodology of the Intervention Analysis

The therapists, in using each approach, were working from a kind of recipe, based partly on the models of therapy as published (e.g., Skynner, 1969; Stuart, 1969) and partly on the need to have the approaches as far as possible mutually exclusive. The outlines of the three therapeutic approaches are given in the next section, and it may be seen there that, as far as possible, therapists were asked to avoid interpretations in the directive and supportive approaches, and to avoid advice in the interpretative and supportive approaches, as well as making the appropriate types of intervention in all three.

The intervention analysis is presented in two parts: This section concerns the assignment of tapes according to the type of therapy being carried out, and the following section provides an analysis of content of the interventions in greater detail.

Description of the Treatment Approaches

The approaches were outlined for the therapists in order to keep the technique in each approach as pure as possible. The outlines were as follows.

DIRECTIVE APPROACH (AFTER STUART, 1969)
Insist on clear communication and on listening to each other.

Emphasize that each partner must change his/her own behavior before expecting the other partner to change his/hers.

Explain the principle of rewarding each other for behavior that is requested and carried out: This should then become mutual (the "give to get" principle).

Insist on an exchange of positive behaviors (whether important or trivial; e.g., decorating a room or having intercourse more often). Do not allow decrease of negative behavior as a target.

Insist on specific descriptions that both partners understand (when and where the behavior should occur, and what exactly is wanted): Do not accept general descriptions (e.g., to be "more manly" or "more loving").

Make the partners tell each other unequivocally what they want; don't allow them to expect the partner to be clairvoyant (e.g., do not accept the statement "If he loved me, he would sense what I want").

In describing interaction, make each partner begin with his/her own behavior, followed by the partner's response; do not allow them to present themselves as making reasonable responses to the partner's inexplicable or hostile acts.

Having elicited three desired behaviors each, write these on a behavioral monitoring form with a space for each day of the week. They should each rate each other's frequency of carrying out the desired behavior, and this should produce an increase in such behavior.

If necessary, arrange a token system, in which the partner behaving in the desired way can obtain a concrete reward.

As desired behavior increases, set new targets in joint discussion with the couple during subsequent sessions.

For sexual problems, if these are largely related to motivation, proceed as above, finding out what part of the sexual process is most satisfying to each partner, and arrange an exchange of "satisfying interactions" on a *quid pro quo* basis.

For specific sexual problems (e.g., premature or delayed ejaculation, impotence, vaginismus, lack of orgasm), use Masters and Johnson's approach — nondemanding pleasurable stimulation of each other, combined with specific techniques and positions.

Do not make interpretations in the traditional sense, for example, of intrapsychic conflict, infantile wishes, transference, feelings in the session, envy, hostility, or hopelessness.

In discussing reported and observed behavior, think and speak in terms of reward, nonreward, attention for behavior, and ways of getting what one wants. A general statement of principle would be "He/she will do what you want him/her to, as long as you make it worth his/her while."

INTERPRETATIVE APPROACH (AFTER SKYNNER, 1969)

It is advisable to be quite active in a conjoint marital interview. This approach, as opposed to the "blank screen" approach of individual or group therapy, inhibits the establishment of too much transference to the therapist and keeps it firmly within the marital couple. It is often beneficial to show emotion oneself, both as a catalyst to the couple and as an example to them that one can be angry, frustrated, depressed, or pleased without losing effectiveness as a person.

In interpretation, work on the material that they bring, on the here-and-now interaction, on communication and emotions. Interpret what the partners are doing to each other in terms of impossible demands, avoiding responsibility, manipulation, splitting between good and bad, projection of good and bad aspects into the other partner, avoiding important issues such as anger or sex for fear of dangerous retaliation, and the unspoken conflicts that lie behind apparently trivial annoyances and disagreements. "Classical" intrapsychic interpretations, even though often valid, do not add much to the ongoing conjoint therapy and are more appropriate to long-term individual therapy in which transference is encouraged.

Bear in mind that, in a marriage, the partners are not "equal" in all respects, but that a division of labor and an implied authority structure are to be accepted and encouraged.

Try not to give advice or direction. Sometimes it is legitimate to do this by implication (e.g., "You don't seem to," "Why is it that you don't?"), or it may be possible to model the desired behavior in the session (e.g., getting angry with a castrating wife). It may be necessary from time to time to take sides, but this should be done so as to achieve overall balance over a few sessions of therapy, and too much criticism is likely to lead the criticized partner to refuse to come for more therapy. On the other hand, the more verbally fluent partner should not be allowed to dominate the session and the therapist, and the less fluent one may have to be encouraged to speak up.

The overall aim of the approach is to understand the communications and relationships between the partners, and to communicate your understanding to them, both verbally and by example.

SUPPORTIVE APPROACH

In this conjoint approach the aim is to be a peacemaker and to try to get the couple to talk to each other. Accept the material they bring up, not ferreting for information or clarification but accepting their statements at their own valuation. When they quarrel in the session, intervene only so far as to prevent physical violence. If long silences occur, come in with a noncommittal, open-ended question. Do not try to give advice or direction, or any "unconscious" interpretation; simply try to show empathy at all times to both partners. The expectation is that, in such an atmosphere, couples will say things to each other that they cannot say when alone. This by itself may produce as much change in the relationship as the more elaborate interpretative or directive approaches.

Reliability Study and Details of Time Sampling

Three blind raters took part in the rating exercise (one clinical psychologist and two social workers). The author (who treated 37 of the 42 cases) and the two other psychiatrists (who treated three and two cases, respectively) joined the three raters for a preliminary exercise designed to develop categories of therapist statement to use during the ratings. A preliminary series of categories was considered in the early meetings, and some representative tape recordings of interviews were listened to by all six workers simultaneously to reach a consensus on each intervention, or the best approximation to this. It was in this way that the 15 statement categories emerged; these are shown in Table 4.2. It will be seen that five of these categories were designated as nonspecific interventions, five as interpretations, and five as directive interventions. It was not expected that interventions in the directive approach would all fall into Categories 11–15, or that all interventions in the interpretative approach would fall into Categories 6–10; but it was expected that these two approaches would be relatively "pure" in style, in other words, that the directive approach would contain many more 11- to 15-type interventions than 6- to 10-type interventions, and vice versa for the interpretative approach.

TABLE 4.2. Categories of Therapist Intervention

A. Nonspecific interventions
  1. General comments
     Light conversation (e.g., "Rather cold today.")
     Answer questions factually (e.g., "Yes, I had a good holiday.")
     Agree with statements (e.g., "Yes, I can see that.")
  2. Empathic comments
     Showing understanding of what has just been said, or the implied emotional tone of
     it, but not bringing a new idea or interpretation (e.g., "So it seems you are quite anx-
     ious when it comes to sex," or "That would be upsetting, wouldn't it?")
  3. Questions
     General or specific, either open-ended or eliciting specific pieces of information; but
     excluding interpretations in the form of questions and specific questions seeking for
     an exchange of behavior on the give-to-get principle (e.g., "How have things been
     since last time?" or "Did you find her attractive when you first married?" but not
     "Surely you must have felt angry at that!" or "What specifically do you want her to
     do each morning?")
  4. Reassurance
     Including taking the couple's side against an outside person (e.g., "Don't worry
     about it, it will come right," or "You can't expect things to succeed 100%.)
  5. General opinion
     Usually on a medical or psychiatric matter (e.g., "Not everyone with agoraphobia
     gets depressed," or "That sounds like the right treatment for your sore throat.")
B. Interpretations
  6. Interactional interpretation
     Relabeling or pointing out unspoken emotions toward the partner or manipulation of
     each other—for example, impossible demands, avoiding responsibility, fears of retali-
     ation, role reversal, avoidance of issues; but excluding give-to-get explanations (e.g.,
     "Perhaps you feel not only scared but extremely angry toward her," or "Why do
     you insist on him dominating you? You want to be dominated, but you don't act
     submissively.")
  7. Personal interpretation
     Pointing out aspects of one partner's personality, way of dealing with relationships,
     or nonverbal expression of emotion in the session (e.g., "This perfectionism of
     yours—if things don't go right you give up the whole thing—that is how you have
     approached sex," or "You look as if you are very miserable.")
  8. Provocative or challenging interpretation
     Showing emotion oneself, reprimanding or teasing the couple, insulting them, etc.

As part of the reliability study, it was also established that the 15 categories were jointly exhaustive and to a large extent mutually exclusive. Clearly
there were exceptions to the latter statement, for instance, the fact that raters
often experienced difficulty in distinguishing among Category 2 (empathic
statements), Categories 6 and 7 (interactional and personal interpretations),
and Category 15 (comments on interaction in terms of give-to-get principles).
However, as shown by the reliability study results (discussed later), a reasonably good agreement was achieved between raters and categories.

The definition of a therapist "intervention" was needed, and eventually
an intervention was defined as an utterance of the therapist that was preceded

TABLE 4.2. (continued)

(e.g., "I just can't imagine you two inhibited people in bed together," "I don't want to hear any more about your boring symptoms," or "It's just an excuse for not facing responsibility.")

9. Transference interpretation
   Pointing out anything which has to do with feelings of either partner toward the therapist, with manipulation of him or putting him in the parental role toward either partner (e.g., "It seems you feel quite angry at me for not helping you to produce an erection—as if I were a parent who should give a child what he wants immediately.")

10. Historical interpretation
    Referring to childhood or family of origin (e.g., "This is similar to the way your mother made you feel guilty when you couldn't perform on the pot," or "You must have felt just as scared and angry when your father came between you and your mother.")

C. Directive interventions

11. Advice and education on general relationships
    Mostly on the subject of give-to-get negotiation (e.g., "You see, most successful couples do things for each other without asking, for example . . . ," "I want you to fill in his side of the chart daily, according to whether he has carried out that piece of behavior or not," or "Try and be more forceful toward her, because that is what she has said she wants.")

12. Education, advice, or explanation about sexual relationship
    (e.g., "I want you to practice the sensate focus in bed each night: but no genital contact or intercourse yet," or "It's unhelpful to be a spectator of your own sexual performance—you must get involved, lose yourself in it.")

13. Praise
    Or similar comment on progress (e.g., "I'm very pleased with your progress," or "Well, you haven't achieved all our goals, but you've made a few real gains.")

14. Questions leading to behavior exchange
    (e.g., "What do you want him to do more of?" or "What part of the sexual foreplay is most enjoyable for you?")

15. Comment on and explanation of the couple's behavior
    In terms of give-to-get, reward, and effective influence (e.g., "You want to change his behavior, but your method of doing this seems to be ineffective—it doesn't produce the result you want," "If his efforts around the house are not rewarded, no wonder he has given them up," or "Well, that was rewarding, wasn't it—it must have made you feel more like doing her a favor another time.")

and followed by an utterance of either spouse or by a silence of more than 5 seconds. Monosyllabic or purely negative or affirmative statements were not rated, however, either as therapist interventions or (if made by either spouse) as terminating a therapist intervention. Interventions that lasted more than 15 seconds were subdivided into 15-second blocks, and each block of 15 seconds or less was scored as a separate intervention of the same or another category.

Following these preliminary meetings the training phase began, in which tapes were listened to by all three raters simultaneously in an effort to agree on categories of statement. Disagreements were discussed, with an attempt to formulate better ways of deciding among statement categories in cases where the statement could be construed in two or more ways. Early reliability figures at this stage were low, with agreement between pairs of raters of only 43% for each category (1-15) and agreement on broad categorization of statements (1-5, 6-10, or 11-15) at only 60%. These levels improved somewhat throughout the exercise, and the definitive reliability study was then carried out.

Six tapes—two of each type of therapy, which were not subsequently used in the rating study—were listened to by two raters working alone at different times. Their ratings were then compared. The mean agreement on exact ratings between pairs of raters was 57%, and the mean agreement on broad groups of ratings was 73%. Although these levels were less than ideal, it was considered that no better accuracy could be achieved with further practice, in that agreement had not been improved during the last few tapes listened to by all three raters in the training phase. It was thought that the level achieved was adequate to the main purpose of the study.

From that point on, the main study was carried out, in which no tape was listened to by more than one rater.

Methodology of the Rating Exercise

The definitive rating study was then carried out as follows. For each couple 10 tape-recorded interviews were potentially available, although this was lower for some couples owing to (1) lack of equipment in the early stages and (2) the fact that seven couples had a shortened series of five interviews as opposed to the full 10 (Crowe, 1978). It was decided not to rate all interviews for all couples but to choose, according to a semirandom system, four tapes only from each couple for rating. The departure from randomization was designed to test two hypotheses. First, two tapes were chosen from Sessions 1-5 and two from Sessions 6-10 of each therapy series (the "early" and "late" tapes) to see whether therapist technique became more blurred or inconsistent as therapy proceeded. Second, two of the four tapes for each couple were rated on the first 40 therapist interventions on the tape (the "beginning" tapes), and the other two were rated using 40 statements starting from 20 minutes after the beginning of the interview (the "middle" tapes). Again, the hypothesis in this case was that interventions would be more specific and consistent at the beginning of any session than in the middle. The randomization then proceeded, with an equal number of "early" and "late" tapes, an equal number of "beginning" and "middle" tapes, and an otherwise random choice of 4 tapes out of the potential 10 per couple.

The instructions to the raters were not only to categorize therapist statements into Categories 1-15 but also to decide for each tape whether it was of directive, interpretative, or supportive therapy. They were to do this partly on a numerical analysis of their own ratings and partly on the general impression they received of the type of approach. There was also an opportunity for them to point to any particular aspect of the tape that had informed their decision as to the type of approach being used.

Care was taken to ensure that the raters had no extraneous clues to the type of therapy being carried out. Each tape was identified only by a code number, and the number bore no relation to the type of therapy, to the couple being treated, or to whether the therapy session was early or late in the couple's treatment. The tapes were given to each rater in batches of six, and no rater received more than one tape of a particular couple in the batch to be rated.

The raters' findings were recorded on a form on which they wrote a few words to identify each statement and the number of the category for each of the 40 statements. Each statement was then put into one of the 15 categories. They then wrote down what treatment they thought was being carried out, and their reasons for this. Their guesses as to treatment were finally compared with a key in which the actual treatment type for each tape was recorded.

The rating procedure can be summarized as follows.

1. Four out of the 10 available tape-recorded sessions for each couple were chosen for rating.

2. Forty therapist statements on each tape were rated, each statement being given a category (1–15).

3. Each tape was assigned by raters to one of the three treatment types, based on the categories of statement rated and on general impression.

4. Raters' opinions on type of treatment were compared with actual treatment being carried out in each case.

Results of Assignment

The answer to the important question "Could the raters accurately assess what type of treatment was being given?" is shown in Tables 4.3 and 4.4. The tables show that 91.4% of the directive tapes, 74.4% of the interpretative tapes, and 72.0% of the supportive (control) tapes were correctly assigned. Overall, the raters correctly assigned 78% of the tapes. It also appears from these tables that, while directive therapy and interpretative therapy were misassigned equally to the other two types of treatment, there was a tendency for the misassigned supportive tapes to be put in the interpretative rather than the directive category.

From the chi-square analysis (see Table 4.4) it may be appreciated that the raters did very much better than chance would have predicted in assign-

TABLE 4.3. Tape-Recorded Interviews: Comparison
between Type of Treatment Carried Out and Type of
Treatment as Judged by Raters

Treatment as judged by raters	Treatment being carried out		
	D	I	S
D	32	5	5
I	2	32	9
S	1	6	36

Note. D = directive therapy; I = interpretative therapy; S = supportive therapy.

ing tapes to the correct category ($p < .001$). However, this test is not all that useful procedurally, as a 22% disagreement indicates some difficulty in being sure what kind of therapy was being carried out, and this has some negative implications for the outcome study itself.

From Table 4.5 it may be seen that the three raters did not differ significantly in their ability to assign tapes correctly.

The tapes rated from the beginning were compared with those rated from 20 minutes into the interview. There was no significant difference in the accuracy of raters' assignment of tapes as between these two starting points (see Table 4.6).

The tapes made early in therapy (Sessions 1–5) were compared, in terms of assignment to therapy type, with those made late in therapy (Sessions 6–10). Again, there was no difference in accuracy of raters' assignment of tapes as between these two periods of therapy (see Table 4.7).

TABLE 4.4. Comparison of Correctly Assigned Tapes and Wrongly Assigned Tapes within Treatment Groups

	Treatment being carried out			
	D	I	S	Total
Correctly assigned	32	32	36	100
Wrongly assigned	3	11	14	28
Total	35	43	50	128
Tests of significance to judge whether this distribution could have arisen by chance	$\chi^2 = 22.45$ $p < .001$	$\chi^2 = 13.71$ $p < .001$	$\chi^2 = 14.44$ $p < .001$	$\chi^2 = 50.47$ $p < .001$

Note. D = directive therapy; I = interpretative therapy; S = supportive therapy.

TABLE 4.5. Accuracy of Each Rater in Assigning Tapes to Treatment Categories

	Rater 1 (E.S.)	Rater 2 (V.G.)	Rater 3 (C.L.)	Total
The three treatment groups combined[a]				
Correctly assigned	34	34	32	100
Wrongly assigned	11	10	7	28
Total	45	44	39	128

	The three treatment groups separately[b]								
	D	I	S	D	I	S	D	I	S
Correctly assigned	13	11	10	9	9	14	10	12	12
Wrongly assigned	0	3	8	3	4	0	0	4	6

[a]Test of significance among raters: $\chi^2 = .21$ (NS).
[b]D = directive therapy; I = interpretative therapy; S = supportive therapy.

TABLE 4.6. Accuracy of Raters in Assigning Tapes to Treatment Categories According to the Sample's Place in the Tape

	Beginning of tape	Middle of tape	Total
The three treatment groups combined[a]			
Correctly assigned	48	52	100
Wrongly assigned	13	15	28
Total	61	67	128

	The three treatment groups separately[b]					
	D	I	S	D	I	S
Correctly assigned	16	13	19	16	19	17
Wrongly assigned	0	8	5	3	3	9

[a]Test of significance of table: $\chi^2 = .12$ (NS).
[b]D = directive therapy; I = interpretative therapy; S = supportive therapy.

TABLE 4.7. Accuracy of Raters in Assigning Tapes to Treatment Categories According to the Stage of Treatment at Which the Interview Took Place

	Early in therapy	Late in therapy	Total
The three treatment groups combined[a]			
Correctly assigned	46	54	100
Wrongly assigned	17	11	28
Total	63	65	128

The three treatment groups separately[b]						
	D	I	S	D	I	S
Correctly assigned	14	15	17	18	17	19
Wrongly assigned	2	6	9	1	5	5

Note. "Early" = Sessions 1–5; "late" = Sessions 6–10.
[a]Test of significance of table: $\chi^2 = 1.34$ (NS).
[b]D = directive therapy; I = interpretative therapy; S = supportive therapy.

Content Analysis Results

Overall content analysis shows (see Table 4.8) that in all types of treatment, the majority of interventions were in fact nonspecific. The percentages of broad categories are also given, and it may be seen that in all types of treatment, the majority of interventions fell into the nonspecific category. However, this was much more marked in the supportive treatment (84.0%) than in the other two (54.3% and 51.5%). The other two treatment approaches each had considerably more appropriate than inappropriate interventions. Thus, in the directive approach, 42.9% of the interventions were appropriately directive (i.e., Categories 11–15), whereas only 5.6% were inappropriately interpretative. Similarly, in the interpretative approach, 35.6% of the interventions were interpretative, and only 10.1% were inappropriately directive.

TABLE 4.8. Therapist Statements in the Three Broad Categories That Occurred in the Three Types of Therapy

	Nonspecific	Interpretative (I)	Directive (D)	Total
Treatment D	667	72	556	1295[a]
Treatment I	913	596	170	1679
Treatment S	1485	189	93	1767

Note. Tests of significance, compared with chance distribution: the whole table—$\chi^2 = 2168$, $p < .001$; for Group D—$\chi^2 = 462.0$, $p < .001$; for Group I—$\chi^2 = 495.0$, $p < .001$; for Group S—$\chi^2 = 2049$, $p < .001$.
[a]Fewer tapes from Group D were rated than from Groups I and S.

It will be seen from the chi-square analysis in Table 8 that such a distribution rejects to a highly significant degree the null hypothesis that the three therapeutic approaches were indistinguishable as regards content.

Table 4.9 shows the distribution of the interventions into each of the 15 specific categories (five in each of the broad categories). Most of the categories are well represented, but it is of interest to note the infrequent use of "transference" and "historical" interpretations, even in the interpretative tapes.

It should be remembered that the content analysis was carried out as a blind exercise, so that the "halo effect" should have been minimized.

A further exercise in discrimination is shown in Table 4.10, in which it can be seen that therapist activity tends to change as the session proceeds. Thus, comparing sessions rated from the beginning with those rated from the middle of the interview, it may be seen that in directive tapes, directive interventions increase at the expense of the interpretative. In interpretative tapes, interpretations increase as the interview proceeds, at the expense of nonspecific interventions. In supportive tapes, on the other hand, both interpretations and directive interventions increase at the expense of nonspecific interventions. In all cases these differences are significant statistically.

Similar significant differences are found between sessions recorded in the first half of therapy and those recorded in the second half (see Table 4.11). In Group D both interpretative and directive interventions increased later in therapy. In Group I a slight decrease in interpretations occurred, both other cate-

TABLE 4.9. Tape-Recorded Interviews: Breakdown of Therapist Statements in the Three Types of Therapy According to the Category of Statement Rated

	Directive	Interpretative	Supportive
A. Nonspecific			
1. General conversation	58	82	162
2. Empathic	237	332	518
3. Questions (general)	323	440	653
4. Reassurance	11	27	46
5. General opinion	38	32	106
B. Interpretative			
6. Interactional	37	331	113
7. Personal	20	173	66
8. Provocative	9	71	6
9. Transference	6	4	0
10. Historical	0	17	4
C. Directive			
11. General advice + education	162	70	53
12. Sexual advice + education	155	13	27
13. Praise	51	29	3
14. Questions for behavior exchange	79	11	1
15. Explanations of behavior in terms of behavioral exchange	109	47	9

TABLE 4.10. Therapist Statements Divided into the Three Categories within Treatment Types, According to the Place in the Tape from Which the Interview Was Taken

	Nonspecific	Interpretative	Directive	Total
Beginning of tape				
Treatment D	257	44	195	496
Treatment I	548	235	103	886
Treatment S	764	77	31	872
Middle of tape				
Treatment D	396	28	338	762
Treatment I	358	372	91	821
Treatment S	718	128	61	907

Note. Tests of significance, comparing observed distribution with an identical distribution between "beginning" and "middle": all groups together—$\chi^2 = 152.1$, $p < .001$; Group D—$\chi^2 = 18.1$, $p < .001$; Group I—$\chi^2 = 38.2$, $p < .001$; Group S—$\chi^2 = 24.1$, $p < .001$.

gories increasing. In Group S there was a marked increase in directive interventions and a slight decrease in interpretative interventions. Thus in all groups, directiveness increased later in therapy.

Regarding the tapes misassigned by raters, the differences between these and the tapes correctly assigned are shown in Table 4.12. All the tapes misassigned were, predictably enough, less typical of the therapeutic approach being carried out than the correctly assigned tapes. Tapes misassigned as Group D contained far more statements rated as directive than correctly assigned Group I and Group S tapes, but still less than correctly assigned Group D tapes. A similar pattern was found for tapes misassigned as Group I and Group S, compared both with their actual group of origin and their group of assignment. As can be seen from Table 4.13, statistical analysis of

TABLE 4.11. Tape-Recorded Interviews: Therapist Statements in the Three Broad Categories within Treatment Types, Divided into Early Interviews and Late Interviews

	Nonspecific	Interpretative	Directive	Total
Early				
Treatment D	309	16	223	548
Treatment I	429	308	76	813
Treatment S	805	127	21	953
Late				
Treatment D	358	56	333	747
Treatment I	484	288	94	866
Treatment S	680	62	72	814

Note. "Early" = Sessions 1–5; "late" = Sessions 6–10.

Note. Tests of significance, comparing the observed frequencies with an identical distribution of statements in early and late sessions: Group D, early versus late—$\chi^2 = 16.4$, $p < .001$; Group I, early versus late—$\chi^2 = 3.9$, $p < .05$; Group S, early versus late—$\chi^2 = 48.4$, $p < .001$; combined groups, early versus late—$\chi^2 = 234.0$, $p < .001$.

TABLE 4.12. Tape-Recorded Interviews: Differences between Correctly and Wrongly Assigned Tapes in Terms of Therapist Statements, Divided into the Three Broad Categories

	Nonspecific	Interpretative	Directive
Tapes of directive therapy: Group D			
Correctly assigned as Group D	581	65	547
Incorrectly assigned as Group I	62	11	7
Incorrectly assigned as Group S	34	4	2
Tapes of interpretative therapy: Group I			
Correctly assigned as Group I	579	559	81
Incorrectly assigned as Group D	105	6	74
Incorrectly assigned as Group S	189	23	18
Tapes of supportive therapy: Group S			
Correctly assigned as Group S	1120	86	33
Incorrectly assigned as Group D	143	9	48
Incorrectly assigned as Group I	284	132	13

Note. See Table 4.13 for statistical analysis.

TABLE 4.13. Statistical Analysis of Table 4.12: Therapist Statements Comparing Wrongly with Correctly Rated Tapes

	Nonspecific	Interpretative	Directive	Significance Tests
Correctly rated tapes compared with those tapes that should have been assigned to that group but were not				
Group D				
D assigned as D	581	65	547	$\chi^2 = 64.9$,
D assigned as I and S	96	15	9	$p < .001$
Group I				
I assigned as I	579	559	81	$\chi^2 = 229.0$,
I assigned as D and S	294	29	92	$p < .001$
Group S				
S assigned as S	1120	86	33	$\chi^2 = 145.9$,
S assigned as D and I	427	141	61	$p < .001$
Correctly rated tapes compared with those tapes that were incorrectly assigned to that group				
Group D				
D assigned as D	581	65	547	$\chi^2 = 27.9$,
I and S assigned as D	248	15	122	$p < .001$
Group I				
I assigned as I	579	559	81	$\chi^2 = 59.3$,
D and S assigned as I	346	143	20	$p < .001$
Group S				
S assigned as S	1120	86	33	$\chi^2 = 16.7$,
D and I assigned as S	223	27	20	$p < .001$

content shows that in all cases the misassigned tapes were significantly different in content both from their correct origin group and from the group of tapes to which they were misassigned.

Finally, it seemed (though unconfirmed statistically due to small numbers) that when therapy with a couple produced one tape that was misassigned, it quite often produced another; this gives an interesting sidelight on the way that clients influence the approach of the therapist.

Discussion

The process research reported here was carried out simply because the outcome study required it in order to establish that three different types of therapy were being carried out. The analysis of process was therefore of a rather limited kind, restricted to therapist activity, and concentrated on a division of interventions according to whether they were general (supportive), interpretative, or directive. However, it is of interest to compare the methods and results with those of other studies analyzing therapist activity in family and marital therapy, which have been recently reviewed by Pinsof (1980).

Postner, Guttman, Sigal, Epstein, and Rakoff (1971) were the first group to publish research on the analysis of therapist activity in family therapy. They used a simple binary system of categorization, in which therapist interventions were labeled either "Drive" (stimulating interaction, obtaining information, or providing support) or "Interpretation" (clarifying motivation, enlarging understanding about the family, labeling unconscious motives, or suggesting alternative behaviors). Some of these categories bear a clear resemblance to those used in the present study. They concluded that a high Drive–Interpretation ratio in therapists' early sessions with the families correlated with a good outcome.

Another group working in Montreal (Sigal, Lasry, Guttman, Chagoya, & Pilon, 1977) cross-validated the Drive–Interpretation category system for the behavior of 19 family therapist trainees. This study showed some consistency for each trainee, in that the Drive scores correlated positively within therapists as among three sample points in the course of family therapy. Similarly, Interpretation scores were positively correlated at three points in simulated family therapy exercises. However, no correlations were found within therapists for the comparison of behavior in real family therapy and behavior in the simulated family therapy exercise.

Pinsof (1979) used a 19-category analysis of therapist intervention in family therapy. The categories of this scale (Family Therapist Behavior Scale) are mutually exclusive and divide activities rather differently from the Montreal scales or the scale used in the present study. Such categories as "Support" and "Intention Desire" clearly have some similarities, but other categories such as "Control-Structure" and "Block Expectation" would be hard to correlate with the foregoing two scales. The scale showed adequate interrater reliability and discriminated reliably between experienced and inexperienced therapist styles. However, correlations of process with outcome were not made.

Alexander, Barton, Schiavo, and Parsons (1976) used an eight-scale category system to rate family therapist behavior. A mixed collection of verbal and nonverbal behaviors was rated, but it appears that the ratings were for overall impression of therapist behavior rather than a statement-by-statement analysis. Such categories as "Humor," "Warmth," and "Self-Confidence" were used. Alexander *et al.* found that some of the scales (labeled "Relationship" and "Structuring" scales) correlated well with some aspects of outcome.

Allred and Kersey (1977) reported on the use of the Allred Interaction Analysis for Counselors (AIAC). Seven of their scales relate to therapist activity, and again these show some similarities to those used in the present study. For instance, their categories of "Educates," "Gathers Information," "Interprets/Confronts," and "Supports" have fairly clear equivalents in the present 15-category scale. No correlations with outcome were made, but the reliability and concurrent validity of the scales were good.

Dowling (1979) evolved a system for assessing therapist activity in family therapy with a special emphasis on the comparison of techniques among cotherapists. As in the present study, tapes from the beginning, middle, and end of therapy were rated, but in her case there was only one rater, and reliability issues were not addressed. Most of the 15 categories were somewhat similar to the first two groups of categories in the present study (e.g., "Building," "Supporting," "Challenging," "Enlarging," and "Pointing Out"); only one category appeared similar to the last group (i.e., "Proposing," which includes all kinds of advice giving). Therapists were found to be consistent in the pattern of categories they used in their personal style of intervention: Their individual styles were consistent even when working with different cotherapists and different families.

Thus, despite the small number of studies in the field of family therapist behavior during therapy, a rather wide variety of ratings have been used, depending on the theoretical orientation of the research group and the exact purpose for which the analysis of behavior was being carried out. All except the method used by Alexander *et al.* (1976) were similar to the present one in that a statement-by-statement analysis of therapist activity was carried out, and therapist "style" was based on a numerical profile made up of frequencies of the various categories of statement. The approach of Alexander *et al.*, however, seems to have been more a matter of observers' global impressions of therapist style. But in none of the studies so far reported was there a systematic attempt, as in the present study, to vary therapist activity and to monitor whether that activity was indeed distinguishable as among three approaches. Perhaps the nearest approach to the present methodology was that used in individual therapy by Sloane, Staples, Cristol, Yorkston, and Whipple

(1975), where the authors analyzed the verbal behavior of dynamically and behaviorally oriented therapists, and found both some interesting differences and some surprising similarities in approach between the two types of therapists.

The levels of interrater reliability in the present study were 57% for exact category and 73% for broad group (nonspecific, interpretation, or advice). This is considerably lower than that found by Allred and Kersey (1977) in the AIAC but about the same as that reported by Alexander *et al.* and higher than that found by Pinsof. No reliability figures were reported by Sigal *et al.* (1977) or Dowling (1979). Certainly, during the reliability exercise of the present study, a plateau was reached, which it was felt could not be exceeded owing to the nature of the task.

The accuracy in assigning tapes to treatment groups was of a fairly high order but clearly less than the desired 100%. Directive tapes were easier to assign than the other types, and indeed two of the raters were without error in detecting directive tapes (see Table 4.5). However, interpretative and supportive tapes were harder to detect, and there was misassignment in all directions (see Table 4.3). This may have related to the difficulty, already mentioned, in distinguishing "empathic" statements from "interpretations." It is also likely that, in the process of rating any particular tape, a kind of halo effect began to obtain, whereby as soon as some clue as to the type of therapy was picked up, interventions from that point on would be interpreted to fit the selected therapy approach rather than in an unbiased and objective way.

Some collateral evidence for this view comes from a study of the content of misassigned tapes. Here the tapes appeared to have an intermediate content: For example, a supportive tape assigned as directive would have a proportion of directive statements greater than a correctly assigned supportive tape but less than a correctly assigned directive tape. The tapes were thus harder to assign on their content, and guesses had to be made on the basis of either the toss of a coin or emphasis on one particular intervention as to the type of treatment being carried out.

It was of interest to note that in all three approaches there was a predominance of nonspecific statements. Perhaps this might be seen as a fault in the two specific types of therapy: The directive approach should perhaps have been more pure than it was in its directiveness; and the interpretative approach, more pure in its use of dynamic interpretations. However, Liberman (1970) adjured the behavioral marital therapist to use a "warm human approach developed during his training as a therapist," and Skynner (1969) stressed the role of the therapist as a "real person, expressing his own thoughts and feelings" rather than a blank screen interpreter. It might therefore be argued that the use of nonspecific interventions freely in both approaches indicated that both these pieces of advice were being followed.

More serious, perhaps, is the demonstrable overlap in techniques, in which some directive advice appeared to be given in the interpretative and

supportive approaches, and some interpretations in the supportive and directive approaches. The fact that such aberrations were relatively few (see Table
4.8) may be seen as reassuring, but one should not underestimate the difficulties of keeping within a "pure" style in a research project such as the
present study. There was a tendency, which was noticed more impression-
istically than numerically, for tapes from particular couples to be misassigned
more than once. Numbers were not great enough in the misassigned group
to assess the significance of this observation, but it certainly did seem harder
with some couples than with others for the therapist to stick to the prescribed
therapeutic regimen.

Conclusions

The study reported here was undertaken in order to confirm that three different kinds of therapy were indeed being carried out. This was confirmed,
despite the percentage of tapes that were misassigned. Such confirmation
should be a routine part of any study in which, as in the present study (Crowe,
1978), different therapeutic approaches are being compared with each other.

Implications for the future of this kind of analysis in general are less
clear, and it seems unfortunate that so many different rating methods have
been used in the studies carried out to date. The indications for its use are
probably four in number: (1) as in the present study, to control for content
differences; (2) as in Postner *et al.* (1971) and Alexander *et al.* (1976), to correlate process with outcome; (3) as in Dowling (1979), to examine the effect
of different settings on therapist style; and (4) as in Sigal *et al.* (1977), to evaluate the effect of training on therapist style. The choice between sentence-
by-sentence analysis of therapist activity, as in most of these studies, and
overall impression of style, as used by Alexander *et al.*, is not resolved, but
it is probable that the greater possibilities of reliability analysis in the former
approach will commend it to researchers in the field. However, it is difficult
to see how (even if they had been available) the more reliable general rating
methods such as that of Pinsof (1979) could have been applied in the present
work, and no doubt, for specific purposes, new rating methods will continue
to be evolved.

REFERENCES

Alexander, J., Barton, C., Schiavo, R. S., & Parsons, B. V. Systems-behavioral intervention
    with families of delinquents: Therapist characteristics, family behavior and outcome. *Jour-
    nal of Consulting and Clinical Psychology*, 1976, *44*, 656–664.
Allred, G. H., & Kersey, F. L. The AIAC, a design for systematically analysing marriage and
    family counseling: A progress report. *Journal of Marriage and Family Counseling*, 1977,
    3, 17–25.
Crowe, M. J. Conjoint marital therapy: A controlled outcome study. *Psychological Medicine*,
    1978, *8*, 623–636.

Dowling, E. Co-therapy: A clinical researcher's view. In S. Walrond-Skinner (Ed.), *Family and marital therapy*. London: Routledge & Kegan Paul, 1979.

Liberman, R. P. Behavioral approaches in family and couple therapy. *American Journal of Orthopsychiatry*, 1970, *40*, 106–118.

Pinsof, W. M. The Family Therapist Behavior Scale (FTBS): Development and evaluation of a coding system. *Family Process*, 1979, *18*(4), 451–461.

Pinsof, W. M. Family therapy process research. In A. S. Gurman & D. P. Kniskern (Eds.), *Handbook of family therapy*. New York: Brunner/Mazel, 1980.

Postner, R. S., Guttman, H., Sigal, J., Epstein, N. B., & Rakoff, V. Process and outcome in conjoint family therapy. *Family Process*, 1971, *10*, 451–474.

Sigal, J. J., Lasry, J. C., Guttman, H., Chagoya, L., & Pilon, R. Some stable characteristics of family therapists' interventions in real and simulated therapy sessions. *Journal of Consulting and Clinical Psychology*, 1977, *45*, 23–26.

Skynner, A. C. R. A group analytic approach to conjoint family therapy. *Journal of Child Psychology and Psychiatry*, 1969, *10*, 81–106.

Sloane, B. B., Staples, F. R., Cristol, A. H., Yorkston, N. J., & Whipple, K. Short term analytically orientated psychotherapy versus behavior therapy. *American Journal of Psychiatry*, 1975, *132*, 373–377.

Stuart, R. B. Operant-interpersonal treatment for marital discord. *Journal of Consulting and Clinical Psychology*, 1969, *33*, 675–682.

5

The Active Ingredients of Behavioral Marital Therapy: The Effectiveness of Problem-Solving/ Communication Training, Contingency Contracting, and Their Combination

DONALD H. BAUCOM

In the past decade, there has been increasing empirical evidence to support the effectiveness of behavioral marital therapy (BMT) in aiding maritally distressed couples. Different BMT investigators and therapists have varied in the emphasis they have placed upon specific techniques (cf. Azrin, Naster, & Jones, 1973; Liberman, Levine, Wheeler, Sanders, & Wallace, 1976; Stuart, 1969, 1980; Tsoi-Hoshmand, 1976; Turkewitz & O'Leary, 1981), yet the various treatments have in common a focus on teaching skills to produce behavior change. The BMT approach developed by Weiss, Patterson, and their associates at the University of Oregon and Oregon Research Institute is one treatment format that has received widespread attention, and it served as the basis for the current investigation. In a series of replicated case studies, Weiss *et al.* found that teaching distressed couples communication skills followed by behavioral contracting skills resulted in improved communication and increased satisfaction with the relationship (Patterson & Hops, 1972; Patterson, Hops, & Weiss, 1972; Weiss, Hops, & Patterson, 1973).

Using a set of treatment strategies derived from the Oregon model, Jacobson (1977, 1978) conducted the first well-controlled experimental investigations of the effectiveness of BMT. In the first investigation, maritally distressed couples were randomly assigned to a BMT treatment or a waiting-list condition. The results indicated that BMT was more effective than no treatment on all self-report and behavioral measures. In the second study (Jacobson, 1978), distressed couples were randomly assigned to one of four

Donald H. Baucom. Psychology Department, University of North Carolina at Chapel Hill, Chapel Hill, North Carolina, U.S.A.

treatment conditions: (1) problem-solving/communication training followed by good faith contracting; (2) problem-solving/communication training followed by *quid pro quo* contracting; (3) a nonspecific treatment condition; (4) a waiting-list condition. Couples in the two BMT conditions improved significantly more than the waiting-list couples, and significantly more than the couples receiving the nonspecific treatment. There were no significant differences between the two BMT conditions on any dependent measures.

The purpose of the current investigation was to provide further understanding of these same BMT procedures. BMT as described in Jacobson's studies comprises two sets of techniques taught sequentially: (1) problem-solving/communication training and (2) behavioral contracting. Based on the previously described findings, it can be concluded that this entire treatment is of assistance to distressed couples. However, whether the changes result from problem-solving/communication training, from contracting, or from the combination of procedures is unknown. A major focus of the current study was to isolate the change-inducing techniques included in the entire treatment program.

At the International Symposium on Marital Interaction and Marital Therapy in Munich, investigators from several countries concurred that results of outcome investigations would be clearer if information was presented in addition to means and standard deviations on dependent variables. More specifically, reporting the percentage of couples who improved, remained unchanged, or deteriorated would assist in evaluating the effects of treatment. Therefore, in this chapter, not only is treatment effectiveness analyzed through the couples' means and standard deviations on the dependent variables, but also the percentages of couples showing improvement following treatment are examined.

Furthermore, in addition to isolating the active ingredients of the treatment itself, treatment effectiveness might also be enhanced if we can predict which couples will respond more favorably to which techniques. Findings of a recent outcome investigation by Turkewitz and O'Leary (1981) suggest that age of the couple might be a potent moderator variable in the relationship between type of marital treatment and successful outcome. They compared the effectiveness of BMT, communication therapy (CT), and a waiting-list condition for assisting distressed couples. The results indicated no significant differences in the overall effectiveness of the two therapy conditions. However, additional analyses revealed a significant though unpredicted interaction effect between the couple's age and the treatment they received, with younger couples showing more improvement under BMT and older couples responding better to CT. This is one of our few pieces of empirical data to consider in attempting to match couples with treatment. Exploring age by treatment interactions will be an additional focus of the current study.

The basic methodology of the current investigation and the findings regarding the relative effectiveness of the four treatment conditions are presented rather concisely here since a more extensive account, which includes detailed psychometric reporting of many of those analyses, is available elsewhere (Baucom, 1982). The issues of percentage of couples showing improvement after treatment and couple age as a moderator variable are newly introduced and are therefore treated more thoroughly in this chapter.

Method

Subjects

The subjects for the investigation were 72 married couples requesting assistance for their marital problems, excluding couples who listed either sexual dysfunctions or alcohol abuse as their major problem. All couples were seen through an outpatient clinic in a university psychology department, which was available to the general population. The mean individual pretest score on the Marital Adjustment Scale (MAS) (Locke & Wallace, 1959) was 83.56, placing the couples within the range typically considered maritally distressed. The average age of the individuals in the study was 32, with a range from 20 to 59. The average number of years of education was 14, with a range from 10 to 21; the couples averaged having 1.5 children, with a range from 0 to 7.

Therapists

Two doctoral students in clinical psychology, one male and one female, served as the therapists for the study. The therapists received approximately 60 hours of training prior to the study's initiation and continued to receive weekly supervision from the author. Each therapist treated a total of 36 couples, nine couples from each of the four treatment conditions.

Measures

The dependent measures included two behavioral measures related to problem-solving/communication skills and two self-report measures, one focusing on requested behavioral changes in various areas of marital interaction and the other serving as a measure of overall marital satisfaction. All dependent measures were completed immediately prior to and at the end of treatment (or waiting period). Three months after the termination of treatment, the two self-report measures were mailed to the couples to complete and return.

REVISED MARITAL INTERACTION CODING SYSTEM

The Marital Interaction Coding System (MICS) (Marital Studies Center, 1975) is a system for categorizing couples' verbal and nonverbal interaction into 29 categories. Based on Patterson, Hops, and Weiss's (1975) recommendations, these categories were collapsed into two measures: Positive Behaviors (Pos. MICS) and Negative Behaviors (Neg. MICS). Pos. MICS included the following categories: accept responsibility, compromise, positive solution, agree, approval, laugh, and positive physical contact. The following categories comprised Neg. MICS: criticize, disagree, complain (no score for husbands), deny responsibility (no score for wives), excuse, interrupt, not track, and put down.

The MICS was used to code each couple's attempts at resolving two problems at a given measurement session (e.g., pretest). For the first problem, each couple selected what they considered to be one of their moderate-sized relationship problems and spent 5–6 minutes attempting to resolve the problem. For the second problem, each couple attempted to resolve in 5–6 minutes a hypothetical problem from the Inventory of Marital Conflicts (Olson & Ryder, 1970).

The problem solving was videotaped, and the same two raters rated each tape using the MICS. Since the total Pos. MICS score and the total Neg. MICS score served as the units of analysis in the results, these two summary scores were the bases for calculating interrater reliability. Pearson correlations indicated an interrater reliability of $r = .87$ for Pos. MICS and $r = .83$ for Neg. MICS across all 72 couples. The scores were combined across the two problems and averaged across raters for the purpose of analysis.

AREAS OF CHANGE QUESTIONNAIRE

The Areas of Change Questionnaire (A-C) (Weiss et al., 1973) is a self-report inventory in which a person indicates the amount of behavior change desired of the spouse in 34 specific areas of marital interaction (e.g., handling of finances). The individual also indicates whether the specific area is viewed as a major problem area.

MARITAL ADJUSTMENT SCALE

The MAS (Locke & Wallace, 1959) is a frequently used, traditional, self-report inventory that serves as an overall measure of marital satisfaction. It was completed by each spouse at each measurement session.

Procedure

Each couple was randomly assigned to one of the two therapists and one of the four treatment conditions. Each couple completed the A-C and MAS prior to the initial session. At the initial session, a marital history was obtained, problem areas were listed and briefly clarified, and each couple attempted to resolve the two problems which were later coded using the MICS. The waiting-list couples were then asked to return after 10 weeks. Each treatment couple was then seen by the therapist for 1- to 1½-hour sessions weekly for the next 10 weeks. All sessions were conducted with the two members of the couple and single therapist present.

PROBLEM-SOLVING/COMMUNICATION TRAINING PLUS CONTRACTING

Couples in this condition (PS/C + CON) were taught problem-solving and communication skills for the first 5 weeks of treatment; contracting was introduced in Session 6 and practiced for the remainder of the treatment sessions. Couples were asked to spend 15 minutes each night selecting a problem and applying the skills from the previous session. In problem solving, couples were taught to state a problem behaviorally, consider alternative solutions, select an agreed-upon solution, implement the solution for a specific time period, and then reevaluate the acceptability of the solution. Communication training focused on skills to help the couple become effective problem solvers. For example, they were taught to avoid interrupting each other, avoid becoming sidetracked onto other problem areas, and avoid inducing guilt in the partner as a way of getting the partner to agree to a solution.

In Session 6, the couples began learning the principles of *quid pro quo* contracting. The couple reached solutions on two problem areas such that the solution to one problem involved behavior change on the wife's part, and the solution to the other problem involved behavior change from the husband. The two solutions were then interwoven such that the husband's behavior change was contingent upon the wife's behavior change and vice versa. A more detailed description of how these treatment procedures were implemented in the current investigation is given elsewhere (Baucom, 1982; Lester, Beckham, & Baucom, 1980).

PROBLEM-SOLVING/COMMUNICATION TRAINING ONLY

Couples in this treatment condition (PS/C Only) received the same problem-solving/communication training as the PS/C + CON group. However, couples in this condition practiced these skills for all 10 weeks of treatment without exposure to contracting.

CONTRACTING ONLY

This treatment (CON Only) consisted of training only in *quid pro quo* contracting for 10 weeks. Thus, the couples were not taught the specific order of steps in problem solving, nor did they receive communication training.

WAITING LIST

Couples in this condition (WL) waited 10 weeks to receive treatment after they had completed the pretest measures. Following this waiting period, each of these couples again completed the dependent measures and then received 10 weeks of PS/C + CON, since this entire treatment was previously shown to be effective (Jacobson, 1977, 1978). Although these couples completed the dependent measures again after treatment, the changes occurring after delayed treatment are not presented in this discussion (see Mehlman, Baucom, & Anderson, 1983, for a discussion of the effects of delayed vs. immediate treatment of distressed couples).

Results

When the relative effectiveness of different treatments is examined in the following analyses, "adjusted" posttest scores are used as the dependent measures unless stated otherwise. These adjusted scores were obtained by developing linear regression equations to predict a dependent variable's posttest score from that variable's pretest score. The residual score (actual posttest minus predicted posttest) served as the adjusted score. In all multivariate analyses of variance (MANOVAs), the dependent variables were A-C, MAS, Pos. MICS, and Neg. MICS.

Therapist Effects

A 2 × 3 MANOVA (female therapist, male therapist × PS/C + CON, PS/C Only, CON Only) was conducted using adjusted posttest scores to determine whether the two therapists were differentially effective in administering BMT. The findings indicated no significant multivariate effects for therapist, $F(4,45) = .95, p > .05$; and no significant multivariate interaction effect between therapist and treatment condition, $F(8, 90) = .89, p > .05$. Since the particular therapist was not a salient factor in producing treatment effects, in the appropriate remaining analyses the data were collapsed across therapists.

Effects of BMT versus No Treatment

A one-way MANOVA with four levels of the independent variable treatment (PS/C + CON, PS/C Only, CON Only, WL) and adjusted posttest scores was conducted as an overall test of whether the four experimental conditions differentially affected the couples. A significant multivariate effect, $F(12, 172) = 3.02, p < .001$, was obtained. Univariate tests revealed a significant effect on all of the dependent measures except Pos. MICS. Planned contrasts of the three BMT treatment conditions together compared to the WL indicated that BMT was more effective than no treatment on all four dependent measures.

*Changes from Pretest to Posttest within Each Experimental
Condition*

The means and standard deviations of each treatment condition at pretest,
posttest, and follow-up are presented in Table 5.1. To determine what changes
occurred within each treatment condition, *t* tests of correlated means were
conducted comparing a treatment's pretest and posttest scores. PS/C + CON
improved significantly on all dependent measures; PS/C Only improved on
all measures except Pos. MICS; CON Only improved only on A-C and MAS.
The WL couples showed significantly more negative interaction on Neg.
MICS at the end of the waiting period but no other significant changes.

Relative Effectiveness of Three BMT Conditions

A major focus of the study was to isolate the effective components of BMT.
To explore this issue, the three BMT treatment conditions were compared in
the 2×3 MANOVA (male therapist, female therapist $\times$ PS/C + CON, PS/C
Only, CON Only) described previously under "Therapist Effects." There was
no significant multivariate main effect for therapy condition, $F(8, 90) = 0.66$,
$p > .05$, indicating no differential effectiveness of the treatments. This conclusion was further supported when corresponding univariate tests showed
no significant main effects on any of the four dependent variables. As stated
earlier, there also was no significant multivariate treatment $\times$ therapist interaction.

Percentage of Couples Showing Improvement Following Treatment

There are no clear, agreed-upon standards for determining whether a particular couple has improved or deteriorated by the end of treatment. As argued
elsewhere, since the couple's self-report of marital distress (either the couple's
informal verbal statement that they are distressed or the couple's score on a
written self-report measure of marital satisfaction) has been the typical criterion for selection as a distressed couple for BMT outcome investigations,
a similar focus on self-reported marital satisfaction should remain central in
BMT outcome evaluation (Baucom, in press). Therefore, in the current investigation, the couples' scores on the MAS were employed in deriving a statement of percentage of couples who improved by the end of treatment. The
MAS is scored such that higher scores reflect greater marital satisfaction. The
magnitude of change was considered by calculating the percentages of couples
whose MAS scores improved (gained at least 10 points), deteriorated (lost
at least 10 points), and showed no change (gained or lost 9 or fewer points)
from pretest to posttest. The results for pretest to posttest change were as
follows:

TABLE 5.1. Means and Standard Deviations of Treatment Groups on Dependent Measures

Treatment condition	Session[a]	Areas of Change		Marital Adjustment Scale		Positive MICS		Negative MICS	
		M	SD	M	SD	M	SD	M	SD
Problem-solving/communication training plus contracting	Pretest	54.28	19.19	158.06	20.74	3.76	2.06	0.99	0.48
	Posttest	35.56	19.14	176.11	32.15	4.85	2.39	0.42	0.35
	Follow-up (n = 14)	38.57	19.60	176.79	32.44	—	—	—	—
Problem-solving/communication training only	Pretest	56.50	24.21	160.67	25.96	4.40	1.55	1.07	1.39
	Posttest	34.72	19.33	180.00	26.10	4.88	1.85	0.43	0.38
	Follow-up (n = 12)	32.33	17.73	191.58	29.86	—	—	—	—
Contracting only	Pretest	49.33	14.64	179.06	25.03	4.62	2.26	1.01	1.04
	Posttest	28.61	21.17	204.44	39.23	5.03	1.86	0.78	1.23
	Follow-up (n = 13)	33.62	25.71	202.77	44.58	—	—	—	—
Waiting list	Pretest	52.28	18.46	170.72	30.32	3.41	1.21	0.91	0.83
	Posttest	46.78	16.62	172.78	33.17	3.62	1.71	1.46	1.19

Note. From D. H. Baucom, A comparison of behavioral contracting and problem-solving/communications training in behavioral marital therapy. *Behavior Therapy*, 1982, *13*, 162–174. Copyright 1982 by the Association for Advancement of Behavior Therapy. Reprinted by permission of the publisher and the author.

[a] n = 18 for each treatment condition group for pretest and posttest scores.

  • PS/C + CON: 12 of 18 (67%) improved, 2 of 18 (11%) deteriorated, 4 of 18 (22%) showed no change
  • PS/C Only: 13 of 18 (72%) improved, 0 of 18 (0%) deteriorated,
5 of 18 (28%) showed no change
  • CON Only: 15 of 18 (83%) improved, 1 of 18 (6%) deteriorated,
2 of 18 (11%) showed no change
  • WL: 6 of 18 (33%) improved, 2 of 18 (11%) deteriorated, 10 of
18 (56%) showed no change

Unfortunately, there are no standards for what is considered a meaningful
clinical change on the MAS. Therefore, these analyses of percentages cannot be interpreted as necessarily indicating clinically meaningful changes; however, they do provide some clarity regarding the degree of improvement obtained by couples under different treatment conditions.

Maintenance of Treatment Effects

Of the 54 couples in the three BMT treatment conditions, 39 couples (72%)
returned the completed A-C and MAS at the 3-month follow-up. As can be
seen in Table 5.1, as a group the couples tended to maintain their treatment
gains. t tests of correlated means from posttest to follow-up confirmed this
observation; there were no significant mean changes on A-C and MAS within
any of the three treatment conditions.

To investigate maintenance of change in terms of percentages, each couple's MAS 3-month follow-up scores were compared to MAS pretest scores
using the criteria described previously. The following results were obtained:

  • PS/C + CON: 8 of 14 (57%) improved, 2 of 14 (14%) deteriorated, 4 of 14 (29%) showed no change
  • PS/C Only: 7 of 12 (58%) improved, 1 of 12 (8%) deteriorated,
4 of 12 (33%) showed no change
  • CON Only: 10 of 13 (77%) improved, 1 of 13 (8%) deteriorated,
2 of 13 (15%) showed no change

Since WL couples were treated immediately following their 10-week wait, no
3-month follow-up data were available for these couples.

Role of Age in Treatment Effectiveness

A median split on couples' ages resulted in a younger-couple group with a
mean age of 25.1 and an older-couple group with a mean age of 37.2. A
$2 \times 3 \times 2$ MANOVA (female therapist, male therapist $\times$ PS/C + CON, PS/C
Only, CON Only $\times$ younger couples, older couples) using adjusted posttest
scores showed a significant multivariate main effect for age, $F (4, 39) = 2.62$,

$p < .05$. There were no other significant multivariate main or interaction effects. Univariate tests corresponding to the significant multivariate effect for age indicated that younger couples improved significantly more than older couples on A-C, F (1, 42) = 4.30, $p < .05$; and on Pos. MICS, F (1, 42) = 6.44, $p < .01$. There were no significant effects of age on MAS or Neg. MICS.

Discussion

Overall, the findings indicate that BMT is more effective than no treatment in aiding distressed couples. This investigation and Jacobson's work (1977, 1978) provide three controlled studies that affirm the utility of these specific BMT techniques. The fairly large sample size in the current study ($n = 72$ couples) helps to increase confidence in the effectiveness of the techniques.

In addition to exploring the overall effectiveness of BMT, the present investigation focused on isolating the change-inducing components of the complete BMT treatment. A direct comparison of the three BMT conditions strongly indicated no differential effectiveness of the three treatments. Thus, from the current data there is no strong empirical basis for recommending one set of treatment strategies over the other.

This finding of no meaningful differences among BMT conditions is consistent with results of other investigations. When comparing two BMT conditions, each of which contained identical problem-solving and communication skills training but differed in the form of behavioral contracting employed, Jacobson (1978) found no significant differences between the two BMT treatment conditions on any dependent variables. Although their two treatment conditions differed in the use of written behavior change agreements, Turkewitz and O'Leary's (1981) BMT and CT conditions overlapped somewhat in their use of communication training; however, they also found no significant differences between their two treatment conditions on any dependent measures. Finally, when Margolin and Weiss (1978) compared two BMT treatment conditions in a study that included four treatment sessions (one BMT treatment condition was actually the same as the other condition plus cognitive restructuring), they found significant differences between these two treatment conditions on only two of nine dependent variables. Thus, from the outcome studies published to date there is little evidence to suggest that one behavioral technique is more effective than another in aiding distressed couples.

One interpretation of the lack of differences between and among BMT conditions is that the changes result from factors not specific to BMT; therefore, when BMT treatments are compared, no significant differences are found. There are some data bearing on this issue. Using a BMT treatment analogous to PS/C + CON in the current investigation, Jacobson (1978) included a nonspecific treatment condition to control for therapist activity level and directiveness, amount of treatment, and number of homework assignments (Jacobson & Baucom, 1977). As mentioned earlier, the results of that study showed BMT to be more effective than the nonspecific condition on three of the four dependent measures. However, on the basis of one investigation, we must be cautious before concluding that nonspecific factors are unimportant in BMT.

Another interpretation of the results of these investigations is that there are factors common to different behavioral techniques, but not included in other marital approaches, that are of assistance to couples. On the most general level, essentially all BMT procedures focus directly on having spouses behave in more effective ways with each other, whether it be verbal and nonverbal communication behavior or instrumental behaviors such as accomplishing chores. Observing one's spouse and oneself behaving in positive ways within the relationship may be a crucial variable in treatment success. Different behavioral techniques focus on different aspects of behavior and use different strategies to produce behavior change, yet a focus on producing positive interaction in important areas of the marital relationship is the crux of BMT.

Although the direct comparison of the three BMT treatment conditions indicates no differential effectiveness, the pretest to posttest changes within each BMT treatment condition should not be ignored. PS/C + CON was the only treatment to show significant improvement on all dependent measures. CON Only, on the other hand, did not show significant improvement on either of the two communication measures. Thus, when couples were not taught communication skills, their communication did not improve significantly. These findings seem to indicate that when communication changes are viewed as important, contracting alone is not the treatment of choice.

The data were also examined in terms of the number of couples who improved by the end of treatment. Of BMT couples, 74% increased at least 10 points on MAS, whereas only 33% of waiting-list couples changed to this degree at posttest. Previous nonbehavioral marital investigations have used various criteria for determining whether a couple improved by the end of therapy. Therefore comparison of results across investigations is difficult. However, with this caution in mind, it should be noted that based on a 10-point MAS change, 74% of the treated couples improved, compared to Gurman and Kniskern's (1978) estimate of 65% improvement for couples in nonbehavioral marital outcome studies.

The results indicate that the CON Only condition exhibited the highest improvement rates of the various treatment conditions at posttest (83%) and at 3-month follow-up (77%). At present the basis for these findings is unclear, but some speculation may be helpful in providing areas on which to focus in future investigations. CON Only differs from the other two behavioral treatment conditions in that CON Only allows couples to devote virtually all of their attention to altering behaviors in various areas of marital discord;

on the other hand, PS/C Only and PS/C + CON include time for learning process skills, that is, problem-solving steps and communication skills to aid in resolving problems. Thus, the issue is raised of whether, in a restricted number of treatment sessions, time is best spent focusing almost entirely on the couple's content problems, or whether an emphasis should also be placed on teaching process skills. This question could be partially answered if data were available to indicate whether CON Only couples actually resolved more of their problems than did couples in the other conditions. Such data are not present in the current study. Although defining whether a presenting problem has been successfully resolved might be a difficult task, future investigators should consider attempting to systematically gather data on the extent to which couples have altered their behavior outside of the therapy sessions. No currently published BMT outcome investigations provide data on whether couples have actually followed through on their problem solutions and contracts.

    Whereas two findings—the percentage of couples improving after receiving BMT and the significant differences on outcome measures between BMT and WL couples—point to the usefulness of behavioral strategies with distressed couples, the couples' absolute levels of satisfaction at the end of treatment should not be ignored. Typically, a score of 200 on the MAS has been considered the cutoff point for differentiating between distressed and nondistressed couples. If this criterion is adopted, the results indicate that the only group whose average posttest MAS score was in the nondistressed range was CON Only; couples in the other two BMT treatment conditions had average posttest MAS scores in the distressed range. Similar results have been found in previously published BMT investigations. For example, in one comparative outcome study in which distressed couples were treated with BMT in a group format, the average posttest score on MAS was in the distressed range (Liberman et al., 1976). Likewise, from the data presented on Turkewitz and O'Leary's (1981) investigation, it appears that the couples receiving BMT also averaged in the distressed range on the MAS at posttest; similar results were obtained for their couples receiving communication therapy. Margolin and Weiss's (1978) couples also had average MAS scores in the distressed range at posttest for both BMT treatment conditions. On the other hand, in each of the three BMT conditions in Jacobson's (1977, 1978) two investigations, the MAS posttest mean was in the nondistressed range.

    In considering these MAS posttest levels, at least two factors need to be kept in mind: the MAS as a criterion for distress, and the format, goals, and effects of treatment. No single measure can serve as an adequate measure of all marital distress, and the current results must be interpreted only in terms of the MAS. Although other criticisms of the MAS might be raised, focal to the current investigation is the use of a cutoff score of 200 for couples (or 100 for individuals) to be considered in the nondistressed range. This cutoff score has become accepted rather routinely, yet a closer look at the derivation of this cutoff score raises some questions. The cutoff score of 100 for individuals was selected because it optimally differentiated persons considered maritally distressed (based on case data) from individuals considered "exceptionally well adjusted in marriage by friends who knew them well" (Locke & Wallace, 1959, p. 254). Whereas it would be preferable to help distressed couples become exceptionally well adjusted through BMT, in many cases more moderate goals must be sought. Requiring couples to reach a cutoff point that originally indicated exceptionally well-adjusted marriages might be an unrealistically stringent criterion to set for any form of marital therapy.

Moreover, in considering absolute levels of MAS posttest scores, it is important to remember that due to experimental requirements, the BMT treatments were conducted in a standardized way for a given number of sessions. Thus the therapist was not allowed to deviate from the treatment format, as might be considered appropriate at times in a clinical setting. Also, treatment was automatically terminated after 10 treatment sessions. In a clinical context treatment might be continued for additional sessions if deemed appropriate. Whereas the relative effectiveness of different treatment approaches is not affected greatly by these experimental constraints, since all treatments would have the same constraints, these constraints become more relevant when the absolute level of functioning of the couple at posttest is considered. Since the therapist in an outcome investigation cannot significantly tailor the treatment to the couple, the research findings are likely to be an underestimate of treatment effectiveness in a more applied clinical context where the treatment can be adapted to the needs of the specific couple.

Furthermore, it may be that in some instances when a couple is dissatisfied with their relationship at the termination of therapy, perhaps even contemplating divorce, they should not necessarily be viewed as a treatment failure. At times these decisions seem well considered, and from the standpoint of the happiness of the individuals involved, such a decision sometimes seems reasonable. Marital therapy might have been useful to such a couple in helping them obtain a realistic appraisal of their relationship and their options. Appropriate goals of marital therapy in outcome investigations constitute a complex issue that is dealt with in more detail elsewhere (Baucom, in press). The main point here is that we should be cautious in assuming that a low MAS score indicates that therapy was not of benefit to the couple. In spite of these cautions, the results of the current investigation, in combination with findings from other studies, do suggest that BMT is not a panacea for all maritally distressed couples.

The final issue addressed in the study was the effect of the couple's age on treatment effectiveness. The results indicated that, overall, younger couples benefited more from treatment than did older couples. In Turkewitz and O'Leary's (1981) study, a similar finding was obtained. In addition, the latter investigators found that age interacted with treatment in determining out-come. Such an interaction was not found in the current investigation, but the findings are not necessarily inconsistent with Turkewitz and O'Leary's find-ings. In their investigation younger couples benefited more from BMT than did older couples. Since all of the treatments in the current investigation were forms of BMT, the present finding that younger couples benefited more from treatment than did older couples is consistent with Turkewitz and O'Leary's finding that younger couples responded more favorably to BMT than did older couples. Since the current investigation did not include a treatment con-dition consisting of communication training only, the relative impact of such a treatment on older and younger couples could not be explored. What can be stated is that there now exist two studies suggesting that younger couples respond more favorably to BMT than do older couples.

Implications

In conclusion, the results indicate that BMT is of assistance to many maritally distressed couples and, overall, is more effective than no treatment. However, it must be recognized that some couples were still experiencing some marital distress at the end of treatment. There are at least two directions for future research to proceed in an attempt to improve the effectiveness of BMT. First, data are needed on efforts to match couples with particular treatments. If a person sought individual therapy for individual psychological distress, the treatment would consist of specific strategies tailored to meet the particular problems presented. We have not yet researched a wide range of behavioral techniques for aiding distressed couples; as a result, we have not been able to match couples with specific types of behavioral interventions. Certainly, investigating the effectiveness of additional behavioral techniques, and subse-quently matching the treatments with the couple's complaints, are worthy goals.

Second, cognitive and emotional interventions for distressed couples need to be researched and integrated with behavioral interventions. Margolin and Weiss (1978) have already conducted an analogue investigation suggesting that cognitive restructuring might fruitfully be added to BMT. Weiss (1980) has presented a general model for combining cognitive and behavioral strategies, and Epstein (1982) has discussed how several specific cognitive-restructuring techniques might be integrated with BMT. The author is currently exploring, in an outcome investigation, the effectiveness of the treatment that integrates cognitive restructuring with the combined treatment of problem-solving/communication training and contracting employed in the investigation re-ported here (Baucom & Lester, 1981).

In essence, we have a strong basis of treatment in the behavioral inter-ventions that have been investigated to date. As we recognize the complexity of marital interaction and marital distress, we also realize that we will need to broaden our treatment to include other behavioral strategies and devote more explicit attention to cognitive and emotional factors.

ACKNOWLEDGMENTS

This research was supported by NIMH Grant No. MH 30905-01 and grants from the Institute of College Research at Texas Tech University. Data for the study were gathered while the author was at Texas Tech University. I wish to thank Susan Mehlman and Daniel Anderson, who served as therapists; and Holly Garrett and Shaun Callison, who were coders for the study.

REFERENCES

Azrin, N. H., Naster, B. J., & Jones, R. Reciprocity counselling: A rapid learning-based procedure for marital counselling. *Behaviour Research and Therapy*, 1973, *11*, 365-382.

Baucom, D. H. A comparison of behavioral contracting and problem-solving/communications training in behavioral marital therapy. *Behavior Therapy*, 1982, *13*, 162-174.

Baucom, D. H. Conceptual and psychometric issues in evaluating the effectiveness of behavioral marital therapy. In J. P. Vincent (Ed.), *Advances in family intervention, assessment and theory: A research annual* (Vol. 3). Greenwich, CT: JAI Press, in press.

Baucom, D. H., & Lester, G. W. *The effects of complementing behavioral marital therapy with cognitive restructuring techniques.* Research in progress, 1981.

Epstein, N. Cognitive therapy with couples. *American Journal of Family Therapy,* 1982, *10*, 5-16.

Gurman, A. S., & Kniskern, D. P. Research on marital and family therapy: Progress, perspective, and prospect. In S. L. Garfield & A. E. Bergin (Eds.), *Handbook of psychotherapy and behavior change: An empirical analysis.* New York: Wiley, 1978.

Jacobson, N. S. Problem-solving and contingency contracting in the treatment of marital discord. *Journal of Consulting and Clinical Psychology,* 1977, *45*, 92-100.

Jacobson, N. S. Specific and nonspecific factors in the effectiveness of a behavioral approach to the treatment of marital discord. *Journal of Consulting and Clinical Psychology*, 1978, *46*, 442-452.

Jacobson, N. S., & Baucom, D. H. Design and assessment of nonspecific control groups in behavior modification research. *Behavior Therapy*, 1977, *8*, 709-719.

Lester, G. W., Beckham, E., & Baucom, D. H. Implementation of behavioral marital therapy. *Journal of Marital and Family Therapy,* 1980, *6*,189-199.

Liberman, R. P., Levine, J., Wheeler, E., Sanders, N., & Wallace, C. J. Marital therapy in groups: A comparative evaluation of behavioral and interactional formats. *Acta Psychiatrica Scandinavica,* 1976, *266*, 3-34. (Suppl.)

Locke, H. J., & Wallace, K. M. Short marital-adjustment and prediction tests: Their reliability and validity. *Marriage and Family Living,* 1959, *21*, 251-255.

Margolin, G., & Weiss, R. L. Comparative evaluation of therapeutic components associated with behavioral marital treatments. *Journal of Consulting and Clinical Psychology*, 1978, *46*, 1476-1486.

Marital Studies Center. *Marital Interaction Coding System* (Rev. ed.). Unpublished manuscript, University of Oregon, 1975.

Mehlman, S. K., Baucom, D. H., & Anderson, D. Effectiveness of cotherapists vs. single therapists and immediate vs. delayed treatment in behavioral marital therapy. *Journal of Consulting and Clinical Psychology,* 1983, *51*, 258-266.

Olson, D., & Ryder, R. G. Inventory of Marital Conflicts (IMC): An experimental interaction procedure. *Journal of Marriage and the Family,* 1970, *32*, 443-448.

Patterson, G. R., & Hops, H. Coercion, a game for two: Intervention techniques for marital conflict. In R. E. Ulrich & P. Mounjoy (Eds.), *The experimental analysis of social behav-*

ior. New York: Appleton-Century-Crofts, 1972.

Patterson, G. R., Hops, H., & Weiss, R. *A social learning approach to reducing rates of marital conflict.* Paper presented at the annual meeting of the Association for Advancement of Behavior Therapy, New York, October 1972.

Patterson, G. R., Hops, H., & Weiss, R. L. Interpersonal skills training for couples in early stages of conflict. *Journal of Marriage and the Family,* 1975, *37,* 295–303.

Stuart, R. B. Operant-interpersonal treatment for marital discord. *Journal of Consulting and Clinical Psychology,* 1969, *33,* 675–682.

Stuart, R. B. *Helping couples change: A social learning approach to marital therapy.* New York: Guilford Press, 1980.

Tsoi-Hoshmand, L. Marital therapy: An integrative behavioral-learning model. *Journal of Marriage and Family Counseling,* 1976, *2,* 179–191.

Turkewitz, H., & O'Leary, K. D. A comparative outcome study of behavioral marital therapy and communication therapy. *Journal of Marital and Family Therapy,* 1981, *7,* 159–169.

Weiss, R. L. Strategic behavioral marital therapy: Toward a model for assessment and intervention. In J. P. Vincent (Ed.), *Advances in family intervention, assessment and theory* (Vol. 1). Greenwich, CT: JAI Press, 1980.

Weiss, R. L., Hops, H., & Patterson, G. R. A framework for conceptualizing marital conflict, a technology for altering it, some data for evaluating it. In L. A. Hamerlynck, L. C. Handy, & E. J. Mash (Eds.), *Behavior change: Methodology, concepts, and practice.* Champaign, IL: Research Press, 1973.

6

Predicting Marital Status following Behavioral Marital Therapy: A Comparison of Models of Marital Relationships

DONALD H. BAUCOM AND SUSAN KAPLAN MEHLMAN

During the past decade there has been rapid growth in behavioral marital therapy (BMT) as an area of research. Important advances have occurred in the development of treatment techniques for use with distressed couples. Parallel advances have taken place in the construction of new assessment devices to use as dependent measures in BMT outcome investigations. Thus, numerous techniques for measuring marital interaction and marital distress are now available to researchers investigating the outcome of BMT, including sophisticated coding systems and self-report inventories.

This proliferation of measures has resulted in part because it has become apparent that marital distress is not a monolithic entity. There are many aspects of marital interaction, and a couple might function effectively in one aspect of marriage, such as allocating chores, but may have difficulty in another area, such as communicating with each other. Since BMT has taken the tack of teaching skills to couples in order to change specific aspects of interaction, it is logical that measures of specific areas of marital interaction have been developed and included in treatment outcome criteria. In addition to these more specific measures, most outcome investigations have also included a rather global measure of marital satisfaction.

Whereas a number of dependent measures to assess numerous aspects of marital interaction have been developed and typically included in BMT outcome investigations, there has been less emphasis to date on how to interpret patterns of dependent measures or how to combine the data for analysis. In this chapter we examine some of those specific and global measures, both individually and in various combinations, and their effectiveness in predicting marital status after treatment by BMT. Some implica-

Donald H. Baucom. Psychology Department, University of North Carolina at Chapel Hill, Chapel Hill, North Carolina, U.S.A.

Susan Kaplan Mehlman. Springfield Hospital Center, Sykesville, Maryland, U.S.A.

tions for therapy are noted and possible directions for future research suggested.

Interpretation of Various Outcome Measures

As argued elsewhere, in most BMT investigations all outcome criteria are not created equal (Baucom, in press). Different strategies can be taken to decide how to interpret the results of various dependent measures in BMT outcome studies. For example, one might decide on a theoretical basis that certain skills are necessary in defining a satisfactory relationship; from this perspective, the dependent measures focal to those relationship skills would be of primary importance. Or one might compare distressed and nondistressed couples empirically on various behaviors, skills, cognitions, and so on, and find those areas in which the two groups differ. Subsequently, treatment strategies could be developed to alter the behavior of distressed couples in the areas where they differ from nondistressed couples, and dependent measures particular to those areas would become the focus. In either of these two strategies, which are not necessarily contradictory, the relationship between measures of specific domains of marital interaction and global marital satisfaction would be of importance in order to determine whether learning new skills improved the couples' satisfaction with their relationships.

In this chapter a third approach is taken to help clarify the interpretation of various outcome measures: An investigation was made of the extent to which different outcome measures obtained at the termination of therapy can predict important future relationship behaviors, decisions, or attitudes. Certainly one important marital decision, and its accompanying behavior, is whether the spouses decide to maintain their relationship and continue to live together, or whether they decide to separate from each other. It has been suggested elsewhere (Baucom, in press) that a couple's decision to divorce or remain married should not be equated with the usefulness of therapy; one's position on that issue is likely to be related to one's values and views on whether divorce is an acceptable solution to an unhappy marriage. However, leaving this value judgment aside, the decision of whether to maintain a marriage is an important relationship decision that will have a considerable impact on the remainder of the spouses' lives. Therefore, it is of importance to know whether there is an empirical relationship between BMT outcome and later marital status, and if so, what the nature of that relationship is.

Initially, logic might seem to dictate that if basic research has shown that distressed couples have certain skill deficits compared to nondistressed couples, then posttherapy measures of these skills might be good predictors of future relationship interaction. For example, if distressed couples do not exhibit the same communication patterns as nondistressed couples, then distressed couples who undergo therapy and then demonstrate improved communication patterns at the end of therapy would likely be the couples who would consequently be less distressed and maintain their marriages. However, at present we have no data to substantiate this logic. It is possible that various behaviors that result from therapy could have different meanings compared to the same behaviors shown by a nondistressed couple who has not undergone treatment. For instance, couples who as a result of communication training show certain verbal and nonverbal behavior may still be very different from nondistressed couples who show similar behavior. Complimenting one's spouse and making eye contact could be indicative of caring and love in a nondistressed, nontreated couple, whereas the same behaviors from a couple who has completed therapy might be what "one is supposed to do because the therapist explained how it would help the relationship." The current study attempted to predict future marital status based on posttreatment outcome measures from couples who had undergone BMT.

Combining Husbands' and Wives' Outcome Measures

In the study of marital interaction and marital distress, data are typically gathered from both spouses, and some decision must be made regarding how the data from the two spouses will be combined to provide an index of the couple's functioning. The second major focus of this study was to explore various ways of combining the spouses' data and the underlying models of marital relationships accompanying each approach to data combination. There are numerous models for combining spouses' scores that have some intuitive appeal, and six of these are examined here.

Models

SUMMATIVE MODEL

On most measures in BMT outcome investigations, the husband receives a score and the wife receives a score; most typically, the spouses' scores have been summed or averaged to provide a single couple's score for a particular measure (Summative Model). O'Leary and Turkewitz (1978) recommended this strategy in their discussion of methodological errors in marital outcome research. The rationale for this strategy is that the marital relationship is seen as the focus of treatment in BMT, and the unit of measurement among dependent variables should reflect this focus.

DIFFERENCE MODEL

The Summative Model makes certain assumptions about a relationship, which should be recognized and evaluated. One conceptual difficulty with it is that it omits potentially meaningful configural information about the couples.

Adding the two spouses' scores together on a marital satisfaction scale evokes a model of a relationship in which one spouse's dissatisfaction can be directly compensated for by the other partner's high level of satisfaction (Baucom, in press). As a result, Couple A, in which the two partners each scored 100 (200 total) on a marital satisfaction inventory, would be treated identically to Couple B, in which the husband scored 130 and the wife scored 70 (200 total). Certainly a clinician who interacted with the two couples would observe a meaningful difference between these two couples regarding their satisfaction with their relationships. Clearly, when the partners' scores are simply added together, information is lost about how one partner scored relative to the other. It might be important that the husband in Couple B scored almost twice as high as the wife. Such differences in satisfaction could be predictive of an unstable relationship. Consequently, a second model of relationships might focus on discrepancies in attitudes or behaviors between the spouses as important; in such a model, one would calculate difference scores between spouses rather than summed scores (Difference Model).

SUM PLUS DIFFERENCE MODEL

Theorists who would view discrepancies as important would likely view the overall level of score for the couple as important as well. Therefore, another relationship model would be to combine the two models discussed thus far and consider both sum and difference scores (Sum Plus Difference Model). Although this model would be of major theoretical importance, the small number of divorced couples (13) in the data base for this chapter, relative to the large number of predictor variables (8) that would be involved in the model, made the investigation of this model implausible in this study. Therefore, the Sum Plus Difference Model is merely introduced here but omitted from the subsequent analyses in this chapter.

TWO-GENDER MODELS

Another model focuses on the possibility that the two genders might show differential relationships between predictor variables and later marital status. For example, it may be that regardless of the magnitude or configuration of scores, the wife's scores considered alone are better predictors of later marital status than the husband's scores. Both variants of the Two-Gender Model were used here: that is, the Husbands' Scores Model and the Wives' Scores Model.

WEAK LINK MODELS

Just as a chain is no stronger than its weakest link, a relationship might be considered no more successful than the more dissatisfied member of the relationship. For example, it is possible that if one spouse is extremely dissatisfied with the relationship, then the marriage is in serious difficulty regardless of the level of marital satisfaction displayed by the other spouse. Likewise, if the husband is unable to make behavior changes requested by the wife but the wife is able to change in ways that her husband requested, then the husband's lack of behavior change may be the most salient aspect to consider regarding the adaptiveness of the relationship. The Weak Link Model takes such possibilities into account. Two variants of the Weak Link Model were employed herein. One variant would suggest that the more maladaptive behavior or more distress indicated by either spouse in each area of marital interaction, the more likely the couple would be to separate. This is referred to as the Less Adaptive Model. Second, it may be that the spouse who has the lower overall marital satisfaction is the better index of the relationship. The second variant reflects this assumption and is labeled the Distressed Spouse Model.

Selecting a Model

Each of these models, with its corresponding approach to data handling, has some logical basis and appeal. How then is one to decide which approach to use in considering couples' data? Again, one resolution would be to consider the extent to which each approach is predictive of some important relationship decision or behavior. Consequently, in this chapter, posttherapy treatment measures were combined into each of the models to predict future marital status—whether the spouses separated from each other or maintained their marital relationship. There is no suggestion that the results of this one investigation will indicate the way in which couples' data should generally be treated. It may be that the utility of a specific model will vary, depending upon the question being addressed in a particular study. The current analyses were conducted to see whether, in this one particular predictive situation, one model seems more appropriate than others. It is hoped that investigators will begin to question the Summative Model, which has become somewhat routinely used in BMT outcome investigations.

Method

Subjects

Out of 79 couples who had received BMT as part of a 4-year project investigating several parameters of BMT, 71 served as the subjects for this investigation. All couples received BMT for 10 weeks. Treatment included either (1) problem-solving/communication training, (2) *quid pro quo* contracting, or (3) problem-solving/communication training followed by *quid pro quo* contracting. Couples also varied in terms of whether they were treated by single therapists or cotherapists, and whether they were seen immediately after requesting treatment or were delayed 10 weeks before beginning treatment (see Baucom, Chapter 5, this volume; Baucom, 1982; and Mehlman, Baucom, & Anderson, 1983, for detailed descriptions of this project). Findings from that project indicated that BMT was more effective than no treatment; moreover, there were no significant differences among couples receiving BMT as a function of the BMT treatment techniques employed, single therapists versus cotherapists, or immediate versus delayed treatment. As a result, couples from the various BMT conditions were combined for the current investigation. The 71 couples in the current investigation were those who responded to a 6-month follow-up query inquiring into the status of their marital relationships. Eight couples who had moved from the area could not be contacted to provide follow-up information.

Materials

The purpose of the study was to predict whether or not couples had continued to live together or had separated, within 6 months after BMT terminated, using the measures gathered at the end of BMT as predictors. The variables that served as outcome measures for the therapy project and consequently as the predictor variables for the current investigation were two self-report and two behavioral observation measures obtained immediately after the termination of treatment.

AREAS OF CHANGE QUESTIONNAIRE
The Areas of Change Questionnaire (A-C) (Weiss, Hops, & Patterson, 1973) is a self-report measure with a behavioral focus; each spouse indicates the degree of behavior change desired in 34 specific areas of marital interaction. In this investigation, a spouse's score was the total amount of change requested.

MARITAL ADJUSTMENT SCALE
The Marital Adjustment Scale (MAS) (Locke & Wallace, 1959) is a commonly used self-report inventory that provides an overall measure of marital satisfaction. Each spouse completes the MAS individually.

REVISED MARITAL INTERACTION CODING SYSTEM
The Marital Interaction Coding System (MICS) (Marital Studies Center, 1975) is a system for coding verbal and nonverbal dyadic interaction into 29 categories. Based on Margolin and Weiss's (1978) scoring system, these categories were combined into two larger categories as follows: Positive Behaviors (Pos. MICS) consisted of agree, approval, accept responsibility, assent, attention, compromise, humor, laugh, positive physical contact, problem solution, and smile; Negative Behaviors (Neg. MICS) consisted of complaint, criticize, deny

responsibility, excuse, interrupt, no response, not tracking, put down, and turn off. At the posttherapy measurement session, each couple was asked to solve two problems, which were then coded according to the MICS by two trained raters. First, each couple was asked to resolve one of their own moderate-sized problems in 5–6 minutes. In the second problem couples were asked to spend 5–6 minutes resolving a hypothetical problem from the Inventory of Marital Conflicts (Olson & Ryder, 1970). For purposes of analysis, the data for these two problems were combined. Based on Pearson correlations, coders showed interrater reliabilities of $r = .89$ for Pos. MICS and $r = .86$ for Neg. MICS posttherapy measures.

Procedure

Six months after couples had completed BMT, each couple was contacted by mail and asked to return a response that included an indication of whether they were still married and living together, or whether they had separated. Couples who did not respond received telephone reminders. Seventy-one couples responded to this follow-up request, and each of these couples was then categorized either as (1) married and living together (MAR) or (2) separated from each other (SEP) 6 months after treatment terminated.

Results

In all of the following analyses, the A-C, MAS, Pos. MICS, and Neg. MICS measured at the termination of BMT (see Table 6.1) were used to predict marital status (MAR vs. SEP) 6 months after the termination of therapy.

Correlations between Husbands' and Wives' Predictor Scores

Across the different relationship models, the posttreatment measures involve various combinations of husbands' and wives' scores. To the extent that husbands' and wives' scores are highly correlated for a given variable, redundant information is carried by those two scores. If the husbands' and wives' scores provide highly redundant information, then combining them differently according to the various models would likely lead to little differential predictability of marital status. For example, in the hypothetical situation in which the husbands' scores were correlated with the wives' scores using $r = 1$ for each predictor variable, then the Husbands' Scores Model, Wives' Scores Model, Summative Model, Difference Model, and Weak Link Models would predict marital status with identical accuracy. Consequently, it was important to determine the correlations between the husbands' and wives' scores on the four predictor variables. The results were as follows: A-C, $r = .31$, $p < .005$; MAS, $r = .71$, $p < .001$; Pos. MICS, $r = .69$, $p < .001$; Neg. MICS, $r = .37$, $p < .001$.

TABLE 6.1. Posttherapy Means and Standard Deviations for Predictor Variables

Spouse	Marital status 6 months after therapy	Areas of Change		Marital Adjust-ment Scale		Positive MICS		Negative MICS	
		M	SD	M	SD	M	SD	M	SD
Husband	Living together[a]	14.40	10.73	96.69	18.23	5.13	1.47	0.44	0.76
	Separated[b]	14.46	9.13	89.08	14.61	6.34	2.40	0.33	0.35
Wife	Living together[a]	17.88	13.08	95.03	18.77	5.18	1.45	0.40	0.43
	Separated[b]	14.00	8.85	83.92	20.33	5.72	2.02	0.75	0.69

[a]n = 58.
[b]n = 13.

These correlations are all statistically significant, and for MAS and Pos. MICS the correlations are substantial. However, for none of these variables do the linear relationships between the husbands' and wives' scores account for more than 50% of the common variance. Therefore, it is possible that marital status might be differentially predicted by the posttreatment measures when they are scored according to the various models.

Correlations between Single Predictor Scores and Marital Status

To determine how well each of the four predictor variables (A-C, MAS, Pos. MICS, Neg. MICS) predicted marital status, the predictor variables were scored in several different ways to reflect the various relationship models described previously. First, the frequently used Summative Model was employed; that is, for each predictor variable, the husband's and wife's scores of a couple were added together. To investigate the importance of discrepancy between a husband's and wife's score, the Difference Model was used; here the wife's score was subtracted from the husband's score for a given predictor variable. For the Two-Gender Model, two procedures were used: The Husbands' Scores Model employed the husbands' scores separately, and the Wives' Scores Model used wives' scores separately. Two Weak Link Models were employed: In the Less Adaptive Model, for a given predictor variable, the spouse's score that showed more marital distress or less adaptive behavior on that variable was used to represent the couple's score on that variable (i.e., the lower MAS score, the higher A-C score, the lower Pos. MICS score, and the higher Neg. MICS score for the husband or wife of a couple). Thus, the husband's score on MAS and Neg. MICS would represent the couple if he scored less adaptively than his wife on those variables, whereas the wife's A-C and Pos. MICS scores would serve as the couple's scores if she scored less adaptively than her husband on those variables. Finally, the Distressed Spouse Model was employed by selecting the spouse with the lower MAS score and using that individual's scores on all four predictor variables as the couple's scores on those variables.

Point biserial correlations were calculated between marital status (MAR vs. SEP) and these single predictor variables (scored according to each of the six models). The results are presented in Table 6.2.

These findings indicate that future marital status can be predicted better than chance from single measures gathered at the termination of BMT. However, the reader should be aware that marital status was coded such that only some of the results were in the direction that would be expected. In four of the six models (see Table 6.2) MAS was significantly correlated with marital status, as expected; also, the wives' Neg. MICS scores were correlated in the predicted direction. However, the findings for Pos. MICS indicated that increased Pos. MICS was correlated with a greater likelihood of separation in

TABLE 6.2. Correlations between Marital Status and Single Predictor Variables in Six Models

Model	Areas of Change	Marital Adjust-ment Scale	Positive MICS	Negative MICS
Summative Model	−.08	−.21*	.23*	.09
Difference Model	.11	.10	.20*	−.25*
Husbands' Scores Model	.00	−.17	.27**	−.06
Wives' Scores Model	−.12	−.22*	.13	.27**
Less Adaptive Model	−.15	−.20*	.25*	.10
Distressed Spouse Model	−.17	−.20*	.27**	.07

*$p<.05$.
**$p<.01$.

four models. MICS difference scores were also correlated with marital status, but how these difference scores would be expected to be related to marital status is unclear. A-C was unrelated to marital status in all models.

Predicting Marital Status from Multiple Measures

The preceding analysis was conducted to provide more understanding of the meaning of single measures of marital interaction that are commonly used in outcome studies. That is, when a couple scores at a certain level on MAS at the end of treatment, does that help us predict whether the couple will be likely to separate in the near future? The next analysis focused on the utility of the various models in predicting marital status when taking all of the predictor variables into account. For that purpose, six discriminant analyses were conducted, one for each of the six models. In each analysis, A-C, MAS, Pos. MICS, and Neg. MICS obtained at the termination of therapy were used as predictor variables.

The results are presented in Table 6.3. Four of the six models significantly predicted marital status: Distressed Spouse Model, Wives' Scores Model, Less Adaptive Model, and Summative Model.

Comparable analyses were conducted using couples' pretherapy scores as the predictors. None of the models significantly predicted marital status at 6 months after therapy. Thus, the findings are comforting in indicating that it is a couple's status at the end of therapy, rather than initial status, that is related to a decision regarding whether to continue to live together. Likewise, comparable analyses were conducted using change scores (posttherapy minus pretherapy scores), and none of the models significantly predicted

TABLE 6.3. Discriminant Analysis Predicting Marital Status from A-C, MAS, Pos. MICS, and Neg. MICS Based on Different Relationship Models

Model	Canonical correlation	Wilks's λ after function 0	χ^2	Standardized discriminant function coefficients				Group means on discriminant function	
				A-C	MAS	Pos. MICS	Neg. MICS	MAR	SEP
Summative Model	.38	0.86	10.40*	0.78	1.00	-0.52	-0.12	0.19	-0.85
Difference Model	.32	0.90	7.32	0.38	0.24	0.51	-0.64	-0.16	0.71
Husbands' Scores Model	.33	0.89	7.85	0.19	0.65	-0.79	0.31	0.16	-0.73
Wives' Scores Model	.44	0.80	14.70***	0.83	0.87	-0.24	-0.58	0.23	-1.03
Less Adaptive Model	.44	0.81	14.38**	0.95	0.96	-0.48	-0.31	0.23	-1.02
Distressed Spouse Model	.45	0.79	15.40***	0.89	0.91	-0.57	-0.12	0.24	-1.06

Note. Degrees of freedom = 4 for each model.

*$p < .05$.

**$p < .01$.

***$p < .005$.

marital status. It appears that it is the level of functioning at the end of therapy rather than the degree of change brought about by therapy that is predictive of future marital status.

Comparing the magnitudes of correlation between marital status and the six models, as shown in Table 6.3, only two models have smaller correlations than the frequently used Summative Model.

Some understanding of the way in which the married/living together and separated couples are discriminated can be obtained by a look at the standardized discriminant function coefficients. However, caution is necessary, since the predictor variables are correlated with each other; therefore, the coefficients are functions of the intercorrelations among the predictor variables, as well as the correlations between a given predictor variable and the criterion of marital status. With this caution in mind, it is apparent that the two self-report measures are weighted more heavily than the two observational measures in the models that provide significant discrimination. Perhaps more surprising, among the models that significantly discriminate, some of the measures appear to operate in the opposite direction from what would be expected. For example, the discriminant coefficients indicate that a decision to maintain the marital relationship is predicted by desiring more behavioral change (A-C) from one's spouse and by making fewer positive communications (Pos. MICS) at the termination of therapy. As would be expected, deciding to maintain the relationship is also predicted by self-reports of higher marital satisfaction (MAS) and by making fewer negative communications (Neg. MICS).

Discussion

Among the 24-point biserial correlations relating single posttherapy measures to marital status, 11 were significant at $p < .05$, although none of the correlations was above .27. Thus, marital status can be predicted at a low yet statistically significant level of accuracy from single predictor variables. The most consistent single predictors were self-reported marital satisfaction (MAS) and positive communication (Pos. MICS). Elsewhere it has been suggested on a conceptual basis that a couple's self-report of how satisfied they are with their relationship must be considered a primary dependent measure in BMT outcome studies in which the goal of the investigations is to improve the quality of the relationship (Baucom, in press). That is, as BMT investigators we can demonstrate through various specific outcome measures that we have taught the couples specific skills and altered certain behaviors. Further, it seems important to determine whether these newly learned skills and behaviors have been accompanied by an increase in the couple's subjective satisfaction with the marital relationship. To the extent that future marital status is a meaningful focus, the current results provide an empirical basis for affirming the importance of self-reported marital satisfaction, since this is one of the most consistent predictors of the couple's decision to separate or remain together 6 months after therapy has terminated.

The relationship between positive communication and marital status is perplexing. The findings generally indicated that the more positive the communication at the end of therapy, the more likely the couples were to separate. This finding, combined with previous results, may indicate that positive communication is an elusive variable that does not operate as we would expect in marital interaction. Several studies have explored whether distressed couples exhibit less positive communication than do nondistressed couples, and many investigators have found no difference between the two groups. Birchler, Weiss, and Vincent (1975) had the spouses of distressed and nondistressed couples interact in a laboratory setting. They found that in both free conversation and problem solving, distressed couples showed significantly more negative communication than nondistressed couples. However, distressed couples showed significantly less positive communication only during problem solving; the two groups did not differ on positive communication during free conversations. Klier and Rothberg (1977) confirmed the findings of Birchler et al. (1975) regarding negative communication but found no differences in positive communication between distressed and nondistressed couples during either problem solving or free conversation. Also, Robinson and Price (1976) found that distressed and nondistressed couples did not differ on the display of positive behavior at home, as recorded by raters. In addition to these observational studies, some BMT outcome investigations have been less successful in altering positive communication than negative communication. Whereas Jacobson (1977, 1978) found positive communication to increase with different BMT treatments, both Baucom (Chapter 5, this volume) and Margolin and Weiss (1978) found more consistent changes in negative communication compared to positive communication as a result of BMT programs that included communication training. These various results do not explain the relationship between positive communication and marital status in the current investigation; however, the combined findings suggest that we must be cautious in our thinking about the role of positive communication in marital distress.

The current findings regarding positive communication could result from the approach to data analysis employed here. Although various relationship models were employed, all data analyses were conducted in terms of number of positive and negative communications per minute. This approach to data analysis does not consider the order or sequencing of communication. Recently, more complex sequential analyses of communication data have been performed that take into account the specific response a spouse makes to a particular communication from the partner (see Margolin & Wampold, 1981). Such analyses might yield different results using the current data, but even so it is puzzling that, overall, a greater rate of positive communication is seen among couples who later separate.

As an alternative interpretation, Markman (1979, 1981) has presented evidence that communication among nondistressed couples is predictive of their relationship satisfaction 2½ and 5½ years later, but that it does not predict marital satisfaction 1 year after the initial communication. Consequently, the impact of communication may change over longer time periods. Couples in the current investigation are now being followed up at an interval of 2 years after the termination of therapy; those 2-year findings will be important in assessing the stability of the 6-month results reported here.

As a final attempt at understanding the relationship between positive communication and marital status, it should be noted that good communication skills are not sufficient for a satisfactory marriage. Teaching couples an effective communication style does not dictate what the content of the communication will be. Indeed, through clearer communication, the therapy may have helped some couples realize that separation was their most appropriate option. Consequently, the relationship between communication and future marital status is likely to be influenced by other dyadic strengths and potentials of the couples; that is, if communication skills are taught to spouses who are highly incompatible, then clearer communication may bring into focus those incompatibilities and a subsequent decision to separate.

The second major focus of this study was a comparison of the various scoring systems for couples' data and the implicit accompanying relationship models. At present, appropriate multivariate techniques have not been developed to directly compare these models, which across models contain correlated yet not identical predictor variables (e.g., in one prediction model, only the husbands' scores were used as predictors, and in another model, only the wives' scores were used). Although statistical tests have been developed for the two-variable case (e.g., Howell, 1982), these techniques do not generalize to the multivariate situation. Therefore, we must be content to observe the relative magnitudes of the canonical correlations. These various correlations do not vary widely, yet it is clear that the sum of the husband's and wife's scores is not the most effective scoring procedure for predicting future marital status. As can be seen in Table 6.3, both Weak Link Models—the Less Adaptive Model and the Distressed Spouse Model—predicted better than the Summative Model. The findings from the Distressed Spouse Model indicate that therapists must be concerned if either spouse leaves therapy with a global feeling of marital dissatisfaction (MAS), regardless of the other spouse's attitude toward the marriage; such couples have an increased likelihood of separating soon after therapy is terminated.

The results also indicate Wives' Scores Model is better than the Husbands' Scores Model in predicting future marital status. In fact, the Wives' Scores Model alone is a better predictor than the Summative Model, in which the husbands' and wives' scores are summed. This pattern of findings is consistent with results from previous investigations that indicated that the wife can be viewed as the "barometer" of a relationship, and that wives' scores are better predictors of relationship satisfaction than are husbands' scores (see Bentler & Newcomb, 1978; Burgess & Wallin, 1953; Floyd & Markman, 1981). Whereas analyzing couples' data separately by gender will likely be fruitful in helping us understand gender differences in marital relationships (Markman, Floyd, & Dickson-Markman, in press), such analyses do not allow us to understand configural patterns within a particular couple. The findings from the Weak Link Models suggest that one spouse's scores relative to the other spouse's scores can be helpful in predicting future marital status.

In summary, although the canonical correlations do not vary widely in magnitude, the findings from the comparison of models suggest that we should not necessarily routinely use the typical scoring procedure for handling couples' data, in which husbands' and wives' scores are simply added together. This model of a marital relationship appears conceptually simplistic, since configural information about the two spouses is disregarded. The current findings suggest that when configural information about the couple is considered, prediction of future marital status is somewhat improved. These results are not intended to indicate that we should now adopt a particular new scoring system or relationship model. It is hoped, however, that these findings will build on previous advances in BMT treatment and measurement by suggesting and exploring some new possibilities for combining and interpreting outcome data. Certainly, much more investigation is necessary before the relative merits of the models mentioned here or other models can be definitively established. At the least, we should be aware that our evaluation of the effectiveness of BMT is gauged relative to a particular relationship model and scoring system; we may do ourselves as investigators and our future clients a disservice unless we evaluate our treatment techniques using a relationship model that captures the complexity of marital interaction.

ACKNOWLEDGMENTS

The authors are grateful to NIMH (Grant No. MH 30905-01) and the Institute of College Research at Texas Tech University for the support they provided for the investigation on which this chapter is based. Portions of the data were gathered while the authors were at Texas Tech University. We wish to thank Daniel Anderson, who served as a therapist; and Holly Garrett and Shaun Callison, who were coders for the study. We would also like to thank Mark Appelbaum and Elliot Cramer for their consultation on certain statistical issues.

REFERENCES

Baucom, D. H. A comparison of behavioral contracting and problem-solving/communications training in behavioral marital therapy. *Behavior Therapy,* 1982, *13,* 162–174.
Baucom, D. H. Conceptual and psychometric issues in evaluating the effectiveness of behavioral marital therapy. In J. P. Vincent (Ed.), *Advances in family intervention, assessment and theory: A research annual* (Vol. 3). Greenwich, CT: JAI Press, in press.

Bentler, P., & Newcomb, M. Longitudinal study of marital success and failure. *Journal of Consulting and Clinical Psychology,* 1978, *46,* 1053-1070.

Birchler, G. R., Weiss, R. L., & Vincent, J. P. Multimethod analysis of social reinforcement exchange between maritally distressed and nondistressed spouse and stranger dyads. *Journal of Personality and Social Psychology,* 1975, *31,* 349-360.

Burgess, E., & Wallin, P. *Engagement and marriage.* Philadelphia: J. B. Lippincott, 1953.

Floyd, F. J., & Markman, H. J. *Insiders and outsiders assessment of distressed and nondistressed marital interaction.* Paper presented at the annual meeting of the Association for Advancement of Behavior Therapy, Toronto, November 1981.

Howell, D. C. *Statistical methods for psychology.* Boston: Duxbury Press, 1982.

Jacobson, N. S. Problem-solving and contingency contracting in the treatment of marital discord. *Journal of Consulting and Clinical Psychology,* 1977, *45,* 92-100.

Jacobson, N. S. Specific and nonspecific factors in the effectiveness of a behavioral approach to the treatment of marital discord. *Journal of Consulting and Clinical Psychology,* 1978, *46,* 442-452.

Klier, J. L., & Rothberg, M. *Characteristics of conflict resolution in couples.* Paper presented at the annual meeting of the Association for Advancement of Behavior Therapy, Atlanta, December 1977.

Locke, H. J., & Wallace, K. M. Short marital-adjustment and prediction tests: Their reliability and validity. *Marriage and Family Living,* 1959, *21,* 251-255.

Margolin, G., & Wampold, B. E. Sequential analysis of conflict and accord in distressed and nondistressed marital partners. *Journal of Consulting and Clinical Psychology,* 1981, *49,* 554-567.

Margolin, G., & Weiss, R. L. Comparative evaluation of therapeutic components associated with behavioral marital treatments. *Journal of Consulting and Clinical Psychology,* 1978, *46,* 1476-1486.

Marital Studies Center. *Marital Interaction Coding System* (Rev. ed.). Unpublished manuscript, University of Oregon, 1975.

Markman, H. J. The application of a behavioral model of marriage in predicting relationship satisfaction of couples planning marriage. *Journal of Consulting and Clinical Psychology,* 1979, *4,* 743-749.

Markman, H. J. Prediction of marital distress: A 5-year follow-up. *Journal of Consulting and Clinical Psychology,* 1981, *49,* 760-762.

Markman, H. J., Floyd, F., & Dickson-Markman, F. Toward a model for the prediction and primary prevention of marital and family distress and dissolution. In S. Duck (Ed.) *Personal relationships 4: Dissolving personal relationships.* London: Academic Press, 1982.

Mehlman, S. K., Baucom, D. H., & Anderson, D. Effectiveness of cotherapists vs. single therapists and immediate vs. delayed treatment in behavioral marital therapy. *Journal of Consulting and Clinical Psychology,* 1983, *51,* 258-266.

O'Leary, K. D., & Turkewitz, H. Methodological errors in marital and child treatment research. *Journal of Consulting and Clinical Psychology,* 1978, *46,* 747-758.

Olson, D. H., & Ryder, R. G. Inventory of Marital Conflicts (IMC): An experimental interaction procedure. *Journal of Marriage and the Family,* 1970, *32,* 443-448.

Robinson, E. A., & Price, M. G. *Behavioral and self-report correlates of marital satisfaction.* Paper presented at the annual meeting of the Association for Advancement of Behavior Therapy, New York, December 1976.

Weiss, R. L., Hops, H., & Patterson, G. R. A framework for conceptualizing marital conflict, a technology for altering it, some data for evaluating it. In L. A. Hamerlynck, L. C. Handy, & E. J. Mash (Eds.), *Behavior change: Methodology, concepts, and practice.* Champaign, IL: Research Press, 1973.

7

Evaluation of a Communication Skills Training Program with Groups of People Living Together

CLIVE REUBEN, MONIKA WIECH, AND DIRK ZIMMER

In recent years community living has become an increasingly popular alternative to living in the traditional small family. What was originally fashionable only among students and young people has now become a viable alternative for a broader spectrum of the population.

Up to now, these "natural groups" have rarely been the focus of psychological research. However, casual observations seem to show that the problems that arise in community living, in general, are more comparable with marital discord than with generation conflicts in family therapy.

Previous investigations of behaviorally oriented group therapy focused on specific behavioral goals (e.g., assertive behavior — see Ullrich, Ullrich, Grawe, & Zimmer, 1980). In all cases groups were formed explicitly for therapeutic purposes and ceased to exist after termination of treatment. In contrast to this, our study deals with therapy in natural groups existing outside of the therapeutic situation.

The basis of our study is a communication skills training program for couples; this program adopted the ideas of K. H. Mandel, who introduced behavioral principles into marital therapy in Germany (Mandel, Mandel, Stadter, & Zimmer, 1971). Following his ideas, we formulated a semistandardized program for couples (Anneken, Echelmeyer, Kaluza, Klein, Klockgeter-Kelle, & Zimmer, 1977). It has been shown to be effective in the treatment of dyadic interactional problems (Zimmer, 1977) and to produce stable results at a 1-year follow-up (Thanner, 1979). This program was adopted for a group setting.

We set out to answer the following questions: (1) Does a structured com-

Clive Reuben. Clinical Psychologist, General Hospital, Boeblingen/Baden-Württhenberg, Federal Republic of Germany.

Monika Wiech. Private practice, Freiburg/Baden-Württhenberg, Federal Republic of Germany.

Dirk Zimmer. Psychological Institute, University of Tübingen, Federal Republic of Germany.

munication skills training program lead to the improvement in communication skills that is necessary for the satisfactory resolution of problems and conflicts in small groups? (2) Are these postulated changes accompanied by a subjective increase in individual satisfaction with group living? (3) Do changes measured after termination of therapy remain stable over time?

Method

Description of Treatment Procedures

The program employed accentuated explicit training in specific target behaviors and, in particular, training for adequate coping skills in conflict situations. The training consisted of seven 2-hour sessions. Each member of the group had the opportunity to rehearse new and alternative ways of sending and reacting to the reception of information of the following kinds: (1) expression of positive feelings (contingent or noncontingent to the behavior of group members); (2) expression of negative emotions, such as anger, aggressive feelings, disappointment, and anxiety; (3) reformulation of negative feelings into concrete wishes and the expression of realistic demands. Furthermore, we rehearsed the integrative use of the newly learned skills in dealing with divergent interests, thus making possible a constructive approach to the resolution of group conflicts. We did not attempt to treat specific group problems, but rather rehearsed new ways of handling difficulties in general. In the last two sessions, however, we did practice the use of the communication skills by working through specific and pressing group conflicts.

During the role-playing exercises each member of the group was encouraged to act as both sender and recipient of expressed feelings. Learning to react to negative feelings expresssed by others proved to be at least as important as learning new sender skills.

The therapists made use of instruction, behavior rehearsal, or role playing as well as contingent feedback and homework assignments to facilitate behavioral change. Contingent feedback between and among group members was encouraged and reinforced. We discussed with the group adequate ways of self-expression, and used principles deduced by us to provide further instruction and to aid consolidation of learned skills.

Experimental Design

The groups were recruited through advertisement. The treatment group (TG) consisted of three "natural groups" of people living together (TG: $n = 14$ subjects) and was compared to the data of three untreated groups (no-treatment control group — CG: $n = 13$). The TG received seven sessions, which took between 5 and 7 weeks to treatment termination. The TG was tested at the beginning, after termination of the training period, and at a 3-month follow-up; while the CG was tested twice, with a 6-week interval.

There were no significant differences in demographic data between the groups. All were recruited from a predominantly academic environment; mean age was 24.

All three groups of the TG were treated by two of the authors, who are trained clinical psychologists (C. R. and M. W.).

Dependent Measures

We sought to measure changes both on the behavioral and the subjective level.

BEHAVIORIAL ASSESSMENT

The behavioral test was used to evaluate directly changes in communicative skills of individual subjects in group conflict discussion: Subjects in each group were asked to "discuss the character of their current conflicts in the group and to come to an agreement as to which issues were of greatest importance to the group." All behavior tests were tape-recorded, and these taped conversations were evaluated by 15 blind raters (trained psychology students). Table 7.1 includes these dimensions, as well as interrater agreement for reliability on each dimension.

We decided to use qualitative scales (from +3 to −3), because the time and length of individual speech varied in the group discussions. The interrater reliabilities shown in Table 7.1 reflect the difficulty of rating individuals in a group discussion setting.

SUBJECTIVE MEASURES

Communication Skill Inventory. The Communication Skill Inventory (KIP) (Zimmer, Raschert, & Weinert, 1978) is a questionnaire devised to measure individual communication competence. A short description is given in the Appendix. It has been found to be reliable (internal consistency: .83), able to differentiate between happy and distressed couples (Zimmer *et al.,* 1978), and sensitive to changes due to therapy (Lueg, Walker, & Zimmer, 1980). The KIP was adopted for group situations. A few items had to be reformulated.

Marital Pre-Counseling Inventory. Scales from the Marital Pre-Counseling Inventory (MPI) (Stuart & Stuart, 1973) were extracted and reformulated for the group setting to assess satisfaction in day-to-day living (housekeeping, responsibilities, leisure activities, and level of conflict).

Additional Items. In addition to the questionnaires mentioned, we developed some general questions specifically relevant to individual experiences in the group.

TABLE 7.1. Dimensions of the Behavioral Assessment

Dimension	Interrater reliability
1. Concreteness in the expression of personal wishes, goals, and intentions	.61
2. Open expression of personal feelings	.56
3. Empathic understanding of communication by other group members	.43
4. Willingness to help others in the expression of their feelings and wishes	.60
5. Clear and open expression of conflicts and problems	.59
6. General style of communication relevant to successful conflict resolution	.50

Results

Intergroup comparisons were made with the Mann–Whitney U test, and intragroup changes were tested for significance by means of the Wilcoxon test — both of which are nonparametric statistical tests. The raw data, changes, and comparisons on the behavioral test are given in Table 7.2.

Behavioral Test

The behavioral test showed that the subjects in the TG were significantly more able to express "concrete wishes and intentions" and also to communicate feelings more "directly and openly" at the end of the treatment as compared to pretreatment data. These improvements were shown to be stable at the 3-month follow-up test. The follow-up revealed further significant improvement in the "concreteness" dimension. Marginal positive changes on other dimensions did not reach statistical significance.

The CG showed some deterioration over time on several dimensions. The intergroup comparison revealed a significant superiority of the TG on Dimension 5 ("clear and open expression of conflicts and problems") after treatment had been completed.

These data are backed up by the KIP results, which show a significant increase in communicative competence of the TG. No such changes were seen in the CG. The follow-up test showed no significant deterioration in the newly learned skills.

Ratings of the group atmosphere by external raters revealed noticeable improvement in two of the three training groups. The control groups were judged to have deteriorated slightly. Intergroup comparisons cannot be calculated in this case, because of the nature of the data (interdependency of individual ratings).

TABLE 7.2. Results of the Behavioral Ratings and the KIP

| Dimensions | Means and standard deviations | | | | | Intragroup changes | | | Between-group differences | |
| | CG | | TG | | | Pre–post | | Post–FU:TG | Pretreatment | Posttreatment |
	Pre	Post	Pre	Post	FU	CG	TG			
Concreteness										
M	4.2	3.3	3.2	4.2	5.4	D*	I**	I**	CG>TG*	TG>CG**
SD	2.0	1.9	1.9	1.5	1.8					
Openness										
M	4.6	3.7	2.6	3.6	3.4	D*	I**	—	CG>TG***	—
SD	1.6	1.7	1.8	1.5	1.9					
Understanding										
M	5.7	5.2	4.9	5.0	4.4	D*	—	—	CG>TG*	—
SD	0.9	1.2	0.9	1.3	1.1					
Willing to help										
M	4.3	3.9	3.6	3.9	3.6	—	—	—	—	—
SD	1.4	1.5	1.3	1.7	1.4					
Clear conflict expression										
M	5.2	4.9	4.6	4.0	3.2	—	—	—	—	—
SD	1.4	1.5	1.8	1.7	2.0					
Communicative style										
M	4.6	3.8	3.9	3.5	3.4	D**	—	—	—	—
SD	1.3	1.2	1.3	1.6	1.7					
KIP, communicative competence										
M	4.4	4.2	4.6	5.2	5.2	—	I**	—	—	TG>CG***
SD	1.0	0.9	0.7	1.0	0.9					

Note. Data have been transformed to a 6-point scale. FU = follow-up; TG = treatment group; CG = control group; D = deterioration; I = improvement.

*p = .10.
**p = .05.
***p = .01.

Changes in Subjective Experience

Because of the lack of any significant improvement in the CG over time on any subjective level, we refer here only to changes in the TG. We found significant positive changes for the TG on the following levels: (1) experience of consideration and interest in others, (2) mutual understanding, (3) experience of openness and less constraint in the expression of agreement and disagreement, (4) general satisfaction with group living, (5) trust and closeness, and (6) increase in joint activities and satisfaction during this time.

An interesting result was that positive changes were seen more clearly in the other group members, in comparison to evaluations of personal changes. Although a few deteriorations on these scales were seen at follow-up, the open-ended questions at follow-up showed a general stability in openness and in positive attitudes toward feelings, wishes, and criticism.

Discussion

In general, the results confirm our experimental hypotheses, although we did not detect significant positive changes on all the expected dimensions. The fact that changes took place both on the behavioral test and on the level of subjective experiences, feelings, and attitudes demonstrates the clinical significance of this training program.

This study raises some practical considerations to be kept in mind when working with natural groups. The basic competencies of the therapists reflect the data presented by Alexander, Barton, Schiavo, and Parsons (1976): It was highly important to build up a positive and anxiety-reducing relationship to the group members and to impose structure, in order to move away from fruitless avoidance discussions in the group and to encourage active role playing and new behavioral experiences. Role playing and behavioral tests proved to be very helpful in increasing motivation and facilitating a behavioral orientation to problem solving. The experience of behavioral improvement and concomitant changes in feeling demonstrated the usefulness of this approach.

In our experience the highest impact on the development of mutual trust came from exercises that focused on the expression of positive feelings as well as anxiety, and on training in how to react to the expression of negative emotions by others (e.g., anger).

Finally, we want to share a clinical impression, which may also be relevant for marital therapy. An improvement in communication skills often leads to heightened willingness to deal with problems that could not otherwise have been discussed. This may give the impression of an increased conflict load, but it probably reflects a greater preparedness to bring up more important issues. This may explain the disappointing results on Dimension 6 of our behavioral assessment ("global judgment of communication style"). Here the raters detected no improvement, possibly because the trainees were more willing to discuss more serious conflicts. It should be noted here that the CG deteriorated significantly over time on this scale.

The various methods of measurement show consistently that stable changes in communicative competence and attitudes toward group living can be achieved by a short-term communication skills training program on a behavioral basis.

Appendix: Description of the Communication Skill Inventory (KIP)

The KIP consists of 22 items; these describe critical situations of partner interaction and provide for choices among alternative reactions. One item is given here, as an example of the inventory's content.

Item No. 17

Your spouse expresses that he/she would like to take you in his/her arms and hug you. But you feel angry and do not feel like hugging. You are afraid that he/she might feel put down by your refusal.

Alternative Reactions

- You do not say anything, but you do not respond to the hugging.
- "Don't be angry, but I don't feel like hugging you right now."
- "I don't feel like hugging right now. I am still a little bit mad at you because . . . "
- "I am sorry I can't react to your wish right now because I'm still angry at you. Couldn't we take some time to talk it over first?"
- "Oh, let me alone! Don't you see I'm busy?"
- "Be careful, that hurts!"

Instructions

Choose among these alternatives for the following questions:

1. What is your typical and most often chosen verbal reaction?
2. What reaction would your spouse most likely choose?

Evaluation

Scoring

Each alternative reaction was judged by eight experienced marital therapists for "communicative competence" and weighted accordingly (from 1 to 8). The "individual score of communicative competence" was calculated as the average value of the chosen alternatives.

Specific Communication Strategies

We are currently comparing therapy couples, nondistressed couples, and couples who came for sex therapy, and analyzing the data with more detailed categories. Each verbal reaction (see "Alternative Reactions") can be seen to represent one or several different aspects along the following dimensions: avoidance (general), empathic reaction to partner, specific avoidance of emotional content, paradoxical reactions, self-acceptance versus self-putdown, partner acceptance versus partner putdown, and open versus indirect communication of emotions, especially direct, indirect, and hostile expression of anger (Zimmer, 1983).

REFERENCES

Alexander, J. F., Barton, C., Schiavo, R. S., & Parsons, B. V. Systems-behavioral intervention with families of delinquents: Therapist characteristics, family behavior and outcome. *Journal of Consulting and Clinical Psychology,* 1976, *44,* 656–664.
Anneken, R., Echelmeyer, L., Kaluza, K., Klein, H., Klockgeter-Kelle, A., & Zimmer, D. *Kommunikationstraining für Paare* (Materiale Nr. 2). Tübingen: DGVT (German Association for Behavior Therapy), 1977.
Lueg, L., Walker, C., & Zimmer, D. Das paradoxe Rollenspiel: Eine erste empirische Überprüfung. *Partnerberatung,* 1980, *17,* 201–211.
Mandel, K. H., Mandel, A., Stadter, E., & Zimmer, D. *Einübung in Partnerschaft durch Kommunikationstherapie und Verhaltenstherapie.* Munich: Pfeiffer, 1971.
Stuart, R., & Stuart, F. *Marital Pre-Counseling Inventory.* Champaign, IL: Research Press, 1973.
Thanner, J. *Nachuntersuchung zu einem Kommunikationstraining für Paare.* Unpublished master's thesis, University of Tübingen, 1979.
Ullrich de Muynck, R., Ullrich, R., Grawe, K., & Zimmer, D. *Soziale Kompetenz* (Vol. 2). Munich: Pfeiffer, 1980.
Zimmer, D. Beschreibung und erste Überprüfung eines Kommunikationstrainings für Paare. *Mitteilungen der DGVT,* 1977, *9,* 566–576.
Zimmer, D. Interaction patterns and communication skills in sexually distressed, maritally distressed, and normal couples: Two experimental studies. *Journal of Sex and Marital Therapy,* 1983, *9*(4), 251–265.
Zimmer, D., Raschert, K., & Weinert, M. *Fragebogen und Manual zum Fragebogen "Kommunikation in der Partnerschaft" (KIP)* (Materialen Nr. 11–12). Tübingen: DGVT, 1978.

8

Outcome Research on Behavioral Marital Therapy: A Methodological and Conceptual Reappraisal

NEIL S. JACOBSON, WILLIAM C. FOLLETTE, AND RICHARD W. ELWOOD

One of the most laudable features of behavior therapy has been its unprecedented commitment to the experimental evaluation of its treatment technology (Kazdin & Wilson, 1978). Compared to other schools of psychotherapy, behavior therapy has been unique in the history of psychotherapy in its documentation of treatment efficacy. This dedication to controlled and rigorous investigation of treatment outcomes has paid rich dividends, resulting in the accumulation of massive amounts of data that support the general utility of behavioral approaches for a wide variety of problems in living. This dedication to experimental scrutiny carries with it certain risks that can be avoided by treatment approaches confined to the use of testimony and anecdote as evaluative criteria. One risk is that when an application of behavior therapy is ineffective, knowledge of the failure is inescapable. The self-serving biases of advocacy lose their credibility when confronted with hard data documenting the absence of a treatment effect in a well-controlled outcome investigation. In contrast, advocates of a particular model of therapy can wax poetic in the absence of controlled research, unencumbered as they are by potentially damaging data that have not as yet been collected. They can compensate for missing data with unbridled optimism, relying on the inevitable "true believers" to perpetuate the use of their model.

A second risk entailed by a model of therapy dedicated to empirical scrutiny is that self-criticism is unavoidable. As our methodological and conceptual sophistication advances, so must our insight into the limitations of our previous work. Yesterday's important finding becomes today's seriously

Neil S. Jacobson, William C. Follette, and Richard W. Elwood. Department of Psychology, University of Washington, Seattle, Washington, U.S.A.

flawed study. As the quality of our research improves, so must our capacity for retrospective self-criticism. The more ambitious our methodological aspirations become, the more humble must our interpretations of our findings be.

Behavioral marital therapy (BMT) has been very much a part of this legacy of rigorous self-scrutiny. In an area of clinical practice that has been, for most of its history, a veritable wasteland for controlled outcome research (Jacobson, 1978, BMT stands alone in its proliferation of data regarding treatment efficacy. Since one of us first reviewed the literature 7 years ago (Jacobson & Martin, 1976), there have been no less than 16 published, controlled outcome studies evaluating the efficacy of BMT. No other approach to marital therapy, with the possible exception of Guerney's (1977) Relationship Enhancement Model, has been shown to be demonstrably effective for couples who are distressed.

Yet, following in the tradition outlined in the preceding paragraphs, it is time to evaluate the research of the past 8 years from the vantage point of 1984. In that brief period of time, research strategies, standardized treatment techniques, and measurement devices have been informally canonized by our unquestioning adherence. This chapter reconsiders some of these conventions for designing our treatment manipulations, reporting and analyzing our data and measuring the quality of a relationship. Our basic contention is that, despite the obvious payoffs from the last 8 years, our research strategies may be beginning to pay diminishing returns. Further developments in both clinical practice and theories of behavior change may require some innovations in the design and methodology of research investigations.

The first two sections of this chapter address the issue of how we examine and report our data. The first deals specifically with the concern that our conventions for analyzing and reporting data disguise rather than illuminate important information regarding treatment efficacy. By relying primarily on conventional tests of statistical significance to evaluate treatment effects for groups of subjects, we learn very little about the variability of response to BMT within our samples. The second section addresses a more specific issue in regard to client variability, an issue that can be broadly translated into "clinical significance." To state it colloquially, How many of our couples are happily married following exposure to BMT, as opposed to simply "less miserable"?

The third section discusses the problems of comparative outcome studies as a vehicle for advancing knowledge. Then, in the fourth section, some issues are raised regarding the merits and limitations of standardized treatment packages employed by BMT outcome researchers. Finally, the fifth section raises some concerns regarding our measurement of marital relationship quality.

We conclude the chapter with a skeletal outline of recommendations for future research. These constitute a meager effort to begin a dialogue regarding ways to enhance our research strategies so that we can both evaluate our treatment techniques more definitively and refine them when necessary to enhance their potency.

Variability in Response to BMT

The vast majority of published outcome studies on BMT have based their inferences regarding treatment efficacy on statistical comparisons between treatment and control groups, or between or among alternative treatment groups. Yet, as many recent commentators have noted, group differences in mean performance provide only limited information for clinicians attempting to evaluate the effects of a particular form of therapy (Barlow, 1980; Garfield, 1981; Hugdahl & Ost, 1981; Kazdin & Wilson, 1978). Based as they are on the average amount of change for the subjects in a treatment group, they tell us nothing about the response to treatment on the part of individual couples comprising the sample. Group averages may or may not be representative of the amount of change exhibited by particular couples in the treatment group.

Conventional statistical comparisons based on group means treat variability as error rather than as information. At first glance, it might appear that the sum of squares within groups might allow one to make inferences regarding variability. Unfortunately, the sum of squares within groups does not contain information regarding the percentage of clients who are responding positively to treatment.

One attempt to improve upon the standard way of reporting outcome data has been the determination of "effect size" by Smith and Glass (1977). This statistic is the mean difference between the treated and control subjects divided by the standard deviation of the control group. It is an improvement over the simple reporting of group means, F tests, and p values, since it does provide an estimate of the magnitude of change. However, we have the remaining problem of translating this summary statistic into a description of variability in outcome across a sample of subjects. Ultimately, there is no adequate substitute for reports that include the proportion of treated couples who improve. If the reader is provided with these proportions, then it is possible to estimate the probability that treatment will be successful for a particular client, assuming that this client resembles the clients in the treatment study on relevant characteristics. If one wished, these proportions could be supplemented by a chi-square test; however, the descriptive data would serve as an estimate of the treatment's clinical significance and would, we would argue, provide the clinician with information that is considerably more useful than that typically reported in treatment studies.

In order to report percentages of improved clients, criteria for improvement need to be established. Obviously, the criteria should be as free from bias as possible. As a starting point, we propose that the determination of improved status be based on the same measure(s) used to calculate treatment effects. The more difficult problem is how much change a couple needs to demonstrate on a particular measure in order to be designated as improved. It seems clear that a change of one point on the Dyadic Adjustment Scale is an insufficient amount of change, since changes of minimal magnitude do not exceed chance fluctuations on most measures. More generally, criteria for improvement must take into account the reliability of the particular instrument. Jacobson, Follette, and Revenstorf (1983) proposed a criterion called the reliable change index *(RC)* based on the standard error of measurements *(S_E)*. According to this criterion, change on the part of an individual (or a couple) is deemed statistically significant if it exceeds 1.96 S_E. Changes of this magnitude are unlikely ($p < .05$) to be merely a function of measurement error. Although this criterion has some disadvantages (Jacobson, Follette, & Revenstorf, 1983), it is offered as one example of a nonarbitrary, psychometrically sound method of determining whether a couple has improved from pretest to posttest.

We have begun to reanalyze data from previously published outcome studies to examine variability of outcome within samples of treated couples (Jacobson, Follette, Baucom, Hahlweg, & Margolin, 1983). In most studies, a majority of couples demonstrate improvement. But the results are variable, not only from study to study but also across different measures within the same study. Moreover, marked improvement tends to be limited to a minority of couples. A substantial percentage of treated couples do not change in either direction, and a few (about 5%) actually deteriorate during the course of therapy. Thus, the outcome of BMT is highly variable, and one must be careful to qualify the interpretation of significant treatment effects.

We have also begun to look at variability within couples by calculating improvement rates separately for husbands and wives. If improvement means that both spouses show improved relationship satisfaction at the conclusion of therapy, the success rate of BMT is considerably less impressive. Quite often, it appears that only one of the spouses is exhibiting or reporting substantial relationship improvement as a function of BMT. It should be pointed out that in many cases only one spouse is unhappy with the relationship prior to therapy. Therefore, one might expect improvement only in one spouse, at least for this type of couple. However, these findings serve as a reminder that we tend to disguise variability not only by confining our reports to group means, but also by reporting data only for the couple as a unit (cf. Baucom, in press). Further comments are provided later on this issue.

To summarize, when we examine variability in couples' response to BMT, it becomes clear that outcomes are highly variable. Moreover, although a majority of couples improve their relationships during therapy, the improvement is substantial for only a minority. If we consider intracouple variability as well, the assessment of efficacy becomes even more murky. Clearly, summary statistics based on group means, even when contributing to statistically significant treatment effects, provide, at best, incomplete information or, at worst, misleading information regarding the impact of therapy on couples in the sample.

They're Better, but Are They Nondistressed?

Another consideration in evaluating the outcome of BMT has to do with the clinical significance of the changes undergone by couples in therapy. Above and beyond the proportion of couples whose relationships improve, how common is it for distressed couples to leave therapy with a "nondistressed" relationship? Rather than quibbling about the difficulties in making such a determination, which we acknowledge, let us operationalize a "nondistressed" relationship as one in which spouses score within the nondistressed range on one or more preselected measures of marital functioning.

We recognize that by posing this question we imply that conformity to a norm set by the nondistressed population is desirable. Despite the implication, we are not advocating that norms be viewed as the optimal standards for evaluating the effects of BMT. Nor do we believe that the characteristics of nondistressed couples necessarily serve as a starting point for designing marital therapy treatment programs. However, on some measures (e.g., measures of subjective relationship satisfaction), the questions posed by such comparisons are directly relevant to evaluating the effects of therapy — regardless of the particular presenting problem. Criteria having to do with satisfaction derived from the relationship are universally relevant, unless the goals of therapy are not to improve relationship quality.

It might also be argued that a criterion for efficacy based on joining the ranks of the nondistressed is too stringent. This may, indeed, be the case. But if BMT (or any form of therapy) does not typically lead to couples describing themselves as "happy," this is certainly important information for the consumer as well as the scientific community. Clients often expect treatment to eliminate the presenting problem. In marital therapy, if this is an unrealistic expectation, then it needs to be more clearly communicated. Our position is that clients typically, although not always, enter therapy defining "success" to mean that they will be happy together by the time therapy is over. It is questionable whether anything less than this is clinically meaningful. Revenstorf, Hahlweg, Schindler, and Kunert (see Chapter 12, this volume) present data suggesting that the amount of change is relatively unimportant compared to where the couple ends up. They suggest that couples characterized as treatment failures often changed considerably in the positive direction, although they remained in the distressed range even when therapy was over. Though one must be cautious in inferring that couples who show large change scores experienced strong treatment effects, as opposed to weak treatment effects plus regression effects (Nesselroade & Stigler, 1980), there is the clear suggestion that the magnitude of change may be relatively meaningless unless the end result is that couples fall within "nondistressed limits." Similarly, Baucom and Mehlman (see Chapter 6, this volume) report that change scores from pre- to posttest were not predictive of separation at a 6-month follow-up, whereas posttest scores were correlated with marital status at follow-up. It is possible that this finding is due, in part, to the fact that the more highly correlated the pre- and posttest measures are, the less reliable the difference score is (Cronbach & Furby, 1970). Hence, the observation that the posttest alone is more useful may be partially a statistical phenomenon. Still, there is evidence that where the clients end up after therapy, instead of how much they change during therapy, may be important in predicting long-term outcome.

We have been looking at proportions of couples in previous outcome studies who fall within the nondistressed range by the time therapy is over. Obviously, such calculations are possible only for those measures on which adequate norms exist. If one excludes from these analyses those couples who were already within the nondistressed range at pretest, in three out of the four studies less than half of the treated couples actually moved from the distressed to the nondistressed ranges by the end of therapy. Thus, of those couples who were moderately to severely distressed at pretest, less than half reported scores within the maritally satisfied range at posttest. As we have already seen, a majority of them are reporting an improved relationship relative to their pretherapy reports, but they are still reporting more distress than their nondistressed married counterparts.

BMT versus Alternative Approaches

Most recent outcome research on BMT has been comparative in nature. Rather than simply comparing BMT to a control group, the studies have involved comparisons between BMT and one or more alternative treatments. Some of these studies have utilized dismantling strategies, where a BMT treatment package is compared to one or more components of that package in isolation. These studies are typically aimed at uncovering the procedures that are most responsible for treatment efficacy; they may, in addition, provide indirect tests for competing theoretical accounts of the change process in BMT. Other studies compare BMT with a treatment approach derived from an alternative theoretical framework.

With some isolated exceptions on certain measures, in virtually every comparative study thus far reported, the result has been the same: no differences. BMT as a treatment package has not been shown to be more effective than its component parts (Baucom, Chapter 5, this volume; Hahlweg, Schindler, Revenstorf, & Brengelmann, Chapter 1, this volume; Jacobson,

1978), nor have investigators found it possible to reject null hypotheses regarding comparisons between BMT and other approaches (Crowe, Chapter 4, this volume; Emmelkamp, van der Helm, MacGillavry, & van Zanten, Chapter 3, this volume; Hahlweg et al., Chapter 1, this volume; Liberman, Levine, Wheeler, Sanders, & Wallace, 1976). These null findings have occurred with such consistency that they themselves require explanation. First, it may, indeed, be the case that there are no differences between BMT and the various comparison treatments. Unfortunately, since null hypotheses can never be accepted, this cannot be proven. The absence of real differences becomes a more compelling hypothesis when the finding is independently replicated. However, this is true if and only if there is adequate statistical power to detect treatment differences, should they really exist. Unfortunately, to date we are not aware of power calculation reports in published comparative studies. This criticism does not exclude the possibility that treatment effects, as they are currently tested, are weak or nonexistent. There are a number of factors which might contribute to the disguising of a treatment effect in a comparative outcome study. Unfortunately, none of them can be ruled out, given the present state of knowledge.

First, comparative outcome studies often involve comparisons between treatments that share a number of characteristics. Although they may differ on one or more dimensions, the commonalities may more than compensate for these differences. Even if the dimensions on which the treatments differ are important, the more overlap between the treatments on other relevant dimensions, the more likely it will be that a Type II error is made. For example, in Baucom's comparison (see Chapter 5, this volume) between communication/problem-solving training (C/PS) and behavioral contracting (BC), both treatments share the end product of a negotiated solution to the problems being discussed. This step-by-step accumulation of change agreements may provide those two treatments with a common element that swamps the more subtle effects of the independent variable. This possibility is even more likely in outcome studies comparing treatments derived from different theoretical perspectives. Invariably, such comparisons involve complex treatment packages that share many common elements. The problem of therapies sharing common elements becomes potentially even larger when the same therapists do more than one type of treatment in the study. That is, across time therapists may inadvertently adopt elements of one treatment package and insert them into another, thus further diluting our ability to detect treatment differences.

The best solution is to compare truly distinct treatments while implementing procedures to maintain the differences between them during the course of the study. For example, if one is really to compare a treatment component focusing on process (communication training) with one focusing on behavior change, the pure communication-training treatment would be devoid of behavior change instigations, whereas the former would avoid any discussion of process. Yet the purer the comparison treatments, the less relevant they are to clinical practice. Therefore, external validity is often the price that one pays for designing pure or sensitive outcome manipulations.

In short, the commonalities shared by various treatments detract from the ability of a comparative outcome study to detect any remaining differences between them.

Second, comparative outcome studies are often designed to ferret out main effects, when in fact the phenomenon being studied is sufficiently complex that one or more additional variables need to be isolated before the relationship between the independent and dependent variables can be elucidated. For example, in a hypothetical comparison between communication training and behavior exchange treatments, the investigator might find no main effects for treatment. Yet, it may be that communication training is more effective than behavior exchange for older couples whose presenting problems include arguing, provided that they have a traditional relationship and are treated by an inexperienced male–female cotherapy team. On the other hand, to carry this hypothetical example further, behavior exchange might be more effective than communication training when the clients are young and communicate well, and the therapist is experienced but lousy and has taken a graduate course in BMT (with Jacobson & Margolin, 1979, used as the text, of course). Despite the exaggerated, quasi-facetious example, the relationship between a treatment variable and outcome could easily be buried in a three-way interaction involving client and therapist variables as well as technological variables. We do not think that this level of complexity is farfetched.

Efforts to cope with the complexity of interactions among technical, therapist, and client characteristics have ranged from using multiple therapists to investigating various demographic or personality variables and relationship predictors of outcome. Unfortunately, most efforts are limited by small sample sizes. Indeed it is probably neither feasible nor practical to conduct outcome studies of sufficient scope to adequately test hypotheses in comparative outcome studies regarding differential treatment effects. There may be relatively few such effects in nature, that is, real differences between widely used treatments that would emerge across the entire population of clients and therapists.

Intermodel comparative outcome studies tell us little about the process of therapeutic change, even in the event that significant differences were to emerge between treatments. Conclusions regarding the process of change are possible only with carefully controlled intramodel component studies that creatively combine dismantling, constructive, and parametric research strategies. Unfortunately, such studies on BMT have not produced conclusive findings. We believe that their failure has to do with the complex interactions that qualify the treatment–outcome relationship. Experimental designs can theoretically be extended to uncover relationships between variables regardless of the degree of complexity. Unfortunately, what is theoretically possible is not always practical.

Standardized versus Flexible Treatments

In virtually all outcome research on BMT, the effects of a standardized treatment package are evaluated. Between-group designs require that each couple in a given treatment condition receive the same treatment program. These standardized treatment packages, while necessary from a methodological perspective, contradict notions such as functional analysis and idiographic assessment — notions that characterize BMT in clinical practice (Jacobson & Margolin, 1979). It would seem on the face of it that this lack of clinical flexibility imposed by the constraints of outcome research might lead to a very conservative estimate of the effectiveness of BMT. The research enterprise might also detract from clinical advances, since investigators begin to conceptualize treatment issues in a standardized fashion. After all, what good are technical innovations in the midst of an outcome study? Our research designs, in other words, might be squelching creativity.

Marital distress is no more a monolithic entity than is individual distress. Couples enter therapy with problems spanning a wide range: Bickering, jealousy, orgasmic dysfunction, and emotional disengagement may require different treatment plans, even though they all lead to similarly low levels of marital satisfaction. It is inevitable that any standardized treatment will compromise the needs of a portion of the distressed couples in their sample. Thus, one might hypothesize that treatment effects in outcome research underestimate the effectiveness of BMT in clinical practice.

On the other hand, there are those who advocate a standardized treatment package for virtually all marital problems. Stuart (1980), in recommending a standardized treatment program for most marital problems, argues that "we are more alike than different, and that the process of relieving marital distress is generic. . . ." It seems clear that the belief in the importance of individualized treatment plans is not universally shared among BMT experts. And there is another argument that has been put forth to support the advocacy of standardized treatment programs (see Emmelkamp, 1981). In the absence of empirically documented relationships between the matching of client characteristics with treatment plans, on the one hand, and outcome, on the other hand, these idiographic treatment plans are based almost exclusively on clinical lore and intuition. The alterations or variations in our treatment plans from couple to couple may, in fact, be trivial, to the extent that our clinical lore departs from reality. If, for example, nontechnological factors account for a preponderance of the outcome variance, then the specific content of the treatment program is relatively unimportant.

The pros and cons of standardized treatment packages constitute a very important clinical issue. If, in fact, couples are no more likely to benefit from an individually tailored program than they are from a standardized treatment package, the standardized package becomes the preferred treatment. Not only do standardized treatments simplify the process of pretreatment assessment, but they greatly reduce the complexity of the decision-making process for the therapist during treatment sessions. Standardized treatments are also more easily disseminated, and they offer enhanced opportunities for training paraprofessionals to conduct the therapy.

In summary, there are good points on both sides of this controversy, and virtually no extant data from which to render a verdict.

The Measurement Problem

There seem to be at least three basic reasons why we need precise measures of marital distress and interaction. First, as scientists we need precise measures of marital interaction in order to advance our theoretical understanding of relationships. Second, as clinicians we need measures to discover "what is wrong" when a couple seeks therapy. Third, as applied scientists we need to measure relationship change as a function of therapy. Discussions of marital assessment do not typically distinguish between these different purposes of assessment, yet the ideal instrument for one purpose may not occupy similar status when it comes to serving the second or third. The following applies exclusively to the assessment of treatment efficacy.

Baucom (in press; see also Chapter 5, this volume) has covered the topic of measurement in some detail, and we confine our remarks here to a couple of issues that seem particularly important. First, there is no empirical basis for trusting one measure more than another in evaluating the efficacy of a treatment program. All of the commonly used measures are flawed, although the flaws differ to some degree from one to the other; but all are limited by the fact that relevant psychometric research has not been conducted. As behaviorists, we tend to favor behavioral measures, which leads to a bias in favor of observational coding systems as primary dependent measures. This bias seems to us rather arbitrary, since, although observational coding systems are — by definition — observational, they do not exemplify "behavioral assessment" any more than do self-report measures of global satisfaction. Although at first glance this point may seem counterintuitive, consider the definition and domain of behavioral assessment (see Cone & Hawkins, 1977; Hersen & Bellack, 1981). The essence of behavioral assessment is its adoption of a "sample" rather than a "sign" approach to the analysis of dysfunctional behavior. This means that a behavioral measure is a direct reflection of the target problem, and the relationship of the former to the latter is self-evident, requiring no inferences or even empirical demonstrations. If the presenting problem is "smoking," the rate of cigarette consumption requires no assessment of psychometric properties; its validity is self-evident. Observational coding systems that directly measure the presenting problem in the natural environment are similarly valid *a priori*: A reliable frequency count of a tantruming child is necessarily a valid measure of temper tantrums. As one departs from this direct correspondence between problem behavior and its measurement, one moves away from a sample approach and toward a sign approach, that is, away from a behavioral assessment. The currently available observational coding systems measure behavior whose relationship to relevant marital problems is unclear. Some investigators "assume," and others "observe," that distressed spouses put each other down, look away from each other, deny responsibility, and the like. But in no sense are these behaviors direct measures of the presenting problem unless the couple actually enters therapy complaining of low agreement–disagreement ratios, insufficient paraphrasing, and the like. These are seldom the presenting problems of distressed couples.

Couples do, of course, often enter marital therapy complaining of "communication problems." But even in those instances one cannot assume that the Marital Interaction Coding System (MICS) or the Couples Interaction Scoring System (CISS) measures these communication problems any more directly than the Dyadic Adjustment Scale (DAS) or the Spouse Observation Checklist (SOC). The MICS categories were not empirically derived, and the construct validity of the instrument has not been established. Data on the construct validity of the CISS are similarly unavailable. Discriminant validity is well established for both instruments; however, the ability of observational coding systems to identify couples with low DAS scores is absolutely irrelevant to questions pertaining to their utility as behavioral measures of marital distress.

It makes little sense to rely on data from observational coding systems to assess the degree of change produced by BMT on the basis of statistically significant correlations with much cheaper and more efficient questionnaires. Reliance on observational coding systems as dependent measures in outcome research will be justified only when it is demonstrated that these systems measure relevant constructs that are not adequately measured by less expensive means. In addition to the issues already raised, recent studies have suggested that observational coding systems are relatively insensitive to relationship changes produced during BMT (Baucom, Chapter 5, this volume; Hahlweg, Reisner, Kohli, Vollmer, Schindler, & Revenstorf, Chapter 11, this volume; Turkewitz & O'Leary, 1981).

To summarize, there seems to be no justification for currently available behavioral measures' serving as the ultimate criterion measures in outcome research on BMT. However, we cannot agree with Baucom (in press) that currently available measures of global adjustment (Locke & Wallace, 1959; Spanier, 1976) are superior to other currently available measures. It is certainly true, as Baucom argues, that the bottom line is how satisfied the couple is with their relationship subsequent to therapy. However, it is not clear to us that either the DAS or the Locke–Wallace instrument is a valid measure of relationship satisfaction. The potential for bias in the completion of these instruments and their susceptibility to social desirability are well documented (Jacobson, Elwood, & Dallas, 1981; Jacobson & Margolin, 1979; Margolin & Jacobson, 1981; Weiss & Margolin, 1977). As measures of the outcome of marital therapy, they are particularly susceptible to demand characteristics. Moreover, since one consequence of successful marital therapy is open, honest communication, DAS or Locke–Wallace scores can actually disguise the effects of treatment when couples enter therapy with a pretest score inflated by social desirability and depart with a score deflated by candor and a willingness to accept a relationship's imperfections.

Thus, there does not seem to be any currently justifiable decision rule for trusting one outcome measure more than another in the event that results are inconsistent. If we had to choose, we would opt at present for the measure that taps the couple's presenting (or emergent) problems most directly. Problem checklists and goal attainment scales—particularly when amount of change is inferred from multiple sources (impressions of each spouse, questionnaire data, etc.)—seem to be the most direct possible means of evaluating whether or not couples "got what they came for." The issue of what dependent measures to use and how to analyze them is complex and has not received the close scrutiny it warrants. It may be that the multitrait–multimethod approach discussed by Campbell and Fiske (1959) would be useful in helping BMT researchers choose which measures to use and which to discard.

Recommendations

In this section we present some indications and contraindications for our efforts to understand the sources of variability in outcome and ultimately to reduce it.

First, we need to report and analyze our data in ways that highlight client variability in response to BMT. Group summary statistics are inadequate to the task. At the very least, group treatment effects should be supplemented by descriptive data indicative of outcome variability. Data should also be reported for each spouse, rather than simply for the couple as a unit, and data analyses should be augmented by an investigation of differential treatment effects as a function of spouses. Despite the problems with this type of analysis (see O'Leary & Turkewitz, 1978), these problems are not insurmountable. Potential solutions include dividing the number of degrees of freedom in half; treating individual spouses as repeated measures, with the unit of analysis remaining the dyad (Kraemer & Jacklin, 1979); and viewing each spouse as a separate univariate component in a multivariate analysis of variance (Baucom, in press). Unfortunately, we do not have an idea to propose that adequately addresses all these points. One idea that we find useful is to represent the treatment effects graphically. Figure 8.1 is a scatterplot of pretreatment versus posttreatment DAS scores for the more distressed partner of the dyad. In this particular study, couples were either placed on a waiting list (WL) or treated with behavior exchange alone (BE), problem-solving training alone (PS), or a combination of the two (CO). Stunkard and Penick (1979) used this method for reporting follow-up data in weight reduction research. Points falling above the line represent improvement, points on the line represent no change, and points below the line indicate deterioration. One can see that there are no obvious group differences among the active treatment conditions, but there are

FIGURE 8.1. DAS scores for more distressed partner, pretreatment versus posttreatment.

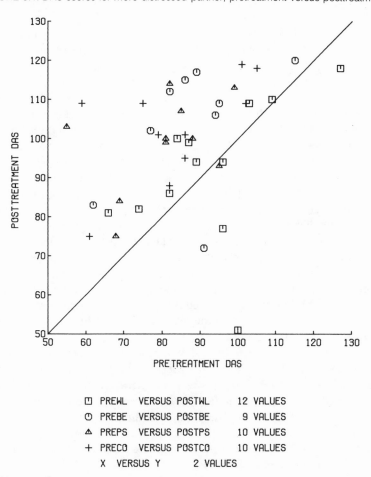

some striking individual treatment differences within conditions among subjects with comparable pretest scores. One can also see the proportion of clients who move into the "nondistressed" range at posttest. This includes subjects whose data points fall above a line parallel to the abscissa and intersecting the ordinate at 100. A plot such as this would probably contain the most useful information when the abscissa represents posttest data and the ordinate represents 1-year follow-up data. If there are differential effects among treatments in the ability of clients to continue to benefit from treatment by themselves, such a graph should help one see these differences. Of course, graphic representation allows one to clearly see outliers, which may be introducing artifacts into the data analysis or which may contain useful information for identifying different typologies of clients. We are not suggesting that this approach is devoid of problems, but it is one example of a method of presenting data in a manner preserving both group and individual difference information.

Second, predictors of positive outcome must be vigorously pursued. In addition to correlations based on demographic and severity variables, real efforts should be made to categorize clients according to type of presenting problem or type of relationship. Since there are a number of possible ways to classify couples, classification systems should be derived from current theory, empirical investigation, and clinical impressions. At this stage of our knowledge, it would be unnecessarily restrictive to exclude hunches, clinical intuition, and other subjective criteria as building blocks for a model that predicts the responses of particular types of client couples to specific clinical intervention strategies. This attempt to identify variance in outcome attributable to couple characteristics constitutes a necessary precursor to actuarial matching of couple and treatment technique.

It seems that developing a system of typologies to understand variance can include a wide range of approaches. This might include specific types of communication deficits, differing needs for affiliation, different developmental histories leading up to the present distress, different family histories for violence or substance abuse, or any number of other dimensions. It may even be possible to build a typology based not on current deficits but instead on what strengths are still extant in the relationship, and subsequently to build therapeutic strategies upon these strengths.

Third, therapist characteristics should be studied as they relate to positive outcome. We have begun to identify a set of dimensions (Jacobson, Berley, Melman, Elwood, & Phelps, in press) of therapist performance that are hypothesized to be important in facilitating a positive response to BMT. These could be evaluated either by observational coding systems or by clinical ratings. Once identified, these dimensions could be incorporated into existing BMT technology. To some extent, this process is already occurring (Jacobson, 1983; Jacobson et al., in press).

Fourth, these efforts toward correlating therapist as well as couple characteristics with outcome have as their ultimate purpose a reduction in the variability of outcome. Toward that end, it will be necessary to demonstrate that variability is reduced, and/or overall outcome enhanced, by changes resulting from these procedures. For example, can outcome be improved by matching specific treatments to couple characteristics? Moreover, it may be that we can already enhance outcome simply by assigning treatments to clients based on clinical judgment. Perhaps assigning couples at random to "different" standardized treatments leads to a conservative estimate of BMT's potency. If treatment strategies were determined on the basis of client characteristics, and these determinations were left to the discretion of the therapist, overall outcome might be enhanced relative to subjecting all couples to randomly assigned standardized treatments. Comparing BMT as it is applied during an outcome study to BMT as it is utilized in clinical practice would be highly instructive — even in the absence of empirically based criteria for matching.

Comparative Outcome Studies

We recommend that low priority be given to comparative outcome studies. For reasons discussed earlier, they are almost guaranteed to produce null findings. This holds especially for intermodel comparisons. Studies of the process of therapy, or investigations of interactions among therapist, client, and technological variables, are much more likely to enhance our knowledge in the immediate future.

Measurement Issues

First, experimenters should distinguish between primary and secondary outcome measures in advance of data collection. Primary measures are those that are expected to show improvement to the extent that treatment is effective. Secondary measures are those being examined for exploratory purposes and hypothesis generation. Primary measures should be few in number, and the experimenter should justify the inclusion of each individual measure. In the absence of construct validity, the conservative assumption should be made that all measures are components of the same construct. Multivariate analyses (e.g., MANOVAs) should be used when multiple measures are intercorrelated.

Second, even in group studies, measures should include some assessment of whether the presenting problem(s) has (have) been solved.

Third, distinctions must be made among the various assessment domains. For theoretical research requiring careful description of marital interaction (see Gottman, 1979), data on marital communication based on standardized observational coding systems are essential. However, for outcome research — in the absence of evidence for construct validity and given the costs of training and utilizing coders — observational coding systems are difficult to justify. What is needed are less costly, less time-consuming observation-based rating scales, validated according to the criteria for which they are to be used. For example, if the experimenter wants to measure problem-solving effectiveness, the coding system can be justified only if its construct validity as a measure of problem-solving effectiveness is established.

We think that it is time to cease the mechanical repetition of psychotherapy research conventions that have stopped bearing fruit. Both "independent" and "dependent" variable issues should be reexamined from a fresh perspective. Global questions such as "Is BMT effective?" are relatively meaningless. Our data suggest that sometimes it is, and sometimes it is not. But we have almost no data allowing us to predict the response to therapy of a particular couple. The development of such predictive power would comprise a major contribution.

REFERENCES

Barlow, D. H. Behavior therapy: The next decade. *Behavior Therapy*, 1980, *11*, 315–328.
Baucom, D. H. Conceptual and psychometric issues in evaluating the effectiveness of behavioral marital therapy. In J. P. Vincent (Ed.), *Advances in family intervention, assessment and theory: A research annual* (Vol. 3). Greenwich, CT: JAI Press, in press.
Campbell, D. T., & Fiske, D. W. Convergent and discriminant validation by the multitrait-multimethod matrix. *Psychological Bulletin*, 1959, *56*, 81–105.
Cone, T. D., & Hawkins, R. P. (Eds.). *Behavioral assessment: New directions in clinical psychology*. New York: Brunner/Mazel, 1977.
Cronbach, L. J., & Furby, L. How we should measure "change" — Or should we? *Psychological Bulletin*, 1970, *74*, 68–80.
Emmelkamp, P. M. G. The current and future status of clinical research. *Behavioral Assessment*, 1981, *3*, 249–253.
Garfield, S. L. Evaluating the psychotherapies. *Behavior Therapy*, 1981, *12*, 295–307.
Gottman, J. M. *Marital interaction: Experimental investigations*. New York: Academic Press, 1979.
Guerney, B. G. (Ed.). *Relationship enhancement*. San Francisco: Jossey-Bass, 1977.
Hersen, M., & Bellack, A. S. (Eds.). *Behavioral assessment: A practical handbook* (2nd ed.). London: Pergamon Press, 1981.
Hugdahl, K., & Ost, L. On the difference between statistical and clinical significance. *Behavioral Assessment*, 1981, *3*, 289–295.
Jacobson, N. S. A review of the research on the effectiveness of marital therapy. In T. J. Paolino & B. S. McCrady (Eds.), *Marriage and marital therapy: Psychoanalytic, behavioral, and systems theory perspectives*. New York: Brunner/Mazel, 1978.
Jacobson, N. S. Clinical innovations in behavioral marital therapy. In K. Craig (Ed.), *Clinical behavior therapy*. New York: Brunner/Mazel, 1983.
Jacobson, N. S., Berley, R., Melman, K. N., Elwood, R., & Phelps, C. Failure in behavioral marital therapy. In S. Coleman (Ed.), *Failures in family therapy*. New York: Guilford Press, in press.
Jacobson, N. S., Elwood, R. W., & Dallas, M. Assessment of marital dysfunction. In D. H. Barlow (Ed.), *Behavioral assessment of adult disorders*. New York: Guilford Press, 1981.
Jacobson, N. S., Follette, W. C., Baucom, D. H., Hahlweg, K., & Margolin, G. *Variability in*

outcome and clinical significance of behavioral marital therapy: A reanalysis of outcome data. Unpublished manuscript, 1983.

Jacobson, N. S., Follette, W. C., & McDonald, D. W. Reactivity to positive and negative behavior in distressed and nondistressed married couples. *Journal of Consulting and Clinical Psychology*, 1982, *50*, 706–714.

Jacobson, N. S., Follette, W. C., & Revenstorf, D. *Psychotherapy outcome research: Methods for reporting variability and evaluating clinical significance.* Unpublished manuscript, 1983.

Jacobson, N. S., & Margolin, G. *Marital therapy: Strategies based on social learning and behavior exchange principles.* New York: Brunner/Mazel, 1979.

Jacobson, N. S., & Martin, B. Behavioral marriage therapy: Current status. *Psychological Bulletin*, 1976, *83*, 540–566.

Kazdin, A. E., & Wilson, G. T. *Evaluation of behavior therapy.* Cambridge, MA: Ballinger, 1978.

Kraemer, H., & Jacklin, C. Statistical analysis of dyadic social behavior. *Psychological Bulletin*, 1979, *86*, 217–224.

Liberman, R. P., Levine, J., Wheeler, E., Sanders, N., & Wallace, C. J. Marital therapy in groups: A comparative evaluation of behavioral and interactional formats. *Acta Psychiatrica Scandinavica*, 1976, *266*, 3–34. (Suppl.)

Locke, H. J., & Wallace, K. M. Short-term marital adjustment and prediction tests: Their reliability and validity. *Journal of Marriage and Family Living*, 1959, *21*, 251–255.

Margolin, G., & Jacobson, N. S. Assessment of marital dysfunction. In M. Hersen & A. S. Bellack (Eds.), *Behavioral assessment: A practical handbook.* London: Pergamon Press, 1981.

Nesselroade, J. R., & Stigler, S. M. Regression toward the mean and the study of change. *Psychological Bulletin*, 1980, *88*, 622–637.

O'Leary, K. D., & Turkewitz, H. Methodological errors in marital and child treatment research. *Journal of Consulting and Clinical Psychology*, 1978, *46*, 747–758.

Smith, M. L., & Glass, G. V. Meta-analysis of psychotherapy outcome studies. *American Psychologist*, 1977, *32*, 752–760.

Spanier, G. B. Measuring dyadic adjustment: New scales for assessing the quality of marriage and similar dyads. *Journal of Marriage and the Family*, 1976, *38*, 15–28.

Stuart, R. B. Helping couples change: *A social learning approach to marital therapy.* New York: Guilford Press, 1980.

Stunkard, A. J., & Penick, S. B. Behavior modification in the treatment of obesity: The problem of maintaining weight loss. *Archives of General Psychiatry*, 1979, *36*, 801–806.

Turkewitz, H., & O'Leary, K. D., A comparative outcome study of behavioral marital therapy. *Journal of Marital and Family Therapy*, 1981, *7*, 159–170.

Weiss, R. L., & Margolin, G. Assessment of marital conflict and accord. In A. R. Ciminero, K. D. Calhoun, & H. E. Adams (Eds.), *Handbook of behavioral assessment.* New York: Wiley, 1977.

PART TWO

ASSESSMENT AND ANALYSIS OF MARITAL INTERACTION

9

A Comparison of the Interaction of Distressed and Nondistressed Married Couples in a Laboratory Situation: Literature Survey, Methodological Issues, and an Empirical Investigation

CAS SCHAAP

When reviewing studies investigating the effectiveness of communication training and behavioral marital therapy (Van Den Heuvel & Schaap, 1979), we were struck by the "ideal" relationship that is reflected in the goals of the different programs (see also Schaap, 1982b).

The studies reviewed and presented in this chapter tried to answer the following question: "What are the differences in verbal and nonverbal communication between the interaction of nondistressed couples and that of distressed couples?"

The first section ("Literature Survey") gives a summary of a comprehensive survey of studies investigating the interaction of married couples in a laboratory situation, described more extensively elsewhere (Schaap & Romijn, 1982). The second section ("Methodological Issues") describes some methodological issues raised when one tries to summarize the results of the studies reviewed in the first section. The issues center around (1) subject characteristics, (2) data-generating characteristics, (3) coding scheme, and (4) methods of analysis. The third section ("An Empirical Study") describes an empirical investigation, more fully presented in Schaap (1982a).

Literature Survey

An extensive search of the literature led to the identification of 26 studies comparing distressed and nondistressed married couples. Excluded were some "special" groups, as well as those whose marital distress was explicitly or im-

Cas Schaap. Department of Clinical Psychology, Catholic University Nijmegen, Nijmegen, The Netherlands.

plicitly considered a by-product of such problems as alcoholism or physical handicaps. Also excluded were studies where a comparison between distressed and nondistressed couples could not be made, for instance, because factor analysis was used (Ryder, 1968). Included in the sample are "clinic" couples — that is, distressed couples who sought or were referred for marital therapy — but only if the data were obtained using the behavioral observation method, and when a control group was available. This sample of 26 studies is extensively described in Schaap and Romijn (1982).

Affect (Love–Hate, Positiveness–Aversiveness, Support–Defensiveness)

As one scans the 26 studies, one obtains a lasting impression: that distressed couples are predominantly negative in their attitudes and behavior (even in low-conflict tasks), and that nondistressed couples are more positive. We see this in their emotional expression, behavior exchange, and problem-solving behavior. Further, we note this particularly in their nonverbal behavior, but also in their verbalization. To be more explicit, compared to distressed couples, nondistressed couples show more behaviors variously called "positive cues of affect" (e.g., empathic smile; warm, tender voice; attention) (Gottman, 1979; Rubin, 1977); "social reinforcement" (e.g., approval, agreement, assent) (Birchler, 1972; Hahlweg, Helmes, Steffen, Schindler, Revenstorf, & Kunert, 1979; Revenstorf, Vogel, Wegener, Hahlweg, & Schindler, 1980; Vincent, 1972); "reconciling acts" (e.g., changing the subject, using humor, accepting the other's ideas) (Barry, 1968; Raush, Barry, Hertel, & Swain, 1974); "facilitative behaviors" (e.g., positive description of partner, paraphrasing) (Wegener, Revenstorf, Hahlweg, & Schindler, 1979); and "supportive behaviors" (e.g., outcome agreement, process agreement, self-confidence) (Sprenkle, 1975). Apparently nondistressed couples sit closer to each other, touch themselves less, and use more "open" positions than distressed couples do (Beier & Sternberg, 1977).

In contrast, distressed couples show more negative affect (e.g., inattention, staccato voice, arms akimbo) (Gottman, 1979; Rubin, 1977); more coercive acts (e.g., leaving the field, using an outside power to force the other to agree) (Barry, 1968; Raush et al., 1974); more negative social reinforcement (e.g., turn off, put down, disagree, criticize) (Birchler, 1972; Hahlweg et al., 1979; Revenstorf et al., 1980; Vincent, 1972); and more defensive behaviors (e.g., outcome disagreement, process disagreement, disapproval of other) (Sprenkle, 1975). In some studies, they exhibit more silence (Birchler, 1972; Hahlweg et al., 1979; Vincent, 1972), and in others they talk more (Beier & Sternberg, 1977); they also speak more loudly (Foy, 1977). Some studies report that they use less eye contact (Beier & Sternberg, 1977; Birchler, 1972; Hahlweg et al., 1979; Vincent, 1972), others that they use more (Haynes, Follingstad, & Sullivan, 1979). Finally, they keep more interpersonal distance and touch themselves more (Beier & Sternberg, 1977). The distressed partners are far more negative in their coding of the behavior (i.e., impact) of their spouses than the nondistressed partners (Fiorito, 1977; Gottman, 1979).

Status (Power, Dominance–Submission, Control, Assertiveness)

The results on the status dimension are far less clear than those on the affect dimension, according to Sprenkle (1975), due to a failure in the literature to make a careful conceptual distinction among aspects of power. It is clear that the problems of distressed couples center around the relationship aspect of communication versus the content aspect (Mendelson, 1971; Morse, 1972); or, in other words, the presence of a status struggle is characteristic. Further, nondistressed couples change more easily between acceptance and rejection of mutual control in the relationship (Busch, 1975).

Nonclinic couples have a higher control efficiency (the ratio of the directions, instructions, suggestions, or requests that actually modify the behavior of a spouse relative to the number of attempts to modify that spouse's behavior) than clinic couples (Sprenkle, 1975). Sprenkle also reports that equalitarian power in conjunction with high support was most satisfying, echoing the conclusions of Mendelson (1971) and Morse (1972) that the status dimension should be interpreted in conjunction with the affect dimension of interaction.

Problem Solving (Conflict Resolution)

The problem-solving behavior of distressed couples is more negative (Billings, 1979), and they engage in much longer conflict scenes (Barry, 1968; Raush et al., 1974). Nondistressed couples emit more problem-solving acts (e.g., compromise, offer to collaborate in planning) and more cognitive acts (e.g., probe, seek information, give information) and almost no coercive acts (e.g., demand compensation, induce guilt) or personal attacks (e.g., threaten the other, disparage the other) (Barry, 1968; Raush et al., 1974). They develop a more neutral problem discussion (Wegener et al., 1979) and show more positive problem-solving behaviors (e.g., positive solution, compromise) (Birchler, 1972; Hahlweg et al., 1979; Koren, 1978; Revenstorf et al., 1980; Vincent, 1972).

Nondistressed couples are more responsive (Dewitt, 1977; Koren, 1978) and deliver more acknowledgments (Barry, 1968; Holzman, 1973; Raush et al., 1974) and assents (Birchler, 1972; Gottman, 1979; Revenstorf et al., 1980; Rubin, 1977; Vincent, 1972).

Exchange and Reciprocity

There is a positive exchange (i.e., a high baserate of positive behaviors for both spouses) among nondistressed couples and a negative exchange among distressed couples. Also, negative reciprocity seems to be characteristic of distressed spouses, though this is never very significant, especially for affect (Billings, 1979; Gottman, 1979; Revenstorf et al., 1980). There is no evidence for positive reciprocity among nondistressed couples for affect; there is some evidence for positive reciprocity with regard to verbalizations (Revenstorf et al., 1980).

Rigidity (Creativity, Flexibility)

Gottman (1979), in his structural model, uses the meta-concept of "rigidity," operationalized as a "high degree of predictability." Unfortunately, at least two other definitions are encountered in the literature under review. Sprenkle (1975) is among those for whom rigidity is equated with a low productivity of problem solutions, that is, the opposite of creativity. In some studies using frequency analysis (Mendelson, 1971; Morse, 1972), rigidity is equated with a high baserate of positive behavior. This last definition is identical to an operationalization of "exchange."

Sprenkle (1975) reports that nonclinic and nondistressed spouses, especially husbands, are more flexible spouses; "flexibility" was operationalized as the number of new modes of play either suggested or actually tried while playing the Simulated Family Activity Measure (SIMFAM) game in the crisis trials. Gottman (1979) reports more rigidity (i.e., high predictability) among his clinic and distressed couples, as was anticipated by him on the basis of family interaction literature.

Husband–Wife Differences

Raush et al. (1974) report no great sex differences in interaction styles. Where differences occur, they are in a direction that, they say, implies a "traditional" complementary relationship: The husbands are independent and supportive; the wives coerce and appeal. Raush et al. noticed a striking sequential aspect in their "discordant" couples' management of conflict. In the first two scenes the wives attacked, while the husbands responded rather calmly and benignly; in the last two scenes, where the level of conflict aroused was highest, this pattern was reversed. Suggestive is the finding by Gottman (1979) that in the low-conflict situations the nondistressed husbands take care that negative affect does not escalate. In the high-conflict situations, it is the wife who takes that role. Generally, the wives were more negative during the Fun Deck Task (a low-conflict task!), Sex, and In-Laws. The husbands were most positive during the Sex Situation. Margolin and Wampold (1981) report more Smile/Laugh, Complain, and Criticize for the wives; and more Excuse for the husbands in their study. Beier and Sternberg (1977) also report more smiling among the wives of their subjects.

Sprenkle (1975) reports that an interaction style where the wife is dominant is associated with low marital satisfaction scores of both spouses. The egalitarian style is associated with the highest satisfaction scores.

Summary of Literature Survey

REPLICATED FINDINGS

Effective discriminators between nondistressed (and nonclinic) and distressed (and clinic) couples are:

- Nonverbal communication in general, even when the spouses are instructed to fake positive communication (Vincent, Friedman, Nugent, & Messerly, 1979).
- Negative affect or emotional atmosphere (Fiorito, 1977; Gottman, 1979; Mendelson, 1971; Morse, 1972; Rubin, 1977).
- Negative impact; that is, the negative manner in which the behavior of the distressed spouses is experienced by their (distressed) partners (Fiorito, 1977; Gottman, 1979).
- Negative verbal (or content) categories like put down, criticize, disagree (Birchler, 1972; Gottman, 1979; Hahlweg et al., 1979; Koren, 1978; Vincent, 1972).
- Presence of a status struggle for distressed couples (Busch, 1975; Mendelson, 1971; Morse, 1972).
- Agreement/disagreement ratio (Gottman, 1979; the recoding of Raush et al., 1974; Rubin, 1977).
- Responsiveness, including acknowledgment and assent (Birchler, 1972; Dewitt, 1977; Gottman, 1979; Holzman, 1973; Koren, 1978; Raush et al., 1974; Revenstorf et al., 1980; Vincent, 1972).
- Sequential patterns of "validation loops" (problem describing followed by agreement) (Gottman, 1979; Revenstorf et al., 1980).
- Revenstorf et al. and Gottman also seem to agree that nondistressed couples are able to counteract negative escalations; that is, negative nonverbal behavior as a listener is not continued when the person changes to the speaker's role.

UNREPLICATED FINDINGS

The following variables were found to discriminate distressed and nondistressed couples in only one study:

• Gottman (1979, p. 113) distinguishes three phases in interaction: "agenda building" (the task of this phase is getting problems out for subsequent discussion), "arguing" (the task of this phase is airing disagreements and exploring common ground in opinion and feelings about a problem), and "contracting" (the task of this phase is coming to a mutually satisfying agreement on how to solve the problem).

• A higher congruence between the coding of observers and nondistressed couples than between the coders and distressed couples is reported by Fiorito (1977).

• Distressed couples code their own behavior as less negative than do observers (Fiorito, 1977).

• Positive affect only discriminates distressed and nondistressed couples during a low-conflict task (Gottman, 1979).

• Distressed couples need more time to come to a solution than do nondistressed couples (Raush et al., 1974).

• Revenstorf et al. (1980) report certain patterns of "attempts of reconciliation" (a sequence of negative code by A and a positive and "filler" code by B) and "acceptance" (positive code of A after a positive code of B) as characteristic of nondistressed couples.

• The patterns of "devaluations" (negative code of B after a positive code of A), "fight backs" (negative code of B after a negative code of A), and "yes-butting" (sequence of positive–filler–negative) are characteristic of distressed couples (Revenstorf et al., 1980).

• These last authors also report the generalized sequential patterns of "problem acceptance" (sequences — often longer than an interact, i.e., a behavior of A followed by a behavior of B — of problem descriptions followed by positive codes), "problem escalation" (sequences of problem descriptions followed by a negative code), "attraction" (series of positive codes), and "distancing" (series of negative codes).

CONTRADICTORY FINDINGS

The following variables are reported in some studies to be indicative of nondistressed couples and in other studies to be indicative of distressed couples, or are otherwise difficult to interpret:

• The status dimension, as operationalized by the Interpersonal Checklist, generates results that can be interpreted only by taking into account the affect dimension (Mendelson, 1971; Morse, 1972).

• "Cross-complaining" (i.e., feelings about a problem followed by an expression of feelings about a problem by the spouse) is reported by Gottman (1979) to discriminate his groups; Revenstorf et al. (1980) did not find this. (This is probably directly the result of the fact that they used different coding systems. In the system used by Gottman, the category Problem Feeling includes the code Talk, which is somewhat strange.)

• Gottman (1979) and Margolin and Wampold (1981) report that positive reciprocity does not discriminate distressed and nondistressed couples, whereas Revenstorf et al. (1980) report that it did discriminate their couples. It is difficult to relate this to the results reported in Billings (1979), since he used a different coding scheme.

• There is also no consensus whether interruptions, silence (pauses, no response), and eye contact are more characteristic of distressed or nondistressed couples.

Methodological Issues

Subject Characteristics: Homogeneity

A total of 20 studies used groups of couples homogeneous with regard to critical demographic variables such as age (phase in the family life cycle), number of children, and socioeconomic status (Barry, 1968; Bayard, 1975; Beier & Sternberg, 1977; Birchler, 1972; Busch, 1975; Fiorito, 1977; Gottman, Notarius, Markman, Bank, Yoppi, & Rubin, 1976, Studies 1 and 2; Gottman, 1979; Hahlweg et al., 1979; Jamrozy, 1975; Koren, 1978; Mendelson, 1971; Morse, 1972; Rubin, 1977; Vincent, 1972; Vincent et al., 1979); in six of these studies the homogeneity was tested statistically (Bayard, 1975; Busch, 1975; Jamrozy, 1975; Koren, 1978; Morse, 1972; Rubin, 1977). Heterogeneous samples were used in six studies (Billings, 1979; Foy, 1977; Hofman, 1970; Revenstorf et al., 1980; Sprenkle, 1975; Wegener et al., 1979); in three of these studies this was tested statistically (Billings, 1979; Hofman, 1970; Sprenkle, 1975). One study (Dewitt, 1977) gives insufficient information.

Homogeneity is very important, since the number per group is rather low (an average of 10–15 couples).

One of the factors that influences this homogeneity is the recruiting strategy. Four different ways of recruiting subjects can be identified. They may be described as follows:

1. Recruitment via acquaintances of the researcher or of other subjects
2. Referral by marital therapists, clergy, or clinics ("clinic" couples)
3. Recruitment via advertisement (TV, newspaper)
4. Recruitment via marriage license records

No studies could be identified that tried to determine whether the recruiting strategy affects the actual communication of couples. The strategy of recruiting as subjects persons who are acquaintances of the researcher and/or others subjects—as practiced by Bayard (1975), Billings (1979), Foy (1977), and Sprenkle (1975)—seems to us a questionable method. Moreover, one might assume that subjects recruited by Method 2 ("clinic") will differ from those recruited by Methods 3 and/or 4. However, more research needs to be done.

LENGTH OF MARRIAGE OR STAGE IN THE FAMILY LIFE CYCLE

The distribution of the length of the period the subjects have been married shows two peaks; one occurs around the first year, and the second one occurs in the interval from 6 to 10 years. Thus subjects in research on differences between distressed and nondistressed couples are mainly newlyweds and couples married 6-10 years. It is unclear whether this represents an artifact (e.g., due to the recruiting strategy) or whether these stages are most critical in the family life cycle. The older marriage (from 10 years onward) is not represented. Generalization of the results of these studies to marriages of longer duration is no problem, if it is shown that the length of marriage (or phase in the family life cycle) does not affect the interaction of couples. However, there exists some evidence that it does (Corrales, 1974; Frenken, 1976; Gottman, 1979; Raush et al., 1974).

THE PRESENCE OF CHILDREN

The studies reviewed generally report an average number of children. It is therefore impossible to search for an effect of this factor. One might suppose that the presence (vs. absence) of children is more important than the mere number. We do not know of studies that have tested the influence of this factor on the actual interaction of married couples. It is certain, however, that this factor will influence the content of problems in marriage; the more so, since problems between parents are often hidden underneath the problems that parents have with their child(ren).

SOCIOECONOMIC STATUS OF THE COUPLES

Only one study (Jamrozy, 1975) of all 26 analyzed the communication of couples from lower socioeconomic classes. Many of the studies reviewed do not give information on the socioeconomic status of their couples or use somewhat heterogeneous groups. There exists some evidence that this factor influences the actual interaction of couples (Hawkins, Weisberg, & Ray, 1977; Jamrozy, 1975; Mark, 1970; Scarlett, 1978; Schaap, Mencke, & Jacobs, 1982) but, apparently, not their problem-solving effectiveness (Cohen, 1974; Henggeler, 1977).

INSTRUMENTS TO MEASURE MARITAL ADJUSTMENT

Finally, an important factor in comparing results across studies is the method of measuring marital adjustment. Evidence for the influence of this factor on communication comes from Gottman (1979). He recoded the tapes of

Raush *et al.* (1974) and found that the agreement–disagreement ratios of all their couples fell within the range of his distressed couples. Earlier he had shown the high positive correlation between scores on a combination of distress criteria and the ratio of agreement to disagreement.

The implications of this are that cross-cultural comparisons (e.g., the studies by the Max-Planck group; Van Den Eijnden, Handelé, & Meeuwisse, 1978; the study reported in the third section of this chapter) should be practiced with caution, since the instruments to measure distress–satisfaction are quite different.

Data-Generating Characteristics

DATA-GENERATING TECHNIQUES

For an extensive description of the tasks, the reader is referred to Schaap and Romijn (1982). In this discussion we concentrate on two questions: (1) the effect of the relevancy of the data-generating task on the interaction, and (2) the effect of different conflict resolution techniques on the interaction.

Crump (1978) provides evidence for the proposition that the relevancy of the task for the couples does influence the ensuing interaction. He notes, however, that the relevancy of the task does not influence more formal and structural characteristics of the interaction (pauses, speech rate).

With regard to the second question, the studies of Van Den Eijnden *et al.* (1978) and Schaap, Mencke, and Jacobs (1982) are relevant.

Van Den Eijnden *et al.* concentrated on the differences in interaction generated by the Inventory of Marital Conflicts (IMC) and a Marital Problem Discussion (MPD). They found a higher frequency of the following codes of the Marital Interaction Coding System (MICS) in the IMC condition: Talk, Not Tracking, Disagree, Interrupt, Problem Description, Compliance, Compromise, Positive Physical Contact, Positive Solution, Laugh, Question, Turn Off, Agree, Assent, and Accept Responsibility. The MPD resulted in a higher frequency of the codes Attention, Complain, Criticize, Deny Responsibility, Excuse, Smile, Put Down, Approve, Negative Solution, No Response, Noncompliance, and Humor.

Schaap, Mencke, and Jacobs (1982) compared the effect of an MPD and the Assessment Task. (In this task, the couples discuss the "state" of their marriage in a number of role areas—household, children, social activities, finances, sex, communication, work, and the autonomy of each partner.) Using multivariate analyses of variance, the latter was characterized by significantly more Problem Descriptions, Paralinguistic Features, Positive Solution, No Response, and Normative. The couples in the MPD delivered significantly more Accept Responsibility, Deny Responsibility, Command, Put Down, Criticize, and (to a somewhat lesser extent) Assent. Our suggestion is that the

Assessment Task generates more neutral interaction by giving the couples an opportunity to "escape."

Gottman (1979) reports that his improvisation scenes evoked conflict (as measured with the agreement–disagreement ratio) in the following order: Sex, Getting Children, Finances, In-Laws, Discussing Events of the Day, Disciplining Children, and the Fun Deck. He also presents evidence that positive reciprocity discriminates the groups only when the level of conflict induced is high. Other sequential patterns remain stable. Other authors reporting a task effect are Foy (1977) and Hofman (1970).

THE LENGTH OF THE OBSERVATION PERIOD

Most authors employ a period of observation of 10–15 minutes or less. There is some evidence that the length of the observation period influences the results (Gottman, 1979; Schaap, Mencke, & Jacobs, 1982; Wegener *et al.*, 1979; Revenstorf *et al.*, 1980). The shorter this period, the more neutral codes are observed.

Coding Scheme

THE CODING SYSTEMS

In this section we focus on the category systems used in the literature, because they provide a stream of discrete events where the temporal order is retained. They usually code the verbal channel in interaction. Sometimes nonverbal behaviors are included — for example, in the Marital Interaction Coding System (Hops, Wills, Patterson, & Weiss, 1971). In the reviewed literature, seven relevant category coding systems are used:

- The Analysis of Relational Communication (Busch, 1975; Ericson, 1972; Mark, 1970; Rogers, 1972)
- The Coding System for Interpersonal Conflict (Barry, 1968; Billings, 1979; Raush *et al.*, 1974)
- The Marital and Family Interaction Coding System (Crump, 1978; Miller, 1971)
- The Kategoriensystem für interpersonelle Kommunikation (KIK) (Schindler, 1981; Wegener *et al.*, 1979)
- The Behavior Coding System (Koren, 1978)
- The Couples Interaction Scoring System (CISS) (Gottman, 1979; Rubin, 1977)
- The Marital Interaction Coding System (MICS) (e.g., Birchler, 1972; Hahlweg *et al.*, 1979; Revenstorf *et al.*, 1980; Vincent, 1972)

RELIABILITY

Some authors (Bayard, 1975; Beier & Sternberg, 1977; Foy, 1977) give insufficient information about the type of reliability index. Further, various indices and scores for reliability of the observations are reported. Remarkable is the popular use of a simple percentage agreement score. Gottman (1979) devotes a whole chapter to the issue of reliability. He concludes that simple percentage agreement scores inflate the reliability. Moreover, if the data are to be analyzed sequentially, and the position of the codes in the sequence is important, he advises the use of the kappa statistic.

Methods of Analysis

FREQUENCY ANALYSIS

MICS codes are usually cast in rate per minutes, in contrast to CISS codes. These are transformed into proportions. It is possible that these data are not comparable, if an appreciable difference in verbal output rate between distressed and nondistressed couples is present.

Differences between distressed and nondistressed couples in communication are commonly tested by analysis of variance techniques (including multiple t tests) and multivariate analysis of variance, or by nonparametric techniques. Hahlweg *et al.* (1979) decided to test the differences in MICS codes between their nondistressed and distressed groups with the Mann–Whitney U test. They point out that one disadvantage of applying the U test several times on the same sample is that alpha increases (this capitalization on chance is also a problem in t tests and univariate analysis of variance). Nevertheless, they used this nonparametric test rather than an analysis of variance because of their small sample (10 couples per group) and failing homogeneity of variance.

Since the data of the husbands and wives are correlated, sex is considered a repeated measure in the analysis of variance design.

SEQUENTIAL ANALYSIS

Patterson (1974) identified the specific behaviors of three family members (father, mother, sister) that controlled the initiation and maintenance of the subject's (an aggressive boy) hostile behavior; these were operationally defined as "yell," "whine," and "disapproval" responses. A scrutiny of the boy's hostile behavior confirmed the existence of a relationship between the behavior of the family and that of the boy. Patterson found that the use of such a sequential analysis approach doubles the predictive power, compared to information based merely on the frequency of occurrence of hostile behavior. In a sense, Patterson's study may be construed as a replication of findings reported one decade earlier (Raush, 1965).

Since these pioneering efforts, the importance of sequential analysis has gained momentum among researchers interested in the patterning of communication, normal and abnormal. As a result, existing models of sequential analysis were adapted for use in studying family communication and new methods were developed. Among the approaches used are Markov analysis (Hertel, 1968), multivariate informational analysis (Raush *et al.,* 1974; Van

Den Bercken, 1979; Revenstorf *et al.*, 1980), N-gram analysis (Revenstorf, Hahlweg, & Schindler, 1979), behavior grammars (Bodnar & Van Baren-Kets, 1974; Rodger & Rosebrugh, 1979), and the lag sequential method (Sackett, 1978).

For further issues related to sequential analysis, we refer to Gottman (1979), Notarius, Krokoff, and Markman (1981), and Schaap (1982a).

Summary of Methodological Issues

It is important that the researcher sample a homogeneous group of couples, especially with regard to their stage in the family life cycle or length of marriage, the presence or absence of children, and socioeconomic status. These couples should be recruited in an identical way. Since the instruments that are used to measure marital adjustment in the American studies are not available in a reliable and valid version for the Dutch population, we have to take special care in forming the distressed and nondistressed groups. The technique to generate the interaction should preferably come from the conflict resolution tasks with high relevancy, and a longer period of interaction should be observed than is usual in this type of research. The scheme to code this interaction should be adequate for measuring problem-solving behavior and affect exchange of couples in a conflict resolution task in a laboratory setting. The data should be checked for reliability with the kappa statistic, particularly if they are to be analyzed sequentially.

An Empirical Study

Compared to the studies summarized in the first section, this study differs with regard to the following points:

- The data of the "in-between" group ("conflict group") were included in the analysis.
- A neutral habituation period was included, preceding the MPD.
- The observation period was appreciably longer than is usual (25 minutes).
- The anxiety or stress generated by the experimental task was measured by the "Speech Disturbance Ratio" (Mahl, 1956).
- Both verbal and nonverbal channels were measured; the verbal codes of the MICS and the Affect Code (AC) of the CISS were used.
- The data were analyzed by frequency and by sequence, using the lag sequential method (Sackett, 1978).
- Behavioral observational methods were complemented by having the spouses comment on the nonverbal facets of their partners' behavior.

Method

SUBJECTS AND PROCEDURE

Subjects were recruited via an advertisement in the local newspapers. The newspaper entry explained that subjects were sought for participation in a study on marital communication. The entry indicated that couples who considered their relationship to be mutually satisfying as well as those who considered themselves to be experiencing marital problems were welcome to contact the author. However, in order to attract a homogeneous group of subjects, the following criteria were explicitly stated: couples should be married 10 to 15 years, should have two or three children, should be living in the local vicinity, and should not be undergoing psychiatric or psychological treatment. Finally, in order to maximize the chances of securing the couples needed for this study, the newspaper advertisement explained that at completion of the investigation, subjects would have the option of receiving marital therapy or participating in a "marital enrichment program," if they wished to do so.

A total of 35 couples responded. Of these, eight were excluded (five for loss of contact, one for deafness of one spouse, and two for being much older than the rest of the subjects), leaving 27 couples who constituted the sample finally used in this investigation. One-third of this sample was defined as "distressed," one-third was defined as "nondistressed," and one-third fell in between, labeled the "conflict" group.

The partners were assisted to feel at ease and adapt to the experimental situation by having them, while the taping equipment was on, talk for the first 5 minutes about their initial acquaintance before marriage and the first ensuing years (Habituation Phase). This was followed by videotaping the interaction on the experimental task (i.e., the MPD). When this was over, the wife was taken to the adjacent room to view the session that had just been videotaped and to comment on the behavior of her husband. Her comments were audiotaped. After the wife finished her comments, the husband was asked to make his comments in the same manner. Each "commenting" session took roughly 30 to 40 minutes. Results of this task are not reported in this article. The reader is referred to Schaap, Mencke, and Van Der Lippe (1982) for these results.

INSTRUMENTS

The following instruments were used for assessing marital distress and satisfaction; they were the main, though not the exclusive, means used for forming the three groups: the Sexuality Experiencing Scales (Frenken, 1976), the Marital Deprivation Scale (Frenken, 1976), and the Maudsley Marital Questionnaire (Boelens, Emmelkamp, MacGillavry, & Markvoort, 1980).

For the purposes of this investigation, we have decided to include among the nondistressed those couples of whom the husband has a score above the mean of the males and the wife has a score above the mean of the females. Those couples of whom the husband and the wife scored below the mean of their sex group were considered to be distressed. Nine couples, out of the 27, met this criterion of classification as distressed. Six couples did not meet the criterion for classification as either distressed or nondistressed. Twelve couples were classified as nondistressed. However, of these, three couples were among those who have explicitly expressed the desire to receive marital therapy. These three couples were dropped from the nondistressed group and, along with the six couples who did not meet the classification criteria, were placed in the conflict group. There were thus nine couples in each group.

In selecting an appropriate task, a balance had to be found between, on the one hand, a reasonably wide sampling of couples' interaction, involvement, and freedom from the constraints of the situation; and, on the other hand, products which lend themselves to breakdown into reliably codable and meaningful units. Of all methods used in pilot work for generating communication, the one calling on subjects to discuss their problems, as they see them, was found to yield the most animated yet focused interaction.

As a result of early efforts and much trial and error, a decision was made to use three coding systems: the MICS (Hops, Wills, Patterson, & Weiss, 1971), the Speech Disturbance Ratio (Kasl & Mahl, 1958; Mahl, 1956) and the AC of the CISS (Gottman, 1979; Rubin, 1977).

The MICS is derived from the Family Interaction Coding System (Patterson, Ray, Shaw, & Cobb, 1969), a method for analyzing family communication in the context of social learning theory. Its validity and utility have been shown in a number of studies: comparing distressed and nondistressed couples (Birchler, 1972; Birchler, Weiss, & Vincent, 1975; Hahlweg, Helmes, Steffen, Schindler, Revenstorf, & Kunert, 1979; Margolin & Wampold, 1981; Revenstorf, Hahlweg, & Schindler, 1979; Revenstorf, Vogel, Wegener, Hahlweg, & Schindler, 1980; Vincent, 1972; Vincent, Weiss, & Birchler, 1975; Wieder & Weiss, 1980); defining characteristics of the communication of distressed/"clinic" couples (Schaap, Mencke, & Jacobs, 1982; Van Den Eijnden et al., 1978); and in the assessment of outcome of marital therapy (Boelens, Emmelkamp, MacGillavry, & Markvoort, 1980; Emmelkamp, van der Helm, MacGillavry, & van Zanten, Chapter 3, this volume; Hahlweg, Schindler, & Revenstorf, 1981; Jacobson, 1978; Liberman, Levine, Wheeler, Sanders, & Wallace, 1976; Margolin & Jacobson, 1976; Patterson, Hops, & Weiss, 1975). The reliability of the MICS is consistently high in these various studies (above .70; usually quite higher). The MICS codes were, a priori, reduced to a three-category (Scheme I) and a nine-category (Scheme II) system, as shown in Table 9.1.

The Speech Disturbance Ratio reflects the stress people experience in certain interactional situations. It consists of counting the occurrence of specific speech disturbances per number of words in a particular segment of interac-

TABLE 9.1. Reduction of the MICS Codes into Categories

Scheme I	Scheme II	MICS codes
Positive	Joking	Laugh, Humor
	Consenting	Approve, Agree, Compromise, Accept Responsibility, Assent
Neutral	Problem describing	Normative, Problem Description, Question
	Contributing to a solution	Positive Solution, Negative Solution, Compromise
	Blurping	Talk
Negative	Dissenting	Disagree, Noncompliance, Deny Responsibility, Command
	Nagging	Criticize, Complain, Put Down, Excuse
	Interrupting	Interruption
	Pausing	No Response

tion. "Speech disturbances" include the following: (1) stuttering, (2) repetitions, (3) sentence changes, (4) sentence incompletions, (5) intruding incoherent sounds, (6) omissions, and (7) tongue slips. Due to its high reliability and the fact that it yields quantitative scores, the Speech Disturbance Ratio has been extensively used in a wide range of psychological investigations of interaction. Its validity has been affirmed again recently in a review dealing with, among others, studies similar to our own (Harper, Wiens, & Matarazzo, 1978).

The AC provides the coder with a number of descriptive categories, each dealing with a specific channel of nonverbal behavior: (1) the face, (2) the voice, and (3) the body. In addition to categorization, the AC calls for rating each nonverbal behavior on a scale for the positiveness of the communication. Gottman (1979) devotes a whole chapter to the reliability of the AC. Its validity has been shown in studies discriminating distressed from nondistressed couples (Gottman, 1979; Rubin, 1977) as well as studies investigating the effectiveness of marital therapy (Gottman, 1979, Chapter 14).

CODING AND ANALYSIS

The audiotapes of the couple's interaction in the 5-minute Habituation Phase and the 25-minute MPD were transcribed verbatim in a manner that closely resembles the method of Labov and Fanshel (1977). Prosodic and paralinguistic features were also indicated. These transcripts were then checked for accuracy by a different person. Speech disturbances were coded in the text by a separate team of three independent coders. The transcripts, with time codes, speech disturbances, and paralinguistic features, were then keyed on a computer disk (PDP 11/34). This material was processed under the edit program (EM), running under the operating system UNIX.

Using the audiotapes (and then the videotapes for ascertaining accuracy), the protocol was coded by a team of four independent coders on the basis of the verbal codes of the MICS. The reliability was consistently high (with κ ranging from .68 to .98 for codes, and from .75 to .98 for categories).

Using the video, a protocol was then coded on the basis of the AC of the CISS, which deals exclusively with nonverbal communication. Three independent coders were used for this purpose. The reliability was also high (with κ ranging from .71 to .85).

It was decided to use nonparametric statistics, because of our small sample and failing homogeneity of variance, for the frequency analysis; and the lag sequential method for the analysis of sequences (Sackett, 1978).

Results

In the tables, used to present the results of the frequency and sequence analyses, the data are presented on the husband–wife level, whereas in the text the data are interpreted on the couple level. Although it would make sense to present average values, it was nevertheless decided to present "individual" data as an illustration of the differences between husbands and wives that we encountered in our study.

Mann–Whitney U tests revealed no difference among the three groups in the "Non-Ah" Speech Disturbance Ratio. It can therefore be concluded that the stress, caused by the couples having to discuss their problems in front of the cameras (and assuming that the Non-Ah Speech Disturbance Ratio measures this stress), is more or less the same for all couples regardless of their satisfaction–distress status. Furthermore, the interaction of the conflict couples is the liveliest (they delivered significantly more words and less pauses), and that of the distressed couples is the flattest.

FREQUENCY ANALYSIS

Table 9.2 summarizes the results of the frequency analysis of the content codes. The nondistressed couples deliver significantly more Humor, Laugh, Agree, Approve, Assent, and Negative Solution. The distressed and conflict couples resemble one another. They both deliver significantly more Disagree, Criticize, and Put Down than the nondistressed couples, with the distressed couples delivering significantly more Command and Excuse, and the conflict couples delivering significantly more Deny Responsibility and Interrupt.

Table 9.3 summarizes the results of the analyses of the AC. Generally, the nondistressed and conflict couples are very similar during the (low-conflict) Habituation Phase. In this situation, negative affect (!) especially discriminates the distressed couples. During the MPD the conflict couples resemble the distressed couples. Both groups are more negative and less positive than the nondistressed couples.

TABLE 9.2. Results of the Mann–Whitney U Tests on the Content Codes of Nondistressed, Distressed, and Conflict Couples during Marital Problem Discussion

	DD	CF	ND	Mean		Rank		Mann–Whitney U test	
MICS codes	M SD	M SD	M SD	ND	DD	ND	CF	ND–DD	ND–CF
Humor	1 1	0 0	1 1	22	14	24	12	−3.41**	−3.44**
Laugh	1 2	3 3	5 4	24	12	22	14	−2.59**	−2.02*
Agree	3 1	4 2	6 3	23	13	22	14	−2.78**	−2.24*
Approve	1 1	0 1	1 1	22	14	21	15	−2.18*	−1.97*
Accept Responsibility	2 2	2 3	1 2	16	20	16	20	−1.01	−0.99
Assent	10 7	9 6	18 9	23	13	23	13	−2.99**	−3.06**
Compliance	1 1	0 1	0 0	14	22	19	17	−2.60**	−0.47
Normative	0 1	0 0	0 1	20	16	20	16	−0.95	−1.37
Problem Description	29 8	27 9	33 7	21	15	21	15	−1.61	−1.89
Question	6 6	5 4	6 7	17	19	17	19	−0.60	−0.53
Negative Solution	0 1	0 1	1 1	22	14	21	15	−2.20*	−2.02*
Positive Solution	3 3	2 2	3 3	18	18	19	17	−0.18	−0.79
Compromise	0 0	0 0	0 0	19	17	19	17	−1.43	−1.43
Talk	7 5	9 5	7 5	18	18	16	20	−0.18	−1.13
Command	1 1	0 1	0 0	13	23	19	17	−2.96**	−0.62
Disagree	8 4	8 6	3 2	10	26	12	24	−4.42**	−3.14**
Noncompliance	0 0	0 0	0 0	17	20	18	18	−1.78	0.0
Deny Responsibility	1 1	3 3	1 2	15	21	12	24	−1.57	−3.27**
Complain	2 2	2 4	1 2	15	21	16	20	−1.74	−1.42
Criticize	3 4	5 6	1 1	15	21	14	22	−1.98*	−2.49**
Excuse	0 1	1 2	0 1	15	21	16	20	−2.11*	−1.46
Put Down	4 4	4 5	1 1	12	24	11	25	−3.36**	−3.87**
Interrupt	5 3	7 4	4 3	17	19	14	22	−0.69	−2.37**
No Response	5 5	3 3	3 3	16	20	19	17	−0.87	−0.52

Note. DD = distressed couples; CF = conflict couples; ND = nondistressed couples. Means and standard deviations in percentages.

$*p = .05.$

$**p = .01.$

RECIPROCITY

In this section we present the results of the analyses on exchange and reciprocity.

We defined "positive exchange" as a high baserate of positive and "negative exchange" as a high baserate of negative behaviors for both partners. The results of the frequency analysis already suggest that such a mechanism is present. However, to test exchange properly, the baserates within couples should be compared. As Gottman (1979) points out, this definition of exchange as "similar rates" is identical to the concept of *"quid pro quo"* (Stuart,

TABLE 9.3. Results of the Mann–Whitney U Tests on the Affect Codes of Nondistressed, Distressed, and Conflict Husband and Wife

	DD		CF		ND		ND–DD		ND–CF	
	M	SD	M	SD	M	SD	Ranks	z	Ranks	z
Habituation phase										
Husband										
Negative	27	33	0	0	0	0	5 13	−3.16**	8 10	−1.45
Neutral	37	31	32	37	30	38	8 10	−0.50	9 9	−0.22
Positive	37	31	68	37	70	38	11 7	−1.86	9 9	−0.22
Wife										
Negative	52	44	3	8	11	26	6 12	−2.14*	10 8	−1.39
Neutral	16	33	25	20	33	31	11 7	−1.61	9 9	−0.30
Positive	32	35	73	22	56	35	11 7	−1.54	8 10	−1.14
Marital problem discussion										
Husband										
Negative	68	26	34	40	11	21	5 13	−3.28**	7 11	−1.46
Neutral	17	25	40	32	28	32	10 8	−0.66	8 10	−1.10
Positive	15	19	25	26	61	35	13 5	−2.78**	12 6	−2.25*
Wife										
Negative	63	34	57	35	18	26	6 12	−2.52**	6 12	−2.52**
Neutral	26	34	28	29	38	24	11 7	−1.28	10 8	−0.88
Positive	11	10	16	12	44	25	13 5	−3.04**	12 6	−2.69**

Note. DD = distressed couples; CF = conflict couples; ND = nondistressed couples. Means and standard deviations in percentages.

*p = .05.

**p = .01.

1969, p. 675) and "reciprocity" as operationalized by Birchler (1972) and Alexander (1973).

For the sake of completeness, two analyses were performed. In the first analysis the proportion of behaviors that are concurrent with similar behaviors of the partner was calculated for positive, neutral, and negative nonverbal behavior. Essentially, this proportion gives an indication of the simultaneity of affect. These results might therefore be referred to as "simultaneity-based reciprocity." The higher this value, the more responsive the partners are. Since this ratio implies coding of behavior of the spouses in parallel tracks, such a ratio cannot be calculated for the content categories. The results, presented in Table 9.4, show that positive simultaneity is highest for the nondistressed spouses and the conflict wife, that neutral simultaneity is highest for the nondistressed and conflict spouses, and that negative simultaneity is highest for the distressed and conflict spouses, with the conflict husband scoring almost maximum.

Remarkable is the fact that positive simultaneity is for all wives higher than for their husbands. Table 9.4 is interesting because it is the only place where positive reciprocity is so clearly found to be characteristic of nondistressed couples; and negative reciprocity, of distressed couples.

The second analysis performed was a correlation within couples between the baserates of MICS categories and ACs of both spouses. This reciprocity might be referred to as "baserate-based reciprocity." The results are presented in Table 9.5. Notice the different pattern of correlations for the MICS and the AC. Concentrating on the first, Table 9.5 reveals very high correlations for the distressed and conflict couples for all categories. Surprising is the fact that the amounts of positive MICS categories delivered do not correlate for the nondistressed couples. So, an absence of positive reciprocity is actually found.

When we inspect the correlations for the amounts of affect, Table 9.5 reveals high positive correlations for the nondistressed spouses, in particular with regard to positive affect. Remarkable are the negative correlations for the distressed couples with regard to negative affect. So here, apparently, positive reciprocity is indeed a characteristic of nondistressed couples, as is the absence of negative reciprocity for the distressed couples.

Gottman (1979) defines what he calls "contingency-based reciprocity" as follows:

> if we know that organism Y has given behavior A to organism X, there is a greater probability that organism X will, at some later time, give behavior A to organism Y than if the prior event had not occurred. . . . (p. 63)

We define "at some later time" as "immediately." If reciprocity is defined in this way, we stay close to the rest of the literature (Billings, 1979; Gottman, 1979; Revenstorf et al., 1980).

The first analyses we did are identical to the ones presented by Gottman (1979, pp. 111–112). The nonverbal behavior of the speaker (for which Gottman reserved the term "Affect") is the criterion behavior. The results of these analyses are presented in Schaap (1982a) and are summarized here.

Results indicate that negative reciprocity (at lag = 1) is characteristic of all couples, but especially of the conflict husband and wife. We find no evidence for negative affect cycles (long sequences, up to 6 lags, of negative af-

TABLE 9.4. Simultaneity of Negative, Neutral, and Positive Affect

	Nondistressed		Distressed		Conflict	
	Husband	Wife	Husband	Wife	Husband	Wife
Positive affect	.59	.82	.25	.34	.29	.53
Neutral affect	.61	.47	.19	.13	.43	.50
Negative affect	.36	.23	.62	.66	.93	.59

TABLE 9.5. Correlations between MICS Categories and ACs of Spouses within Couples

	Nondistressed	Distressed	Conflict
MICS			
Positive	0	.61	.73
Neutral	.61	.91	.88
Negative	.90	.87	.85
Affect			
Positive	.77	.33	.23
Neutral	.73	−.32	.55
Negative	.43	−.25	.93

fect by one partner followed by negative affect by the spouse), as reported in Gottman (1979).

The results further indicate that positive reciprocity (at $lag = 1$) is characteristic of all couples. Positive affect cycles are characteristic of the non-distressed couples.

However, reciprocity may be operationalized in a number of different ways. For instance, we might distinguish affect–affect reciprocity, content–content reciprocity, content–affect reciprocity, affect–content reciprocity, and even category–category reciprocity.

As already indicated, Gottman (1979) defines the nonverbal behavior of the speaker as "Affect." If this is taken as the criterion and the nonverbal behavior of the listener ("Context") is taken as the behavior, we get the following results, as presented in Table 9.6. We find very high positive, neutral, and negative reciprocities for the nondistressed couples. The conflict couples show the same tendency, but it is not so extreme. Remarkable is the low neutral reciprocity among the distressed husbands and wives.

Another operationalization of reciprocity is the immediate exchange of affect after positive, neutral, or negative verbal categories. The results, presented in Table 9.7, indicate negative reciprocity for the nondistressed and conflict spouses. Positive reciprocity is found only for both conflict spouses.

Conversely, a third operationalization of reciprocity is the immediate exchange of positive, neutral, or negative MICS codes after positive, neutral, or negative affect. The results, presented in Table 9.8, again point toward negative reciprocity for the nondistressed and conflict couples. Positive reciprocity is again found only for the conflict couples.

The fourth, and final, operationalization of reciprocity presented here is the immediate exchange of positive, neutral, or negative MICS categories after such categories delivered by the partner. Table 9.9 presents the results. These analyses reveal that nondistressed couples are characterized by an absence of positive reciprocity. Negative reciprocity is shown by the distressed and conflict couples.

TABLE 9.6. Results of Analyses of Nonverbal–Nonverbal Sequences with Speaker's Affect as the Criterion and Listener's Affect as the Reaction

	Affect–affect sequences[a]					
	Positive–positive		Neutral–neutral		Negative–negative	
	H-W	W-H	H-W	W-H	H-W	W-H
Nondistressed	+ +	+ +	+ +	+ +	+ +	+
Distressed	+ +	+ +	0	0	+ +	+ +
Conflict	+ +	+ +	+ +	+ +	+ +	+ +

Note. In this and the following tables, significant z values are not given. Instead, + + stands for a positive z value, significant at the .01 level; and + for a positive z value, significant at the .05 level. They both refer to increased conditional probabilities. Further, − − stands for a negative z value, significant at the .01 level; and − for a negative z value, significant at the .05 level. These refer to decreased conditional probabilities. Finally, 0 refers to a nonsignificant z value. Tables 9.6–9.9 present only the diagonals (i.e., a positive behavior followed by a positive behavior of the spouse, a neutral behavior followed by a neutral behavior of the spouse, and a negative behavior followed by a negative behavior of the spouse). The relationship between, for example, a positive behavior and a neutral or negative behavior of the spouse, although interesting, is not relevant for reciprocity.

[a]H-W = husband–wife sequences; W-H = wife–husband sequences.

TABLE 9.7. Results of Analyses of Verbal–Nonverbal Sequences with MICS Categories of One Partner as the Criterion and Affect Categories of the Spouse as the Reaction

	MICS–affect sequences[a]					
	Positive–positive		Neutral–neutral		Negative–negative	
	H-W	W-H	H-W	W-H	H-W	W-H
Nondistressed	0	+ +	+	0	+ +	+ +
Distressed	+ +	0	0	0	0	−
Conflict	+ +	+ +	+	0	+ +	+ +

[a]H-W = husband–wife sequences; W-H = wife–husband sequences.

TABLE 9.8. Results of Analyses of Nonverbal–Verbal Sequences with Affect Categories of One Partner as the Criterion and MICS Categories of the Spouse as the Reaction

	Affect–MICS sequences[a]					
	Positive–positive		Neutral–neutral		Negative–negative	
	H-W	W-H	H-W	W-H	H-W	W-H
Nondistressed	+ +	0	0	+ +	+ +	+ +
Distressed	0	+ +	0	0	+ +	0
Conflict	+ +	+ +	0	+ +	+ +	+ +

[a]H-W = husband–wife sequences; W-H = wife–husband sequences.

TABLE 9.9. Results of Analyses of Verbal–Verbal Sequences with MICS Categories of One Partner as the Criterion and MICS Categories of the Spouse as the Reaction

	MICS–MICS sequences[a]					
	Positive–positive		Neutral–neutral		Negative–negative	
	H-W	W-H	H-W	W-H	H-W	W-H
Nondistressed	– –	– –	– –	– –	+ +	0
Distressed	0	0	+ +	+ +	+ +	+ +
Conflict	0	0	– –	– –	+ +	+ +

[a]H-W = husband–wife sequences; W-H = wife–husband sequences.

Discussion and Conclusion

In this chapter, we have tried to review the behavioral observation literature, comparing the interaction of distressed and nondistressed married couples in a laboratory situation. Although the literature can be distilled into some characteristic differences between distressed and nondistressed couples, some difficulties in interpretation remain. This is certainly influenced by the fact that the studies differ in a number of important ways. Some of these are discussed in the second section of the chapter.

The third section is devoted to a description of an empirical study. The main results were that on both verbal (MICS) and nonverbal (AC) measures, the distressed and nondistressed couples can be discriminated. Generally, the nonverbal channel is the best discriminator, as is repeatedly shown in the literature. (The code Not Tracking also discriminated strongly between the nondistressed and both the distressed and the conflict couples.)

We have also focused on the concepts of exchange and reciprocity. Our results do not reveal that positive reciprocity is characteristic of the nondistressed couples, nor that negative reciprocity is characteristic of the distressed (or of the conflict) couples. It does seem to depend on (1) the time dimension (its importance is also suggested by Conger and Smith, 1981); (2) the channel of communication; and (3) the impact of the categories (positive, neutral, negative). We would therefore like to propose the following three types of reciprocity:

- "Simultaneity-based" reciprocity
- "Baserate-based" reciprocity
- "Contingency-based" reciprocity

For the second and the third form of reciprocity, we have to distinguish between verbal (content) and nonverbal (affect) reciprocity. For all three forms of reciprocity, we have to take into account the impact of the behaviors under consideration.

Interestingly, in most analyses (except for the MICS–MICS reciprocity), the conflict couples show the clearest evidence of both positive and negative reciprocity. This might mean that reciprocity is more of an index of a "heated" discussion where, apparently, partners tend to "mirror" each other's behavior. This is particularly so for negative reciprocity.

The interested reader is referred to Schaap (1982a) for the analysis of the Commenting Task, the sequential analyses of the MICS categories, the analyses of styles of interaction, the analysis of the "attractiveness" or "aversiveness" of the MICS categories, and for a presentation of the differences between husbands and wives. Implications of these results for clinical practice are also discussed in that volume.

REFERENCES

Alexander, J. F. Defensive and supportive communication in normal and deviant families. *Journal of Consulting and Clinical Psychology,* 1973, *40,* 223–231.

Barry, W. A. *Conflict in marriage: A study of the interaction of newlywed couples in experimentally induced conflicts.* Unpublished doctoral dissertation, University of Michigan, 1968.

Bayard, R. T. *Nonverbal communication between spouses.* Unpublished doctoral dissertation, University of Pittsburgh, 1975.

Beier, E. G., & Sternberg, D. P. Subtle cues between newlyweds. *Journal of Communication,* Summer 1977, pp. 92–97.

Billings, A. Conflict resolution in distressed and nondistressed married couples. *Journal of Consulting and Clinical Psychology,* 1979, *47*(2), 368–376.

Birchler, G. R. *Differential patterns of instrumental affiliative behavior as a function of degree of marital distress and level of intimacy.* Unpublished doctoral dissertation, University of Oregon, 1972.

Birchler, G., Weiss, R., & Vincent, J. Multimethod analysis of social reinforcement exchange between maritally distressed and nondistressed spouses and strangers. *Journal of Personality and Social Psychology,* 1975, *31,* 349–360.

Bodnar, F. A., & Van Baren-Kets, E. J. Sequentiele analyse van gedragsobservaties bij jonge kinderen. *Nederlands Tijdschrift voor de Psychologie,* 1974, *29,* 27–66.

Boelens, W., Emmelkamp, P., MacGillavry, D., & Markvoort, M. A clinical evaluation of marital treatment: Reciprocity counseling versus system-theoretic counseling. *Behavior Analysis and Modification,* 1980, *4,* 85–96.

Busch, L. L. *Strategies of marital communication.* Unpublished doctoral dissertation, University of Southern California, 1975.

Cohen, R. L. *Social class differences in the problem solving process: An integration of social organization, language, and nonverbal communication.* Unpublished doctoral dissertation, University of Minnesota, 1974.

Conger, R. D., & Smith, S. S. Equity in dyadic and family interaction: Is there any justice? In E. E. Filsinger & A. R. Lewis (Eds.), *Assessing marriage: New behavioral approaches.* Beverly Hills, CA: Sage, 1981.

Corrales, R. G. *The influence of family life cycle categories, marital power, spousal agreement and communication styles upon marital satisfaction in the first six years of marriage.* Unpublished doctoral dissertation, University of Minnesota, 1974.

Crump, L. D. *A comparative analysis of couples' verbal communications during nonsalient versus salient conflict resolution tasks.* Unpublished doctoral dissertation, University of Tennessee, 1978.

Dewitt, K. *Intimate communications and marital adjustment: Examining the connection.* Unpublished doctoral dissertation, University of California, 1977.

Ericson, P. *Relational communication: Complementarity and symmetry and their relation to dominance–submission.* Unpublished doctoral dissertation, Michigan State University, 1972.

Fiorito, B. *Marital interaction among high and low adjusted couples: A comparison of participant and observer perceptions.* Unpublished doctoral dissertation, Syracuse University, 1977.

Foy, J. O. *The interpersonal conversation: Nonverbal communication and marital interaction.* Unpublished doctoral dissertation, University of Rochester, 1977.

Frenken, J. *Afkeer van sexualiteit: Sociaal–seksuologisch onderzoek onder 600 gehuwden.* Deventer: Van Loghum Slaterus, 1976.

Gottman, J. M. *Marital interaction.* New York: Academic Press, 1979.

Gottman, J. M., Notarius, C., Markman, H., Bank, S., Yoppi, B., & Rubin, M. E. Behavior exchange theory and marital decision making. *Journal of Personality and Social Psychology,* 1976, *34*(1), 14–24.

Hahlweg, K., Helmes, B., Steffen, G., Schindler, L., Revenstorf, D., & Kunert, H. Beobachtungssystem für partnerschaftliche Interaktion. *Diagnostica,* 1979, *25,* 191–207.

Hahlweg, K., Schindler, L., & Revenstorf, D. *Partnerschaftsprobleme: Diagnose und Therapie. Reziprozitaetstraining. Handbuch für Therapeuten.* Heidelberg: Springer Verlag, 1981.

Harper, R. G., Wiens, A. N., & Matarazzo, J. D. *Nonverbal communication: The state of the art.* New York: Wiley, 1978.

Hawkins, J. L., Weisberg, C., & Ray, D. L. Marital communication styles and social class. *Journal of Marriage and the Family,* 1977, *39,* 479–490.

Haynes, S. N., Follingstad, D. R., & Sullivan, J. C. Assessment of marital satisfaction and interaction. *Journal of Consulting and Clinical Psychology,* 1979, *47*(4), 789–792.

Henggeler, S. W. *Normative effects of race and social class in family interaction styles.* Unpublished doctoral dissertation, University of Virginia, 1977.

Hertel, R. K. *The Markov modeling of experimentally induced marital conflict.* Unpublished doctoral dissertation, University of Michigan, 1968.

Hofman, K. *Marital adjustment and interaction, related to individual adjustment of spouses in clinic and non-clinic families.* Unpublished doctoral dissertation, Michigan State University, 1970.

Holzman, C. G. *Patterns of verbal interaction in couples seeking marital therapy.* Unpublished doctoral dissertation, Columbia University, 1973.

Hops, H., Wills, T. A., Patterson, G. R., & Weiss, R. L. *Marital Interaction Coding System* (Technical Report 8). Unpublished manuscript, University of Oregon, 1971.

Jacobson, N. A stimulus control model of change in behavioral couples' therapy: Implications for contingency contracting. *Journal of Marriage and the Family,* 1978, *4*(3), 29–37.

Jamrozy, L. H. *An investigation of the relationship of communication, adjustment in marriage and socioeconomic status.* Unpublished doctoral dissertation, University of Miami, 1975.

Kasl, S. V., & Mahl, G. F. Experimentally induced anxiety and speech disturbances. *American Psychologist,* 1958, *13,* 349.

Koren, P. E. *Marital conflict interaction: Relationships among subjective and objective measures.* Unpublished doctoral dissertation, University of Utah, 1978.

Labov, W., & Fanshel, D. *Therapeutic discourse: Psychotherapy as conversation.* New York: Academic Press, 1977.

Liberman, R. P., Levine, J., Wheeler, E., Sanders, N., & Wallace, C. J. Marital therapy in groups: A comparative evaluation of behavioral and interactional formats. *Acta Psychiatrica Scandinavica,* 1976, *266,* 3–34. (Suppl.)

Mahl, G. F. Disturbances and silences in the patient's speech in psychotherapy. *Journal of Abnormal and Social Psychology,* 1956, *53,* 1–15.

Margolin, G., & Jacobson, N. S. The assessment of marital dysfunction. In M. Hersen & A. S. Bellack (Eds.), *Behavioral assessment: A practical handbook.* New York: Pergamon Press, 1976.

Margolin, G., & Wampold, B. E. Sequential analysis of conflict and accord in distressed and nondistressed marital partners. *Journal of Consulting and Clinical Psychology,* 1981, *47*(4), 554–567.

Mark, R. A. *Parameters of normal family communication in the dyad.* Unpublished doctoral dissertation, Michigan State University, 1970.

Mendelson, L. A. *Communication patterns in high and low marital adjustment.* Unpublished doctoral dissertation, Florida State University, 1971.

Miller, S. L. *The effects of communication training in small groups upon self-disclosure and openness in engaged couples' systems of interaction: A field experiment.* Unpublished doctoral dissertation, University of Minnesota, 1971.

Morse, B. L. *An investigation of the relationship between marital adjustment and marital interaction.* Unpublished doctoral dissertation, University of North Carolina, 1972.

Notarius, C. I., Krokoff, L. J., & Markman, H. J. Analysis of observational data. In E. E. Filsinger & R. A. Lewis (Eds.), *Assessing marriage: New behavioral approaches.* Beverly Hills, CA: Sage, 1981.

Patterson, G. R. A basis for identifying stimuli which control behaviors in natural settings. *Child Development,* 1974, *45,* 900–911.

Patterson, G. R., Hops, H., & Weiss, R. L. Interpersonal skills training for couples in early stages of conflict. *Journal of Marriage and the Family,* 1975, *37,* 295–303.

Patterson, G. R., Ray, R. S., Shaw, D. A., & Cobb, J. A. *A manual for coding family interactions, 1969 revision* (document No. 01234). Unpublished manuscript, 1969. (Available from ASIS/NAPS, c/o Microfiche Publications, 304 East 46th Street, New York, N.Y. 10017.)

Raush, H. L. Interaction sequences. *Journal of Personality and Social Psychology,* 1965, *2,* 487–499.

Raush, H. L., Barry, W. A., Hertel, R. K., & Swain, M. A. *Communication, conflict and marriage.* San Francisco: Jossey-Bass, 1974.

Revenstorf, D., Hahlweg, K., & Schindler, L. Interaktionsanalyse von partnerkonflikten. *Zeitschrift für Sozialpsychologie,* 1979, *10,* 183–196.

Revenstorf, D., Vogel, B., Wegener, C., Hahlweg, K., & Schindler, L. Escalation phenomena in interaction sequences: An empirical comparison of distressed and non-distressed couples. *Behavior Analysis and Modification,* 1980, *2*(4), 97–116.

Rodger, R. S., & Rosebrugh, R. D. Computing a grammar for sequences of behavioral acts. *Animal Behavior,* 1979, *27,* 737–749.

Rogers, L. E. *Dyadic systems and transactional communication in a family context.* Unpublished doctoral dissertation, Michigan State University, 1972.

Rubin, M. E. Y. *Differences between distressed and nondistressed couples in verbal and nonverbal communication codes.* Unpublished doctoral dissertation, Indiana University, 1977.

Ryder, R. G. Husband–wife dyads versus married strangers. *Family Process,* 1968, *7,* 233–238.

Sackett, G. P. (Ed.). *Observing behavior* (Vol. 2): *Data collection and analysis methods.* Baltimore: University Park Press, 1978.

Scarlett, H. R. H. *Communication exchange behaviors of men and women from middle and lower socioeconomic class backgrounds.* Unpublished doctoral dissertation, Clark University, 1978.

Schaap, C. *Communication and adjustment in marriage.* Lisse: Swets & Zeitlinger, 1982. (a)

Schaap, C. Gezinsdiagnostiek. In B. Baarda & L. Zwaan (Eds.), *Alternatieven in de diagnostiek.* Nijmegen: Dekker v.d. Vegt, 1982. (b)

Schaap, C., Mencke, E., & Jacobs, H. *The analysis of the interaction of clinic couples.* Internal Report, Catholic University, Nijmegen, 1982.

Schaap, C., Mencke, E., & Van Der Lippe, G. *Interpreting the partner's behavior: Analysis of the commenting task.* Internal Report, Catholic University, Nijmegen, 1982.

Schaap, C., & Romjin, C. *Marital interaction observed: A literature survey of laboratory studies comparing the interaction of distressed and nondistressed married couples.* Internal Report, Catholic University, Nijmegen, 1982.

Schindler, L. *Empirischer Analyse partnerschaftlicher Kommunikation: Konfliktloeseverhalten zufriedener und unzufriedener Paare und dessen Veraenderung durch therapeutische Training.* Unpublished doctoral dissertation, University of Tübingen, 1981.

Sprenkle, D. H. *A behavioral assessment of creativity, support, and power in clinic and nonclinic married couples.* Unpublished doctoral dissertation, University of Minnesota, 1975.

Stuart, R. B. Operant-interpersonal treatment for marital discord. *Journal of Consulting and Clinical Psychology,* 1969, *33,* 675–682.

Van Den Bercken, J. H. L. *Information-statistical analysis of social interaction in Java-monkeys applied in the neuro-ethology of the caudate nucleus.* Unpublished doctoral dissertation, Catholic University, Nijmegen, 1979.

Van Den Eijnden, P., Handelé, C., & Meeuwisse, B. *Observatiemethoden in het evalueren van echtpaartherapie.* Doktoraalskriptie klinische psychologie, Rijksuniversiteit Leiden, 1978.

Van Den Heuvel, M., & Schaap, C. Een overzicht van evaluatiestudies van partnerrelatietherapie (in het bijzonder van communicatie- en gedragstherapie). *Tijdschrift voor Psychotherapie,* 1979, *5,* 44–56.

Vincent, J. P. *The relationship of sex, level of intimacy, and level of marital distress to problem-solving behavior and exchange of social reinforcement.* Unpublished doctoral dissertation, University of Oregon, 1972.

Vincent, J. P., Friedman, L., Nugent, J., & Messerly, L. Demand characteristics in observation of marital interaction. *Journal of Consulting and Clinical Psychology,* 1979, *47*(3), 557–567.

Vincent, J. P., Weiss, R. L., & Birchler, G. R. A behavioral analysis of problem solving in distressed and nondistressed married and stranger dyads. *Behavior Therapy,* 1975, *6,* 475–487.

Wegener, C., Revenstorf, D., Hahlweg, K., & Schindler, L. Empirical analysis of communication in distressed and nondistressed couples. *Behavior Analysis and Modification,* 1979, *3,* 178–188.

Wieder, G. B., & Weiss, R. L. Generalizability theory and the coding of marital interaction. *Journal of Consulting and Clinical Psychology,* 1980, *48,* 469–477.

10

Interaction Analysis of Marital Conflict

DIRK REVENSTORF, KURT HAHLWEG,
LUDWIG SCHINDLER, AND BERND VOGEL

Introduction

Each of two people living together constitutes an important part of the other's environment. The marital "environment" basically *is* the spouse. One spouse controls the responses of the other in that he/she delivers discriminative stimuli and provides consequences. This mutual control is not well depicted by a linear stimulus–response–consequence (S-R-C) chain, since S and C are both Rs of the other partner. The two organisms responding to each other and thereby mutually controlling each other may more adequately be described as a circular system. During a rapid exchange, a systems property is likely to occur that is technically described as "positive feedback." This may include either increasing mutual attraction or aversion. The former is exemplified by sexual approach; the latter is what Patterson (1977) calls the "coercion process." Since humans also think, they tend to interpret the responses of their spouses. This may result in a discrepancy between intent and impact. It has been shown that distressed couples have a negative bias: They tend to overlook the positive intent (Gottman, 1979). But spouses may also reinterpret the responses of the other in order to reduce the negative impact – as cognitivists remind us (e.g., Ellis & Harper, 1975). Both events lead to what is technically called "negative feedback": In the former case, attraction is weakened; in the latter case, problem escalation is avoided.

We were interested in studying these processes with distressed and nondistressed couples in order to see how indicative they are of marital distress, and the extent to which changes take place subsequent to therapy. We have seen from the analysis of daily satisfaction ratings that a high interdependence of these processes is predictive of distress (see Revenstorf, Hahlweg, Schindler, & Kunert, Chapter 12, this volume). Besides these long-range effects, we wanted to investigate short-range developments in the relationship. For this

Dirk Revenstorf. Psychological Institute, University of Tübingen, Tübingen, Federal Republic of Germany.

Kurt Hahlweg, Ludwig Schindler, and Bernd Vogel. Max-Planck-Institute for Psychiatry, Munich, Federal Republic of Germany.

purpose we observed couples in problem-solving situations, coded their behavior, and analyzed it on a microscopic level.

In the therapy outcome study (see Hahlweg, Schindler, Revenstorf, & Brengelmann, Chapter 1, this volume), we collected data from couples' problem discussions. Using standardized vignettes from the Inventory of Marital Conflict (IMC) (Hahlweg, Helmes, Steffen, Schindler, Revenstorf, & Kunert, 1979; Olsen & Ryder, 1970) as well as topics of their own choice, the couples were asked to jointly find solutions to the problems.

In Table 10.1 the different samples are shown. The videotapes were taken from 20 couples treated by behavioral marital therapy (BMT) before (TH-1) and after (TH-2) therapy, and from 10 control couples before (WL-1) and after (WL-2) a 3- to 4-month waiting period. The subsample demographic characteristics are practically identical to those of the total sample as described by Hahlweg et al. (Chapter 1, this volume). In addition, we included a sample of 10 nondistressed couples. Their demographic characteristics are described in Hahlweg et al. (1979). In general these samples constitute middle-class couples with a mean age of 33 years and an average marriage duration of 8 years. Statistical analyses revealed no significant differences among the groups on the main demographic variables.

The discussions of their own problems lasted about 10 minutes and were coded by independent observers using the Marital Interaction Coding System (MICS), developed by Hops, Wills, Patterson, & Weiss (1972). By this method we gathered data from about 70 problem discussions, as listed in Table 10.1. An average of 10 codes covered a minute of discussion. Roughly 18,000 observations were collected, and these form the basis for the following analysis.

Our aims in analyzing marital patterns are twofold. In comparing distressed and nondistressed couples, discriminating features in the interaction are sought. For example, is it a preponderance of negative reactions or a lack

TABLE 10.1. Samples of Couples Observed in Problem Discussions

Group	No. of couples	Total no. of codes in the sample
Normal	10	3,308
WL-1	10	1,426
WL-2	10	1,547
TH-1	20	6,306
TH-2	20	5,402
Total	70	17,989
	(Problem discussions)	(Coded observations)

Note. WL = waiting list; TH = therapy; 1 = pre; 2 = post.

of positive reactions that best indicates distress? The findings could have a direct bearing on therapy goals. A second point of interest is the locus of therapy effects. Which interaction patterns change due to therapy? Does the tendency to escalate in a problem discussion decrease, and if so, does it approach the level found in nondistressed couples?

The Coding of Interaction

The Coding System

Many researchers have developed observational categories in order to objectify human interactions. Well known from the general area of social psychology is the Interaction Process Analysis (IPA) system of Bales (1950), which is used in problem-solving groups. The IPA appears to be inadequate for the present purpose. Observational instruments are tools for screening certain information—but this screening has to be selective. The tools have to provide the necessary information for testing the hypotheses under consideration. The system (one hopes) taps relevant information, and therefore it has to be fitted to that purpose. But if the fit is too tight, the system might extract just the information necessary to maintain the hypotheses of the author and not the information that would allow for an alternative interpretation of the situation. This particular objection has been raised against the IPA by Merkens and Seiler (1978). A serious candidate for a sufficiently broad but still relevant observational system for marital interaction is the Marital and Family Interaction Coding System (MFICS) (Olson & Ryder, 1970), which was developed for the evaluation of problem discussions. Since we used these scenes, the MFICS appeared to be appropriate. An empirical analysis showed, however, that the MFICS did not discriminate between distressed and nondistressed couples (Steffen, 1977). We then chose the MICS, which served our purpose as a first approximation: It discriminated between the two groups of couples (Hahlweg *et al.*, 1979) and enabled us to show a variety of interesting interaction patterns (Revenstorf, Hahlweg, & Schindler, 1979; Revenstorf, Vogler, Wegener, Hahlweg, & Schindler, 1980). The observational categories of the MICS and some of its features in our sample are shown in Table 10.2 and Figure 10.1.

Columns (1) through (4) of Table 10.2 contain information about the original 28 MICS categories. There are 20 verbal and (besides Interruption and No Response) six nonverbal categories (Assent, Positive Physical, Laugh, Attention, Not Tracking, Turn Off). The remaining columns of Table 10.2 contain information about a reduced system, which we discuss later in this chapter.

The coding of the videotape discussions is done in an alternating fashion.

TABLE 10.2. Original Behavioral Coding System (MICS) and Two Collapsed Coding Systems, with Average Occurrence of Category per Minute of Discussion and Significance of Student's t Test for the Discrimination of 10 Distressed and 10 Nondistressed Couples

(1)	(2)	(3)	(4)	(5)	(6)	(7)	(8)	(9)	(10)
						Reduced systems			
Original 28 MICS categories				System I (11 categories)			System II (6 categories)		
Categories		Freq.	t	Categories	Freq.	t	Categories	Freq.	t
1 Approve		0.01							
2 Agree		0.30	**	1' Positive Reply	0.81	*	1" Positive Reaction (+)	1.80	***
5 Comply		0.01							
23 Assent (N)		0.50	*						
26 Positive Physical (N)		0.01							
12 Humor		0.01	*	7' Humor	0.43	*			
22 Laugh (N)		0.42	**						
21 Attention (N)		0.56	*	8' Attention	0.56				
3 Accept Responsibility		0.01							
8 Compromise		0.01							
16 Problem Solution		0.01		2' Problem Solution	0.01		2" Problem Solution (S)	0.01	
4 Command		0.01							

162

Code / Category	Value	Sig.
6 Complain	0.01	*
7 Criticize	0.35	*
10 Deny Responsibility	0.01	*
11 Excuse	0.13	
14 Negative Solution	0.01	
17 Put Down	0.12	*
24 No Response	0.01	**
25 Not Tracking (N)	0.45	*
27 Turn Off (N)	0.01	
9 Disagree	0.70	
20 Noncompliance	0.01	
13 Interrupt	0.26	
15 Problem Description	1.50	*
18 Question	0.28	
19 Talk	0.27	*
28 Normative	0.26	*
29 Filler, more than one		
30 Filler, continuous		

Code / Category	Value	Sig.
3' Negative Counteraction	0.49	**
9' Blocking	0.58	***
10' Reject	0.71	
11" Interrupt	0.26	
4' Problem Description	1.77	*
5' Neutral Reaction	0.53	**
6' Filler		

Code / Category	Value	Sig.
3" Negative Reaction (−)	2.04	***
4" Problem Description (P)	1.78	*
5" Neutral Reaction (O)	0.53	*
6" Filler (v)		

$*p = .05.$
$**p = .01.$
$***p = .001.$

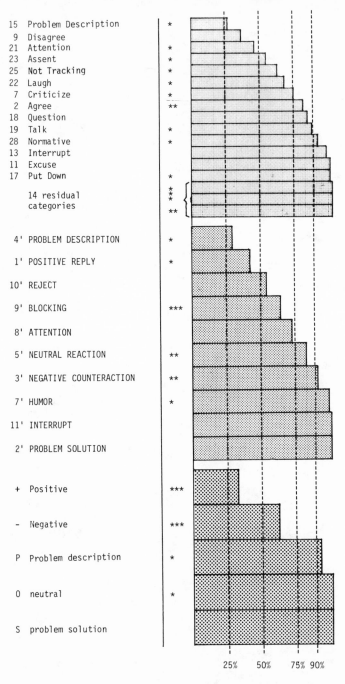

FIGURE 10.1. Main codes in the original MICS observation system and two collapsed versions, with the cumulative frequency of occurrence. (*, **, and *** indicate significant differences between nondistressed and distressed couples at the .05, .01, and .001 levels, respectively; see Table 10.2.)

In a sequence beginning with the female responses, the codes in even positions are those of the males. To allow for two consecutive different codes by one speaker, the other is formally assigned code 29 ("in between"). If one speaker is continuing the same code for more than 1 minute, the other is coded "in between" with Code 30. Codes 29 and 30 therefore are filler coes (v). The alternation with an artificial category (filler) precludes a sequence of two consecutive codes from one spouse. The following results are therefore not directly comparable with the common coding system used, for example, by Margolin and Wampold (1981).

The interrater reliability of all codes was above 70% when two independent raters were compared response by response. This was checked for 150 randomly selected coding intervals.

As others have found, it was not necessary to distinguish between male and female, since in most categories there was no significant sex difference (Hahlweg et al., 1979; Margolin & Wampold, 1981). As indicated in Table 10.2, Column (4), 14 categories discriminated the two groups of 10 normal and 20 therapy couples (TH-1). From the discriminant validity of at least one-half of the categories, it may be concluded that the coding system is relevant to the observation of couples in problem-solving situations.

Column (3) of Table 10.2 contains the average frequencies of the categories per minute. Figure 10.1 depicts cumulative frequencies, with the categories listed in descending order. It may be seen that Problem Description (Code 15), Disagree (9), Attention (21), and Assent (23) are the most frequent categories. These four cover about 50% of the observations. Actually, 90% of the observations are accounted for by 11 out of the 28 categories (in order of descending contribution, Codes 15, 9, 21, 23, 25, 22, 7, 2, 18, 19, and 28). Since four codes cover 50% of the emitted responses and eight cover 75%, it may be concluded that the system might profitably be collapsed. Collapsing is also necessary for the purpose of analyzing longer sequences of codes.

Collapsing the Coding System

As indicated in Table 10.2 and Figure 10.1, two attempts were made to collapse the category system, to 10 codes and then to 5 codes plus a filler. In the first reduction, System I, 7 out of 10 codes are necessary to cover 90% of the data; and in the second, System II, 3 out of 5 codes are necessary, compared with 11 out of 28 in the original system. The collapsing obviously makes the coding system more economical while still retaining the ability to discriminate between the two criterion groups (see significance levels in Table 10.2 and Figure 10.1). The reduction was based on content similarity rather than statistics. However, informational analysis (Revenstorf et al., 1979) showed how much information is lost by this reduction.

The measure of transinformation (Atneave, 1959) may be used to evaluate the connectedness of two parts in a system. It tells us how much predictability of the behavior of one party (information) is gained by knowing the antecedent response of the other party. Transinformation is a nonparametric analogue to correlation. In the case of spouses engaged in an argument, the unconditional redundancy (predictability without knowledge of the antecedent) of the responses was moderate, due to the unequal frequencies of occurrence of the categories (see Table 10.2 and Figure 10.1): The information was 3.5 bits; that is, knowing which code occurs at a particular point in time saves 3.5 binary questions on the average (3.5 binary questions would have been necessary to guess what behavior occurred). If the 28 codes were equally likely, the information of the responses would have been 1d (28): roughly 5 binary questions would be necessary. Therefore 3.5/5, or 70%, of the information that it is possible to record by this coding system is used by the couples (30% redundancy).

This information may be completely irrelevant with respect to what happens in the discussion. However, if we consider the transinformation—that is, the proportion of the 3.5 bits that may be predicted from the antecedent behavior of the spouse—then we are tapping something more relevant, at least something to which the spouse reacts. This transinformation is 30% with the full system of 28 categories. There was no difference between the transinformation from husband to wife and vice versa. (In a similar investigation with interactions between mother and child, the transinformation was 25% in both directions; see Revenstorf et al., 1979.) By collapsing the coding system, the transinformation decreased by 7% each time:

28 categories	30% transinformation
10 categories	23% transinformation
5 categories	16% transinformation

We concluded that some of the relevant information (15%) is lost by collapsing the system. On the other hand, we needed more reliable data for larger sequences. The reader will recognize the well-known validity–reliability dilemma.

Our collapsed system differs somewhat from the one used by Margolin and Wampold (1981). The positive and negative summary categories are the same except for one code. The main difference is the neutral category, which is more narrowly defined by the present authors. Margolin and Wampold include in the neutral category what we call Rejection, Interruption, Problem Description, and Question.

Since in later sections of this chapter we consider sequences up to a length of six items, even 10 categories would be too many to give reasonable figures. For instance, there are a million (10^6) possible patterns with length of six. Too many patterns would be empirically empty, even with millions of data points, let alone the 18,000 data points we were able to collect. Therefore, in later paragraphs Reduced Category System II is used (five categories).

Results

Baserates and Contingencies

As a first view of the data let us inspect the baserates and the contingencies (order-2-sequence) in the distressed and nondistressed samples. Table 10.3 contains the baserates for the waiting-list control group measured before (WL-1) and after (WL-2) waiting, the therapy group measured before (TH-1) and after (TH-2) therapy, and the nondistressed, normal sample for Reduced Category System II. The neutral code (0) and Problem Solution (S) occurred so rarely (.5, .01) that they were dropped from further consideration.

Not unexpectedly, positive responses are more frequent in the nondistressed (.35) compared to the distressed samples (.24–.27). Negative responses are more frequent in the distressed samples (.34–.37) than in the normal sample (.24). The figures for distressed couples after therapy are close to the normal sample. Problem Description is comparatively frequent in all samples (.20), which seems to be natural in the test situation. The tendency to utter a problem is raised after therapy (.26), which is plausible due to the fact that couples are trained in communication and problem solving.

Besides being more negative and less positive in their baserates, the two groups of couples are also distinguished by their contingencies. Table 10.4 contains the more frequent transitions in terms of conditional probabilities. These sequences of two exchanges have been tentatively named, as can be seen from Table 10.4. The most frequent positive sequences (first three items), negative sequences (last three items), and a neutral sequence (PP) are given in the table. A sign following a datum indicates whether the conditional probability is higher (+) or lower (−) than the unconditional probability of the response. The conditional probability may be used to evaluate the impact of the antecedent on the response. All three positive conditional probabilities are smaller in the distressed samples than in the nondistressed (posttherapy and normal). The opposite is true for negative patterns. Typically, the conditional probabilities differ from the unconditional probabilities. For instance,

TABLE 10.3. Baserates of Simple Observation Categories in Different Samples

	WL-1 ($n = 1462$)	WL-2 ($n = 1547$)	TH-1 ($n = 6306$)	TH-2 ($n = 5402$)	Normal ($n = 3951$)
+ : Positive	.27	.24	.27	.35	.35
− : Negative	.35	.37	.34	.21	.24
P : Problem	.21	.21	.21	.26	.24
v : Filler	.17	.19	.18	.18	.18

Note. WL = waiting list; TH = therapy; 1 = pre; 2 = post; Normal = nondistressed couples.

TABLE 10.4. Conditional Probabilities (Simple Transitions) for Waiting-List, Therapy, and Normal Samples (labels after Gottman, 1979)

		WL-1 (n = 1462)	WL-2 (n = 1547)	TH-1 (n = 6306)	TH-2 (n = 5402)	Normal (n = 3951)
+ +	: Acceptance	.26	.14 −	.23 −	.30 −	.29
− +	: Reconciliation	.20 −	.22	.24 −	.31 −	.15 −
P +	: Validation loop	.41 +	.41 +	.45 +	.60 +	.43 +
PP	: Cross-Complain	.20	.17	.17 −	.20 −	.14
+ −	: Devaluation	.18 −	.20 −	.17 −	.11 −	.08 −
− −	: Fight Back	.47 +	.42 +	.41 +	.29 +	.28
P −	: Problem Rejection	.33	.41	.38 +	.18 −	.38

Note. WL = waiting list; Th = therapy; 1 = pre; 2 = post. A sign after an entry indicates that probability is significantly above (+) or below (−) the baserate.

a negative response after a negative antecedent (Fight Back) is more frequent in distressed couples (.41–.47) than the unconditional negative (.35).

Testing of Differences

In order to statistically test the differences between various probabilities, four types of questions should be distinguished:

1. Do certain baserates differ from one group to another? For instance, are distressed couples more negative than nondistressed couples in their response? In a more general sense, the whole distribution of baserates over all categories may be compared among groups.

2. Do the conditional probabilities — that is, the contingencies — differ from one group to another? For instance, is the frequency of "acceptance" (+ +) different before and after therapy? In a more general sense, the whole matrix of transition probabilities may be compared from one group to another.

3. Is the conditional probability in a particular group different from the baserate? That is, is there an impact of the antecedent on certain responses? For instance, is a negative response after a positive antecedent less likely than a negative response in general?

4. The most intricate statement would be that the impact of an antecedent on a certain response is different from one group to another. Since the impact would be tested by evaluating a difference (between baserate and conditional probability), this question implies the test of a difference or differences between probabilities. For instance, is the impact of a negative response on the next negative response greater in nondistressed couples?

Questions 1–3 can be answered by an appropriate critical ratio (see Gottman & Bakeman, 1979; McNemar, 1949, p. 60):

$$z = (\text{Obs } F - NP)/\sqrt{NP(1 - P)}$$

In this z value the difference between observed frequency (Obs F) and expected frequency (NP) is divided by the standard deviation of expected frequency. For example, is the probability of a positive response in a "validation loop" $(P+)$ smaller than the positive baserate in the waiting list (WL-1)? Observed frequency here is 126. The expected frequency is $1462 \times .27 = 395$. The standard deviation is easily seen to be 16.9. The resulting statistic is $z = -15.8$, which is highly significant, with N larger than 25 approaching the normal distribution. In this example, conditional and unconditional probabilities were compared.

If two unconditional or conditional probabilities from different samples are to be compared, the formula is slightly modified. Here the expected frequency is that observed in one sample, and the observed frequency is that of the other sample. In the same way, conditional probabilities of two samples may be compared.

If the reader is interested in testing the difference of several probabilities in a compound test, then the common chi-square test may be used. For instance, consider the following frequencies:

Following P	+	−	Sum
Nondistressed	251	159	410
Distressed	181	251	432
Sum	432	410	842

This subtable gives $\chi^2 = 29$ with $df = 1$, which is highly significant. With a similar test it is possible to look for a statistically significant difference between two transition matrices, where each matrix contains all the possible conditional probabilities (Anderson & Goodman, 1957). These more global tests indicate that there are differences in the contingencies; the z values provide information about particular differences of interest.

However, as pointed out by Margolin and Wampold (1981), the use of this z statistic is not completely legitimate, since we use aggregate data from several couples. The observations within each sample are not independent. A better statistic is a normalized z, whose critical value (5% in a one-tailed test) is 4.36. In large samples, however, both methods lead to the same conclusion.

Looking back to Table 10.4, it is realized that most of the conditional probabilities are different from the baserate of the response; that is to say, the antecedent has a certain impact on what follows during an argument. Also, distressed couples react in a way that is statistically different from nondistressed couples for the contingencies listed. Therefore we may conclude that the antecedent has an immediate effect on the response of the partner. This is a strong indication of stimulus control. The distressed and nondistressed couples may be distinguished by their baserates of both positive and negative responses, and in most of their contingencies. However, it is not clear whether the impact of the antecedent is different in the two samples (Question 4). There is no way to statistically analyze this question, as far as the authors know. But it is not important to answer this simple question, because two responses in a sequence hardly represent a meaningful interaction. The consideration of longer sequences is in order.

Sequential Analysis

Sequences

Since the responses as coded last only 6 seconds on the average, contingencies cannot depict a meaningful interaction. Therefore longer sequences are considered in the following. The difficulty with this type of analysis is the increasing paucity of data points with longer sequences. For example, having 5000 observations in a sample (as in the posttherapy group) implies that the most frequent single event is +, with a frequency of 1539. The highest frequency for longer sequences decreases with each lag: double, 541; triple, 301; quadruple, 199; quintuple, 57; sextuple, 33; septuple, 22. That is, the more meaningful a sequence, the fewer data are available.

There are two ways to overcome this handicap: One is to use lag sequential analysis (Gottman & Bakeman, 1979), where the responses are considered in relation to antecedents more than one step back in time, irrespective of what happens in between. The other possibility is to combine simple patterns, in order to arrive at broader sequential patterns. We consider both methods here.

Table 10.5 contains sequences up to the length of five for the different samples of data mentioned before. In this table the sequences have not been named, as is done in Table 10.4. Rather, they are tentatively sorted into *a priori* positive patterns (interactions that counteract negative escalation; see first group of codes for each sequence length in Table 10.5) and negative patterns (enhancing escalation; see second group of codes for each sequence length in Table 10.5). A sign following a proportion in the body of the table indicates whether the conditional probability is greater or less than expected. For example, in the waiting-list sample (WL-1), positive reciprocity had a conditional probability .26 of occurring after a plus (which is not different from the unconditional plus; see Tables 10.3 and 10.4). A third positive response now has a heightened conditional probability of .40, which is a significant increase over a simple contingency.

Some of the patterns are worth consideration. The positive response after two negative responses (− − +) is rare in all of the samples. If aversive con-

TABLE 10.5. Sequences of Interaction, Lengths 3 to 5

Frequent sequence				WL-1	WL-2	TH-1	TH-2	Normal
Length 3								
(1)	+	+	+	.40+	.22	.38+	.45+	.42+
(2)	−	−	+	.18−	.20	.21−	.25−	.16−
(3)	+	v	−	.65+	.71+	.62+	.44+	.38+
(4)	−	v	+	.54+	.49+	.47+	.50+	.57+
(5)	+	v	P	.33+	.29	.37+	.56+	.62+
(6)	P	+	+	.23	.15	.21−	.26−	.19−
(7)	P	+	P	.20	.22	.15−	.18−	.20
(8)	P	P	+	.46+	.37	.44+	.65+	.40
(9)	−	−	−	.57+	.52+	.46+	.42+	.39+
(10)	−	v	P	.43+	.48+	.52+	.50+	.42+
(11)	−	P	−	.46+	.48	.46+	.32+	.56+
(12)	−	P	P	.13	.21	.17	.17	.07−
(13)	P	−	−	.34	.34	.33	.25	.19
Length 4								
(14)	+ +	+	+	.53+	.−	.40+	.47+	.46+
(15)	+ v	P	+	.49+	.45+	.49+	.57+	.51+
(16)	+ v	−	+	.16	.26	.22	.24−	.11−
(17)	+ v	P	P	.20	.15	.16	.29	.28
(18)	P +	v	−	.68+	.71+	.64+	.40+	.43+
(19)	P +	v	P	.37	.29	.36+	.59+	.56+
(20)	− +	v	−	.77+	.73+	.65+	.58+	.51+
(21)	− −	−	+	.17	.18	.22	.21−	.11−
(22)	− −	−	−	.60+	.61+	.49+	.55+	.53+
(23)	+ v	−	−	.46	.36	.40	.25	.28
(24)	P −	v	+	.50+	.38	.38	.52	.62+
(25)	+ v	P	−	.30	.38	.34	.13−	.33+
Length 5								
(26)	+ + +	+	+	.67	.−	.−	.57+	.49+
(27)	+ v P	P	+	.50	.63	.−	.72+	.47
(28)	P + v	P	+	.53	.33	.54+	.57+	.47+
(29)	P + v	P	P	.18	.22	.−	.31	.16
(30)	+ P +	v	P	.58	.33	.−	.61+	.68+
(31)	− − +	v	−	.93	.78+	.68+	.68+	.−
(32)	+ v −	v	+	.52	.71+	.61+	.46	.49+
(33)	− − −	−	−	.60+	.63+	.54+	.62+	.49+
(34)	+ v −	−	−	.46	.50	.43	.−	.23
(35)	P + v	−	−	.42	.29	.30	.18	.17
(36)	− + v	−	−	.49	.41	.54+	.42+	.44
(37)	P + v	P	−	.29	.39	.−	.−	.36+
(38)	− v +	v	−	.58	.70	.59+	.59+	.49+
(39)	+ v −	v	P	.38	.29	.39+	.53+	.50+

Note. Numbers are conditional probabilities of the last response, given the foregoing sequence of length $n-1$. A sign after an entry indicates that conditional probability is significantly (5%) smaller or larger than the unconditioned probability of the particular response.

trol takes over, a recovery does not take place immediately. Another pattern is the "Yes, but" (Code 3: $+v-$). This is popular in distressed couples (.62–.71) and decreases after therapy (.44) to a level close to normal (.38). The constructive problem description $+vP$ (Code 5), which indicates that the spouse precedes a problem description by a positive statement and is not interrupted by the partner, ranges from .29 to .37 in the distressed samples; it increased to .56 by the end of therapy, close to the normal sample (.61). The negative escalation pattern (Code 9: $---$) is slightly reduced by therapy. Another obviously disruptive pattern of problem escalation is $P--$ (Code 13), which is also slightly reduced by therapy.

Among the quadruples, the patterns $P+v-$ (Code 18), $-+v-$ (Code 20), and $+v--$ (Code 23) decrease in frequency as a result of therapy. A comparison of distressed and nondistressed samples indicates that these patterns are normally of low likelihood, probably because of their disruptive character. On the other hand, sequences like $P-v+$ (Code 24) and $P+vP$ (Code 19) are rare in distressed couples and frequent in the normal sample. (To be precise, the likelihood of the last event in the sequence is high, given the foregoing three responses.) These patterns obviously characterize non-escalating problem discussion, where the problem description is followed by a positive statement of the spouse, who then follows through with his/her own problem description (Code 19); or a problem description is followed by a negative remark, but this critique is followed by a positive statement from that same spouse (Code 24).

To illustrate the course of the problem discussion, the response chains following a problem description (P) are drawn in Figure 10.2 as a probability tree before (PRE) and after (POST) therapy. The heavy lines indicate the more frequent sequences of interaction. As can be seen, the immediate positive response to a P is almost the same before and after therapy, but the immediate negative response has been weakened considerably. Also, the pause to let the other continue (v) is more likely after therapy. Generally, the branch beginning with a positive response is not much changed by therapy, but the branch beginning with the negative response and changing to a problem description does change after therapy. After therapy, branches do not end as often with a negative response. The remaining two branches are similar and not much changed after therapy (starting with a pause and with a problem description after the initial statement). Therefore, some of the changes effected by therapy in the interaction sequence can be seen in Figure 10.2.

Lag Sequential Analysis

To overcome the problem of fewer data points with increasing length of sequences, Bakeman proposed a lagged sequential analysis of interaction patterns (Gottman & Bakeman, 1979). Here the response distributions are con-

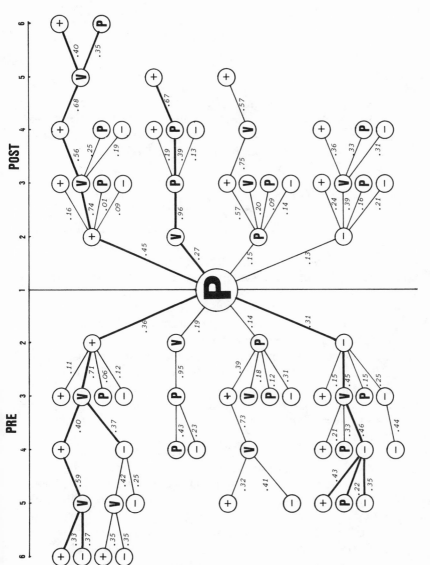

FIGURE 10.2. Probability trees of interaction sequences following a problem description (P): left, before treatment (PRE); right, after treatment (POST). The numbers indicate the conditional probability of the consecutive response after the foregoing sequence. Heavy lines indicate the main routes of the problem discussion. (Sample slightly different from Tables 10.4 and 10.5.)

173

sidered with increasing lag times from a selected antecedent ($+$, $-$, P). For instance, for Lag 7 the response probabilities are conditional responses, given that a particular antecedent has taken place. Therefore we are not considering chains of behavior, but events that are simply more and more distant from the initial antecedent. The data base remains the full sample throughout.

Other authors (Gottman & Bakeman, 1979; Patterson & Moore, 1979) infer characteristics of behavior sequences from these lagged probabilities. The present authors hesitate to do so, since it is unclear from these data what is happening in the time between the antecedent and the lagged response. The consecutive conditional distributions do not constitute a chain of behavior; instead, in each case they refer back to the antecedent rather than to the preceding lagged distribution. To tackle the problem of fading data when considering longer sequences, the present authors retreated to defining generalized interaction patterns. This is dealt with in the next section.

Generalized Interaction Patterns (Escalation and Deescalation)

We have considered baserates and contingencies of coded behavior in problem discussions of distressed and nondistressed couples before and after therapy. There are differences among the groups in conditional probabilities as well as baserates. Longer sequences, however, provide more adequate pictures of the couples' interaction. To consider those, we have to face the problem of fewer data points. Many of the sequences in Table 10.5 have a similar meaning; therefore lumping them together results in generalized interaction patterns that at the same time have a more solid data base.

We sorted out four patterns of interest, comprising superclasses of interaction: *Distancing,* which is basically an alternation of negative responses; *Problem Escalation,* basically an alternation of problem description and negative responses to it; *Acceptance,* basically problem descriptions and positive responses in alternation; and patterns of alternating positive responses, called *Attraction.*

In these generalized patterns, filler codes (v) have been ignored. Neutral responses and problem solutions have been treated as identical to positive responses. The Problem Escalation pattern contains sequences of Ps alternating with negative responses as well as consecutive Ps. Figures 10.3–10.6 give these generalized interaction patterns in terms of conditional probabilities of the last response for three groups: distressed couples before therapy (PRE), distressed couples after therapy (POST), and nondistressed couples (NORM).

The pattern of Problem Escalation (Figure 10.3) shows that in distressed couples before treatment (PRE), a negative response following a problem description is likely (.53), as is a restatement of the problem by the first spouse (.55). Thereafter, the likelihood of further negative responses and problem

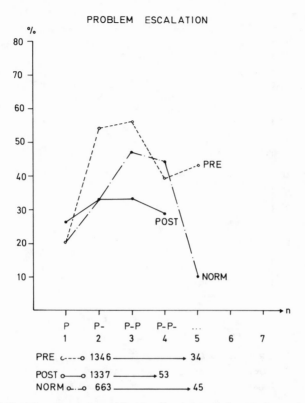

FIGURE 10.3. The interaction pattern of Problem Escalation. Ordinate indicates the conditional probability of the responses after the foregoing sequence ($n - 1$). Decreases in the number of observations are given below the graph.

descriptions goes down to .40. That is, there is a high likelihood of escalating the problem by one partner stating it, the other responding negatively, having it restated again, and so forth. Nondistressed (NORM) people, too, show a tendency to escalate, but to a lesser extent, and they are more likely to de-escalate. After therapy (POST) this pattern is completely changed. Treated couples now respond with even less escalation than nondistressed couples. This change is not surprising, because the handling of problem solving is one of the main topics of therapy.

Figure 10.4 shows the sequence of a "well-behaved" problem discussion. Acceptance of a problem statement by a positive response reinforces the problem statement, and the likelihood of a continuation decreases. This positive interaction pattern breaks down earlier with untreated distressed couples and moves to a certain extent in the direction of nondistressed couples after treatment. Comparing Figures 10.3 and 10.4, one can see that the treatment is

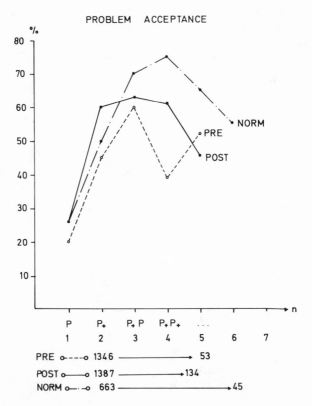

FIGURE 10.4. The interaction pattern of Problem Acceptance. Decreases in the number of observations are given below the graph.

more effective in reducing Problem Escalation than in establishing well-behaved problem discussions, but that some change is visible in both patterns.

Another form of Problem Escalation is the continuing Fight Back, as reflected in alternating negative statements (Distancing). In Figure 10.5 it can be seen that there is an increasing tendency to fight back even in nondistressed couples. The well-known phenomenon of revenge, or the "coercion process," is depicted by these data. The distressed couples before treatment show this tendency to a greater degree than do nondistressed couples, but they also show a lesser slope. In addition, the negative exchange continues much longer. The treatment effect here is that in the first few steps of the argument, the treated couples respond like nondistressed couples. However, after a certain development in the argument, they continue almost as long as they did before treatment, and they produce an even larger slope. If these patterns could be analyzed statistically, it would mean that couples learn to behave well in arguments for a while but then are even more likely to fight than before treatment.

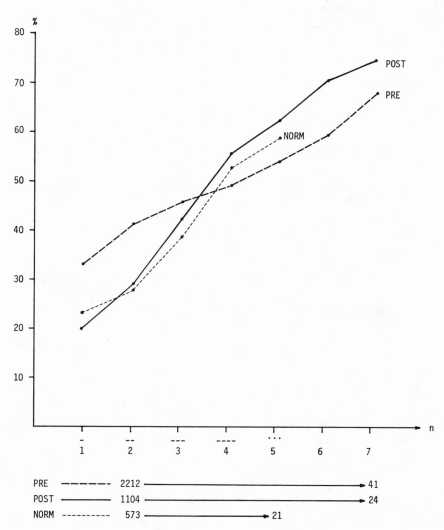

FIGURE 10.5. The interaction pattern of Distancing. Decreases in the number of observations are given below the graph.

Figure 10.6 shows the opposite interaction sequence: Whereas untreated distressed couples tend to replicate their positive regard (Attraction) for a while, nondistressed couples continue it much longer. The treatment effect here transgresses the norm: After treatment the mutual attraction starts at a higher level, lasts even longer, and reaches a higher maximum than is the case for nondistressed couples.

Discussion

In summary, distressed and nondistressed couples may be distinguished by their interaction patterns in arguments. Four such patterns have been defined here: Attraction, Problem Acceptance, Distancing, and Problem Escalation. Marital counseling as described by Hahlweg *et al.* (Chapter 1, this volume) changes each of these patterns considerably in the direction of the behavior of nondistressed couples. In two of the patterns (Attraction and the avoidance of Problem Escalation), treated couples even excel relative to nondistressed couples. In Distancing and Problem Acceptance, the treatment works in the direction of normal behavior. We have seen that groups may be discriminated by the patterns shown in this analysis. Moreover, therapy changes these patterns of interaction toward normal behavior. Since in these samples of observations, several couples are lumped together, statistical evaluations of these differences must be treated with caution. We prefer to consider these data as exploratory (in the sense of Tukey, 1979).

These interaction patterns may be used as diagnostic instruments. Diagnostic instruments serve several purposes: Mate selection is certainly not the goal, since no one can decide for a couple that they are right for each other. Neither is classification appropriate, since no one can decide for a couple whether they should continue their marriage, consider divorce, or see a marriage counselor. Evaluation of therapy studies is the appropriate place to use this kind of data analysis. Individual behavior analysis could also profit from such observations; however, it would be prohibitive in cost to evaluate the development of therapy for a specific couple by these means. Eventually, more economical ways to produce these kinds of observations may be developed. For now, the interaction patterns show some basic features of a good diagnostic instrument. The reliability, here in terms of objectivity, seems to be established. Norms are easily assessed (see Figures 10.3–10.6). And validity seems to be obtained to some extent by the comparison of extreme groups (distressed and nondistressed couples) as well as the comparison of couples before and after treatment.

The method described here, and used for the evaluation of a therapy study, is not particularly economical at the present time, but it is nonetheless promising from the standpoint of validity. It seems to be a first approach to the analysis of couples' interactions in terms of the marital system. There

ATTRACTION

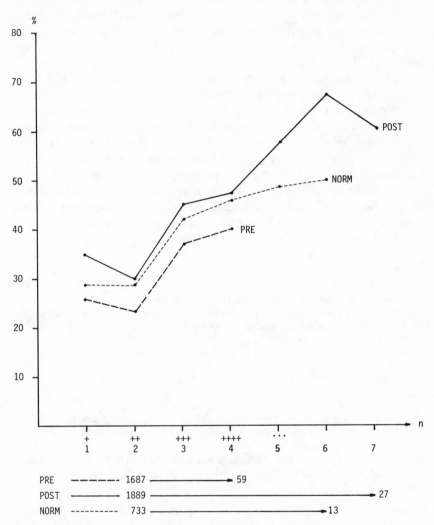

FIGURE 10.6. The interaction pattern of mutual Attraction. Decreases in the number of observations are given below the graph.

are many more ways to look at these data. One is to use the paradigm of bi-directional communication theory (Marko, 1966). Here the mutual influence of two parts of a system is considered in terms of transinformation (discussed in a preceding section). This depicts mutual interdependence and control on a nonparametric level. Also based on the information measure is multivariate analysis of the influence of antecedents (positive and negative responses of the spouse), groups (nondistressed, distressed), and so forth, as done by Raush, Barry, Hertel, and Swain (1974).

It may also be possible to consider the response probabilities observed here as a measure of response strength. Then Bertalanffy's (1968) proposals for analyzing a system's properties by using differential equations may be considered. Here the change in quality of one part of a system is considered a function of the status of two (or more) parts of the system.

In general, we think, the analysis of interactions as a system's properties has just begun, although it has been postulated by many authors before in a less tangible way (Bateson, Jackson, Laing, & Lidz, 1978; Watzlawick, Beavin, & Jackson, 1967).

REFERENCES

Anderson, T. W., & Goodman, L. A. Statistical inference about Markoff chains. *American Journal of Mathematical Statistics*, 1957, *28*, 89–110.
Atneave, F. *Informationstheorie in der Psychologie*. Bern/Stuttgart/Vienna: Huber, 1959.
Bales, R. F. *Interaction process analysis: A method for the study of small groups*. Reading, MA: Addison-Wesley, 1950.
Bateson, G., Jackson, D. D., Laing, R. D., Lidz, T., & Wynne, L. C. *Schizophrenie und Familie*. Frankfurt: Suhrkamp, 1978.
Bertalanffy, L. von. *General system theory*. New York: Braziller, 1968.
Ellis, A., & Harper, R. A. *A new guide to rational living*. Los Angeles: Wilshire, 1975.
Gottman, J. M. *Marital interaction*. New York: Academic Press, 1979.
Gottman, J. M., & Bakeman, R. The sequential analysis of observational data. In M. E. Lamb, S. J. Suomi, & G. R. Stephenson (Eds.), *Social interaction analysis*. Madison: University of Wisconsin Press, 1979.
Hahlweg, K., Helmes, B., Steffen, G., Schindler, L., Revenstorf, D., & Kunert, H. Beobachtungssystem für partnerschaftliche Interaktion. *Diagnostica*, 1979, *25*, 191–207.
Hops, H., Wills, T., Patterson, G. R., & Weiss, R. *Marital Interaction Coding System (MICS)*. Unpublished manuscript, University of Oregon, 1972.
Margolin, G., & Wampold, B. E. Sequential analysis of conflict and accord in distressed and nondistressed marital partners. *Journal of Consulting and Clinical Psychology*, 1981, *49*, 554–567.
Marko, H. Die Theorie der bidirektionalen Kommunikation und ihre Anwendung auf die Nachrichtenübermittlung zwischen Menschen. *Kybernetik*, 1966, *3*, 128–136.
McNemar, Q. *Psychological statistics*. New York: McGraw-Hill, 1949.
Merkens, H., & Seiler, H. *Interaktionsanalyse*. Stuttgart: Kohlhammer, 1978.
Olson, D. H., & Ryder, R. G. Inventory of Marital Conflict (IMC): An experimental procedure. *Journal of Marriage and the Family*, 1970, *32*, 443–448.
Patterson, G. R. A performance theory for coercive family interaction. In R. Cairns (Ed.), *Social interaction: Method, analysis and illustration*. Society for Research in Child Development Monograph, 1977.

Patterson, G. R., & Moore, D. Interactive patterns as units of behavior. In M. E. Lamb (Ed.), *Social interaction analysis.* Madison: University of Wisconsin Press, 1979.

Raush, H. L., Barry, W. A., Hertel, R. K., & Swain, M. A. *Communication, conflict and marriage.* San Francisco: Jossey-Bass, 1974.

Revenstorf, D., Hahlweg, K., & Schindler, L. Interaktionsanalyse von Partnerkonflikten. *Zeitschrift für Sozialpsychologie,* 1979, *10,* 183-196.

Revenstorf, D., Vogel, B., Wegener, C., Hahlweg, K., & Schindler, L. Escalation phenomena in interaction sequences: An empirical comparison of distressed and non-distressed couples. *Behavior Analysis and Modification,* 1980, *4,* 97-115.

Steffen, G. *Beobachtungssystem für partnerschaftliche Interaktion.* Unpublished master's thesis, University of Munich, 1977.

Tukey, J. *Exploratory data analysis.* New York: Academic Press, 1979.

Watzlawick, P., Beavin, J. H., & Jackson, D. *Pragmatics of human communication.* New York: Norton, 1967.

11

Development and Validity of a New System to Analyze Interpersonal Communication: Kategoriensystem für partnerschaftliche Interaktion

KURT HAHLWEG, LILLITH REISNER, GULJIT KOHLI, MARGRIT VOLLMER, LUDWIG SCHINDLER, AND DIRK REVENSTORF

In this chapter a new system for coding marital or dyadic interaction is presented, despite the fact that at least five behavioral observation systems for coding marital interaction have been reported in the literature:

    1. Coding System for Interpersonal Conflict (CSIC) (Raush, Barry, Hertel, & Swain, 1974)

    2. Marital and Family Interaction Coding System (MFICS) (Olson & Ryder, 1975)

    3. Marital Interaction Coding System (MICS) (Hops, Wills, Patterson, & Weiss, 1972)

    4. Couples Interaction Scoring System (CISS) (Gottman, 1979)

    5. Kategoriensystem für interpersonelle Kommunikation (KIK) (Schindler, 1981; Wegener, Revenstorf, Hahlweg, & Schindler, 1979)

As these coding systems have been extensively reviewed and critiqued either by Jacobson, Elwood, and Dallas (1981), Markman, Notarius, Stephen, and Smith (1981), or Schaap (see Chapter 9, this volume), here we add only a few additional comments on the conceptual or psychometric problems associated with the use of some of these systems, in order to justify the development of a new one.

Kurt Hahlweg, Lillith Reisner, Guljit Kohli, and Ludwig Schindler. Max-Planck-Institute for Psychiatry, Munich, Federal Republic of Germany.

Margrit Vollmer. Psychosomatic Clinic, Windach, Federal Republic of Germany.

Dirk Revenstorf. Psychological Institute, University of Tübingen, Tübingen, Federal Republic of Germany.

Conceptual and Psychometric Problems

Coding Unit

One of the major decisions in devising a system is the definition of the coding unit. Both the CSIC and the MFICS employ the "floorswitch" as a coding act, which is defined as "the statement or action of one person bounded by the statement or action of another" (Raush *et al.*, 1974, p. 214). This is a very behavioral definition of a coding unit, but unfortunately it leads to difficult problems with regard to double coding, which in turn may lower the reliability and validity of the system. Therefore the coding unit should be defined as a "thought unit" or "utterance," as used by the CISS, the MICS, and the KIK.

Criterion or Differential Validity

A coding system should discriminate between distressed and nondistressed couples. In a pilot study by Steffen (1977) using the MFICS to analyze problem discussions, only one significant difference between the groups was found: Distressed couples showed more "relevancy information" than nondistressed ones. Therefore the criterion validity of the MFICS is highly questionable, a finding corresponding to that of Weiss and Margolin (1977). The CISS content (verbal) codes *alone* did not discriminate between distressed and nondistressed couples, despite the fact that extreme groups from the distressed and nondistressed couples were used (Gottman, 1979).

Independent Nonverbal Coding

Nonverbal behavior in general has been shown to be a very powerful discriminator between distressed and nondistressed couples (Gottman, 1979), but only the CISS assesses this dimension independently. While the CSIC, the MFICS, and the KIK focus more or less exclusively on verbal behavior, the MICS is tapping nonverbal aspects. These codes can be clustered *a priori* into negative or positive behavior (e.g., Birchler, Weiss, & Vincent, 1975; Hahlweg, Helmes, Steffen, Schindler, Revenstorf, & Kunert, 1979; Jacobson, 1977). Unfortunately, the definition of some codes does not exclude double meanings: While, for example, TO (Turn Off) is clearly a "negative" code, LA (Laugh) or AT (Attend) is certainly not a clearly "positive" one. LA is defined as "occurrence of laughter or smile" with no further qualification; therefore an ironic laugh (which should be regarded as negative) is coded explicitly as positive. AT (maintaining eye contact longer than 3 seconds) is also counted as positive — What do we do with glaring at the other person? NT (looking away for more than 3 seconds) may or may not qualify as negative, depending very much on the other nonverbal cues of the listener. For these reasons, independent coding of nonverbal behavior as positive, negative, or neutral should be employed (see Gottman, 1979).

Content Validity

In order to establish content (or construct) validity for a system, it is necessary to describe the theoretical assumptions underlying the development of the various code definitions. With the exception of the KIK, unfortunately, none of the other systems gives a rationale for defining the codes. This perhaps reflects the "state of art" in that there is no empirically derived "communication" or "problem-solving" theory. To date the KIK has been the only system explicitly developed to examine the communication skills proposed by Guerney (1977) and Berlin (1975), thus giving a rationale for defining the codes.

Double Coding

When analyzing stimulus–response chains by interaction analysis, double coding should be avoided. It occurs when one person changes the content of his/her speech one or more times while the other partner is listening. For interaction analysis the responses of the two partners have to be coded in an alternating manner. As none of the systems explicitly avoids double coding, several ways of handling this problem have been proposed: (1) "Considering each code of a multiple code as a stimulus for immediate subsequent responses, yielding different frequencies of codes when compared to single counting of codes" (Wieder & Weiss, 1979); (2) insertion of a neutral "filler code" (Revenstorf, Vogel, Wegener, Hahlweg, & Schindler, 1980); or (3) defining *a priori* the most important code within a multiple code as the stimulus or response code to be used in the analysis (Schindler, 1981). None of these approaches seems to satisfactorily handle the problem of double coding appropriately.

Summary Codes

At least seven different schemes for summarizing the MICS categories have been published (Birchler *et al.*, 1975; Hahlweg, Schindler, & Revenstorf, 1982; Jacobson, 1977; Margolin, 1978; Margolin & Wampold, 1981; Margolin & Weiss, 1978; Vincent, Weiss, & Birchler, 1975). Some of the major differences are: (1) inclusion of Interrupt (IN) as a "negative" (e.g., Birchler *et al.*, 1975; Jacobson, 1977) or "neutral" summary code (Margolin & Wampold, 1981); (2) inclusion of Negative Solution (NS) as a "problem description" (Vincent *et al.*, 1975) or a "negative" (Hahlweg *et al.*, 1982) or a "neutral" summary code (Margolin & Wampold, 1981), or total exclusion of this category from statistical analysis (Birchler *et al.*, 1975; Margolin, 1978); (3) inclusion of

Attention (AT) as a "positive" summary code (Hahlweg *et al.*, 1982; Margolin & Weiss, 1978) or total exclusion of this category from statistical analysis (Birchler *et al.*, 1975; Margolin & Wampold, 1981); (4) inclusion of Problem Description (PD) as a "negative" (Jacobson, 1977) instead of as a "neutral" summary code as usual.

Because of the use of these heterogeneous summary codes, one should be extremely careful in interpreting results from different studies, especially when apparently identical summary names are used. As regards the problems mentioned above, some conclusions can be drawn with respect to the different coding systems:

1. CSIC: Definition of coding unit unsatisfactory, unknown differential validity, nonverbal behavior not assessed.
2. MFICS: Definition of coding unit unsatisfactory, does not seem valid for discriminating between distressed and nondistressed couples, nonverbal behavior not assessed.
3. MICS: Definition of some nonverbal codes questionable, no common definition for summary codes.
4. CISS: No differential validity for verbal codes.
5. KIK: Nonverbal behavior not assessed.

These conclusions have led to the development of a new coding system for marital or dyadic interaction: Kategoriensystem für partnerschaftliche Interaktion (KPI).

Development and Description of the KPI

Rationale

The aim of the KPI is to assess empirically the speaker and listener skills that are the basis of our communication and problem-solving treatment package (see Hahlweg, Schindler, Revenstorf, & Brengelmann, Chapter 1, this volume). These skills have been derived by combining different sources: communication skills training (Berlin, 1975; Guerney, 1977), systems theory (Watzlawick, Beavin, & Jackson, 1967), and behavioral marital therapy (BMT) (Liberman, Wheeler, & Sanders, 1976; Stuart, 1976; Weiss, Hops, & Patterson, 1973). (The KPI Manual can be obtained from the first author of this chapter.) It was hypothesized that the following skills facilitate general communication and problem solving within a couple (see Hahlweg *et al.*, Chapter 1, this volume, for a complete list and discussion).

1. Speaker skills.
   a. Use "I" messages
   b. Describe specific situations

    c. Describe specific behaviors
    d. Stick to the "here and now"
2. Listener skills
    a. Listen actively
    b. Paraphrase
    c. Ask open-ended questions
    d. Give positive feedback
    e. Disclose your own feelings

Partners who employ these skills in turn should avoid blaming, criticizing, and side tracking; increase their mutual understanding; and generate specific solutions to their problems. The core skills are reciprocal self-disclosure of feelings, attitudes, and thoughts, either about a specific problem in the relationship or about a general point of discussion; and accepting (not necessarily agreeing to) the speaker's utterances. The codes of the system were defined along these lines, using also codes and definitions from the MICS, CISS, and KIK.

Coding Unit

The basic unit is a verbal response that is homogeneous in content without regard to its duration or syntactical structure. For each content code, a nonverbal rating (negative, neutral, positive) is assigned (Gottman, 1979). In case of multiple coding of the speaker, a listening code (ZH) with the nonverbal rating is assigned to the listener, thus guaranteeing alternate coding.

Content Codes

The following 12 positive, neutral, and negative summary codes have been defined.

    1. Self-Disclosure (SO = *Selbstöffnung*): There are two types of SO: (*a*) direct expression of feelings (e.g., "I am too angry to listen to you at the moment" or "I was very happy reading your note"), and (*b*) direct expression of wishes and needs (e.g., "I would like to go fishing tomorrow" or "I prefer to decide this on my own").

    2. Positive Solution (PL = *Positive Lösung*): There are two types of PL: (*a*) specific, constructive proposals (e.g., "I'll do the dishes in the evening" or "Let's save money for the holiday from now on"), and (*b*) compromise (e.g., "I'll sweep the floor if you'll play with the kids").

    3. Acceptance of the Other (AK = *Akzeptanz*): There are three types of AK: (*a*) paraphrase (e.g., "You are thinking that the kids are too young"), (*b*) open question (e.g., "Are you still unhappy?"), and (*c*) positive feedback (e.g., "I liked the way you started the discussion").

4. Agreement (ZU = *Zuhören*): There are three types of ZU: (*a*) direct agreement (e.g., "Yes, that is right"), (*b*) acceptance of responsibility (e.g., "I was responsible for the quarrel"), and (*c*) assent ("yes" or "o.k.").

5. Problem Description (PB = *Problembeschreibung*): This code includes neutral descriptions of the problem (e.g., "I think we have got a problem with the kids" or "The car broke down yesterday").

6. Meta-Communication (MK = *Metakommunikation*): There are two types of MK: (*a*) clarification requests (e.g., "Would you say that again, please?"), and (*b*) meta-communication related to topic (e.g., "We are getting away from the issue").

7. Rest (RK = *Restkategorie*): RK is coded when a statement does not fit any of the other verbal codes; for example, comments irrelevant to the topic or statements that the coder cannot understand because of a poor tape recording.

8. Listening (ZH = *Zuhören*): ZH is coded for the listener when double coding of speaker occurs.

9. Criticize (KR = *Kritik*): There are two types of KR: (*a*) when the speaker's intention is to hurt, demean, or embarrass the listener in a global way (e.g., "You are lazy" or "You are foolish"), and (*b*) when the speaker expresses his/her dislike or disapproval of a specific behavior of the listener (e.g., "Yesterday you wasted money" or "The car broke down because you forgot to take it to the garage").

10. Negative Solution (NL = *Negative Lösung*): NL is coded when the speaker describes something he/she would like the other not to do in order to solve a problem (e.g., "You shouldn't sleep all day" or "Stop smoking, and we'll save money").

11. Justification (RF = *Rechtfertigung*): There are two types of RF: (*a*) excuses for one's own behavior (e.g., "I had a lot of things to do yesterday"), and (*b*) denying of responsibility (e.g., "That is not my job").

12. Disagreement (NU = *Nicht-Übereinstimmung*): There are three types of NU: (*a*) direct disagreement (e.g., "No I won't" or "No, that is not true"), (*b*) "Yes, but" (e.g., "Yes, you are right, but we don't have the money"), and (*c*) short disagreeing statements (e.g., "No" or "What?").

Nonverbal Codes

All of the foregoing content codes receive a nonverbal rating (see Gottman, 1979). In a hierarchical order, first, the facial cues are evaluated as positive, neutral, or negative using a list of descriptions (see Table 11.1). If the coder is unable to code the utterance as positive or negative, he/she scans the voice tone cues. If the coder is still unable to code the utterance as positive or negative, the body cues are scanned, and then the rating is applied.

TABLE 11.1. Cues Used to Code Nonverbal Behavior

Nonverbal channel	Cue	
	Positive	Negative
Face	Smile, empathetic expression, head nod	Frown, sneer, fearful, glare, angry expression
Voice	Caring, satisfied, warm, soft, happy	Cold, blaming, sarcastic, tense, accusing, depressed
Body	Touching, attention, forward lean	Rude gestures, pointing, inattention, arms akimbo

Note. Adapted from J. M. Gottman, *Marital interaction: Experimental investigations.* New York: Academic Press, 1979.

Coding Procedure

The following example illustrates the coding procedure (1 = husband; 2 = wife).

(2) "I was very angry last night with the kids." (SO^0, neutral nonverbal behavior)

(1) "I said to them that they should go to bed." (PB^0, neutral nonverbal behavior)

(2) "That is right, they told me that." (ZU^+, smiling)

(1) "Are you still angry?" (AK^+, warm and soft voice)

(2) "Yes, a little bit." (ZU^0, neutral)

(1) "But you came home too late again." (KR^-, accusing voice)

(2) ZH^0 (neutral)

(1) "So I believe we should change our time schedule. You start off at 5 o'clock, I'll go at 7." (PL^0, neutral)

This interaction would be recorded along a time dimension in the following way:

(1)		PB^0		AK^+		KR^-		PL^0
(2)	SO^0		ZU^+		ZU^0		ZH^0	

Method

In the studies described here, we were investigating the reliability and validity of the KPI, in particular the criterion or differential validity aspects. In Study 1 we used distressed/nondistressed groups of couples to establish the discriminating power of the KPI. In Study 2 we compared treated and untreated couples in order to investigate the sensitivity of the KPI as a measure of change.

Study 1

SUBJECTS

Two criterion groups were assessed: distressed couples who asked for marital therapy ($n = 29$) and nondistressed couples ($n = 12$) who rated their relationship as happy. Couples were volunteers and were solicited either by an advertisement in a local health center or by personal contact via friends and colleagues. However, none of these subjects was connected with a university. The demographic characteristics of the samples are shown in Table 11.2.

Statistical analysis revealed no significant difference between the two samples on age, duration of marriage, number of children, income, or level of education. All couples were middle-class.

Several questionnaire measures were used as criteria for marital satisfaction:

1. Partnership Questionnaire (PFB) (Hahlweg, 1979), consisting of three scales: Quarreling, Tenderness, and Togetherness/Communication
2. Conflict Score (on the Problem List — PL; see Hahlweg, Kraemer, Schindler, & Revenstorf, 1980)
3. Happiness Rating (see Hahlweg, 1979)

These variables are described elsewhere in this volume (see Hahlweg *et*

TABLE 11.2. Means and Standard Deviations for Demographic Characteristics of Distressed and Nondistressed Couples

Variables	TC	NC	Level of significance[a]
Age			
M	34.1	32.2	NS
SD	5.5	5.7	
Duration of marriage			
M	8.3	7.4	NS
SD	4.0	5.6	
Children			
M	1.5	1.4	NS
SD	1.1	0.9	
Income[b]			
M	1670	1920	NS
SD	1270	2190	

Note. TC = distressed; NC = nondistressed.

[a]Test of significance either by *t* test or χ^2.

[b]Housewives are excluded from analysis. Income is in Deutsche marks.

al., Chapter 1). The means and standard deviations as well as the level of significance are shown in Table 11.3.

Statistical analysis (*t* tests) revealed highly significant and predicted differences between the two groups on every variable.

PROCEDURE

Couples were seen conjointly by the investigators and completed the questionnaires. Following this, they were interviewed to explore possible problem areas of the relationship, and finally, two problem discussions were videotaped.

1. The couple had to solve 4 out of the 18 standardized conflict situations from the Inventory of Marital Conflict (IMC) (Hahlweg *et al.*, 1979; Olson & Ryder, 1970). This lasted about 10 minutes.

2. Following these vignettes, the couples discussed for another 10 minutes a problem of their own, selecting a moderate problem from the PL (Hahlweg *et al.*, 1980) or from the list that was compiled during the interview.

Only the free discussions were analyzed using the KPI. The ongoing interaction was coded in parallel 30-second intervals by two trained observers who were blind to the experimental conditions. In contrast to the coding procedure of the CISS (Gottman, 1979), no transcript of verbal exchanges was prepared. Instead, verbal and nonverbal interactions were coded from the videotape.

TABLE 11.3. Means and Standard Deviations for Distressed and Nondistressed Couples on Criterion Variables

Variables	TC	NC	Level of significance (*t* test)
PFB			
Quarreling			
M	11.6	4.6	*
SD	5.7	3.7	
Tenderness			
M	11.9	20.2	*
SD	6.5	5.4	
Communication			
M	14.1	20.8	*
SD	4.8	4.6	
PL Conflict Score			
M	6.9	0.7	*
SD	3.1	1.6	
Happiness Rating			
M	2.1	4.3	*
SD	0.9	0.6	

Note. TC = distressed; NC = nondistressed.
*$p = .001$.

TABLE 11.4. Reliability of the KPI: Agreement for Six Observers and Two Observers

	Six observers			
Code	Frequency[a]	%[b]	α	Two observers: κ
SO	138	93.0	.91	89.6
PL	62	79.1	.95	92.1
AK	217	91.0	.92	89.0
ZU	353	88.0	.89	89.0
KR	286	82.4	.97	87.4
NL	—	—	—	—
RF	138	94.0	.96	85.1
NU	349	82.2	.99	93.0
PB	329	78.8	.85	86.0
MK	237	91.4	.90	92.0
ZH	469	92.7	.99	96.0
RK	57	77.5	.85	—
NV+	1130	71.7	.82	86.0
NV−	528	68.6	.89	84.0
NV0	977	75.3	.52	70.0

[a]"Frequency" refers to how often this code was used by all observers.
[b]Point-to-point agreement.

RESULTS OF STUDY 1

Reliability of KPI. In order to investigate the interobserver agreement, four randomly selected tapes were coded by one reliability checker and five coders. As a first analysis, place-to-place agreement (Bijou, Peterson, & Ault, 1968) was computed, showing averages of 85.7% agreement for verbal and 76.3% for nonverbal codes. The average agreement for the verbal codes ranged from 77.5% (RK) to 94% (RF). NL was not coded. (See Table 11.4.)

In a second analysis, Cronbach's alpha (see Gottman, 1979, Chapter 5) was computed using the same four tapes and six coders. For the verbal codes α ranged from .85 (PB, RK) to .99 (NU, ZH), showing that all verbal codes have high generalizability coefficients (see Table 11.4). For the nonverbal codes the results are quite satisfying for positive (.82) and negative behavior (.89) but not for neutral behavior (.52). This may be due to the fact that the nonverbal codes are not independent of one another, thus enhancing residual (error) variance for the neutral code.

Because only two raters coded the tapes for both validity studies, a separate reliability analysis was performed, using these two coders and 125 randomly selected 30-second intervals from six couples. In Table 11.4 Cohen's kappa coefficients (Gottman, 1979) are presented; these range from .70

(neutral behavior) to .96 (ZH). In general, the studies show that the interobserver reliability of the KPI is satisfactory for frequency and sequential analysis.

Differences between Nondistressed and Distressed Couples. Table 11.5 shows the means (relative frequency) and standard deviations as well as the results of the significance tests (Mann–Whitney U tests). Nonparametric statistics were applied because of nonhomogeneity of variances and because the data were not representative of a normal distribution.

Out of the positive cluster, PL and MK showed no significant difference, whereas nondistressed couples showed significantly more SO, ZU, and AK than distressed couples. Within the negative cluster, distressed couples yielded significantly higher relative frequencies on every variable. Out of the neutral cluster, only PB revealed a significant difference, indicating that nondistressed couples are more neutral in their interactions than distressed couples.

Regarding the nonverbal behavior, statistical analysis revealed highly significant differences. Nondistressed couples are far more positive and neutral, and less negative than distressed couples.

There were three significant sex differences. Females showed more SO, t (40.3) = 4.1, p = .000, and KR, t (48) = 2.2, p = .03, and less RF, t (48) = 1.9, p = .05, when compared to men, irrespective of level of distress.

Study 2

The aim of Study 2 was to investigate the sensitivity of the KPI as a measure of change.

SUBJECTS

The couples used in this study were all distressed and required marital therapy. After an initial interview the couples were randomly assigned to the experimental group (BMT) or the waiting-list control group (WLCG). BMT couples were treated behaviorally, conjointly, or in a conjoint group for 15 sessions. WLCG couples waited for 3–4 months. The demographic characteristics, the treatment, and the results are described elsewhere in this volume (see Hahlweg *et al.*, Chapter 1). The mean age of clients was 33 years; the average duration of marriage, 7.7 years; and the mean number of children, 1.4. There was no significant difference between the groups regarding the demographic characteristics.

PROCEDURE

The procedure for the pretest was the same as described for Study 1. For the posttest a different set of standardized IMC scenes was used.

TABLE 11.5. Means and Standard Deviations of Codes for Nondistressed and Distressed Couples.

Codes	NC	TC	Significance test[a]	
			z	p
SO: Self-Disclosure				
M	10.6	5.6	2.9	.003
SD	7.3	4.3		
PL: Positive Solution				
M	1.7	2.2	0.01	.99
SD	2.1	3.7		
AK: Acceptance of Other				
M	5.1	2.7	2.7	.006
SD	4.7	4.0		
ZU: Agreement				
M	13.5	9.4	2.0	.05
SD	8.8	6.6		
KR: Criticize				
M	7.9	15.8	3.3	.001
SD	8.9	9.3		
NL: Negative Solution				
M	0.1	0.7	2.1	.03
SD	0.3	1.7		
RF: Justification				
M	2.3	4.9	2.6	.009
SD	3.8	5.0		
NU: Disagreement				
M	11.6	17.6	2.9	.004
SD	8.0	9.3		
PB: Problem Description				
M	27.1	18.4	3.0	.002
SD	13.0	8.6		
MK: Meta-Communication				
M	1.6	2.3	0.8	.42
SD	2.0	3.1		
ZH: Listening				
M	15.4	16.4	0.4	.66
SD	11.1	10.7		
RK: Rest				
M	3.3	4.1	1.3	.21
SD	4.1	4.2		
NV$^+$: Nonverbal, positive				
M	91.7	32.8	6.5	.000
SD	13.6	28.9		
NV$^-$: Nonverbal, negative				
M	0.9	31.0	6.3	.000
SD	2.8	28.7		
NV^0: Nonverbal, neutral				
M	7.4	36.2	5.6	.000
SD	12.2	21.6		

Note. NC = nondistressed; TC = distressed.

[a]Mann–Whitney U test: unit = couple; two-tailed.

The following outcome was predicted: After therapy, BMT couples will respond more positively and less negatively to each other when compared to controls. In particular, there will be increases in positive nonverbal behavior (NV⁺), SO, PL, AK, ZU, and MK.

On the negative side, there will be decreases in negative nonverbal behavior (NV⁻), KR, NL, RF, and NU. A slight increase of neutral PB was expected as well.

RESULTS OF STUDY 2

The pre and post group means and standard deviations for the verbal and nonverbal codes, as well as the results of the statistical analysis, are shown in Table 11.6. Mann–Whitney U tests were calculated using the average couple-difference score (pre–post).

Statistical analysis revealed the following significant changes: After therapy, BMT couples showed more NV⁺, SO, and AK, and less NV⁻, KR, NU, and NL. Statistical significance was approached (10%) regarding increases of MK and ZH, and decreases of RF and PB. Within-couple analysis for the WLCG couples showed no significant results (Wilcoxon test). Overall, results confirmed the hypothesis that the treated couples would use the newly learned skills after therapy.

Discussion

When comparing these results with other results that have been published, the following conclusions can be drawn.

Distressed–Nondistressed Comparisons

When distressed and nondistressed couples were compared using single (not summary!) codes, nondistressed couples showed significantly more (1) positive nonverbal behavior – CISS (Gottman, 1979); MICS: Assent, Laugh, Attention (Hahlweg *et al.*, 1979), and Assent, Positive Physical, Laugh (Margolin & Wampold, 1981); (2) positive verbal behavior – MICS: Agree, Humor (Hahlweg *et al.*, 1979), and Problem Solution, Agree (Margolin & Wampold, 1981); KIK: Expressing Positive Feelings, Approve, Acceptance of Other (paraphrase), Showing Interest toward Other (Schindler, 1981); and (3) neutral behavior – MICS: Problem Description (Hahlweg *et al.*, 1979; Margolin & Wampold, 1981).

Distressed couples showed significantly more (1) negative nonverbal behavior – CISS (Gottman, 1979); MICS: No Response, Not Tracking (Hahlweg *et al.*, 1979), and Not Tracking (Margolin & Wampold, 1981); and (2) negative verbal behavior – MICS: Criticize, Put Down, Deny Responsibility, Complain

TABLE 11.6. Pre and Post Comparisons for BMT and WLCG Couples on Criterion Variables

	BMT		WLCG		Significance test[a]	
Codes	Pre	Post	Pre	Post	z	p
SO						
M	5.4	10.1	6.4	5.7	3.2	.001
SD	3.0	5.2	2.9	3.2		
PL						
M	2.1	3.3	2.6	1.9	1.1	.15
SD	2.6	4.1	3.0	2.2		
AK						
M	2.8	9.7	2.1	2.1	3.4	.0003
SD	3.0	6.6	1.8	1.9		
ZU						
M	9.4	11.6	9.3	8.7	0.9	.19
SD	4.4	4.8	5.6	2.9		
KR						
M	15.1	9.0	15.6	15.5	2.1	.02
SD	6.2	7.5	7.5	4.4		
NL						
M	0.8	0.4	0.5	1.2	2.5	.007
SD	1.3	0.9	0.8	1.6		
RF						
M	4.8	2.7	5.5	5.4	1.5	.07
SD	3.2	3.1	3.1	2.9		
NU						
M	17.4	9.2	15.5	18.6	3.1	.001
SD	8.7	7.6	5.6	6.5		
PB						
M	18.6	16.7	16.7	18.2	1.6	.06
SD	7.0	7.9	6.0	8.1		
MK						
M	2.3	3.6	3.1	2.4	1.5	.07
SD	2.6	3.3	2.8	1.9		
ZH						
M	16.4	19.4	14.1	13.6	1.5	.07
SD	7.9	7.8	4.9	6.4		
RK						
M	4.1	3.8	7.1	6.1	0.03	.50
SD	3.8	2.9	4.5	4.8		
NV+						
M	33.6	60.5	41.6	34.7	2.5	.006
SD	23.3	21.9	40.3	32.1		
NV-						
M	30.8	14.1	32.5	37.0	2.5	.006
SD	26.6	32.0	34.9	25.7		
NV0						
M	35.6	25.4	25.9	28.3	1.5	.08
SD	18.2	20.6	20.5	19.2		

[a]Mann–Whitney U test on the average couple = difference score; one-tailed.

(Hahlweg *et al.*, 1979), and Command (Margolin & Wampold, 1981); KIK: Criticize and Justification (Schindler, 1981).

In general, these findings were replicated in our study. Again, nonverbal behavior was the most powerful discriminator between the criterion groups. Considering the verbal content, nondistressed couples were more self-disclosing, accepting, agreeing, and neutral in problem description than distressed couples, thus empirically supporting the basic assumption that these behaviors facilitate communication and problem solving. Distressed couples, on the contrary, were more critical, disagreeing, and self-justifying, and offered more negative solutions. The negative verbal behaviors were more powerful in discriminating between the two groups than the positive content codes. These results provide strong evidence for the criterion or differential validity of the KPI system.

However, one finding regarding the nonverbal behavior is difficult to explain: Our relative frequencies are very different from those of Gottman (1979) (see Table 11.7). Our couples, irrespective of level of distress, were far more positive and far less neutral than the couples in Gottman's study. With regard to negative behavior, however, the samples seem to be quite comparable. These findings may indicate that there are major differences between the subjects in the two studies. Another explanation could be that there are important cross-cultural differences in rating nonverbal behavior. German observers perhaps rate the defined facial, voice, or body cues as positive, while American observers rate the same cues as neutral. According to this assumption, the definitions should be revised to yield better comparability. These results need further investigation and emphasize the necessity to publish means and standard deviations as well as significance levels.

Treatment Evaluation

The results of Study 2 provide strong evidence that the KPI is a sensitive assessment tool for monitoring change. Couples treated by BMT (Hahlweg, Schindler, & Revenstorf, 1982) significantly reduced the amount of negative nonverbal behavior, Disagreement, Negative Solutions, and Criticism when compared to untreated controls. More important are the findings that the BMT couples showed significantly more Self-Disclosure, Acceptance, and positive nonverbal behavior, indicating that the treatment was successful in teaching these basic communication skills.

The reported results of both studies obviously need confirmation by cross-validation studies. Furthermore, the construct and predictive validity of the system need to be investigated. In summarizing the results, one can conclude that the KPI seems to be a reliable and valid system to assess marital interaction.

TABLE 11.7. Percentages of Neutral, Positive, and
Negative Nonverbal Behavior of Distressed and
Nondistressed Couples in Two Studies

	Distressed		Nondistressed	
	A	B	A	B
Neutral	65	36	85	7.5
Positive	10	33	12	91.5
Negative	25	31	03	01

Note. Data in A columns from Gottman (1979); data in
B columns from the present study.

ACKNOWLEDGMENTS

This research was supported by the Deutsche Forschungsgemeinschaft (DFG), Grant No.
402/6. The authors extend their thanks to Ian Bennun and Tom Stachnik for helping with the
translation.

REFERENCES

Berlin, J. *Das offene Gespräch: Paare lernen Kommunikation* (Ein programmierter Kurs).
Munich: Pfeiffer, 1975.

Bijou, S. W., Peterson, R. F., & Ault, H. M. A method to integrate descriptive experimental
field studies at a level of data and empirical concepts. *Journal of Applied Behavioral
Analysis,* 1968, *1,* 175-191.

Birchler, G. R., Weiss, R. L., & Vincent, J. P. A multimethod analysis of social reinforcement
exchange between maritally distressed and non-distressed spouse and stranger dyads.
Journal of Personality and Social Psychology, 1975, *31,* 349-360.

Gottman, J. M. *Marital interaction: Experimental investigations.* New York: Academic Press,
1979.

Guerney, B. G. (Ed.). *Relationship enhancement.* San Francisco: Jossey-Bass, 1977.

Hahlweg, K. Konstruktion und Validierung des Partnerschaftsfragebogens PFB. *Zeitschrift für
Klinische Psychologie,* 1979, *8,* 17-40.

Hahlweg, K., Helmes, B., Steffen, G., Schindler, L., Revenstorf, D., & Kunert, H. Beobachtungssystem für partnerschaftliche Interaktion. *Diagnostica,* 1979, *25,* 191-207.

Hahlweg, K., Kraemer, M., Schindler, L., & Revenstorf, D. Partnerschaftsprobleme: Eine
empirische Analyse. *Zeitschrift für Klinische Psychologie,* 1980, *9,* 159-169.

Hahlweg, K., Schindler, L., & Revenstorf, D. *Partnerschaftsprobleme: Diagnose und Therapie.
Reziprozitätstraining. Handbuch für Therapeuten.* Heidelberg: Springer Verlag, 1982.

Hops, H., Wills, T. A., Patterson, G. R., & Weiss, R. L. *Marital Interaction Coding System.*
Unpublished manuscript, Research Institute, University of Oregon, 1972. (Available from
ASIS/NAPS, c/o Microfiche Publications, 305 E. 46th Street, New York, NY 10017)

Jacobson, N. S. Problem solving and contingency contracting in the treatment of marital discord.
Journal of Consulting and Clinical Psychology, 1977, *45,* 92-100.

Jacobson, N. S., Elwood, R. W., & Dallas, M. Assessment of marital dysfunction. In D. H.
Barlow (Ed.), *Behavioral assessment of adult disorders.* New York: Guilford Press, 1981.

Liberman, R. P., Wheeler, E., & Sanders, N. Behavioral therapy for marital disharmony: An
educational approach. *Journal of Marriage and Family Counseling,* 1976, *2,* 383-385.

Margolin, G. A. A multilevel approach to the assessment of communication positiveness in distressed couples. *International Journal of Family Counseling,* 1978, *6,* 81–89.

Margolin, G. A. & Wampold, B. E. Sequential analysis of conflict and accord in distressed and non-distressed marital partners. *Journal of Consulting and Clinical Psychology,* 1981, *49,* 554–567.

Margolin, G. A., & Weiss, R. L. Communication training and assessment: A case of behavioral marital enrichment. *Behavior Therapy,* 1978, *9,* 508–520.

Markman, H. J., Notarius, C., Stephen, T., & Smith, R. Behavioral observation systems for couples: The current status. In E. Filsinger & R. Lewis (Eds.), *Observing marriage: New behavioral approaches.* Beverly Hills, CA: Sage, 1981.

Olson, D. H., & Ryder, R. G. Inventory of Marital Conflict (IMC): An experimental interaction procedure. *Journal of Marriage and the Family,* 1970, *32,* 443–448.

Olson, D. H., & Ryder, R. G. *Marital and Family Interaction Coding System (MFICS).* Unpublished manuscript, Unversity of Minnesota, 1975.

Raush, H. L., Barry, W. A., Hertel, R. K., & Swain, M. A. *Communication, conflict and marriage.* San Francisco: Jossey-Bass, 1974.

Revenstorf, D., Vogel, B., Wegener, C., Hahlweg, K., & Schindler, L. Escalation phenomena in interaction sequences: An empirical comparison of distressed and nondistressed couples. *Behavior Analysis and Modification,* 1980, *4,* 97–115.

Schindler, L. *Empirische Analyse partnerschaftlicher Kommunikation.* Unpublished doctoral dissertation, University of Tübingen, 1981.

Steffen, G. *Beobachtungssystem für partnerschaftliche Interaktion.* Unpublished master's thesis, University of Munich, 1977.

Stuart, R. B. An operant interpersonal program for couples. In D. H. L. Olson (Ed.), *Treating relationships.* Lake Mills, IA: Graphic Press, 1976.

Vincent, J. P., Weiss, R. L., & Birchler, G. R. A behavior analysis of problem solving in distressed and nondistressed married and stranger dyads. *Behavior Therapy,* 1975, *6,* 475–487.

Watzlawick, P., Beavin, J. H., & Jackson, D. D. *Pragmatics of human communication.* New York: Norton, 1967.

Wegener, C., Revenstorf, D., Hahlweg, K., & Schindler, L. Empirical analysis of communication in distressed and nondistressed couples. *Behavior Analysis and Modification,* 1979, *3,* 178–188.

Weiss, R. L., Hops, H., & Patterson, G. R. A framework for conceptualizing marital conflict, a technology for altering it, some data for evaluating it. In L. A. Hamerlynck, L. C. Handy, & E. J. Mash (Eds.), *Behavior change: Methodology, concepts, and practice.* Champaign, IL: Research Press, 1973.

Weiss, R. L., & Margolin, G. Assessment of marital conflict and accord. In A. R. Ciminero, K. S. Calhoun, & H. E. Adams (Eds.), *Handbook for behavioral assessment.* New York: Wiley, 1977.

Wieder, G. B., & Weiss, R. L. *Marital Interaction Coding System: II. User's guide.* Unpublished manuscript, University of Oregon, Marital Studies Program, 1979.

12

The Use of Time Series Analysis in Marriage Counseling

DIRK REVENSTORF, KURT HAHLWEG, LUDWIG SCHINDLER,
AND HANS KUNERT

Introduction

The focus of this chapter is on how to use a simple device, a diary, in counseling and evaluation of marital distress. The data presented are part of a larger research program on marital therapy (see Hahlweg, Schindler, Revenstorf, & Brengelmann, Chapter 1, this volume). Besides having pre–post measurements of questionnaires and behavioral observations, we were interested in continuous data surveying the process and development of the relationship of the couple under treatment. To this end, we asked each spouse to give daily ratings on six aspects of the relationship. The data were used in several ways. We asked the couples to bring their data sheets to the weekly sessions. These data sheets contained the ratings for the past week. By looking at the ups and downs of their estimated tenderness, for example, a résumé of the week was facilitated. Moreover, we asked the couples to note important events, such as arguments, pleasant events, separations, and dreams, on the back of the sheet. So the first purpose of the diary was to provide a standardized monitoring device for the events occurring between therapy sessions (see Figure 12.1).

The counseling approach we used in the study is comprised of communication skills training and the enhancement of mutual positive exchange, as well as skills of problem solving. As a result the spouses should talk in a more open and self-disclosing manner, and they should express feelings more directly, avoiding accusation and blame. They are also trained to listen more empathically and in a supportive way in order to facilitate self-disclosure. Besides talking, the couples are taught to bargain for concrete and fair solutions to their problems and are stimulated to share more positive activities. As a result, the couples should talk more and quarrel less, and should feel

Dirk Revenstorf. Psychological Institute, University of Tübingen, Tübingen, Federal Republic of Germany.

Kurt Hahlweg, Ludwig Schindler, and Hans Kunert. Max-Planck-Institute for Psychiatry, Munich, Federal Republic of Germany.

| | | Weekday | | | | | | |
		Mo	Tu	We	Th	Fr	Sa	Su
1. Time spent together	A great deal	6	6	6	6	6	6	6
		5	5	5	5	5	5	5
		4	4	4	4	4	4	4
		3	3	3	3	3	3	3
		2	2	2	2	2	2	2
	None	1	1	1	1	1	1	1
2. Feeling understood	A great deal	6	6	6	6	6	6	6
		5	5	5	5	5	5	5
		4	4	4	4	4	4	4
		3	3	3	3	3	3	3
		2	2	2	2	2	2	2
	None	1	1	1	1	1	1	1
3. Talked to each other	A great deal	6	6	6	6	6	6	6
		5	5	5	5	5	5	5
		4	4	4	4	4	4	4
		3	3	3	3	3	3	3
		2	2	2	2	2	2	2
	None	1	1	1	1	1	1	1
4. Tenderness	A great deal	6	6	6	6	6	6	6
		5	5	5	5	5	5	5
		4	4	4	4	4	4	4
		3	3	3	3	3	3	3
		2	2	2	2	2	2	2
	None	1	1	1	1	1	1	1
5. Attentiveness	A great deal	6	6	6	6	6	6	6
		5	5	5	5	5	5	5
		4	4	4	4	4	4	4
		3	3	3	3	3	3	3
		2	2	2	2	2	2	2
	None	1	1	1	1	1	1	1
6. Feeling accepted	A great deal	6	6	6	6	6	6	6
		5	5	5	5	5	5	5
		4	4	4	4	4	4	4
		3	3	3	3	3	3	3
		2	2	2	2	2	2	2
	None	1	1	1	1	1	1	1
7. Glad to attend therapy	A great deal	6	6	6	6	6	6	6
		5	5	5	5	5	5	5
		4	4	4	4	4	4	4
		3	3	3	3	3	3	3
		2	2	2	2	2	2	2
	None	1	1	1	1	1	1	1

FIGURE 12.1. Diary sheet for 1 week.

closer and increase their joint activities. With regard to these considerations, we chose a standardized diary with the following six categories: (1) time spent together, (2) feeling understood, (3) time talking to each other, (4) feeling tender, (5) attending to the spouse, (6) feeling accepted. (Therapy motivation was also assessed but is not considered here.) Each category is to be rated daily and independently by each spouse (ratings range from 1 to 6; see Figure 12.1).

The weekly data sheets are collected and combined in a summary evaluation at the end of the therapy. These diaries typically result in a time series of 90–150 data points on each of the six categories. At the end of the therapy we look at the plotted time series of wife and husband, and discuss with the couple the developments, breakdowns, rises, and falls in the several categories. For instance, the graphs might indicate that there was no change in the extent to which the husband felt accepted during the course of therapy, whereas his wife felt increasingly accepted over time. There might be a continuous increase in time spent talking for both spouses, easily detectable from their respective time series. In other words, the final plot provides a concrete summary of the changes in the relationship during therapy. The diary, therefore, is a convenient device to make the couples more conscious about changes and stagnations in their relationship. At the same time it helps us monitor the events of therapy in a systematic way. (Although it may appear burdensome to complete the diaries, most couples did not object; some of them even continued to send the diaries for 6 months after therapy terminated.)

Besides being a monitoring device, these standardized diaries provide a continuous data base for the evaluation of the therapy process. One way of evaluating a time series is by inspection. By mere "eyeballing," one can see whether there is a general positive or negative trend in the data. One can see whether there is a rise in the time series due to treatment after an initial baseline (in terms of a step function). One can see whether the daily fluctuations are so large that any detection of change seems questionable. One can also see whether the ups and downs in the several categories of the diary covary (i.e., whether the time series are correlated). All of these evaluations are done individually, as opposed to in groups. By counting positive and negative trends or shifts in level, the effects of therapy may be evaluated without the risk of falling victim to the fallacies of group statistics. It is well known that in group statistics, opposite trends in individual cases may cancel each other out, thus contributing to the variability but not to the average level, and thereby rendering the data analysis statistically inefficient. It is also well known that simple pre–post measurements may not be sensitive to the actual changes that took place. According to the hypothesis of an evolutionary operating characteristic of the therapy process (Gottman & Markman, 1978), there may be an initial deterioration effect (sensitization), followed by an over-optimistic view of the therapy success. It is only after a period of settling down that the net effect of the treatment becomes visible — see Figure 12.4 (e) in the section on statistical evaluation.

Since little is known about which phase couples are in when the pre and post measurements are typically taken, and since the time scale for such developments may differ from one couple to another, it is rather unlikely that a standardized pre–post measurement procedure will be sufficiently sensitive to change. In other words, a time series gives a more complete picture of the developments in therapy and avoids some of the shortcomings of group evaluation.

There are limitations to the inspection method of evaluating time series. First, variation in the time series may be considerable, and therefore trends and shifts may not be easily detected (signal-to-noise ratio is low). Further, as has been repeatedly shown (Glass, Wilson, & Gottman, 1975; Gottman & Glass, 1977) the sequential dependence of consecutive measurements from one data generator makes it difficult and misleading to judge changes in the time series. Due to the inertia of the system, consecutive data points are not independent of each other (the system — i.e., the spouse or the couple — has a "memory" that influences behavior ratings sequentially). This sequential dependence works against the random fluctuations of the residuals about their local mean. That is, not only inspection but also traditional statistical evaluation (of, say, a level difference in two phases of therapy) is misleading.

An elaborate statistical methodology has been developed to analyze time series with proper tools to take into account the sequential dependence (Box & Jenkins, 1970; Glass, Wilson, & Gottman, 1975; Keeser, 1980; Revenstorf, 1979). The statistical time series, besides being a technical tool to handle this kind of data, provides a number of interesting parameters on its own. Time series analysis results in estimates of, as well as shifts in, mean and trend. One can also estimate the variation of the time series, autocorrelation of the measurements, and indices of periodicity. There is another interesting feature of time series analysis: cross-correlation. By computing cross-correlations, the time series makes it possible to consider cross-lagged relations. That is, we may compute the correlation of "joint activity" today with the "feeling of being accepted" the next day. Temporal covariation between two events in a series allows for a tentative causal interpretation of correlational data. Finally, for research purposes, the validity of the various time series parameters may be tested by comparing them with parallel or follow-up data from other sources, such as questionnaires.

Inspection of Time Series

Diaries were collected during therapy for 100 days, on the average, from each couple. All 78 couples in the program completed the diaries. However, 14 couples used an earlier version of the diary and were excluded from most of the present analyses. Of the remaining 64 couples, 47 provided diaries that had no more than 10% of the data missing and were included in the present analyses. Since each spouse filled in six ratings every day, we are dealing here with roughly $50 \times 6 \times 2 = 600$ time series.

In our initial approach to evaluation, these time series were plotted and inspected visually. Features that are obvious from time series such as these are general level, slope, and variation. Figures 12.2 and 12.3 give two opposite examples of time series, each depicting the process of therapy: Figure 12.2 depicts a case with a generally positive outcome, while Figure 12.3 depicts one with a generally negative outcome.

In Table 12.1 the frequencies (in terms of proportion) of the main characteristics of these time series are compared for the four treatment groups: behavioral marital therapy (conjoint modality), behavioral marital therapy (group modality), communication skills training (conjoint modality), and communication skills training (group modality). As can be seen from Table 12.1, low (−), medium (0), and high (+) initial ratings on the various categories are almost evenly distributed. The four groups do not differ in their initial ratings, except for the group receiving communication skills training (conjoint modality). This group seems to contain fewer couples with a poor initial relationship. Concerning the slope, it can be seen that a positive slope predominates (46%). That is, in all four treatment conditions, the six relationship categories under consideration increased more often than they decreased. Ony 19% of the time series showed decreases such as those depicted in Figure 12.3. However, a great number of the time series stayed at the initial level. Summarizing this rough analysis, it can be said that the couples in treatment showed considerable variability in their pretreatment relationship quality, with about 74% showing either low or medium ratings at the beginning. Almost half of the clients increased their ratings during treatment. Only 19% deteriorated. It is interesting to note that the distribution of increases, decreases, and no changes in the series was the same for all three levels of initial ratings.

Table 12.2 gives the joint distribution of initial level and slope, and it can be seen that the only rare combination has an initially low level of relationship quality combined with a decrease in quality during the course of therapy.

Since a relationship can obviously be enhanced regardless of its initial quality (low, medium, or high), it might be interesting to look for differences between successes and failures in therapy. To this end, 13 couples were selected, each of whom showed an increase from the premeasurement to the 6-month follow-up on the General Happiness Rating Scale (Terman, 1938) for both spouses. (We did not consider here the increase from pre- to postmeasurement, since we wanted to avoid confounding therapy success and the "hello–good-bye" effect.) These 13 couples approximate the uppermost quartile; they were contrasted with 11 couples in which at least one spouse had

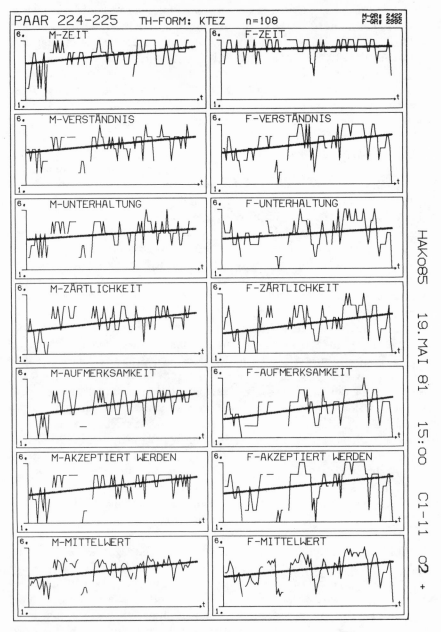

FIGURE 12.2. Sample time series for one couple from beginning to end of therapy: couple improving with respect to diary variables.

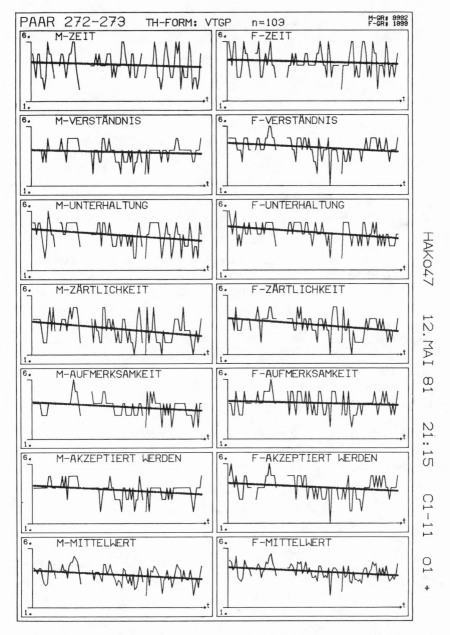

FIGURE 12.3. Sample time series for one couple from beginning to end of therapy: couple deteriorating with respect to diary variables.

TABLE 12.1. Percentages of Time Series with Low, Medium, and High Level; and Increasing, Zero, and Decreasing Slope in the Four Treatment Groups

		Level (%)			Slope (%)		
	n	Low (−)	Medium (0)	High (+)	Increasing	Zero	Decreasing
BMT-C	13	39	30	31	43	40	17
BMT-G	15	44	40	16	51	32	17
CT-C	9	19	50	31	52	28	20
CT-G	10	34	38	28	48	32	20
Totals							
n	47	201	213	150	261	198	105
%	—	36	38	26	46	35	19

Note. BMT-C = behavioral marital therapy (conjoint); BMT-G = behavioral marital therapy (conjoint group); CT-C = communication training (conjoint); CT-G = communication training (conjoint group).

a decrease on the General Happiness Rating Scale from premeasurement to the 6-month follow-up (roughly the lowest quartile).

Table 12.3 contains the distribution of the joint patterns of initial level and slope for these two extreme groups. As can be seen from Table 12.3, two patterns are particularly predictive of therapy success: improving from a medium pretreatment level (0/), and maintaining an initially high level of relationship quality (+ 0). Another two patterns are predictive of therapy failure: maintaining an initial medium level (00), and, interestingly, starting therapy with a low level of happiness but increasing the quality of the relationship (− /). Although an increase from a low level of quality might appear promising, the fact that it does not predict therapy success in the long run (6 months) shows that even significant change from an initially low level is not always sufficient. In other words, the initial ratings are more indicative of ultimate outcome than the amount of change during therapy, at least for

TABLE 12.2. Distribution of Level and Slope as Detected by Inspection of 564 Time Series (47 Couples: Two Spouses and Six Diary Variables Each)

	Level			
Slope	−	0	+	Total
Increasing (/)	95	96	70	261
Zero (0)	43	84	71	198
Decreasing (\ )	12	33	60	105
Total	150	213	201	564

TABLE 12.3. Percentage Distribution of Level and Slope in 13 Successful and 11 Nonsuccessful Couples

Slope	Level −	0	+	Q⁺	Q⁻	
Increasing (/)	7%	23%	12%	42%		Q⁺
	20%	10%.	14%		44%	Q⁻
Zero (0)	3%	7%	25%	35%		Q⁺
	9%	19%	16%		44%	Q⁻
Decreasing (\ )	3%	5%	15%	23%		Q⁺
	1%	2%	9%		12%	Q⁻
Q⁺	13%	35%	50%	100%		
Q⁻	30%	31%	39%		100%	

Note. Q⁺ = successful; Q⁻ = Nonsuccessful. Patterns predictive of success and failure are in boxes to distinguish them from nonpredictive patterns.

some couples. Comparing the marginal proportions from Table 12.3, positive versus zero slope does not discriminate between successes and failures. Negative slopes are slightly more frequent with successful patients—a somewhat puzzling result. More discriminating, as already mentioned, is a low or a high initial level: Unsuccessful patients are characterized by low initial ratings; successful patients, by high ratings on the diary categories investigated here. This simply means that initially difficult cases are more difficult to treat successfully.

Considering the data in Table 12.3, simple level and slope may be compared with configural scoring to predict therapy success. By configural scoring, the combination of level and slope is meant. Furthermore, the two patterns having the same meaning in Table 12.3 may be combined in a predictor.

- Pattern 1(failure): Low level/increase, or medium level/no change
- Pattern 2 (success): Medium level/increase, or high level/no change

As can be seen from Table 12.4, roughly 50% of successful clients show Pattern 2, whereas roughly 40% of therapy failures show Pattern 1. Pattern 1, moreover, discriminates slightly better than the simple low level (Pattern 3), with a failure–success ratio of 2.8, as compared to 2.3. There is also a slight advantage in the prediction of therapy success by Pattern 2 (ratio = 1.8), as compared with the simple high level (Pattern 4: ratio = 1.4). In other words, there is a slightly better prediction of success and failure by configural scoring, taking into account level and slope, than by simple initial level of the time series; but the most distinct feature is that the initial level alone is a better predictor than the slope.

TABLE 12.4. Comparison of Configural Patterns
(1, 2) and Simple Patterns (3, 4) in Time Series and
Their Prediction of Success and Failure

	Pattern (%)			
	1^a	2^b	3^c	4^d
Success	14	48	13	50
Failure	39	26	30	39
Ratio	2.8	1.8	2.3	1.4

[a]Pattern 1 = low level/positive slope, or
    medium level/no slope.
[b]Pattern 2 = medium level/positive slope, or
    high level/no slope.
[c]Pattern 3 = low level.
[d]Pattern 4 = high level.

Statistical Evaluation of Change

Besides using the time series of the diaries to monitor and evaluate therapy
process through visual inspection, sophisticated tools have been devised to
analyze time series statistically. The special feature of time series is that the
sequential dependence of the data must be taken into account before a statistical analysis of level, level shifts, trends, variations, and correlations can be
conducted. The sequential dependence may be due to several sources: A consistent upward or downward trend in the data alone disturbs the local independence of the time series data. Since they are bound to increase or decrease
steadily they may not vary freely, as would be the case if the data points were
drawn at random. Another source of sequential dependence is periodicity.
In the diary data considered here, weekly fluctuations are very likely — for
instance, "time spent together" is probably higher on weekends than on
workdays. A further reason for sequential dependence is a day-to-day relationship in the data. Consecutive data points may either be close together,
due to an inertia of the system (positive autocorrelation), or they may tend
toward alternating extremes (negative autocorrelation). Trends, periodicities,
and day-to-day dependence may take several forms, which are discussed com-
prehensively by Box and Jenkins (1970). Moreover, the time series may not
be stationary, showing gross fluctuations over large segments of time; these
fluctuations may not be predictable from trend, periodicity, or day-to-day
dependence. We do not detail the techniques for analyzing time series here
(see Anderson, 1975; Box & Jenkins, 1970; Glass et al., 1975; Keeser, 1980;
Revenstorf, 1979). The basic procedure is to build a mathematical model for
the sequential dependence in the data, eliminate the model from the empirical

data, check the sequential independence of the residuals, and then treat them as independent sample points by classical statistics — if independence is achieved.

A versatile model for time series is the so-called ARIMA (*A*uto*R*egressive-*I*ntegrated-*M*oving *A*verage) process (Box & Jenkins, 1970): It contains in its most general form nonstationarity, periodicity, and two kinds of sequential dependence. The behavior of the system today may be partly determined by its behavior yesterday, either by continuation (growth process, autoregressive model) or by compensating random fluctuations (homeostatic process, moving-average model). On top of it, a linear (polynomial) trend may be fitted.

For the purpose of analyzing time series in the present study, a grossly simplified procedure was used, in order to effectively handle the large number of time series considered here. For all time series, the following steps of a preliminary data analysis were performed:

1. Linear trend: Being most conspicuous from the therapy context, a linear trend was eliminated by a linear regression procedure (ignoring serial dependence at this stage). The resulting parameters were general level and slope.

2. Periodicity: Since most joint activities of marital interaction are ruled by a weekly schedule, our time series probably have a periodicity of 7. To eliminate this periodicity, an artificial cyclical time series was constructed of the season means (Monday through Sunday). This artificial model is the same for all weekly segments. This model was eliminated from the empirical time series by a linear regression procedure, analogous to eliminating the linear trend in point 1.

3. Autoregression: To take into account the sequential day-to-day dependence, which might still be in the residuals after the first two components (1 and 2) are eliminated, the first-order autoregressive process was estimated: It was assumed that the behavior of the individuals depends just on the day before. No longer was "latent memory" assumed. This is an obviously simple model for human behavior. However, in combination with the linear trend and the weekly periodicity, in practically all cases the simple autoregressive model

$$Z(t) = aZ(t-1) + e$$

absorbed the sequential dependence in the data *(Z)*, so that independent residuals resulted (*a* is the autoregressive coefficient and *e* is the random error).

The independence of the residuals may be checked by a simple chi-square test (Portemonteau test). It may also be indicated by vanishing autocorrelations in the residuals. Independence was achieved in all cases by the foregoing procedure. After the raw data were treated this way, such treatment effects as shifts in level or trend were preserved, as were substantial cross-correlations.

All three parameters of the initial analysis of the data (trend, periodicity, and autoregressive process) may be expressed in correlation coefficients, which tell us to what extent the trend, the periodicity, and the day-to-day dependence explain the variation in the data. Table 12.5 gives an overview of these parameters in the 51 couples for each of the six diary categories. A seventh time series was added, being the average of the other six $(\overline{X})$.

A weekly periodicity was present in practically all time series (100%). Linear trends were significant in about 30% of the time series (note the difference between the statistical evaluation and the number of trends detected by eyeballing in the preceding section). In another 30% of the time series

TABLE 12.5. Characteristics of the Distribution for Trend, Periodicity, and First-Order Autoregression Parameters in the Time Series of 51 Couples for Six Diary Catgegories and Their Average Time Series

Diary variables	Correlations				
	Range	Mean	SD	Skewness	Kurtosis
Trend					
Time together	− .34/ + .60	.07	.20	+ .62	+ .52
Understood	− .38/ + .57	.10	.21	+ .13	− .50
Joint talk	− .30/ + .51	.06	.20	+ .27	− .59
Tenderness	− .32/ + .67	.12	.21	+ .38	− .08
Attention	− .29/ + .64	.15	.21	+ .14	− .17
Feeling accepted	− .30/ + .55	.15	.22	− .28	− .25
$\overline{X}$	− .31/ + .66	.14	.22	+ .21	− .33
Periodicity					
Time together	+ .22/ + .76	.49	.13	+ .00	− .84
Understood	+ .12/ + .53	.28	.11	+ .43	− .66
Joint talk	+ .11/ + .57	.33	.12	− .06	− 1.08
Tenderness	.00/ + .57	.30	.13	+ .09	− .65
Attention	+ .10/ + .50	.37	.11	+ .19	− .82
Feeling accepted	+ .10/ + .57	.25	.10	+ 1.09	+ 1.30
$\overline{X}$	+ .08/ + .58	.36	.14	− .37	− 1.00
AR (1)					
Time together	− .12/ + .66	.32	.17	− .29	− .39
Understood	− .16/ + .85	.33	.24	− .12	− .43
Joint talk	− .14/ + .89	.32	.22	+ .10	− .54
Tenderness	− .16/ + .70	.25	.19	+ .19	− .43
Attention	− .20/ + .75	.30	.23	+ .05	− .46
Feeling accepted	− .20/ + .81	.32	.24	− .08	− .42
$\overline{X}$	− .13/ + .84	.37	.24	− .10	− .78

Note. AR(1) = first-order autoregression; $\overline{X}$ = average time series of the six diary variables. Average length of the time series is about 100 days.

a day-to-day dependence was present, after elimination of the first two components.

For our initial analysis, we wanted to see whether there was a change in the time series after active treatment began. During the first 3 weeks initial interviews were performed; these included explaining the program, talking to each spouse separately, and observing the clients. This period of time may be considered a baseline period. After this, a change may take place, which is most simply described by either a shift in level or a shift in slope (see Figure 12.4).

The shifts in level and in trend were evaluated by a t test. To give an example of this analysis, a subsample of only 10 couples was used. The results are presented elsewhere (Revenstorf, Kessler, Schindler, Hahlweg, & Bluemer, 1980) and are repeated here only briefly. The couples analyzed in this subsample were treated with communication skills training and used an earlier type of diary. In it the clients had to estimate the time spent talking, in joint activities, tenderness, and togetherness, and had to rate the feeling of closeness on a 5-point scale.

Table 12.6 gives an overview of the various combinations of changes in trend and level. It can be seen that about 35 (45%) of the 78 time series showed no significant change. Another 24 (31%) showed a significant positive change at the .05 level. This positive change may take various forms: It may be an upward-step function — see Figure 12.4 (c) — or it may be an initial slope with a maintenance at the level that is reached after the baseline. Whereas the first may be interpreted as a true treatment effect, the second change might be characterized as an initial placebo effect. A third form of positive change showed an initial decrease and then an increase after the baseline — see Figure 12.4 (b). This might be interpreted as an initial sensitization because of the couples becoming more conscious of the problems. Besides the positive changes, there were a large number of negative changes, namely in 19 (24%) of the individual time series. The 24% deterioration effects in the time series do not mean that 24% of the couples actually deteriorated. Instead, the deteriorations (as well as the positive effects) were largely clustered within the individual and also within the couple.

The following conclusions may be tentatively drawn from the data and must be confirmed by more thorough analyses of diaries. With communication skills training, feelings of closeness, time spent together, and time spent in joint activities are seldom negatively affected, whereas time spent talking and time with tenderness may be positively or negatively affected. And time spent together is generally enhanced. Since talking is a main focus of the training, it is of interest that it may lead to less talking at home. Perhaps talking becomes aversive with too much practice. Tenderness is not emphasized in the program and consequently does not show much of an effect. It might be worthwhile to include more active components of this sort in the training.

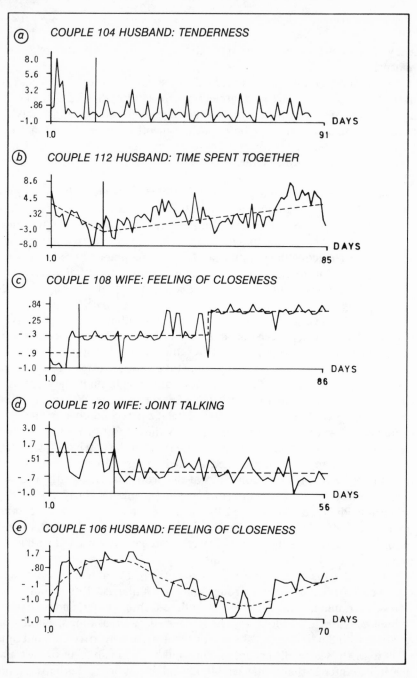

FIGURE 12.4. Several forms of changes detectable in time series: (a) periodicity (heightened level on weekends); (b) increase of level after active treatment begins; (c) shift in level (step up); (d) shift in level (step down); (e) time course comparable to the evaluation operating characteristic.

TABLE 12.6. Positive and Negative Treatment Effects in 78 Time Series from Diaries of 10 Couples over 80–120 Days: Number of Significant Results on Two Levels

	n at .05 and .10 levels										
	Talk		Tenderness		Close-ness		Joint activity		Togetherness		Sum	
Level of sign	.05	(.10)	.05	(.10)	.05	(.10)	.05	(.10)	.05	(.10)	.05	(.10)
Step up	6	(7)			2	(3)	2	(3)	2	(6)	12	(19)
Placebo					1	(2)		(3)		(2)	1	(7)
Sensitization	1	(2)	6	(6)	1	(3)	2	(4)	1	(1)	11	(16)
Positive effects total	7	(9)	6	(6)	4	(8)	4	(10)	3	(9)	24	(42)
Step down	6	(6)	5	(8)	2	(2)	3	(3)	3	(3)	19	(22)
Significant effects total	13	(15)	11	(14)	6	(10)	7	(13)	6	(12)	43	(64)

Note. An older type of diary was used in this analysis; see text for explanation.

Statistical Evaluation of Relationships

Changes in the time series, like those mentioned in the preceding section, may be interpreted as effects of the training on the couple. Another point of interest is the interrelation of the various time series in the diaries. Do changes in one aspect of the relationship go along with similar changes in other areas? Or do certain events in the relationship precede others?

Questions related to this type of dependence and interdependence may be analyzed by means of cross-correlations (Revenstorf, Kunert, Hahlweg, & Schindler, 1981; Revenstorf, Schindler, & Hahlweg, 1978). Whereas in normal correlational analysis the direction of causality may not be inferred, time series allow for a special kind of correlation. Two time series may be correlated synchronously, for example, today's "feeling accepted" with today's "being attentive." If this correlation is substantial, no causal inference is warranted, because of the synchronicity (interdependence). However, one also might correlate today's "feeling accepted" with tomorrow's "being attentive," or yesterday's "being attentive" with today's "feeling accepted." These time-lagged correlations have direction, insofar as it can be excluded that events of today usually influence events of yesterday (dependence).

Figure 12.5 gives a concrete example from two time series. It can be seen that there is a substantial synchronous correlation (.51) and a significant association between being attentive tomorrow and feeling accepted today (.27). The other direction of dependence is not significant. So this individual (male) is more attentive the next day if he feels accepted by his wife today.

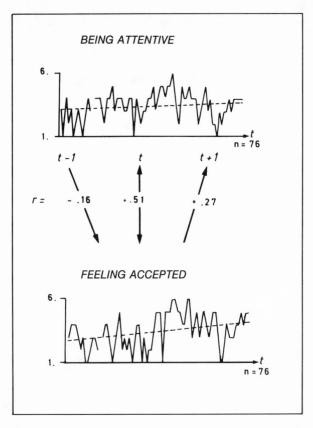

FIGURE 12.5. Example of synchronous and cross-lagged correlations between two time series ("being attentive" and "feeling accepted").

Table 12.7 describes a set of synchronous cross-correlations within and between spouses in the sample of 51 couples. All these cross-correlations were computed after the individual time series were rectified by eliminating linear trend, periodicity, and first-order autoregressive process. As can be seen from Column 1 there is a strong synchronicity between the same diary categories of wife and husband, averaging about .45. There is also strong consistency among the time series within each spouse, as indicated by the correlation of the single time series (x) with their average $(\overline{X})$ (Columns 2 and 3 of Table 12.7). These correlations roughly correspond to the factor loadings of the first principal component, thus indicating that about 30% of the variance in the time series is absorbed by their common first factor.

We computed cross-correlations between time series within one spouse as well as between spouses. Here we consider only time lags of 1 day and synchronous correlations. We now turn to the consideration of the time-lagged relations between different aspects of the relationship. First, the effect of antecedents *within* each spouse is investigated. Table 12.8 contains the means and standard deviations of those cross-correlations, lagged for 1 day. In order to avoid having to consider all possible combinations of the six diary categories, we computed only the influence of the single time series x on the average time series $(\overline{X})$ and vice versa. As can be seen from this table, there is a connectedness in the behavior and feelings of each spouse that is more pronounced when considering single variables influencing the summary time series – (1) in Table 12.8.

Last, let us turn to the time-lagged relationship *between* both spouses. As can be seen from Table 12.9, these cross-lagged correlations (1-day lag)

TABLE 12.7. Synchronous Relations: Means and Standard Deviations of the Synchronous Cross-Correlations of the Diary Variables

Diary variables (x)	Synchronous cross-correlations		
	$(1)^a$ $x(M) \leftrightarrow x(F)$	$(2)^b$ $x(M) \leftrightarrow \overline{X}(M)$	$(3)^b$ $x(F) \leftrightarrow \overline{X}(F)$
Time together			
M	.58	.42	.41
SD	.23	.16	.18
Understood			
M	.50	.63	.62
SD	.18	.12	.18
Joint talk			
M	.46	.55	.59
SD	.20	.13	.14
Tenderness			
M	.51	.58	.59
SD	.21	.16	.17
Attention			
M	.28	.57	.58
SD	.17	.16	.17
Feeling accepted			
M	.42	.56	.61
SD	.18	.14	.12
$\overline{X}$			
M	.62		
SD	.16		

[a]Cross-correlations between husband and wife.

[b]Correlations of the separate diary variables (x) for the husband, Column (2), and the wife, Column (3), with the average time series $(\overline{X})$. This corresponds to the usual item–test correlation in test theory.

TABLE 12.8. Time-Lagged Relations between Time Series of One Spouse:
Means and Standard Deviations of the Cross-Lagged Correlations of the Diary
Variables (Lagged 1 Day)

Diary variables (x)	(1)[a] $x \to \overline{X}$		(2)[b] $\overline{X} \to x$	
	Male	Female	Male	Female
Time together				
M	.19	.15	.04	.03
SD	.15	.17	.16	.14
Understood				
M	.23	.24	.09	.07
SD	.21	.17	.09	.11
Joint talk				
M	.25	.24	.06	.07
SD	.10	.14	.13	.12
Tenderness				
M	.27	.25	.03	.04
SD	.16	.18	.12	.09
Attention				
M	.22	.23	.09	.08
SD	.19	.16	.11	.09
Feeling accepted				
M	.21	.24	.07	.04
SD	.20	.18	.10	.12

Note. x = separate diary variables; $\overline{X}$ = average time series.
[a]For the prediction of the average time series by the separate aspects of the diary.
[b]For the prediction of separate aspects by the average time series.

are generally low, averaging about .05 with considerable variation (*SD* averages about .12). That is, there are positive and negative cross-lagged correlations. This means that the spouses influence each other positively and negatively in different aspects of their relationship.

The cross-correlations vary greatly from one individual to another. It therefore might be worthwhile to look separately at individual cases. Table 12.10 contains cross-correlations for one couple in the group of spouses using the earlier version of the diary. As a criterion variable of the diary categories, the "feeling together" may be used, and the relationship between this variable and the other categories of the diary was investigated. It may be seen from Table 12.10 that there was a conspicuous difference between husband and wife here: While all activities, talks, tenderness, and other categories for the husband synchronously meant togetherness (the synchronous correlation is higher than the lagged correlations), this was not so for the wife. She had the higher correlations with lag 1; that is, her feeling of togetherness was followed by increased joint activity, tenderness, time spent together, and so forth. This may indicate that the wife initiated more joint experiences after she felt good in the relationship. In fact, the husband had a different view of the relationship than she had. He felt good all of the time and considered her to be the patient. She, on the other hand, longed for joint experience and closeness. So the discrepancies in their expectations have a parallel in the cross-correlations of the diary variables.

Analyses like this may shed some light on the dynamics of the individual relationship. Let us contrast two couples whose differences are clear from the statistical data as well as phenomenologically. At the moment we are only considering dependence and interdependence between time series within one individual, although the relation between the spouses might also be of interest. For the time being we are taking "feeling understood" (FU), "tenderness" (TD), and "feeling accepted" (AC) as criteria of the relationship and relating these to the other aspects of the diary, namely "talking" (TA) and "time spent to-gether" (TT). We do not consider the synchronous correlations; these are all

TABLE 12.9. Time-Lagged Relations between Time Series of Both Spouses: Means and Standard Deviations of the Cross-Lagged Correlations (Lagged 1 Day)

Diary variables (x)	(1)[a] Male→female		(2)[a] Female→male	
	$x(M)→x(F)$	$\overline{X}(M)→x(F)$	$x(F)→x(M)$	$\overline{X}(F)→x(M)$
Time together				
M	.00	.03	.03	.00
SD	.12	.12	.14	.13
Understood				
M	.05	.06	.05	.10
SD	.14	.12	.15	.13
Joint talk				
M	.05	.06	.00	.03
SD	.12	.14	.12	.13
Tenderness				
M	.04	.03	.03	.06
SD	.09	.13	.12	.13
Attention				
M	.05	.05	..06	.08
SD	.12	.13	.11	.10
Feeling accepted				
M	.03	.03	.06	.09
SD	.13	.13	.14	.12
$\overline{X}$				
M	.03	—	.05	—
SD	.12	—	.10	—

Note. x = separate diary variables; $\overline{X}$ = average time series.

[a]For the prediction of the diary variables of the wife through those of the husband (1), and vice versa (2).

TABLE 12.10. Synchronous and Lag 1 Cross-Correlations for Residuals of Several Variables in One Couple

| | | Cross-correlations | | | | | |
| | | Husband | | | Wife | | |
X	Y	$X \rightarrow Y$	$X \leftrightarrow Y$	$X \leftarrow Y$	$X \rightarrow Y$	$X \leftrightarrow Y$	$X \leftarrow Y$
1 Time together	— Time undertaken	.05	.45	.22	.03	.69	.24
2 Time together	— Time in conversation	.01	.54	.16	.00	.68	.20
3 Time together	— Time in tenderness	.01	.38	.15	-.10	.46	.01
4 Time together	— Feeling together	.25	.33	.10	.03	.10	.27
5 Time undertaken	— Time in conversation	.01	.64	.19	.00	.63	.14
6 Time undertaken	— Time in tenderness	.22	.35	-.19	-.14	.50	-.10
7 Time undertaken	— Feeling together	.14	.35	.23	.07	.21	.09
8 Time in conversation	— Time in tenderness	.02	.28	.02	-.14	.50	-.10
9 Time in conversation	— Feeling together	.15	.48	.22	-.08	.17	.41
10 Time in tenderness	— Feeling together	.15	.24	.11	.12	.16	.29

Note. Correlations for Couple 106/107, using the earlier version of the diary. Two-tailed level of significance: .25 (.05) and .33 (.01).

relatively high, varying from .40 to .80. Figures 12.6 and 12.7 illustrate how cross-lagged correlations between the criteria and each of the other diary variables are marked when significant. This is done for the preceding and the following 3 days, separately for male and female. For example, consider the "acceptance" portion of Figure 12.6 (bottom): Here it is indicated that for the female the "feeling of being accepted" is preceded by "time spent together (TT), "feeling understood" (FU), and "tenderness" (TD) in the days before today. It is followed by more "time spent together" (TT).

In these plots, the significant antecedents and consequences of certain aspects of the relationship are indicated. If we now compare Figure 12.6 and Figure 12.7, you will see that for the wife in Couple 1 (Figure 12.6), there are a number of antecedents that predict she will feel understood and feel accepted. There are a number of consequences when she experiences tenderness. This is less pronounced in the male. In Couple 2, in contrast (Figure 12.7), there are very few antecedents and very few consequences to important feelings such as being understood, being tender, and being accepted. The emotional landscape, so to speak, appears to be more impoverished in Couple 2.

Table 12.11 summarizes the significant cross-lagged correlations from Figures 12.6 and 12.7. For Couple 1 there are 32 positive significant emotional antecedents and consequences. For Couple 2 there are only 10 consequences and antecedents that are positive, and a further four that are negative. Here negative cross-correlations occurred, which means, for instance, that after being tender, this woman feels less accepted (AC) and less understood (FU).

So much for statistical evaluation. With regard to therapy, in the first case the treatment was successful, while Couple 2 separated 1 year after completion of the therapy.

In the first couple, the husband was calm, shy, and tender. He had a strong tendency to pay attention to his wife and appeared to be very caring. The wife was rather shy, too, tended to be desperate, and had strong emotional reactions in such situations. Although she had a job (like the other wife), she was less interested in the career and more interested in the relationship. The second couple had a less caring and warm relationship even at the time of assessment. The husband was introverted, controlled, friendly, but not very emotional. He tended toward sarcasm and was able to fulfill his own wishes. The wife was self-critical and ambitious. She wanted to be a superb mother as well as professionally successful. She was often dissatisfied with herself and her performances, tended to render all-or-none judgments, and had strong emotional reactions. Those, in turn, put her husband under pressure.

Although this is a *post hoc* analysis, it illustrates the potential for analyzing the structure of the diaries to gain some insight into the dynamics of a marital relationship.

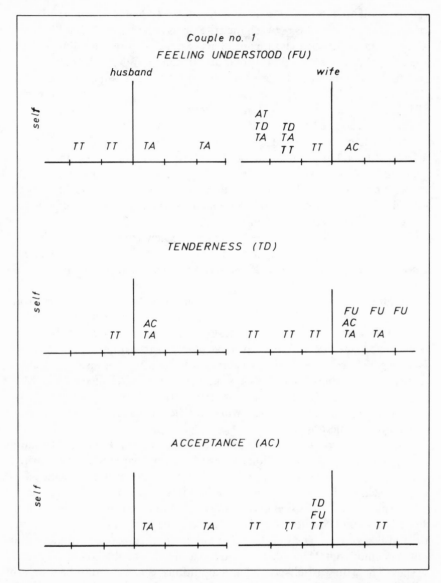

FIGURE 12.6. Case study of cross-lagged correlations within the spouses of Couple 1 with respect to the criterion variables "feeling understood," "tenderness," and "acceptance." Abscissa indicates lag 1 and lag 3, forward and backward; ordinate indicates magnitude of correlation. These plots predict the diary variables TT (time spent together), TA (time spent talking together), TD (tenderness), AT (attentiveness), AC (feeling accepted), and FU (feeling understood).

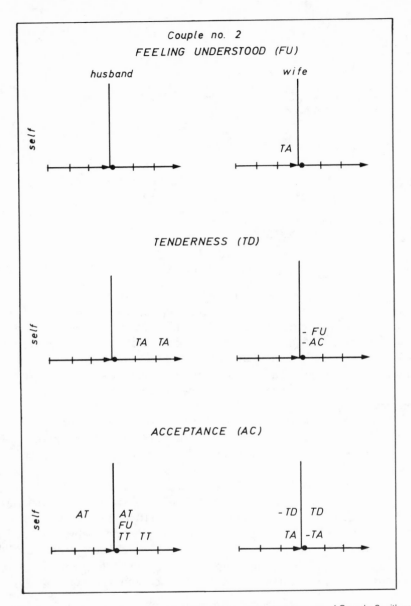

FIGURE 12.7. Case study of cross-lagged correlations within the spouses of Couple 2 with respect to the criterion variables "feeling understood," "tenderness," and "acceptance." Abscissa indicates lag 1 and lag 3, forward and backward; ordinate indicates magnitude of correlation. These plots predict the diary variables TT (time spent together), TA (time spent talking together), TD (tenderness), AT (attentiveness), AC (feeling accepted), and FU (feeling understood).

TABLE 12.11. Number of Significant Cross-Lagged Correlations (.05 Level) in Two Couples

	Antecedents	Consequences	Totals
Couple 1			
Husband	3 +	6 +	
Wife	15 +	8 +	
Total			32 +
Couple 2			
Husband	1 +	6 +	
Wife	2 + /1 −	1 + /3 −	
Totals			10 + , 4 −

Note. The correlations were computed between the three criteria "feeling understood," "tenderness," and "feeling accepted" and the rest of the diary variables.

Predictive Utility of Time Series Parameters

Figures 12.2 and 12.3 as well as Table 12.6 provide evidence for some changes that take place in the relationship of the couples, as assessed by the diaries. There are positive and negative trends or shifts in level, or both, which gives some impression of face validity regarding the process depicted by the time series. However, Tables 12.3 and 12.4 remind us that therapy success is not always accompanied by an increasing slope in the time series. In the following paragraphs we systematically try to evaluate the validity of various parameters resulting from time series analysis.

As external criteria for success, we chose four indices from our assessment battery. At the beginning (B) and the end (E), and at 6-month (FU-6) and 12-month (FU-12) follow-ups, questionnaires were given to each couple, resulting in four measures of the quality of the relationship (Partnership Questionnaire − PFB) (Hahlweg, 1979; Hahlweg *et al.*, Chapter 1, this volume): Happiness (0–5 rating scale), Quarreling (10-item questionnaire), Tenderness (10-item questionnaire), and Communication (10-item questionnaire).

While the diaries were assessed only during therapy (between B and E), the questionnaires provide data 6 and 12 months later. Thus, predictive validity may be assessed. To evaluate the concurrent and predictive validity of the various time series parameters, we discuss them in three groups:

1. Effect parameters: Level and trend
2. Process parameters: Variability, autocorrelation, and periodicity
3. Relation parameters: Synchronous and cross-lagged correlations between spouses and within spouses

First, let us examine the cross-sectional (classical) correlations, which were computed between questionnaire indices and time series parameters across the sample of individuals. These validity correlations should not be confused with the auto- and cross-correlations resulting from the time series. The time series correlations were computed for each individual in a longitudinal fashion. They were then treated as simple scores for each individual, analogous to a test score. These time series parameters were computed from each of the six diary variables as well as the average time series.

Validity of Effect Parameters

As one might guess from earlier discussions regarding Tables 12.3 and 12.4, the slope of a time series (trend) is less indicative of therapy success than is the level. Only the slope of the average time series $(\overline{X})$ correlates with at least some questionnaire measures: Happiness after 12 months, and Tenderness at all four points in time (B, E, FU-6, FU-12).

The level parameter is more consistently associated with questionnaire measures. For the average time series $(\overline{X})$, correlations with three of the criterion measures are shown in Table 12.12. As can be seen from this table, the correlations are substantial even 6 and 12 months after the end of the time series (the end of the therapy). The level of the time series therefore has some predictive validity, but more impressive is the concurrent validity, as reflected in correlations with the questionnaire data at the beginning and the end of therapy.

Validity of the Process Parameters

The parameter of periodicity (the weekly cycle) did not correlate substantially with the questionnaire data, although some of the correlations were significant. However, the variability of the time series — here measured by the standard deviation — correlated markedly with Quarreling, as may be seen from Table 12.13. This is especially true for the diary category "feeling understood." Interestingly, the predictive validity is higher than the concurrent validity here, and it even increases from FU-6 to FU-12. In other words, temporal variation in the subjective feeling of being understood indicates a risk for quarrel-

TABLE 12.12. Validity of the Time Series Parameter: General Level (Average of Six Different Time Series) $(n = 94)$

	B	E	FU-6	FU-12
Happiness	.42	.59	.29	(.06)
Tenderness	.33	.36	.42	.35
Communication	.29	.49	.40	.44

Note. B = beginning of therapy; E = ending of therapy; FU-6 = 6-month follow-up; FU-12 = 12-month follow-up.

TABLE 12.13. Validity of the Time Series Parameter:
Standard Deviation

	B	E	FU-6	FU-12
Quarreling	.31	.29	.41	.45

Note. B = beginning; E = ending; FU-6 = 6-month follow-up;
FU-12 = 12-month follow-up. This example uses the correlation of the time series "feeling understood" with Quarreling.

ing even a year later. Other diary variables also predicted Quarreling (FU-12),
with correlations averaging about $r = .35$. Other questionnaire measures (Happiness, Tenderness, and Communication) did not correlate significantly with
variability in the time series.

The autoregressive dependence is assessed here by the first autocorrelation in the time series. This parameter correlated negatively with the measure
of Happiness 6 and 12 months after therapy had ended. That is, the autocorrelation in the time series was high for people who later showed low Happiness. The data are shown in Table 12.14 for the average time series $(\overline{X})$.
Other diary variables correlated with Tenderness, the correlations at FU-12
averaging about $-.25$. The correlation of the average time series $(\overline{X})$ with
Quarreling was $+.30$.

These results are amazing. Whereas it seems plausible that the variation
in the diary categories may be deleterious to the relationship, it is less plausible for the autocorrelation. Positive autocorrelation means day-to-day stability of feelings and activities of the spouses. According to these findings, high
stability in these aspects of the relationship is associated with less happiness
and greater conflict at later points in time. A possible explanation for this
could be that stability as measured by autocorrelation from day to day reflects
unresponsive stability of the spouses. The spouses do not react to each other,
but simply continue in their present mood or activity. Perhaps in a good relationship, responsiveness is more desirable: Being attentive, tender, or understanding in response to some behavior of the spouse is more desirable than
always being attentive, tender, or understanding, and particularly not always so.

Validity of the Relation Parameters: Synchronous

Time series may be correlated in a synchronous or a time-lagged fashion (cf.
Figure 12.5). That is, in addition to analyzing interdependent correlations,
as in classical statistics, antecedents and consequences among the diary variables can be evaluated. Here, time series analyses provide a more advanced
tool than any cross-sectional investigation. Although one cannot infer causal-

TABLE 12.14. Validity of the Time Series Parameter: Autocorrelation (First Order)

	B	E	FU-6	FU-12
Happiness	(−.15)	(−.11)	−.34	−.26

Note. B = beginning; E = ending; FU-6 = 6-month follow-up; FU-12 = 12-month follow-up. This example uses the correlation of the average time series $(\overline{X})$ with Happiness.

ity until alternative third-variable explanations are ruled out, a time-lagged correlation precludes a causal interpretation in the direction against time. But first, let us consider synchronous correlations between the time series of husband and wife. These correlations indicate to what extent the diary ratings are low or high for both spouses at the same time. As can be seen from Table 12.15, Happiness and Tenderness scores correlate with the synchronicity of the diary categories in the spouses. For the sake of completeness, the correlations with the questionnaire data for husbands and wives have been listed separately. As can be seen, these correlations are positive and have substantial values after 6 and 12 months.

TABLE 12.15. Validities of Synchronous Relations between Spouses: Correlation of the Cross-Correlations in Table 12.7, Column (1), with the Questionnaire Data

Diary variables (x)	Questionnaire							
	Happiness				Tenderness			
	B	E	FU-6	FU-12	B	E	FU-6	FU-12
Time together	<u>.26</u>	.32		<u>.31</u>	<u>.32</u> .29	<u>.24</u>		
Understood			.29	<u>.32</u>	.35			
Joint talk			.30	<u>.36</u>			.37	
Tenderness				<u>.46</u>	.34			
Attention	.37	<u>.32</u> <u>.42</u>						<u>.38</u>
Feeling accepted							.25	
$\overline{X}$			.32	.39				.31

Note. B = beginning; E = ending; FU-6 = 6-month follow-up; FU-12 = 12-month follow-up. Data for women are underlined.

Validity of the Relation Parameters: Cross-Lagged

More interesting are the cross-lagged correlations between the diary categories within each spouse. They indicate the connectedness between behaviors and feelings of today and tomorrow. Since there are many possible cross-correlations between the six categories of the diary, only those correlations between the categories and the average time series $(\overline{X})$ are considered. Table 12.16 reports the validity of these time series parameters, and it can be seen that positive correlations between different categories of the diary from one day to another are negatively related to Happiness and positively to Quarreling. The latter is more true for females. Again, predictive validity is more substantial than concurrent validity. This result is puzzling in a similar way to the finding that a positive autocorrelation corresponds to low Happiness. We have no clear idea as to what this means. However, if it is not an artifact (as are

TABLE 12.16. Validities of the Antecedent Relations within Each Spouse: Correlation of the Cross-Correlations in Table 12.8, with the Questionnaire Variables Happiness and Quarreling

Diary variables (x)	Questionnaire							
	Happiness				Quarreling			
	B	E	FU-6	FU-12	B	E	FU-6	FU-12
Female								
Time together			−.30 / −.28			.45	.32 / .50	.35
Understood		−.27	−.24 / −.26	−.27	.26	.39	.28 / .36	.31
Joint talk						.27	.25 / .33	.30
Tenderness			−.21				.41	
Attention	−.26				.25	.39	.35 / .32	.27
Feeling accepted			−.28 / −.27			.34	.34 / .35	.27
Male								
Time together								
Understood	−.26 / −.34	−.25		−.33				
Joint talk		−.27 / −.27	−.30	−.40			.24	.31
Tenderness								
Attention								
Feeling accepted	−.29 / −.35	−.28		−.36				

Note. B = beginning; E = ending; FU-6 = 6-month follow-up; FU-12 = 12-month follow-up. Only correlations significant at the .05 level are given. Correlations with women's questionnaire data are underlined.

perhaps the autocorrelation findings), this cross-lagged correlation means stability and predictability in the behavior of each spouse. This stability is not contributing to joint Happiness; this might be especially true if the relationship is generally negative. Again, it could mean that the behavior of each partner is basically noncontingent.

Finally, we consider the validities of cross-lagged correlations between the spouses. To simplify the evaluation, the average time series $(\overline{X})$ of one spouse was correlated with each category of the diary of the other spouse for the next day. These data are contained in Table 12.17. As with the synchronous correlations between the spouses, here we consider a systems property of the relationship. Again we find a puzzling result. There are negative correlations with Happiness and positive correlations with Quarreling. In other words, if feelings and behaviors in one spouse are preceding those in the other spouse, this indicates less Happiness and more Quarreling in the relationship. This is more pronounced when the feelings and the behavior of the female are the antecedents. There are also some less substantial correlations in the areas of Tenderness and Communication at the 12-month follow-up. These are also negative. Since for most couples the diaries are reflective of generally negative relationships, the dependence of feelings of today on those of the spouse yesterday could be indicative of lingering resentment, as opposed to feelings that are contingent on today's experiences. Therefore, here stability in a negative sense again turns up as an indicator of later conflict and unhappiness.

Discussion

A standardized diary was used in this study as a monitoring and evaluation device to accompany a marital counseling program. As presented in this chapter, the inquiry into the usefulness of this kind of diary leads us to several conclusions. Assuming that the ratings contained in the diary tap some relevant aspects of relationships, the diary may serve several purposes.

As a monitoring device, it keeps track of the developments of the relationship during therapy. It provides a standardized basis for discussing changes with the couple. It also sensitizes the spouses to their problems and helps them maintain an awareness of the aspects of their relationship that they want to change. Plotted as a complete graph, it serves as a résumé of the changes at the end of therapy. By mere inspection of these time series (Figures 12.2 and 12.3), one can easily spot improvement, stagnation, and deterioration in separate categories of the relationship. This way one can see where changes have taken place and where they have not.

A more sophisticated evaluation of the data gathered by the diaries is provided by time series analysis. It allows for statistical tests of changes in single-case data. This is of interest to the clinical researcher, who is not con-

TABLE 12.17. Validities of the Antecedent Relations between Two Spouses

	Questionnaire															
	(1)[a] $\overline{X}$(F)→x(M)								(2)[b] $\overline{X}$(M)→x(F)							
	Happiness				Quarrelling				Happiness				Quarrelling			
Diary variables (x)	B	E	FU-6	FU-12	B	E	FU-6	FU-12	B	E	FU-6	FU-12	B	E	FU-6	FU-12
Time together	-.23 <u>-.34</u>				.25				-.24 <u>-.26</u>							
Understood					.31	.28						-.35	.24	.30	.27	.33
Joint talk	-.24			-.32	.34	.32										
Tenderness				<u>-.53</u> -.30		.28 <u>.26</u>	.25 <u>.24</u>	<u>.33</u>				-.37				.31
Attention																
Feeling accepted		-.27		<u>-.34</u>	.37 <u>.29</u>	.40	.29	<u>.40</u>		-.23						
$\overline{X}$				-.41	.47	<u>.25</u>		<u>.33</u>			-.24	-.30				.30

Note. B = beginning; E = ending; FU-6 = 6-month follow-up; FU-12 = 12-month follow-up. Data for the woman are underlined.
[a] Average time series of the wife precedes the diary variables of the husband.
[b] Average time series of the husband precedes the separate time series and separate diary variables of the wife.

tent with outcome evaluation by group statistics. This researcher may look for improvements as well as deteriorations in several ways. In fact, there were a substantial number of significant increases as well as significant decreases in terms of steps or changes in slope. These would have at least partly canceled each other out if we had averaged the data. In summary, it can be said that a marital therapy program comprised only of communication skills training does lead to deterioration in a number of couples, especially with respect to Communication and Tenderness. This kind of analysis also shows that in some respects the program does not change the relationship very much. In other words, the single-case evaluation by statistical time series gives a much more detailed picture of the therapy outcome and the therapy process than does evaluation by group statistics.

A number of programs for time series analysis have been issued. A complex one is that compiled by Box's co-worker D. Pack, now contained in the program package BMD-P, available from most computer software distributors. The program of Glass *et al.* (1975) is easier to use. It would perhaps be more convenient, however, to write an individual program, in a simplified version tailored to any special purposes. (Part of our analysis was programmed by one of the authors — H. K.)

The use of statistics to analyze time series is worthwhile if a researcher is interested in changes that may be hidden in large fluctuations. Another research purpose of time series analysis is the exploration of relationship structure. By analyzing cross-correlations (synchronous and cross-lagged) between several aspects of the relationship and between the spouses, dependencies and interdependencies may be detected. These structures, if they emerge, are valid only for the individual couple. Analyses like these do not lend themselves to general laws. They therefore may appear to be too cumbersome and inefficient. On the other hand, research that alternates between generalizable results from experiments and single-case studies may be optimal for understanding complex human behavior.

A tentative single-case analysis has been presented in this chapter to illustrate how the results from the statistical analysis can be related to details of the case report. However, it would be premature to conclude that this kind of analysis is valid. Further replication and cross-validation are necessary. Questions could be raised about the quality of the data in the first place, and also about the validity of the more refined indices that are extracted from the data by statistical time series analysis. Since the derived indices have some validity (see below), it is implied that the basic data are also valid. The inspection of the time series in the second section of this chapter shows that a positive slope in some aspect of the diary does not necessarily mean therapy success. The analysis of the concurrent and predictive validities of several time series parameters in comparison to questionnaire data did provide three noteworthy findings.

First, parameters computed from time series depicting therapy process can predict Happiness, Tenderness, Communication, and Quarreling to some extent. This is noteworthy because indices such as periodicity, autocorrelation, and cross-correlations are distant from the original empirical data source. Statistical manipulation does not necessarily mean a loss of substance. The opposite may be true, since those indices are certainly much harder (if not impossible) to fake, compared with level and trend of time series.

Second, we found evidence not only for concurrent validity but also for predictive validity. The time series indices correlated with Happiness reported 12 months after the time series ended. In fact, for some of the indices (variability, autocorrelation, and some cross-correlation) the predictive validities are more substantial than the concurrent ones. Perhaps the daily monitoring of the relationship reveals underlying trends that do not show up in the concurrent questionnaire responses. In fact, questionnaire responses at the end of therapy may well be faked to please the experimenter and to reduce the cognitive dissonance of having spent so much effort with only minor results. This tendency may be reduced 6 to 12 months later.

Third, some of the time series indices, such as general level and synchronicity of feelings and behaviors in the spouses, predict Happiness. Less plausible at first glance is the fact that other indices such as variability, autocorrelation, and cross-lagged correlations within and between spouses predict lack of Happiness and Quarreling. These findings may be explained as follows: Positive autocorrelation could mean stability in the sense of nonresponsiveness. Positive cross-lagged correlations within each spouse could mean stability and consistency even in the sense of righteousness. And positive cross-lagged correlations between spouses could indicate a long-term contingency consisting of resentment and vengeance. This is especially true if the relationship is in the negative realm of the scale. All these phenomena would mean that the spouses are not responsive to each other on a short-term basis within a day's time span. This type of behavior might, indeed, be deleterious to a relationship. However, we are awaiting cross-validation before giving weight to all these observations.

Diaries as monitoring devices may be worthwhile and simple to use. Diaries and resulting time series to evaluate therapy outcome and process, on the other hand, may be cumbersome to use. However, this is a convenient way to continuously collect data that seem to warrant consideration for research purposes, as well as to analyze the therapy process and outcome in more detail on a single-case basis.

ACKNOWLEDGMENT

This research was supported by the Deutsche Forschungsgemeinschaft Grant No. (DFG-Re 40212-6).

REFERENCES

Anderson, O. D. *Time series analysis and forecasting: The Box-Jenkins approach*. London: Butterworths, 1975.

Box, G. E. P., & Jenkins, G. M. (Eds.). *Time series analysis: Forecasting and control*. San Francisco: Holden-Day, 1970.

Glass, G. V., Wilson, V. L., & Gottman, J. M. (Eds.). *Design and analysis of time series experiments*. Boulder: Colorado Associated University Press, 1975.

Gottman, J. M., & Glass, G. V. Analysis or interrupted time series experiments. In T. Kratochwill (Ed.), *Strategies to evaluate change in single subject research*. New York: Academic Press, 1977.

Gottman, J. M., & Markman, H. Experimental designs for psychotherapy research. In A. E. Bergin & S. L. Garfield (Eds.), *Handbook of psychotherapy and behavior change*. New York: Wiley, 1978.

Hahlweg, K. Konstruktion und Validierung des Partnerschaftsfragebogens PFB. *Zeitschrift für Klinische Psychologie*, 1979, *8*, 17-40.

Keeser, W. *Zeitreihenanalyse in der klinischen Psychologie*. Unpublished doctoral dissertation, University of Munich, 1980.

Revenstorf, D. *Zeitreihenanalyse für klinische Daten*. Weinheim: Beltz, 1979.

Revenstorf, D. Kessler, A., Schindler, L., Hahlweg, K., & Bluemer, H. Time series analysis: Clinical applications evaluating intervention effects. In O. D. Anderson (Ed.), *Proceedings of the 2nd ITSM Conference*. Amsterdam: North-Holland, 1980.

Revenstorf, D., Kunert, H., Hahlweg, K., & Schindler, L. The use of cross-correlations and other time series parameters in clinical analysis. In O. D. Anderson (Ed.), *Proceedings of the 3rd ITSM Conference (Valencia)*. Amsterdam: North-Holland, 1981.

Revenstorf, D., Schindler, L., & Hahlweg, K. Lead and lag in aspects of marital interaction. *Behavior Analysis and Modification*, 1978, *2*, 174-184.

Terman, L. *Psychological factors in marital happiness*. New York: McGraw-Hill, 1938.

13

Cognitive and Behavioral Measures of Marital Interaction

ROBERT L. WEISS

Behavioral marital therapy (BMT) has made a substantial contribution to the assessment of marital interactions. Associated with these advances are new questions about the interface between objective (outsider) and subjective (insider) measures of such interactions. Judgments about interactions are complex, but judgments about interactional intimacy are even more complex. Not only does the topography of the behavior exchange provide information to the two sets of observers, but there is the additional issue of the extent to which the participants utilize the information provided by their own inter-actional behaviors. It is often possible in social psychological experiments to create sufficient ambiguity about one's experience to force an outward search for context cues, thereby providing an explanation for one's experience (e.g., (Bem, 1965; Schachter & Singer, 1962). With intimates, on the other hand, there is seldom such ambiguity about the "meaning" of the other's behavior; rightly or wrongly, each feels in possession of perfect knowledge of the other! When we ask a married couple to provide a sample of their conflict-resolving interactional behaviors, as in a negotiation of some conflict, and we then ask them to make a judgment about the outcome — whether it was successful or unsuccessful — their judgment is composed of different sources of informa-tion. We might expect that, just as outsiders do, they would use the informa-tion provided by the interaction. But because of their belief in perfect knowl-edge, the partners utilize their familiarity with each other as a data base. These preexisting cognitions (and associated affects) function as a "sentiment over-ride" (Weiss, 1980) to the impact of the behavioral data base. Such preexisting cognitions are themselves based upon actual experiences with one another in conflict-resolving situations, but they also reflect private expectations about the goodwill and intent of the other. A further complication, even assuming the best of intent, is that couples may simply lack the skills to report accurately.

The present study was formulated precisely because of this entanglement of the objective and subjective bases for making judgment calls about inter-

Robert L. Weiss. Department of Psychology, University of Oregon, Eugene, Oregon, U.S.A.

actional outcomes. The entanglement led us to define a model that might clarify the various sources of data available to couples and observers when each made judgments about the nature of an interaction. This chapter summarizes the basis for the model, together with some preliminary findings from a correlational analysis of data germane to the model.

A Model of Context, Process, and Outcome

When asked to evaluate the outcome of their interaction, a couple can draw upon two sources of information: their previous history with each other, and the immediate experience provided by the interaction itself. Their history is the "context" of variables preexisting to their interaction. It includes cognitive and affective influences as well as actual competencies and resources available to the couple. In a word, "context" includes everything that the couple brings with them to the interaction.

By "process" we refer to the behavioral data generated by the interaction itself, should the couple choose to avail themselves of these data. During the course of a conflict-resolving interaction, certain things are said and done. These may be available to an outside observer (e.g., may be encoded by some system of behavior codes), and they may be available to the couple themselves (e.g., noting that something said by one was helpful in moving the discussion to a point of agreement). But it may also be true that because of preformed beliefs, one partner does not "read" the constructive behavior of the other (e.g., he/she "never supports my point of view").

Finally, by "outcome" we refer to the judgments made by partners and outside observers of the immediately preceding interaction. Typically these are evaluative judgments of outcome—for example, "Did we (they) resolve the issue?" or "Did we (they) make any progress toward resolution?" or "How satisfied were you (they) with the outcome?"

Each of the three panels—context, process, outcome—forms a unit in a sequential process. All subsequent judgments must filter through the first panel, that is, context. The issue then becomes one of discerning the relative influence of one panel on its sequentially adjacent neighbor—that is, context as an influence on process, and process as an influence on outcome. Thus, for example, it might be shown that context variables are better predictors of outcome than process variables; that is, behavior based on the process is, in this instance, overriden by preexisting cognitions, affects, beliefs, etc. If such were the case, it might lead us to conclude that expectations override the input of behavioral evidence. Certainly we would not expect couples to completely ignore the impact of their present interactional behaviors; that is, they probably do not "gate out" such information entirely.

Yet it is important to recognize that a couple's ability to access information from their interaction is also at issue. We know relatively little about how couples encode their interactions. Gottman (1979) and his associates have shown that distressed (relative to nondistressed) couples rate the impact of messages sent by the partner as significantly more negative than the partner intended, whereas both marital status groups intended to send essentially positive messages. In a related study, Notarius, Vanzetti, and Smith (1981) demonstrated that distressed (relative to nondistressed) husbands intended their messages to be more negative, rated messages received from their wives as more negative, and predicted that their own messages would be received negatively. Distressed wives did not receive their husbands' messages as negatively as husbands had predicted, although nondistressed wives rated messages somewhat less positively than their husbands had predicted. Gottman and Porterfield (1981) found that wives' marital satisfaction predicts to both husbands' and strangers' ability to decode nonverbal messages sent by the wives. Husbands of maritally distressed wives have greater difficulty (in terms of greater number of errors made) with their wives' nonverbal messages than stranger-husbands have with these same messages. Husbands of nondistressed wives, on the other hand, do much better (make fewer errors) with their wives' messages than do stranger-husbands with these same messages. The authors take these findings – and related findings from Gottman (1979) – as support for the hypothesis that nondistressed couples have a private or idiosyncratic communication system.

In the two studies just considered, couples were selected on the basis of an important context variable, namely, marital satisfaction. The finding that outside observers were more accurate, than the spouses from distressed relationships, in their rating of the connotative meaning of messages sent by the latter suggests that accuracy in using process data is determined, in part, by context variables. Although these data do not clarify the exact nature of the filter, they do suggest that one is operating.

The current approach does not answer more "molecular" questions about information processing as such, but focuses rather on context and couples' performance as predictors of both their process and outcome evaluations. We might expect, for example, that certain aspects of context would account for outcome ratings simply on the basis of expecting confirmation of one's beliefs. Consistencies in evaluating verbal behaviors are likely across situations.

Thus far we have considered both perceptual and performance functions of the couple. Let us consider next the relationship between the outsider and the couple. Our interest here is in a comparison between how well couples' and outsiders' judgments can be accounted for by parallel processes. For example, how well are outcome judgments predicted by process ratings within each set of process raters (i.e., couple-to-couple measures and coder-to-coder measures)? Similarly, how well do cross-modality variables predict to outcome measures? That is, do couple process ratings predict to outside outcome judgments? In this sense we are asking whether couples utilize information similar to the ways in which outsiders utilize information, acknowledging that we do not have a direct isomorphism between the two encoding systems.

With these considerations in mind, we turn to a discussion of the study itself.

A Correlational Study of Context, Process, and Outcome

Our attempt to establish the links between and among the panels, as described by the model, required, first, defining a relevant set of context measures, that is, those that conceptually would be expected to account for variance in both process and outcome ratings. Next, we required samples of conflict-resolving interactions that could be rated on process measures by both couples and outside coders. Finally, outcome ratings by both groups were required, such that both couples and outside observers could rate the outcome (e.g., satisfaction, progress, etc.) of the interaction.

Method

SUBJECTS

Couples were solicited from newspaper and radio announcements offering a marital communications research project designed to provide extensive feedback about patterns of communication in intimate relationships. Of those responding to the ads, 25 couples were selected who, based upon an initial screening interview and response to assessment tests, were judged not to be in immediate need of individual marital therapy and who reported a positive expectation that the communication awareness focus would be beneficial to them. Participation required a $25 deposit, $15 of which was refundable when all phases of the project were completed.

The mean ages of husbands and wives were 33.4 and 31.4 years, respectively ($SD = 6.4$), and they had been living together for an average of 7.8 years (range: 1–29 years); one-third of the sample was childless. For husbands and wives, respectively, 44% and 32% had some college, and the sample was biased toward the more highly educated. Marital adjustment scores as measured by the Dyadic Adjustment Scale (DAS) ranged from 72 to 135 (mean = 102.2), and the Marital Status Inventory (MSI) means were 2.7 and 2.6 (range: 0–7). (MSI scores greater than 3 indicate a clinically noteworthy potential for dissolution.) The sample was well educated, represented a wide range of marital satisfaction, and was generally similar to couples in this community who elect to participate in marital enrichment offerings of the Oregon Marital Studies Program.

MEASURES

Context. Two categories of context measures were employed: namely, sentiment or satisfaction measures, and efficacy expectation or perceived competence measures.

As used here "marital satisfaction" refers to test scores on the DAS (Spanier, 1974), the MSI (Weiss & Cerreto, 1980), and Rubin's Love–Liking Scale (L-L) (Rubin, 1970). The DAS is a widely used self-report measure of marital satisfaction not too dissimilar in content and form from the more familiar Locke–Wallace (1959) measure of marital satisfaction. The MSI is a 14-item self-report measure of likelihood of divorce, identifying steps that bring one closer to actual termination of the relationship (e.g., from "Thoughts of divorce occur to me frequently" to "I have filed for a divorce"). Not all marital dissatisfaction leads to divorce, so the MSI provides still another view of the sentiment of the relationship. The L-L self-report, although most appropriate for young unmarried adults, was included in order to add still another dimension to the sentiment variable, that is, degree of positive feeling toward the spouse.

The efficacy expectation or perceived competence measures were all designed to capture expectations about likely outcomes of conflict-resolving interactions in general, as well as those involving particular content. The main efficacy measure designed for this study was a rationally derived 34-item expectancy scale that asks about likely acts and feelings during a discussion. Twenty-four of the items have an individual focus; they are answered on a 7-point Likert scale, ranging from "extremely likely" to "extremely unlikely," for both the self role and the partner role. Typical items are: "propose constructive solutions," "feel appreciated," "feel understood," and "criticize, disagree, show disapproval." The 10 team-focused items include "work as a team," "turn the discussion into an argument," and "be unable to stay on the topic." A total score was derived by summing the scores on the three subscales; these may range from a low of 58 to a high of 406. Alpha coefficients for the subscales were found to be .82, .87, and .86.

Expectations that a conflict would be resolved and measures of conflict severity were obtained on a single form entitled the Problem Intensity Form (PIF), adapted from a similar instrument designed by Gottman (1979). Couples first rated the severity of conflicts defined by 14 areas (sex, communication, money, etc.) on a scale ranging from 0 (not problematic) to 100 (extremely problematic). For each content area rated as problematic, subjects also indicated on a 0- to 100-point scale their estimate of how likely it would be for them to resolve that issue.

The conflict severity measures were converted to z scores for each subject, thereby making it possible to select a moderate and a high conflict topic for each couple to discuss. Degree of topic severity was made uniform across couples. The topic severity score used for statistical analyses included only ratings for topics actually discussed.

Process. Two categories of process measures were employed: a subjective or couple-based evaluation of the process of the interaction, and an outsider's evaluation of the process. The outsider was trained in coding the Marital Interaction Coding System (MICS) (Hops, Wills, Patterson, & Weiss, 1972). The subjective measure, Video Rating Scale (VRS), was similar to Gottman's (1979) Impact Rating Scale. Unlike in Gottman's procedure, couples made individual ratings (from the videotape of their interaction, every 15 seconds) on a 5-point Likert scale ranging from + + through 0 to − − to reflect the degree of perceived helpfulness of their partner's behavior during that interval. For example, a + + rating would indicate that the partner was judged to be extremely helpful during that 15 second interval, whereas a − rating would indicate that partner was unhelpful; and so on. Two scores were derived from the VRS measure, percentage positive (+ %) and percentage negative (− %), by combining either the two positive or the two negative scale points.

The MICS was employed by trained coders, who coded the same video-taped couple interactions rated by the couples. The MICS provides many behavior codes and possibilities for combining codes into categories (see Jacobson, Elwood, & Dallas, 1981; Wieder & Weiss, 1980). Our interest in this study was to look at two levels of MICS process information: (1) baserate occurrence of Positive, Negative, and Problem Solution categories, and (2) sequential or conditional scores. The latter refer to changes over baserate probability in the form: "Given a Problem Solution code, what is the probability that it will be followed by PS, CP, or AG?" where PS is Problem Solution, CP is Complaining, and AG is Agreement. Thus, MICS process measures were defined either in terms of total frequencies of specific groups of codes or in terms of response sequences. The latter were defined as a particular behavior sequence, for example, PS followed by supportive, critical, or counterproposal responses. The specific codes included in the base rate and z score categories are presented in Table 13.1.

Outcome. As with the process measures, there were also two categories of outcome measures, a subjective or couple-based set and an outside-observer-based set of measures.

Couples were asked to make outcome ratings immediately after each interaction. The Interaction Rating Scale (IRS) was devised for this purpose. Two sets of questions assessed (1) the degree of satisfaction with the interaction and (2) the amount progress the rater felt they had made. Six items were rated on a 7-point Likert rating scale of agreement reflecting satisfaction with the interaction, for example, "Overall, I am satisfied with the discussion," "I did not feel understood," "We worked well as a team," and so on. Two items were rated for progress, for example, "We made progress toward solving the problem" and "We agreed on a workable solution to the problem."

The outside outcome raters were also trained MICS coders, but for purposes of this study no coder both coded and rated outcome for the same taped interaction. Thus, while outsiders in this case were not unsophisticated observers, they were not familiar with the interactions they judged on outcome. The outcome observers answered 10 questions grouped into three categories:

TABLE 13.1. Description of MICS Code Categories

Category name/designation	Code descriptions
MICS baserate	
Positive (MICS +)	Agree, Approve, Assent, Attend, Humor, Smile/Laugh, Positive Physical Contact
Problem Solution (PS)	Accept Responsibility, Compromise, Paraphrase, Positive Solution
Negative (MICS −)	Complain, Criticize, Disagree, Deny Responsibility, Excuse, Mind Read, No Response, Not Tracking, Put Down, Turn Off
MICS z scores	
PS→AG (supportive)	Problem Solution, Negative Solution: Agree, Approve, Compromise
PS→CP(critical)	PS, NS: Complain, Criticize, Deny Responsibility, Excuse, Put Down, Disagree, Interrupt, No Response
PS→PS (counterproposal)	PS, NS: PS, NS

(1) "outcome" — number of attained resolutions, quality of attained resolutions, number of problems resolved; (2) "satisfaction" — the extent to which the couple worked together, how satisfied each spouse was with the interaction, how adjusted the couple seemed; and (3) "progress" — how much progress did the couple make toward resolving the problem? The mean rating across observers for each item for each couple was used as the score.

PROCEDURES

Couples were seen weekly over a period of 6 weeks by a male and female pair of consultants who were advanced clinical graduate student members of the Marriage Practicum at the University of Oregon. Prior to the first interview, couples were sent self-report forms (DAS and MSI) to complete before their first meeting. During the first interview the general purpose of the study was explained, as well as what the couple could expect to gain in the way of communication skills and how their data would be incorporated in a special final feedback session with them. All other self-report instruments used in the study were assigned during this session.

In weeks 2 and 3 couples made two 10-minute conflict-resolving interactions that were videotaped. They first discussed a problem rated at medium severity, and during the second session, one rated at high severity. Immediately after each interaction the spouses independently completed the IRS which was used for their outcome ratings. (During each of the two videotaping sessions, couples also made a "fake good" and a "fake bad" videotaped interaction. When it was desired to give couples practice in rating their own videotapes, a portion of the "fake good" tape was used. These data are not otherwise included in this report.)

During the fourth session the couples made process ratings of their two previously videotaped interactions, using the VRS. Couples practiced by making 15-second impact ratings on one of their tapes not used in this report. The order of tape presentation for VRS process ratings was randomized with regard to level of conflict severity. In the final session the consultants summarized the couple's strengths and weaknesses as indicated by the couple's data. The aim was to provide positive feedback whenever possible but to be realistic in the assessment of problems and offer suggestions as to what the couple might choose to do to improve their difficulties. Although many forms of data were collected, the consultants in each case became very familiar with their couple(s) and were able to fulfill their agreement to provide useful feedback about how each couple communicated.

Objective process coding was done by seven trained MICS coders who had successfully completed an extensive training program. Coder pairs were randomly constituted and assigned randomly to the 50 tapes. A subsample of tapes was assigned to a master coder for reliability checking. Intercoder agreement was figured on a code-by-code basis and ranged from 78% to 95% (mean = 84%). As a check on observer drift, each coder coded an additional three tapes that the master coder also coded. Interobserver agreement with this criterion ranged from 78% to 82% (mean = 79.4%).

The outside outcome observers were six undergraduates associated with the project either as MICS coders or as research assistants. Outcome rating data from a coder who had coded a tape were eliminated from statistical analyses.

Results

The results are presented first for the within-panel relationships (i.e., association between and among variables within each panel) and then for relationships between panels (i.e., the extent to which context predicts to process and to outcome). Couple scores, summed over the two interaction sessions, rather than individual analyses for husbands and wives, are reported here.

WITHIN-PANEL ANALYSES

Context. The intercorrelations among the context variables are presented in Table 13.2. Within each of the two sets of context variables, only the DAS and MSI were related, and the so-called efficacy measures did not form a single construct, (i.e., r was nonsignificant in all cases). The correlations between measures of each set indicated that marital satisfaction and perceived effectiveness were related ($r = .59$, $p < .01$), and that closeness to divorce and both perceived effectiveness ($r = -.39$) and severity of problem ($r = -.52$) were

TABLE 13.2. Within-Context-Measure Correlations (Pearson's r)

	2	3	4	5	6
1. DAS	−.68	—	.59	—	—
2. MSI		—	−.39	—	−.52
3. L-L			—	—	—
4. Efficacy				—	—
5. Severity					—
6. Outcome					—

$r = .39$, $p < .05$; $r = .50$, $p < .01$

Note: DAS = Dyadic Adjustment Scale; MSI = Marital Status Inventory; L-L = Love–Liking Scale; Efficacy = expectancy measure; Severity = problem severity score; Outcome = likelihood of resolving problem.

related. Thus the greater the marital satisfaction, the greater the expectation that problems can be resolved satisfactorily; and the more strongly one has considered terminating the relationship, the less likely it is that positive outcomes are expected and the more likely that problem severity will be rated high. Although all of the outcomes were as expected, not all relationships were significant: Our grouping of these context measures was only partially correct.

Process. The intercorrelations among the process variables are listed in Table 13.3. In this table r values are listed for within- as well as between-process measures (i.e., subjective and objective measures).

There was a strong tendency for couples to use extreme ratings of partner helpfulness—the r value between $+\%$ and $-\%$ VRS ratings was $-.81$ ($p < .01$)—and a lesser (yet significant) tendency for those making high helpfulness ratings not to use neutral rating options. (Because of the ipsative nature of these helpfulness scores, only $+\%$ and $-\%$ VRS scores are considered.)

The baserate Positive MICS and Negative MICS scores were also related ($r = -.59$), but to a lesser degree than was the case with the subjective couple ratings. PS, defined *a priori* as a positive type of behavior, was not related to the more affectively defined Positive and Negative MICS codes.

For the MICS sequential (z score) scores, there was a slight tendency ($r = .39$) for either a positive or a negative behavior to follow a PS; that is, if a PS occurs within an interaction and someone responds to it positively, it is also likely that other PSs will be responded to negatively. A couple is likely to be evaluative of their PS statements.

Thus far we have focused on within-method correlations (i.e., with subjective and objective measures). The between-process measure r values are informative because they clarify the overlap between couples and outsiders as raters.

Positive behaviors in the MICS system were also seen subjectively by couples as being helpful ($r = .57$) and as not unhelpful ($r = -.42$). However, MICS Negative codes did not map well onto subjectively rated unhelpful behaviors; that is, Negative MICS and $-$% VRS scores were not related. Thus couples and coders may be in agreement about positive behaviors yet hold different views of what is truly negative.

The disparity between what couples and MICS coders view as negative is further illustrated by the sequential z scores and the subjective impact ratings, as seen in Table 13.3. Note that the relationship between unhelpful ratings ($-$% VRS) and PS→PS was $r = .62$ ($p < .01$), indicating that the more PS immediately followed PS in a session, the greater the overall negative impact rating was for that session. This suggests that a pattern of proposal–counterproposal is not a particularly helpful sequence. (We do not have an event-for-event comparison for these data, only session totals.) Similarly, from the table it can be seen that PS→PS and *a priori* defined helpful scores were negatively related ($r = -.42$). Finally, it may be seen that an Agree response is more likely after a PS than either a Disagree or a counterproposal. It is important to recall that these z scores are net after the baserate frequencies have been accounted for; for example, a high PS→AG score means that Agree responses occur with PS at a much greater frequency than the unconditional probability for Agree would indicate.

TABLE 13.3. Within-Process-Measure Correlations (Pearson's r)

	VRS			Baserate MICS			z scores		
	1	2	3	4	5	6	7	8	9
1. Help. %	—								
2. Unhelp. %	$-.81$	—							
3. Neutral %	$-.42$	—	—						
4. MICS +	.57	$-.42$	—	—					
5. MICS PS	—	—	—	—					
6. MICS −	—	—	—	$-.59$	—	—			
7. PS→AG	—	—	—	—	.46	—	—		
8. PS→CR	—	—	—	—	—	—	.39		
9. PS→PS	$-.42$	.62	—	—	—	—	—	—	—

$r = .39$, $p < .05$; $r = .50$, $p < .01$

TABLE 13.4. Within-Outcome-Measure Correlations (Pearson's *r*)

	IRS		Outside		
	1	2	3	4	5
Subjective					
1. Satisfaction	—	.75	.46	.52	.45
2. Progress		—	.77	.55	.64
Objective					
3. Outcome			—	.55	.77
4. Satisfaction				—	.79
5. Progress					—

$r = .39$, $p < .05$; $r = .50$, $p < .01$

Note. Subjective = IRS ratings; Objective = observer outcome ratings.

Outcome. The results for the outcome measures are presented in Table 13.4, where it can be seen that generally there is better agreement within modalities than between; that is, subjects' ratings were more similar on the two outcome measures than they were between subjects and outsiders. Outsiders tended to rate progress, outcome, and satisfaction more alike than they did satisfaction and outcome. Satisfaction was less similar to number of solutions (for the outsiders) than it was to their estimate of the amount of progress made; they were weighting process more than product in estimating outcome and satisfaction of the couples.

Again, the comparisons between the two sources, couples and outsiders, are noteworthy. That which couples called progress, outsiders also rated as outcome and progress; agreement on these two variables between the two sources was quite high. The agreement on satisfaction ($r = .52$) was higher than agreement on outcome or progress. Overall, these correlations suggest a moderate amount of overlap between couples and observers on the outcome measures. While noting the greater magnitude of within-modality *r* values, those for between-modality correlations were not unimpressive, suggesting overlap in perceptions at this level.

BETWEEN-PANEL ANALYSES

The format used to present results on how well the variables from one panel predict the scores in each of the other panels is a series of multiple regression tables showing the relative contribution of the various sets of variables. Because of the large number of correlation coefficients involved, we have greatly simplified the tables to highlight only major relationships. Only statistically significant models are shown in the tables in this section.

Context-to-Process Comparisons. To what extent do context variables account for variance in process variables? Do context scores constrain the kinds of values we obtain on process measures? (Comparisons within and between methods are highlighted by the design of the tables; major quadrants of the tables display self-report to self-report measures, while others display self-report to objective measures. These mono- and heteromethod distinctions are noted in evaluating the data.)

The box scores for the methods were as follows: Four out of four of the regression models comparing self-report measures were significant, whereas only 3 of 12 heteromethod models reached statistical significance, as can be seen from Table 13.5.

Looking first at sentiment variables as predictors of process, we note that substantially more of the negative impact variance ($-$ % VRS) than positive impact variance ($+$ % VRS) was accounted for by the regression model that used sentiment measures as predictors (54% vs. 39%, respectively). The situation was reversed for the efficacy variables: The efficacy variable model accounted for 44% of positive and only 33% of negative impact variance. Problem severity did not enter the model as a variable predictive of negative impact variance. Inspection of the zero-order *r* values associated with these variables indicates that the efficacy scale was the major factor in these predictions.

TABLE 13.5. Context Variables as Predictors of Process Variables (Summarized Multiple Regression Models)

	Process							
	+ Impact		− Impact		MICS +		PS→AG	
Context	R^2	r	R^2	r	R^2	r	R^2	r
DAS	36	.61	37	− .61	29	.54	26	− .51
MSI	38	− .32	48	.17	30	− .44	27	.41
L-L	39	.26	54	− .35				
	39%		54%		30%		27%	
Efficacy	42	.65	24	− .49	41	.64		
Severity[a]	44	− .01			59	− .56		
Outcome	44	.10	33	.04	60	.30		
	44%		33%		60%			

Note. F for all models significant at $p < .05$. Only models with significant predictors are shown.
[a]Variable not significant in all models.

Couples' ratings of their interactional process, in a conflict resolution task, are expressed in behaviors that can be coded by outsiders. It was also noted above that couples and coders overlapped in their assignment of positive ratings ($r = .57$, or 32% of the variance). One estimate, then, would be that approximately one-third of the process is used by couples as their behavioral ("true skill") data base for judging positive behaviors. Negative behaviors, as noted before, may have a more idiosyncratic meaning for couples and are not as readily available to coders.

But the situation for the expectancy variables was quite straightforward. Couples who have high expectations of favorable outcomes emit behaviors that are coded as MICS Positive. (This is true only for baserate MICS Positive measures.) The model using all of the expectation variables accounted for 60% of the MICS Positive variance. It appears from examination of the actual codes that make up the MICS Positive variable that nonverbal positive behaviors are related to positive expectations. Nonverbal behaviors are least susceptible to instructional manipulation to fake good or bad (Vincent, Friedman, Nugent, & Messerly, 1979). Problem severity was also an important factor in the model predicting MICS Positive ($r = -.56$), relating to how the couple interacts affectively, but not for actual PS behaviors. Severity is an important factor in the prediction model ($r = -.56$) of MICS Positive, but not for actual PS behaviors.

As already suggested, the context variables did not predict variance in the sequential MICS scores. The model presented in Table 13.5 indicates that sentiment variables (DAS and MSI) were negatively related to PS→AG sequences, which was also noted before as a discrepancy in meaning between insiders and outsiders for PS→AG sequences.

Process-to-Outcome Comparisons. The major findings for the two sets of process variable predictors (subjective and objective) of the two sets of outcome variables are presented in Table 13.6.

The subjective impact ratings (VRS % scores) accounted for 59% of the variance in subjective satisfaction and approximately 33% of the variance in subjective rating of outcome. Between methods, these same subjective impact ratings were predictive only of the objective rating of satisfaction, accounting for 48% of the variance. There was a noteworthy degree of overlap in what the couples and raters saw in satisfaction ratings.

The three MICS baserate scores predicted quite well in both modalities; their prediction models accounted for 42% to 55% of the variance in objective outcome ratings. The within-method models yield box scores of 2 for 2 and 3 for 3.

MICS baserate models did a fair job of predicting subjective outcome ratings (a far less obvious result), accounting for 46% and 63% of the variance in subjective satisfaction and outcome ratings, respectively. The MICS predicted reasonably well what couples said about their interaction. When com-

TABLE 13.6. Process Variables as Predictors of Outcome Variables (Summarized Multiple Regression Models)

Process	Outcome									
	Subjective				Objective					
	Satisfaction		Outcome		Satisfaction		Outcome		Progress	
	R^2	r	R^2	r	R^2	r	R^2	r	R^2	r
− Impact	58	−.76	30	−.55	42	−.65				
+ Impact	59	.68	32	.51	48	.52				
	59%		32%		48%					
MICS +	33	.58	41	.64	38	.62	41	.64	36	.60
MICS PS	46	.47	63	.59	42[a]	.23	55	.49	41	.33
MICS −	46	−.33	63	−.35	40[a]	−.48	55	−.22	43	−.45
	46%		63%		42%		55%		43%	
PS→PS							12	−.35		
PS→CP							27	.30		
PS→AG							27%			

Note. F for all models significant at $p < .05$. Only models with significant predictors are shown.
[a]Variable associated with lower R^2 entered before next higher R^2.

245

pared to the couples' own process ratings as predictors of their own outcome ratings (the 59% and 32% noted above), the MICS does a much better job of matching what the couples said about their progress (but not satisfaction) than the couples' own process judgments. (Possible reasons for the superiority of the MICS baserate scores over couple impact ratings are considered later.)

The results for the sequential MICS measures were essentially negative; in a marginally significant model, PS→PS and PS→CP predicted a small amount (27%) of the variance in objectively rated outcome variance.

Box scores for the heteromethod comparisons were: 1 out of 3 for subjective impact to objective outcome, and 2 out of 4 objective process predicting subjective outcome.

Context Variables as Predictors of Outcome. The last set of panel comparisons is presented in Table 13.7. How well do conceptually preexisting variables, sentiment and efficacy, predict to outcome ratings? Obviously, if outcome is highly constrained by these front-end variables, there would be little point in looking further for the contribution of process variables.

Somewhat more than one-third (40% and 38%) of subjective outcome measures were accounted for by satisfaction context measures. As much as 55% of outsider ratings of satisfaction is predicted by the context sentiment variables. This suggests that marital distress status is communicated to raters independently of the highly molecular (e.g., MICS) encoding system used with the interactions. Once again the pattern for sentiment and efficacy variables was reversed: The prediction model using efficacy variables predicted slightly better to objective outcome ratings than to subjective outcome ratings.

Discussion

One of the purposes of this correlational study was to provide data relevant to the proposed model. Specifically, we wished to determine the relative effects of context on process and outcome, bearing in mind that self-report correlations tend to be high because of common method variance. Therefore, we added the additional feature of outside process and outcome measures, making possible comparisons between methods of observation.

We found that sentiment and expectancy variables accounted for more than one-third of the variance in subjective impact (process) measures. To that extent, couples "saw" what they expected to see. These same predictor variables (sentiment and expectancy) differentially accounted for variance in two of the objective process measures: approximately 30% of variance in sentiment and 60% for expectancy. It would seem from this that couples who expect to work well together and to feel understood and so forth, emit behaviors that are coded positively in our system. The specific behaviors in the MICS Positive category are largely nonverbal positive affective behaviors, and as already noted, they are least responsive to direct manipulation (Vincent

TABLE 13.7. Context Variables as Predictors of Outcome Variables (Summarized Multiple Regression Models)

	Outcome									
	Subjective				Objective					
	Satisfaction		Outcome		Satisfaction		Outcome		Progress	
Context	R^2	r	R^2	r	R^2	r	R^2	r	R^2	r
DAS	39	.62	30	.55	38	.62				
L-L	40	.10	38	−.10	55[a]	.33				
MSI	40	−.39			50[a]	−.16				
	40%		38%		55%					
Efficacy			39[a]	.42	24	.49	40[a]		28	.53
Severity			33[a]	−.42			25[a]	−.46	38	−.43
Outcome			21[a]	.45				.50	44	.38
			39%				40%		44%	

Note. F for all models significant at $p < .05$. Only models with significant predictors are shown.
[a]Variable associated with lower R^2 entered before next higher R^2.

247

et al., 1979). Even more noteworthy is the fact that self-reporting on one occasion predicted to interactional behaviors on another occasion.

But the analysis is further complicated by the fact, also noted earlier, that "seeing" what one expects to "see" is confounded by what there is to be seen! If satisfied couples are more skilled when they interact, outside coders read this, but so do the couples; that is, they, too, may "see" this skillfulness. The correlations between efficacy and MICS Positive scores are affected by uncontrolled variations in marital satisfaction (DAS) scores. Differences in satisfaction scores can be held constant statistically by use of partial correlation techniques. When we look at the relationship between efficacy and MICS Positive scores, holding constant the DAS scores, the partial $r = .48$ ($p < .05$), whereas when we look at the relationship of DAS to MICS Positive, holding efficacy constant, the resulting partial $r = .26$ ($p > .05$). From this we conclude that the expectation of future understanding in a discussion accounts for behaviors independently of the couple's satisfaction level. When we control for level of marital satisfaction, expectancy still predicts to process.

Before turning to the overlap in subjective and objective perceptions, namely the process comparisons, consider an interesting issue that figured largely in the study by Koren, Carlton, and Shaw (1980), namely that the context sentiment variable (here, the DAS; the L-W in their study) accounted for 32% of the variance in outcome ratings made by couples. "These findings suggested that the distress measure alone was sufficient to predict couples' satisfaction with conflict outcomes" (p. 465). The present results are consistent with this finding: Sentiment accounted for 38% and 40% of variance, respectively, in subjective outcome and satisfaction measures. Our interpretation of these findings differs from that offered by Koren *et al.,* (1980), since in that study they did not make crucial comparisons both within and between methods. Thus sentiment and self-report outcome variance do have common elements, since the same evaluative process may be involved in both methods. When these authors sought the unique contribution of marital distress in predicting objective outcome ratings, there was only an 8% net gain in variance accounted for beyond that already accounted for by behavioral measures; the zero-order r between distress and objective measures was $-.56$, accounting for 26% of outcome variance. Our outside observers (who, like Koren *et al.,* were also coders) seemed to be responding more accurately to couples' distress status, since their ratings of outcome satisfaction accounted for 55% of DAS scores and a range of 40% (outcome) to 44% (progress) using expectancy variables as predictors. It would seem that Koren *et al.*'s (1980) conclusion about the significant role of context variables must be viewed in a broader context than we believe they intended: Marital distress and expectancies about interactional outcomes predict to both methods of measuring outcome variables, but we found a slight edge for predictions to the objective (between-method) predictions.

The case for couples' displaying behaviors that outside observers read can be made even more strongly when context-to-outcome effects are demonstrated between different methods, that is, when capitalizing on method variance. How the couples describe themselves overlaps with how the outside raters rate the couples' performances. Caution demands, however, that we limit this conclusion to trained undergraduate coders. In the Royce and Weiss (1975) study, untrained undergraduate observers were used, and their "hit rate" (correct identification of marital distress) was not much greater than 50% correct, although it was significantly different from chance. Of considerable interest would be the judgments of couples as outside raters, that is, whether married judges can read context measures of distress from interactional behaviors. Some of the perception studies by Gottman and Porterfield (1981) and Noller (1980) are germane to this point.

The process-to-outcome results indicated an interesting interaction pattern: The two subjective outcome ratings, satisfaction and progress, were predicted differently by the subjective and objective process measures. Impact predicted subjective outcome satisfaction (59% of the variance), whereas MICS baserate measures predicted to subjective outcome (progress) 63% of the variance. Similarly, impact accounted for 32% of outcome, and MICS baserate accounted for 46% of satisfaction variance. Couples' judgments of satisfaction and progress seemed to be based upon different data sets: In the former instance, impact predicting to satisfaction, subjective variables shared common variance, whereas when the judgment was about progress made, the MICS data shared common variance with the couples' judgments. In this sense, the MICS did a better job of accounting for couples' judgments than their own subjective process ratings did.

Some Methodological Cautions

An apparent curiosity of the present study was the decision to have couples make impact ratings in a session held 2 weeks after participating in the first interaction (and 1 week after the second), while the outcome ratings were made immediately after each interaction.

The aim was to provide couples the same context for viewing the taped interactions as that provided to the objective coders. Coders rate the ongoing videotaped interaction at a time after it was made, and so we wanted the couples to make their ratings in a similar way. We intentionally sought to separate participation and observation; the former was the basis for the outcome ratings, and the latter was the basis for the impact ratings. An alternative to the impact ratings would be along the lines of Gottman's (1979) procedure that requires subjects to rate the impact on-line. This procedure would confound participation and observation, and thus make the results less comparable to outside coding.

The impact coding system used here certainly put undue demands on couples. Each spouse was told to view the other, not the self, and developing the appropriate hand–eye coordination is difficult even with practice given beforehand. Nor is it clear from our study whether subjective impact ratings would predict better to subjective outcome ratings, had the two measures been obtained on the same occasion.

Implications

Our aim was to provide initial data on a heuristic approach to couples' perceptions of their own behaviors and how these perceptions map onto those of outside observers. The subjective–objective interface requires much further analysis. One implication is that subject-defined units may not agree with laboratory-defined units. In this way our indices of agreement between sources may always be lower than would be the case if we were able to use more naturalistic units (i.e., those chunks used by couples). Thus, negative behavior was not found to map well onto coders' judgments. Couples are limited by the situation itself in the ways that they may express themselves; that is, they do not walk out of the room or yell as they might at home. They are forced by the situation to rely on more subtle cues of intended meaning. The coded positives may be the easier responses, in the sense that anyone would see them, and for this reason (popularity) they may be less informative. Further exploration of idiosyncratic meaning is needed.

Clearly, one implication of our findings is that expectancies play an important role in behavior, and we need to zero in on these occurrences. Given the caveats about what the MICS actually encodes, there is good reason to conclude that expectancies do predict to interactional behavior and not just self-report. This study helps ground the scientific merit of these variables.

The separation of progress and satisfaction should be maintained in future work; couples as well as outsiders do keep these separate. These results lend further support to Gottman's (1979) distinction between content and affect codes. Future work should focus more clearly on rated progress and rated satisfaction as separate entities of the process as well as outcome.

Finally, the study supports the notion of sentiment override. We know such a phenomenon exists, but we need to define more precise methods for measuring it. More than one-third of the variance in context measures of sentiment do predict to subjects' outcome ratings, but more than one-half of the variance in outcome raters' judgments of satisfaction with an interaction is predicted from couples' context sentiment scores. We have known that distressed and nondistressed couples behave differently in terms of coded measures like the MICS, but it is interesting to see that outsiders can globally read interactional behavior quite well. Perhaps we need to turn to outside observers to understand the cues they are using, similar to the approach taken by Royce and Weiss (1975). The present results may be distorted by our use of trained MICS coders; that is, we do not know how much the training added to their global accuracy.

The model proposed here offers a workable approach to couples' and outsiders' perceptions of interactional behavior. The interface between these two sources is what defines idiosyncratic perception, which in turn is what makes a relationship unique. Surely romance will be able to withstand the scrutiny of these harsh objective measures!

ACKNOWLEDGMENTS

The work presented here was based on the joint effort of the author and his graduate students, notably Gary B. Wieder, Kendra Summers, and David Wasserman. Some of the assessment devices are described more fully in Wieder's dissertation (1982). A special note of thanks to Kendra Summers and Darien Fenn for their generous help in programming and data analyses.

REFERENCES

Bem, D. An experimental analysis of self-persuasion. *Journal of Experimental Social Psychology,* 1965, *1,* 199–218.

Gottman, J. M. *Marital interaction: Experimental investigations.* New York: Academic Press, 1979.

Gottman, J. M., & Porterfield, A. L. Communicative competence in the nonverbal behavior of married couple. *Journal of Marriage and the Family,* 1981, *43,* 817–824.

Hops, H., Wills, T. A., Patterson, G. R., & Weiss, R. L. *Marital Interaction Coding System.* Eugene: University of Oregon, Oregon Research Institute, 1972.

Jacobson, N. S., Elwood, R. W., & Dallas, M. Assessment of marital dysfunction. In D. H. Barlow (Ed.), *Behavioral assessment of adult disorders.* New York: Guilford Press, 1981.

Koren, P., Carlton, K., & Shaw, D. Marital conflict: Relations among behaviors, outcomes, and distress. *Journal of Consulting and Clinical Psychology,* 1980, *48,* 460–468.

Locke, H., & Wallace, K. Short marital adjustment and prediction tests: Their reliability and validity. *Marriage and Family Living,* 1959, *21,* 251–255.

Noller, P. Misunderstandings in marital communication: A study of couples' nonverbal communication. *Journal of Personality and Social Psychology,* 1980, *39,* 1135–1148.

Notarius, C. I., Vanzetti, N. A., & Smith, R. J. *Assessing expectations and outcomes in marital interaction.* Paper presented at the meeting of the Association for Advancement of Behavior Therapy, Toronto, November 1981.

Royce, W. S., & Weiss, R. L. Behavioral cues in the judgment of marital satisfaction: A linear regression analysis. *Journal of Consulting and Clinical Psychology,* 1975, *43,* 816–824.

Rubin, Z. Measurement of romantic love. *Journal of Personality and Social Psychology,* 1970, *16,* 263–273

Spanier, G. B. Measuring dyadic adjustment: New scales for assessing the quality of marriage and similar dyads. *Journal of Marriage and the Family,* 1976, *38,* 15–28.

Schachter, S., & Singer, J. E. Cognitive, social and physiological determinants of emotional state. *Psychological Review,* 1962, *65,* 379–399.

Vincent, J. P., Friedman, L. C., Nugent, J., & Messerly, L. Demand characteristics in observations of marital interaction. *Journal of Consulting and Clinical Psychology,* 1979, *47,* 557–566.

Weiss, R. L. Strategic behavioral marital therapy: Toward a model for assessment and intervention. In J. P. Vincent (Ed.), *Advances in family intervention* (Vol. 1). Greenwich, CT: JAI Press, 1980.

Weiss, R. L., & Cerreto, M. C. The Marital Status Inventory: Development of a measure of dissolution potential. *American Journal of Family Therapy,* 1980, *8,* 80–85.

Wieder, G. B. *Toward an empirically-based model of marital conflict resolution.* Unpublished doctoral dissertation, University of Oregon, 1982.

Wieder, G. B., & Weiss, R. L. Generalizability theory and the coding of marital interactions. *Journal of Consulting and Clinical Psychology,* 1980, *48,* 469–477.

14

The Longitudinal Study of Couples' Interactions: Implications for Understanding and Predicting the Development of Marital Distress

HOWARD J. MARKMAN

Introduction

Interest in research on the factors predictive of marital satisfaction and stability dates back to the earliest sociological studies on marital and family relations (Burgess & Cottrell, 1939; Terman, 1938). Part of the fascination with this topic stemmed from the 20th-century Western cultural tradition of free choice in mate selection and the attendant importance of marital satisfaction as the ultimate criterion of evaluating the success or failure of one's choice. More recently, rising divorce rates in Western societies have focused attention on the factors associated with marital distress and success.

Two distinct research traditions have contributed to our knowledge of predictors of marital satisfaction and stability: (1) the sociological tradition that uses large-scale survey methods to examine characteristics of husbands and wives associated with current or future marital adjustment (e.g., Bentler & Newcomb, 1978), and (2) the mate-selection tradition that uses questionnaires to examine amount and type of husband–wife similarity associated with future relationship stability (e.g., Levinger, Senn, & Jorgensen, 1970; Lewis, 1972, 1973).

Taken together, the results of studies representing these two traditions indicate that marital distress and stability can be predicted from measures taken before or in the early stages of marriage (see Markman, Floyd, & Dickson-Markman, 1982, for a review). However, the results of these studies have had little implication for understanding the development of marital problems and for developing intervention programs to help couples. The reason for this is

Howard J. Markman. Department of Psychology, University of Denver, Denver, Colorado, U.S.A.

that studies have not been designed to test conceptions of the development of marital distress and have focused upon dimensions of relationships (e.g., demographic characteristics) that are difficult to modify in intervention programs. It is not surprising that the number of prediction studies in these traditions has dwindled in the past decade, given the time and expense of conducting longitudinal research. The major objectives of this chapter are: (1) to present a way of thinking about prediction research with couples based on current conceptual models for understanding close relationships, and (2) to discuss some research relevant to the goals of predicting and understanding marital distress. In addition, several issues in prediction research are addressed, and future directions for research are reviewed. These include: (1) risk and prevention, (2) prediction research as premarital intervention, (3) demand characteristics and longitudinal research, and (4) understanding the social ecology of marriage.

Prediction and Development

The primary objective of prediction research with couples is to study relationship development in order to provide information on the prediction and understanding of the problems we would like to treat and prevent. For the purposes of the present chapter, prediction research with couples is best considered as a systematic study of change in couples' relationships. From this perspective, one major objective of prediction research is to increase our understanding of the normal developmental changes in couples. Two research traditions have shed light on developmental changes in couples' relationships: the longitudinal approach and the cross-sectional approach. The cross-sectional approach compares the associates of "normal" (i.e., a happy marriage) and "abnormal" (an unhappy marriage) development. There are three general types of cross-sectional investigations: (1) studies using objective observers (e.g., Billings, 1979; Birchler, Weiss, & Vincent, 1975; Gottman, Markman, & Notarius, 1977), (2) studies using couples as observers in laboratory settings (e.g., Gottman, Notarius, Markman, Yoppi, Bank, & Rubin, 1976), and (3) studies using couples as observers in home settings (e.g., Wills, Weiss, & Patterson, 1974) (see Schaap, Chapter 9, this volume, for a review of these studies). The longitudinal approach follows premarital couples over time in order to identify the developmental antecedents of distressed and nondistressed relationships.

A second major objective of prediction research is to increase our understanding of the role of external variables in normal and abnormal development. Many explanations of the currently high divorce rates suggest that societal changes (e.g., women working, economic stress) are at the root of marital distress. There are obviously many approaches to capturing environmental or situational factors. For couples, perhaps the best approach is to consider the effects of passage through normal family transition periods (e.g., planning marriage, birth of first child). In these stages, couples are faced with new demands that call for the modification or acquisition of coping skills to master the demands. Perhaps the best point in time to assess relationships in terms of predictive goals is at transition periods. This chapter discusses the results of studies that have examined the longitudinal relationship between couples' interaction during the transition-to-marriage period and couples' future satisfaction and stability.

To summarize at this point, one main objective of prediction research is to provide information concerning the etiology of marital distress. In other words, we are not interested in prediction for its own sake; we are interested in prediction in the service of understanding and explaining. A second objective is to apply this information in prevention programs that intervene in relationship development to increase couples' chances of developing successful relationships. Specifically, prediction research should identify both the coping skills and external stressors, relevant to all couples and families, as they progress through the normal stages of family development. Ideally, the products of research should be translated into components of primary prevention programs for couples and families. We have developed a research model that makes progress toward achieving these goals. This model fits prediction research into the context of a larger research program on the treatment and prevention of marital and family distress.

Behavioral-Competency Model

Consistent with Goldfried and D'Zurilla's (1969) behavioral-competency approach to assessment, the model involves assessing the behavior of groups independently identified as either competent or incompetent in specific situations. Comparisons of behavioral characteristics of population members who have developed disordered behaviors with those who have not, generate variables that may discriminate between the social skills of the two groups. Once variables that have discriminative validity are identified using cross-sectional studies, longitudinal studies can assess questions relevant to predictive validity. For example, do these variables (e.g., social skills) predict positive outcomes later in development? To the extent that longitudinal studies identify variables that have predictive power, the variables can then be used as behaviors to be modified in preventive intervention programs. Note that the focus of study is on behavioral or cognitive indices of future dysfunction, which can be modified in subsequent interventions — unlike personality or demographic indices, which may be good predictors but are not easily modifiable in interventions. Thus, ideally, prediction research has direct implications for both a theory of marital and family distress and for prevention (see Markman, Floyd, & Dickson-Markman, 1982, for further details). This model provides a structure for a research program; however, a theoretical framework is needed to guide the questions to be asked by researchers.

The theoretical focus of this volume, and of current conceptions of close relationships, is on couples' interaction in general and on communication in particular. The next section of this chapter presents an integration of social exchange and communication theories that focus on perceptual and behavioral characteristics of couples' interactions as predictors of current and future relationship stability and satisfaction.

A Social Exchange/Communication Model of Marital Distress

During the past few years my colleagues and I have conducted a series of studies designed to increase our understanding of marital distress (e.g., Gottman, Notarius, Gonso, & Markman, 1976; Markman, 1979, 1981). We have drawn on social exchange theory (e.g., Kelley & Thibaut, 1978; Thibaut & Kelley, 1959) to develop a framework linking a model of good communication and problem solving with a developmental model of marital distress. "Good communication" is defined as occurring when the speaker's intended message during problem-solving discussions matches the impact on the listener. Based on this model, it is predicted that two factors—(1) The exchange of messages with positive impacts and (2) perceptual accuracy (i.e., intent = impact)— are associated with developing and maintaining a happy relationship. The emphasis on perception of communication, rather than on the content of communication (e.g., behavioral communication skills), is consistent with social exchange theory (Kelley & Thibaut, 1978; Thibaut & Kelley, 1959) and current conceptions of social skills (Trower, 1979). The use of communication skills (as measured by behavioral observation systems, e.g., Marital Interaction Coding System—MICS; Couples Interaction Scoring System—CISS) is assumed to underlie perceptual accuracy and positive impact; however, the behavioral observation literature is not considered in the present chapter (the interested reader is referred to Markman, Notarius, Stephen, & Smith, 1981; and Schaap, Chapter 9, this volume, for a review). We should note, however, that no published studies have yet examined the predictive validity of communication skills (we are currently analyzing data from a longitudinal study that examines the predictive validity of communication skills). The following sections describe a series of studies designed to test the predictions presented above.

Cross-Sectional Studies

Consistent with the behavioral-competency research model described earlier, we first conducted a series of cross-sectional studies to assess how well the intent and impact variables discriminated distressed from nondistressed couples (Gottman, Notarius, Markman, Yoppi, Bank, & Rubin, 1976). Intent and impact were defined by having couples rate their own problem-solving interactions using a device called the "talk table." The talk table was a double-sloping box equipped with a toggle switch and two rows of buttons on each side. Couples sat at opposite sides of the talk table and were instructed that the toggle switch must be facing the side of the person who had the floor to speak. A light, controlled by the toggle switch and facing the speaker, indicated who had the floor. A row of five buttons on the person's left was used to rate the intended impact of the message by the speaker ("intent"), and a row of five buttons on the right was used to rate the actual impact of the message by the listener ("impact"). The five buttons were labeled "supernegative," "negative," "neutral," "positive," and "superpositive." The procedure for using the talk table was: (1) One person spoke; (2) the speaker then rated the intent of the statement using the five buttons; (3) the listener, before speaking, rated the impact of the statement on the buttons; (4) the listener then spoke, and the rating process continued throughout the interaction. The couples could not see each other's ratings. The impact ratings are a measure of the perceived positivity of the interaction from the listener's perspective; the intent ratings, a measure of intended positivity from the speaker's perspective.

The couples completed several interaction tasks including a discussion of their top problem area and vignettes from Olson and Ryder's (1970) Inventory of Marital Conflicts (IMC). The results indicated that distressed couples rated the impact of each other's behaviors (impact ratings) significantly less positively than nondistressed couples. There were no differences in intent ratings; all couples rated their intentions as highly positive. We hypothesized that distressed couples were less accurate in communication than nondistressed couples since the speakers' intent ratings were not consistent with the listeners' impact ratings, whereas this seemed to be the case with nondistressed couples. However, intent–impact comparisons were based on overall ratings rather than on point-by-point comparisons. Nevertheless, this study established the link between couples' coding of their own behaviors and marital distress.

Subsequent studies using similar procedures in different research laboratories (Floyd & Markman, 1983), including studies with Black couples (Markman & Baccus, 1982) and deaf couples (Ferraro & Markman, 1981), have established the reliability and generalizability of the positive impact results. In all of these studies, nondistressed couples had significantly higher impact ratings than their distressed counterparts. However, these studies did not test hypotheses concerning the etiology of marital distress, since interaction was measured after the development of marital discord.

Prediction Studies

One of the major goals of prediction research with couples is to demonstrate that couples' premarital interaction is predictive of future outcomes. Specifically, previous research suggested that developing a satisfying exchange pattern (as measured by impact ratings) before marriage is predictive of future marital satisfaction. Longitudinal studies, starting before marital distress develops, are clearly needed to test this and other etiological hypotheses. As noted by Huston and Levinger (1978), "Few studies have examined on-going relationships at more than one point in time; there has been very little sound longitudinal research [due to] . . . its heavy cost and lengthy time commitment . . . " (p. 133).

The next step in our research program was to conduct a longitudinal study designed to provide a test of the assertion that negative communication patterns, measured by intent and impact ratings, preceded the development of marital distress (Markman, 1979, 1981). There were four stages in the design of this study: initial interview and laboratory sessions (Time 1), 1-year follow-up (Time 2), 2.5-year follow-up (Time 3), and 5.5-year follow-up (Time 4). In addition to intent and impact ratings, the major predictor variables assessed at Time 1 were problem intensity and relationship satisfaction. The major outome variables, assessed at Times 2, 3, and 4, were the couples' relationship satisfaction as measured by the Marital Relationship Inventory (MRI) (Locke & Williamson, 1958) and relationship status. The MRI overlaps completely with the more commonly used Marital Adjustment Test (MAT) (Locke & Wallace, 1959), but it contains additional questions concerning sexual adjustment. Correlations between the MAT and MRI exceed .80.

Briefly, the procedure involved the couples completing five tasks that required problem-solving discussions and rating their interaction using the talk table. The tasks were selected to sample across high- and low-conflict situations. High-conflict tasks required discussion of emotionally engaging issues (e.g., the couple's major problem area), while low-conflict tasks required discussion of less emotional and less personal issues (e.g., the IMC; Olson & Ryder, 1970).

Couples were invited back to the laboratory 1 year (Time 2) and 2.5 years (Time 3) later to complete a similar session. Those who could not return completed measures of relationship status and relationship satisfaction by mail. At Time 4, 5.5 years later, all intact couples were contacted by mail and asked to complete the two outcome measures. Since the major goal of the study was to provide information on the same set of couples over time, the Time 2 and Time 3 results were based on data from the 14 intact couples who provided Time 1 interaction data and both Time 2 and Time 3 relationship satisfaction scores. The Time 4 results were based on nine intact couples who provided data at all four points in time.

MAJOR FINDINGS

For purposes of data analysis of the communication ratings, the five impact categories were considered as a 5-point Likert scale ranging from 1 (supernegative) to 5 (superpositive). In our earlier studies we found no conflict effect (i.e., personal problem discussion vs. impersonal problem discussion) for young married couples, and therefore the couples' impact ratings were combined across the tasks for analysis. The Time 2 results, summarized in Table 14.1, revealed significant correlations between Time 1 problem intensity and Time 2 relationship satisfaction, $r = -.47, p < .05$, and between Time 1 relationship satisfaction and Time 2 relationship satisfaction, $r = .82, p < .01$ (Markman, 1979). All significance tests were two-tailed tests.

The lower the couples' problem intensity and the higher their relationship satisfaction at Time 1, the more satisfied they were at Time 2. In contrast, there was virtually no association between Time 1 impact ratings and Time 2 relationship satisfaction, $r = .06$. This was consistent with the Time 1 (cross-sectional) results, which showed no correlation between relationship satisfaction and impact rating, $r = .06$. Taken together, the Time 2 results support what have been called the faulty mate-selection hypotheses: Dissatisfaction at Time 2 seems to be related to a continuation of Time 1 problems and relationship dissatisfaction.

In contrast to the Time 2 results, the Time 3 results revealed a nonsignificant correlation between problem intensity at Time 1 and relationship sat-

TABLE 14.1. Pearson Product–Moment Correlations between Time 1 Predictor Variables and Relationship Adjustment at Times 2, 3, and 4

| | Time | | |
Predictor variable	2	3	4
Impact ratings	.06	.67**	.59*
Problem intensity	-.47*	-.27	-.10
Relationship adjustment (MRI)[a]	.82**	-.02	-.18

Note. From H. J. Markman, The prediction of marital distress: A five-year follow-up. *Journal of Consulting and Clinical Psychology*, 1981, *49*, 760–762. Copyright 1981 by the American Psychological Association.
[a]MRI = Marital Relationship Inventory.
*$p < .05$.
**$p < .01$.

isfaction at Time 3, $r = -.27$, and virtually no correlation between Time 1 and Time 3 relationship satisfaction, $r = .02$ (Markman, 1979). Thus, the significant Time 2 correlations between the problem intensity and relationship satisfaction predictors and the relationship satisfaction criterion did hold up at Time 3.

However, in support of the predictions, there was a highly significant correlation between impact ratings at Time 1 and relationship satisfaction at Time 3, $r = .67$, $p < .01$. The more positively the couples rated their exchanges at Time 1, the more satisfied they were with their relationships 2.5 years later, at Time 3. Thus, the results provide evidence that negative communication, as measured by impact ratings, precedes the development of relationship dissatisfaction.

The 5.5-year follow-up results (Time 4) revealed a significant correlation between Time 1 impact ratings and Time 4 relationship satisfaction, $r = .59$, $p < .05$ (Markman, 1981). The more positively the couples rated their premarital interaction, the more satisfied they were 5.5 years later. In contrast, as seen in Table 1, the Time 1 problem intensity and relationship satisfaction scores had no predictive validity. Thus, the predictive relationships seen at the 2.5-year follow-up were found again 3 years later.

The stability of these predictive relationships suggests that communication patterns (as measured by impact ratings) remain stable over time. To provide a preliminary test of this hypothesis, an evaluation of the stability of impact over time was conducted. An estimate of the consistency of impact ratings over time was obtained from the couples who completed the interaction sessions at Times 1, 2, and 3. The results indicated that the correlations of impact ratings over time are generally consistent: r T1, T2 $= .39$, $p < .10$, $n = 12$; r T1, T3 $= .78$, $p < .05$, $n = 6$; r T2, T3 $= .82$, $p < .05$, $n = 6$ (Markman, 1981). These results provide evidence for the stability of communication patterns, as measured by the talk table, over time. The results also indicate that there is greater stability later in relationships. This suggests that once interaction patterns are established, they are resistant to change, a familiar observation among marital therapists and distressed couples. This finding is consistent with the results of the only other longitudinal study of couples' interaction (Raush, Barry, Hertel, & Swain, 1974), which also documented the consistency of couples' communication patterns.

PREDICTING BREAKUP

The study also examined predictions of relationship breakup. Descriptively, the "fate" of the 26 couples at time 4 was: 18 (69%) married, 4 (15%) broken up prior to marriage, 3 (12%) divorced, and 1 (4%) separated. The best predictor of future breakup was the couple's confidence that they would get married. The second best predictor was a measure of power derived from the IMC task. The lower the couples' confidence that they would in fact marry and the less give and take in discussions, the more likely the couples were to break up at both Time 2 and Time 3. These results are consistent with W. Mischel's (1972, 1977) claim that simply asking people about future behavior is an excellent source of information. Further, the results indicate that different factors are associated with relationship stability as opposed to relationship satisfaction. This suggests that both breakup and satisfaction should be used as criteria to evaluate relationship outcomes in future studies.

Additional Predictors of Time 4 Relationship Satisfaction

The results also indicated that other measures of communication derived from the talk table at Time 1 are predictive of relationship satisfaction. These data are reported here for the first time.

INTENT

The reader will recall that "intent" is a measure of how positive the speakers intended their messages to be. For the male intent variable (summed across the five tasks), there was no significant relationship with Time 1, $r = -.27$, or Time 2, $r = .29$, couple relationship satisfaction. However, there was a significant relationship with Time 3 relationship satisfaction, $r = .55, p < .01$. At Time 4 the relationship was still positive, but no longer significant, $r = .39$. For the female intent variable, the patterns were the same — Time 1, $r = -.13$; Time 2, $r = -.38, p < .07$; Time 3, $r = .38, p < .07$; Time 4, $r = -.23$ — but the Time 3 correlation failed to reach the .05 level. It is interesting to note that at Times 1 and 2, the female intent ratings were unexpectedly negatively correlated with relationship satisfaction. The Time 3 results were surprising, since intent ratings did not discriminate between distressed and nondistressed couples in an earlier study (Gottman, Notarius, Markman, Yoppi, Bank, & Rubin, 1976). The clearest interpretation of these data is that the more positive the males intended their communication to be at Time 1, the more satisfied the couple was at Time 3 (2.5 years later). This same pattern holds at Time 4 but is not as strong.

The predictive power of intent ratings considered in terms of the relative frequency of each button press (superpositive, positive, negative, supernegative) was also examined. The findings were dramatic. The best predictors of Time 3 relationship satisfaction were the relative frequency of male negative intent, $r = -.73, p < .001$, and female negative intent, $r = -.62, p < .005$. Using the negative buttons at Time 1, when rating intent, was the single best predictor of Time 3 relationship satisfaction. This finding also held for impact ratings, although the correlations were not as high: males, $r = -.37$, $p < .08$; females, $r = -.47, p < .03$. This finding becomes even more intriguing when the cross-sectional relationship between rating negative intent and relationship satisfaction is examined. The Time 1 results showed that there was a positive correlation for both males, $r = .31$, NS, and females, $r = .43$, $p < .05$. This means that using the negative button is associated with both currently happy premarital relationships and future unhappy marital relationships. We see once again that predictors of premarital happiness are different from predictors of future marital happiness.

PERCEPTUAL ACCURACY

To assess perceptual accuracy, discrepancy scores were derived for each couple and averaged over tasks. This method of comparing intent and impact ratings provides point-by-point analysis and thus does not suffer from the problems mentioned earlier regarding our first study. The results showed no predictive power for discrepancy scores for relationship satisfaction at Time 1, $r = -.07$, NS; Time 2, $r = -.05$, NS; Time 3, $r = -.07$, NS. However, 5.5 years later (Time 4), the correlation between Time 1 discrepancy scores and relationship satisfaction for the nine couples who completed all four stages of the study approached significance, $r = -.49$, $p < .10$. When three couples who provided Time 4 data but missed Time 2 or 3 were added, the relationship was strongly significant, $r = -.66$, $p < .01$. The more accurate the couples' Time 1 communications (intent = impact), the more satisfied they were at Time 4. It is not at all clear why this relationship did not emerge at Time 3. These results should be interpreted with caution until they are replicated, since they were not predicted.

A Partial Replication

The same basic patterns of results between the major predictor variables and relationship satisfaction emerged in a recent study (Markman, Floyd, Stanley, & Stephen, 1983). The major differences between this second study and the first study were that the second study had a posttest 6 weeks after Time 1 and that half the couples participated in a premarital intervention program called PREP (Markman & Floyd, 1980; Markman *et al.,* Chapter 22, this volume). Table 14.2 presents the results of correlations between the three major predictor variables in the first study and the relationship satisfaction criterion variable at Time 1 (pretest), Time 2 (posttest, 6 weeks later), and Time 3 (1 year later). In the second study, relationship satisfaction was measured by a premarital version of the Locke and Wallace (1959) inventory. Further, the talk table was replaced by a "communication box" (Markman & Floyd, 1980; Markman & Poltrock, 1982). The couples still rated their partners on a 5-point scale using similar procedures; however, in this study they rated only impact.

Consistent with the results of the first longitudinal study, the cross-sectional findings indicated that communication box impact ratings were not significantly predictive of relationship satisfaction, whereas problem intensity scores were significantly related, $r = -.55$, $p < .01$. At Time 2 (posttest),

TABLE 14.2. Correlations between Time 1 Predictor Variables and the Locke–Wallace Criteria at Times 1, 2, and 3, for 10 Couples

	Mean Locke–Wallace scores		
Predictor variable	Time 1[a]	Time 2[a]	Time 3[b]
Individual Locke–Wallace	—	.54**	.45*
Individual problem intensity	− .55**	− .47	− .24
Individual communication box	.25	.20	.35

[a] $n = 20$ individuals.
[b] $n = 18$ individuals.
*$p < .05$.
**$p < .01$.

as expected, the same pattern of results was found. Finally, at Time 3 the only significant predictor of relationship satisfaction was Time 1 relationship satisfaction, $r = .45$, $p < .05$. These findings essentially replicated those obtained 4 years earlier with a different sample of couples planning marriages. Further, as seen in Table 14.2 and consistent with Study 1, communication box ratings were more predictive as time progressed, and relationship satisfaction and problem intensity scores were less predictive. It is expected that when the next follow-up is conducted, the Time 1 communication box impact ratings will be significantly predictive of relationship satisfaction for stable couples.

Discussion of Results

The findings indicate that the negative communication behaviors rated by the speaker (intent) or listener (impact), and the global similarity between positivity of speaker and listener behaviors, are related to future marital discord. Three major explanations of the results have been considered: communication skills, global reciprocity versus immediate reciprocity, and good communication and perceptual accuracy. The differences between these explanations relate to how the couples' ratings are interpreted.

COMMUNICATION SKILLS

To the extent that a couple's impact ratings reflect the use of communication skills by the speaker, the results provide evidence for differential use of communication skills predicting later marital satisfaction. Premarital couples with high levels of communication skills were more satisfied with their marriage 2.5 and 5 years later, as compared with couples with low levels. Unfortunately, there has been no research comparing, for the same unit of interaction, couples' talk table ratings and objective observers' ratings of communication skills. Gottman (1979) compared talk table impact ratings with affect codes from the CISS (see Notarius & Markman, 1981) and found no relationship for nondistressed couples and a significant relationship for distressed couples. This finding provides evidence for a "private message system" operating for happy couples, but it does not directly address the relationship of impact ratings and skill use. Such a study is currently underway. In addition, we are directly testing the predictive validity of communication skills. These studies should shed more light on the communication skill hypothesis.

GLOBAL VERSUS IMMEDIATE RECIPROCITY:
THE BANK ACCOUNT MODEL

Taken together, the talk table studies indicate that current and future non-distressed relationships are characterized by an exchange of high rates of non-contingent positive behaviors. The exchange does not seem to follow the model of a "tit for tat" positive reciprocity (i.e., positive behaviors followed by positive behaviors). The pattern that emerges is best described in terms of a "bank account" model. It is as if all couples start with a sizable "bank account" and that couples who become distressed start "withdrawing" from the "account" before marriage and continue to do so afterward. In contrast, couples who do not become distressed continually make "deposits" to the "account" through mutually rewarding interaction. The lack of predictive power of the impact ratings at the 1-year follow-up point in both studies suggests a "sleeper effect" in that the "withdrawals" do not reach a critical point for a relatively long time.

Applied to relationship development, the bank account model predicts that all premarital couples begin their marriage with a history of positive interactions (or they probably would not be planning marriage). However, these positive interactions are not necessarily the product of good communication. For example, premarital couples may be "in love with love" and the idea of getting married, and these romantic feelings may screen out negative events and highlight positive events. The major task confronting couples is to maintain this high level of positive exchange through establishing (1) good communication and (2) mutually rewarding patterns of interdependence.

These data are also consistent with a global positive reciprocity model, which predicts that the exchanges of positive behavior balance out over the long run. However, with the exception of self-report equity studies (e.g., Walster, Berscheid, & Walster, 1973), there is no direct evidence supporting a global reciprocity model. In contrast, a recent study (Margolin & Wampold, 1981) does provide some support for immediate positive reciprocity operating in marital relationships. However, their use of objective observers makes direct comparisons with studies using couples as raters somewhat problematic.

GOOD COMMUNICATION AND PERCEPTUAL ACCURACY

The predictive power of discrepancy scores may indicate that good premarital communication, defined as intent = impact, is associated with future marital happiness. The validity of this interpretation depends, to a large extent, on the interpretation of intent ratings. To the extent that intent ratings reflect the prediction by the speaker of the listener's response, the intent ratings may be measuring perceptual accuracy or empathy. There is evidence that perceptual accuracy is related to marital happiness (e.g., Knudson, Sommers, & Golding, 1980; Murstein & Beck, 1972). Notarius and his colleagues at Catholic University (Notarius & Vanzetti, 1981), and our research group (Farrell & Markman, in press), are currently comparing intent ratings with prediction ratings in order to shed light on this question.

Alternatively, the discrepancy results may be due to high ratings reflecting a socially desirable response ("we should say nice things to our partner"). Thus, in the marital studies, the lack of discriminative validity of intent ratings may reflect the distressed couples not being "honest" about their intent. As noted by Jacobson (1982), distressed couples "often do intend to be negative: They are pissed, vengeful — self-centered. . . . Their unwillingness to admit to their motivations is one of the factors that makes marital therapy so difficult." In the premarital studies, the predictive validity of both intent ratings and low discrepancy scores then suggests that acting in a socially desirable manner or being "polite" may be an indicator of a positivity screen or high levels of idealism. As noted by Gurman (1980), idealism may be an important determinant of future satisfaction for premarital couples. The issue of idealism is discussed in detail elsewhere (Markman, Jamieson, & Floyd, 1983). The interpretation of talk table ratings as representing perceptual screens is discussed in a later section of this chapter.

Summary on Social Exchange/Communication Research

Future studies of couples' interaction research should attempt to test these three alternative models (i.e., communication skills, bank account, perceptual accuracy). There are, however, difficult conceptual and methodological problems to be overcome. These problems include: (1) developing operational definitions of concepts such as exchange and reciprocity, which are widely used but rarely adequately defined; (2) developing agreed-upon measures of these concepts and using the same measures across studies; (3) increasing our understanding of what objective observers' (outsiders) and couples' (insiders) ratings are measuring; and (4) increasing our understanding of what the differences between these two perspectives mean. Additionally, both the bank account model and the positive reciprocity model can be criticized, like most social exchange hypotheses, for not specifying the content of rewarding or reciprocal exchanges. Research is needed that attempts to identify the types of interactions associated with marital distress. Marital interaction studies (e.g., see Schaap, Chapter 9, this volume) using objective observers provide one step toward identifying typologies of marital interaction. Alternatively, Foa and Foa (1974) suggest six different types of reward (e.g., love, money, sex) exchanged by intimates that can be explored in future research with couples.

In the next section, I discuss some of our most recent work designed to increase our understanding of what couples' ratings in general, and the impact ratings in particular, were measuring. Although the research was designed to consider social exchange and communication hypotheses, the results led us toward more cognitive-perceptual conceptualizations of marital relationships.

Beyond Social Exchange and Communication Theories

In a series of recent studies, we have compared couples' ratings with two types of objective ratings of the same interaction sequence. Floyd and Markman (1983) had untrained observers rate the interactions of a group of distressed and nondistressed couples. Distressed couples ($n = 6$) were defined on the convergent bases of seeking marital therapy and scoring below 100 on the Locke–Wallace test (1959). Similarly, nondistressed couples ($n = 10$) identified themselves as happily married and both spouses scored above 100 on the Locke–Wallace test. Both observers and couples used a revised version of the talk table, the communication box (Markman & Floyd, 1980), to rate the couples' communication. The communication box is a hand-held plastic box that has five buttons ranging from supernegative to superpositive. The buttons trigger a set of lights and tones, which are recorded on video- and audiotape, respectively. A computerized version of this procedure is now available (Markman & Poltrock, 1982). Couples were instructed to speak one at a time and to use a "floor" switch to indicate when they were finished talking. Ratings were made by both the couples and the objective raters when the floor was passed from one partner to the other. Couples completed two problem-solving tasks: the IMC (Olson & Ryder, 1970) and a personal problem discussion. Observers' evaluations of the same units of each couple's interaction assessed the degree to which a spouse's ratings reflected the "objective value" of their partner's behaviors.

The results, summarized in Figure 14.1, revealed some very interesting spouse–observer differences. Distressed wives rated their husbands' communications significantly lower than observers, and distressed husbands rated their wives' significantly higher than observers. These same couples' interactions were coded with an objective coding system using verbal and nonverbal codes from the Coding System for Interpersonal Conflict (CSIC) (Raush *et al.*, 1974) and CISS (Notarius & Markman, 1981). The distressed wives used more coercive and negative nonverbal behaviors than any other of the four groups (Sullivan & Markman, 1983).

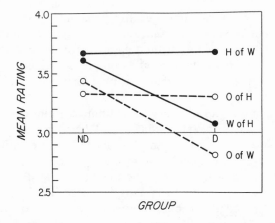

FIGURE 14.1. Comparison of spouses' and observers' communication box ratings of nondistressed (ND) and distressed (D) couples, with husbands rating wives (H of W), wives rating husbands (W of H), observers rating husbands (O of H), and observers rating wives (O of W). (From F. Floyd & H. Markman, Observational biases in spouse interaction: Toward a cognitive/behavioral model of marriage. *Journal of Consulting and Clinical Psychology,* 1983, *51,* 450–457. Copyright 1983 by the American Psychological Association.)

Taken together, these studies may indicate that distressed husbands are ignoring (i.e., are not responsive to) negative behavior from their wives, and that wives are "projecting" their negative feelings onto their husbands' behavior. This does not mean that wives are the cause or the victims of marital distress, but rather that wives' behavior may be viewed as a barometer of dysfunction, at least in some couples (Floyd & Markman, 1983).

These results led us to hypothesize a negativity screen for distressed wives and a positivity screen for distressed husbands. That is, distressed spouses were not being reactive or responsive to each other's behaviors, but, rather, their impact ratings may have been a reflection of their subjective feelings about the relationship. Differences in reactivity between distressed and nondistressed couples have also been reported and discussed by other researchers (e.g., Jacobson & Moore, 1981). A better test of the existence of perceptual screens would involve point-by-point comparisons (rather than the global mean level comparisons used in the Floyd & Markman study) of couples' and observers' ratings.

We have thus obtained preliminary evidence for perceptual screens operating in relationships. As noted by Weiss (1980), researchers and practitioners need to expand their models to integrate the interaction of cognitions with behaviors. The developmental role of perceptual screens is clearly an important issue, and we are currently conducting studies to test several hypotheses concerning potential biases in rating that have emerged in previous research (e.g., females rate more negatively than males; distressed vs. non-distressed couples are more accurate at monitoring negative vs. positive behaviors). We will also use this methodology to provide an outcome measure for evaluating the effects of intervention programs with couples. For example, since we train couples to monitor their partners' behaviors, their responsiveness should increase.

These preliminary results suggest that impact ratings are jointly determined by the partner's objective behavior and the rater's subjective "screens" (cognitive sets) about the relationship. Applied to the premarital results and prediction research, we can generate several hypotheses concerning the etiology of marital distress. Couples who maintain a satisfying relationship, compared to couples who do not, (1) display more positive communication behaviors (skills), and (2) attribute negative behaviors to external factors and positive behaviors to internal factors. Thus, objectively negative behaviors are seen as neutral or positive (rating made according to positive view of relationship), and objectively positive behaviors are rated even more positively. Christensen (1981) finds that this attributional pattern diminishes as length of the relationship increases. Thus, we would predict impact ratings to decline over time. If couples are rating negative impact when, in fact, the objective value of their partners' communications is positive, this may result in a decline in the objective value of their partners' communications ("No matter what I do, I can't please you").

To summarize, I have reviewed a program of research that examined the role of the couples' perceptions of each other's communications in the development of marital distress. The findings have highlighted the importance of the couples' perceptions of their interactions in predicting future outcomes. These findings are consistent with current conceptualizations of social skills that consider accurate perception of relationship events to be an important component of social skills (Trower, 1979). The next section examines areas that should provide fertile ground for future research in cognitive-perceptual processes in marital interaction.

Future Directions: Examining Perceptual Components of Couples' Interactions

There is a largely untapped resource in the social perception literature that can help us understand marriage partners' perceptual processes. In my opinion, we should attempt to apply these principles to the understanding, treatment, and prevention of marital distress. Three traditions in social perception research are particularly relevant: perceptual readiness, attribution theory, and sex differences.

Perceptual Readiness

According to Bruner (1957), accurate perception of social cues is based on an actor's (A) readiness to react to (i.e., perceive, construe) his/her partner's (B) behaviors and make accurate inferences about unobservables (e.g., intent, emotional state, attitudes). A's perceptual readiness to perceive B accurately is dependent upon A's previous experiences, which provide a "cognitive set" predisposing A to expect that certain events will occur with certain probabilities. In addition, A's current emotional state (e.g., anger) and A's perceptual biases (i.e., wishes, fears) affect accurate perception. Finally, the extent to which B's behavior is an accurate representation of B's inner state determines A's perceptions. We can define perceptual readiness in terms of one's construct system (Kelly, 1955) by viewing constructs as a cognitive set. T. Mischel (1964) argues that constructs provide rules about the world that guide behavior. Applied to premarital relationships, for example, an unhappy bachelor who cannot find the right mate may have a powerful domination–submission construct that dictates that potential mates should be very submissive. This man may be very skillful (behaviorally) but may have a "foolish rule" (T. Mischel, 1964). Thus, he is viewing his relationship world through a screen that presents a "picture" of the world different from his potential partners'. Weiss's (1980) concept of "sentiment override" can be viewed as one form of perceptual readiness. Partners with a positive sentiment override are predisposed, at the time, to perceive (rate) events positively, and vice versa with negative sentiment.

Applied directly to partners' observing relationship events, the concept of perceptual readiness predicts that: (1) accurate perception is limited by the degree of perceptual readiness of the partners, (2) partners may select each other in terms of dimensions of their construct systems, (3) partners develop together a joint construct system that results in a shared relationship world image (Stephen & Markman, 1983), and (4) relationship events are processed through cognitive screens that determine how the events are perceived.

From this perspective, the goal of therapy is to "reeducate perceptual experience," as opposed to getting people to take a "closer look" at their social interactions. Kelly's (1955) cognitive interventions are a good example of such an intervention strategy (e.g., fixed-role therapy in order to change the rules guiding behavior). The goal of prevention is to educate or prepare couples to be accurate social perceivers, with perhaps a slight positivity bias. Specifically this involves: (1) being accurate communicators of relationship information, (2) developing a shared world image through sharing their individual perceptions, and (3) tuning conceptual systems to each other and building in periodic checkups.

Future research needs to develop strategies to assess the perceptual readiness of partners and categorize the various dimensions relevant to construing relationships. Then tests of the many predictions generated by this perspective can proceed. Personal relationship researchers (e.g., Duck, 1977) have long found Kelly's (1955) construct theory useful to the study of friendships. Marital researchers should examine and benefit from these efforts.

Attribution Theory

The regularities in partners' attributions concerning the cause of relationship events can be considered a form of perceptual readiness. Attribution theory and research have provided some interesting "laws" about differential perceptual biases of actors and observers (e.g., Jones & Davis, 1965; Kelley, 1971). Applied to premarital relationships, one partner is the actor and the other is the observer (of the actor's behavior). Observers can be participant observers (i.e., the partner) or objective observers (e.g., objective coders).

Actors (A) are predisposed to attribute their own behaviors to external factors (e.g., situations — "I had a bad day at work," or to others — "my partner made me do it"), while observers (O) are predisposed to attribute the cause of observed behaviors to A. As noted by Heider (1958) and confirmed by numerous studies (e.g., Jones & Davis, 1965), behavior "engulfs" O's perceptual field. We must be careful, however, in generalizing the results of these attribution studies, where A and O are usually strangers to intimate relationships. Fortunately, couple interaction researchers have recently turned their attention to attributional processes between intimates.

Christensen's (1981) research suggests an interesting interaction between positivity and attributions for couples' attributions. The longer the couple is together, the greater the tendency to attribute positive behaviors to situational factors (contrary to earlier attribution research) and to attribute the cause of negative behavior to internal factors. If these findings are replicated and demonstrated through longitudinal research, they can provide fascinating insights into the cause of marital distress.

Similarly, the research of Braiker and Kelley (1979) suggests that attributional conflicts over the cause of relationship problems may underlie many relationship conflicts and arguments. Attributional conflict is defined as a situation "in which the partner explains behavior in a way the actor cannot accept" (Kelley, 1979, p. 100). A tends to explain his/her own negative behavior in terms of concern for the partner, while O (partner) makes the attribution that A is not concerned with him/her. In general, Kelley and associates have found "the strong tendency to interpret specific negative behaviors in interaction in terms of stable, general causal properties of the Actor (i.e., traits)" (Kelley, 1979, p. 96). The interpretations of negative events, but not positive events, were in disagreement. This is consistent with the greater importance of negative events than positive events in predicting distress, which has been reported in previous marital interaction research (e.g., Gottman, 1979).

In terms of our communication model, attributional conflicts may be a case of an intent–impact discrepancy concerning the explanation of behaviors. A's intent is generally positive or neutral, while B's impact is generally negative (for "objectively" negative events). Thus, A's ability to communicate his/her intent to B (i.e., low discrepancy), or alternatively, B's ability to discuss his/her negative reaction in a way that enables clarification of A's intent, may be important in overcoming conflict-producing attributional tendencies. Unfortunately, there is also evidence for a remarkably high level of disagreement between spouses in just the occurrence of both positive and negative relationship events, let alone interpretation of these events (e.g., Christensen & Nies, 1980; Jacobson & Moore, 1981).

From an attributional perspective, prevention programs can be designed to increase the cognitive complexity of couples around relationship issues, increase or decrease the "range of convenience" (Kelly, 1955) of the couples' constructs in order to increase perceptual accuracy, and help couples cope with their attributional tendencies. This involves increasing (1) awareness, (2) situational attributions (e.g., most couples planning marriage experience conflicts over their wedding plans), and (3) communication skills to clear up intent–impact discrepancies. Research needs to focus on the development of attributional tendencies as well as on increasing our understanding of the associates of different types of attributional biases in interaction (e.g., Jacobson, McDonald, & Follette, 1981).

Sex Differences

Numerous studies spanning different content areas (e.g., empathy, marital adjustment, loneliness, personality) have converged to indicate that there are systematic gender differences in partners' sensitivity or reactivity to relationship events. Females are socialized to respond to events (e.g., problems, conflicts) by finding out how the other person feels (empathy, problem discussion) and may be better at this; males, on the other hand, are socialized to respond to events (problems) by searching for solutions (problem solution) and may be better at it (Hoffman, 1977). Moderators of this gender difference include sex role orientation (androgeny), self-esteem level, career orientation, and in general, the dependency on the relationship for rewards. Thus females may be more likely than males to perceive and respond to relationship events (other factors being equal). Thus we have theoretical support for the clinical lore of wives' being more concerned about relational distress than husbands.

Future research on sex differences is needed to better understand a growing body of findings that indicate that marriage is better for men than for women. For example, several studies have demonstrated that married females, especially traditional females (measured by femininity scores on androgeny scales), are at high risk for psychological and physical problems, and that married males are at low risk for problems (e.g., Olds & Shaver, 1980). These findings have been interpreted in terms of women's providing more interpersonal resources to men than vice versa. While differential social (intimacy) skills have been suggested as an explanation for these findings (e.g., Wheeler, Reis, & Nezlek, 1983), recent data from our laboratory suggest that there are no differences in intimacy skills between males and females in premarital relationships. Rather, our data suggest that the females' nonverbal expressivity may be related to current levels of relationship satisfaction. However, interview studies with married couples suggest that females may act as the "directors" of relationships, using "meta-skills" to facilitate their partners' use of intimacy skills. For example, one happily married male described his wife "as helping me disclose my deepest feelings."

Future research should examine sex differences in marital and premarital interaction systematically. A particularly exciting question concerns the development of the sex differences reported in marital interaction studies (e.g., Floyd & Markman, 1983) but not observed in premarital interaction studies (Markman, 1979, 1981).

A Final Note: Let's Not Reinvent the Wheel

To summarize, the behavioral tradition has come a long way from the initial operant conceptualizations of marriage (e.g., Stuart, 1969). It now encompasses behavior exchange, social learning, attribution theory, social skills, and strategic constructs in its conceptualization of the development and treatment of marital distress (e.g., Birchler & Spinks, 1980; Vincent, 1980; Weiss, 1980). Thus, it is not uncommon to find a mixture of terms from these five models, to which I apply the label "cognitive-behavioral." All five models have in common the assertion that aspects of the couples' interaction and/or perception of their interaction are the primary determinants of marital distress or success, and also the primary targets for intervention.

It is interesting to note that interest in cognitive-perceptual factors in marriage seems to cycle (e.g., Tharp, 1963), and it is important not to reinvent the wheel in the sense of ignoring previous contributions. Our research program represents the recent history of the marital field in general, in that we have been led by our data to consider the role of cognitive-perceptual factors, in addition to behavioral-interactional variables. It is likely that affect, motivation, and needs will reemerge as well, as constructs in marital research in the near future (e.g., Graziano, in press). By maintaining a historical perspective and building on the work of our theoretical and empirical forefathers and mothers, we can separate advances from recapitulations as we proceed into the 1980s. In particular, we should not lose our focus on relationship phenomena. Thus, tests of relationship theories and laboratory studies should not lose connection with the phenomena that represent the mysteries of marital interaction that we are trying to unravel (Markman, Alvarado, Buhrmeister, Furman, Reis, Shaver, & Sorrel, 1982).

Issues in Prediction Research with Couples

There are many important conceptual, methodological, and pragmatic issues confronting researchers interested in studying the development of relationships. This section briefly identifies and discusses four of these.

Risk and Prediction Research

An important, though controversial, future use of prediction research may be to develop procedures for identifying couples at risk for developing relationship distress. However, despite our ability to make theoretical predictions about the development of marital distress, it may be unreasonable to expect single predictor variables to account for a large proportion of the variance in marital distress, given the complexities of intimate relationships. Researchers interested in understanding the etiology of psychopathology (e.g., Heller & Monahan, 1977; Mednick & McNeil, 1968; Price, 1974) have argued that we lack adequate theory development, empirical data, and methodological tools for the admittedly ambitious task of causal prediction, given the current state of the art in psychology. They recommend searching for "risk factors" that predict the development of psychological disorders. If risk factors of marital distress can be reliably identified, then couples at risk for developing marital distress can be invited to participate in prevention programs early in their relationship in order to enhance their chances of developing a successful relationship.

Two intervention strategies are implied by this approach. First, if couples at risk for developing marital and family problems can be identified before marriage, then these couples can be discouraged from marrying. This strategy was perhaps best summarized by Ellis (1948), who stated that "Our current divorce rates are generally considered to be alarmingly high; and any technique which might help to weed out doomed marriages before they were actually consummated would be enthusiastically welcomed" (p. 710). Second, couples or families can be screened on the basis of predictor variables (risk indicators), and then intervention can be offered only to those who are "at risk." These are examples of secondary prevention (as opposed to primary prevention) and carry with them the problems typically associated with such programs. Prediction research can provide only probability estimates of the development of relationship distress, estimates accurate only for groups of couples or families rather than for an individual couple or family. For example, evidence from child studies (e.g., Anthony, 1974) indicates that some high-risk children are invulnerable to disorders, while some low-risk children are vulnerable. Further, without the data base to accurately classify couples and families as high-risk and low-risk, ethical considerations preclude making this designation known to them. Primary prevention avoids the problems associated with secondary prevention interventions based on risk factors, since targets are identified by progress through transition periods rather than by potentially biased screening procedures. Thus, in my opinion, at least for the time being, prediction research is best used to provide a data base for primary prevention programs rather than for screening purposes and secondary prevention programs.

Prediction Research as Premarital Intervention

Many couples in our studies have reported that just being in the study helped their relationships. For example, one woman said that she and her partner talked about important issues in their relationship that they never got around to discussing at home. It seems likely that, for some couples, participation in the research served as a helpful intervention. Rubin and Mitchell (1976) found that many of their dating couples found participation in the research project helpful, and these authors suggested that couples research should be considered as a form of premarital counseling or intervention. In our studies, couples experience conditions similar to those recommended by existing premarital intervention programs (Markman, Floyd, & Dickson-Markman, 1982; Rutledge, 1968). They were asked to talk about their relationship, how they met, and how the future looked; to identify problem areas and discuss the problems until they reached a mutually satisfying solution; and to talk to each other in a situation conducive to face-to-face communication (e.g., sitting opposite each other in a room with no potential distractions like television or friends), and to use the talk table or communication box, which ensured that each person would be listened to, since interruptions and simultaneous talk were discouraged (in a way, these devices serve a role similar to that played by a therapist). However, it is also possible that this experience may have negative effects as well. In general, we have little information concerning the short- or long-term negative or positive effects of programs specifically designed as premarital intervention programs (see Markman, Floyd, & Dickson-Markman, 1982, for a review).

There are also ethical and methodological issues that need to be considered in this context. First, researchers must carefully consider the effects on a couple's relationship of research participation. Clearly, informed consent about potential negative (or for that matter, positive) effects must be obtained from couples. From a methodological perspective, the pretest (Time 1) measures may be interacting with subsequent development and therefore masking "true" developmental changes. A Solomon four-group design would be a good, but very expensive, solution to at least some of the problems raised here (Campbell & Stanley, 1963).

Problems with Longitudinal Research

OVERCOMING BARRIERS TO LONGITUDINAL RESEARCH

Despite many calls for increased longitudinal research in the close-relationships field (e.g., Huston & Levinger, 1978; Weiss, 1980), there have been surprisingly few such endeavors. There seems to be an attitude that longitudinal research is just too time-consuming and difficult to even attempt. Typical of this attitude is a quote from Calderone (1978) concerning a different research area: "we have no way of showing in the near future *short of the laborious, longitudinal studies that at this time it is unrealistic to hope for,* what the 'good' or preventative effects might be of planned sex education . . ." (p. 152; italics added). However, longitudinal research is not as hard as the lack of such studies may suggest. In the hope of stimulating more longitudinal studies, particularly possible collaborative efforts among relationship researchers, I would like to offer several suggestions for dealing with some of the problems that we have encountered in our research program. You should: (1) have research participants provide information on several people who "will always know where to contact you" (e.g., parents, friends); (2) inform the participants about the longitudinal objectives of the study and attempt to establish an alliance with them that gets them reasonably interested in the study (though not to the point of providing biased data); (3) maintain frequent (e.g., yearly) follow-up contacts with the participants; and (4) provide periodic reports on the progress of the study and general results that are of interest to the participants but do not bias future data collection.

DEMAND CHARACTERISTICS AND LONGITUDINAL STUDIES

One paradox associated with longitudinal research is that a positive alliance with subjects is necessary to keep motivation, interest, and commitment at high levels, yet these same factors introduce potentially severe bias problems into the interpretation of results. A discussion of demand characteristics inherent in longitudinal research is beyond the scope of this chapter. Suffice it to say that these problems exist and need to be considered when evaluating both the internal and external validity of longitudinal research with couples.

The Social Ecology of Marriage

As noted earlier, longitudinal research on marriage should consider the role of external variables that affect couples and families. There are numerous societal changes that all couples and families must react to and attempt to master. These external factors define the social ecology of contemporary marriage in the sense that they provide constraints within which couples and families function. These changes include changing definitions of gender roles, the increase in career orientation of women and the number of working women, psychological insecurities from factors such as the poor economy and threat of nuclear war, and the increase in awareness of demographic trends in family life (e.g., continuing high rates of divorce, dramatic increase in one-parent families). In addition, there is increasing evidence that family transition periods (e.g., planning marriage, first year of marriage, parenthood, children leaving home, divorce, widowhood) are stressful in themselves (e.g., Nock, 1981). Each of these periods provides a set of common tasks that couples and families need to master in order to maintain a well-functioning relationship (Markman, Floyd, & Dickson-Markman, 1982).

The research presented in this chapter focuses on the transition-to-marriage period. We have completed studies on other transition periods, including the transition to parenthood (Kadushin & Markman, 1982), and on couples planning remarriage (Farrell & Markman, in press). We are also investigating the role of the wife's working on marital interaction and satisfaction.

Future research should head in four directions in order to increase our understanding of these important external factors. First, studies should focus on couples and families as they progress toward, enter, and emerge from family transition periods. Ideally, longitudinal components should be built into these studies in order to better understand the etiological impact of coping with transitions on future functioning.

Second, studies are needed on couples and families who are grappling with the external changes noted above. For example, studies should focus on dual-career families, couples living apart, single-parent families, families with handicapped children, divorcing couples, and children of divorce, to name but a few. In addition, we must expand our studies to include minority groups for whom these external changes are most salient.

Third, all studies of couples and families should include an assessment of the specific external factors that might affect the dependent variables of interest. For example, measures of stage of family life cycle, economic stress, and recent life changes (e.g., death of a relative, birth of a handicapped child, moving, job change), to name just a few, should be included in all studies. To the extent that measures of these factors are not available, they should be developed.

Finally, we should not ignore the role of individual factors (e.g., psychological adjustment) as both causes and effects of relationship functioning in our future research. For example, when examining the impact of divorce on couple members, it is possible that divorce causes psychological problems and that psychological problems cause divorce.

To summarize, external factors have not been systematically examined in the present chapter and in marital research in general. Since it is likely that the impact of external factors on contemporary marriages is striking, we must correct this deficiency in future research.

Conclusions

This chapter has argued that longitudinal research on the development of marital distress can help us understand the factors involved in the etiology of marital discord and provide an empirical basis for developing intervention (treatment and prevention) programs. For example, longitudinal studies testing the cognitive-behavioral model hypothesis that interactional deficits precede the development of marital distress have implications for both a cognitive-behavioral theory of marital distress and the development of prevention programs. However, there is a pressing need for additional longitudinal research with a wider range and larger numbers of couples over longer periods of time to replicate and extend the results of the preliminary research described here. Currently we are conducting a longitudinal study of family development with more than 150 couples in order to accomplish these objectives. Further, there is a need to examine the specific types of perceptual–interactional deficits associated with various outcomes. I have briefly discussed three areas of research already providing fertile ground for research and helping us increase our understanding of the development of marital distress. Finally, there remain numerous conceptual, methodological, ethical, and pragmatic issues that need attention and resolution.

ACKNOWLEDGMENTS

Preparation of this chapter was supported by Grant No. MH35525-01 from the National Institute of Mental Health. I would like to thank Phillip Shaver, Neil Jacobson, and Marshall Haith for their helpful comments on earlier drafts.

REFERENCES

Anthony, J. The syndrome of the psychologically invulnerable child. In J. Anthony & C. Koupernik (Eds.), *The child in his family: Children at psychiatric risk*. New York: Wiley, 1974.

Bentler, P., & Newcomb, M. Longitudinal study of marital success and failure. *Journal of Consulting and Clinical Psychology,* 1978, *46*, 1053–1070.

Billings, A. Conflict resolution in distressed and nondistressed married couples. *Journal of Consulting and Clinical Psychology,* 1979, *47*, 368–376.

Birchler, G., & Spinks, S. Behavioral systems marital and family therapy: Integration and clinical application. *American Journal of Family Therapy,* 1980, *8*, 6–28.

Birchler, G. R., Weiss, R. L., & Vincent, J. P. Multimethod analysis of social reinforcement exchange between maritally distressed and nondistressed spouse and stranger dyads. *Journal of Personality and Social Psychology,* 1975, *31,* 349–360.

Braiker, H. B., & Kelley, H. H. Conflict in the development of close relationships. In R. L. Burgess & T. L. Huston (Eds.), *Social exchange in developing relationships.* New York: Academic Press, 1979.

Bruner, J. On perceptual readiness. *Psychological Review,* 1957, *64,* 123–152.

Burgess, E., & Cottrell, L. *Predicting success or failure in marriage.* Englewood Cliffs, NJ: Prentice-Hall, 1939.

Calderone, M. Is sex education preventive? In C. Qualls, J. Wincze, & D. Barlow (Eds.), *The prevention of sexual disorders: Issues and approaches.* New York: Plenum Press, 1978.

Campbell, D. T., & Stanley, J. C. *Experimental and quasi-experimental designs for research.* Chicago: Rand-McNally, 1963.

Christensen, A. *Perceptual biases in couples' reports of their own interaction.* Paper presented at the meeting of the Association for Advancement of Behavior Therapy, Toronto, 1981.

Christensen, A., & Nies, D. C. The Spouse Observation Checklist: Empirical analysis and critique. *American Journal of Family Therapy,* 1980, *8,* 69–79.

Duck, S. *The study of acquaintance.* London: Saxon House, 1977.

Ellis, A. The value of marriage predictions tests. *American Sociological Review,* 1948, *13,* 710–718.

Farrell, J., & Markman, H. Individual and interpersonal factors in the etiology of marital distress: The example of remarital couples. In R. Gilmour & S. Duck (Eds.), *Personal relationships.* Hillsdale, NJ: Erlbaum, in press.

Ferraro, B., & Markman, H. *Application of the behavioral model of marriage to deaf marital relationships.* Paper presented at the annual meeting of the Midwestern Psychological Association, Detroit, 1981.

Floyd, F., & Markman, H. *Insiders' and outsiders' assessment of distressed and nondistressed marital interaction.* Paper presented at the meeting of the Association for Advancement of Behavior Therapy, Toronto, 1981.

Floyd, F., & Markman, H. Observational biases in spouse interaction: Toward a cognitive/behavioral model of marriage. *Journal of Consulting and Clinical Psychology,* 1983, *51,* 450–457.

Foa, V., & Foa, E. *Societal structures of the mind.* Springfield, IL: Charles C Thomas, 1974.

Goldfried, M. R., & D'Zurilla, T. J. A behavioral analytic model for assessing competence. In C. D. Spielberger (Ed.), *Current topics in clinical and community psychology.* New York: Academic Press, 1969.

Gottman, J. *Empirical investigations of marriage.* New York: Academic Press, 1979.

Gottman, J. M., Markman, H. J., & Notarius, C. I. The topography of marital conflict: A sequential analysis of verbal and nonverbal behavior. *Journal of Marriage and the Family,* 1977, *39,* 461–478.

Gottman, J., Notarius, C., Gonso, J., & Markman, H. J. *A couple's guide to communication.* Champaign, IL: Research Press, 1976.

Gottman, J., Notarius, C., Markman, H., Yoppi, B., Bank, S., & Rubin, M. Behavior exchange theory and marital decision-making. *Journal of Personality and Social Psychology,* 1976, *34,* 14–23.

Graziano, W. A developmental approach to social exchange processes. In J. Masters & K. Yarkin (Eds.), *Boundary areas in psychology: Social and developmental psychology.* New York: Academic Press, in press.

Gurman, A. Behavioral marriage therapy in the 1980's: The challenge of integration. *American Journal of Family Therapy,* 1980, *89,* 86–96.

Heider, F. *The psychology of interpersonal relationships.* New York: Wiley, 1958.

Heller, K., & Monahan, J. *Psychology and community change.* Homewood, IL: Dorsey Press, 1977.

Hoffman, M. Sex differences in empathy and relaxed behaviors. *Psychological Bulletin,* 1977, *84*, 712-722.

Huston, T., & Levinger, G. Interpersonal attraction and relationships. In M. Rosenzweg & W. Parker (Eds.), *Annual review of psychology* (Vol. 29). Palo Alto, CA: Annual Reviews, 1978.

Jacobson, N. S. Problem solving and contingency contracting in the treatment of marital discord. *Journal of Consulting and Clinical Psychology,* 1977, *45*, 52-60.

Jacobson, N. S. Personal communication, July 1981.

Jacobson, N. S. Personal communication (letter), February 17, 1982.

Jacobson, N. S., McDonald, D., & Follette, W. *Attributional differences between distressed and nondistressed married couples.* Paper presented at the meeting of the Association for Advancement of Behavior Therapy, Toronto, November 1981.

Jacobson, N. S., & Moore, D. Spouses as observers of events in their relationship. *Journal of Consulting and Clinical Psychology,* 1981, *49*, 269-277.

Jones, E., & Davis, K. From acts to dispositions: The attribution process in personal perception. In L. Berkowitz (Ed.), *Advances in experimental social psychology.* New York: Academic Press, 1965.

Kadushin, F., & Markman, H. *The effects of Lamaze training on marital satisfaction and anxiety.* Paper presented at the annual meeting of the American Psychological Association, Washington, D.C., August 1982.

Kelley, H. Attribution in social interaction. In E. Jones, D. Kanouse, H. Kelley, R. Nisbett, S. Valins, & B. Weiner (Eds.), *Attribution: Perceiving the causes of behaviors.* Morristown, NJ: General Learning Press, 1971.

Kelley, H. *Personal relationships: Their structure and process.* Hillsdale, NJ: Erlbaum, 1979.

Kelley, H., & Thibaut, J. *Interpersonal relations.* New York: Wiley, 1978.

Kelly, G. *The psychology of personal constructs* (Vol. 1). New York: Norton, 1955.

Knudson, R., Sommers, A., & Golding, S. Effect of perceived environmental conditions during cooperation on intergroup attraction. *Journal of Personality and Social Psychology,* 1980, *38*, 751-763.

Levinger, G., Senn, D. J., & Jorgensen, B. W. Progress toward permanence in courtship: A test of the Kerckhoff–Davis hypothesis. *Sociometry,* 1970, *33*, 427-443.

Lewis, R. A. A developmental framework for the analysis of premarital dyad formation. *Family Process,* 1972, *11*, 17-48.

Lewis, R. A. A longitudinal test of a developmental framework for premarital dyadic formation. *Journal of Marriage and Family,* 1973, *35*, 16-25.

Locke, H., & Wallace, K. Short marital adjustment and prediction tests: Their reliability and validity. *Marriage and Family Living,* 1959, *21*, 251-255.

Locke, H., & Williamson, R. Marital adjustment: A factor analysis study. *American Sociological Review,* 1958, *27*, 562-569.

Margolin, G., & Wampold, B. Sequential analysis of conflict and accord in distressed and nondistressed marital partners. *Journal of Consulting and Clinical Psychology,* 1981, *49*, 554-567.

Markman, H. J. The application of a behavioral model of marriage in predicting relationship satisfaction for couples planning marriage. *Journal of Consulting and Clinical Psychology,* 1979, *4*, 743-749.

Markman, H. J. The prediction of marital distress: A five-year follow-up. *Journal of Consulting and Clinical Psychology,* 1981, *49*, 760-762.

Markman, H. J., Alvarado, A., Buhrmeister, D., Furman, W., Reis, H., Shaver, P., & Sorrel, G. *Recent trends in the study of close relationships: Are we about to reinvent the wheel?*

Paper presented at the International Conference on Personal Relationships, Madison, WI, July 1982.

Markman, H. J., & Baccus, G. *The application of behavioral model of marriage to Black couples.* Unpublished manuscript, Bowling Green State University, 1982.

Markman, H. J., & Floyd, F. Possibilities for the prevention of marital discord: A behavioral perspective. *American Journal of Family Therapy,* 1980, *8,* 29–48.

Markman, H. J., Floyd, F., & Dickson-Markman, F. Toward a model for the prediction and prevention of marital and family distress and dissolution. In S. Duck (Ed.), *Personal relationships 4: Dissolving personal relationships.* London: Academic Press, 1982.

Markman, H. J., Floyd, F., Stanley, S., & Stephen, T. *Baby steps toward the primary prevention of marital distress.* Unpublished manuscript, 1983.

Markman, H. J., Jamieson, K., & Floyd, F. The assessment and modification of premarital relationships: Preliminary findings on the etiology and prevention of marital and family distress. In J. Vincent (Ed.), *Advances in family interventions, assessment, and theory* (Vol. 3). Greenwich, CT: JAI Press, 1983.

Markman, H. J., Notarius, C., Stephen, T., & Smith, R. Behavioral observation systems for couples: The current status. In E. Filsinger & R. Lewis (Eds.), *Observing marriage: New behavioral approaches.* Beverly Hills, CA: Sage, 1981.

Markman, H. J., & Poltrock, S. E. A computerized system for recording and analysis of self-observations of couples' interactions. *Behavior Research Methods and Instrumentation,* 1982, *14,* 186–190.

Mednick, S. A., & McNeil, T. F. Current methodological research on the etiology of schizophrenia: Serious difficulties which suggest the use of the high-risk method. *Psychological Bulletin,* 1968, *70,* 681–693.

Mischel, T. Personal construct, rules, and the logic of clinical activity. *Psychological Review,* 1964, *71,* 180–192.

Mischel, W. Direct versus indirect personality assessment: Evidence and implications. *Journal of Consulting and Clinical Psychology,* 1972, *33,* 319–324.

Mischel, W. On the future of personality measurement. *American Psychologist,* 1977, *32,* 246–254.

Murstein, B. I., & Beck, G. D. Person perception, marriage adjustment, and social desirability. *Journal of Consulting and Clinical Psychology,* 1972, *39,* 396–403.

Nock, S. Family life-cycle transitions: Longitudinal effects on family members. *Journal of Marriage and Family Living,* 1981, *43,* 703–714.

Notarius, C. I., & Markman, H. J. The Couples Interaction Scoring System. In E. Filsinger & R. Lewis (Eds.), *Assessing marriage: New behavioral approaches.* Beverly Hills, CA: Sage, 1981.

Notarius, C. I., & Vanzetti, N. *Communication process in distressed and nondistressed couples: The role of expectancies.* Paper presented at the annual meeting of the Association for Advancement of Behavior Therapy, Toronto, 1981.

Olds, D., & Shaver, P. Masculinity, femininity, academic performance and health: Further evidence concerning the androgeny controversy. *Journal of Personality,* 1980, *48,* 323–341.

Olson, D. H., & Ryder, R. G. Inventory of Marital Conflicts (IMC): An experimental interaction procedure. *Journal of Marriage and Family Living,* 1970, *32,* 443–448.

Price, R. H. Etiology, the social environment, and the prevention of psychological disorders. In P. Insel & R. H. Moos (Eds.), *Health and the social environment.* Lexington, MA: D. C. Heath, 1974.

Raush, H. L., Barry, W. A., Hertel, R. K., & Swain, M. A. *Communication, conflict and marriage.* San Francisco: Jossey-Bass, 1974.

Rubin, Z., & Mitchell, C. Couples research as couples counseling. *American Psychologist,* 1976, *31,* 17–25.

Rutledge, A. A systematic approach to premarital counseling. In J. C. Heston & W. B. Frich (Eds.), *Counseling for the liberal arts campus.* Yellow Springs, OH: Antioch Press, 1968.

Stephen, T., & Markman, H. The Relationship World Index: An instrument for the measurement of symbolic interdependence in developing intimate relationships. *Family Process,* 1983, *22,* 15–25.

Stuart, R. B. Operant-interpersonal treatment for marital discord. *Journal of Consulting and Clinical Psychology,* 1969, *33,* 675–682.

Sullivan, M., & Markman, H. J. *Coercive interaction in marriage.* Manuscript in preparation, 1983.

Terman, L. *Psychological factors in marital happiness.* New York: McGraw-Hill, 1938.

Tharp, R. Psychological patterning in marriage. *Psychological Bulletin,* 1963, *60,* 97–117.

Thibaut, J. W., & Kelley, H. H. *The social psychology of groups.* New York: Wiley, 1959.

Trower, P. Fundamentals of interpersonal behavior: A social psychological perspective. In A. Bellack & M. Hersen (Eds.), *Research and practices in social skills training.* New York: Plenum Press, 1979.

Vincent, J. The empirical clinical study of families: Social learning theory as a point of departure. In J. Vincent (Ed.), *Advance in family intervention, assessment and theory* (Vol. 1). Greenwich, CT: JAI Press, 1980.

Walster, E., Berscheid, E., & Walster, G. New directions in equity research. *Journal of Personality and Social Psychology,* 1973, *25,* 151–176.

Weiss, R. Strategic behavioral marital therapy: Toward a model for assessment and intervention. In J. Vincent (Ed.), *Advances in family intervention, assessment and theory* (Vol. 1). Greenwich, CT: JAI Press, 1980.

Wheeler, L., Reis, H., & Nezlek, J. Loneliness, sex roles, and social interaction. *Journal of Social and Personality Psychology,* 1983, *45,* 943–953.

Wills, T. A., Weiss, R. L., & Patterson, G. R. A behavioral analysis of the determinants of marital satisfaction. *Journal of Consulting and Clinical Psychology,* 1974, *42,* 802–811.

PART THREE

CLINICAL EXTENSIONS AND INNOVATIONS

15

The Modification of Cognitive Processes in Behavioral Marital Therapy: Integrating Cognitive and Behavioral Intervention Strategies

NEIL S. JACOBSON

One way of assessing the maturity of a research area is by noting its capacity for self-criticism. When advocates of a particular model of therapy become critics of that same model, when advocacy gives way to enlightened, sober appraisals of limitations, one can often be sanguine about the continuing contributions of that model. By these criteria, behavioral marital therapy (BMT) seems to be in the midst of a maturation process. BMT has been criticized in recent years not only by outsiders (Gurman & Knudson, 1978; Knudson, Gurman, & Kniskern, 1979) but also by those identified with the area (Birchler & Spinks, 1980; Gottman, 1979; Jacobson, 1979a; Jacobson, Berley, Elwood, Melman, & Phelps, in press; Jacobson & Moore, 1981a; Weiss, 1980). These criticisms, while continuing to acknowledge the contribution of BMT to the understanding and treatment of distressed relationships, also acknowledge limitations in both the conceptual model and the treatment technology. We know that BMT is not always effective. At times, the primary obstacles to successful treatment seem to reside in the characteristics of intractable clients; at other times, limitations in therapist skill and performance account for failure. But there is little doubt that some couples are not successfully treated because BMT, as it is currently practiced, is limited.

The thesis of this chapter is that both the success rate of BMT and the quality of relationships embodied in our successfully treated cases can be improved by a more systematic focus on the modification of spouses' cognitive processes. In the first section, a rationale is established for the inclusion of a cognitive focus in BMT. This rationale is based upon the observations of experienced marital researchers and clinicians, as well as recent analogue research. The second section then focuses on behavior exchange procedures.

Neil S. Jacobson. Department of Psychology, University of Washington, Seattle, Washington, U.S.A.

Suggestions are put forth for designing behavioral interventions in ways that foster desirable cognitive changes along with behavioral changes. In the third section, following a review of cognitive-restructuring interventions already discussed in the BMT literature, some guidelines are offered for the systematic incorporation of cognitive interventions within a behavioral treatment program. A fourth section briefly discusses the application of cognitive self-control strategies to problems involving bickering and impulsive anger expression.

The Need for Cognitive-Restructuring Procedures: Clinical Observations and Research Findings

Despite the philosophical preference for focusing on overt behavior, BMT has always utilized theoretical concepts explicitly acknowledging the role of internal mediational processes in influencing marital distress. The theoretical foundations of BMT, social learning theory and social psychological exchange theories, both emphasize the dual roles of external and internal environments in regulating interpersonal interaction. For example, the highly influential concept of "comparison level for alternatives" (Thibaut & Kelley, 1959) describes an internal evaluation process where spouses compare the gratification derived from their current relationship with the perceived gratification that they would attain in available alternative relationships, and on that basis continue or discontinue their present relationship. This concept has been central to social learning conceptions of marriage, and it views spouses as rational, information-processing organisms who make decisions about relationships on the basis of their perceptions. Both explicitly and implicitly, social learning and behavior exchange notions emphasize that spouses are not simply passive receptors of environmental stimuli, but rather actively evaluate and interpret such stimuli based on their idiosyncratic cognitive sets and schemata. Jacobson and Margolin (1979), among others (cf. O'Leary & Turkewitz, 1978; Stuart, 1980; Weiss, 1978, 1980), have discussed the importance of cognitive and perceptual processes in mediating the reinforcing and punishing impact of marital interactional behavior:

> People talk to themselves, they appraise their environments, and they make attributions and interpretations of their world. These self-statements, appraisals, and attributions mediate and moderate the effects of environmental stimuli on behavior, and can serve either as eliciting or discriminative stimuli. Attributions on the part of one spouse regarding the "intent" of the partner's behavior can moderate the reinforcing effects of that behavior. . . . Emotional reactions can be elicited by specific self-statements, which often serve as interpretations of an environmental event. . . . The inclusion of cognitions as possible mediators of behavior will have important implications for the analysis and treatment of distressed relationships. (Jacobson & Margolin, 1979, p. 12)

Similarly, behavioral marital therapists have argued from the beginning that cognitive and perceptual deficiencies can serve as vexing impediments to successful therapy, and that they often require direct attention (Stuart, 1969; Weiss, Hops, & Patterson, 1973). This emphasis on internal changes as well as behavior changes is reflected in early papers specifying subjective "satisfaction" as the fundamental goal of marital therapy, despite the focus on behavior change as a means to achieve increments in satisfaction (Weiss & Margolin, 1977; Wills, Weiss, & Patterson, 1974). Jacobson, Elwood, and Dallas (1981) went so far as to suggest that marital distress is a multidimensional construct that is evaluated by the therapist through a variety of means: overt behavioral transactions observed by the therapist and measured by observational coding systems (Gottman, 1979; Hops, Wills, Patterson, & Weiss, 1971; Patterson, 1976); reports from spouses regarding the behavioral transactions that occur between them in the natural environment, measured by instruments such as the Spouse Observation Checklist (SOC) (Patterson, 1976; Weiss & Perry, 1979); and subjective reports from spouses regarding their attitude toward and degree of satisfaction derived from the relationship, measured by self-report instruments such as the Dyadic Adjustment Scale (Spanier, 1976). It has long been recognized that treatment success depends upon change in cognitive and affective domains, and that behavior change is best thought of as a means to an end rather than an end in itself.

There are at least three ways that dysfunctional cognitive processes can subvert the process of change in BMT. First, and most simply, cognitive and perceptual processes can remain dysfunctional, despite successfully induced behavior change. Positive behavior changes may not be noticed, they may be interpreted in such a way that their impact is negligible, or they may not be regarded as permanent. In such cases, marital satisfaction will not be substantially altered, despite behavior changes that correspond to the couple's stated treatment goals. Second, dysfunctional cognitive and perceptual processes can interfere with the behavior change itself, such that spouses will avoid complying with therapeutic directives or in other ways refuse to enact positive behavior changes. For example, a spouse complaining of "mistrust" may withhold potentially reinforcing behaviors with the expressed desire that the partner change "first." Third, dysfunctional cognitive and perceptual processes can become functionally autonomous from any behavioral referent. In such cases, the cognitive and perceptual processes constitute the problem, and an exclusive focus on behavior change would be fruitless and unproductive.

Behavioral clinicians have long suspected that standard BMT technology may be insufficient to modify cognitive and perceptual processes that interfere with change in any of the ways enumerated here (Gurman, 1978; Gurman & Knudson, 1978; Knudson, Gurman, & Kniskern, 1979; Margolin, Christensen, & Weiss, 1975; O'Leary & Turkewitz, 1978; Stuart, 1969, 1980;

Weiss, 1978, 1980; Weiss *et al.*, 1973). Even if the technology is sufficient to induce behavior change, traditional contingency management procedures may often prove to be self-defeating. Contingency contracts, for example, may help to maintain dysfunctional cognitions through the very act which is assumed to be the active mechanism for change—the specified reinforcer (Jacobson, 1978b; Jacobson & Margolin, 1979). Since many spouse-provided behaviors are reinforcing only when they are accompanied by certain attributions on the part of the recipient, the specification of reinforcers contingent upon desirable changes may in some cases lead to attributions that undermine the reinforcing impact of the change. Changes that would otherwise be well received and attributed to internal factors such as "love" might be attributed instead to the exigencies of the contract. These concerns are not pure speculation; in addition to social psychological research in the area of attribution theory (Jones, Kanouse, Kelley, Nisbett, Valins, & Weiner, 1972), our research has produced findings that distressed couples are more likely than nondistressed couples to attribute their partners' positive behaviors to external factors (Jacobson, McDonald, Follette, & Berley, in press). In other words, even when distressed spouses perceive positive behaviors emitted by their partners, they are likely to deny them credit for those behaviors or in some other way devalue them.

Research findings over the past few years provide support for the proposition that distressed couples have cognitive and perceptual biases that have implications for the practice of BMT. These and other research findings illustrate the inadequacy of the early social learning models as applied to marital distress, and they suggest novel treatment strategies involving more careful attention to the modification of internal events.

A number of studies suggest that differences between distressed and nondistressed couples cannot be reduced simply to discrepancies in the frequencies of rewarding and punishing exchanges (Billings, 1979; Gottman, Markman, & Notarius, 1977; Gottman, Notarius, Markman, Bank, Yoppi, & Rubin, 1976; Jacobson, Follette, & McDonald, 1982; Jacobson, Waldron, & Moore, 1980; Margolin, 1981; Margolin & Wampold, 1981). Research in our laboratories has identified a difference in "reactivity" between distressed and nondistressed couples (Jacobson *et al.*, 1980, 1982). This means that distressed spouses are hypersensitive on a subjective, affective level to their partners' immediate behavior; for example, not only does punishing behavior occur more frequently in the exchanges of distressed couples, but when it does occur, it has a deleterious effect on their marital satisfaction. In contrast, generally happy couples are relatively "robust" in the face of negative behavior; even when punishing behavior does occur, it does not seem to have a deleterious effect on subjective marital satisfaction. Our interpretation of these findings is that punishing behaviors have a negative impact on distressed couples not simply because they occur but because of the extreme reaction that each spouse has to the partner's delivery of punishing behavior. Somehow, happy couples have devised a mechanism to neutralize the impact of negative behavior, and this mechanism is lacking in distressed couples. Gottman's (1979) research provides further evidence of such an "editing" function in the repertoire of nondistressed couples. The clinical implications of this phenomenon are that reducing the frequency of negative behavior will be insufficient unless distressed spouses also learn, during the course of therapy, to react less strongly to it when it does occur. Although it is possible that the reactivity will decrease as a concomitant to a reduction in the frequency of negative behavior, the contention here is that independent attention needs to be paid to the reactivity process itself, that these strong emotional reactions tend to be cognitively mediated, and that purely behavioral interventions are likely to be insufficient in the modification of reactivity.

In addition to their heightened reactivity to negative behavior, distressed spouses are significantly more likely to reciprocate negative behavior (Billings, 1979; Gottman, 1979; Jacobson & Moore, 1981a; Margolin & Wampold, 1981; Revenstorf, Hahlweg, Schindler, & Vogel, Chapter 10, this volume). In distressed couples, negative behavior tends to occur in chains, and this process suggests a tendency toward escalation. The clinical implications of this process are that distressed couples must be taught strategies for interrupting these escalating chains of negative behavior, and the strategies for controlling and neutralizing conflict expression involve training in cognitive self-control (Epstein, 1982; Mahoney & Arnkoff, 1978; Meichenbaum, 1977; Schindler & Vollmer, Chapter 16, this volume).

Thus far, our brief literature review has focused exclusively on negative behavior. But it is not simply the control of negative behavior that leads to a satisfying relationship (Margolin & Weiss, 1978; Weiss, 1978). Happy couples also provide one another with high rates of rewarding behavior (see Jacobson, 1979a). Traditionally, BMT has sought to provide for increased rates of positive behavioral exchanges through the use of contingency management procedures based on positive control. But Gottman, Notarius, Markman, Bank, Yoppi, and Rubin (1976) have interpreted their data as supporting a "bank account" model of marital satisfaction. According to this model, happy couples exchange high rates of positive behaviors noncontingently. It is the very absence of contingent exchanges of positive behavior, combined with high rates of such behavior, that distinguishes happy couples. To the extent that this model is correct, it suggests that training couples to provide higher rates of positive behavior in an overtly contingent manner may be self-defeating. I would argue that contingencies exist to regulate the positive behavior of nondistressed couples, but that the contingencies are long-term rather than immediate. The clinical implications of these observations are that marital therapy will be successful only when spouses perceive each other as responding positively in the absence of any obvious or immediate return. The fostering of such perceptions not only requires appropriate cognitive and perceptual changes, but it has implications for how behavioral interventions are designed.

Finally, a number of studies have suggested that distressed spouses are particularly unreliable as observers of the events in their marriage (Christensen & Nies, 1980; Elwood & Jacobson, 1982; Jacobson & Moore, 1981b). Robinson and Price (1980) reported that distressed spouses underestimate the frequency of positive behavior, relative to objective observers. The studies point to the existence of cognitive and perceptual biases in distressed couples and suggest the need to pay attention to those biases in the designing of treatment interventions.

To conclude this section, clinical observations, theoretical formulations, and recent research findings all point to the necessity for supplementing, and in some cases substantially modifying, our behavioral treatment programs with couples. To effectively modify cognitive and affective components in the marital distress constellation, three types of deviation from a pure behavioral approach appear to be necessary. First, behavioral interventions must be designed not simply to change behavior but also to concurrently facilitate desirable cognitive and perceptual changes. Second, cognitive-restructuring procedures are necessary to change dysfunctional internal processes that remain refractory to even carefully designed behavioral interventions. Third, since negative reciprocity and reactivity are so prevalent in distressed couples, cognitive self-control strategies appear necessary in training couples to regulate the escalation process. In the following section, procedural modifications are considered that expand the flexibility of BMT to deal effectively with cognitive and affective processes.

Behavior Exchange Procedures

In the previous section it was argued that insufficient attention has been paid to designing behavioral intervention strategies that foster the concomitant modification of dysfunctional cognitions. In fact, some intervention procedures, such as contingency contracting, may actually be counterproductive in this regard. The challenges facing behavioral marital therapists are twofold: to instigate behavior changes that are accompanied by supportive cognitive changes, and to induce positive changes that undermine the dependency of distressed spouses on immediate contingencies for their maintenance. In this section some examples are offered regarding possible expansions of traditional BMT technology designed to meet both of these challenges. In presenting these suggestions, the goal is to expand the flexibility of behavior exchange procedures so that a greater proportion of distressed couples may be successfully treated. These intervention strategies will be unnecessary for some couples; some couples will respond positively to traditional behavioral interventions even when the emphasis is on maintaining immediate contingency control, and even when the interventions are designed in the absence of a direct attention to internal processes. It is for those couples who remain refractory to such interventions that these suggestions are offered.

In designing behavioral and instigative tasks to promote desirable cognitive changes, the following guidelines must be observed. First, behavior changes that occur at the giver's initiative are more likely to be favorably evaluated by the receiver than behavior changes that have been initially requested by the receiver. Second, the fewer the constraints on the behavior-changing spouse, the more choice he/she has (or appears to have) in deciding whether or not to deliver a desired behavior, the more positive impact the enactment of this behavior will have on the receiver. Third, the more specifically the behavior change directive emanates from the therapist, the more likely it is that the therapist, rather than the spouse, will receive credit for any behavior changes that do occur. Fourth, parallel but unilateral behavior changes — that is, changes with "no strings attached" — are more likely to be perceived as internally motivated, and therefore to be highly valued, than bilateral changes or changes that are part of a *quid pro quo* contingency arrangement.

We always begin our interventions by directing each spouse to focus on the self and how he/she can change his/her own behavior to increase the quality of the relationship for the partner (see Jacobson, 1981). The rule that is imposed on spouses applies both to their behavior during the therapy sessions and to their behavior at home between sessions. The notion is that, instead of complaining about what one is not getting from the partner or requesting change from the partner, each spouse must direct attention to pinpointing — without input from the partner — behaviors that are likely to enhance the quality of the relationship for the partner, and then increase the frequency of those behaviors and examine their impact. Each spouse is working independently, in consultation with the therapist, to enhance the partner's relationship satisfaction.

Prior to the initiation of formal therapy sessions, each spouse makes the commitment to "focusing on yourself" (for an elaboration of the rationale that is presented to couples for this self-focus, see Jacobson & Margolin, 1979, Chapter 5). Therapy does not begin until this commitment is obtained, but there is rarely any difficulty in obtaining it from both spouses. Once they have made the commitment, subsequent rule violations can be easily enforced simply by the therapist's referring back to the commitment. The first few therapy sessions are then spent consulting with each spouse, training him/her in pinpointing the functional relationship between his/her own behaviors and the partner's day-to-day marital satisfaction. We rely heavily on the SOC, developed by Weiss and his associates (Patterson, 1976; Weiss & Perry, 1979), for this purpose. Using the SOC, each spouse tracks the partner's frequency of positive and negative behaviors on a daily basis. Concurrently, each partner records his/her daily satisfaction rating (DSR) for the marriage, a global subjective rating on a scale of 1 to 7. Using these data from the SOC, the therapist teaches each spouse to monitor his/her daily impact on the partner by regularly perusing the partner's data. By determining the behaviors that discriminate between relatively satisfying and relatively unsatisfying days, each spouse learns to pinpoint those behaviors that maximize their reinforcing impact on the partner. Usually, an early homework assignment requires each to generate a list of those behaviors that seem to be the best discriminators between the partner's high and low DSRs. Then, after each spouse has mastered these functional analytic skills, he/she is directed to test the hypotheses by escalating the frequency of those behaviors hypothesized to be reinforcing, and examining their impact on the partner's DSRs. Each spouse selects from the pool of hypothesized reinforcers and "decides" which ones to accelerate. To the extent that a partner's DSR increases, the hypotheses are confirmed. Subsequent therapy sessions are spent debriefing the homework assignment, with each spouse critiquing his/her own performance over the previous week. If one or both spouses are unsuccessful in increasing the partner's DSR, the therapist initiates a "troubleshooting" exercise, the purpose of which is to correct any deficiencies in the way the assignment was carried out. This may involve responding to noncompliance (Jacobson, 1981); simply clarifying the assignment; or, most often, identifying alternative behaviors that might prove to be more reinforcing.

This initial exercise in accelerating the frequency of positive relationship behaviors is similar to Weiss's concept of "love days" (Weiss et al., 1973) and Stuart's (1980) concept of "caring days." However, rather than concentrating on particular days of the week, the spouses are asked to focus on maximizing the other person's satisfaction each day. Another distinction involves our emphasis on teaching spouses a strategy for empirically generating and testing hypotheses on how to please their partners more effectively. The goal, as in much of BMT, is to teach spouses skills in tracking and systematically reinforcing each other. A subgoal is to introduce the notion that maintaining relationship satisfaction requires daily vigilance and careful attention (Jacobson, Berley, Melman, Elwood, & Phelps, in press). The rule that each spouse is to work independently and to focus only on his/her own behavior undercuts spouses' tendencies to blame one another for the problems in their marriage and to use that blame as a justification for not changing their own behavior. Throughout this exercise, each partner works independently and unilaterally, such that he/she must continue regardless of what the partner is doing.

Notice how this exercise incorporates the guidelines mentioned at the beginning of the section. First, all positive behaviors that are increased occur at one's own initiative, rather than in response to requests from the partner. The fact that the initiative comes from the giver rather than the receiver undercuts one type of devaluing attribution ("She changed because I asked her to") and fosters a more relationship-enhancing internal attribution ("She changed on her own, out of an internal, spontaneous desire to please me and improve the relationship"). Any particular positive behavior is more likely to be received as a relatively unanticipated, pleasant surprise, and as a sign of caring and commitment. Second, each spouse has a maximum amount of freedom regarding which positive behaviors to accelerate, usually choosing from a large pool of behaviors rather than responding to a directive to change any particular behavior. Since the spouses have such freedom and so few external constraints are placed upon them, it is highly likely that the changes that do occur will be perceived as resulting from "free choice" rather than from external demands. Third, there is no directive coming from the therapist to change any particular behavior. Therefore, another source of "external attribution" is undermined, namely that the spouse is responding to the external demand of a therapist. Fourth, since there is no contingency contract and the assignment requires parallel but unilateral changes on the part of each spouse, it is unlikely that the changes will be attributed to the requirement of a contingency. The external attribution that "he changed only because he wanted to get me to be good to him" is less likely to occur.

In our behavior exchange assignments, there is a gradual evolution toward a focus on the more central behavioral problems in the relationship. The previously described assignment emphasizes "low-cost" behavior changes, with each spouse deciding from a number of options, thereby maximizing the amount of choice. Inevitably, as the therapy tasks move closer to those central issues, the potential costs of behavior change increase for each spouse, and to some degree the options for how to satisfy the partner become more restricted. With this evolution comes the ever-increasing risk that self-defeating cognitions will interfere with each spouse's reception of even successfully enacted behavior changes. However, if this progression from minor to major relationship issues is gradual enough, and if previous therapeutic tasks have been successful, the partners will be highly motivated to take risks and maintain a collaborative focus.

There is an analogy between the graded movement toward central relationship tasks in BMT and the use of hierarchies in systematic desensitization. As relatively low-cost ventures yield positive outcomes and increased relationship satisfaction, there is a corresponding diminution of anxiety regarding the investment in more risky commitments to therapy. Each spouse is more confident that such risks will have payoffs for him/her personally. Both the therapist and the treatment program have enhanced credibility. In addition, if behavior changes during the early treatment sessions are received positively by each spouse, and attributed to the partner's motivation to change and his/her commitment to therapy, there will be increased trust, and future changes will be more likely to be accompanied by relationship-enhancing attributions. Moreover, despite the inevitable restriction in behavior change options and increment in costs that accompany the latter stages of therapy, adherence to these principles — (1) self-focus, (2) general rather than specific directives, and (3) parallel but unilateral rather than *quid pro quo* changes — maximizes the likelihood that cognitive changes will support the occurring behavior changes.

For example, at some point it becomes self-defeating to require that each spouse work independently to increase the partner's satisfaction without input from the receiver. But requests from the receiver do not inevitably neutralize the impact of subsequent positive responses. The initiative regarding what, when, and how to change can still be left to each partner. The receiver's input can be presented as "information" rather than as a "request for change." In fact, this distinction can become more than mere semantics without jeopardizing the behavior change process as long as there is an implicit directive to continue one's efforts toward enhancing the partner's satisfaction. The therapist might ask the wife to give some suggestions as to how the husband might "support your efforts toward improving your education." Assuming that the wife produces five suggestions, the husband now has the "information," without being requested to offer any particular manifestation of support. As long as the therapist continues to emphasize and enforce each spouse's initial commitment to focus on becoming a more satisfactory spouse, there is an implicit directive to implement at least a portion of the wife's suggestions, while still maintaining an emphasis on the freedom to choose among various options. And as long as no explicit contingencies are agreed to that link one spouse's behavior changes to those initiated by the partner, the principle of parallel but unilateral change is maintained.

Dysfunctional attributions are not the only type of cognitive process that interferes with the receptivity to behavior change. "Selective negative tracking" can also bias spouses toward experiencing the relationship as more dissatisfying than need be the case. If spouses fail to notice positive behaviors that do occur, their impact will be inconsequential. BMT researchers have long recognized this problem, and BMT interventions are structured in order to encourage "positive tracking" (Jacobson, 1981; Jacobson & Margolin, 1979; Stuart, 1980; Weiss *et al.*, 1973). The rationale of many of our intervention strategies is to increase the salience of positive events that already occur so that their impact will be more positive. Positive tracking strategies include interviews that focus on elucidating relationship strengths, questionnaires that pull for such information, homework assignments that direct spouses to selectively track and report on positive behavior, therapy sessions structured to emphasize and accentuate relationship-enhancing behaviors that occur during the sessions and between sessions, and behavior change efforts that focus on increasing positive relationship behaviors rather than decreasing negative relationship behaviors.

This discussion has emphasized one dimension of the behavior exchange approach: the emphasis on fostering cognitive and affective change as well as behavior change. Those internal changes, it is argued, cannot be left to chance, because both recent research and clinical observations suggest that they do not inevitably follow successful behavior changes. Some of the very basic procedures associated with BMT can be seen as high-risk for producing cognitions that are destructive to the long-term outcome of therapy, including the emphases on one spouse requesting change from the other, on contingency management procedures, and on specific behavior change tasks. We have been attempting to maintain the focus on behavior change while at the same time paying direct attention to how each spouse perceives and reacts to those behavior changes. I am optimistic that behavioral interventions, if designed and engineered appropriately, can go a long way toward accomplishing dual goals.

Cognitive-Behavioral Marital Therapy

Cognitive therapy has proven to be a valuable adjunct to behavior therapy techniques for a number of clinical problems, including anxiety and stress (Meichenbaum, 1977), depression (Beck, Rush, Shaw, & Emery, 1979), addictive behaviors (Marlatt, 1978), and family dysfunction (Barton & Alexander, 1981). Up until now, little has been written about the applications of cognitive approaches such as rational emotive therapy (Ellis, 1962) or self-instructional training (Meichenbaum, 1977) to the treatment of marital problems. However, from examining the literature it is apparent that cognitive interventions have been utilized unsystematically (Jacobson & Margolin, 1979; Margolin et al., 1975), and many have argued for a more systematic inclusion of cognitive strategies within a BMT framework (O'Leary & Turkewitz, 1978; Weiss, 1980). There are several reasons why such an inclusion would be desirable. First, there is no guarantee that even carefully designed behavioral interventions will successfully modify dysfunctional cognitions for all couples. If the technology of BMT is broadened to include cognitive interventions, it is likely that more couples will be successfully treated. Second, an imbalance exists in the current practice of BMT, placing an implicit value on behavior change as the solution to all marital conflict. When one spouse is unhappy about a partner's behavior that is occurring at either an excessive or deficient rate, there is a strong tendency to use BMT technology to serve the complainant, with not much attention paid to the validity or reasonableness of the complaint. Yet it is obvious that not all behavioral complaints are fair, reasonable, or justified. Although virtually all behavior therapists would pay lip service to this truism, we tend to be so avoidant of making explicit value judgments that we end up making an implicit value judgment: Whenever one spouse is upset about some aspect of the other's behavior, the concern is *a priori* valid.

Furthermore, any spouse who is unwilling to change or collaborate is "resisting" therapy. Consider the husband who was so sensitive to being rejected that he was inclined to inappropriately interpret a variety of his wife's behaviors as signifying rejection. During one treatment session, he defined the problem of his wife "going to bed earlier" than he did. This behavior was aversive to him because he interpreted her early retirement as an attempt to avoid sex and intimacy. Furthermore, he retired at 2 A.M., and her compliance with his request would have meant that she would have to limit her sleeping to 5 hours per night. His request was not only irrational and based on an unrealistic expectation, but it stemmed from a faulty and unwarranted interpretation of the meaning of her behavior. Without a method for uncovering and modifying such irrational thoughts, not only would a therapist be condoning unrealistic demands made by one partner, but he/she would be ignoring an important factor in the perpetuation of marital discord.

In this section I examine the traditional, unsystematic use of cognitive-restructuring techniques in BMT, and follow with some suggestions for integrating cognitive therapy more systematically. The section concludes with a mention of some of the pitfalls and clinical hazards of a cognitive approach.

Traditional Use of Cognitive-Restructuring Procedures in BMT

Throughout the BMT literature, there are frequent references to the *ad hoc* use of reframing and relabeling interventions (Jacobson & Margolin, 1979; Margolin *et al.*, 1975; Markman & Floyd, 1980; O'Leary & Turkewitz, 1978; Weiss, 1980; Weiss *et al.*, 1973). The use of cognitive relabeling can be traced back to the early application of systems and communications theories to marital and family problems (Bodin, 1981; Haley, 1963; Sluzki, 1978; Watzlawick, Weakland, & Fisch, 1974), and it has been a major addition to models that seek to integrate behavioral and systems approaches to marital and family therapy (Barton & Alexander, 1981; Birchler & Spinks, 1980; Spinks & Birchler, 1982; Weiss, 1980). These interventions are designed to provide couples with alternative frameworks in which to view their distress, to debunk destructive myths that couples hold about their relationship or about marriages in general, and to increase positive outcome expectancies.

The model of marital discord that is presented to couples in BMT can be viewed as a cognitive-restructuring intervention. Spouses enter therapy with biased perspectives or theories regarding the problems in their marriage. Each spouse adheres to an adversarial position, which not only blames the relationship problems on deficiencies in the partner, but also attributes the partner's undesirable behavior to malevolent intent or other pejorative personality traits. Behavior therapists offer spouses an alternative framework that emphasizes the dyadic nature of their difficulties and presents more benign interpretations for each spouse's undesirable behavior. Although it is unlikely that spouses will immediately "buy into" an interpretation of their problems based on reciprocity and mutual responsibility, the offering of an alternative framework serves two important functions at the beginning stages of therapy. First, it gives them something to think about, since the therapist is both an expert and presumably an objective observer. Second, it establishes a rationale for their commitment to a treatment program that assumes that the therapist is correct. In other words, whether or not this alternative framework actually influences their view of the relationship, it seems to serve as part of the constellation of discriminative stimuli that produce collaborative behavior.

Behavior therapists also make frequent use of attributional relabeling interventions. Most of these consist of interpreting displeasing relationship behavior in such a way as to make it appear to be more benign. Behaviors that are viewed by spouses as implying negative intentions are reinterpreted as representing skill deficits or ineffectual attempts to achieve desirable goals. A recent example involves Jack and Jane (Jacobson et al., in press). Jane was frequently upset by Jack's apparent unwillingness to assert himself. One example involved a friend of his who frequently intruded on their time together by dropping in uninvited during the evening. Although Jane urged Jack to tell his friend to cease his intrusive and unannounced visits, Jack was reluctant to do so. Jane interpreted this reluctance as proof that he cared more about the feelings of third parties than he did about hers. The therapist reframed Jack's behavior as a skill deficit in assertiveness. Another example involved the husband who lied to his wife about their debts. She chose to view his deception as caused by the trait of dishonesty. The therapist relabeled it as an indication of caring and concern: "He was so worried about what you might think of him and so afraid that he would lose you that he was afraid to tell you."

In addition to these cognitive relabeling interventions, the BMT literature is replete with examples of other cognitive interventions employed on an *ad hoc* basis, whenever necessary, to counter expressed attitudes and beliefs on the part of spouses that are counterproductive to the tasks of therapy. Some of these interventions take the form of debunking unrealistic expectations or myths held by spouses regarding their partners, the institution of marriage, or the process of therapy (Jacobson & Margolin, 1979). Examples of such myths include the notion that the joys and pleasures of courtship can be maintained throughout the duration of married life, the notion that successful therapy should result in a return to that idealization phase where the spouses are "in love," or the belief that one's partner should know "intuitively" that one is upset and therefore that direct expression of feelings is unnecessary. The skillful behavior therapist engages in "search and destroy" missions to ferret out and challenge beliefs and attitudes that decrease motivation and detract from therapeutic progress. By frequently probing spouses as to their reactions to therapy, and by tracking their nonverbal behavior to detect concerns or affective reactions that seem unexplainable given the manifest content of the treatment session, such beliefs and attitudes can often be elicited. For example, some spouses react negatively to the structure of BMT and to the mechanical nature of some of the therapeutic tasks. The painstaking, step-by-step skill training often runs counter to their beliefs that change should occur spontaneously, or that the "feelings" of wanting to change should precede the efforts to change. Once elicited, these myths are countered by statements such as "We have found that the only way to make real and permanent changes is to start by being mechanical. Old habits die hard, and we need to be mechanical for a while in order to counter your tendencies to do things the old way. Our ultimate goal is the same as yours, but it will take some time before we get there. Think of this as a means to an end."

Cognitive interventions have also been aimed at maintaining spouses' positive outcome expectancies (Jacobson & Margolin, 1979). Behavior therapists are typically "upbeat" regarding the likelihood of a positive outcome in therapy, although their optimism is tempered by the proviso that, ultimately, improvement is in the hands of the spouses and will require their firm dedication as well as collaborative effort. These statements are designed to induce optimism in couples, so that they will work productively during therapy. At times, paradoxically, positive expectancies are best maintained by warnings that spouses should not expect improvement for a while. Since relapses during the course of therapy are so common, the therapist is wise to predict them; otherwise, spouses may become demoralized when they occur and are unanticipated. If no relapse occurs, so much the better; but a predicted relapse should not interfere substantially with positive expectancies regarding the overall outcome of treatment. Moreover, there are times during therapy when no progress is expected for a limited period of time, such as during the assessment phase or during the early stages of problem-solving training. The skillful therapist will remind spouses of this so that positive expectancies are maintained despite the lack of immediate benefit.

Thus, in the course of working effectively with couples, a number of clinical guidelines have been established over the years for a strategic interposing of cognitive interventions. What is proposed here is that we advance our clinical flexibility by programming cognitive interventions more systematically into BMT. The next section establishes some guidelines for what may be termed cognitive BMT (C-BMT).

Clinical Guidelines for Cognitive-Behavioral Marital Therapy

C-BMT is based on the integration of BMT with the therapeutic models of Beck *et al.* (1979), Ellis (1962), and Meichenbaum (1977). It contains a number of different foci. First, C-BMT exposes and challenges irrational and dysfunctional cognitions that underlie specific complaints. Second, C-BMT can expose and modify the cognitions that inhibit spouses from changing in ways that conform to their partners' requests. Third, C-BMT teaches spouses an additional set of skills that can be combined with the functional analytic skills forming the core BMT package.

The preceding discussion has already illustrated how mediating cognitions can exacerbate a situation or, in some cases, can even cause a behavior on the part of the partner to be experienced as aversive. By carrying on a dialogue with the complaining spouse, the skillful therapist can expose these cognitions and thereby subject them to scrutiny and perhaps modification. This dialogue can assume a myriad of forms. One is illustrated in the following transcript (H = husband; T = therapist; W = wife):

H: You never show any interest in my work. It's gotten to the point where I don't bother to talk to you about it any more.

T: What is it about that that bothers you?

H: I just don't like it. I work hard all day and she doesn't appreciate it.

T: So you feel unappreciated when she doesn't show interest in your work.

H: Yes.

T: Now I presume you are referring to the fact that she doesn't ask you any questions about your work when you come home.

H: Hardly ever. And if I bring something up, she doesn't sit down and listen. She just keeps puttering around the kitchen.

T: So Harriet seldom asks you questions about your day at work, and when you offer information about it she doesn't sit down and listen. Does she make any comment?

H: Only "That's nice, dear." Or some other bullshit.

W: How am I supposed to get dinner ready and keep Chip and Dale out of your hair if I'm sitting around talking to you?

T: Hold it a minute, Harriet. Let me finish talking to Ozzie. I want to hear from you in a little while. Ozzie, let me see if I have this right. Harriet seldom asks you questions about your day at work. When you bring things up, she seldom stops what she's doing to listen. And she doesn't say much in response. Does that about do it?

H: Yes.

T: And on the basis of that you assume that she isn't interested.

H: Of course. Isn't that obvious?

T: I'm not sure. What else do you think that says about her besides not being interested in your work?

H: What do you mean?

T: It seems to me that you see her as making some kind of statement about you and her. I'm trying to get at what it is.

H: Well, I think that she cares about getting what she wants and needs from me, but she doesn't care about me as a person. I'm a meal ticket and a security blanket for her, and that's about as far as her interest goes.

T: O.K., now we're getting somewhere. Let me point out that there are two things going on. You're noticing certain things about Harriet. That's one thing. And then you're making some interpretations about what she does. That's something else. If I was in your home, and saw Harriet in action, I'm not sure that I would conclude that she is not interested in your work or that she does not care about you as a person.

H: What else could it mean?

In this example, the therapist establishes the behaviors that are upsetting the husband and then distinguishes between those behaviors and the inferences the husband draws regarding the meaning of those behaviors. Spouses often are not aware of the fact that they are making such inferences, and they are so insensitive to the distinction between observation and interpretation that they think that the former inevitably implies the latter. In extreme cases, the interpretations are reified to such an extent that they become autonomous. When this happens, the partner will respond with an interpretation, even when asked for a behavioral description, as in the following example.

T: Tell me what he did that upset you so much.

W: He was completely insensitive to my feelings. He knew that I was upset and he didn't even care.

By carrying on a dialogue with the complaining spouse, the cognitions become exposed. The therapist then has a number of options. One possibility would be to check out the validity of the complaining spouse's interpretation with the partner.

T: Is he right, Harriet? That you're not interested in his work or him as a person?

W: No, that's not right. I've been assuming that he doesn't want to talk about his work. As a matter of fact, I would like to hear a lot more. But not right when he comes home. That's the time of day I feel most hassled.

Another possibility would involve continuing the dialogue with the husband and having him explore some alternative interpretations himself, after being prompted to do so by the therapist. Or the therapist can suggest his/her own alternative interpretations. These more benign interpretations—whether they are originally suggested by the therapist, the husband, or the wife—will then compete with the complaining spouse's interpretation, even if the alternatives are not immediately accepted by the spouse. This reconsideration is more likely to occur if the therapist throws the weight of his/her authority behind the more benign interpretation. The possibility of a more positive view of the partner can have a number of favorable consequences. In some cases, a more benign interpretation will do away with the problem. Some behaviors, as mentioned earlier, are aversive simply because of the meaning that the partner attributes to them. When the door to alternative interpretations is opened, the impact of the behavior changes. In other cases the behavior may still be targeted for change, but collaboration will be fostered. The alternative perspective for viewing the behavior diffuses some of the emotional intensity associated with it and allows for a smoother problem-solving session. Both spouses are more likely to be empathic and therefore more open to compromise.

I recommend that behavior therapists integrate cognitive exploration within a BMT framework. I have begun to conduct such explorations as a prelude to negotiation or problem-solving sessions for a particular problem. In addition to the potential benefits of such an integration that have already been mentioned, these individual dialogues foster increased sensitivity on the part of the therapist to the internal workings of each spouse. This addition to the structure helps guard against the tendency to focus one's attention exclusively on the construct of the couple's relationship.

Cognitive interventions are not confined to exploring the basis for complaints; they can also be applied to the inhibitions to change experienced by the complainee. The exploration of cognitions that accompany the complainee's displeasing behavior often creates more empathy and an increased willingness to compromise on the part of the complainant. Moreover, the verbalization of inhibitions and catastrophic expectations held by the complainee can likewise facilitate collaboration, and the ensuing discussion can aid in transcending those expectations and fears. This is illustrated in the following example:

T: When you are jealous and have a tantrum, what do you think you gain?

W: He knows that I'm watching him and that he can't pull anything on me.

T: What do you think would happen if you stopped being jealous?

W: I can't help being jealous.

T: But, I mean, let's say you just stopped showing it—hid it from him so he had no idea that you felt jealous.

W: I don't think I could do that. But assuming that I could, I guess I'm afraid that he would start messing around.

T: Has he given you any basis for worrying about that?

W: No.

T: Then you're stuck. The only way you can find out whether he's faithful because he wants to be, is by not being jealous and seeing what happens.

When cognitive factors act to inhibit behavior change, exposing them and subjecting them to reality testing can often lead to cognitive restructuring. When exposure and reality testing prove to be insufficient for cognitive change, they still might lead to hypothesis testing. Challenging clients to definitively test their formulations can often lead to an effective instigation for behavior change, where other behavioral interventions have met with resistance.

Cognitive-restructuring interventions need not be confined to the therapist–client dialogues. Spouses can be trained to include cognitive explorations with one another as part of the process of problem-solving training. The inclusion of such a dialogue during both the problem definition and problem solution phases of a problem-solving session fosters increased empathy, facilitates collaboration, and provides an increased number of options in the resolution of the conflict. Using the problem-solving format suggested by Jacobson and Margolin (1979), there are two points where cognitive explorations by the spouses could be particularly useful. During the definition phase, the complainee could probe the complainant for the cognitions surrounding a particular complaint.

W: I enjoy spending time with you on weekends, and that is why it upsets me so much when you work on Saturdays.

H: You're saying that you like spending time with me, but you don't like it when I work on Saturdays. Is that right?

W: Yes.

H: I do end up working a lot of Saturdays, and I don't like it either. What does it mean to you when I work on Saturdays?

W: I think that you don't view our relationship as a priority.

H: So, when I spend extra time working on weekends, you see that as an indication that work is more important to me than we are.

W: That's right.

During the solution phase of a problem-solving session, as the spouses discuss the costs and benefits of various brainstormed proposals for conflict resolution, the complainant has an ideal opportunity to explore the complainee's inhibitions or catastrophic expectations surrounding behavior change.

W: What would be the costs to you of scheduling yourself so that all office work could be done during the week, and weekends would be reserved for us? Then if you had too much to do, you could at least do the excess at home.

H: I guess my fear is that you would not accept, even at home, work on weekends. That would put extra pressure on me.

W: So you're afraid that I would still be upset even if the work you did on weekends was at home.

H: Um-hum.

W: I really don't think I would mind. Maybe I'm being naive, but at least we could test it out.

Teaching couples to explore each other's cognitions is consistent with the secondary-prevention component of BMT. To the extent that spouses are capable of learning to do the therapist's job, they will be better fortified to resolve further conflicts on their own, subsequent to the termination of therapy.

Cognitive Self-Control Training

Among the most difficult interaction patterns to modify in distressed relationships are those characterized by impulsive, destructive exchanges of anger. This is not to say that expression of angry feelings is inherently destructive; clearly, angry feelings are inevitable in even the most satisfying marriages, and the expression of such feelings is not only necessary but often constructive and capable of enhancing intimacy (Gottman, Markman, Notarius, & Gonso, 1976; Guerney, 1977; Jacobson & Margolin, 1979; O'Leary & Turkewitz, 1978). But distressed couples are often plagued by extremely destructive and apparently impulsive exchanges of anger. This bickering and reciprocal verbal abuse is often refractory to typical behavioral interventions. Change agreements are often relatively easy to negotiate, only to be forgotten and ignored when conflict situations arise. The dilemma for the therapist is that, although during periods of tranquility spouses recognize the destructive impact of these interchanges and are highly motivated to control the outbursts, when the situations arise the spouses react impulsively. Even when they are aware of what they are doing, in the short run the salience of whatever short-term reinforcers derive from destructive anger expression seems to outweigh the benefits of anger control.

There has been some discussion in the literature on how to teach couples to interrupt these hostile chains (Epstein, 1982; Liberman, Wheeler, deVisser, Kuehnel, & Kuehnel, 1980; Margolin, 1981; Schindler & Vollmer, Chapter 16, this volume). Cognitive self-control strategies may prove to be the optimal solution to this clinical problem. Epstein (1982) and Schindler and Vollmer (Chapter 16, this volume) have advocated teaching couples how to instruct themselves to behave more positively during times of conflict, adapting the techniques of Meichenbaum's (1977) self-instructional training. Epstein (1982) has suggested that individual or concurrent therapy sessions may enhance such training. This is one area of BMT where individual therapy sessions may be necessary, particularly during the acquisition phase of anger control training, since the presence of the other spouse may often function as an S^Δ for practicing the necessary adaptive skills.

In the area of anger control as well as in other areas of BMT, the most effective approach may be the creative combination of cognitive and behavioral intervention strategies. From our preliminary work at the University of Washington, it often seems helpful to focus attention on the spouse who must respond to an aversive initiation from the partner. Our assumption is that negative initiations and provocations are inevitable in intimate relationships, but that their destructive impact will be minimized if the initiation can be contained. We further note that marital distress is associated with heightened reactivity to negative behavior (Jacobson *et al.*, 1980; Margolin, 1981) and with a tendency, not found in happy couples, to reciprocate negative behavior (Billings, 1979; Gottman, 1979; Margolin & Wampold, 1981). Finally, we note the "editing" function performed primarily by wives in non-distressed couples (Gottman, 1979). Following this literature, our goals in anger control are to teach both wives and husbands to "edit" their responses to negative behavior by exerting cognitive control over their "reaction" to it and thereby decreasing the tendency to reciprocate. Retrospectively, couples can be taught to debrief recent quarrels during therapy sessions by recreating them and then discussing alternative responses available to each spouse at every step during the interchange. Each spouse focuses on himself/herself by examining alternative responses that could have been used to diffuse the situation and on self-statements that might have been employed to modify one's affective reaction and set the stage for a more constructive behavioral response. Examples of such self-statements are "I don't have to zap him back," "It would be better if I stay calm and control myself," and "She's in a bad mood, and I can be nice."

Self-instructional strategies can also be integrated into problem-solving training by training spouses to talk to themselves in ways that maintain their focus on collaboration and conflict resolution. They can be presented with coping self-statements to use when they find themselves becoming angry and drifting into an adversarial position. These self-statements should first be modeled by the therapist, then rehearsed overtly by clients, and finally practiced covertly as they are integrated into the problem-solving repertoire.

Finally, cognitive self-control strategies can be used prospectively to rehearse situations that are likely to become problematic in the future; the preventative work will in some cases involve recurring trouble spots such as frequent situations in which conflict is likely, or it may involve unusual, one-shot, high-risk situations such as an impending visit with troublesome in-laws. Preparation involves rehearsal of both cognitive and behavioral coping strategies for anticipated stressful situations (e.g., "What will you do if you start to get angry?" or "How will you feel and what can you do if your mother-in-law starts to insult you?").

Conclusion: Caution and Further Research

This chapter has suggested that BMT will be more powerful if its focus is expanded to include cognitive interventions, and some strategies are suggested for modifying dysfunctional cognitions in distressed couples. However, it should be noted that the success of those strategies remains unproven. Despite the considerable research that has been conducted in recent years (see Mahoney & Arnkoff, 1978), our technology for changing cognitions is relatively primitive, compared to the technology for changing behavior. Therefore, it would be premature to assume that cognitive exploration and relabeling interventions actually change the dysfunctional cognitive sets and inferences at which they are aimed. The more important issue, from a clinical standpoint, is whether or not these interventions facilitate the outcome of BMT, regardless of whether they actually do so through cognitive change. It could be, for example, that these therapeutic tactics, to the extent that they are effective, work not by modifying cognitions but by prompting more collaborative behavior independent of the client's cognitive functioning. The challenge of empirically demonstrating the efficacy of C-BMT relative to BMT, and the more intricate challenge of demonstrating that these techniques actually modify cognitions, await the ingenuity of future investigators.

It remains to be seen whether or not cognitive strategies are compatible with BMT. One of the advantages of BMT in its pure form is that it counters distressed spouses' strategies to avoid change. Distressed spouses often enter therapy with highly sophisticated skills in denying responsibility for problems, pleading that they are helpless and cannot help the way they are, and intellectualizing or analyzing their problems rather than focusing on the resolution of them. BMT counters these tendencies by its focus on mutual responsibility, problem solving, and behavior change. Despite the criticisms that I have leveled against the exclusivity of this emphasis, there is potential danger in the dilution inherent in C-BMT. The fostering of a cognitive focus can reinforce spouses' tendencies to rationalize, intellectualize, and analyze their problems instead of modifying their behavior. For example, when the therapist focuses on the complainant's irrational cognitions, the complainee can opportunistically use this focus to justify a maintenance of the status quo. Although the skillful behavior therapist can subvert this maneuver during therapy sessions, it may not always prove to be containable when spouses are working on their problems at home, particularly after therapy has ended. In order for distressed couples to successfully integrate cognitive and behavioral strategies, they must learn that, while exposing and modifying dysfunctional cognitive processes can facilitate and at times can even obviate the necessity for behavior change, these processes are not generally a substitute for behavior change. The challenge facing BMT is one of augmenting behavior procedures in a benign manner, without allowing the cognitive focus to become malignant.

REFERENCES

Barton, C., & Alexander, J. Functional family therapy. In A. S. Gurman & D. P. Kniskern (Eds.), *Handbook of family therapy*. New York: Brunner/Mazel, 1981.

Beck, A. T., Rush, A. J., Shaw, B. F., & Emery, G. *Cognitive therapy of depression*. New York: Guilford Press, 1979.

Billings, A. Conflict resolution in distressed and nondistressed married couples. *Journal of Consulting and Clinical Psychology*, 1979, *47*, 368-376.

Birchler, G. R., & Spinks, S. Behavioral systems marital and family therapy: Integration and clinical application. *American Journal of Family Therapy*, 1980, *8*, 6-28.

Bodin, A. M. The interactional view: Family therapy approaches of the Mental Research Institute. In A. S. Gurman & D. P. Kniskern (Eds.), *Handbook of family therapy*. New York: Brunner/Mazel, 1981.

Christensen, A., & Nies, D. C. The Spouse Observation Checklist: Empirical analysis and critique. *American Journal of Family Therapy*, 1980, *8*, 69-79.

Ellis, A. *Reason and emotion in psychotherapy*. New York: Lyle Stuart, 1962.

Elwood, R. W., & Jacobson, N. S. Spouses' agreement in reporting their behavioral interactions: A clinical replication. *Journal of Consulting and Clinical Psychology*, 1982, *50*, 783-784.

Epstein, N. Cognitive therapy with couples. *American Journal of Family Therapy*, 1982, *10*, 5-16.

Gottman, J. M. *Marital interaction: Experimental investigations*. New York: Academic Press, 1979.

Gottman, J., Markman, H., & Notarius, C. The topography of marital conflict: A sequential analysis of verbal and nonverbal behavior. *Journal of Marriage and the Family,* 1977, *39*, 461-477.

Gottman, J., Markman, H., Notarius, C., & Gonso, J. *A couple's guide to communication*. Champaign, IL: Research Press, 1976.

Gottman, J., Notarius, C., Markman, H., Bank, S., Yoppi, B., & Rubin, M. E. Behavior exchange theory and marital decision making. *Journal of Personality and Social Psychology*, 1976, *34*, 14-23.

Guerney, B. G. (Ed.). *Relationship enhancement*. San Francisco: Jossey-Bass, 1977.

Gurman, A. S. Contemporary marital therapies: A critique and comparative analysis of psychodynamic, systems, and behavioral approaches. In T. J. Paolino, Jr., & B. S. McCrady (Eds.), *Marriage and marital therapy: Psychoanalytic, behavioral, and systems theory perspectives*. New York: Brunner/Mazel, 1978.

Gurman, A. S., & Knudson, R. M. Behavioral marriage therapy: I. A psychodynamic-systems analysis and critique. *Family Process*, 1978, *17*, 121-128.

Haley, J. *Strategies of psychotherapy*. New York: Grune & Stratton, 1963.

Hops, H., Wills, T. A., Patterson, G. R., & Weiss, R. L. *Marital Interaction Coding System*. Eugene: University of Oregon, Oregon Research Institute, 1971. (Order from ASIS/NAPS, c/o Microfiche Publications, 305 E. 46th Street, New York, NY 10017.)

Jacobson, N. S. Specific and nonspecific factors in the effectiveness of a behavioral approach to the treatment of marital discord. *Journal of Consulting and Clinical Psychology*, 1978, *46*, 442-452. (a)

Jacobson, N. S. A stimulus control model of change in behavioral marital therapy: Implications for contingency contracting. *Journal of Marriage and Family Counseling*, 1978, *4*, 29-35. (b)

Jacobson, N. S. Behavioral treatments for marital discord: A critical appraisal. In M. Hersen, R. M. Eisler, & P. M. Miller (Eds.), *Progress in behavior modification*. New York: Academic Press, 1979. (a)

Jacobson, N. S. Increasing positive behavior in severely distressed adult relationships. *Behavior Therapy*, 1979, *10*, 311-326. (b)

Jacobson, N. S. Behavioral marital therapy. In A. S. Gurman & D. P. Kniskern (Eds.), *Handbook of family therapy*. New York: Brunner/Mazel, 1981.

Jacobson, N. S., Berley, R., Melman, K. N., Elwood, R., & Phelps, C. Failure in behavioral marital therapy. In S. Coleman (Ed.), *Failures in family therapy*. New York: Guilford Press, in press.

Jacobson, N. S., Elwood, R. W., & Dallas, M. Assessment of marital dysfunction. In D. H. Barlow (Ed.), *Behavioral assessment of adult disorders*. New York: Guilford Press, 1981.

Jacobson, N. S., Follette, W. C., & McDonald, D. W. Reactivity to positive and negative behavior in distressed and nondistressed married couples. *Journal of Consulting and Clinical Psychology*, 1982, *50*, 706–714.

Jacobson, N. S., & Margolin, G. *Marital therapy: Strategies based on social learning and behavior exchange principles*. New York: Brunner/Mazel, 1979.

Jacobson, N. S., McDonald, D. W., Follette, W. C., & Berley, R. A. Attributional processes in distressed and nondistressed married couples. *Cognitive Therapy and Research*, in press.

Jacobson, N. S., & Moore, D. Behavior exchange theory of marriage: Reconnaissance and reconsideration. In J. P. Vincent (Ed.), *Advances in family intervention, assessment, and theory* (Vol. 2). Greenwich, CT: JAI Press, 1981. (a)

Jacobson, N. S., & Moore, D. Spouses as observers of the events in their relationship. *Journal of Consulting and Clinical Psychology*, 1981, *49*, 269–277. (b)

Jacobson, N. S., Waldron, H., & Moore, D. Toward a behavioral profile of marital distress. *Journal of Consulting and Clinical Psychology*, 1980, *48*, 696–703.

Jones, E. E., Kanouse, D. E., Kelley, H. H., Nisbett, R. E. Valins, S., & Weiner, B. *Attribution: Perceiving the causes of behavior*. Morristown, NJ: General Learning Press, 1972.

Knudson, R. M., Gurman, A. S., & Kniskèrn, D. P. Behavioral marriage therapy: A treatment in transition. In C. M. Franks & G. T. Wilson (Eds.), *Annual review of behavior therapy* (Vol. 7). New York: Brunner/Mazel, 1979.

Liberman, R. P., Wheeler, E. G., deVisser, L. A. J. M., Kuehnel, J., & Kuehnel, T. *Handbook of marital therapy: A positive approach to helping troubled relationships*. New York: Plenum Press, 1980.

Mahoney, M. J., & Arnkoff, D. Cognitive and self-control therapies. In S. L. Garfield & A. E. Bergin (Eds.), *Handbook of psychotherapy and behavior change* (2nd ed.). New York: Wiley, 1978.

Margolin, G. Behavior exchange in happy and unhappy marriages: A family cycle perspective. *Behavior Therapy*, 1981, *12*, 329–343.

Margolin, G., Christensen, A., & Weiss, R. L. Contracts, cognition, and change: A behavioral approach to marriage therapy. *Counseling Psychologist*, 1975, *5*, 15–26.

Margolin, G., & Wampold, B. E. Sequential analysis of conflict and accord in distressed and nondistressed marital partners. *Journal of Consulting and Clinical Psychology*, 1981, *49*, 554–567.

Margolin, G., & Weiss, R. L. Comparative evaluation of therapeutic components associated with behavioral marital treatments. *Journal of Consulting and Clinical Psychology*, 1978, *46*, 1476–1486.

Markman, H. J., & Floyd, F. Possibilities for the prevention of marital discord: A behavioral perspective. *American Journal of Family Therapy*, 1980, *8*, 29–48.

Marlatt, G. A. Craving for alcohol, loss of control, and relapse: A cognitive-behavioral analysis. In P. E. Nathan, G. A. Marlatt, & T. Loberg (Eds.), *Alcoholism: New directions in behavioral research and treatment*. New York: Plenum Press, 1978.

Meichenbaum, D. H. *Cognitive-behavior modification*. New York: Plenum Press, 1977.

O'Leary, K. D., & Turkewitz, H. The treatment of marital disorders from a behavioral perspective. In T. J. Paolino & B. S. McCrady (Eds.), *Marriage and marital therapy: Psychoanalytic, behavioral, and systems theory perspectives*. New York: Brunner/Mazel, 1978.

Patterson, G. R. Some procedures for assessing changes in marital interaction patterns. *Oregon Research Institute Bulletin*, 1976, *16*(7).

Robinson, E. A., & Price, M. G. Pleasurable behavior in marital interaction: An observational study. *Journal of Consulting and Clinical Psychology*, 1980, *48*, 117–118.

Sluzki, C. Treatment of marital disorders from a systems theory perspective. In T. J. Paolino & B. S. McCrady (Eds.), *Marriage and marital therapy: Psychoanalytic, behavioral, and systems theory perspectives*. New York: Brunner/Mazel, 1978.

Spanier, G. B. Measuring dyadic adjustment: New scales for assessing the quality of marriage and similar dyads. *Journal of Marriage and the Family*, 1976, *38*, 15–28.

Spinks, S. H., & Birchler, G. R. Behavioral-systems marital therapy: Dealing with resistance. *Family Process*, 1982, *21*, 169–185.

Stuart, R. B. Operant interpersonal treatment for marital discord. *Journal of Consulting and Clinical Psychology*, 1969, *33*, 675–682.

Stuart, R. B. *Helping couples change: A social learning approach to marital therapy*. New York: Guilford Press, 1980.

Thibaut, J. W., & Kelley, H. H. *The social psychology of groups*. New York: Wiley, 1959.

Watzlawick, P., Weakland, J., & Fisch, R. *Change: Principles of problem formation and problem resolution*. New York: Norton, 1974.

Weiss, R. L. The conceptualization of marriage from a behavioral perspective. In T. J. Paolino & B. S. McCrady (Eds.), *Marriage and marital therapy: Psychoanalytic, behavioral, and systems perspectives*. New York: Brunner/Mazel, 1978.

Weiss, R. L. Strategic behavioral marital therapy: Toward a model for assessment and intervention. In J. P. Vincent (Ed.), *Advances in family intervention, assessment and theory* (Vol. 1). Greenwich, CT: JAI Press, 1980.

Weiss, R. L., Hops, H., & Patterson, G. R. A framework for conceptualizing marital conflict, technology for altering it, some data for evaluating it. In L. A. Hamerlynck, L. C. Handy, & E. J. Mash (Eds.), *Behavior change: Methodology, concepts, and practice*. Champaign, IL: Research Press, 1973.

Weiss, R. L., & Margolin, G. Assessment of marital conflict and accord. In A. R. Ciminero, K. D. Calhoun, & H. E. Adams (Eds.), *Handbook of behavioral assessment*. New York: Wiley, 1977.

Weiss, R. L., & Perry, B. A. *Assessment and treatment of marital dysfunction*. Eugene: Oregon Marital Studies Program, 1979. (Available from R. Weiss, Department of Psychology, University of Oregon, Eugene, OR 97403.)

Wills, T. A., Weiss, R. L., & Patterson, G. R. A behavioral analysis of the determinants of marital satisfaction. *Journal of Consulting and Clinical Psychology*, 1974, *42*, 802–811.

16

Cognitive Perspectives in Behavioral Marital Therapy: Some Proposals for Bridging Theory, Research, and Practice

LUDWIG SCHINDLER AND MARGRIT VOLLMER

The contributions to this volume impressively illustrate how behavioral marital therapy (BMT) has developed since its beginning in 1969, when Stuart introduced exchange theory to the field of couples therapy. On the basis of this empirical summary, we believe that it is appropriate to consider perspectives for further expansion of theory, research, and practice. This seems necessary if we remind ourselves about the existing limitations of the therapeutic help we can offer. In summarizing the critical discussions included in this volume, we have to realize the following:

1. Although we have established the effectiveness of BMT strategies, we are not able to account for the variation in therapeutic outcome.

2. We usually observe some deterioration at follow-up 1 year after therapy; only 64% of the treated couples report that they are still experiencing benefit from the therapy 1 year after treatment (see Hahlweg, Schindler, Revenstorf, & Brengelmann, Chapter 1, this volume).

3. Our knowledge is limited to the treatment of only moderately distressed couples.

So the major tasks for BMT in the future are to provide help for severely distressed couples and to establish greater generalization and stability of treatment success. We cannot accomplish this simply by elaborating our hitherto existing technology; rather, we have to pay attention to other aspects of marital interaction and thereby broaden our theoretical model of marital distress and change. Such a reconsideration of theory building and testing should lead us to therapeutic innovations. Starting with an analysis of existing discrepancies between theoretical formulations and clinical practice, we want to offer some suggestions for bridging theory, research, and practice with respect to cognitive phenomena.

Ludwig Schindler. Max-Planck-Institute for Psychiatry, Munich, West Germany.
Margrit Vollmer. Psychosomatic Clinic, Windach, Federal Republic of Germany.

Present Status of BMT

The description of distressed couples as having a low rate of mutual positive reinforcement, a high rate of aversive interactions, and inadequate problem-solving behavior has received considerable empirical support (e.g., Gottman, 1979; Wills, Weiss, & Patterson, 1974). According to present theoretical assumptions these characteristics are the result of deficits in communication skills and/or erosion of positive reinforcement (Jacobson & Margolin, 1979; Patterson & Reid, 1970). However, as Murphy and Mendelson (1973) and Jacobson (1979) have pointed out, whether those characteristics represent causes or effects of marital distress remains unresolved.

There is evidence that spouses in a distressed relationship do have the proper skills but do not emit them when interacting with each other. Vincent, Weiss, and Birchler (1975) and Birchler, Weiss, and Vincent (1975) have shown that in a conflict discussion with a stranger the spouses are separately able to interact in a constructive manner. Moreover, Vincent, Friedman, Nugent, and Messerly (1979) reported that distressed spouses can alter their communication style with each other in a positive manner simply by following the experimenter's instruction to do so. This means that the spouses do have the skills in their repertoire, but they represent to each other an S^Δ for emitting these skills. Accordingly, the mere mention of certain conflict issues by one spouse is an S^D for the other to emit aversive behavior (see also Weiss, 1980). The skill deficit hypothesis does not offer a satisfying explanation for this phenomenon, and that limitation has important consequences for therapeutic intervention. Within an interaction process, the reaction of spouse A represents a stimulus for the subsequent response of spouse B. B's response will depend on the perceived stimulus quality of spouse A's behavior. With distressed couples we observe a noticeable discrepancy between the sender's intent and the impact on the receiver (Gottman, 1979; Gottman, Notarius, Markman, Bank, Yoppi, & Rubin, 1976). By training the spouses in communication skills we hope they will be able to reduce the incidence of such misunderstandings. In the natural environment, however, the use of these skills is hindered by perceived aversive stimuli that set the stage for competing behaviors (Marholin & Touchette, 1979). The task of therapy, therefore, is not only to train skills but also to change stimulus qualities in order to foster the use of such skills (see Morrison & Bellack, 1981).

Up to now only training in constructive skills has been systematically included in therapy. It is assumed that the spouses practicing the skills under the control of the therapist will experience positive consequences and that this will lead to a higher frequency of these behaviors. Yet common experience in the application of BMT is that the transfer from the therapeutic setting to the natural environment is quite difficult to achieve for most couples. If we look critically at our inventory of homework assignments, we have to realize that until now there have been few available self-control procedures for facilitating generalization to the home situation and to new conflict areas. This becomes particularly evident when difficult phases arise during the course of therapy. Furthermore, the focus of our intervention strategy is on establishing positive interactions; there has been little in the way of systematic attempts to influence the decrease of aversive behavior. This emphasis on increasing positives assumes that negatives will automatically be eliminated when constructive skills are acquired. However, Wills *et al.* (1974) have already demonstrated that a change in the frequency of pleasing behavior does not necessarily include a stimultaneous change in displeasing behavior. We know that the satisfaction level for distressed couples depends predominantly on the amount of perceived aversive stimuli (Jacobson, Waldron, & Moore, 1980). This indicates a need for therapeutic attention to the reduction of aversive exchanges, along with efforts to build positive reciprocity.

There are several weak points in the technology of BMT. We need to generate new hypotheses in order to find additional techniques by which we can maximize treatment effects. There are at least two ways of developing such hypotheses. The first one, a very pragmatic strategy, is described by Jacobson (1981b), who suggests that we should investigate the tactics used by successful therapists when implementing therapy technology. By making these elements of "good BMT" subject to systematic research, we will generate further techniques and thereby enrich our intervention format. This is in keeping with Weiss (1980), who noted: "It is often the case, when a technology-based program is first presented, that many significant details of 'practice' are omitted" (p. 230). Certainly it is necessary to define and to investigate such therapist behaviors. Only in this way is it possible for the researcher to learn how the effectiveness of BMT is maximized, and for the practitioner to receive a comprehensive therapist training in BMT (Jacobson, 1981a).

However, we should not confine ourselves to these pragmatic approaches, since "practice already has turned out theory" (Glisson, 1976). We should rather strive simultaneously for an integrated and empirically based theoretical model that will enable us to explain causes of and change in marital distress. Failing this, we will remain in the position described by Gottman (1979): "Behavioral Marital Therapy research to date meets the criterion of effectiveness but not the criterion of understanding process, and research is, thus, in the somewhat embarrassing position of having to explain the effectiveness of a complex, multicomponent program the design of which is not based on a sound empirical footing" (p. 262). Therefore we want to pursue another avenue by which we can formulate new research hypotheses, referring to the traditional theoretical framework of BMT, which is exchange theory.

Reappraisal of Exchange Theory

We should recall that exchange theory, which is the original theoretical basis of BMT, is cognitive in nature. Homans (1961) and Thibaut and Kelley (1959) have stressed the subjective estimation of rewards and costs by the individual and the dependence on personal values and plans. Social behavior is oriented to certain individual goals, and therefore behavioral plans are designed on the basis of an anticipated evaluation of the probable outcome (i.e., rewards minus costs) (for a review, see Chadwick-Jones, 1976). The process of anticipation, selection, and decision making in a given situation is determined by the individual learning history and associated attitudes. The anticipation of outcome is not necessarily a calculated process, and as a product of learning it can become quasi-automatic. Kendall (1981) refers to findings of cognitive psychology in order to explain such a learning process: "Research on human learning indicates that there is a negative correlation between the amount of practice on a cognitive learning task and the subject's awareness of the intermediate stages of the learning process. That is, within extended practice, awareness is reduced and automaticity sets in" (p. 6). For example, Dean and Martin (1966) have reported that overlearning of a paired-associated list resulted in a decrease in the number of mediating thoughts reported by subjects.

If we transfer these implications to marital interaction, the reaction of partner B will depend on his/her evaluation of the behavior of partner A. In situations in which unfamiliar elements — such as new conflict issues or new spouse behaviors — are present, the intermediate process will consist of anticipation and decision making. According to Kendall (1981), automaticity will set in after a certain amount of repetition. The result of this process will be that certain behaviors of partner A will elicit immediately negative reactions of partner B. These reactions will acquire a high probability, although there is no obvious contingent reinforcement. This response strength can hinder the performance of alternative skills learned in therapy unless stimulus qualities are changed as well. "Stimulus quality" means B's perception of A's previous response. As the stimulus quality is determined by subjective estimation as well as by objective qualities of the stimulus, therapy requires as much emphasis on modification of perception and evaluation processes as on behavior change (see Jacobson & Moore, 1981). As implied by the assumptions of exchange theory, the cognitive process of evaluation of a given spouse behavior and the resulting decision about the individual's own reaction is influenced by higher-order cognitive structures such as values and attitudes. These include expectations concerning the ideal spouse, concept of marriage, and concept of self (see Figure 16.1).

Of course, such a cognitive-behavioral model contains a number of theoretical constructs that must be further operationalized and subjected to empirical investigation.

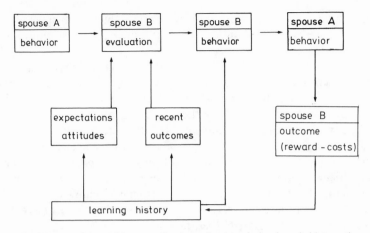

FIGURE 16.1. A model for cognitive-behavioral analysis of marital interaction.

The Need for New Assessment Strategies

The first task for research following a cognitive-behavioral model is the development of appropriate assessment strategies. For this purpose it is useful to examine the literature dealing with other areas of behavior disorders. Kendall and Hollon (1981) provide an excellent review of assessment procedures for cognitive processes that have already been used in different kinds of studies. Some of them seem easily transferable to the assessment of marriages. Let us first remain at the lower level of complexity and consider the assessment of "what clients say to themselves" as antecedents of overt reactions in a given situation.

One possible strategy is the "thinking out loud" method first described by Klinger (1971). This could be used in the therapeutic setting by presenting certain spouse behaviors that are identified as anger-provoking. It could also serve as *in vivo* sampling of evaluation processes in relevant situations. Specific thoughts could be recorded either in writing or on tape. These self-dialogues could later be coded according to categories of constructive or destructive characteristics of the individual evaluation process.

Another assessment strategy has been suggested by Meichenbaum (1975). Here videotaped replays are used to aid the subject in thought recall. For instance, the couple, while engaged in a problem-solving conversation, is videotaped as usual. Afterward the spouses watch themselves separately on the videotape and report the thoughts (which are the perceptions of the other spouse's behavior) they had during certain parts of the interaction sequence. The subject's spoken thoughts are recorded and later coded into categories for further data analysis. A similar procedure has already been used (see

Schaap, Chapter 9, this volume). It seems to represent a promising technique to gain empirical evidence about the role of cognitive processes during couple problem solving.

If we believe in the reduction of the subject's awareness of mediating thoughts as a product of an overlearning process (see Dean & Martin, 1966), we have to face certain difficulties when applying these assessment procedures. Clients, when asked to report about their thoughts, often say, "I'm not really thinking anything at this very moment." It will be necessary to bring to the client's awareness those thoughts or processes that have been so overlearned as to be automatic. Such pretraining could consist of a *post hoc* inquiry into the client's evaluation of a given situation or modeling of spoken thoughts by the therapist (Meichenbaum, 1977). Further guidelines concerning the implementation of these cognitive-behavioral assessment strategies could be derived from the analysis of Nisbett and Wilson (1977).

Finally, one could use self-statement inventories such as those already developed for the assessment of assertiveness (Schwartz & Gottman, 1976) and coping behavior (Kendall, Williams, Pechacek, Graham, Shisslak, & Herzof, 1979). With regard to marital interaction, one could, for instance, define coping behavior as constructive self-statements in situations when conflict arises, that is, self-statements that are used by spouses as a means of handling anger and preventing escalation (Ellis, 1976; Ilfeld, 1980).

All of these assessment strategies are consistent with the traditional behavioral methodology and meet the criterion of being linked with the theoretical model (Jacobson, Elwood, & Dallas, 1981; Weiss & Margolin, 1977). They could also facilitate further basic research on the characteristics of marital dysfunction, in addition to serving as outcome measures.

As we mentioned earlier, the assumptions of exchange theory imply the existence of higher-order cognitive structures such as values and attitudes, which in turn influence the evaluation of a specific spouse behavior. The question now is how can such complex cognitive structures be subjected to an empirically based assessment (Sutton-Simon, 1981)? One hypothesis assumes that unrealistic expectations concerning marriage may cause distress (Lederer & Jackson, 1968). There is already some empirical evidence that irrational beliefs are correlated with an unsatisfying relationship. Epstein, Finnegan, and Bythell (1979) reported that subjects who scored high on the Irrational Belief Test (Jones, 1968) equated disagreement in observed couples with marital maladjustment. Perhaps persons with unrealistic beliefs about marriage perceive mere disagreement as a symptom of a deteriorating relationship. Günther (1981) compared distressed and nondistressed couples on a similar questionnaire. She was able to show that distressed couples have higher scores on measures of irrational beliefs. Of course, these studies offer only hints for further investigation.

Apart from irrational beliefs, spouses in a particular relationship may be distressed because their concepts of what marriage should be like are extremely different. Again, Günther (1981) has shown that distressed couples report greater discrepancies in such attitudes than nondistressed couples. If this result received further empirical support, there would be a more substantial basis for discussing possible separation with severely distressed couples, for with a great discrepancy in their concepts, a mutual approach might be difficult, and continuous conflicts would arise.

All of these strategies for measuring cognitive processes present methodological problems with regard to establishing reliability and validity (see Kendall & Korgeski, 1979). It is impossible to verify the existence of cognitions. As Klinger (1978) has pointed out, validating processes can only "result in ruling out artifacts, in replications, and ultimately in the usefulness of data or theory for making possible other forms of prediction and perhaps control" (p. 227).

Consequences for a Cognitive-Behavioral Intervention Format

Since the challenge for BMT is to provide for greater generalization and stability of treatment gains, the focus has to shift to the modification of stimulus qualities. According to the theoretical model, stimulus qualities are determined by the individual's perception of the spouse's preceding behavior. An additional target for intervention is to change the evaluation processes that represent antecedent events for that spouse's subsequent overt behavior. If we consider an interaction sequence as a cognitive-behavioral chain consisting of a behavior of spouse A (stimulus) and the perception, evaluation, decision, and reaction of spouse B (response chain), a modifying interference at an early link in the chain can prevent an aversive reaction and promote a constructive response (see Meichenbaum, 1976). Such a cognitive intervention can therefore develop as a means for decreasing negative behavior. For therapeutic interventions of this kind there already exists a cognitive-behavioral technology used in several areas of behavior disorders (Mahoney & Arnkoff, 1978).

If we try to classify stimulus qualities, three subgroups can be distinguished in a cognitive-behavioral framework: (1) stimuli that immediately lead to an aversive response as a result of an overlearning process; (2) stimuli that are intended as displeasing by the sender, causing anger and initiating negative reciprocity on the part of the receiver; and (3) stimuli that are neutral but are perceived as negative by the receiver.

In order to illustrate this scheme, we offer some situations and discuss appropriate interventions. For the first category, let us take a conflict presented by John and Mary. The problem is that John complains about the fact that Mary does not show any interest in his work; Mary in turn is annoyed because John works too much. They have had severe quarrels several times because John came home late from work without phoning in advance. While John is approaching his house, his thoughts are as follows:

> O.K., here I am coming home from work late again. I already know she will be wearing a long face and nag all evening. She absolutely doesn't care about my troubles and my tiredness. All she is concerned about is her own comfort. I'm really fed up with this lack of understanding, and I certainly won't give in this time!

One can presume that this kind of self-talk will be incompatible with an affectionate welcome. John cannot be sure that Mary will react in the way he fears, but since several incidents of this kind have occurred during previous weeks, he now anticipates such a response from Mary. One can imagine a more constructive set of cognitions:

> O.K., I am coming home late again. Mary might be angry. But I'm done in and I really don't feel up to an argument right now. So don't start a fight; you know it will end up in shouting and tears. She has probably had a busy day too, so give her a couple of minutes. Maybe she will be more understanding than you think.

This kind of self-referent speech will make positive behavior by John more probable. Since the wife will receive similar training for this problem situation, a successful and positive interaction will be facilitated. This example illustrates the way in which systematic cognitive training may help to promote positive day-to-day interaction by modifying stimuli that quasi-automatically elicit displeasing behavior.

Another crucial instance appears when one spouse exhibits aversive behavior and the other is expected to respond in a constructive and positive way (see also Jacobson, Chapter 15, this volume). As distressed couples show strong reactivity to negative behavior from their partners, this is one of the main reasons why they fail in problem-solving discussions at home (Revenstorf, Hahlweg, Schindler, & Vogel, Chapter 10, this volume). Here, again, training in cognitive restructuring can offer a self-control procedure for preventing or interrupting an escalation of negative and unproductive exchanges.

We therefore have developed a structured cognitive intervention component termed "crisis intervention." It is part of the treatment package called "reciprocity training" (Hahlweg et al., Chapter 1, this volume). This treatment component is introduced at the end of therapy in order to enhance generalization by facilitating the use of the previously acquired problem-solving skills, particularly in conflict or crisis situations. In explaining this intervention to the couple, we call it "crisis intervention." By "crisis" we mean a situation in which aversive exchanges tend to escalate (Schindler, Hahlweg, & Revenstorf, 1980).

If one follows a progressive escalation process, one can identify four stages. For each stage spouses are instructed in the use of an internal dialogue that can help to avoid the escalation of an aversive exchange and support direct communication (see Figure 16.2).

Stage 1 represents the period before one spouse pinpoints a specific behavior pattern in the other that is particularly disliked. In such a case, the following should precede any overt behavior:

1. Do I think this behavior is really important enough to discuss or change?
2. Is this reaction only occasional, and am I usually content with this issue?
3. Have I contributed to the behavior?

If the client decides to discuss the event, the following should be considered: Is it desirable to initiate a discussion of the problem now?

Stage 2 becomes relevant when the spouse decides that the conflict issue should be addressed now. At this point the communication skills learned in treatment should become operational. This means the omission of blaming statements and the direct expression of feelings. Although the other spouse may not immediately react in a constructive manner, responsibility for successful problem-solving discussions resides with the dissatisfied partner.

Stage 3 represents coping with an imminent quarrel. In spite of all efforts to the contrary, a quarrel may ensue. In this case the client should interrupt the conversation in order to avoid escalation. He/she should directly express his/her fears, ask for a time lapse, and suggest the resumption of the discussion later.

If everything has gone wrong and the prevention of escalation has failed (Stage 4), each spouse must accept responsibility for resuming positive interaction. Both should consider whether they are prepared to tolerate 1 or 2 days of tension until the other gives in, or take the first step to reduce the conflict.

This "weighing out," or appraisal, is the essential characteristic of the cognitive training at all four stages. The clients are coached in anticipation of outcome and decision making according to their individual priorities. The inner dialogues based on the described rationale are learned by means of their typical conflict situations. The experience of negative feelings like anger or disappointment should become an S^D for these covert responses, which will elicit the newly acquired skills. At this point we do not know to what extent this component of therapy contributes to overall treatment success, since we have not carried out controlled investigations. However, many spouses report the spontaneous occurrence of these covert events and state that they have found the training helpful for implementing communication skills in the home situation. Our impression is that with the help of modeling, it is possible to train (or retrain) any couple to utilize such cognitive processes.

In our multicomponent treatment package we devote only two sessions to this training (Hahlweg, Schindler, & Revenstorf, 1982). However, from our experience we think it is feasible to expand the cognitive component. One

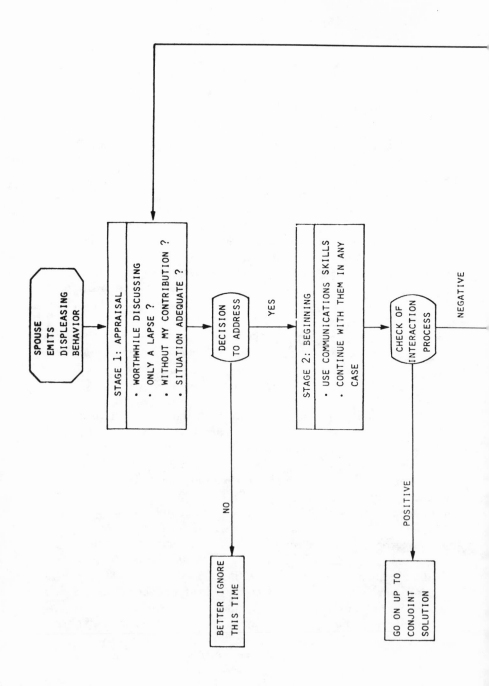

SPOUSE EMITS DISPLEASING BEHAVIOR

STAGE 1: APPRAISAL
- WORTHWHILE DISCUSSING
- ONLY A LAPSE ?
- WITHOUT MY CONTRIBUTION ?
- SITUATION ADEQUATE ?

DECISION TO ADDRESS

NO

BETTER IGNORE THIS TIME

YES

STAGE 2: BEGINNING
- USE COMMUNICATIONS SKILLS
- CONTINUE WITH THEM IN ANY CASE

CHECK OF INTERACTION PROCESS

NEGATIVE

POSITIVE

GO ON UP TO CONJOINT SOLUTION

318

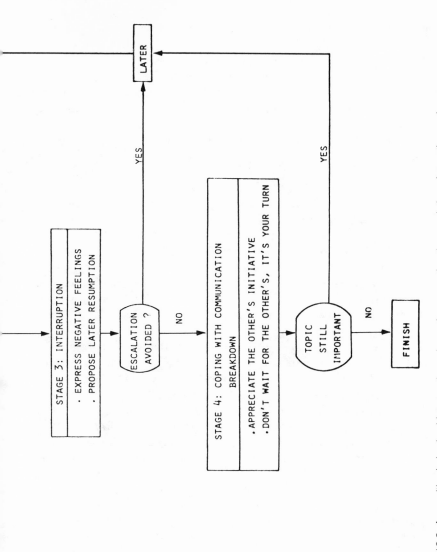

FIGURE 16.2. A cognitive-behavioral intervention scheme for preventing the escalation of negative exchange.

might consider some sessions with each spouse alone for individualized training. At first glance this may seem unusual, since BMT always stresses that a change in the relationship requires both spouses working together; this is why usually only conjoint therapy sessions are held (Jacobson & Margolin, 1979; Liberman, Wheeler, deVisser, Kuehnel, & Kuehnel, 1980). Yet it is also true that each spouse is individually responsible for the modification of his/her behavior as well as for reinforcing the partner's changes. This demands individual learning processes. Especially with spouses in a severely distressed marriage, it seems reasonable to provide additional therapeutic help with concurrent individual sessions. Perhaps the inclusion of such sessions will foster individual behavior change, since the occasional absence of the spouse means a reduction of fear when testing new responses. It must be left to further investigation whether this actually supports treatment success.

Until now we have dealt only with lower-level cognitive processes, that is, the modification of private speech in a given situation. As has been mentioned before, these are influenced by higher-order cognitive structures such as values and attitudes. It might be possible to derive these structures by sampling cognitions from several kinds of situations. Thus one might come upon irrational beliefs such as "We must do everything together" or "My spouse must share all my interests" (Margolin, 1979). This offers an explanation for the third group of stimulus qualities described previously. It includes stimuli that are meant to be neutral by the sender but are perceived as negative by the receiver. The neutral assertion of the wife that she is not interested in football is perceived by the husband as a strong provocation: He cannot understand why his wife is not willing to share his favorite leisure-time pursuit. With the unrealistic expectation that in a good marriage everything is done together, such neutral stimuli will be experienced as displeasing and will elicit aversive reactions. Here, once again, change can be facilitated by seeing each spouse separately in order to modify such beliefs, using the familiar strategies of cognitive restructuring or Socratic dialogue (Ellis, 1962; Meichenbaum, 1977).

However, we agree with Marzillier (1980) that these cognitive interventions can be dangerous, since they remove spouses from the direct connection with overt behavior. Therefore, research for the moment should concentrate on the lower level of private speech, which requires fewer theoretical constructs and allows us to investigate these cognitive interventions within the empirical tradition of BMT.

For research on a cognitive-behavioral format, we do not recommend further comparisons between isolated therapy components. Rachman and Wilson (1980) have reviewed 34 studies evaluating cognitive intervention with various behavioral disorders. When the components of traditional behavior therapy and cognitive treatment are isolated and compared, the two forms of treatment turn out to be equally effective. When both treatments are combined, they lead to greater success as compared with the single component.

The first study in BMT that dealt with a cognitive treatment was done by Margolin and Weiss (1978). They demonstrated that a combination of cognitive and behavioral components is the most effective treatment. Their study also shows that analogous research is a fitting strategy to test theoretical assumptions before they are used in clinical settings.

Summary and Conclusion

There is growing empirical evidence for the overall effectivenss of BMT technology (e.g., Hahlweg, Revenstorf, & Schindler, 1982; Jacobson, 1978). We should now consider the hitherto neglected fact that some couples deteriorate in treatment, do not profit from it, or drop out (Gurman & Kniskern, 1978; Jahn & Lichstein, 1980). In order to account for these circumstances it is insufficient simply to investigate therapist behavior and the nonspecifics of treatment. Of course, research must relate to practical problems, but it must not stick to technological dimensions. Preferably, we should apply ourselves to an expansion of theory and thereby develop guidelines for therapeutic innovations (Olson, 1976).

There are two perspectives for further expanding the behavioral model for marital interaction. One is the dimension of emotion and sentiment (Weiss, 1980), and the other is the role of cognition. As behavior therapy has always involved cognitive assumptions (Kazdin, 1978), one can answer any reproach from radical behaviorists with Wilson's (1980) comment: "It is no longer a question of whether we can afford to introduce cognitive concepts within the scientific analysis of behavior; both developments within experimental psychology and the reality of clinical practice suggest that we cannot afford not to pay serious attention to cognitive processes in human behavior" (p. 5). In regard to BMT, one can observe a growing appeal for a cognitive-behavioral conceptualization of marital satisfaction in the publications of recent years (e.g., Gottman, 1979; O'Leary & Turkewitz, 1978; Weiss, 1978). In the clinical application of BMT, cognitive techniques are already used, however unsystematically (Jacobson, Chapter 15, this volume; Jacobson & Margolin, 1979). Now it is time to use these practical suggestions to instigate further theoretical formulations, which in turn will initiate further research. In this way we can both enrich our technology and answer the urgent need for an integrative theoretical model. It is an empirical question whether or not a therapy approach broadened in this sense will result in better treatment outcome. The question of whether or not we should systematically include cognitive constructs can be answered by data only. Our purpose in this chapter has been to show that the traditional theoretical framework of BMT is quite capable of offering us testable hypotheses about cognitive variables.

ACKNOWLEDGMENT
The authors thank Ian Bennun and Tom Stachnik for their help with the translation.

REFERENCES
Birchler, G. R., Weiss, R. L., Vincent, J. P. A multimethod analysis of social reinforcement exchange between maritally distressed and nondistressed spouse and stranger dyads. *Journal of Personality and Social Psychology*, 1975, *31*, 349-360.
Chadwick-Jones, J. K. *Social exchange theory: Its structure and influence in social psychology.* New York: Academic Press, 1976.
Dean, S. J., & Martin, R. B. Reported mediation as a function of degree of learning. *Psychonomic Science*, 1966, *4*, 231-232.
Ellis, A. Techniques of handling anger in marriage. *Journal of Marriage and Family Counseling*, 1976, *2*, 305-315.
Ellis, A. *Reason and emotion in psychotherapy.* New York: Lyle Stuart, 1962.
Epstein, N., Finnegan, D., & Bythell, D. Irrational beliefs and perceptions of marital conflict. *Journal of Consulting and Clinical Psychology*, 1979, *47*, 603-610.
Glisson, D. H. A review of behavioral marital counseling: Has practice turned out theory? *Psychological Record*, 1976, *26*, 95-104.
Gottman, J. M. *Marital interaction: Experimental investigations.* New York: Academic Press, 1979.
Gottman, J. M., Notarius, C., Markman, H., Bank, S., Yoppi, B., & Rubin, M. E. Behavior exchange theory and marital decision making. *Journal of Personality and Social Psychology*, 1976, *34*, 14-23.
Günther, A. *Ehe- und Partnerschaftsprobleme: Eine Explorationsstudie zu Unterschieden kognitiver Variablen bei glücklichen und unglücklichen Partnerschaften anhand eines Fragebogens zu irrationalen und anderen Einstellungen.* Unpublished master's thesis, University of Tübingen, 1981.
Gurman, A. S., & Kniskern, D. P. Deterioration in marital and family therapy: Empirical, clinical and conceptual issues. *Family Process*, 1978, *17*, 3-20.
Hahlweg, K., Revenstorf, D., & Schindler, L. Treatment of marital distress: Comparing formats and modalities. *Advances in Behavior Research and Therapy*, 1982, *4*, 57-74.
Hahlweg, K., Schindler, L., & Revenstorf, D. *Partnerschaftsprobleme: Diagnose und Therapie. Handbuch für den Therapeuten.* Heidelberg: Springer Verlag, 1982.
Homans, G. L. *Social behavior: Its elementary form.* New York: Harcourt, Brace & World, 1961.
Ilfeld, F. W. Understanding marital stressors: The importance of coping style. *Journal of Nervous and Mental Disease*, 1980, *168*, 375-381.
Jacobson, N. S. A review of the research on the effectiveness of marital therapy. In T. J. Paolino & B. S. McCrady (Eds.), *Marriage and marital therapy: Psychoanalytic, behavioral, and systems theory perspectives.* New York: Brunner/Mazel, 1978.
Jacobson, N. S. Behavioral treatments for marital discord: A critical appraisal. In M. Hersen, R. Eisler, & P. Miller (Eds.), *Progress in behavior modification.* New York: Academic Press, 1979.
Jacobson, N. S. Behavioral marital therapy. In A. S. Gurman & D. P. Kniskern (Eds.), *Handbook of family therapy.* New York: Brunner/Mazel, 1981. (a)
Jacobson, N. S. *Behavioral marital therapy in the eighties: Review of outcome and development of new treatment strategies.* Paper presented at the International Symposium on Marital Interaction Analysis and Modification, Schloss Ringberg, Tegernsee, West Germany, 1981. (b)
Jacobson, N. S., Elwood, R. W., & Dallas, M. Assessment of marital dysfunction. In D. H. Barlow (Ed.), *Behavioral assessment of adult disorders.* New York: Guilford Press, 1981.

Jacobson, N. S., & Margolin, G. *Marital therapy: Strategies based on social learning and behavior exchange principles.* New York: Brunner/Mazel, 1979.

Jacobson, N. S., & Moore, D. Spouses as observers of the events in their relationship. *Journal of Consulting and Clinical Psychology*, 1981, *49*, 269–277.

Jacobson, N. S., Waldron, H., & Moore, D. Toward a behavioral profile of marital distress. *Journal of Consulting and Clinical Psychology*, 1980, *48*, 696–703.

Jahn, D. L., & Lichstein, K. L. The resistive client: A neglected phenomenon in behavior therapy. *Behavior Modification*, 1980, *4*, 303–320.

Jones, R. G. *A factored measure of Ellis' irrational belief system, with personality and maladjustment correlates.* Unpublished doctoral dissertation, Texas Technological College, 1968.

Kazdin, A. E. *History of behavior modification.* Baltimore: University Park Press, 1978.

Kendall, P. C. Assessment and cognitive-behavioral interventions: Purposes, proposals, and problems. In P. C. Kendall & S. D. Hollon (Eds.), *Assessment strategies for cognitive-behavioral interventions.* New York: Academic Press, 1981.

Kendall, P. C., & Hollon, S. D. (Eds.). *Assessment strategies for cognitive-behavioral interventions.* New York: Academic Press, 1981.

Kendall, P. C., & Korgeski, G. P. Assessment and cognitive-behavioral interventions. *Cognitive Therapy and Research,* 1979, *3*, 1–21.

Kendall, P. C., Williams, L., Pechacek, T. F., Graham, L. E., Shisslak, C., & Herzof, N. Cognitive-behavioral and patient education interventions in cardiac catheterization procedures: The Palo Alto medical psychology project. *Journal of Consulting and Clinical Psychology*, 1979, *47*, 48–59.

Klinger, E. *Structure and functions of fantasy.* New York: Wiley, 1971.

Klinger, E. Modes of normal conscious flow. In K. S. Pope & L. Singer (Eds.), *The stream of consciousness: Scientific investigations into the flow of human experience.* New York: Plenum Press, 1978.

Lederer, W. J., & Jackson, D. D. *The mirages of marriage.* New York: Norton, 1968.

Liberman, R. P., Wheeler, E., deVisser, L. A. J. M., Kuehnel, J., & Kuehnel, T. *Handbook of marital therapy: A positive approach to helping troubled relationships.* New York: Plenum Press, 1980.

Mahoney, M. J., & Arnkoff, D. Cognitive and self-control therapies. In S. L. Garfield & A. E. Bergin (Eds.), *Handbook of psychotherapy and behavior change* (2nd ed.). New York: Wiley, 1978.

Margolin, G. Conjoint marital therapy to enhance anger management and reduce spouse abuse. *American Journal of Family Therapy*, 1979, *7*, 13–23.

Margolin, G., & Weiss, R. L. Comparative evaluation of therapeutic components associated with behavioral marital treatments. *Journal of Consulting and Clinical Psychology*, 1978, *46*, 1476–1486.

Marholin, D., II, & Touchette, P. E. The role of stimulus control and response consequences. In A. P. Goldstein & F. H. Kanfer (Eds.), *Maximizing treatment gains: Transfer enhancement in psychotherapy.* New York: Academic Press, 1979.

Marzillier, J. S. Cognitive therapy and behavioural practice. *Behaviour Research and Therapy*, 1980, *18*, 249–258.

Meichenbaum, D. H. Theoretical and treatment implications of developmental research on verbal control of behaviour. *Canadian Psychological Review*, 1975, *16*, 22–27.

Meichenbaum, D. H. A cognitive-behavior modification approach to assessment. In M. Hersen & A. S. Bellack (Eds.), *Behavioral assessment: A practical handbook.* New York: Pergamon Press, 1976.

Meichenbaum, D. H. *Cognitive-behavior modification.* New York: Plenum Press, 1977.

Morrison, R. L., & Bellack, A. S. The role of social perception in social skill. *Behavior Therapy*, 1981, *12*, 69–79.

Murphy, D. C., & Mendelson, L. A. Communication and adjustment in marriage: Investigating the relationship. *Family Process*, 1973, *12*, 317–326.

Nisbett, R., & Wilson, T. D. Telling more than we can know: Verbal reports on mental processes. *Psychological Review*, 1977, *84*, 231–259.

O'Leary, K. D., & Turkewitz, H. Marital therapy from a behavioral perspective. In T. J. Paolino & B. S. McCrady (Eds.), *Marriage and marital therapy: Psychoanalytic, behavioral, and systems theory perspectives.* New York: Brunner/Mazel, 1978.

Olson, D. H. Bridging research, theory, and application: The triple threat in science. In D. H. Olson (Ed.), *Treating relationships.* Lake Mills, IA: Graphic Publishing, 1976.

Patterson, G. R., & Reid, J. B. Reciprocity and coercion: Two faces of social systems. In C. Neuringer & J. L. Michael (Eds.), *Behavior modification in clinical psychology.* New York: Appleton-Century-Crofts, 1970.

Rachman, S. J., & Wilson, G. T. *The effects of psychological therapy* (2nd ed.). New York: Pergamon Press, 1980.

Schindler, L., Hahlweg, K., & Revenstorf, D. *Partnerschaftsprobleme: Möglichkeiten zur Bewältigung: Ein verhaltenstherapeutisches Programm für Paare.* Heidelberg: Springer Verlag, 1980.

Schwartz, R. M., & Gottman, J. M. Toward a task analysis of assertive behavior. *Journal of Consulting and Clinical Psychology*, 1976, *44*, 910–920.

Stuart, R. B. Operant-interpersonal treatment for marital discord. *Journal of Consulting and Clinical Psychology*, 1969, *33*, 675–682.

Sutton-Simon, K. Assessing belief systems: Concepts and strategies. In P. C. Kendall & S. D. Hollon (Eds.), *Assessment strategies for cognitive-behavioral interventions.* New York: Academic Press, 1981.

Thibaut, J. W., & Kelley, H. H. *The social psychology of groups.* New York: Wiley, 1959.

Vincent, J. P., Friedman, L., Nugent, J., & Messerly, L. Demand characteristics in observations of marital interaction. *Journal of Consulting and Clinical Psychology*, 1979, *47*, 557–566.

Vincent, J. P., Weiss, R. L., & Birchler, G. R. A behavioral analysis of problem solving in distressed and nondistressed married and stranger dyads. *Behavior Therapy*, 1975, *6*, 475–487.

Weiss, R. L. The conceptualization of marriage from a behavioral perspective. In T. J. Paolino & B. S. McCrady (Eds.), *Marriage and marital therapy: Psychoanalytic, behavioral, and systems theory perspectives.* New York: Brunner/Mazel, 1978.

Weiss, R. L. Strategic behavioral therapy: Toward a model for assessment and intervention. In J. P. Vincent (Ed.), *Advances in family intervention, assessment and theory* (Vol. 1). Greenwich, CT: JAI Press, 1980.

Weiss, R. L., & Margolin, G. Assessment of marital conflict and accord. In A. R. Ciminero, K. D. Calhoun, & H. E. Adams (Eds.), *Handbook of behavior assessment.* New York: Wiley, 1977.

Wills, T. A., Weiss, R. L., & Patterson, G. R. A behavioral analysis of the determinants of marital satisfaction. *Journal of Consulting and Clinical Psychology*, 1974, *42*, 802–811.

Wilson, G. T. Cognitive factors in lifestyle changes: A social learning perspective. In P. O. Davidson & S. M. Davidson (Eds.), *Behavioral medicine: Changing health lifestyles.* New York: Brunner/Mazel, 1980.

17

The Role of Attribution of
Marital Distress in Therapy

DIRK REVENSTORF

Introduction

Empirical studies in marital therapy have mainly confirmed the efficacy of communication skills training and behavioral marital therapy (Gurman & Kniskern, 1978; Jacobson & Margolin, 1979). Some of the respective intervention strategies are mentioned in this chapter. As a primary goal in behavioral marital therapy and communication skills training, an attempt is made to change the relation toward a more positive exchange. Besides helping people change, acquire new skills, and build a better relationship, it seems reasonable to provide the clients with a causal explanation for their distress. The general reference to learned habits serves this purpose but is far too general and insufficiently personalized. The thesis of this chapter is that if couples can understand their learning history — beginning with their childhood, extending from their parents as models to mate selection, and finally leading to their present distress — then they will be more involved in therapy and much more motivated for change. At the same time this learning history serves as a convincing external attribution for their behavior patterns, which can free the spouses from personal guilt and blame. That is, besides communication skills, positive exchange, and cognitive strategies of restructuring "activating events," this chapter adds another cognitive aspect: reattribution of discord.

Before discussing how the connection between a present crisis in marriage and earlier individual development may be established, I would like to outline a general framework for marital therapy, from which the different intervention strategies may be derived. This is not a claim for the integration of different therapeutic schools. Rather, it is a preliminary view, in which the different aspects of the marital relationship are arranged.

Dirk Revenstorf. Psychological Institute, University of Tübingen, Tübingen, Federal Republic of Germany.

Communication and Exchange

For the sake of exposition let us consider a marital relationship as a closed system. It consists of two interacting units, both functioning as sender and receiver. The first aspect to be discussed is mutual exchange. There are at least three channels through which this exchange may take place: (1) motor action (e.g., giving a present), (2) nonverbal expression (e.g., smiling), and (3) verbal communication (e.g., "I like your dress today").

Although this exchange may be conceived of in terms of stimulus and response, there are significant differences between this and common behavior theory. In the closed system of two human individuals, the response of A is at the same time stimulus and consequence for the response of B:

$$R(A) = S(B) = C(B)$$

That is, the behavior of A controls the behavior of B, which in turn provides stimulus and consequence for spouse A. Stimulus and consequence in this system are rapidly changing and interdependent features of the two spouses. Therefore properties develop such as homeostasis, as well as positive and negative feedback. An example of positive feedback is escalation in marital distress; another example is the mutual sexual attraction in flirting and lovemaking. An example of negative feedback is deescalation during an argument.

Therapeutic interventions deriving from this aspect of the relationship are usually called "communication skills training" and/or "behavioral exchange training." Communication skills training is concerned with the modification of verbal and nonverbal expressive qualities as well as listener characteristics: (1) sender skills (e.g., nonaccusatory critique), (2) receiver skills (empathy, active listening), and (3) meta-communication (the ability to interrupt ongoing interactions and discuss their meaning and impact).

Behavioral exchange programs are more concerned with the motor action channel and attempt changes toward more positive exchange through: (1) increased mutual attraction (e.g., care days), (2) problem-solving skills (executive session), and (3) behavior contracts (balanced give and take).

There are several disturbances that may interfere with smooth and gratifying mutual exchange in these three channels. There may be a lack of positive communication (extinction, lack of positive reinforcement), a predominance of aversive control (negative reinforcement), weak skills in meta-communication, and discrepancy between channels. In many cases such deficits lead to what is called the "coercion process" (Patterson, 1977).

Cognitions

Another important dimension of the marital relationship is the cognitive transformation of communication inputs by the receiver. Often the receiver does not interpret the message as it was intended; at least in distressed couples, there is a discrepancy between intent and impact (see Gottman, 1979). For example:

Intent	Impact
A sighs, meaning:	B thinks:
"What a hard day."	"I am bothering him," or
	"He is overworked."

It is doubtful whether this kind of self-comment is explicitly verbal, as is assumed by some cognitive therapists. Rather, such self-instructions may be overlearned to the extent that they directly trigger aggression, anxiety, or depression without explicit verbalization (see Kendall & Hollon, 1979). Marital interaction may be effectively influenced by training in profitable self-instructions, as has been shown in the treatment of depression, hyperactivity, aggressiveness, social anxiety, stress, pain, and other ailments (Beck, 1979; Davidson, 1980; Ellis, 1977; Meichenbaum, 1979). The training of restructuring skills in marital therapy amounts to establishing safeguards against breakdowns in overt communication. Sometimes even highly skilled couples — who know how to express feelings, how to attend to the other, and how to enter into meta-communication — are not able to handle highly charged situations by responding appropriately. In such instances restructuring strategies may be helpful, as in the following examples.

Cognitive Restructuring
Critical remark: "You don't take any interest in me: It makes me sick."

Self-comments

Facilitating aggression	Inhibiting aggression
"How can she dare to say that?"	"Maybe she has had a bad day; perhaps I can help her." *(displacement of the problem onto the other)*
"This is intolerable."	"She is in a bad mood; maybe I should watch football." *(distraction)*
"I can't take it any more."	"This is an uneasy situation, but we have managed more difficult ones." *(self-reinforcement)*
	"She is not to be taken seriously; maybe she is a little mad." *(devaluation of the other)*
	"It is normal to have fights in marriage. It would be unreasonable to expect harmony always." *(accepting the given state as normal)*

This is not a complete list of possible self-comments. The examples only serve to demonstrate how an activating event (stimulus) emitted by one spouse may be positively or negatively transformed by cognitions. These cognitions in turn facilitate different emotional states — perhaps empathy or even benevolence, but at least distance and calmness (see also Schindler & Vollmer, Chapter 16, this volume).

Entanglement and Escalation

The third aspect of the relationship comprises the motivational structure of each spouse (needs and interests) and their mutual fit. Although behavior therapists do not assert that randomly assigned mates could be made happy by proper training, they take couples as they appear and do not base their treatment on a theory of mate selection. However, each individual has particular characteristics, which may be accepted without difficulties by the spouse, or which may be experienced as difficult and painful. Every marital therapist has experienced those rapidly escalating disputes where the indulgent reminder of a behavior contract or of the proper rules of communication is in vain. Many couples have considerable communication skills and use them up to the critical point where aversive control takes over. A certain response completely turns off the other or drives him/her crazy. He/she drops his/her "good manners" or withdraws. Revenge seems to be the prevailing motive.

In such situations the emotional quality seems largely independent of the current "trigger." If a certain amount of stress is exceeded, it appears that individual response patterns become effective so that the situation gets out of control. Psychoanalysts would classify these responses as "regressive." Transactional analysis calls these reactions "rackets" (Berne, 1972; Goulding & Goulding, 1975). Behaviorists would use the term "learned emotional responses." Some people turn angry when they cut their finger, when they lose a game, when their partner turns away, or when they have an automobile accident. Others, under the same circumstances, become sad and cry. Others begin to withdraw and become depressed, and some people become apprehensive and nervous. In any case, an idiosyncratic response from a long "learning history" sets in. The following two examples may demonstrate how these idiosyncratic patterns may launch an escalating quarrel:

Couple 1. In problem discussion, when it gets difficult, the wife begins to cry and whine and lament. This makes the husband, who likes to be a tough guy, furious. He pushes her to rely on herself and be strong. However, the result is the opposite: She deteriorates. Essentially she gives messages such as: "I am so timid, because you are so angry." And he: "I am so angry, because you get so timid."

Couple 2. When the needs of the spouses clash and frustration seems inevitable, he turns off and becomes stubborn. He says things such as: "I don't get what I deserve; you withhold things for which I have a perfect right." Nonverbally, he appears hurt and demanding. She withdraws, becomes depressive, and cries. Consequently his despair becomes greater; now he doesn't even get her attention. Basically she says things such as: "He wants too much. I don't have room to breathe." And he says: "I want so little, and even this I do not get."

Unfortunately in the heat of argument, the trouble is usually attributed to the spouse, but a sober analysis would make both spouses recognize that their responses are learned patterns, probably dating from before they met.

Therapeutic Interventions

What can be done in situations where both spouses struggle and neither seems capable of disentangling? For example, a problem discussion gets out of control in the way described above. All three, the couple and the therapist, are helpless and unable to change the interaction. At that moment it may be wise to split the therapeutic triad and initiate a dyadic interaction with one of the spouses — probably the one who is more perplexed. The other spouse is asked to sit back for a while and listen. The therapist then concentrates on what is going on in the first client, who is still emotionally aroused:

1. The therapist lets the client explore his/her feelings and try to put them into words.

2. The therapist urges the spouse to utter his/her spontaneous wishes and impulses, possibly in direct "I" sentences ("I want to . . . ").

3. The therapist asks the client to become aware of body sensations and other sensations ("What do you see . . . , what do you feel, where do you feel it?).

4. The therapist points to body movements, patterns of breathing, and other expressive signs that the client shows, in order to make the client aware of what is going on within himself/herself and what it may mean to him/her.

In other words, the therapist tries to keep track of what is happening to the client at the moment — not leaving time for a rational analysis. Since the therapist is accepting any impulse or feeling in the client, he/she behaves contrary to what the spouse would have done in the same situation. Therefore the client has no need to be defensive. The client cannot continue to complain about the spouse, because the therapist urges him/her to explore his/her feelings without explanations. This brings the client in close contact with his/her momentary inner motions, leading to what gestalt therapists call "contact episodes" (Pearls, Hefferline, & Goodman, 1951; Polster & Polster, 1975).

Alternatively, transactional analysts suggest that guided imagery may be used, leading back to childhood experiences (Goulding & Goulding, 1975). Consider the following example. The therapist says:

Imagine that you are between 6 and 10 years old. The whole family has gathered in the house in which you lived. You can see the house in front of you. The family sits in a large circle in one room, or everybody sits in his own room. Imagine this even if they did not all live in the same house. Try to see this vividly. And try to feel as if you were at that age. Now what happens if you imagine the following:

- You got a bad grade at school and come home. . . . *(Pause)*
- You have tumbled and hurt your knee. It is bleeding. . . . *(Pause)*
- You have smashed a window of the neighbor by throwing a ball. . . .
(Pause)

What do you do in these situations? How do the family members react? Do they let you cry? Do they prohibit crying? Do they scold? Do they spank you? Do they call you names? Do they ask you to be brave? Do they reject you? Which of those reactions was usually the most convenient one for you, the most accepted one?

Generally, in such an exploration of momentary awareness or in fantasy trips of former experiences, the client is led to intensify and relive emotional patterns, which he/she identifies as those he/she regularly engages in. The client may see that he/she responded in the same way even as a child; he/she may see connections between his/her present behavior and feelings and his/her emotional development. The client may also recognize how specific constellations in the primary family (being the small one, the adult one, the eldest, "mother's little helper," and so on) shed some light on his/her present response patterns and how they came about. It may turn out that the client's responses were quite adequate at the time of childhood when he/she was small and helpless and had no alternatives. But it may also be clear that these responses are obsolete now and may be "turned in" for other, more creative ways to react in present situations with the spouse.

The following abbreviated excerpt of a therapy session demonstrates what such an exploration might look like. Following a heavily escalating problem discussion of couple 2, who are briefly described above, the following dialogue developed between the therapist and the wife (T = therapist; C = client):

T: What is going on inside you at the moment?
C: I have the feeling that M [the husband] is within my sphere. I feel intruded upon and uneasy.
T: What kind of wish is behind that?
C: I would like to decide about my life: I'd like to be strong and wait prepared for whatever is coming.
T: What do you feel as you say that?
C: I feel that I am doing something that is all right for me but will be a big disappointment for M. I am afraid of tomorrow.
T: What do you want to do; what will be your next step?
C: I'd like to go out on my own.
T: Please say that again. *(Silence)*
T: You are anticipating his reaction.
C: Yes, he will oppose it.
T: Say something like this: "Maybe you will think I am cool, but I can't

change that. Tonight I'd like to go out on my own; don't be irritated about that."

C: Something makes me hold back from saying things like that. If I say that, I can feel a hand, which is going to spank me.

T: Whose hand?

C: My father's hand. [We know from what she has already said that the father had been rude and brutal toward the mother and children when they were young.]

T: Tell you father: "I am going out now!"

C: *(Screaming)* I can't do it! He will kill me.

T: Is there anything you like about him?

C: He doesn't mean as much to me as when I was young. But I do not feel any revenge . . . I feel dizzy. *(Crying)*

T: Can you say that you don't care about him?

C: I can't even think that.

T: What is it that you like about him?

C: He understood me.

T: Can you say a preliminary good-bye to him? Like: "You mean a lot to me but I can stand on my own feet and do without you."

C: *(Role-playing)*) I really love you. It hurts me a lot and it is very difficult for me to say things like that. *(And then to the therapist)* I didn't know that my father still meant so much to me. I would like to talk more about it.

During such an exploration the therapist builds a temporary but strong alliance with one of the spouses and should be aware of this and be able to compensate for it. For instance, later the therapist could treat the other spouse in the same way. Or the therapist could ask the other spouse about his/her feelings after having listened to all of this. Or guided imagery could be done with both of them at the same time; the therapist could let them explore their feelings mutually or sequentially.

Attribution

While this dialogue between the therapist and one of the spouses is going on, the latter is no longer under the stimulus control of his/her partner. During the course of the exploration the client learns that there are other possible causes of his/her momentary arousal and problem responses besides the partner. The client can see that it is not the spouse who has caused his/her stereotyped emotional overreaction. Both spouses can see that from a certain point the escalation is no longer their momentary problem but goes back to their developmental uniqueness. With the other couple described briefly above (couple 1), the history went like this:

The husband was brought up without close contact with his parents. He was seldom supported or taken care of by his parents. Therefore he became independent. He became a sailor at the age of 16, and his ideal man was the "tough guy." Typically his closest friend and model was the first officer on the boat, who approximated this ideal and suggested strategies like "Never give up," "Always keep cool," "Don't show anxiety," and "Try to be superior in all critical situations."

The wife had a good relationship with her mother; her father was a very domineering man. She never had a chance to assert herself with him. So she developed a great deal of resentment and transferred this resentment to other male authority figures, including her present boss. Her mother always consoled her when she was upset and thereby reinforced her feeling of being weak and her tendency to resort to crying.

As soon as a therapist reattributes the present crisis between the two of them to their respective developmental histories, the partner can no longer be blamed for the conflict. In this way the problem of "punctuation" (Watzlawick, Beavin, & Jackson, 1967) is eliminated. After such a journey into the past, the present interaction may be resumed. The ensuing discussion is likely to be more constructive. Mutual empathy and positive regard will increase.

For the treatment of the idiosyncratic response patterns of the two spouses, there are two alternatives: The response pattern might become acceptable to the spouse since now he/she understands its origins. This knowledge may be used by both to foster cognitive restructuring: "My present reaction hasn't too much to do with my spouse. We have just touched my critical point," he may say. And the spouse may comment to herself, "He doesn't mean me; it is his old problem." Similar self-comments are relevant for the idiosyncratic emotional patterns of the other partner. In any case, it is important to initiate discussion about the newly available attributions in the presence of the therapist. The therapist must prevent either of them from using these new causal attributions to manipulate the other by speaking disparagingly about the other's "personal" problem.

The second alternative is to develop an individual treatment plan, such as assertiveness training for the wife in the example above. Individual therapy is indicated if the problem continues to disturb the interaction between the spouses. For example, with couple 1, the wife and therapist worked out possibilities for her to be more assertive. This was done first in a role play with the imagined father, then with the spouse, followed by the therapist, and finally as a homework assignment with the present boss. For the husband, the goal was to be more self-disclosing, to try to show weaknesses and feelings.

This brief description might appear to resemble crisis intervention. However, it may be used in a systematic way, if the therapist is alert to the proper time for such explorations. The advantage of this kind of therapeutic intervention in an escalating problem discussion is that the spouses consider alternative causal explanations for the problem and thus transcend their impasse.

This is contrary to standard communication skills training, which would post-pone the subject of discussion, initiate cognitive restructuring, or move into an "executive session" strongly controlled by the therapist. All these tactics are designed to cool down the discussion. In contrast, here external attributions are made available to the spouses, which, on the one hand, may depict the behavior as a long-standing habit yet, on the other hand, also depict it as changeable by "new learning." In any case the external attribution is prefer-able to global misbehavior on the part of the spouse.

There are probably many ways to explore such idiosyncratic emotional reactions by going back to the developmental history of the individual. It may be done through a contact episode as in gestalt therapy, through the guided imagery used in transactional analysis, or through age regression induced via hypnosis. The main advantage of a genetic exploration relative to a behav-ioral analysis appears to be that an explanation is found which is personally meaningful.

Discussion

Typically, during a distressing problem discussion, both spouses attribute the breakdown of their interaction to the other. In these cases it makes sense for the therapist to pinpoint the idiosyncratic emotional response patterns of each spouse and trace them to his/her individual learning history. That way the causes of his/her behavior may become clear, independent of the present re-lationship. Sometimes the mutual fit of those response patterns is quite clear. It hardly seems necessary to appeal to a psychoanalytic theory of psychosex-ual development. But it may make sense to elucidate how a certain response pattern was reinforced or modeled by the parents and the family of origin. At this point the spouses may appreciate the power of a habit that dates back to long before the present relationship began. This knowledge is a useful sup-plement to measures of cognitive restructuring and communication skills as well as a heightened level of positive mutual exchange. It is an especially use-ful tool when all three, the spouses and the therapist, reach an impasse.

Looking at these escalating problem discussions, the process of escala-tion may be divided into two phases. Initially, for each spouse there is an ac-tivating event, which is either distressing, anger-provoking, depressing, or ter-rifying. (The activating event may be that the spouse forgets an important appointment, is criticizing heavily, is blaming the other, is questioning the continuation of the relationship, and so on.) Gradually, discussion reaches the point where both spouses lose control. From now on irritating words and sentences serve as stimuli for reciprocal escalation. At the same time, arousal is rapidly increasing. A study using observational data (Revenstorf, Hahlweg, & Schindler, 1979; Revenstorf, Hahlweg, Schindler, & Vogel, Chapter 10, this volume; Revenstorf, Vogel, Wegener, Hahlweg, & Schindler, 1980) showed how such problem discussions differ in nondistressed and distressed couples, and also how marital therapy may change it. It was found that escalation is less likely to occur with nondistressed couples, and that it is altered in the direction of a normal pattern by communication skills training for distressed couples. A problem discussion in nondistressed couples appears to indicate that both spouses have methods for countering escalation. They operate like a negative feedback loop, as opposed to the positive feedback loop in problem escalation common to distressed couples.

In my opinion there are at least three factors that influence the process of problem escalation. There is an initial, biologically reasonable, reaction of the organism to stress; this reaction may be anger, sadness, or anxiety. The particular emotional experience depends largely on how the incoming information is processed (see Lazarus, 1968). This spontaneous response of the organism can be seen as a signal by the body, a signal that should be alarming to the spouse as well as to the individual concerned. There is some evidence that suppressing emotional responses to stress leads to psychosomatic complaints. There are data to suggest that psychosomatic patients show alexithymia—that is, the inability to decode and express feelings (Sifneos, 1973). As a second component, both the initial emotional response and, particularly, the ensuing escalation have an idiosyncratic quality, which may be explained from the learning history of the individual. This idiosyncratic quality often has instrumental value; it has been historically successful in manipulating the environment. This factor may play an important role in the second phase of the escalation, when the discussion is out of control for both spouses. Then a third component begins to operate: mutual stimulus control and the coercion process. This is mutually responsive behavior.

This hypothetical tripartite model of escalation calls for different intervention strategies (see Figure 17.1): (1) The spontaneous emotional response should be facilitated as a necessary biological reaction. This is usually done in most communication skills training by the demand of expressing feelings. Sometimes, however, affect is neglected in favor of a controlled dialogue ("executive session"). (2) The instrumental component, which may be traced back to developmental uniqueness, may be made intelligible to both spouses through the interventions described in this chapter. The necessary explorations may be done with one spouse individually. (3) The responsive component in the escalation process is concerned with the mutual facilitation of distressing arguments, blaming, and accusations. This component may be reduced by cognitive restructuring and communications skills.

The use of experiential methods results in a strong emotional experience for the client. This must not be confused with catharsis. Affect is not taken as a healing factor, as in encounter groups (Yalom, 1970), but rather as an indicator of the relevancy of the matter dealt with.

It is important to keep the individual focused on his/her problem and

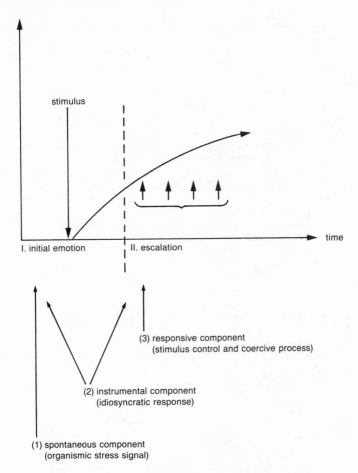

FIGURE 17.1. The escalation process according to the two-phase, three-component model.

the possibility of change. If the therapist is successful in inducing a high emotional level as well as a meaningful explanation of the response pattern shown, the client will not only be motivated to modify his/her behavior, but also will be satisfied with the model provided by the therapist.

REFERENCES

Beck, A. T. *Wahrnehmung der Wirklichkeit und Neurose.* Munich: Pfeiffer, 1979.
Berne, E. *What do you say after you say hello?* New York: Grove Press, 1972.
Davidson, P. O. (Ed.). *Angst, Depression und Schmerz—Methoden zur Prävention und Therapie.* Munich: Pfeiffer, 1980.
Ellis, A. *Rational-emotive therapie.* Munich: Pfeiffer, 1977.
Gottman, J. M. *Marital interaction.* New York: Academic Press, 1979.

Goulding, M., & Goulding, R. L. *Changing lives through redecision therapy.* New York: Brunner/Mazel, 1975.

Gurman, A. S., & Kniskern, D. P. Research on marital and family therapy: Progress, perspective and prospect. In S. L. Garfield & A. E. Bergin (Eds.), *Handbook of psychotherapy and behavior change* (2nd ed.). New York: Wiley, 1978.

Jacobson, N. S., & Margolin, G. *Marital therapy: Strategies based on social learning and behavior exchange principles.* New York: Brunner/Mazel, 1979.

Kendall, P. C., & Hollon, S. D. (Eds.). *Cognitive behavioral interventions: Theory, research and procedures.* New York: Academic Press, 1979.

Lazarus, R. S. Emotions and adaptation: Conceptual and empirical relations. In W. J. Arnold (Ed.), *Nebraska Symposium on Motivation.* Lincoln: University of Nebraska Press, 1968.

Meichenbaum, D. W. *Kognitive Verhaltensmodifikation.* Munich: Urban & Schwarzenberg, 1979.

Patterson, G. R. A performance theory for coercive family interaction. In R. Cairns (Ed.), *Social interaction: Method, analysis and illustration.* Monograph of the Society for Research in Child Development, 1977.

Pearls, F. S., Hefferline, R. F., & Goodman, P. *Gestalt therapy.* New York: Bantam, 1951.

Polster, E., & Polster, M. *Gestalttherapie.* Munich: Kindler, 1975.

Revenstorf, D., Hahlweg, K., & Schindler, L. Interaktionsanalyse von Partnerkonflikten. *Zeitschrift für Sozialpsychologie,* 1979, *10,* 183–196.

Revenstorf, D., Vogel, B., Wegener, C., Hahlweg, K., & Schindler, L. Escalation phenomena in interaction sequences: An empirical comparison of distressed and non-distressed couples. *Behavior Analysis and Modification,* 1980, *4,* 97–115.

Sager, C. J. *Marriage contracts and couple therapy.* New York: Brunner/Mazel, 1976.

Sifneos, P. E. The Prevalence of alexithymic characteristics in psychosomatic patients. *Psychotherapy and Psychosomatics,* 1973, *22,* 255–262.

Watzlawick, P., Beavin, J. H., & Jackson, D. D. *Pragmatics of human communication.* New York: Norton, 1967.

Yalom, J. D. *The theory and practice of group therapy.* New York: Basic Books, 1970.

18

Cognitive and Strategic Interventions in Behavioral Marital Therapy

ROBERT L. WEISS

There appears to be an increasing recognition, on the parts of researchers and practitioners alike, that straightforward skills-training approaches to marital therapy impose restrictions on interventions. Researchers, for their part, have included cognitive variables in conceptualizing behavioral effects (e.g., Gottman, 1979; Margolin & Weiss, 1978; Vincent, Cook, & Messerly, 1980); clinical guides now also incorporate cognitive and strategic considerations (Jacobson & Margolin, 1979; Weiss, 1980). Whether from experience with noncompliance or an instance of the current wave of popularity enjoyed by cognitive psychology, the cognitive bandwagon rolls on. The purpose of this chapter is both to expand upon earlier considerations of cognitive and strategic applications within behavioral marital therapy (BMT) and to bring together some of the informal bits of clinical lore we often find ourselves exchanging informally at conferences. Specifically, I attempt a more systematic view of cognitive and strategic interventions potentially useful in BMT yet not fully elaborated in earlier presentations. The first section briefly summarizes some possibilities for utilizing cognitive variables as conceptualized in general psychology within a BMT framework. The second half of the chapter considers clinical applications and the selection of appropriate techniques at different stages of therapy.

Points of View about Cognitive Variables

One of the fascinations of marital therapy is its epistemological challenge: How do spouses know about each other from their joint behaviors? As outsiders, equipped with coding systems, we often have access to transactional data, yet we often come to conclusions different from those of the actors. Being a participant–observer in a relationship that is broadly evaluative, in the sense of being an ongoing negotiation about self-worth, invites numerous opportunities for distortion of behavioral data.

Robert L. Weiss. Department of Psychology, University of Oregon, Eugene, Oregon, U.S.A.

In my view, intimacy carries with it agreements about "fate control"; that is, one gives fate control over to the partner. By this I suggest that an intimate partner now has the capability to move the other through a wide range of affective states, from dejection to gleeful highs. In this sense one's partner evaluates and defines the value of one's own behaviors. Failures of consideration take on very special meaning in marital transactions. Although I am not endorsing the psychodynamic view of identity or development of self, I am suggesting that we need to be mindful of the special circumstances that may hold otherwise "unsatisfactory" relationships together. To this end I suggested the metaphor of "sentiment override" (Weiss, 1980) as a reminder that spouses do not often respond to behavioral inputs, but rather to some affective–cognitive representation of one another that sets the "value" of any particular bit of behavior.

In working with couples, the encoding processes themselves are of special interest because of the subject matter. An interesting technical literature is now appearing that focuses on differences in "private communications" between distressed and nondistressed couples (e.g., Gottman & Porterfield, 1981; Noller, 1980).

Much of the current literature that describes cognitive variables potentially of interest to clinical work focuses on individual processes. For example, Mischel (1979) posits five "cognitive social learning person variables": (1) competencies for constructing cognitive and behavioral products, (2) encoding strategies and ability to categorize situations, (3) behavior–outcome and stimulus–outcome expectancies (see below), (4) subjective values of outcomes, and (5) self-regulatory systems and plans. These categories cover the gamut of informational processing and response transformations, areas in which we could begin to look for consistencies within persons.

At a level of greater concern to couples, although still focusing on individual psychology, we note the extensive literature on "attributions," that is, the ways in which we generate explanations of causality and conditions under which such explanations may influence subsequent behaviors. Partners experience their marital interactions as intentional acts having motivational significance. The behaviors of one spouse have particularistic significance for the other, and because of this partners easily train each other to engage in explanation contests: for example, who can explain best the reasons for instances of nonmotivated events. There have been a few isolated attempts in the literature to test the applicability of some generalizations from attribution research. Since persons perceive their own behaviors as situationally dependent when in the role of actor, but perceive behaviors of others as trait-dependent when in the role of observer, it was suggested that by encouraging role reversal one could overcome this attributional bias. Fichten (1980) attempted to influence attributional reporting by having spouses view videotapes of their own (prior) interactions under conditions that focused on the self or the other partner. The study failed to show the expected (manipulated) attribution effect, although it did confirm the earlier generalization about self–other attributions.

Attributions (theories of causality) are of importance in working clinically with couples. In recognition of this, one might consider a recent review of the literature by Kelley and Michela (1980). These authors approached the attribution literature by considering both the antecedents and the consequences of attributions (perceived causes). By focusing on the antecedents of attributions (e.g., information, beliefs, motivation), the result is a consideration of *attribution* theories. By focusing on the link between attributions and their consequences (behavior, affect, expectancy), the result is a consideration of *attributional* theories. Although generalizations about attribution theories (antecedents) are numerous, those germane to attributional theories (consequences of attributions) are often equivocal. (We seem to know more about the role of information, beliefs, and motivation as precursors of attributions than we do about the effects of attributions on behavior, affect, and expectancy.)

For illustration, here are two sample generalizations about antecedents: (1) Properties of the cause are assumed to be similar to properties of the effect; that is, if the effect is major (a presidential assassination) the cause must be major (a conspiracy). (2) The good behavior of liked persons and the bad behavior of disliked persons will be attributed to person (rather than environment) factors.

Yet there are difficulties in demonstrating that attributions themselves mediate behavior; it is often difficult to establish independent variable status for attributions. Methodologically the problem is complex, since we must independently manipulate attributions (by context or instruction), and we must also show that a particular attribution was salient at the precise point in time of concern to us. In addition to manipulating the independent variable status of attributions, there is a further complication: "The central point is that properties of the attribution itself elicit behavior that shapes its subsequent informational antecedents" (Kelley & Michela, 1980, p. 491). This is most clearly the case whenever the consequence of an attribution serves to strengthen it, as in so-called exacerbation cycles. Storms and McCaul (1976) define a four-stage exacerbation cycle as follows: (1) Undesirable behavior is attributed to the self, an attribution that in turn (2) increases expectancies of negative consequences, which in turn (3) exacerbates the undesirable behavior; as the behavior becomes more extreme, it is (4) more readily attributed to the negative self.

In earlier papers (Weiss, 1980, 1981) I have adapted Bandura's (1977) self-efficacy model for use with couples, since, as noted above, most of the work in this area (including the exacerbation model) is limited to individual attributional loops. The exacerbation model — which is clinically familiar to those working with cognitive-restructuring techniques—also impacts efficacy expectations as well as behavior. Yet as Kelley and Michela (1980) conclude, research on the links between attributions and consequences has proceeded linearly and generally has not taken cognizance of the circular loops that carry input to antecedents of attributions.

Using the efficacy model, I argued for separating BMT into its cognitive-based and performance-based components (Weiss, 1980). The performance-based component describes our efforts to teach couples skills that alter outcome expectations. Distressed couples clearly demonstrate unhelpful exchanges; teaching appropriate skills reduces their distress by changing their interactions. This approach assumes that attitude change follows from behavioral change. Indeed, the consequences of positive interactions should build positive sentiment, and for many couples who have a strong commitment to staying together, this regime is sufficient. But for the majority of unselected distressed couples, one encounters considerable negative sentiment override, that is, questioning whether the partner intends good faith. It is at this point, then—when "theories of the relationship" are quite negative—that one encounters "resistance" to therapeutic skills training. Either the couple appears not to be listening, or the tasks never seem to get done, or appointment times are forever changing, but things seem to be off track. It is also under these conditions that I suggest we consider the cognitive-based component of BMT.

Based upon Bandura's (1977) model for self-efficacy, I suggested a three-stage model germane to couples (Weiss, 1980): Dyad→Transaction→Outcome. Like Bandura, I define two classes of "expectations" that mediate between the Dyad→Transaction segment and the Transaction→Outcome segment; these are efficacy expectations and outcome expectations, respectively. The cognitive-based component of BMT is reflected in the efficacy expectations at the front end of the sequence. These are, collectively, cognitions and affects that serve to control Transaction→Outcome results, in a fashion that may override outcome expectations. Whereas outcome expectations refer to "knowledge about what leads to what," efficacy expectations refer to whether the couple "sees themselves accomplishing some end," independent of their knowledge about such events. Thus they may understand the lawfulness of some transaction-to-outcome sequence (contingency) but hold the view that such a contingency is not possible in their relationship.

The lore persons have about adult intimacy, the theories they evolve from living with a specific partner, and the consequences of their exchanges with specific partners—all combine into what I am here calling "efficacy expectations" about the relationship. When we refer to developing the cognitive component of BMT, it is with regard to techniques, tactics, and strategies that impact the affective belief systems (efficacy expectations) that couples hold.

Viewed in this perspective, the exacerbation cycle described above is the cognitive equivalent of the coercion process, which BMT has used to explain performance-based dysfunction. Clinically, on a cognitive level, we often see how spouses have driven each other into ever more extreme positions, resulting in a caricature of their former reasonableness. As Watzlawick, Weakland, and Fisch (1974) have so nicely stated the matter, the solution that the couple adopts *is* the problem.

These kinds of theoretical considerations have been addressed in at least two offerings in the marriage literature: in my earlier papers (Weiss, 1980, 1981), and in Doherty's recent model (Doherty, 1981a, 1981b). Here I consider both models briefly and then conclude this section with some considerations of how techniques themselves provide a basis for unintended attributions, that is, those not planned by the therapist.

Doherty's Model

Doherty (1981a, 1981b) offers an integrated model drawing upon attribution and social learning theories, for example, Bandura's self-efficacy approach (Bandura, 1977). Doherty defines two cognitive dimensions, "causal attributions" and "efficacy expectations," both of which are seen as leading to "conflict dimensions." The latter refer to blaming attitudes and persistent problem-solving attempts including learned-helplessness responses. Ongoing family conflict instigates members to ask both attributional questions (e.g., "Who or what is causing this problem?") and efficacy questions (e.g., "Can we solve this problem?"). As to who or what caused the problem, the potential choices are self, others, the relationship, and the external environment, including God's will, luck, chance, or fate. In addition to identifying agents, Doherty draws from a mix of attribution theory sources (Abramson, Seligman, & Teasdale, 1978; Heider, 1958; Weiner, 1974) and includes such attributional dimensions as intent, stability, voluntariness, and specificity. Doherty's model is a bit confusing in that not all terms are used systematically to form the various matrices he suggests for defining different conflict approaches. He may interchange sources (self, external environment) with cognitive dimensions (e.g., intent, stability). The attributional model of learned helplessness proposed by Abramson et al. (1978) is a more simplified version of Doherty's. In this model, it will be recalled, three categories are defined: stable–unstable, internal–external, and specific–global. Thus, a person can attribute some outcome to the self or to the environment (internal–external), to conditions that are more or less changeable (trait-like or capricious, as in luck, the day of the week, etc.), and finally, to a specific or global cause. The Doherty and the Abramson et al. models are similar, but Doherty discusses the additional feature of efficacy expectations.

Weiss's Model

In my earlier discussions of cognitive and strategic factors in BMT, I have suggested a much simpler cognitive–self-efficacy model. I was concerned first with the kinds of attributions that would result as a function of three variables: sentiment, perceived skillfulness, and choice. "Sentiment" is defined as the overriding evaluation of the partner (essentially positive or negative); "perceived skillfulness" refers to whether the partner is judged to possess the requisite skills to produce an outcome, and "choice" refers to whether the partner is seen as having made a deliberate choice to behave in this or that way. Skillfulness and choice are attributions that are made about the partner; sentiment is the affective resting level. Judgments about the spouse involve sentiment and whether the perceiver thinks that the spouse could do X or Y but chooses to do X and not Y.

Both Doherty and I provide a heuristic for viewing the efficacy expectations that spouses hold about themselves, their partners, and, most importantly from our point of view, their relationships. As therapists we can gain an understanding of potential belief barriers if we do our homework and carefully assess the kinds of attributional conclusions that spouses have reached. The entire second section of this chapter is devoted to this issue, but I feel it necessary to mention it here as well. Particular types of attributions lead to specific efficacy expectations, and these in term delimit the acceptability of skills-training options for the spouses. Unlike Doherty, I am assuming that efficacy expectations are relational as well as individual, and that attributions may lead to efficacy expectations, as in the feedback loop mentioned by Kelley and Michela (1980). Doherty sets those two categories (expectations and attributions) as cocontributors.

Only if the therapist assumes that skills training will unseat otherwise tenaciously held beliefs (expectations) will he/she find this approach redundant at best, or trivial at worst. But those expectations, based upon beliefs that partner A is riddled with global, unchangeable traits, are going to be difficult to change simply through skills training. From attribution theory we know that new evidence will be fitted into the already existing schema of the other, and distortions will occur as necessary to allow the new evidence to "fit."

One clinical issue, therefore, appears to be how we deal with efficacy expectations that result from particular attributional relationship theories. It is the rigid, patterned ways of thinking about the relationship that often interfere with skills-based therapy — that is, noncompliance, failure to "understand" the purpose of tasks, and other resistance techniques.

A second clinical issue revolves around the attributions that are conditioned by behavioral enactments themselves, that is, the ways in which behaviors themselves set the stage for specific attributions. It is here that behavioral therapists need to take seriously the principle that says that behavior is the basis for attitude formation. The quality of an act changes with the perceived context for that act; something of objective value (a diamond ring) loses its subjective value if the context is wrong (owned by a former spouse).

Based upon the conceptual distinction between behaviors that are under reinforcement control and those under stimulus control (Weiss, 1980), I attempted to show how systems theory notions about patterned and rule-governed behaviors can be fitted into a cognitive-behavioral schema (Weiss, 1980, 1981). Behavior is under reinforcing control when the immediate consequences of a transaction are responded to by the partners. This is reminiscent of the tit-for-tat immediacy seen in reciprocal negative exchanges. Rule control, on the other hand, involves transactions that are under stimulus control: Partners may invoke cues to bring about a transaction or a specific behavior on the part of another. Agreements, contracts, lists, and so on all serve as explicit forms for ensuring rule control. It is also necessary to consider that behaviors are under greater or lesser symbolic elaboration, that is, more or less in awareness. A written agreement that such and such shall govern some aspect of a relationship transaction is an example of a very explicit, symbolically elaborated form of rule control. Behavior elaborated to a much lesser degree occurs automatically in specific contexts. As an example of this "out of awareness" processing, Langer (1982) cites research she has done on "mindlessness." If the grammatical context is familiar, people will execute even meaningless commands. Thus if a message is sent in a familiar and expected "grammatical" form, the specifics (content) of the message are not processed. For example, an unreasonable request followed by any excuse results in more compliance than an unreasonable request not followed by an excuse. "May I interrupt, because I have something to Xerox?" is an unreasonable request when made to a person now using the Xerox machine, together with a nonsensical justification ("I have something to Xerox"). Many transactions in marriage occur in such highly patterned, seemingly automatic ways without much conscious elaboration as to why the events occur as they do. These kinds of automatic transactions are often the subject of satirical assaults on the institution of marriage, for example, the inattentive yet vocally assenting husband (reading the newspaper) agreeing to his wife's suggestion that he pay for her trip to the Orient.

If we make these two continua (rule to reinforcing control, and high to low elaboration) orthogonal, the resulting four quadrants define likely attributions about the causal or intentional acceptability of any particular behavior. Thus behavior that is under rule control and is also highly elaborated (such as a negotiated written contract) is likely to be seen as deliberative and not spontaneous. At the other (diagonal) extreme we have behavior that is under reinforcing control and is also minimally in awareness. Such behavior would seem to be spontaneous or involuntary. Since not necessarily under the person's control, in some cases it might be seen as most revealing of the person's "true feelings." (We often take the cortically impaired behavior of inebriated friends as representing their true feelings, especially when they say something negative about us!) When using this particular diagonal plane of the quadrants, we see that certain behaviors should not be encouraged under specific quadrant rules; for example, affectionate behaviors that are planned and occur by agreement (explicit rule control) will be devalued, whereas affectionate behaviors that appear spontaneously, "just happen," and that build reciprocally are seen as genuine.

The quadrants formed by the other diagonal are very different; that is, the lower left and upper right quadrants define high elaboration and response control versus low elaboration and high degree of rule control, respectively. Behavior that is highly elaborated and under reinforcing control can run the risk of overgeneralization: This is the situation of a small segment of reciprocal behavior's being used as the basis for a "theory" of intent. Viewed positively, the behavior could be labeled as "thoughtful tokens"—a lot of thought going into a small act. But we are concerned with the tendency to overgeneralize from small reinforcement-controlled acts. The diagonal counterpart to this case involves those acts that are not symbolically elaborated yet are patterned or under rule control; these are ritualized transactions. The point here is that certain behaviors should be excluded from this attributional frame; behaviors that communicate about the worth of the other should never be ritualized.

In this section we have explored some of the possibilities for including cognitive/strategic considerations in behavioral marital therapy. The various models that have been posited all seem to deal with efficacy and attributional considerations. From general attribution theory it is important to distinguish between the antecedents of attributions (factors that influence the development of causal explanations) and the consequences of attributions (outcomes mediated by attributions held). More seems to be known about the antecedents of attribution than about the effects of attributions on behavioral outcomes.

Clinical Applications

There are themes common to the various attempts to implement relationship change systematically. Most approaches recognize that spouses are engaged in highly patterned, often ritualized transactions. Couples present their "story" as if on a cassette that represents their own theories of distress. Those working in a systems perspective look for regularities in how the family members attempt to realign imbalances, as though under a homeostatic rule; as one partner becomes less depressed or less a problem drinker, the other seems to hit upon the exactly correct behavior to send the dyad back to ground zero.

From a behavioral perspective (Jacobson & Margolin, 1979), these events would be construed in terms of the couple's fears of change because of their inadequate skill repertoires; what they are resisting is novelty. From the various psychodynamically based models, the explanation would follow along the lines of inevitable personality dynamics being projected onto the spouse, maintaining a collusion between them based upon their need complementarity.

I find the systems perspective most helpful as a way to encourage focusing on the context of transactions, that is, very much like a functional analysis of behavior. How do spouses organize their movements, and how do these become patterned to accomplish what ends? Performance-based approaches to marital therapy emphasize skills training; intervention is focused on outcome expectations by teaching what acts lead to which outcomes. I see the task of the marital therapist as requiring the skills of a cinema director. The therapist sets goals, selects techniques, and constantly evaluates outcomes, changing techniques in response to outcome changes. It is this directiveness on a grand scale that is "strategic" in the sense used by Haley (1973). All marital behavior therapy is strategic in this sense, and as indicated above, because we are dealing with intimacy it is necessarily concerned with cognitions. One can choose not to acknowledge the role of cognitions in adult intimacy, just as one can choose not to be antiseptic before surgery.

This section attempts to illustrate the ways in which I feel BMT is strategic and takes cognitions seriously. Intervention is strategic in the sense that the therapist develops a coherent plan for making relationship change possible; the tactics and techniques employed are dictated by that plan. The plan in turn is based upon the therapist's conceptualization of the case. I find it useful to distinguish the functional components of intervention according to three sequential phases: (1) initial entry and assessment, (2) early stages of intervention, and (3) termination phase. We shall consider each of these in turn.

Initial Entry and Assessment

The therapist's first directorial task is to define the context in which the relationship will be seen. There are two features in this phase: encouraging behaviors that allow the therapist and couple to work together, and assessing the potential for relationship change.

Persons present themselves to the marital therapist for a host of reasons, very few of which are for relationship change. Often their perception is that the problem resides in the other as a personality or physical limitation. A relationship advocate (the appropriate role for the therapist) is not what is being sought at this stage. Moving from an individually focused rationale to one that makes it possible to work with them as a relationship is a specific therapeutic task.

Assessment of potential for relationship change depends entirely on our conceptualization of (1) therapy, (2) desirable outcomes, and (3) what we know how to do best. These factors combine to determine what we define as informative about a couple. For instance, I am interested in estimating the degree of commitment a couple will have if they and I are to be successful. Are there positive reasons, understandable to me, for them to persist together? Am I likely to be effective with this couple? In order to be effective I must get their attention. I also believe that couples must be able to shift set, step outside of themselves by adopting an "as if" attitude (see Stuart, 1980) or one that suspends judgment. My data base will be my interaction with their interaction, that is, their attempts to deal with the problems I set for them as we interact. Generally I do not expect their verbal communications to provide as much information as their nonverbal (process) communications.

The therapist does need to understand the kinds of attributions spouses use to explain their upset and their efficacy expectations. Although one hears about these in verbal communication, one also needs to determine these from process data, that is, what the couple does in session.

Accommodation and assessment come together when we consider who has responsibility for controlling the context of the meeting. Context will be defined by someone's activity, and I believe it is the therapist's responsibility to provide the context through his/her activity. Typically the spouses present their repertoire of progress-impeding behaviors: They will talk for each other; engage in mind reading; ask questions in a rapid-fire style, presumably to elicit information about caring; and generally pursue unanswerable "why" questions. Some of these behaviors may function to elicit the therapist's support for an individual's position; some are designed to communicate the inevitability of divorce, that the other person cannot (will not) change; and so on. These behaviors are annoying and challenging as to who is the authority on whom! It is essential that the therapist have available tactics for shifting the context of the meeting. This is not the same as saying that the therapist needs ways for protecting himself/herself; it means the therapist is able to blow bigger and more awe-inspiring soap bubbles than the couple.

Context provides meaning to events; if we accept A, then B but not C is true. Therapists often wonder how to "bail out" of a difficult place in an interaction; my suggestion is to not allow those moments to develop. Take the example of the hypothetical young Deadlys and the empathic therapist. The therapist allows the session to proceed with the heaviness and solemnity of a Bergman movie; more important, the therapist's own motor behavior begins to slow down. The context is now defined as a funeral. Something terrible has happened, people are overwhelmed by their loss, and the future cannot be mentioned now out of respect for the intensity and validity of the survivors' sorrow. Short of being a court jester, the therapist must change the context before it envelops him/her. We need to know whether the couple can step out of this context (the funeral), and it is our responsibility to provide them a means for doing so. They may not be able to do so, but we need behavioral evidence either way.

We need to know whether this heavy state results whenever the couple attempts to take themselves seriously, as they are now doing by seeing the therapist. Does their morbidity reflect a prediction of futility in regard to trying to make things better? Are they so totally dependent upon one another that their very caring immobilizes them like quick-drying epoxy? "Empathy" should be of concern in their relationship, as well as the fact that they are unable to attain it in this present state; "empathy" is not provided by the therapist's pretending to understand an ill-defined history of disappointments. By taking what is portrayed in the process as evidence for a larger relationship issue, we actually create a new problem for the couple to solve, a problem they did not have before.

My peculiar solution to the control-of-context issue is to have available a set of "universal truths"; these are relationship generalizations that are designed to stop ongoing action, thereby requiring a searching, thoughtful reply. They take the form of "All couples must do_____; how have you (together) accomplished that goal?" For example, "Since all spouses have an obligation to be attractive to each other, how have you done that?" (or ". . . an obligation to be protective of each other . . . ," or ". . . to enhance each other's self-esteem . . ."). The universal truth (which is meant to sound like the wisdom of the ages) focuses on constructive features of relatedness and defines these cooperatively. Take an apparent exception to this definition: "Since every relationship must allow the partners to be separate people as well as a couple, how have you . . . ?"Note that even here the rules for separateness are defined within the context of their relationship (not by individual whimsy); the challenge is dyadically focused, even though the content is about separateness.

Whatever the answer to a universal truth may be, the therapist gains information. If the spouses don't support each other, if they don't care about each other's self-esteem, if they don't know how to have time alone, or if they are afraid to be attractive, and so on, the therapist has a grasp on a possible goal for therapy. By responding to the universal truth, the individuals legitimize its very existence, and the problem then becomes how they can deal with it. If they do not care about self-esteem, then they must not want to burden themselves with caring for each other, so they can have a nice business-like relationship (or some other unacceptable choice). The therapist has accomplished his/her end, namely, controlling the context by focusing on a relationship issue now made problematic in that it calls attention to how the partners provide mutual benefits.

Contrast this downright manipulative approach with a simple, direct question put to the couple: "Do you provide benefits to one another?" There are at least two problems associated with such a question asked in the initial accommodation phase: (1) It assumes that the couple can step outside of their current anger and comment on pleasurable exchanges; whether they can step outside of their current mind-set is precisely what we are trying to assess, so we should not assume it. (2) There has been no behavioral definition of benefits; that is, benefits could range from a roof over their heads to taking a daily shower. The couple does not need to interact with the therapist's meaning of benefits; rather, like a cinema director, the therapist should establish a context that makes the question poignant. Simply put: I do not ask the benefits question directly, because I cannot believe the answer! During the initial phases of accommodation, neither couple nor therapist has struck a bargain that allows for more than the couple's complaining and expecting validation for their position. My approach is to provide a rationale for a problem by using the couple's own behavior as a justification for noticing the problem. It is their answer to my unanswerable question that allows me to remain a sympathetic observer of their plight, and further, to be in a position to suggest that perhaps the solution to that problem might well occupy us in therapy if we choose to proceed.

If a couple is in great turmoil because of an affair or a history of inconsideration, I will ask something like "Often couples will experiment with separation . . . how have you done this?" Their response to such an implied demand will be informative: One soon sees the degree of their dependency on each other as well as efficacy fears (i.e., fears of being alone, guilt, etc.). It is important to note that these various types of context manipulations are all predicated on increasing the benefits that can be derived from the relationship. Once the bricks have been laid, once it has been established that "mutual care and feeding of self-esteem" is required in all relationships, the assessment focuses on how much of this benefit the relationship provides its members. It also makes it possible to return to this "issue" at a later time in therapy when one encounters noncompliance and indicates that such behavior on their parts does not meet the goal of enhancing self-esteem.

The use of humor is still another tactic for context change. Indeed, humor is often emotionally compelling, just because we find ourselves enmeshed in one predictable context, only to find suddenly that an otherwise familiar but statistically rare context fits the course of events illustrated by the joke or tale. A couple's positive response to humor that involves them (not joke telling!) is a positive indication of their flexibility. It is the first step in being able to take the role of the other. Humor also has another dimension that is consistent with couples therapy: metaphor. Vivid imagery can be used to advantage to either expand or contract the context of a problem. Although many family therapists advocate the use of metaphor as a structured representation of family roles, I prefer the use of colorful images to depict something essential about the quality of the transactions of a particular couple. It is burdensome for the therapist to have to create images anew, but it is a useful test of how well the therapist understands the texture of the couple's lives together. In addition to giving the couple a special status, it invites them to step outside their usual cause–effect construal of themselves and to view their own metamorphosis directed by the therapist.

It should be obvious by now that many of these suggestions are instances of a larger, more familiar attempt at cognitive restructuring. The issue is not whether insight must precede behavior change—a point repudiated by both systems and behavioral therapists—but rather how we affect those efficacy expectations that function as belief barriers. These particular suggestions—such as the use of universal truths, humor, metaphor, and reframing—are all based on the positive, beneficial components of relationships but do not require insight into causes. The use of restraining types of paradoxical messages is based upon encouraging forms of transactions that will be restricted and thereby will result in change. These restraining techniques are not likely to be useful in the early phases of entry and accommodation. Restraining techniques require a thorough knowledge of how a couple functions in their own setting. The therapist simply does not know enough about the couple to rely on admonitions designed to create oppositional reactions. The one possible exception to this can occur with an initial contact defined by considerable vagueness, lack of demonstrated hurt, and a highly competitive interaction between the spouses. If one gets the sense that important issues are not being presented (and probably won't be with repeated meetings), it might be advisable to suggest that their problems simply have not yet gotten to a point that they could change; it would be better, therefore, to wait until things get worse. Whether restraining techniques are ever successful is still based upon clinical testimony rather than empirical results.

Early Stages of Intervention

During the early phases of intervention, the focus is typically on communication skills and training. Typically, something like pinpointing or other objectification skills (see Weiss & Perry, 1979) is begun. Since these techniques represent a major shift from the introspective–complaining–justification recursive loops, couples often "fail to see how this is relevant to our problem." The issue then becomes accommodating the technology to the couple's view of what is required, which is easier to do if they have already accepted the therapist as someone worth paying attention to. During later phases of intervention, when negative and aversive exchanges are reduced, the therapist gets an opportunity to see the spouses express self-doubt about change more fearfully. They will often look to the therapist to normalize their concerns, that is, to provide encouragement that they will be able to master satisfying closeness. In our experience, when couples get close to the problem-solving phase of BMT, there appears to be a rekindling of old hurts, and various crises may be precipitated; smoke screens, acting out, or direct challenges to the therapist are not uncommon manifestations.

Intervention begins formally when the therapist has a coherent plan for the couple; this includes an evaluation of what efficacy expectations operate to impede change and which ones can be depended upon to facilitate change. We need to assess the ways in which attributions are employed, whether causes are seen as external or internal, whether stable or unstable, and so on. (I am restricting myself largely to cognitive factors, since much has already been written on behavioral assessment of the performance components of relationships.)

Intervention requires that the therapist continue to be the controller of context: Individual attacks by spouses are to be reframed as dyadically relevant skill deficits, the presence of which impedes mutual benefits. I think it is important to be able to provide a rationale to the spouses for any and all requests that I might make. I anticipate this need by providing them a written outline of the four goals of marital therapy: objectification, support/understanding, problem solving, and behavior change skills. This immediately allows the therapist to invoke the rule, "You must never get ahead of yourselves." When a couple starts to solve problems prematurely, I can then invoke the rationale and the rule; for example, "See what happens when you get ahead of yourselves? You tried to solve an important issue [who is going to do the dishes!] and it ended up in an argument." This also brings their own behavior under stimulus control; that is, they can invoke the rule as a means of controlling their escalations.

Another example may help to make the point of how cognitive elements are included in early stages of intervention. Pinpointing, paraphrasing, and reflecting exercises are often tortuously difficult for distressed couples. For them, every statement of request is loaded with historical barnacles and so cannot be compacted into a simple declarative pinpointed request. The goal is to keep them on task and to make success and failure always a dyadic event. My colleague Barbara Perry implements this by designing a set of 3 × 5 cards for each couple containing simple one-liners of great relevance to the couple's relationship, for example, "closeness," "working together with the kids," "affection in public," and "initiating recreational activities." The partners take turns drawing from a deck of cards and putting the content into an acceptable pinpointed statement. In addition to the obvious practice in skills training, note how Perry maintains control of the exercise and how, as director, she can comment on their joint successes and failures with dyadic reframes: "The problem you are having is that you are both trying to elaborate too much, all I want now is a simple statement of your desire." She has made the "problem" their ability to meet the demands of the task, not each other's inadequacies as people.

By maintaining control of context, the therapist is in a position to use ongoing transactions as the basis for reframes and rationale-building attempts. It is possible to focus their struggle on learning rather than their concerns about intentionality. But sooner or later we will run headlong into the problem of intentionality; does the partner really mean this or that, or isn't the partner doing something only because the therapist has suggested it? These are the concerns of a person who feels vulnerable, not necessarily malicious. The person is asking whether it is safe to take the risks suggested by the new techniques. The dyadic issue now becomes: How can I help you feel safe as you engage in bilateral disarmament activities? How can you express your desire to be reassured in ways that will ensure your partner's ability to comply?

Couples can often be helped to overcome these concerns by providing them with techniques for bringing the conditions of doubt under their own control. We often assign a joint task that is designed to muddy the waters, to prevent complete accuracy in reading the intent of the other. The plan is to create a context in which verification is difficult at best, and preferably impossible. If knowing the intent of another reduces one's own estimate of that person's interest (since no objective judgment is possible), then it becomes a matter of whether one will choose to ascribe good intent. But such a choice is now unrelated to the behavior of the other. The therapist is now in control, because having removed the external supports for reading intent (correctly), the issue is good faith, more commonly known as "trust." The way is now paved for introducing the basic rule of stimulus control: "DRIVE FRIENDLY." Each individual should remind himself/herself (as does the Texas freeway system) that the spouse is a friend, not an adversary. If in doubt, one should assume good intentions (or "Drive friendly" in the face of contradictory evidence!). We suggest that each person, on some schedule known only to the therapist and the person, purposely say or do something when the intent will be valid or not valid. But the success of this task requires that the partner not know what the true intent is. Thus, "I want you to provide a love day to Sally in such a way that she cannot tell it is an assignment from me. If she does guess correctly, then you are not being subtle enough. Sometimes be especially loving, even when you don't mean it as a love day!"

On other occasions it is useful to predict failure by enlisting the couple's assistance: "How might you purposefully make X or Y fail this week? What would you both have to do to make it not work right?" If neither person can come up with the necessary "commando tactics," then I would suggest it is too soon for them to try the new idea; it will fail because they don't yet know how to make it fail! Control means having the capability of countercontrol. Here, too, we are assuming that countercontrol will equalize the power balance for the relationship: we can make both good and ill outcomes happen. This shifts the focus to outcome, not to intent. Failure to maximize pleasant outcomes is now self-defeating because of the inherently dyadic nature of the exchange.

We mentioned earlier the possible attributions that result when behavior is jointly classified according to rule versus reinforcing control and high versus low symbolic elaboration. It is during intervention that this schema may prove helpful in guiding the choice of rationale for assignments. Take the example of contracting with couples for some behavior change. Because contracting is the most externally controlling of the behavior change devices, it requires a high degree of rule control and considerable elaboration, such as a written agreement. It would be counterproductive to contract for behaviors that are valuable only when they are spontaneous and offered without deliberate choice. Uncontrollable affection that seems to burst forth validates the incredible appeal the other spouse has for the individual! But affection that is doled out on a contractual schedule is invalid, and rightly so.

Negative behaviors, on the other hand, are precisely not the ones to be encouraged for spontaneous expression. Negative reciprocation cycles (escalation of aversiveness) is most often under reinforcing control and occurs with little forethought. These behaviors should be brought under explicit rule control. The issue should not be allowed to become one of dirty socks or specific sexual failures as exemplars of dissatisfaction; but rather, a rule is needed to guide transactions. Then both partners function under the guidance of the rule, not of the moment-to-moment payoff matrix of individual responses.

In this way the rule control–awareness matrix squares with recent theorizing and research. Both Jacobson (1979) and I (Weiss, 1978) have argued that distressed relationships are tied to immediate reciprocity more than nondistressed relationships. That is, marital satisfaction for the former is incremented and decremented by the vicissitudes of daily exchanges of pleasing and displeasing behaviors. We need to be cognizant of those intervention procedures that foster narrowly focusing on immediate reciprocity, such as reinforcing (or more typically rewarding) behaviors in a tit-for-tat fashion. Many of our most interesting techniques for helping couples are based on specific attention to the details of an exchange. This *quid pro quo,* which is often the basis of our behavioral technology, may inadvertently foster unhelpful attributions. It would seem advisable, following this line of reasoning, to assiduously separate mechanics from volition: "First we learn what the response (behaviors) would look like, then we consider the conditions under which you might choose to engage in those behaviors." The issue of choice is used to instill good faith: "Your partner chose to do X or Y for you, which is a sign of good intention."

But as I have suggested elsewhere (Weiss, 1980), judgments of intent may be made before establishing that the partner has the requisite skills to choose to refuse. The therapist should become simplistic in demanding that the partners have necessary behavior capabilities before assuming anything about intentionality. First we establish that the partner has the skill capability to provide X or Y; then we focus on the rate of choosing to do so. Finally, the best strategy is to focus on skills and choice issues dyadically. "Obviously you now know what to do, so the issue becomes how often you are going to signal your regard for one another by doing X or Y." In this way (reframing the issue), the important point is not the consumable behaviors exchanged, but rather their significance to the couple. This shift in emphasis reinforces the view "We do for each other out of our positive regard for us." In my view, our earlier endorsement of strict *quid pro quo* exchanges often failed to acknowledge the implicit meta-message that goes something like "My spouse cares enough to contract for change with me." For many distressed couples this "evidence" may have been a first. Recall that Jacobson (1978) failed to show differential effectiveness of *quid pro quo* over good faith contracting, suggesting that there may be a common factor to both forms. Obviously his results do not establish that the common factor is the one suggested here, but they are not inconsistent with the view expressed here.

In the examples cited above, I have intended to portray the therapist as the magician for the relationship, or, more acceptably, as spokesperson for the relationship. This requires a constant cognitive set to think dyadically, to ask oneself what happens to the transaction if only one person behaves in this or that fashion. Tasks should be framed as having joint, interlocking requirements. If one partner learns to paraphrase and the other does not, we have created the possibility for an iatrogenic effect: The successful partner can now browbeat the unsuccessful partner by impugning intention, motivations, and so on. Success is not additive in the sense of summing partial credits. Success is defined as the dyad's accomplishing an end that will pay off for the relationship.

Termination Phase

I suggest calling termination a *phase* to underscore the transition rather than the abrupt ending. Viewed in this way, the termination phase is a time of great vulnerability, and we need to help couples relabel this vulnerability for themselves. Recurrent failures should be reframed as skill-level problems, not intent or volitional defects. It is wise to provide for how the partners will help themselves get back on track, to label precursors of difficulty. We have already mentioned the device of having them practice failure.

Following this lead, any tactic that increases the couple's estimate of their control of negative exchanges should be encouraged. Specifically, we encourage the use of cueing statments for identifying the locus of problems as internal or external, favoring external construals. Is it an issue of poor planning, inappropriate use of situations (trying to make love when fatigued), physical weakness because of illness, or some other factor? Often very active couples get caught up in their own *macho* ideology and see "slowing down" as a sign of personal weakness. Similarly, we provide couples with a maintenance kit that can be reread when the going gets difficult, problem-solving aids they have found particularly useful in prior sessions, and additional spouse observation rating forms to track daily pleasing events.

Conversely, any tactic that makes affection appear to be spontaneous (not under control) is to be encouraged, whereas joint pleasures (such as coupling activities or shared recreational events) should be encouraged as high-choice options. That is, joint pleasures or presentations as a couple should be seen as under couple control, but affectional responses should remain purposely outside of control in order to enhance the spontaneity thereof. In this regard, the rules for the termination phase are not very different from early stages of intervention.

Finis

Someone once said that the most practical thing is a good theory. BMT needs conceptual refinement, and this will result from our attempts to make explicit our models for change. The fit between academic theories of attribution and other cognitive functions, on the other hand, and what the clinician does with couples, on the other, is still often more a promise than an actuality. This chapter attempts to bring the two closer together by identifying areas of considerable interest to the marital therapist, areas that have received attention in other quarters. For "cognitive restructuring" to be more than a currently fashionable password, we need to examine the tactics that seem to fit this broad notion. More important from the point of view being advocated here, we need to view our work strategically. This is accomplished by an active interplay between assessment and planning. The ideas presented here are intended to facilitate this interplay by discriminating cognitive and performance elements in our therapies with couples. In this form it is hoped that we can address the bigger issues of confirmation or disconfirmation; being correct is wonderful, but being testable runs a close second.

REFERENCES

Abramson, L. Y., Seligman, M. E. P., & Teasdale, J. D. Learned helplessness in humans: Critique and reformulation. *Journal of Abnormal Psychology*, 1979, *87*, 49–74.

Bandura, A. Self-efficacy: Toward a unifying theory of behavioral change. *Psychological Review*, 1977, *84*, 191–215.

Doherty, W. J. Cognitive processes in intimate conflict: 1. Extending attribution theory. *American Journal of Family Therapy*, 1981, *9*, 3–13. (a)

Doherty, W. J. Cognitive processes in intimate conflict: 2. Applications of attribution theory and social learning theory. *American Journal of Family Therapy*, 1981, *9*, 35–44. (b).

Fichten, C. *It's all your fault: Videotape and spouses' causal attributions.* Paper presented at the meeting of the American Psychological Association, Montreal, September 4, 1980.

Gottman, J. M. *Marital interaction: Experimental investigations.* New York: Academic Press, 1979.

Gottman, J. M., & Porterfield, A. L. Communicative competence in the nonverbal behavior of married couples. *Journal of Marriage and the Family*, 1981, *43*, 817–824.

Haley, J. *Uncommon therapy.* New York: Ballantine Books, 1973.

Heider, F. *The psychology of interpersonal relations.* New York: Wiley, 1958.

Jacobson, N. S. Specific and nonspecific factors in the effectiveness of a behavioral approach to the treatment of marital discord. *Journal of Consulting and Clinical Psychology*, 1978, *46*, 442–452.

Jacobson, N. S. Behavioral treatments for marital discord: A critical appraisal. In M. Hersen, R. M. Eisler, & P. M. Miller (Eds.), *Progress in behavior modification.* New York: Academic Press, 1979.

Jacobson, N. S., & Margolin, G. *Marital therapy: Strategies based on social learning and behavior exchange principles.* New York: Brunner/Mazel, 1979.

Kelley, H. H., & Michela, J. L. Attribution theory and research. In M. R. Rosenzweig & L. W. Porter (Eds.), *Annual review of psychology* (Vol. 31). Palo Alto: Annual Reviews, 1980.

Langer, E. H. Automated lives. *Psychology Today*, April 1982, pp. 60–71.

Margolin, G., & Weiss, R. L. Comparative evaluation of therapeutic components associated with behavioral marital treatments. *Journal of Consulting and Clinical Psychology*, 1978, *46*, 1476–1486.

Mischel, W. On the interface of cognition and personality. *American Psychologist*, 1979, *34*, 740–754.

Noller, P. Misunderstandings in marital communication: A study of couples' nonverbal communication. *Journal of Personality and Social Psychology*, 1980, *39*, 1135–1148.

Storms, M. D., & McCaul, K. D. Attribution processes and emotional exacerbation of dysfunctional behavior. In J. H. Harvey, W. J. Ickes, & R. F. Kidd (Eds.), *New directions in attribution research* (Vol. 1). Hillsdale, NJ: Erlbaum, 1976.

Stuart, R. B. *Helping couples change. A social learning approach to marital therapy.* New York: Guilford Press, 1980.

Vincent, J. P., Cook, N. I., & Messerly, L. A social learning analysis of couples during the second post-natal month. *American Journal of Family Therapy*, 1980, *8*, 49–68.

Watzlawick, P., Weakland, J., & Fisch, R. *Change: Principles of problem formation and problem resolution.* New York: Norton, 1974.

Weiner, B. *Achievement motivation and attribution theory.* Morristown, NJ: General Learning Press, 1974.

Weiss, R. L. The conceptualization of marriage and marriage disorders from a behavioral perspective. In T. J. Paolino & B. S. McCrady (Eds.), *Marriage and marital therapy: Psychoanalytic, behavioral, and systems theory perspectives.* New York: Brunner/Mazel, 1978.

Weiss, R. L. Resistance in behavioral marriage therapy. *American Journal of Family Therapy*, 1979, *7*, 3–6.

Weiss, R. L. Strategic behavioral marital therapy: Toward a model for assessment and intervention. In J. P. Vincent (Ed.), *Advances in family intervention* (Vol. 1). Greenwich, CT: JAI Press, 1980.

Weiss, R. L. The new kid on the block: Development of a behavioral-systems approach. In E. E. Filsinger & R. A. Lewis (Eds.), *Marital observation and marital assessment: Recent developments and techniques.* Beverly Hills, CA: Sage, 1981.

Weiss, R. L., & Perry, B. A. *Assessment and treatment of marital dysfunction.* Eugene: Oregon Marital Studies Program, 1979.

19

Marital Therapy with One Spouse

IAN BENNUN

The one-to-one therapist–client relationship dominates the fields of psychiatry and clinical psychology. Consequently, many therapists feel uncomfortable at the thought of being confronted simultaneously by more than one patient. The prohibition on treating more than one person is based largely on the psychoanalytic notion that the relationship between the therapist and patient will be diluted if the therapist sees the family or couple together. In contrast to this dominant perspective is the view that marital therapy should be conjoint, with the important relationship being between the spouses rather than between therapist and patient.

Marital therapy has many different forms. Cookerly (1973, 1976), for the purposes of a comparative analysis, differentiated six major forms of marital treatment:

1. Individual interview marriage counseling
2. Individual group marriage counseling
3. Concurrent interview marriage counseling
4. Concurrent group marriage counseling
5. Conjoint interview marriage counseling
6. Conjoint group marriage counseling

Despite the controversies surrounding individual treatment, it has always been recognized as one form of marital therapy. The effect of psychotherapy with one partner on the untreated spouse has been noted in clinical practice. The best-known account of this was provided by Kohl (1962) in his study of marital partners of inpatients. Several pathological reactions were noted in the untreated partners as a response to the patient's improvement. This reaction has been referred to as a "neurotic complementary reaction" (Mittelmann, 1948) or a "neurotic reciprocity" (Kohl, 1962), and it has been one of the cautions or contraindications of individual treatment with one partner. There are, of course, specific risks for the marital pair when only one partner is being treated. Some of these include a lowered motivation for change by the untreated partner, a collusive alliance between the therapist and the treated spouse (Rice, 1978), distorted reporting by the spouse, and gaps in

Ian Bennun. Institute of Psychiatry, University of London, London, United Kingdom.

reported information (Fibush, 1957). It has also been suggested that the treated partner's gains in therapy tend to make the untreated partner feel inadequate (Hurwitz, 1967). From a psychoanalytic view, the therapeutic transference may complicate the basic relationship between the spouses, resulting in secrecy, a breakdown in couple communication, and sexual problems.

Whatever the merits of having both spouses present, at times the therapist has no choice when one partner simply refuses to attend. Rice (1978) noted that women more commonly initiate therapy and that husbands often feel that they enter treatment in a "one-down" position. Another common occurrence is one partner's refusing to accept any responsibility for the marital difficulty and responding with "straighten him/her out and the marriage will be fine" (Perelman, 1960). The question that the therapist has to consider is whether treating one partner would be a viable form of intervention in helping these couples resolve their distress.

Reservations about individual treatment on both an empirical (Cookerly, 1973, 1976; Gurman, 1978; Gurman & Kniskern, 1978a, 1978b) and a theoretical basis (Ackerman, 1958; Saul, 1953) have been reported. However, these reservations may be questioned because of the confusion relating to the focus of the treatment. Unfortunately, many authors have failed to differentiate between marital therapy with one spouse and individual therapy with the marital relationship as one of the treatment foci (e.g., Giovacchini, 1961). Not only is this distinction unclear, but the goals of therapy, especially in the treatment of one marital partner alone, remain poorly defined. In his discussion on the process of conjoint treatment, Gurman (1978) questions whether therapists in the classical psychoanalytic tradition aim at individual personality change or a change in the relationship. That is to say, is the focus of treatment the underlying conflict in one marital partner or a change in the dynamics of the relationship? The psychoanalytically oriented therapist essentially views a change in the individual and a change in the marital interaction as being mutually dependent.

Are There Arguments in Favor of
Individual Treatment for Marital Problems?

Fibush (1957) contended that conjoint treatment could be recommended if it was the couple's definite choice. She realized that forcing a spouse into treatment would have little effect in improving marital functioning. Psychodynamic theorists have urged caution regarding the indiscriminate use of conjoint interviews. Clients who are immature and who are unable to tolerate the stress of a competitive conjoint interview may best benefit from individual treatment (Blanck, 1965; Nadelson, 1978). Nadelson (1978) recommends individual therapy when unresolved conflicts within one individual interfere with and threaten the marital relationship.

Smith and Hepworth (1967) have taken to task those who dispute the therapeutic effectiveness of individual treatment. They reported improved marital functioning following marital therapy with one partner, but did not present any data to support their assertion. Along with most writers who have considered individual treatment, these authors believe that while conjoint therapy may be desirable, individual therapy need not always result in therapeutic failure.

A symposium on individual marital treatment (Saul, 1953) produced many diverse opinions from marital therapists. Nelson (see Saul, 1953) believed that individual treatment was advantageous with premarital couples where pressures from the new family could be relieved within an individual relationship with the therapist. Other participants indicated that one could initiate therapy with one partner as an intermediate step to later conjoint sessions. Ormsby (see Saul, 1953) noted the usual experience of one partner's not attending. He stressed that the therapist should not listen to the complaints about the nonattending spouse but should examine the attending partner's part in the marriage and move toward changing this, which in turn might result in both partners agreeing to attend together.

Thus far, the arguments in favor of individual treatment have addressed this form of treatment "by default" through the spouse's decision not to attend therapy. There are situations, however, where joint sessions initially may be contraindicated. Jacobson and Margolin (1979) describe couples with affiliation–independence discrepancies where an overtly dependent partner is experienced as being excessively demanding and distances his/her spouse through extreme affiliative–demanding behavior. The therapeutic endeavor to balance affiliation and independence within relationships is seen by these authors to represent one of the rare contraindications to conjoint treatment. Interestingly, one of the important processes in the treatment of this type of difficulty is the enhancement of the relationship between the therapist and the excessively affiliated spouse in order to provide the support to ameliorate the stress of therapy. Part of the treatment would be to develop skills with the affiliative partner that would introduce new and valued reinforcements in the relationship that are independent of the spouse.

Clinical experience has shown that other couples' difficulties can also be treated by seeing one spouse only. A couple whose relationship is characterized by excessive acts of both emotional and physical aggression is a case in point. Although the aim of conjoint sessions would be the reduction of aggressive behavior, some couples respond to joint sessions with increased aggression, often provoked by the therapeutic directives. However determined the therapist's attempts to introduce alternative sources of reinforcement or new behavior may be, the aggression serves some function for the partner, and the presence of the spouse may militate against the exploration of this aspect of the behavior (Wile, 1981).

Another presenting marital difficulty that has responded favorably to individual treatment is one where a partner presents with low self-esteem not necessarily linked to depression. Clinical presentations include lethargy, feelings of worthlessness, and self-deprecation. Frequently, the partner has difficulties in fulfilling what is perceived to be his/her role in the marital relationship. This is often accompanied by a relatively satisfying sexual relationship and no appetite loss or sleep disturbance. At the initial session, the spouse presents as a kind and caring person who genuinely has attempted to alleviate the partner's difficulties. Adopting an exclusively dyadic focus may reinforce these feelings of inadequacy. A more appropriate approach would be to concentrate on the interests of the presenting spouse as an individual within the context of both the marriage and the spouses' extrarelational interests and activities.

A theme that has occurred throughout the literature on individual marital therapy is the use of individual sessions in preparation for later conjoint sessions. Many of the difficulties described, when alleviated in individual sessions, could facilitate later joint sessions. Here, the changes that occurred in the individual sessions could be discussed by the couple together, and then with the therapist. A regime may be investigated that would maintain the positive changes. Marital therapists tend to emphasize observable interaction changes and relationship enhancement as the only acceptable treatment goals. However, it is not unusual for couples to request therapy, wanting to remain in their marriage yet also wishing to be more comfortable in it. At the same time, they do not expect any great change in their relationship. Recently a couple described their problem as the wife's emotional difficulty in accepting an open marriage, although intellectually she felt that an open marriage was acceptable. Both partners had similar views on the advantages of open marriages, but her expressed fear was that the parallel relationship would irretrievably damage the marriage if she, like her husband, developed an extramarital relationship. After a few joint sessions, his continued presence engendered jealousy and frustration in her; thus it was decided to treat her alone until she felt that her husband's attendance would be less aversive.

The arguments presented here suggest that one marital partner can be treated alone and that this could favorably alter the nature of the existing marital relationship. At the same time, the promotion of well-being in each spouse can be enhanced. The introduction and investigation of this form of treatment may guard against the myopic tendencies of marital therapists to see only dyads, as well as introduce some flexibility into the role of the marital therapist in dealing with two-person difficulties. Watters (1982) has described the apparently arbitrary decisions that are sometimes taken when marital discord emerges during a psychiatric consultation. If relationship issues are identified, then couples are referred to a marital therapist on the grounds that the symptoms are not real psychiatric problems. If, on the other hand, the underlying current relationship issues are not identified, then the patient is treated alone. However, the decision whether the relationship or the individual becomes the primary treatment focus, in the final analysis, rests on clinical judgment.

There are precedents in the behavioral marital literature for modifying dyadic difficulties through the treatment of one partner alone. Recently Epstein (1981) noted the increasing use of assertiveness training in the treatment of interpersonal skill problems. The essential goal of this training is the substitution of clear, direct, and appropriate expressions of thought and behavior for inhibited and aggressive behavior. In so doing, the skills introduced are directed toward maximizing need fulfillment and minimizing the alienation of others in the social and interpersonal environment. However, as Epstein (1981) points out, the decision to introduce assertiveness training or skills training must take into account whether the treatment will be conjoint or individual. This remains an empirical issue, with preferences for conjoint treatment being justified theoretically rather than by available research findings. The challenge of individually oriented marital therapy should not be discarded until it has been investigated systematically; otherwise a potentially important form of treatment may be overlooked.

Empirical Considerations

Individual therapy, while remaining controversial, has not been empirically evaluated in the context of marital therapy. The available evidence supporting this form of treatment is largely anecdotal, with the exception of the studies by Goldstein and Francis (1969) and Goldstein (1971). These studies showed that in a small select group, wives could be taught to modify their husbands' behavior. The reviews of marital therapy outcome research have highlighted the poor results of individual therapy (Cookerly, 1973, 1976; Gurman & Kniskern, 1978a, 1978b).

Cookerly (1973, 1976) compared six forms of marital therapy in order to investigate their relative effectiveness. It is necessary at this point to differentiate between treatment form and treatment approach. "Form" relates to the composition or sequence of the therapeutic relationship (e.g., individual, conjoint, collaborative, group, consecutive), whereas "approach" identifies the particular therapeutic perspective (e.g., behavioral, psychodynamic, systemic). In Cookerly's investigations, the therapeutic approach was not considered; only form of treatment was investigated. Following up 773 marriage-counseling clients and 21 therapists, conjoint sessions and conjoint groups were found to be the most effective forms of treatment. For the individual interview "wherein only one spouse receives marriage counseling [this] is generally the modality decried as being least effective" (Cookerly, 1973, p. 610).

Cookerly's results must be interpreted with caution, since the outcome criteria and statistical analyses were far from rigorous.

Gurman and Kniskern's (1978a, 1978b) reviews were based in part on an analysis of deterioration in marital and family therapy. Comparing individual, conjoint, conjoint group, and concurrent treatment, individual treatment for marital problems was found to be the least effective, with only 45% of couples showing positive change. Of a total of 406 patients, 196 (48%) improved, 183 (45%) reported no change, and 27 (7%) deteriorated. Deterioration in the marital relationship was found to be most common in individual and group marital therapy. Combining the couples who received conjoint, conjoint group, and concurrent-collaborative therapy, and comparing these with couples receiving individual marital therapy, the deterioration rates in the combined group were half those resulting from the individual marital therapy. Only 5% of the couples treated individually had a better outcome than those receiving conjoint or conjoint group therapy.

While the reviews leave little doubt about the authors' views on the credibility of individual treatment, it should be noted that some of the individual treatment studies cited included those where one partner had a definite psychiatric diagnosis (e.g., alcoholism). It remains questionable whether one can link relationship difficulties and individual psychopathology when investigating the efficacy of marital therapy when the specific psychopathology is not taken into account. It may be the case that some marital problems complicated by specific pathology may respond better to one particular form of marital therapy.

Goldstein and Francis (1969) and Goldstein (1971) were the first to systematically use behavioral techniques in the treatment of one marital partner. The ideal situation, in which both partners request help and are equally motivated to achieve change, is extremely rare. In their work these researchers employed a behavior modification paradigm that clearly specified the behavioral responses that were to be modified. Objectives of the studies related to marital intervention and behavior analysis and control. Because wives typically initiate the request for treatment (Fox, 1969; Rice, 1978), these studies emphasized the modification of husbands' responses in the natural environment. Wives were trained to record the rate of their husbands' distressing behaviors and then to systematically program new responses to those behaviors, which would then result in a significant change in the behaviors.

Using a small sample of wives and a success criterion of "moving in the right direction," all five couples showed improvement. The targets used in these five cases included the following: decreasing the number of beers consumed, decreasing the occurrence of clothes' being dropped on the floor, eliminating the missing of meals, increasing the number of occasions husband said "I love you," and coming to meals on time. This pilot investigation was extended to a larger study of 10 couples (Goldstein, 1971). Using the same procedures, 8 of the 10 wives successfully altered their husbands' behavior. While these studies were the first to empirically investigate the efficacy of working with one partner, one must question the extent to which one behavioral target change indicates anything more than the potential of this treatment. However, it is clear that spouses can be trained to systematically alter their partners' behavior. If this form of treatment can be replicated with more complex targets and interactional sequences of behavior, then there would be a framework for further study of similar or related intervention procedures.

A Model of Individual Marital Therapy

If one is to engage in individual marital treatment with one partner, then it is important to question the rationale for this choice and how the technique needs to be adapted. It is important to consider the role of the untreated, nonattending spouse and the effect of the intervention on the untreated spouse. The literature on the effect of marital therapy on the untreated spouse is vast (Fox, 1969; Hurwitz, 1967; Kohl, 1962; Sager, Gundlach, Kremar, Lenz, & Royce, 1968), and a full account of it is outside the scope of this discussion. Not only is there an unclear distinction between marital therapy with one partner and individual therapy with the marriage as a treatment focus, but the goals of therapy, especially in the treatment of one marital partner, are poorly defined. An area of study that has been neglected in the marital therapy outcome research is the effect of varying the context of the treatment as the independent variable. Research investigating this independent variable offers a new direction for investigating marital and family therapy.

The form of therapy described here addresses some of these issues and offers some therapeutic guidelines for working with one marital partner. There are four necessary conditions for working with one partner alone:

1. The therapy with the individual will have both a dyadic and an individual focus.

2. The untreated partner is involved in the treatment by being seen as a nonparticipating partner. Although he/she does not attend the sessions, to ignore the nonparticipating partner would be inconsistent with the notion of recognizing his/her role in the marital conflict.

3. The goal of the individual treatment format is for the partners to understand their respective contributions to the problem and what they can do to influence change within the dyad.

4. The various skills (behavioral, cognitive) that are practiced and learned at the individual session are communicated to the nonattending spouse, who in turn learns and practices them.

Individual and Dyadic Focus

Throughout the treatment with one partner, a balance needs to be maintained between the needs of the individual and those of the dyadic relationship. A successful marriage fulfills important needs for each spouse individually and for the couple as a unit. When these needs remain unfulfilled and the positive feelings are weakened, discord sets in. The discord results both from interactional difficulties and from one partner's difficulties. An entirely dyadic focus in marital therapy may ignore the needs of the two individuals comprising the dyad. In this case, frustration and hostility may be exacerbated, and the therapeutic focus may prove to be counterproductive.

One of the major tasks facing the therapist is the successful delineation of the dyadic and individual problems that contribute to marital dysfunction. The treatment of one partner does not preclude discussion of the relationship, and likewise marital therapists should not neglect the needs of the individual partners.

Some of the problems that could be treated in an individual format have been outlined. Although these problems will have a direct bearing on the relationship, one could hypothesize that, for example, the affiliative partner or the fused, enmeshed relationship will not respond to conjoint treatment because the difficulties in separating will be reinforced by joint sessions. Similarly, the inadequate partner faced with a seemingly self-assured spouse may experience his/her own inadequacy all the more within the conjoint session. In these and similar cases the therapy should try to help the partner develop new ways of viewing himself/herself, both as an individual and as a marital partner. In the behavioral and cognitive therapy literature, there are descriptions of appropriate therapeutic interventions (social skills training, assertiveness training, cognitive restructuring, self-control procedures, and the challenging of irrational ideas, etc.) that could be used in the context of a broad-based approach to marital therapy.

The other perspective of the individual approach is the more dyadic focus of the therapy. In practical terms, the dyadic focus demands that the problems be relabeled to focus on the relationship. If the therapist is working toward the resolution of a specific marital problem, this goal needs to be formulated in terms that include both marital partners. For example, if one presenting problem is the wife's depression, the dyadic position adopted by the therapist would necessitate the problem's being understood as both the wife's depression and, for example, the husband's inability to help her overcome this depression.

The presenting partner may spend time during therapy sessions discussing personal difficulties and may neglect or defocus the relationship. Alternatively, he/she may focus entirely on the relationship and attempt to defocus himself/herself. When one partner presents alone, the therapist needs to pay special attention to the focus of the marital difficulty and to direct attention where appropriate, either the individual or the dyad. Thus, although only one partner is seen, both can be the focus of the treatment.

The Nonattending Partner

Successful marital therapy requires that the therapist gain the confidence and cooperation of both partners. At the outset, the nonattending spouse's role must be clearly defined. It is always preferable for both partners to attend the first session (Gurman, 1978) so that the treatment can be explained to both. Moreover, the initial conjoint session provides the therapist with an opportunity to observe the interaction between the spouses. The nonattending spouse is able to meet the therapist, and the therapist can explain that part of the treatment will specifically focus on the relationship. In my experience of treating one partner alone, the nontreated spouse has always kept the initial appointment. This opportunity has been used to discuss the presenting problems, develop therapeutic targets, and explain to both partners how the treatment would proceed. The involvement and inclusion of the nonattending spouse has been obtained in the following way:

1. He/she is given a complete résumé of the session.
2. He/she is included in any joint task or assignment and has a specific role in the accomplishment of specific dyadic tasks.
3. The therapist receives, via the treated partner, feedback regarding the task or anything that the nonattending spouse wishes to share. In turn, the therapist may offer feedback to the nontreated spouse about issues raised by either partner.
4. Both partners practice whatever is learned or discussed in the session if it is relevant to the dyad (e.g., skills).

Jacobson and Margolin (1979) have described a collaborative set whereby both spouses take responsibility for the common problem that can be resolved if both spouses work together. This is emphasized throughout the treatment, but especially at the initial meeting when both spouses are present. Knudson, Gurman, and Kniskern (1979), noting that the wife presents more often as the "identified patient," suggest that a single partner often acts as the couple's "messenger" to the therapist and communicates that the relationship is in distress. Similarly, the nontreated (nonsymptomatic) spouse assumes the role of "caretaker," whose purpose at the initial session may be to present the caring yet judgmental view that the therapy should "help her with her problems and then she'll be o.k." The adopted roles of "messenger" and "caretaker" are functional for the couple, inasmuch as the former indicates the presence of the dysfunction while the latter places the dysfunction in the context of the symptomatic partner.

These two views illustrate an implied task of the therapist and the non-treated spouse, respectively. Jacobson and Margolin (1979) stress the collaborative set as a way of placing some responsibility for change on both partners, whereas Knudson et al. (1979) describe the roles that spouses often adopt in avoiding the shared responsibility.

It is important that therapists avoid accepting this latter presentation. Madanes (1980), using a systems-theoretical approach, has shown how redistributing the power system relieves the symptom and improves the quality of the marriage. In her analysis, the symptomatic partner is seen as weak because he/she has the symptoms, but is also strong because the spouse cannot control the symptom. At the same time, the nonsymptomatic partner is strong, but weak in not being able to change the symptom. In this way two incongruous hierarchies emerge, and the symptoms are used to balance the power relationships. Implicit in the roles of "messenger" and "caretaker" are power relationships that could be one of the foci of the treatment. Both partners need to recognize the identified relationship problem and not just the identified patient problem.

Contribution to Conflict

Marital therapy sessions are often used as a battleground by the two warring partners. The sessions provide the couple with an opportunity to discharge emotions and to blame one another for the problems in their relationship. In the treatment of one partner, the same scenario occurs with equal intensity. Each problem that is discussed needs to be examined in terms of each partner's contribution to the maintenance and possible escalation of that problem. When problems are defined dyadically, the therapist proceeds to help the presenting partner understand his/her contribution to the problem, as well as that of the absent spouse. If during the initial session with both partners their combined contribution can be outlined, this may be hoped to enhance change. Using the terms of Knudson et al. (1979), the "caretaker" will not acknowledge his/her active contribution to the symptomatic partner's problems and may deny that the symptoms imply a dysfunctional relationship. By overemphasizing the relationship dysfunction, the therapist may alienate and antagonize the nontreated spouse.

Knudson et al. (1979) accuse the "task orientated data orientated ahistoric" behavioral approach of presuming that couples acknowledge mutual responsibility for their marital difficulties (p. 545). More correctly, it is one of the aims of the therapist to foster the development of this cognitive set. However, this does not necessarily detract from focusing on the presenting partner's difficulties. Rather than being a presumption on the part of the therapist, the mutual responsibility aspect of the treatment is a therapeutic goal.

If Madanes (1980) is correct in asserting that the symptomatic partner is seen as being weak, then it is likely that he/she will accept most of the blame for the marital conflict. It is nevertheless important to encourage the partner to accept and develop a new understanding of the problem. One could redefine or reframe the problem with a different focus (e.g., including or extricating the spouse) that will alter the couple's interaction in regard to the problem. This new formulation is shared with the nonattending spouse and could be modified once they have discussed it together. The role of the therapist is to ensure that a balance in the responsibility for the problem is maintained so that neither the couple nor one partner is scapegoated.

Marital Skills

Communication training, problem solving, and contingency contracting form the cornerstones of behavioral marital therapy. Distressed marriages are characterized by an inability to solve their problems, an aversive interactional style decreasing the frequency of reinforcing interactions, and the inability to negotiate reciprocal exchanges of positive behavior (Lester, Beckham, & Baucom, 1980). In general, intervention provides the couple or the individual with a chance to acquire the techniques and skills to alter, negotiate, and contain marital distress. However, in the treatment of one partner, the acquisition of skills is not always sufficient. If the aim of therapy is to teach particular skills to just one partner, then the successful acquisition of these skills by the partner may be sufficient, and the focus need not be dyadic. Yet when the focus is on the dyad, the generalization of the skills from the session (between the therapist and partner) to the couple becomes paramount.

Within the individual sessions, the partner must demonstrate that he/she has understood and acquired the necessary competencies to resolve some of the distress and is able to teach them and share them with his/her spouse. Unless both of these conditions are met, any approach (behavioral-structured) will be rendered ineffective. Behavioral interventions develop previously deficient marital skills and must be geared toward generalization within the dyadic relationship.

One way the therapist can ensure some generalization effects is to develop a method whereby the skills can be taught to the nonattending spouse. The presenting partner can teach or outline to the therapist the principles of the intervention and can actively demonstrate his/her ability to use them. Therefore, in the acquisition of particular marital skills by one partner, role playing with the therapist becomes an important element of the treatment. Both the therapist and the partner must demonstrate to each other clear supportive communication (Alexander, 1973). Furthermore, they need to negotiate contracts and attempt to solve distressing problems using the appropriate skills. Within the session the therapist is able to provide feedback to the partner and ensure correct and appropriate use of the skills. At the same time, the therapist, as a model, provides an *in vivo* demonstration of the skills.

Although the present discussion emphasizes skills, one of the critiques of behavioral marital therapy is the apparent deemphasis on cognitive factors (Knudson *et al.,* 1979). Cognitions can influence behavior, and any attempt at behavior change must include some cognitive changes. Segraves (1978) has integrated behavioral and cognitive aspects into a treatment model for couples therapy. In the integrative model, it is noted that cognitive schemas determine how one interprets experiences and events. Chronic discord is seen as the development of schemas about a spouse that are discrepant with that spouse's personality and character. The maintenance of conflict is determined, therefore, by the rigidity of personal misperceptions.

Couples could be given the task of verifying perceptions or beliefs that they hold. Alternatively, they could be asked to explore the mutual distortions or projections that influence their interaction. The therapist can correct or challenge cognitive distortions by pointing out aspects of reality that have been omitted, thereby opening up the possibility for discovering further faulty cognitive patterns. New perceptions of the relationship stimulate growth and maturity in both partners, which, in turn, could generalize beyond the marital dyad (Mannino & Greenspan, 1976). The interruption of cognitive distortions is therapeutic in itself and can be a useful addition to the more orthodox skills approach. Just as skills and tasks are regularly prescribed in behavioral treatments, one could include as a skill an examination of the cognitive factors maintaining marital dissatisfaction and then test them outside of the session.

Within the session the therapist may question the partner's perception and beliefs about himself/herself and his/her spouse. It would be important for the therapist to model how such an inquiry would be carried out. The most obvious type of cognitive investigation is the search for evidence consistent with particular cognitions and attributions. In the absence of such evidence, the validity of the cognitions needs to be questioned. Thoughts and assumptions around particular events can be elicited and tested out against reality. Working within a couple's framework, Rush, Shaw, and Khatami (1980) found that the correction of distorted cognitions improved open communication, decreased hostility, and made explicit private assumptions that each partner had about the spouse. Within the session the therapist can achieve most of this with one partner. Moreover, with the treated partner's therapeutic experience, the nontreated spouse can be encouraged to examine his/her perceptions and also test them out against the reality of the partner and their relationship.

When the dyadic difficulty is defocused, these cognitive interventions can be usefully applied in the individual treatment of one marital partner. The rigidity of particular attitudes and perceptions held by that partner may be perpetuating the marital conflict. Unless these are examined and altered, the distress may escalate and become increasingly resistant to change.

These four elements are axiomatic in the treatment of one spouse. The therapist's input into the marital system is via strict adherence to these aspects within the sessions. The traditional unspecific individual approach to marital therapy may account for its poor therapeutic outcome. What is being presented here is a specific model with clear therapeutic guidelines for working with one spouse alone in the treatment of marital conflict.

Case Illustration and Comment

Vicky and Stan

Vicky and Stan had been married for 14 years at the time they requested therapy. They had three children: a 12-year-old boy, a daughter aged 8 years, and another son aged 5. Stan was a languages graduate and was working in university administration. Vicky left school at 16 and was working in a personnel department.

Stan came from a close, supportive family, all of whom lived in the north of England. His family frequently requested that the couple come up and visit. Vicky came from a deprived family background and was brought up by an aunt after her parents had died before she was 12.

Their marital problems developed following their return to England after having spent 8 years abroad. During the assessment session, Stan said that he felt the problems were essentially his wife's; he did not think that the dilemma he was experiencing (about his parents and his own family) was enough to bring him into therapy. He believed he was functioning well and said that he could not make time to come for weekly sessions. He was convinced more could be achieved if Vicky "sorted herself out."

During the first session with Vicky, the problems that the couple reported had to be reformulated in dyadic terms. This involved formulating the target problems to include both partners with a bilateral focus for change. Although this approach does in part rely on the notion of homeostasis (Jackson, 1957), there is no *a priori* adherence to the idea that a change in one partner will automatically alter the marital problem and bring about a change in the other. More important, the target for change needs to be the relationship and the couple's interaction, rather than just an individual partner.

Presenting problems	*Formulated problems*
1. Vicky complained that they weren't getting on and that things had steadily deteriorated since their return to England. She complained of tension and a "silent marriage."	1. Vicky was feeling very tense in their silent marriage, and Stan needed to help her relax in a way he felt would be effective.

2. Vicky felt ashamed of herself for coming from a different background to that of her husband and felt inferior to him.

2. Vicky believed that she was inferior, and Stan had never questioned this idea with her.

3. There was little communication between the couple, and that which existed was short and sarcastic. Vicky complained that Stan was too quiet, while she saw herself as being active and extroverted.

3. As a couple they had little communication because Stan was quiet, whereas Vicky was more of an extrovert. When they talked, they always argued.

4. Vicky was depressed and often weepy at home. She felt that no one understood her or ever took notice of her.

4. Stan did not know how to comfort and help Vicky when she was feeling low and weepy.

5. Stan was concerned about being forced to choose between his family of origin and his wife and children because Vicky refused to go with him when he visited his parents.

5. They could not negotiate family visits because they were both determined to have their own way.

Having reformulated the important issues, Vicky discussed these targets/problems with Stan. She reported that he realized that there were aspects of the relationship that affected him, and although he would not attend, he would cooperate with the treatment.

Initially the focus was on developing communication skills with Vicky. As she was loud and overpowering in her speech, the therapist attempted to alter the nature of her communication—to slow her down, develop her listening skills, and outline the principles of supportive–defensive communication (Alexander, 1973). The final aspect of the communication training was an impact–intent exercise (Gottman, Notarius, Gonso, & Markman, 1976). Here, after every interchange, the impact of her communication was fed back to her and compared to what she had intended to communicate to the therapist. If there were discrepancies they were clarified, and together Vicky and the therapist examined why the discrepancies had arisen. These often related to voice tone, facial expression, and the phrases she used. She was also encouraged to begin each interchange by acknowledging and paraphrasing Stan's view and feelings, and having made sure she understood him correctly, then constructively express her own.

T: I'm tired, I've had a long day and I don't really want to hear about what's been happening at work. I just want to be left alone to relax and unwind. Can't you understand that?

V: I realize that you've had a long day, but later I would like to share with you something exciting that happened. It can wait for now.

This new way of communicating was achieved after sessions of role playing with Vicky when she practiced both her own reactions and those of Stan. It is not necessary to expand on communication skills training here; what is important is that skills are learned and practiced in the sessions so that they can be relayed back and practiced with the spouse. In the session, the therapist can provide feedback to the partner and practice altering different ways of communication and expression.

One problem that surfaced during the course of treatment was the difficulty Vicky had in initiating a discussion at home about the most recent session. It became necessary to clarify during the session what occurred at home and to practice initiating the "home session." Vicky's initial efforts left something to be desired:

> V: Sit down and listen to what happened today.
> or
> I was told to tell you that . . .
> or
> Do you think I'm inferior because I do not come from the north of England like you?

It is important to relay back to the spouse the context and issues that arose during the session. The partner needs to create a relaxed and intimate atmosphere to share with the spouse what transpired during the session. After practicing the initial part of the conversation with the aim of creating an intimate atmosphere, Vicky tried again:

> V: At some point today I would like to share with you what happened when I went to the hospital.
> or
> Sometimes I wonder if you get a chance to answer me when I talk to you. Do you think I shut you out?
> or
> I wonder what it is that makes me think I'm inferior because I don't come from the north. I can't believe every southerner is inferior to every northerner. Have you ever heard of that before?

Having demonstrated and practiced the various ways of beginning the "home session," Vicky could attempt to share the session with Stan and use the skills in attempting to alter their style of communication. She, in turn, would provide feedback to Stan and the therapist as to how the "home session" proceeded. Various aspects of communication skills were discussed, including the shared expression of feelings, the discrepancy between intent and impact, supportive and defensive communication styles, and listening to and expressing negative feelings and disagreements.

Five sessions focused on developing problem-solving and negotiation skills (Jacobson, 1977, 1978a, 1978b, 1979; Jacobson & Margolin, 1979;

Weiss, Birchler, & Vincent, 1974). One issue that was obviously threatening the marriage was that pertaining to Stan's family. In therapy one can attempt to resolve a particular presenting problem (e.g., problem 5) and together with the couple negotiate the best solution. Alternatively, the couple can choose a less critical or less sensitive problem and use the skills to demonstrate and practice problem solving. Later they can begin to solve their more pressing difficulties, having become efficient in this way of dealing with their problems. If in the session an attempt is made to provide a solution to the problems that are presented, then one runs the risk of the partner's returning home and presenting, rather than negotiating, a solution. Furthermore, to focus on the presenting problem with one partner could create difficulties with the spouse if the dyadic focus is neglected or ignored. The therapist should note that individual sessions with one partner can be seen as a threat to the stability of the marriage. This may emerge as a result of a power coalition between the therapist and the partner, which, at the extreme, may characterize a better marriage than that existing between the partner and his/her spouse. When treating one partner, it is important that the therapist remains aware of his/her potential influence on the marriage.

One way of approaching this delicate power coalition issue is to develop alternatives and then allow the couple to negotiate the best solution. This keeps control with the couple. In the present case, the principles of negotiation were discussed and practiced with Vicky so that she could share them with Stan and apply them to the possible alternatives that had been produced. Together they could search for other alternatives and apply their skills to negotiate the one that would be acceptable to them both. Alternatively, they could negotiate among some of the possible solutions already developed.

With Vicky and Stan, cognitive interventions were used to deal with target problem 2. The issue of Vicky's inferiority was explored by asking her to elaborate on her perceptions of her inferiority. What emerged was a detailed account of her attitude toward some families from the north who had moved into the local neighborhood. Their children were loud and undisciplined, and what was once a quiet area had altered quite considerably. In addition, she was still distressed about having lost her parents when she was young. As a consequence she had felt left out and alone as a child because, unlike the other children, she did not have parents to attend school functions, give her birthday parties, and so on. During these exploratory sessions, Vicky was very sad and weepy, realizing that for the 25 years since her parents' deaths she had never discussed them or the effect of their deaths on her with anyone.

Following these sessions, Vicky realized that her perception of inferiority and her attitude toward her husband resulted from their inability to share some of these intimate and painful feelings. She was encouraged to share them with Stan at their "home session," and at the following session she reported that she was feeling much more positive about herself.

Vicky came to the next session and reported that she and Stan had had a long conversation about how she viewed herself and his family. She felt that during the recent sessions she had gained the confidence to bring out some of these issues. Previously she had kept them to herself for fear of becoming too distressed or aggressive if her husband did not appear receptive to her. The combination of the cognitive and communication-training aspects of the treatment allowed the couple to engage each other in a new and positive way. Just as Vicky was able to be more open with Stan, he in turn was able to express some of his feelings about her. In particular, he shared his feelings about her working and being a successful woman when he had initially wanted to have a wife at home. Finally, Vicky reported that the family had planned a trip to her in-laws during the forthcoming school vacation.

Outcome at Posttreatment and Follow-Up

As this case is one of a series being treated in this way, the outcome can best be represented by clinical description. After the 10 sessions, both partners reported feeling much more at ease with each other. Vicky was planning a trip to see Stan's parents, this being the first joint visit in 6 years. Vicky still felt inferior, but her questioning of her worth was not as extreme as before treatment. Both felt that they were more communicative and open with one another.

At the 6-month follow-up interview, the couple appeared content and were openly affectionate toward each other. They had visited Stan's parents on two occasions since therapy terminated. One month after treatment, Vicky had ceased taking her antidepressive medication. She reported that Stan was very supportive and constructively "monitors my behavior when I go off the deep end."

Summary and Conclusion

The model of individual marital therapy presented here is an attempt to deal with a genuine need in couples therapy. The aim is to offer the couple and the individual the opportunity to explore the issues that contribute to the marital distress. In general, this distress is assumed to result from interaction difficulties. However, as outlined, there may be occasions when it is advantageous to treat one partner alone. The goals of therapy are balanced between the needs of the individual and the couple. In many instances, the conjoint approach overemphasizes the dyad, with the result that each partner's individual needs can be ignored. This may exacerbate marital problems rather than relieve them.

While the "across the board" application of individual marital therapy is not being argued for in this presentation, serious consideration and examination of individual treatment are now warranted. Consideration needs to be given to the situation where one partner refuses to attend the first session (or any sessions) and, by implication, will not cooperate with the treatment. Possibly in these instances it is important to question whether marital therapy would be the treatment of choice. At some point one has to accept that not every distressed marriage will benefit from marital therapy. Whatever the setting, be it the psychiatric hospital, the general practitioner, the marital agency, or private practice, the effect of uninvolved, uncommitted spouses is the same in that intervention will have limited positive outcome. The fact that conjoint marital therapy has only been shown to be effective with mildly distressed couples may indicate that severely distressed couples more often seek an alternative solution to their marital difficulties. As marital therapists, we can only intervene with those who wish it.

REFERENCES

Ackerman, N. *The psychodynamics of family life.* New York: Basic Books, 1958.

Alexander, J. Defensive and supportive communication in normal and deviant families. *Journal of Consulting and Clinical Psychology,* 1973, *40,* 223-231.

Blanck, R. The case for individual treatment. *Social Casework,* 1965, *46,* 70-74.

Cookerly, J. The outcome of the six major forms of marriage counseling: A pilot study. *Journal of Marriage and the Family,* 1973, *35,* 608-611.

Cookerly, J. Evaluating different approaches to marital counseling. In D. Olson (Ed.), *Treating relationships.* Lake Mills, IA: Graphic Press, 1976.

Epstein, N. Assertiveness training in marital therapy. In G. Sholevar (Ed.), *The handbook of marriage and marital therapy.* Lancaster, England: M. T. P. Press, 1981.

Fibush, E. The evaluation of marital interaction in the treatment of one partner. *Social Casework,* 1957, *38,* 303-307.

Fox, R. The effect of psychotherapy on the spouse. *Family Process,* 1969, *7,* 7-16.

Giovacchini, P. Resistance and external object relations. *International Journal of Psychoanalysis,* 1961, *42,* 246-254.

Goldstein, M. Behavior rate change in marriage: Training wives to modify husband's behavior. *Dissertation Abstracts International,* 1971, *32,* 559B.

Goldstein, M., & Francis, B. *Behavior modification of husbands by wives.* Paper presented at the meeting of the National Council on Family Relationships, Washington, D.C., 1969.

Gottman, J., Notarius, C., Gonso, J., & Markman, H. *A couple's guide to communication.* Champaign, IL: Research Press, 1976.

Gurman, A. Contemporary marital therapies: A critique and comparative analysis of psychoanalytic behavioral and systems theory approaches. In T. Paolino & B. McCrady (Eds.), *Marriage and marital therapy: Psychoanalytic, behavioral and systems theory perspectives.* New York: Brunner/Mazel, 1978.

Gurman, A., & Kniskern, D. Deterioration in marital and family therapy: Empirical, clinical and conceptual issues. *Family Process,* 1978, *17,* 3-20. (a)

Gurman, A., & Kniskern, D. Research on marital and family therapy: Progress, perspective and prospect. In S. Garfield & A. Bergin (Eds.), *Handbook of psychotherapy and behavior change.* New York: Wiley, 1978. (b)

Hurwitz, N. Marital problems following psychotherapy with one spouse. *Journal of Consulting Psychology,* 1967, *31,* 38-47.

Jackson, D. The question of family homeostasis. *Psychiatric Quarterly Supplement,* 1957, *31,* 79-90.

Jacobson, N. Training couples to solve their marital problems: A behavioral approach to relationship discord. I. Problem-solving skills. *International Journal of Family Counseling,* 1977, *5,* 22–31.

Jacobson, N. Contingency contracting with couples: Redundancy and caution. *Behavior Therapy,* 1978, *9,* 679. (a)

Jacobson, N. A stimulus control model of change in behavioral couples therapy: Implications for contingency contracting. *Journal of Marriage and Family Counseling,* 1978, *4,* 29–35. (b)

Jacobson, N. Increasing positive behavior in severely distressed marital relationships: The effects of problem solving training. *Behavior Therapy,* 1979, *10,* 311–326.

Jacobson, N., & Margolin, G. *Marital therapy: Strategies based on social learning and behavior exchange principles.* New York: Brunner/Mazel, 1979.

Knudson, R., Gurman, A., & Kniskern, D. Behavioral marriage therapy: A treatment in transition. In C. Franks & G. Wilson (Eds.), *Annual review of behavior therapy* (Vol. 7). New York: Brunner/Mazel, 1979.

Kohl, R. Pathological reactions of marital partners to improvement of patients. *American Journal of Psychiatry,* 1962, *118,* 1036–1041.

Lester, G., Beckham, E., & Baucom, D. Implementation of behavioral marital therapy. *Journal of Marital and Family Therapy,* 1980, *6,* 189–199.

Madanes, C. Marital therapy when a symptom is presented in one spouse. *International Journal of Family Therapy,* 1980, *2,* 120–136.

Mannino, F., & Greenspan, S. Projection and misperception in couples treatment. *Journal of Marriage and Family Counseling,* 1976, *2,* 139–143.

Mittelmann, B. The concurrent analysis of married couples. *Psychoanalytic Quarterly,* 1948, *17,* 182–197.

Nadelson, C. Marital therapy from a psychoanalytic perspective. In T. Paolino & B. McCrady (Eds.), *Marriage and marital therapy: Psychoanalytic, behavioral and systems theory perspectives.* New York: Brunner/Mazel, 1978.

Perelman, J. Problems encountered in group psychotherapy of married couples. *International Journal of Group Psychotherapy,* 1960, *10,* 136–142.

Rice, D. The male spouse in marital and family therapy. *Counseling Psychologist,* 1978, *7,* 64–67.

Rush, A., Shaw, B., & Khatami, M. Cognitive therapy of depression: Utilizing the couple system. *Cognitive Therapy and Research,* 1980, *4,* 103–113.

Sager, C., Gundlach, R., Kremar, M., Lenz, R., & Royce, J. The married in treatment. *Archives of General Psychiatry,* 1968, *19,* 205–217.

Saul, L. Can one partner be successfully counseled without the other? *Marriage and Family Living,* 1953, *15,* 59–64.

Segraves, R. Conjoint marital therapy: A cognitive-behavioral model. *Archives of General Psychiatry,* 1978, *35,* 450–455.

Smith, V., & Hepworth, D. Marriage counseling with one marital partner: Rationale and clinical implications. *Social Casework,* 1967, *48,* 352–359.

Watters, W. Conjoint couple therapy. *Canadian Journal of Psychiatry,* 1982, *27,* 91.

Weiss, R., Birchler, G., & Vincent, J. Contractual models for negotiation training in marital dyads. *Journal of Marriage and the Family,* 1974, *36,* 321–330.

Wile, D. *Couples therapy: A nontraditional approach.* New York: Wiley, 1981.

20

Partners of Psychiatric Outpatients: The Difference between Husbands and Wives on Psychological Well-Being and Its Implications for Marital Therapy

GERDA J. METHORST

Based on the findings of Van Dyck and Van der Ploeg (1976) that wives of psychiatric outpatients report more psychological distress than husbands and score less favorably on measures of emotional stability, a research plan has been developed to verify some hypotheses that can explain these differences. As this research is in progress, the theoretical background underlying the hypotheses is presented in this chapter. Special attention is given to the implications of the sex differences for marital therapy.

Theoretical Background

Sex Differences in Psychiatric Illness

Reviewing the epidemiological literature on the incidence of psychiatric illness among men and women, a general conclusion seems to be that women have a greater chance of becoming psychiatric patients than men (Chesler, 1971; Gove, 1972; Gove & Tudor, 1973; Horwitz, 1977; Ineichen, 1975; Mechanic, 1976; Nathanson, 1975, 1977; Roy, 1978). Several explanations are given, which can be divided broadly into two models, within which specific hypotheses are formulated.

ARTIFACT MODEL

The artifact model states that there are no real sex differences in psychological well-being, but that response biases should be held responsible for the differences found (Allen, Weinman, Lorimor, Claghorn, McBee, & Justice, 1979;

Gerda J. Methorst. Department of Psychiatry, Jelgersma-Kliniek (psychiatric hospital), State University of Leiden, Oegstgeest, The Netherlands.

Dohrenwend & Dohrenwend, 1976, 1977; Phillips & Segal, 1969). The first specific hypothesis within this model is based on the deviation theory and on differences in the socialization process of men and women. This "socialization hypothesis" holds that girls learn to express their feelings more than boys, are more encouraged to do so, and are therefore more capable of recognizing and giving expression to distress. In accordance with this hypothesis, Horwitz (1977) found that women talk earlier and to a greater variety of people about their psychological problems than do men. Women also seemed to be more active in looking for professional help than men; they entered treatment more often on their own initiative and were more likely to label their symptoms as psychological. A second hypothesis within the artifact model is the "power difference hypothesis," put forward by Szasz (1974) and — from a feminist viewpoint — Chesler (1971). Both start from the social reaction theory (Scheff, 1966), which says that more powerful people are more capable of preventing being labeled psychiatrically ill; both assume that men are in a more powerful position than women. According to Szasz, men would lose too much prestige and power by admitting to emotional problems, since such admission would be incompatible with the socially accepted male role expectations. Chesler regards psychological disturbances among women as a reflection of the devaluation of the female role. Because of this devaluation, female ways of expressing emotions would be too quickly labeled as psychological distress by mental health professionals and by significant others, as well as by the women themselves. Support for this hypothesis is derived from the work of Broverman, Vogel, Broverman, Clarkson, and Rosenkrantz (1970), who found that public opinions about the typical man are similar to those about the typical adult, while those about the typical woman are both different and more pejorative from the standpoint of mental health. The third hypothesis within the artifact model is the "role compatibility hypothesis" (Glaser, 1970; Verbrugge, 1976), which states that because of their role obligations, women are more prone to yield to complaints and illnesses. Evidence for this hypothesis is found in the fact that for acute conditions, more days of staying in bed and more restrictions in daily activities are reported by women. In the case of chronic illnesses, however, even though these are more often registered among women, men report more difficulties in living up to their normal duties. Nathanson (1975) notices the contradictory views concerning the compatibility of the sick role and the female role. On the one hand, there is the opinion that the role obligations of women are less demanding than those of men, which in turn gives women more time for being ill. On the other hand, it is said (e.g., Gove, 1972; Parsons & Fox, 1952, as cited in Nathanson, 1975) that women's role obligations are primarily concerned with household chores and family life, which means that the wife's illness is a most disturbing factor in family stability.

NONARTIFACT MODEL

The second explanatory model, we call the "nonartifact model." A specific hypothesis within this model is the "real-difference hypothesis," stating that because of biological and/or psychological "makeup," women are more susceptible to intrapsychic disturbances, while men suffer more from somatic complaints and antisocial behavior (cf. Dohrenwend & Dohrenwend, 1969; Phillips & Segal, 1969; Weitz, 1977). Systematic research attempting to verify this hypothesis is lacking. Gove (1972) advocates the "role-strain hypothesis." This hypothesis explains the higher incidence of psychological complaints in women by appealing to the differences in roles of men and women. The traditional female role of being a spouse, housewife, and mother is characterized by more strain because of lower status, fewer compensating opportunities outside the nuclear family, and fewer possibilities for self-actualization than the male role. Evidence for this hypothesis is given by Gove and Tudor (1973), who found that married women display psychiatric symptoms more often than married men and unmarried women. Unmarried women show even fewer symptoms than their male counterparts. In The Netherlands a similar picture has been found by De Jong-Gierveld (1969) in comparing married and unmarried men and women on life satisfaction and psychological well-being. Later research has indirectly supported this hypothesis. For example, Pratt (1972) and Blumenthal and Dielman (1975) found that psychopathology correlated positively and significantly with marital tension for women but not for men. Research among women who differ in sex role occupation and sex role orientation lends support to the assumption that the traditional female role is negatively associated with psychological health (Nicklaus, 1978; Robison, 1978; Volgy, 1976; Young, 1975, as cited in Amenson & Lewinsohn, 1981). Intervening variables such as number of children, socioeconomic class, responsibility for household chores, and incorporation of the female role influence the strength of this relationship (see also Gove, Hughes, & Galle, 1979; Rivkin, 1972, as cited in Nathanson, 1975).

Analyzing the research on response bias, Clancy and Gove (1974) and Gove and Geerken (1977) rejected the response bias explanation in favor of the role-strain hypothesis. All sex differences showing a greater incidence of mental health problems in women were limited to the married respondents. Data on sex differences in physical health reported by Gove and Hughes (1979) were also in line with the role-strain hypothesis and unsupportive of a response bias hypothesis. After investigating data on the treatment of men and women in The Netherlands between 1977 and 1978, Bauduin (1980) concluded that no inferences regarding a greater vulnerability of women than men to psychopathology are justified. In child guidance clinics male clients were overrepresented. In bureaus for life and family problems, no sex differences were found. In social psychiatric services more married women were treated than married men up to the age of 40, whereas the reverse was found for single clients of this age category. From 40 years on, more single women than men were treated, especially in the age range over 60. Even this finding cannot be explained satisfactorily by vulnerability, since there are more older women than men in the Dutch population at large.

What can we learn from these research findings? In the first place, there is insufficient evidence in support of the real-difference hypothesis. Second, socialization alone cannot account sufficiently for the differences between the sexes. For example, the socialization hypothesis cannot explain the more favorable position of unmarried women as compared to both married women and unmarried men. The role-strain hypothesis provides the most plausible explanation because it begins with the social position that a person occupies. This social position places constraints on both men and women because of the associated expectations concerning their behavior. Thus, it is not one's sex *per se* that accounts for vulnerability to psychopathology, but sociological and sociopsychological factors related to one's role. Sex is, of course, an important determinant of that role.

Psychiatric Symptoms in Married Couples

The role-strain hypothesis states that the role of a married woman accounts for the stress that makes her more vulnerable to psychopathology. This hypothesis leads us to an examination of the incidence of psychiatric symptoms within the marital relationship, the subject of our research.

In a review of research on the incidence of psychiatric illness among married couples, Crago (1972) concludes that when one of the partners shows psychiatric symptoms, the chance that the other partner will also show signs of psychopathology is significant. She cites Penrose (1944, as cited in Crago, 1972) and Gregory (1959, as cited in Crago, 1972), who found that clinical psychiatric treatment of partners of psychiatric patients exceeded chance level. The same situation was found among partners of psychiatric outpatients by Kreitman (1962) and Nielsen (1964). Surveys of the correlations between partners on variables indicative of psychopathology, as operationalized by high scores on neuroticism scales and psychological symptom checklists, point in the same direction (Buck & Ladd, 1965; Hagnell & Kreitman, 1974; Hare & Shaw, 1965; Pond, Ryle, & Hamilton, 1963; Ryle & Hamilton, 1962).

To explain these high interspouse correlations, Slater and Woodside (1951, as cited in Kreitman, 1964) put forward the "assortative mating theory." This theory states that people select partners with characteristics similar to their own. This hypothesis has been confirmed in studies among normal populations with regard to variables such as physical appearance, intellectual abilities, and cultural and social background. Pond *et al.* (1963) and Ovenstone

(1973) failed to find confirming evidence pertaining to similarity in psychological functioning.

In a cross-sectional research design, Kreitman (1962, 1964) compared high- and low-scoring neurotic couples with different marriage durations. In contrast to the assortative mating theory, highly neurotic couples with short marriage duration showed less correlation on neuroticism than high-scoring married spouses of longer duration. Low-scoring couples correlated highly when married for a short time, while low-scoring couples showed less correlation when they were married for a longer duration. Kreitman concludes that assortative mating may exist for sociological characteristics but not for those indicative of psychopathology. He proposes the "interaction hypothesis," stating that exchange of psychopathological behavior results in an increased neuroticism for both partners. Support for this hypothesis, as opposed to the assortative mating theory, was found by Kreitman (1968a, 1968b); Kreitman, Collins, Nelson, and Troop (1970) and Ovenstone (1973).

In an attempt to elaborate the mechanism by which the interaction hypothesis operates, Buck and Ladd (1965) propose the "contagion hypothesis": The patient's deviant behavior infects the partner's emotional stability, who in turn can further infect the former. A negative escalating interaction process has begun.

A Dutch replication by Van Dyck and Van der Ploeg (1976) incorporated couples where either the wife or the husband showed psychiatric symptoms. For the couples in which the man was the identified patient, results were partly in accordance with those of Kreitman: Wives of male patients scored high on neuroticism and psychosomatic complaints. In contrast to what the interaction hypothesis might predict, no differences were found between wives of relatively low-scoring and wives of relatively high-scoring neurotic males. Husbands of female patients, however, scored low on neuroticism and reported fewer psychological but a greater number of somatic symptoms than the wives of male patients. The finding that female partners score high on neuroticism is in accordance with the contagion and interaction theories. However, the similarity in neuroticism between wives of high- and low-scoring patients, and the below-average neuroticism score of the male partners, are contradictory to these views.

An Explanatory Model

Thus, neither the interaction hypothesis nor the contagion hypothesis explains the Dutch results satisfactorily. Consistent with a system-theoretical viewpoint, perhaps there is an interaction between patient and partner psychopathology in the "female-patient couples," but the direction of the interaction is not limited to negative psychological effects on both partners, as is suggested by the interaction hypothesis. The below-average neuroticism score of the male partner can be seen as an antagonistic response to the wife, who is in psychological distress; on the other hand, it could be hypothesized that having such a firm and emotionally stable husband causes the wife to develop psychopathological symptoms. In both cases the husband's behavior is consistent with the socialization hypothesis: Husbands act or react in a rational and independent way with socially accepted male complaints, while their wives act emotionally with socially accepted dependency. The high neuroticism scores of the female partners can be similarly explained. However, as was pointed out before, the socialization hypothesis cannot sufficiently account for sex differences in psychopathology in general, which leaves us in doubt about the plausibility of this hypothesis for the psychological problems of the spouses of psychiatric outpatients.

Thus we still lack a satisfactory explanation for the fact that women in particular report psychological distress when their partners manifest psychiatric problems. As stated before, the role-strain hypothesis is supposed to be a tenable explanation for vulnerability to psychopathology, in this case psychopathology of married women. Concerning the roles that the average married man and woman occupy, there is one important difference that may mean a disadvantage for the woman versus the man when the partner has psychiatric symptoms. This difference is found in the emphasis on family and home events versus experiences outside the home situation in the life of the individual. As the main roles of most married women are those of spouse, housewife, and mother, family life events will take a very central place in their life experiences. These events are more central for wives than for husbands, whose main roles can be defined as spouse, father, and breadwinner. This last role implies that the husband is further away from home in terms of distance as well as time. As a result he is less exposed to family life events but more exposed to the world outside, where he will assume several subroles inherent in the role of breadwinner. Although the wife may also have subroles, this is less often the case with her. This means that compensatory fields outside the nuclear family are less easily accessible to her. Most of her work concerns the house and the family. Because of this, her attention and actual concern with family affairs will be greater, and she will be more dependent upon the well-being of the family. So both positive and negative family events will have a greater impact on her life situation and therefore on her emotional constitution than they will have on her husband. This implies that when negative family life events occur, the wife is in a more stressful and therefore more vulnerable position than the husband.

Psychiatric symptoms that require psychiatric outpatient treatment are examples of these negative family events. So when the patient is the man, his wife will experience more tension than in the reverse situation. Furthermore, the fact that the partner needs psychiatric treatment may cause disappointment in the other, as being married to a psychiatric patient is not considered a desirable state in Western society. This disappointment does not have to be experienced consciously or labeled as such; in fact, such conscious labeling would be rather incongruent with moral standards. It may, however, be reflected in a discrepancy between what one expects the partner to do and how the partner actually behaves. Because of this so-called role discrepancy, the marital relationship can be considered disturbed. Role discrepancy will be experienced by both male and female partners. However, because of the supposed correlation between role discrepancy and marital disturbance, and because of the assumption that the quality of the marital relationship is more important to the psychological well-being of the wife than to the psychological well-being of the husband, it is expected that role discrepancy will be more strongly correlated with emotional instability of the female partners of psychiatric outpatients than with emotional instability of the male partners of psychiatric outpatients. Although these hypotheses still have to be tested, the possible implications for the treatment of married psychiatric outpatients can be considered.

Implications for Marital Therapy

Because of the frequently found concordance of psychological distress between partners when one of them is treated for psychiatric symptoms, it seems necessary to pay attention to the psychological condition of both husband and wife even if only one partner is referred for psychiatric treatment. Particularly when the husband is the identified patient, it seems necessary to investigate possible marital problems, since the psychological well-being of the female partner has been found to correlate positively with a good marital relationship. Very often, however, people will deny that there are marital problems and will state that the only problem is the psychiatric illness of the referred spouse. This calls for an indirect approach, both to discover and to treat marital disturbances. This implies that marital therapy with these couples will be different from marital therapy with couples referred for problems in their relationship. For example, standardized programs such as communication training or training in problem solving are less likely to be used immediately.

Diagnosis

To discover marital problems when only one of the spouses is referred for psychiatric treatment, the diagnostic process must be reconsidered. From the considerations already mentioned, it will be clear that diagnosis of the identified patient alone is insufficient. At the Psychiatric Outpatient Clinic of the Jelgersma-Kliniek (the psychiatric hospital of the State University of Leiden) where the research is carried out, both partners are therefore invited for the first session, during which they are interviewed separately about their life history, their psychological and physical constitution, their work, their hobbies, and their satisfaction with the marriage. Based on the assumption that treatment of one of the spouses will have an impact on his/her behavior and therefore, among other things, on the marital relationship, patients' partners are motivated for conjoint therapy so that they can at least witness and understand the changes taking place in the patients. Thus, very often, interaction patterns have been found that facilitate a patient's symptoms or inhibit his/her recovery. Another way to accomplish the goal of discovering marital problems or pathological interaction patterns is advocated by system-theoretical therapists (e.g., Haley, 1977; Lange & Van der Hart, 1979). They invite both partners directly for a joint first session, during which an inventory of the problems is made. The advantage of this strategy over the first is that from the first moment on it is implicitly clear that problems exceed the psychiatric symptoms of the identified patient. Disadvantageous effects may be that people are not prepared for such an approach, which may result in early dropouts or failure to show up at all. Emphasis therefore lies on the motivation beforehand. This can be done by informing the patient that it is common policy to invite the partner for the diagnostic interview in order to get the necessary information for designing a good treatment program. In case the patient is reluctant or reports difficulties in asking the partner, Lange (1981) proposes the use of role playing to help the clients in motivating their partners and family members to accompany them.

Self-report questionnaires are also helpful ways to get insight into underlying or accompanying problems. At the Psychiatric Outpatient Clinic of the Jelgersma-Kliniek, patients are asked to complete a so-called Admission Questionnaire at home before the first session. This questionnaire covers the same items explored during the first session so that during the interview these items can be elaborated. Questionnaire items concerning the marital relationship have been limited so far to questions about one's own and the partner's activities and about one's own satisfaction with different aspects of the marriage. Because of the hesitation of many people to present a negative image of their relationship, reflected in the generally found artifact of socially desirable response tendencies on questions regarding marital affairs (Edmonds, 1967; Edmonds, Witkers, & Dibatista, 1972; Schumm, Bollman, & Jurich, 1980), it is thought that indirect questions will give better information. Thus by asking the partner what he/she would like to do or would like the spouse to do, compared with what he/she actually does, role discrepancy could be established as an indication of disappointment with the marital relationship. Another way to measure role discrepancy indirectly is by asking the spouses whether they want the marital situation to change, after having asked them how the actual situation is. In order to get a complete picture of the marital relationship, the items will have to cover the roles that a marital partner generally occupies. Marital roles are divided into three areas: the instrumental, the affective, and the interactional role areas. Each role area in turn is divided into marital role behaviors. The instrumental area includes the role behaviors of housekeeping, wage earning, and financial management. Specific marital role behaviors belonging to the affective area are expressions of tenderness and love, expressions of companionship, and expressions of sexual attraction. The interactional area is divided into talking together, decision making, problem solving, child rearing, and social activities. With role discrepancy measured in terms of these behaviors, problem areas in the marriage can be revealed. Further exploration of these problems indicates what changes will have to take place: for example, diminishing misperceptions between the partners about each other's role fulfillment, establishing more satisfactory task allocations, or improving communication patterns. At the moment, research is in progress toward the construction of a self-report questionnaire that measures role discrepancy indirectly in terms of these marital behaviors. Apart from the availability of such a standardized instrument, during the diagnostic interview emphasis could be placed on verbal questions investigating the marital relationship according to role discrepancy related to specific behaviors of the spouses. In that case, marital disturbances would be established through clinical judgment. Based on this information, a treatment strategy could be developed that incorporates marital disturbances into the treatment of the presented symptoms.

Treatment Strategies

After both partners have been successfully motivated for the diagnostic interview, they have to be motivated for further conjoint sessions. This can be done by exploring the impact of the psychiatric illness of the one spouse on the emotional stability of the other and on their family life. Using the information received in the diagnostic interviews, they can be asked, for example, what difference it would make if the symptoms disappeared. Would they do more, fewer, or different things together? Would they have a greater frequency or a smaller number of quarrels? Would role obligations be more equally allocated? A helpful means is to ask them about the coping strategies they have used so far. Probably these have failed, since a psychiatric referral could not be prevented, and they can be asked: So wouldn't it be wise to look for better solutions in which the patient's partner will be of greater help?

These explorations can be made at the end of the diagnostic interview with each spouse separately. Preferably, it should be done in a short joint session directly following the separate interviews, because then it is also possible to identify pathological interaction patterns. Often it is found that the nonreferred partner takes the responsibility of telling what is going on with the patient. Gently stating that the therapist is aware of his/her helping attitude but that it would be more desirable to have the patient tell his/her own story signifies a change in the interaction. Further information about the way they handle the problems at home can result in homework assignments that enable more positive interactions and allow less emphasis on the pathological characteristics of the patient. For example, the husband of an agoraphobic wife could be told to pay no attention to her complaints but to ask what nice things she experienced during the day. Or the wife of an obsessive–compulsive husband could be given the assignment to talk and to do things with him during moments when he is not expressing obsessive thoughts or asking obsessive questions, and to direct him to a special room in moments when he suffers from his symptoms. Especially in these cases it is helpful to have knowledge of coping strategies in the past, which very often will have consisted of too much focusing on the problems, either by means of overprotection, by means of consoling, or by means of forcing the patient to be strong, healthy, or normal. It should be explained that these efforts have probably yielded no effect because they pin the patient down to his/her symptoms and give no room for alternative behavior; they also lead to more and more discouragement on the part of the partner. Through these explanations, they can be motivated to accept the assignments. In case they are hesitant, the assignments can be presented as an experiment worth trying. The fact that the therapist is the one who makes the rules will prevent feelings of guilt in the patient's spouse as well as irritation on the part of the patient.

At the same time, attention has to be given to the presented symptoms, because these constitute the reason for treatment. Various strategies used in individual therapies are available for this purpose. The therapist thereby serves as a model for the partner by not giving direct solutions, but instead concretizing the complaints, asking the patient what he/she thinks can be done, relabeling negative or irrational thoughts, reinforcing positive behavior, and ignoring negative or irrelevant actions.

Summarizing the implications of the concordance of psychological distress between partners when one is a psychiatric patient, and the negative effects this seems to have on the marital relationship, it seems desirable if not necessary to include the partner in therapy. This therapy deviates from marital therapy for couples with manifest marital problems. The marital relationship and interspouse interaction patterns will have to be treated more indirectly, especially during the first phase of the therapy. It has to be approached through the presented symptoms. At the same time the symptoms themselves are to be treated directly, as is done in individual therapy. By attending the sessions, the spouse can learn new modes of reacting to the partner. By changing the interaction pattern that the partners have used to cope with the problems, transfer to other interactional areas can be established. In later phases of the treatment — for example, when the symptoms have been reduced to a more tolerable level — more direct feedback on communication and interaction is possible. This can be accomplished by means of communication training, problem-solving training, or behavioral contracts.

REFERENCES

Allen, R. H., Weinman, M. B., Lorimor, R., Claghorn, J. L., McBee, G., & Justice, B. The effect of response bias on sex differences in a psychiatric population. *Journal of Nervous and Mental Disease,* 1979, *167,* 437–442.

Amenson, C. S., & Lewinsohn, P. M. An investigation into the observed sex differences in prevalence of unipolar depression. *Journal of Abnormal Psychology,* 1981, *90,* 1–13.

Bauduin, J. Vrouwen in tel. *Maandblad Geestelijke Volksgezondheid,* 1980, *6-7,* 464–491.

Blumenthal, M. D., & Dielman, T.E. Depressive symptomatology and role function in a general population. *Archives of General Psychiatry,* 1975, *32,* 985–991.

Broverman, I. K., Vogel, S. R., Broverman, D. M., Clarkson, F. E., & Rosenkrantz, P. S. Sex role stereotypes and clinical judgments of mental health. *Journal of Consulting and Clinical Psychology,* 1970, *34,* 1–7.

Buck, C., & Ladd, K. Psychoneurosis in married partners. *British Journal of Psychiatry,* 1965, *111,* 587–590.

Chesler, P. Women as psychiatric and psychotherapeutic patients. *Journal of Marriage and the Family,* 1971, *33,* 746–759.

Clancy, K., & Gove, W. Sex differences in mental illness: An analysis of response bias in self-reports. *American Journal of Sociology,* 1974, *80,* 205–216.

Crago, M. A. Psychopathology in married couples. *Psychological Bulletin,* 1972, *77,* 114–128.

De Jong-Gierveld, R. *De Ongehuwden: Een Sociologisch Onderzoek naar de Levensomstandigheid en Levensinstelling van Ongehuwde Mannen en Vrouwen.* Alphen a/d Rijn: Samson, 1969.

Dohrenwend, B. P., & Dohrenwend, B. S. *Social status and psychological disorder: A causal inquiry.* New York: Wiley-Interscience, 1969.

Dohrenwend, B. P., & Dohrenwend, B. S. Sex differences and psychiatric disorders. *American Journal of Sociology,* 1976, *81,* 1447–1454.

Dohrenwend, B. P., & Dohrenwend, B. S. Reply to Gove and Tudor's comment on "Sex differences and psychiatric disorders." *American Journal of Sociology,* 1977, *82,* 1336–1345.

Edmonds, V. Marital conventionalization: Definition and measurement. *Journal of Marriage and the Family,* 1967, *29,* 681–688.

Edmonds, V., Witkers, G., & Dibatista, B. Adjustment, conservatism and marital conventionalization. *Journal of Marriage and the Family,* 1972, *34,* 96–103.

Glaser, W. A. *Social settings and medical organization.* New York: Atherton Press, 1970.

Gove, W. R. The relationship between sex roles, marital status and mental illness. *Social Forces,* 1972, *51,* 34–44.

Gove, W. R., & Geerken, M. R. Response bias in surveys on mental health: An empirical investigation. *American Journal of Sociology,* 1977, *82,* 1289–1313.

Gove, W. R., & Hughes, M. Possible causes of the apparent sex differences in physical health: An empirical investigation. *American Sociological Review,* 1979, *44,* 126–146.

Gove, W. R., Hughes, M., & Galle, O. R. Overcrowding the home: An empirical investigation of its possible pathological consequences. *American Sociological Review,* 1979, *44,* 59–80.

Gove, W. R., & Tudor, J. Adult sex roles and mental illness. *American Journal of Sociology,* 1973, *78,* 812–835.

Hagnell, O., & Kreitman, N. Mental illness in married pairs in a total population. *British Journal of Psychiatry,* 1974, *125,* 293–302.

Haley, J. *Problem solving therapy.* San Francisco: Jossey-Bass, 1977.

Hare, E., & Shaw, G. The patient's spouse and concordance on neuroticism. *British Journal of Psychiatry,* 1965, *111,* 102–103.

Horwitz, A. The pathways into psychiatric treatment: Some differences between men and women. *Journal of Health and Social Behavior,* 1977, *18,* 169–178.

Ineichen, B. Neurotic wives in a modern residential suburb: A sociological profile. *Social Science* and Medicine, 1975, 9, 481–487.

Kreitman, N. Mental disorders in married couples. Journal of Mental Science, 1962, 108, 438–446.

Kreitman, N. The patient's spouse. British Journal of Psychiatry, 1964, 110, 159–173.

Kreitman, N. Married couples admitted to mental hospitals: I. Diagnostic similarity and the relation of illness to marriage. British Journal of Psychiatry, 1968, 114, 699–709. (a)

Kreitman, N. Married couples admitted to mental hospitals: II. Family history, age and duration of marriage. British Journal of Psychiatry, 1968, 114, 709–718. (b)

Kreitman, N., Collins, J., Nelson, B., & Troop, J. Neurosis and marital interaction: I. Personality and symptoms. British Journal of Psychiatry, 1970, 117, 33–46.

Lange, A. Het motiveren van cliënten in directieve (gezins-) therapie. Kwartaaltijdschrift voor Directieve Therapie en Hypnose, 1981, 1, 57–74.

Lange, A., & Van der Hart, O. Gedragsverandering in Gezinnen. Groningen: Wolters-Noordhoff, 1979.

Mechanic, D. Sex, illness, illness behavior, and the use of health services. Journal of Human Stress, 1976, 2, 29–40.

Nathanson, C. A. Illness and the feminine role: A theoretical review. Social Science and Medicine, 1975, 9, 55–62.

Nathanson, C. A. Sex, illness and medical care: A review of data, theory and method. Social Science and Medicine, 1977, 11, 13–25.

Nicklaus, C. H. An examination of the relationship between the acceptance of the traditional feminine role by women and the presence of psychological problems in women and their children. Dissertation Abstracts International, 1978, 38, 5097.

Nielsen, J. Mental disorder in married couples. British Journal of Psychiatry, 1964, 110. 683–697.

Ovenstone, I. M. K. The development of the neurosis in the wives of neurotic men: I. Symptomatology. British Journal of Psychiatry, 1973, 122, 35–45.

Phillips, D., & Segal, B. Sexual status and psychiatric symptoms. American Sociological Review, 1969, 34, 58–72.

Pond, D., Ryle, A., & Hamilton, M. Marriage and neurosis in a working class population. British Journal of Psychiatry, 1963, 109, 592–598.

Pratt, L. Conjugal organization and health. Journal of Marriage and the Family, 1972, 34, 85–93.

Robison, E. Strain and the dual role occupation among women. Dissertation Abstracts International, 1978, 38, 4385.

Roy, A. Vulnerability factors and depression in women. British Journal of Psychiatry, 1978, 133, 106–110.

Ryle, A., & Hamilton, M. Neurosis in fifty married couples. Journal of Mental Science, 1962, 108, 265–273.

Scheff, T. Being mentally ill. Chicago: Aldine, 1966.

Schumm, W. R., Bollman, S. R., & Jurich, A. P. Marital communication or marital conventionality?: A brief report on the relationship inventory. Psychological Reports, 1980, 46, 1171–1174.

Szasz, T. The myth of mental illness. New York: Harper & Row, 1974.

Van Dyck, R., & Van der Ploeg, H. M. Psychologisch onderzoek bij echtparen op een psychiatrische polikliniek: Deel I. De besmettingstheorie. Tijdschrift voor Psychiatrie, 1976, 18, 291–312.

Verbrugge, L. M. Females and illness: Recent trends in sex differences in the United States. Journal of Health and Social Behavior, 1976, 17, 387–403.

Volgy, S. S. Sex role orientation and measures of psychological well-being among feminists, housewives, and working women. Dissertation Abstracts International, 1976, 37, 533B.

Weitz, S. Sex roles: biological, psychological, and social foundations. New York: Oxford University Press, 1977.

21

Sexual Dysfunction and Partnership

HERTHA APPELT

Behaviorally oriented sex therapy and marital therapy have remained distinct from each other, despite the fact that a frequent association between sexual dysfunction and marital discord is commonly reported in couples asking for professional help. Kaplan (1974) states that 75% of the patients who presented with a marital problem were found to have a sexual complaint; among those presenting with sexual complaints, some 70% also had nonsexual marital problems. Frank, Anderson, and Kupfer (1976) compared 29 couples seeking marital therapy to 25 couples seeking sex therapy within a clinic where both kinds of therapy were offered in separate specialty units. No significant differences in the incidence of sexual difficulties were found between the two groups, but one-half of the sex therapy couples rated their marriage as "happy," compared with only a quarter of the couples seeking marital therapy. Furthermore, couples seeking sex therapy had a less conservative attitude toward sexuality. Therefore one can assume that other aspects, and not just the symptoms themselves, are relevant for the presentation of marital versus sexual difficulties as the chief complaint and for the decision to approach a marital versus a sex therapist. According to our own experience, we would assume that there are couples with marital and sexual problems who would never ask for sex therapy because of their rather conservative attitude toward sexuality, and other couples who would never ask for marital therapy.

Why, however, do experts perpetuate this distinction between sexual and marital problems, and specialize as either sex or marital therapists? While among sex therapists a growing interest in the relevance of partner conflicts to sexual problems can be observed (e.g., Arentewicz & Schmidt, 1980), there are still books published on marital therapy that do not even mention sexuality in their subject index (e.g., Wile, 1981). We would assume that not only do couples differ with regard to their attitude toward sexuality — and when conservative, prefer marital therapy — but also that therapists differ tremendously in how they conceive marital relationships and the relevance of sexual interaction.

Hertha Appelt. Department of Sex Research, Hamburg University Clinic, Hamburg, Federal Republic of Germany.

Marital therapists seem often to have an unspoken agreement with their patients that sexuality plays only a minor role and can therefore be ignored in the therapy. In this respect the division between sex and marital therapists probably fits in with the patients' own expectations and fears, but these may not be enough to meet their real needs or some of their problems. It seems important that therapists should have a thorough grounding in both sex and marital approaches so that they can respond appropriately and choose the approach best suited to any specific couple.

Although it is perfectly obvious that a couple's nonsexual relationship has a decisive effect on the success or failure of their sexual interaction, surprisingly little work has been done on the interrelationships among partner dynamics, marital discord, and interactional behavior patterns in couples with sexual dysfunction.

It is quite common for a couple with a sexual dysfunction to reveal certain interaction patterns during their very first meeting with the therapist that suggest that the sexual disturbance in some way corresponds with the way they communicate with each other. One common example of this complex interaction pattern is the dominating woman whose partner has erection problems; another is the fatherly man whose spouse suffers from vaginismus. While one should not automatically assume that sexual dysfunctions are matched by equivalent disturbances in the partners' verbal and nonverbal exchanges, the point is that the symptom resembles the interaction, while the felt disturbance is often restricted to the sexual sphere.

After all, notions such as "discord," "dissatisfaction," and the like are purely subjective responses to a given situation; whether the situation itself is regarded as problematic or not depends entirely on the participants' subjective reaction to it. It could well be, for instance, that the dominant behavior of one partner in the sexual sphere is not felt to be disturbing, while in nonsexual situations it may be upsetting, or the other way round.

It is not only the couple who interprets the interpersonal behavior pattern as disturbed or not disturbed; when exploring the functional relevance of sexual or nonsexual partner problems, the therapist gives an interpretation according to his/her theoretical background. The description of the complex phenomenon of the interpersonal relationship of couples with sexual dysfunction therefore has to take the following levels into consideration:

1. The interactional behavior patterns in the sexual and nonsexual spheres

2. Symptom attribution and partner interaction

3. The therapist's interpretation of the interactional process in the couple

Before the pioneering work of Masters and Johnson (1966), which introduced an empirically oriented scientific approach to sexuality, disturbances in sexual functioning were viewed as symptomatic of an underlying conflict, accessible only to traditional psychoanalytic treatment. The increasing interest in the physiology of normal sexual functioning in males and females has had important implications for the understanding of the variety of sexual dysfunctions. Different aspects of the disturbances of "the impotent male" and "the frigid woman" could be specified. This movement away from viewing sexual dysfunction as an etiological factor in the development of psychological distress led to concentration on the symptomatic behavior. This meant often neglecting psychological concomitants such as partner interactional factors. Before formulating our hypotheses on the relevance of the different assessment levels of partner interaction, a short classification of sexual dysfunctions is given.

According to Arentewicz and Schmidt (1980), sexual dysfunctions are those impairments in sexual activity and experience that are attended by absent, diminished, or atypical physiological reactions in the genital area (erection, ejaculation in the male; arousal, orgasm, vaginismus in the female). Normally the partner with the symptom is diagnosed, and this diagnosis is then used to classify the couple's disturbed sexual interactions. Distinctions are usually made according to when exactly in the course of a sexual experience the dysfunction reveals itself, or in other words, at what stage intercourse ceases because of the disturbance (see Table 21.1). A classification of this kind fails, of course, to take into account the situation that triggers all these consequences, including the partners' relationship to each other and any other cognitive considerations — that is, the sexual interaction in the true sense.

Arentewicz and Schmidt stress that this classification represents a very

TABLE 21.1. Sexual Problems in the Different Phases of Sexual Intercourse

	Dysfunction		
Phase	Male	Both genders	Female
Sexual approach		Lack of sexual desire, sexual aversion	
Sexual stimulation	Erectile dysfunction		Arousal difficulties
Insertion of penis			Vaginismus
Coitus		Painful intercourse (dyspareunia)	
Orgasm	Premature ejaculation, ejaculatory incompetence	Orgasm without satisfaction	Orgasmic difficulties
Postorgasmic response		Postorgasmic dysphoria	

Note. Adapted from G. Arentewicz & G. Schmidt (Eds.), *Sexuell gestörte Beziehungen.* Berlin: Springer Verlag, 1980. Used by permission of the editors.

narrow, one-sided approach to the problem, plucking symptoms out of their context and focusing on them in isolation, while ignoring the biographies of the couple involved, their current feelings about each other, and their social environment. However, it is probably necessary to take such a narrow view at the outset to be able to define the physiological and psychological problems with any precision.

Methods to describe sexual interaction patterns (e.g., LoPiccolo & Steger, 1974) are usually restricted to the occurrence and frequency of different behavior patterns between the partners, such as kissing, caressing, sexual intercourse, and so on, but neglect specific aspects of the interpersonal communication that may determine whether a situation is experienced as enjoyable or distressing: What are the expectations in this situation? Who initiates the interaction? In other words, classical S-R behavioral or cognitive patterns often are not analyzed.

It is not really surprising that no standardized methods are available so far that enable us to state with any precision how people interact sexually; after all, it is technically extremely difficult to compose a questionnaire that adequately covers all the details of such an intimate situation. Equally, we have no means of observing the situation "objectively." Nevertheless, we could gain a clearer and more systematic picture of such behavior by detailed exploration; such information would be invaluable in helping us to understand how sexual and nonsexual behavior patterns correlate in couples with sexual dysfunction. This kind of detailed exploration is usually carried out in a nonstandardized way before therapy begins.

While men and women with different dysfunctional behavior may interact differently with their partners, the following examples are meant to back up my contention that there must be marked differences in sexual behavior patterns between those couples where the man has the sexual dysfunction and those where the woman has it.

1. The partner whose symptom appears first in the course of the sexual encounter is very likely to be declared the "patient." In fact, one could say there are some kinds of dysfunction that effectively prevent us from finding out whether the partner suffers from a sexual disturbance too. Close analysis of sexual interaction where the man suffers from premature ejaculation, for instance, can only with great difficulty establish whether the woman has orgasm problems; in a couple where the woman suffers from vaginismus, often nothing can be determined regarding the man's sexual functioning. This fact often becomes relevant during the course of therapy: Once the original "patient" has begun to show an improvement, or when the partner who up until that time never took the initiative begins to do so, the originally "normal" partner begins to become anxious and sometimes even develops a symptom of his/her own. This temporary shift in the balance of power usually manifests itself in the way the couple interacts during the therapy sessions.

2. The men's symptoms — apart from retarded ejaculation — tend to shorten the course of the sexual interaction, whereas women have symptoms that tend to prolong the interaction. Frenken and Vernix (1978) found that in normal couples, 18% of the men complained that their partners took too long to reach orgasm, whereas 16% of the women complained of the opposite in their partners.

3. Sexual intercourse can be "completed" — according to a reproductive model of sexuality — even if the woman suffers from a sexual dysfunction (except in the rare cases of vaginismus); the same does not usually apply to sexual dysfunction in the man.

4. Pain during intercourse is a frequent symptom among women but very rare in men. This means that women can be "punished" by intercourse, while men merely have to forego their "reward."

5. It is rare for a man to be repelled and disgusted by his sexual dysfunction, while this reaction is extremely common among women.

Sexual and Nonsexual Interactional Behavior Patterns

Most studies on partner interaction written from the viewpoint of marital therapists (e.g., Gottman, 1979; Jacobson, Waldron, & Moore, 1980) are concerned with defining in what ways distressed couples differ from nondistressed ones — a subject that is discussed at length in other chapters of this book (see Hahlweg, Schindler, Revenstorf, & Brengelmann, Chapter 1; Hahlweg, Reisner, Kohli, Vollmer, Schindler, & Revenstorf, Chapter 11; Schaap, Chapter 9). Usually the couple is treated as a unit, and less interest is given to the individual, for example, to typical feminine or masculine communication skills.

So far our knowledge on the relationship between sexual and nonsexual interaction patterns in sexually dysfunctional couples is very meager. In a disturbed sexual interaction, we assume attitudes or reactions that are specific to both gender and disturbance, as we have argued above. The following hypotheses seem to us worth examining to clarify the relationship between the sexual and nonsexual spheres: (1) There are systematic interaction patterns that can be found in both the nonsexual and sexual spheres (avoidance behavior, punishment, aversive reaction, etc.); (2) couples with different sexual dysfunctions show different interaction patterns; (3) couples where the woman has the symptom differ in their interaction from those couples in which the man has the symptom; and (4) couples who explicitly mention marital discord differ in their sexual and nonsexual interaction from those couples who do not mention it.

There would be two different approaches to test these hypotheses:

1. Couples with different sexual dysfunctions are observed for differences before treatment in a standardized interactional procedure that has no direct connection to the sexual sphere. Methods used in marital therapy research to distinguish distressed from nondistressed couples can be used in order to look for differences between the diagnostic groups.

2. Independent observers rate a typical sexual interaction pattern recorded in the initial interview and a standardized nonsexual situation using a classification system including factors such as initiation, cooperation, expectations, disappointments, expressions of desires, respect of desires, and so on.

Symptom Attribution and Partner Interaction

Compared with a whole series of studies and methods on how to assess partner relationships, there is very little available on the attribution of symptoms. Madden and Janoff-Bulman (1981), for instance, examined the question whether there is a negative correlation between "blaming one's spouse for marital problems and marital satisfaction." The result was that "the wife perceived her husband as the one who determined how negative marital problems were, while she perceived herself as the major force behind the more positive aspect of resolving and avoiding conflicts" (p. 663).

Harvey, Wells, and Alvarez (1978), discussing attribution in intimate relationships, state:

> [O]ne should differentiate between dispositional, situational and interpersonal attribution. Disloyality for example might comment upon the personal characteristics or trustworthiness of the partner (dispositional attribution). However, at the same time of their partner's "disloyal" behavior subjects might have also viewed their conflicts with respect to the "extramarital affair" or the influence of the "other man/woman" (situational attribution). Similarly they might have interpreted the same disloyal behaviors as signs that "my partner does not care about me any more" or "my partner is going to be unfaithful to me" (interpersonal attribution). (p. 243)

In the few studies so far published on attribution of sexual dysfunction, the authors have limited themselves to questioning individuals. Quadland (1980), for instance, writes that men with secondary erectile dysfunction "tend generally to be more self-conscious, to attribute responsibility for negative outcome situations to themselves . . . than men who are sexually functional" (p. 47). While there are numerous reports in the literature that men tend to attribute their sexual symptoms to organic causes, whereas women much more often attribute their symptom to marital conflict, no one has yet inquired whether their respective partners agree with this attribution.

As far as the attribution of sexual dysfunction is concerned, the following questions seem worth pursuing: (1) To what causes do clients with sexual dysfunctions attribute their symptoms? Is the attribution largely internal (psychic or organic) or external (situational or interpersonal)? (2) Are there any differences between the attributions given by the two sexes, or between groups with different dysfunctions? (3) In what way do the partners with the symptoms differ in their attributions from the partners without the symptoms, and what connection is there among the attributions, the interactional behavior patterns, and the conflicts within the partnership?

These suggestions are intended to help us to arrive at an empirically reliable assessment of the connections between this special aspect of sexual behavior and experience, and the partnership as a whole.

Interpretation of the Interactional Process of a Couple by the Therapist

At first Masters and Johnson (1970) regarded marital discord as sufficient grounds for excluding couples from treatment for sexual dysfunctions, but it soon proved impossible to maintain this attitude. There were too many couples who sought therapeutic assistance for sexual dysfunctions because they felt that their partnerships were severely threatened by this problem, or they listed other marital as well as sexual problems. This naturally led "sex therapists" to reconsider what significance marital discord has in sexual dysfunctions.

Kaplan (1979) has specified which conflicts underlie which sexual disturbances. Looking at the problem from a psychodynamic point of view, she assumes that "the time at which anxiety and the defenses against this anxiety arise within the sexual experience will to some extent determine what kind of symptom the patient will develop" (p. 25). She further suggests that the more severe and intensive the sexual anxiety is, the earlier in the sexual experience it tends to arise. "Thus patients whose anxiety is most severe tend to develop desire-phase problems, while those with the mildest anxieties will tolerate sexual pleasure for a while before they get anxious and typically develop orgasm difficulties" (p. 26). Using this one-dimensional "anxiety" approach, however, it is hard to explain why men and women most commonly develop symptoms at very different times during a sexual encounter. Women suffer significantly more frequently from loss of libido, whereas men suffer above all from erectile dysfunction and premature ejaculation. It would be stretching matters very far to conclude from this that women are more anxious about sexual intercourse than men. The relationships that Kaplan (1979) describes between sexual dysfunctions and psychodynamics could prove an important factor in connection with the mechanisms described by Arentewicz and Schmidt (1980).

Drawing on a comprehensive study of more than 200 couples, Arentewicz and Schmidt (1980) came up with the following hypotheses to explain the connection between sexual dysfunction and the dynamics of partnership:

1. Delegation. The "normal" partner may have his/her own reasons for maintaining the partner's symptom, for it allows him/her to repress his/her own anxieties; as a result he/she is often against therapy, or in the course of therapy may develop a symptom that, as long as his/her partner's symptom was apparent, could not surface.

2. Arrangement. Sexual dysfunction can conceal marital problems at other levels; the sexual disharmony is used as a means of blocking off other fears. Such couples often state that apart from sexual problems the partners are in full accord with each other.

3. Turning against the partner. Sexual dysfunction in one partner enables the couple to join battle with each other, for instance, for dominance and submission. The "normal" partner has one sphere — sexuality — in which he/she can always feel superior. Or the partner with the symptom feels superior by controlling the relationship via his/her symptom.

4. Coping with ambivalence. For some couples the difficult balance between intimacy and keeping one's distance can best be managed via a sexual dysfunction. According to Willi (1975), the ambivalent feelings about intimacy that both share are kept under control in a collusive bond between the partners, in which one takes over the role of the distant partner while the other partner seeks intimacy.

This psychodynamic approach, trying to discover the reasons underlying sexual dysfunction, marks an important step forward from the position of Masters and Johnson (1970), in which they attempted to apply "sex therapy" to the symptoms on their own and neglected the problems of partner dynamics. From a clinical point of view these psychodynamic explanations are certainly very helpful, but they should not distract us from trying to understand and check empirically hypotheses that interlink marital discord with sexual dysfunction.

Aspects of sexual and nonsexual interactional behavior patterns as well as attributional ones should therefore be linked to the psychodynamic explanation of a sexual symptom. Different interactional behavior patterns and symptom attributions can probably be observed, depending on the different functional implication of a symptom.

To sum up, more research has to be done to integrate behavioral, attributional, and psychodynamic aspects to achieve a more comprehensive and satisfactory understanding of the complex interplay of sexual dysfunction and partnership.

REFERENCES

Arentewicz, G., & Schmidt, G. (Eds.). *Sexuell gestörte Beziehungen.* Berlin: Springer Verlag, 1980. (English translation: *The treatment of sexual disorders.* New York: Basic Books, 1983.)
Frank, E., Anderson, C., & Kupfer, D. J. Profiles of couples seeking sex therapy and marital therapy. *American Journal of Psychiatry,* 1976, *133,* 559–562.
Frenken, J., & Vernix, P. *Problemen in tweerelaties: En onderzoek onder 679 manner en vrouwen* (Technical Report No. 1). Amsterdam: Zeist, 1978.

Gottman, J. *Marital interaction*. New York: Academic Press, 1979.

Harvey, J. H., Wells, G. L., & Alvarez, M. D. Attribution in the context of conflict and separation in close relationships. In J. H. Harvey, W. J. Ickes, & R. F. Kidd (Eds.), *New directions in attribution research* (Vol. 2). Hillsdale, NJ: Erlbaum, 1978.

Jacobson, N., Waldron, H., & Moore, D. Toward a behavioral profile of marital distress. *Journal of Consulting and Clinical Psychology,* 1980, *48*, 696-703.

Kaplan, H. S. *The new sex therapy: Active treatment of sexual dysfunctions.* New York: Brunner/Mazel, 1974.

Kaplan, H. S. *The new sex therapy* (Vol. 2, *Disorders of sexual desire*). New York: Brunner/Mazel, 1979.

LoPiccolo, J., & Steger, J. C. The Sexual Interaction Inventory: A new instrument for assessment of sexual dysfunction. *Archives of Sexual Behavior*, 1974, *3*, 585-595.

Madden, M. E., & Janoff-Bulman, R. Blame, control and marital satisfaction: Wives' attributions for conflict in marriage. *Journal of Marriage and the Family*, 1981, *43*, 663-674.

Masters, W. H., & Johnson, V. E. *Human sexual response.* Boston: Little, Brown, 1966.

Masters, W. H., & Johnson, V. E. *Human sexual inadequacy.* Boston: Little, Brown, 1970.

Quadland, M. C. Private self-consciousness, attribution of responsibility and perfectionistic thinking in secondary erectile dysfunction. *Journal of Sex and Marital Therapy*, 1980, *6*, 47-55.

Wile, D. *Couples therapy: A non-traditional approach*. New York: Wiley, 1981.

Willi, J. *Die Zweierbeziehung*. Hamburg: Rowohlt, 1975.

22

A Cognitive-Behavioral Program for the Prevention of Marital and Family Distress: Issues in Program Development and Delivery

HOWARD J. MARKMAN, FRANK J. FLOYD,
SCOTT M. STANLEY, AND KAREN JAMIESON

Harvey and Susan are planning marriage. In a recent conversation they expressed mutual concerns about what the future held for them and what they could do to increase the chances of developing a stable, satisfying marital and family relationship. In other words, given a happy, loving relationship now, what can they do to prevent problems from emerging in the future?

This hypothetical couple is probably reacting to increasing attention, by the professional and lay communities alike, to the high rates of marital and family distress and divorce (e.g., Glick & Norton, 1977). While there has been a dramatic increase in programs to help couples in distress (e.g., Jacobson & Margolin, 1979), little attention has been paid to the needs of couples who, like Harvey and Susan, are interested in prevention programs. Since the focus is on couples who are not currently experiencing problems, we are in the arena of primary (as opposed to secondary or tertiary) prevention. These interventions are usually focused on transition or milestone periods (e.g., entering school, planning marriage) when stress is high and coping skills are needed to deal with the demands of the period.

This chapter is the second in a series of works on the prevention of marital and family distress. The first article presented a conceptual model for understanding prevention with couples and families, and reviewed relevant research (Markman, Floyd, & Dickson-Markman, 1982). The objective here is to describe what answers the cognitive-behavioral perspective can provide

Howard J. Markman, Scott M. Stanley, and Karen Jamieson. Department of Psychology, University of Denver, Denver, Colorado, U.S.A.

Frank J. Floyd. Laboratory of Psychological Studies, VA Medical Center, Brockton, Massachusetts, U.S.A.

to questions about the possibilities of preventing marital and family distress. Specifically, this chapter describes our approach to preventing marital problems using a program we call PREP (Premarital Relationship Enhancement Program). The final article in the series describes a large-scale research project on the prevention of marital distress that uses the PREP program presented and discussed here (Markman, Jamieson, & Floyd, 1983).

Conceptual Underpinnings of PREP

The conceptual underpinnings of PREP are found in three research areas: (1) the theory, research, and clinical practice of traditional behavioral marital therapy (BMT); (2) recent theoretical (e.g., Weiss, 1980), research (e.g., Christensen, 1981; Floyd & Markman, 1983; Jacobson, McDonald, & Follette, 1981) and clinical (e.g., Baucom, 1981) advances in the understanding of the role of cognitive factors in marital relationships; and (3) current conceptualization of social competency and social exchange (e.g., Burgess & Huston, 1979; Curran, 1979; Trower, 1979). We use the term "cognitive-behavioral" to jointly describe these contributions. Cognitive-behavioral approaches to treating marital distress have been shown to be an effective strategy for helping couples (e.g., Jacobson & Margolin, 1979; Weiss, 1980). However, until recently little attention has been paid to the potential preventive usefulness of cognitive-behavioral strategies in helping premarital couples improve their chances of developing and maintaining a successful marital relationship. In contrast to treatment strategies, which can be designed to reduce symptoms and solve problems, prevention strategies need to be based on modifying dimensions that are linked to future outcomes.

Research on the Etiology of Marital Distress

The cognitive-behavioral model predicts that the couple's interaction is important in the maintenance and treatment of marital distress. Research studies comparing distressed and nondistressed couples (e.g., Birchler, Weiss, & Vincent, 1975; Gottman, Markman, & Notarius, 1977) and one longitudinal study of premarital couples (Markman, 1979, 1981, and Chapter 14, this volume) have provided some support for these predictions. These studies provide insights concerning the dimensions of couples' interaction that can be linked to future outcomes and hence targeted for change in prevention programs. However, there are four problems that need to be acknowledged and addressed in future research. First, it is not clear what constructs these studies are measuring, for example, communication skills, patterns of exchange and interdependency, attributions, and reinforcement; or if the studies are not measuring constructs but rather describing interactional differences (Jacobson, Elwood, & Dallas, 1981; Markman, Notarius, Stephen, & Smith, 1981).

Therefore, in this discussion we use the global construct of "dysfunctional interaction patterns" to describe the cause of marital distress suggested by these studies.

Second, Vincent and his colleagues (e.g., Birchler *et al.,* 1975; Vincent, Friedman, Nugent, & Messerly, 1979) have shown that laboratory interactions of couples are subject to situational demand factors. Thus, it is likely that our measures of dysfunctional interaction reflect performance rather than ability. We wonder, however, whether the level of analysis of our studies and interventions should be "performance" in typical interactional situations (e.g., those commonly used in research) or "interactional ability" in any situation.

We should note that the results of a more recent study on demand factors (Cohen & Christensen, 1980) do not replicate Vincent *et al.*'s (1979) findings. Further, pilot work in our laboratory has indicated that there may be sex differences in reactivity to demand effects. Thus, the issue of demand effects is complicated, and more research is clearly needed.

Third, as suggested by Curran (1979), the causes of dysfunctional marital interaction are "multiple and not mutually exclusive" (p. 9). Of particular interest is the role of individual factors in the etiology of dysfunctional interactions. For example, our use of the construct of dysfunctional interaction does not imply that we believe that there must be something "wrong" with the individual partners if the relationship is bad. As noted by Jacobson (1981), this would be similar to a psychoanalytic model assumption that a person's neurosis is the cause of marital problems (Blanck & Blanck, 1968). Consistent with Masters and Johnson (1970), we consider the "relationship" to be the problem, not the individuals. We view the couple's relationship as providing an environment or setting that increases or decreases the probability of individuals' expressing aspects of their personalities and using their skills. Further, the relationship is seen as influencing the physical and mental health of the individuals, and vice versa. Future research needs to explore how individual factors (e.g., level of social skill) are expressed in relationship functioning, and vice versa. Thus, the focus for intervention is the couple as a unit or system. Unfortunately, our research methods have not kept pace with our theoretical advances. As noted by Baucom (see Chapter 5, this volume), we continue to rely on summing individual measures to arrive at a "couples" measure rather than developing and using measures that allow us to "capture" the couple's system as our unit of study.

To summarize, our efforts to understand the etiology of marital distress are at a primitive stage, constrained by problems in construing and measuring social interaction. Increased knowledge about the etiology of marital distress, in general, and dysfunctional marital interaction, in particular, is clearly needed (see Markman, Chapter 14, this volume; Schaap, Chapter 9, this volume). Preventive efforts with couples, however, need not wait until these data are in. As already mentioned, there is a vast array of impressive empirical and clinical suggestions concerning elements of distressed and nondistressed marriages that relate to the couples' interactions, and these provide a preliminary data base for premarital intervention. Further, Weiss (1980; Chapter 18, this volume) has recently synthesized research findings within a theoretical framework that provides a conceptual rationale for early intervention in cognitive-behavioral dimensions of a couple's relationship.

Principles of Premarital Intervention

Our thinking in designing the current version of PREP can only be briefly described here due to space limitations (see Markman & Floyd, 1980, for further details). Our interventions are based on interpretations of the available, empirical, theoretical, and practical knowledge about what makes for a well-functioning, happy marriage. Thus, the components of our program have been designed to counteract known or suspected causes and associates of marital distress that are amenable to change, as well as to enhance the couple's ability to maintain intimacy in their relationship. Another way of stating this is that we are providing couples with information, skills, and strategies associated with marital competency. The general competencies that we stress throughout the program include: learning communication and problem-solving skills, learning how to use self-statements as discriminative cues to guide the use of skills, increasing perceptual accuracy, learning to recognize attributional tendencies or cognitive sets that may lead to false inferences, developing a joint "relationship world image" (i.e., a shared framework) for the relationship, acquiring information about marriage and intimacy, and developing a sense of mastery over future problems.

In general, we attempt to help couples acquire a perceptual and behavioral readiness (Bruner, 1957) to respond to each other in a mutually rewarding way, now and in the future. Implicit in our general model of perceptual and behavioral readiness is that couples need to be as flexible as possible in responding to the stresses and strains inherent in marital and family interactions. These stressors include those internal to the relationship, stemming from the problems of interdependency of the couple (Kelley & Thibaut, 1978), and those external to the couple, stemming from the predictable transition periods (e.g., birth of first child) that most couples and families experience (Markman, Floyd, & Dickson-Markman, 1982). Couples need to have access to resources (e.g., skills, information) to help them cope with these stressors.

In addition to enhancing the competencies described above, there are two nonspecific factors that are important facets of the program. First, the program provides opportunities for exposure to and discussion about issues that most lay people and experts consider important for couples planning marriage to address (e.g., expectations, future plans). Second, the program provides couples with positive experiences "working" on their relationships and thus sets the stage for working on issues when they arise in the future.

Several principles are imbedded throughout our program. These principles reflect our thinking about how to motivate healthy, well-functioning couples, the potential consumers of our program, to acquire the specified competencies. These principles, which are described in detail later, include: maximizing the hedonic relevancy of the sessions, providing a "preventive cognitive set," emphasizing the fit between the problems that we are trying to prevent and the competencies we are teaching, maximizing the current as well as the future usefulness of the competencies we are teaching, and enhancing the couples' sense of mastery or efficacy (Bandura, 1977) over future marital problems.

Each session is structured according to the following outline:

1. Describe the content area (component)

2. Present a rationale for including the component in a prevention/enhancement program (i.e., define the problem to be prevented or skill to be enhanced)

3. Present research/clinical evidence to support the rationale

4. Teach the skill or strategy and provide information (provide competencies to deal with the problem and a sense of mastery over the problem)

5. In-session exercise with consultants to practice ("experiment with") the new skills, information, or orientation

6. Homework to provide more practice and enhance generalization of the newly acquired skill or strategy

The informed reader will note the surface similarity between the program described here and traditional cognitive-behavioral marital therapy programs (you know how far we have come during the past decade when we can use the term "traditional" in this context without raising eyebrows). However, while some of the skills and strategies are similar, teaching them in a preventive framework to nondistressed, healthy couples requires the development of different skills/strategies to help these couples anticipate and cope with potential problems.

The problem we faced in developing PREP was similar to that faced by public health researchers and practitioners who try to educate healthy people to change habits or develop new habits to prevent health problems from developing (e.g., stop smoking to prevent cancer). Public health research has indicated that scare tactics (e.g., showing pictures of diseased lungs) by themselves are not effective preventive strategies (Evans, Henderson, Hill, & Raines, 1979). This result should not be surprising for those acquainted with behavior modification research. Numerous studies have showed that decreasing the probability of a response without providing alternative responses is not an effective intervention strategy for achieving long-lasting results. Knowing what to do to replace potentially harmful responses not only provides alternatives, but also provides a sense of mastery (efficacy) over the negative outcome (Evans *et al.,* 1979). Applied to the area of marital distress, just scaring couples by presenting divorce statistics and/or risk tables is not likely to be an effective preventive strategy. Therefore, the implicit goals of the program are to provide couples with a shared orientation toward their relationship, including: (1) knowing some common pitfalls, (2) how to avoid these areas, and (3) how to get out of them if they do occur. A critical aspect of this orientation involves helping a couple to take an active stand toward constructing the kind of relationship they want to develop and to feel empowered to achieve this goal. Further, if and when barriers develop or are encountered, the couple's "inoculation" against the barriers provides the attitude that these barriers can be overcome.

The PREP Program

The original version of the PREP program was presented in an earlier article (Markman & Floyd, 1980); it has been constantly changing, based on our data, clinical experiences, and feedback from couples. The program currently involves five group or individual meetings, each of which lasts approximately 2 to 2.5 hours. A trained consultant works with each couple throughout the program. Consultants have been graduate students, advanced undergraduates, and paraprofessionals drawn from community groups (e.g., churches). They receive approximately 20 hours of training and receive ongoing supervision. A training manual has recently been developed and is available from the authors.

Each session is devoted to one or two major content areas of the program: Session 1—communication skills training I; Session 2—communication skills training II; Session 3—behavior change; Session 4—examining expectations; Session 5—relationship and sexual/sensual enhancement. The five sessions are described in detail below.

Session 1—Communication Skills Training I: Talking to Each Other

GOALS AND EXPECTATIONS FOR THE PROGRAM

At the beginning of Session 1 the goals of the program are summarized for the couples. The program is presented as an educational/experimental program designed to enhance their relationships. Couples are told that the overall goals are to teach them communication and problem-solving skills, to provide information about relationships, and to facilitate the examination of expectations. We highlight that the content is based on relationship enhancement and marital therapy programs, as well as on the results of research with many types of couples. We tell couples that although we do not have a prescription for successful relationships, we believe that a meaningful, growing, rewarding relationship does not just happen: It is the product of a process of togetherness, sharing, respect, and work done by both people. We clearly distinguish prevention/enhancement programs like ours from therapy programs. We emphasize that entry into our program is based on having a happy, satisfying relationship and that the program is designed to keep it that way. The intent here is to ensure that couples do not make attributions concerning problems in their relationship based on being involved and/or deciding to participate in the program.

We then share a few basic assumptions that we have made about marriage and intimacy to clarify our values for the couples:

1. All couples encounter problems — some specific to various stages of the family life cycle.

2. One major difference between happy and unhappy married couples is how they deal with the problems they face. Unhappy couples seem to have less skill in problem solving and communication, and therefore problems that are encountered become sources of conflict and negative interactions, rather than opportunities for growth.

3. Our focus is on the couple's partnership, not on individual partners. When issues arise, we view both partners as involved in both the problem and the solution.

4. Learning communication skills, like learning other skills (e.g., driving a stick-shift car), may at first seem unnatural, but with practice the new behaviors and strategies will become more and more part of everyday patterns.

5. Adapt an "experimenting set" (i.e., try it, you may like it) toward the program, and then afterward decide what makes sense for you.

Consultants then meet with their couples to discuss how it feels to be in the program and to help each couple identify specific goals for the program. Our intent here is to enhance alliance building with the couple and match our expectations with theirs.

COMMUNICATION SKILLS

The first three sessions are designed to provide a framework for communication and problem solving that involves separating the process of problem discussion from problem solution. In Session 1, we start by teaching couples a model of good communication. First, speaker and listener roles are defined, and then good communication is defined as occurring when a message is exchanged and the speaker's intent equals the listener's impact (Gottman, Notarius, Gonso, & Markman, 1976). Barriers to good communication include "filters" that interfere with the delivery and reception of messages and the complexities of matching verbal and nonverbal elements of communication.

We find that this simple model is very valuable to couples because it provides a useful operational definition of the often used and rarely defined construct of "communication." Using this model as a guide, couples are taught the skills associated with what we term "expressive speaking" and "active listening."

The following speaker skills are presented: speaking for self (using "I" statements) and expressing feelings; staying focused on one issue at a time (staying on "beam"); maintaining eye contact; using body positions that communicate respect and interest; announcing filters (e.g., "I had a bad day at work and that's why I may seem mad"); asking for feedback (e.g., "Please tell me what you heard me saying"); and checking out (e.g., "This is what I heard you saying, am I right?") instead of mind reading (e.g., "You always hated my mother"). The following listener skills are presented: attending to partner using eye contact, head nods, and so on; summarizing the partner; reflecting feelings; asking questions; checking out; and "stopping the action" when discussions are going badly or negative interaction cycles are developing.

Next we teach couples the difference between the process of problem discussion and that of problem solution. We tell couples that there is a tendency in problem solving interactions to skip the important first stage of problem discussion and go for what we call the "problem solution jugular." Thus, the important first steps of getting the issues and feelings on the table, via expressive speaking and active listening skills, are missed. We stress that the goal of problem discussion is to understand each other's position and validate each other, not to change feelings and opinions. We tell partners that they can disagree with each other and still communicate respect for each other's feelings and opinions. We highlight that many psychologists and family therapists feel that self-esteem is linked to validation received from others (e.g., Satir, 1967).

The preventive intent here is to have couples use the speaker and listener skills to avoid or short-circuit negative interaction cycles. The reason for this focus is that research has indicated that negative (not positive) interactions are the most powerful discriminators of distressed and nondistressed couples (Gottman, 1979). These findings are presented to the couples, and the use of skills such as "stop action" and "checking out intent = impact" is highlighted as a strategy to combat negative interactions.

ENGAGING THE SKILLS

We distinguish between "fun" discussions and discussions preceding problem solving. This distinction is important when considering the beneficial effects of skill utilization: Although skills are useful in nonconflict discussions, it is very important to "engage the skills" in conflict situations. We point out that many individuals seem to possess good communication skills but do not seem to use them with their partners during problem-oriented discussions (Birchler et al., 1975). These are usually situations when motivation to communicate well is lowest and anger is highest. Unfortunately, for many couples, it is also the time when good communication and problem-solving skills are most important. Thus, the "meta-skill" of being able to engage already existing communication skills and strategies is of prime importance in preventing problems from escalating and for productive problem discussion, problem solution, and behavior change. We suggest that the onset of a negative interaction cycle can be used as a discriminative cue for couples to "engage the skills" (i.e., call a "stop action") and then to use skills to promote a more productive resolution of the current problem. Other strategies for engaging the skills that are presented include verbally stating that an important topic needs to be discussed and convening a "family meeting" to promote use of positive skills. We note that using clearly defined times and settings for problem discussions can also provide discriminative cues for engaging the skills.

The intent here is to alert couples to the dangers of negative interactions and, more importantly, to provide them with the ability to recognize and deal with negative interaction cycles when they occur. Thus we hope to instill a sense of mastery over future problems, by having couples anticipate the type of problems that may occur and by letting them know that these problems can be solved. It seems likely that many distressed couples feel a sense of helplessness about relationship problems due to a lack of successful experience. As one distressed married partner recently said "Once things started going downhill, there was no hope for changing things. That's the way it is with all marriages."

During the session, couples practice using the new skills. First, they pick a minor issue and are instructed to be "bad" communicators, doing their best to do it all wrong. This makes an excellent icebreaker. Couples then watch videotapes of their interactions, recorded in an earlier session as part of a larger program of research (see Markman, Jamieson, & Floyd, 1983, for details). This exercise is used both to increase the couples' awareness about their use of skills and to offer springboards to further interaction between partners in the current session. Consultants provide ample positive social reinforcement when reviewing the tapes with the couples.

Homework for the first session involves setting up a time and choosing an issue that will be discussed and recorded on a cassette tape. Couples are encouraged to use the skills as much as possible. Additionally, couples are asked to read Chapters 1 and 2 in *The Couple's Guide to Communication* (Gottman *et al.*, 1976) and to complete the exercises in each chapter.

Session 2—Communication Skills Training II:
Videotape Feedback and Practice Problem Discussions

SELF-DISCLOSURE, EDITING, AND LEVELING

The more complex speaker and listener skills are introduced in this session. First, we present self-disclosure skills in the form of X-Y-Z statements (e.g., "When you do X, in situation Y, I feel Z"). Using X-Y-Z statements helps individuals get away from global trait descriptions of their partners, which they all have a tendency to use (Braiker & Kelley, 1979). As an alternative, individuals are taught to describe what their partners do that pleases and displeases them. Weiss (1981), cautions about having happy couples pinpoint too much, since it may decrease positive "sentiment override" and/or make the relationship too mechanical. However, we have not found this to be a problem.

The complex skills of leveling and editing are then presented. "Leveling" involves using the speaker skills to talk about issues and feelings that are hard to discuss. Individuals are advised to let their partners know in advance when they want to level. The rationale is to provide a joint cognitive set that this will be a meaningful, and possibly painful and difficult, conversation. Requesting or setting a time for the discussion allows the partner to prepare for the conversation or request that the conversation wait until a better time. We have found that leveling is particularly important to couples for whom a lack of intimacy may be a current or future problem.

"Editing" is the opposite of leveling and involves conscious control over statements to one's partner. Editing involves the skills of predictive empathy (i.e., knowing how the partner might react to certain statements) and affective empathy (i.e., being sensitive to the partner's emotional reactions). Operationally, editing is not saying things that would unnecessarily hurt one's partner. Couples are told that the rationale for knowing how to edit is that sometimes things are best left unsaid (or at least until another time and place). We stress that editing is particularly important when couples are under a lot of strain and may not be motivated to "engage their skills." It is a way of dealing with problems of anger expression that may lead to spouse or child abuse. Finally, we discuss research that suggests that couples tend to be nicer to strangers than to their partners. In this context we present a list of common "polite" behaviors that tend to diminish over time in marriage relationships (see Gottman et al., 1976, p. 47).

During the session, couples again watch videotapes of a previous interaction. Partners practice giving each other feedback under supervision of the consultant, using both the language system taught in the program and a skills behavior checklist. The contents of this checklist are presented in Table 22.1. Consultants continue to provide positive specific feedback as much as possible. When negative behaviors are observed or communication skills are omitted, consultants work with the couple to discuss and then practice alternative responses. Consultants and couples use a "stop action" button on the tape player to break into the ongoing interaction stream to provide immediate feedback and to practice the skill of "stop action" and to provide immediate feedback to each other. Finally, the difficulty in separating problem discussion from problem solution is emphasized, since most couples omit the problem discussion stage in their videotaped interaction. Couples then discuss an issue and receive immediate ongoing feedback from their consultant.

TABLE 22.1. Skills Checklist Items Used in Videotape Feedback

Speaker/expressor skills	Listener skills
Nonverbal	
Attending to listener (eye contact)	Attending to speaker (eye contact)
Positive affect (e.g., voice tone)	Head nods (facilitators)
Body position	Positive affect (e.g., voice tone)
	Body position
Verbal	
Staying on task (on beam)	Congruency (verbal and nonverbal consistency)
Speaking for self (use of "I")	Active following (assents—uh-huh, hmmm, etc.)
Congruency (verbal and nonverbal consistency)	Asking questions (probing, exploring)
Checking out (avoiding mind reading)	Checking out (asking for clarification)
Brief messages	Paraphrasing (summarizing)
Expression of feelings	Ensuring understanding (paraphrasing and checking out)
Expression of when behavior occurs	Reflecting feelings
Brief self-summaries at end of message	"Stop action" (meta-communication)
"Stop action" (meta-communication)	

INTRODUCTION TO PROBLEM SOLVING: MONITORING BEHAVIORS

The last part of the session focuses on the beginning of problem solution: recognizing pleasing and displeasing behaviors. In order for couples to solve their problems, they must first be capable of identifying and discussing behaviors that occur in their relationships (Jacobson, 1977). We first define constructive behavior change in relationships as involving an increase in positive behavior and a decrease in negative behavior. We discuss research findings that negative change attempts (e.g., coercion) are associated with distress (e.g., Sullivan & Markman, 1982). For example, nagging gets reinforced and starts negative interaction cycles. This is due to a tendency toward a *quid pro quo* or negative reciprocity in relationships (Gottman *et al.*, 1977). We stress to all couples that they have control over the process, through prevention or early intervention. Couples are provided with an orientation that one way of looking at relationships is as an exchange of behaviors that have a pleasing or displeasing impact on one another. We introduce the skill of monitoring behavior, the goal of which is to increase ability to identify and monitor problem behaviors so that they can be changed. During the session individuals fill out forms that help them identify self-behaviors and partner behaviors that can be increased or decreased in order to make their relationship better. Individuals are asked to pick one self- and one partner behavior that they will monitor during the next week, without telling their partners. In addition, they are also to pick an individual behavior that they will change. Monitoring behavior and behavior change is an essential component of the homework for this session. The rationale here is to help couples develop the following expectations:

1. Behaviors can be changed.
2. Behaviors are not the same as traits/dispositions (e.g., my partner can still love me and act in a way that is displeasing).
3. Relationships are always in flux, and couples can take control over changes using the skills discussed in the program.
4. Change can and needs to be negotiated, and compromise is an important ingredient of successful negotiations.

In addition to monitoring and changing behaviors, "homework" for this session includes reading Chapters 3 and 4 in the *Couple's Guide* (Gottman *et al.*, 1976). Couples may also be asked to set up another family meeting to discuss an issue. This discussion is tape-recorded. Following the discussion, partners may be asked to review the tape and provide each other with positive and constructive feedback.

Session 3—Problem-Solving Training

The goals of this session are to teach couples to negotiate agreements concerning how to solve relationship problems and to summarize the skills taught thus far in the program.

LEARNING HOW TO REQUEST CHANGE

Initially, couples are introduced to the topic of negotiating relationship change. We start by telling couples that change is natural and reflects growth and reactions to new demands both on the individuals (e.g., job stress) and on the relationship (e.g., birth of first child). We note that during the premarital period in particular, and transition stages in general, couples are unusually amenable to negotiating changes through discussion and compromise. We highlight that patterns set during the premarital period (like the "wonder years" of childhood) influence the relationship for many years to come. We then present our "bank account model" of relationship development: Couples start their relationship with a large "account" but need to balance "withdrawals" (negative exchanges) with "deposits" (positive exchanges). We tell couples that if they maintain a large account, negative events (which inevitably occur) can be easily tolerated and even used for growth.

We define the goal of change, in this context, as increasing the frequency of positive exchanges and decreasing the frequency of negative exchanges. Couples are told that negative exchanges frequently start with a negative, nebulous complaint (e.g., "you're lazy"). We inform couples that these statements, with their implicit negative attribution about causality, are common statements from couples in conflict (Braiker & Kelley, 1979). Part of our intent here is to inoculate individuals against the tendency to make global, stable, negative attributions about intent to their partners. The danger is that once developed, these attributions are hard to change (Baucom, 1981). We suggest to couples that one way to avoid the tendency to be negative and vague is to recognize such statements when they occur and to counter them with positive and specific statements. To achieve this goal, couples are taught how to take negative, nebulous complaints that have no implication for relationship change (e.g., "you're a slob") and form them into positive, specific statements that have clear implications for relationship change. They accomplish this by using X-Y-Z statements to label when an event occurs, what happens, and how it makes them feel (e.g., "When I come home from work and see your coat on the floor, I feel that you are not doing your share around the house and I feel abused"). In the session, partners take turns transforming nebulous statements into well-formed X-Y-Z statements that provide specific positive requests for change. Couples also complete the "What is irritating?" exercise, which involves each partner's discussing an irritating thing about the other and turning this into a specific, changeable request for behavior change.

We then introduce the final step of the problem-solving process: negotiating agreements (contracting). Couples are told that contracting is simply the last step of the problem discussion–solution cycle. They have already discussed an issue, specified the situational determinants, avoided blaming each other, and transformed global complaints into specific solutions. The last step is mutually agreeing to make the changes already discussed. Couples have initially reacted negatively to contracting terminology, saying that the approach seems too cold and not very humanistic. We encourage couples to distinguish between the terminology and personal application: If they are able to increase positivity in their relationship, what could be more humanistic? Another way to discuss contracting with couples is to avoid the language of social exchange theory and talk about helping the partners "push each other's buttons" in a way that enhances satisfaction and intimacy (Markman, Floyd, & Dickson-Markman, 1982).

Regardless of the language, we teach couples how to develop "good-faith" contracts of the form "We will both change, I will do X and you will do Y, you'll support me doing X, and I'll support you doing Y" (or, in other words, "We'll both push each other's buttons"). We teach couples to use good-faith (vs. *quid pro quo* — Jacobson, 1977) contracts in order to instill the set that a willingness to compromise and accommodate to each other will result in maximizing joint outcomes. We contrast this with a win–lose set in which one person wins at the expense of the other. In addition, we provide the set that the chronic issue of "who goes first" in the change process is not important because the responsibility for change is a couple issue, calling for the use of skills. Couples are told that feeling as if a power issue is at hand (e.g., thinking "I won't give in this time") should be used as a cue that something is wrong. In such instances, editing or "stop action" is called for in order to prevent further negative interactions and to signal the couples to engage their communication skills. We also stress that couples should engage their problem-solving skills when they think and/or make statements such as "I hate it when you do_____" and/or "I wish you would change." These overt or covert statements are presented as discriminative cues that should stimulate engaging the skills. Additionally, it is suggested that couples use mastery-inducing self-statements such as "We can solve this problem" and "We did it; good work!"

MARRIAGE CONTRACT GAME

We use a modified version of Rabin, Blechman, and Milton's (1981) Marriage Contract Game to teach couples how to negotiate contracts. Blechman and Rabin (1981) have found that the game helps nondistressed couples increase positive problem-solving skills and report that couples find it enjoyable. The hedonic relevancy of this task makes it well suited for our purposes, since some of our couples have been put off by contracting exercises based on traditional BMT procedures. More important than just contract negotiation, the current version of the game calls for couples to use all the skills developed to this point. Thus, couples go through the stages of raising, discussing, and then solving an issue.

We have made two major changes in the game. First, we have modified the language to make it compatible with the terminology used in our program. Second, we have built in time for problem discussion and listening prior to contract negotiation. One purpose of the game, as developed by Rabin *et al.* (1981), was to facilitate the quick negotiation of contracts. For our purposes, we wanted to highlight and reinforce the two-step process of problem discussion and problem solution, rather than teach couples to reach a quick solution without discussion. We have maintained the contingency in the game to reward quick contracts, but only after some discussion. An outline of the first part of the modified game is presented in Figure 22.1.

A couple plays the game twice so that each partner has the opportunity to select an issue, discuss it, and negotiate an agreement. Afterwards, couples discuss how they feel about the contracts, and the consultants emphasize again the preventive aspects of the exercise.

INTRODUCTION TO EXPECTATIONS

In the last part of the session, couples are presented with a brief introduction to the existence and effects of the multileveled expectations that partners have regarding each other and marriage. The couples are given copies of the Marriage Expectation Workbook (MEW), which provides a framework

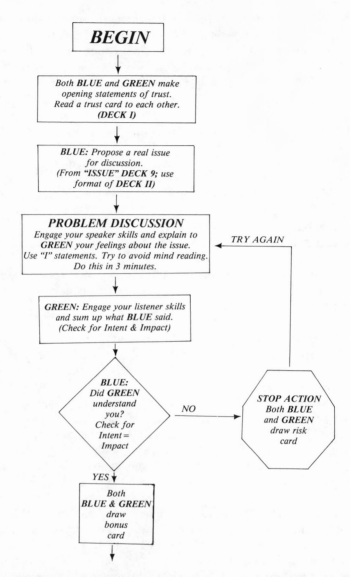

FIGURE 22.1. Outline of the first part of the revised Marriage Contract Game. (Adapted from E. Blechman & C. Rabin, *Concepts and methods of explicit marital negotiation training with the Marriage Contract Game.* Unpublished manuscript, Wesleyan University, 1981.)

for their examination of expectations. Couples are asked to complete the MEW for homework, so that the material can be used in the next session. In addition, the homework for this session includes fulfilling the terms of the contracts negotiated during the Marriage Contract Game. When reviewing the homework in the next session, consultants assess and resolve possible *quid pro quo* problems (i.e., "I didn't do mine because my partner did not do his/hers").

Session 4—Putting It All Together and Examining Expectations

PUTTING IT ALL TOGETHER

In the first part of the session, couples are presented with a summary of the skill and strategy components of the program and given the opportunity to "put all the skills and strategies together." This is accomplished by each couple's taking an issue, discussing it, and reaching a solution. During this exercise, consultants monitor the use of skills as before, but now emphasize the fit between the use of skills and the couple's own interactional style. The intent here (as with homework assignments) is to enhance generalization effects from the program to current and future everyday use.

EXAMINING EXPECTATIONS

The rest of this session is devoted to the area of marital expectations. The rationale for examining expectations is that developing and sharing realistic expectations of each other and marriage has been linked to developing and maintaining successful marriages (Baucom, 1981; Edelson & Epstein, 1981; Sager, 1976). Sager's (1976) theory of unexpressed marital contracts and marital distress provides the conceptual framework underlying our approach to increasing realistic and shared marital expectations. His theory on the role of expectations in marriage predicts that:

> One's expectations may comprise a personal, unstated contract for one's marriage. Sometimes each person acts as if the other knew the terms of the contract and feels angered, hurt, betrayed, etc., when he/she feels that the partner did not fulfill his/her part of the contract. Expectations are not only what you want from your partner, they are also what you are willing to give. Many marital problems arise between spouses who have very different, unstated contracts for marriage. (Sager, 1976, p. 26)

Sager (1976) further asserts that we all have expectations that fall into three types. First are verbalized expectations, which are relatively easy to think of and talk about. Examples include "I expect that we will share a lot of activities together" and "I expect that we will have two children" (Sager, 1976). The second type of expectations includes those of which one is aware but that one does not verbalize because of concern for hurting feelings, fear of starting a fight, or embarrassment (Sager, 1976). Examples may include "I expect my career will be more important than your career" and "I expect that we will have children as soon as we are married." The third type of expectations includes those of which one is unaware or that are very hard to think about and talk about. Clues to the existence and content of these expectations are often found by examining "hidden agendas" (Gottman et al., 1976) that emerge during interactions. These are issues that frequently arise and do not get resolved. While the content varies, hidden agendas frequently revolve around themes of control (power), postivity (love/affection), and status (roles). Self-statements such as "here we go again" may be associated with the existence of hidden agenda issues. Feelings of anger, frustration, and helplessness also provide cues to hidden agenda issues and the existence of hidden expectations concerning one's self and partner.

Our objective in this session is to increase both awareness and communication about hopes and expectations that most couples have about each other and marriage. As the couples progress in their relationships, they can then use their skills to negotiate solutions to divergent expectations that, if not resolved, could lead to dissatisfaction and distress. As noted by Sager (1976), partners often differ in their awareness of expectations and in how easy it is to discuss these expectations. Further, he states that divergent expectations, in their own right, are not necessarily bad; in fact, they are to be expected. Another way of looking at what Sager's framework assesses is in terms of Kelly's (1955) personal construct theory. The exercise helps the couples clarify the constructs they use to guide their thinking about, and their interaction in, their relationships.

During the session couples work with consultants using the MEW, which has been completed for homework. The MEW has two parts: expectations of marriage (e.g., insurance against loneliness) and expectations concerning one's own needs (e.g., dominance and submission). Listed under each category are common expectations held by premarital (and married) couples. This focus on common expectations communicates the orientation that expectations, like problems, come from many sources, including stages of the family life cycle. Each partner considers the list and indicates which of the three types of expectations each statement represents for himself/herself. Each person also writes his/her feelings about the expectations that are most personally meaningful. Thus, the list of common expectations provided by the MEW (e.g., how many children to have, whose career is more important) stimulates the partners' in-depth exploration of their specific expectations.

The MEW is used as a stimulus to discuss the expectations each individual has for himself/herself, the partner, and the relationship. Consultants have couples discuss their hopes and expectations for their marriages. The discussion proceeds to many different areas, depending on the couple (e.g., defining the "rules" for their relationship). Consultants are sensitive to areas of potential conflict, and they do not encourage discussion of issues that couples do not want to discuss at this time. In other words, the goal is to provide an

orientation and opportunity for couples to discuss and ponder their expectations, not to force couples to confront difficult issues. Couples are told that
the exercise may increase awareness of contradictory expectations in one's own
mind, as well as of divergent expectations between couple members (e.g.,
wanting to be independent of one's partner while also desiring his/her approval). To prevent distress, at this point we tell couples that "contradictions
are usual for most people and most couples" (Sager, 1976). The consultants
are trained to fit the exercise to each couple's current level of awareness concerning the areas of expectations tapped by the exercise.

To illustrate this process, we describe how one couple recently used the
exercise to talk about their expectations of the involvement of in-laws in their
relationship.

Susan felt that Harvey's mother frequently overstepped her bounds by giving Susan
advice in the form of commands. Interestingly, Susan had the expectation that she
would not succumb to her mother-in-law's intrusiveness and that Harvey should help
her out, being her ally in the matter. Susan was reluctant to voice this unstated expectation but was pleasantly surprised that when she did, her partner supported her
100%, and that he, too, expected that he would ally with her against his mother's intrusiveness. Thus, a potentially dangerous "hidden agenda" was diffused in a highly reinforcing manner.

Our evaluations of this component indicate that couples find the MEW
exercise to be one of the most rewarding and interesting aspects of the program. We have not had any couple discover or share expectations that resulted in far-reaching negative effects. To the contrary, couples increase
awareness about themselves and their relationships, and find their discoveries
insightful, useful, and at times fascinating. These discussions also provide
for consolidation of the skills that each couple has learned earlier.

The homework for this session is to continue discussions stimulated by
the MEW and to do something different together that will be fun.

*Session 5—Making a Good Thing Better (Relationship Enhancement)
and the Prevention of Sexual Problems*

RELATIONSHIP ENHANCEMENT

The last session is devoted to the final two components of the program: relationship enhancement and the prevention of sexual problems.

The first part of the enhancement section is devoted to linking the use
of skills to enhancing and improving relationships. The couples are taught
how to use the "fun deck" (Gottman *et al.*, 1976), an ever-expanding list of
fun things that couples have told us that they do together. Concepts are presented regarding experimentation with new ideas, being spontaneous, building in positive reinforcers, and how to avoid ruts. Most importantly, we

communicate the idea that people and interests change. Each individual is inoculated against the tendency to assume (mind read) that the partner's attitudes and interests are constant, rather than ever-changing. Thus, we provide the set that partners need to build in time to "touch base" and stay on top of each other's worlds. The intent here is to help couples recognize the early signs of diminishing mutual reinforcement in their relationships. They can then actively respond to the need to construct new activities and/or to resurrect previously enjoyable activities in which they no longer engage.

Jacobson (1981) believes that a diminishing of "positives" (e.g., love, romance) in relationships is the major dimension that needs to be inoculated against in prevention programs with couples. The strategies described above have been designed to accomplish, at least in part, this goal. Some components of the program are based on skills and strategies to maintain fun and intimacy, culled from interviews with happily married couples who have maintained satisfying and close relationships. We hypothesize that using the communication skills and strategies learned in the program will help each couple continue to "make deposits to their relationship bank account" and counteract both the "inflationary pressures" (e.g., attributional tendencies) to devalue positive events and the negative events (e.g., situational stress from transition periods) that inevitably occur.

We end this section by telling the parable of Herman and Lisa, which highlights how boredom develops in a relationship:

After a fun-filled premarital period, Herman and Lisa settled into a very structured daily, weekly, and monthly routine. They played bridge with the Hoyles every Saturday night, watched *Nightline* every night before bed, ate at the same Chinese restaurant (with the exquisite lemon chicken and really hot, spicy soup) once a month, and spent their summer vacations in Milwaukee and their winter vacations in Buffalo. After several years of relative marital bliss, they found themselves bored and thinking (in very behavioral terms, of course) that the reinforcing value of their partner was just "not the same," and that "perhaps they were not right for each other."

These global, negative internal attributions eventually grew to be a stable part of their "theory about their relationship." However, there was an alternative attribution for their increased boredom, which was just as (if not more) logical. This alternative attribution was that "the situations (settings) that we have been in are boring or have lost their reinforcing value." Such external attributions lead to quite specific suggestions for change: change the situations! For example, Herman and Lisa could go to Chinese dinner with the Hoyles, read a story out loud to each other at bedtime, and so on. The moral of the parable is: "If the diamond doesn't look right in the ring, change the setting and keep the diamond."

PREVENTION OF SEXUAL PROBLEMS (SENSUAL/SEXUAL
ENHANCEMENT)

During this final stage of the program, we provide couples with information about human sensual/sexual functioning and dysfunctioning. In addition, we teach the couples several simple techniques that can be used to help prevent sensual/sexual problems from developing and to intervene early if problems do develop. We use the term "sensual/sexual" for two reasons: First, approximately 20% of our couples are not sexually active, and second, it conveys the notion that sensuality is an important component of sexuality. When developing this component, we asked ourselves: "Given all the information covered in human sexuality courses and what is known about treating sexual problems (e.g., Heiman, LoPiccolo, & LoPiccolo, 1976; Kaplan, 1974, 1979; Masters & Johnson, 1970) and enhancing sexual functioning (LoPiccolo & Miller, 1975), what can we teach our couples that will help them in their sexual/sensual relationships now and in the future?"

We start this section by linking communication and sexual functioning (Masters & Johnson, 1970), noting the "chicken–egg" puzzle of which problem comes first. We provide the cognitive set that good communication may be the best strategy for preventing sexual problems. However, we also acknowledge that communicating openly about sexual issues is generally hard even if communication is very good in other areas.

Next, we use LoPiccolo and Miller's (1975) verbal disinhibition game and slides to help desensitize couples to discussing sexual material. Then we present information on the following topics, using a film, slides, and diagrams to assist the presentation:

1. Sex education and miseducation
2. Anatomy and physiology
3. Conception
4. Contraception
5. Human sexual response
6. Norms of sexual behavior
7. Sexual dysfunction

The film *The Sexually Mature Adult* (available from Planned Parenthood) does an excellent job of describing the sexual response cycle and people's feelings about their own sexuality. Couples are told in advance that the film has a few explicit scenes and are given the opportunity not to view the film or these scenes (no couple has chosen this option). After showing the film, we teach the couples about the cause, treatment, and prevention of the major male and female sexual dysfunctions: premature ejaculation, erectile dysfunction (impotency), and orgasmic dysfunction. In particular, we present the techniques of sensate focus, stop–start, squeeze technique, masturbation therapy (Heiman *et al.*, 1976; LoPiccolo & Lobitz, 1972), and the Kegel (1952) technique for strengthening the woman's pubococcygeal muscle. Interwoven with the slides, film, and didactic material, we present and discuss the following points about sexual enhancement:

1. Communicate.
2. Communication and sensuality are related.
3. Sex is more than intercourse; it involves being sensual.
4. Sensuality involves touching/massaging (pleasuring).
5. Pleasuring is important because touching tends to diminish over time.
6. It's not how much, how often, where, when, or what positions; it's what is mutual and enjoyable that counts.
7. Ask each other what feels good.
8. Learn to receive with no demand for reciprocity or orgasm.
9. Actively deal with performance anxiety.
10. Recognize that all couples have sexual problems to a certain degree.
11. Do not create problems by overreacting or causing self-fulfilling prophecy.
12. If you do not respond sexually, engage in pleasuring.

After all questions have been addressed, the couples are taught a sensate focus exercise involving giving and receiving feedback about light touching on the arm or hand. The goal here is to provide a nonthreatening example of how to talk about sensual/sexual interactions. Finally, each couple is left alone and asked to write down and then discuss with each other ways to improve their sensual/sexual relationship (*not* to solve problems).

Evaluation of PREP

To adequately evaluate any premarital prevention program, longitudinal studies comparing randomly assigned intervention with appropriate control groups are necessary. The long-term goals of prevention programs (e.g., preventing dissolution, promoting satisfaction) require that longitudinal studies be conducted. As noted elsewhere (Markman, Floyd, & Dickson-Markman, 1982), the vast majority of studies evaluating premarital interventions have used either single-group designs (e.g., Meadows & Taplin, 1970) or nonrandom assignment to experimental and comparison groups (e.g., Druckman, Fournier, Robinson, & Olson, 1980) both of which are inadequate to evaluate even the short-term (pre–post) effects of premarital intervention. No published study to date has conducted a follow-up longer than 1 year, therefore precluding a test of the long-term preventive effects of the programs. Finally, most studies rely on self-report data, and only a few studies use behavioral observation strategies. Self-report data are subject to numerous biases, while behavioral observation techniques are needed to adequately evaluate changes in communication skills or patterns. We have attempted to respond to some of these problems in our research program on the evaluation of PREP.

Thus far, studies have indicated that, as compared to control couples, PREP couples show higher levels of communication skills (Markman, Jamieson, & Floyd, 1983) and that PREP couples are more satisfied with their relationships 1 year later (Markman, Floyd, Stanley, & Stephen, 1983). Further, Blew and Trapold (1982), in a different laboratory, have replicated and extended these findings. The pattern of the results suggests that the positive effects of the intervention program are due to the prevention of worsening in couples' relationships. A more detailed discussion of the short- and long-term effects of PREP is presented in Markman, Jamieson, and Floyd (1983). Comprehensive evaluations of the effects of the specific components of the program have yet to be completed. One small step toward this important goal was taken at the conference that stimulated the present book.

Issues in Program Development:
Results of Conference Survey

During the conference, a survey was conducted of the participants' opinions of "the importance of skills and/or components included in current premarital prevention programs." In addition to rating a list of skills, participants were asked to add skills that had not been included. The participants were all behaviorally oriented and had serious interest in research and therapy with couples. Twelve participants, nine males and three females, responded to the survey. Eleven were clinical psychologists or trainees in clinical psychology, and one was a psychiatrist. The participants were from four countries (United States, Germany, Holland, and England) and had been in their respective fields for an average of 8.8 years (range: 5–23). The results of the survey are presented in Table 22.2.

Table 22.2 provides the means and ranges of the ratings (made on a 7 = point Likert scale) of the importance of each component (1 = not important at all; 7 = very important). The results indicate that "examining expectations about marriage" and "information about human sexuality" were the two highest-rated components, just edging out "training in communication skills" and "training in problem-solving skills." These results are somewhat surprising, since these behavioral marital therapists rated cognitive factors as being more important than the *sine qua non* of traditional BMT, communication and problem-solving training. This may reflect the increasing importance of cognitive factors in BMT (as reflected by other chapters in this volume), and if a similar survey about BMT were to be conducted, it might reveal the same pattern of findings. Alternatively, the results suggest that par-

TABLE 22.2. Results of Survey on the Importance of Components of Premarital Prevention
Programs

Rank	Component	Rating[a] Mean	Rating[a] Range
1	Examining expectations about marriage	6.7	4–7
2	Information about human sexuality	6.5	4–7
3[b]	Communication skills training	6.1	3–7
3[b]	Problem-solving training	6.1	2–7
5	Information about common problem areas that premarital couples are experiencing	5.8	4–7
6	Increased awareness of partner	5.6	2–7
7	Increased personal awareness	5.3	2–7
8[c]	Videotape feedback on level of skills	4.6	2–7
8[c]	Information about marital relationships (e.g., research results)	4.6	1–7
8[c]	Increased awareness of the role of the family of origin in one's relationships	4.6	1–7
11	Information about the cognitive-behavioral model of marriage	4.4	1–6
12	Using "family meetings" at home to discuss problems	3.7	1–7

[a]1 = not important; 7 = very important.
[b]Items tied for third place.
[c]Items tied for eighth place.

ticipants felt that expectations and sexuality are more important for "healthy"
premarital couples than distressed marital couples, because these factors may
be more causally involved in development of marital distress than social skill
deficits. For example, one prominent BMT researcher and therapist wrote,
"I'm not convinced about training skills for these couples. I am totally convinced about couples discussing issues that they may face which need not necessarily demand skills to negotiate." Also noteworthy about the results is the
importance placed on traditionally nonbehavioral goals such as increasing
awareness of partner and self. Finally, the results indicate that, in general,
all components were considered reasonably important and that all components
received at least some strong support from at least one person.

Taken together, these findings suggest that the conference experts felt
that the components in current premarital prevention programs are generally appropriate. These experts also suggested other potentially important components not included in the survey. These components include: how to cope

with individual problems, anger management, stress control, goal attainment skills, value clarification, skills in home economics, examining religious and philosophical differences, child-rearing skills, how to foster individual growth in the context of an intimate relationship, skills in dealing with jealousy, increasing tenderness and how to ask for it, accepting and coping with life crises that generally occur, recognizing that "alone time" is important, talking about previous meaningful relationships, discussing boundary issues in forming a couple identity, discussing perceptions of their own sexuality, discussing career plans and expectations, and providing information about mate selection. These additional components seem to fall into three general categories: (1) those related to skill training that fosters individual growth in areas that indirectly affect couple functioning (e.g., anger management), (2) those related to thinking about future transition periods (e.g., having children), and (3) those related to increasing the couples' understanding of how they function in relationships (e.g., value clarification). Underlying these three areas is the belief by some that "individual psychological health is a precursor to dyadic happiness." While it is not possible to include all of these components in a premarital prevention program, when it is possible to fit programs to couples' needs, these components can serve as valuable adjuncts to other aspects of the program. As noted by Qualls (1978), the decision as to what to include in prevention programs should be based on what the developers think are causal factors of the negative end state to be prevented.

Finally, comments indicated that such programs either are not available (e.g., Holland) or might not be considered acceptable (e.g., England) outside of the United States. This raises the very interesting issue of differences in societal support for the delivery of prevention services to couples and families.

Clinical Issues in Delivering Prevention Programs to Couples

We conclude this chapter by addressing five issues that seem to be unique to the development and delivery of prevention (as opposed to treatment) programs to couples and families.

Motivation

The objectives of premarital intervention are to enhance relationships so as to better prepare couples to cope with the complexities of family development and to prevent marital and family distress. The rationale underlying these objectives is that couples are inadequately prepared because of deficient communication skills, lack of information, or idealistic expectations for marriage. Premarital studies indicate that couples planning marriage are satisfied with their relationship, idealistic, and high in perceived similarity of needs, values, personality, and expectations. Unfortunately, these characteristics are not predictive of later satisfaction (see Markman, 1979, 1981, and Chapter 14, this volume). Further, these characteristics are not going to provide the motivation needed to come to an intervention program. Thus, the motivation for participation in prevention/enhancement programs is significantly less than for treatment.

One of the major dilemmas facing the field, and encountered by us in our research, is how to motivate couples planning marriage to take advantage of the intervention program. The question for investigators is how to communicate to "targets" the potential benefits of participation in a way that increases motivation. Rather than maintaining a passive stance and winding up with a very highly select group of targets, researchers can educate potential consumers and community resources concerning the potential benefits of prevention. Unfortunately, we do not possess adequate empirical justification, in terms of well-evaluated successful programs, to "sell" prevention programs on such merits. Targeting interventions at transition periods, such as the transition to marriage and parenthood stages, should help in reaching couples who are in the midst of coping with current changes in their relationship.

We are currently recruiting couples to participate in a longitudinal study of the development of healthy premarital relationships, rather than to participate in a premarital intervention program. We then randomly assign matched pairs of couples to PREP or control conditions. We have found that over 85% of the couples to whom we offer our program express interest in participating. However, when it comes down to actually attending our sessions, approximately 50% of these couples eventually complete the program. The usual reason given is "We are too busy." This reflects the fact that our program is not the highest priority in their busy lives. On the other hand, once a couple starts the program, over 90% complete the five sessions. It would be interesting to compare these dropout rates to those from marital and family therapy programs. Unfortunately, these rates do not seem to be available.

To enhance initial participation, we have found it useful to describe our program and the rationale in detail, emphasizing the importance of learning skills that may be useful in the future. The conference survey also addressed the issue of motivating couples, and the participants generated some interesting suggestions:

1. "Sell" the program as an opportunity to increase understanding of each other and to increase awareness of the "real possibilities of relationships."
2. Announce the program as oriented toward "enrichment" rather than "prevention."
3. Offer chances to discuss anxiety about marriage in general and permanence in marriage in particular.

4. Focus on special groups that may be at risk or have "anticipatory fears" concerning marital problems, including people with divorced parents, from distressed families, or with a single parent.

5. Provide services to individuals (not couples) who would like to marry sometime in the future.

As our work progresses, we will continue to modify the components of PREP to increase their intrinsic reward power. A good example of this was our decision to use Blechman and Rabin's (1981) Marriage Contract Game with our couples to achieve the goals of contracting. Nevertheless, we still struggle with the crucial issue of motivation. Research specifically addressed to the question of enhancing motivation for prevention programs is sorely needed.

In view of our problems with the high decline rate, we have recently expanded our research to couples planning to *remarry*. The rationale was that remarital couples might be more motivated to participate in a premarital intervention program given their experience with marital distress. Gurman (1980) also suggests that remarital couples would be an ideal population for premarital intervention. Remarital couples are an interesting group, since there is evidence that there is a lack of societal supports (e.g., language systems) for these "blended" couples and families (Farrell & Markman, in press). Consistent with this formulation, the divorce rates for remarital couples are higher than those for first-time couples (44% vs. 38%) (Glick & Norton, 1977). Thus, remarital couples may be more at risk for future marital distress. We have recently completed a study comparing premarital with remarital couples, designed to address two questions: First, are there differences in idealism between groups? And, second, Do remarital couples have lower decline rates and better outcome than first-timers? Preliminary results indicate that the groups are similar on these dimensions, but that remarital couples have higher levels of communication deficits.

Idealism

Couples planning marriage, especially "first-timers," are likely to be very idealistic and motivated to view their relationships through a "positivity screen" (Floyd & Markman, 1983). We use the term "positivity screen" (and its converse, "negativity screen") similarly to the way Weiss (1980; Chapter 13, this volume) uses the concepts of positive and negative "sentiment override." In more behavioral terms, these couples may not be "responsive" to each other's behaviors during interactions (i.e., positive behaviors being responded to positively), but may react in accordance with a positivity screen, regardless of the "objective value" of the partner's behavior. Idealism (positivity screens) may function to keep couples from focusing on their relationships and thereby may decrease motivation to participate in prevention programs.

Additionally, Gurman (1980) argues that idealism is a positive force in young relationships that should not be disturbed, since idealism "fuels the passion of courtship" (Gurman, 1980, p. 93). He argues that programs like PREP may have explicit or implicit deidealization effects that may hinder or attack the emotional bonding. Suggesting that such bonding may be very important in the early stage of the marital relationship, Gurman argues that PREP and other similar programs may be dangerous to young premarital couples to the extent that idealization is "attacked" in the intervention. While we obviously disagree with Gurman's position on conceptual grounds (see Markman, Jamieson, & Floyd, 1983, for full discussion of this issue), the issue of the impact of idealization on relationship development is an important empirical question that needs evaluation. Thus far, our results indicate that although participation in PREP may result in a decrease in idealism, this decrease does not seem to have a negative influence on couples' relationships. In fact, the decrease may be an important component of the positive effects of the program (Markman, Jamieson, & Floyd, 1983).

Should We Change Sex Roles?

Sociologists (e.g., Waller & Hill, 1951) have defined two types of roles in a relationship: expressive (e.g., relationship maintenance functions, emotional expression, sensitivity) and instrumental (e.g., task orientation). Many researchers have defined traditional relationships as those in which husbands assume the instrumental role, and wives assume the expressive role. Egalitarian or companionate relationships, on the other hand, are those in which husbands and wives share these roles. Classic sociological studies have indicated that traditional relationships are happier and more stable (e.g., Burgess & Wallin, 1953). However, in sharp contrast, recent social psychology research has indicated that when both partners have traditionally masculine (e.g., instrumental) as well as traditionally feminine (e.g., expressive) characteristics, the individuals involved score higher on physical and mental health adjustment measures (e.g., Wheeler, Reis, & Nezlek, 1983). There is also evidence that traditional females are at risk for numerous physical and mental health problems (Olds & Shaver, 1980) and that women meet the needs of their partners more than vice versa (Wheeler *et al.*, 1983).

Despite the fact that the research reviewed above has a number of problems, we must consider the possibility that many traditional relationships best serve the needs of men and may be harmful to women. Thus, as noted by Jacobson (1981), perhaps prevention programs like PREP should facilitate couples' sharing expressive and instrumental roles (see the later section on ethics for a discussion of the ethical questions raised by the sex role issue).

To complicate matters, as noted by Jacobson, when considering sex roles we are operating in a political as well as a psychosocial arena.

Currently in PREP, while we do not directly teach couples how to share sex roles, the skills taught set the stage for sharing expressive and instrumental functions. Communication skills, such as expressing feelings and sensitivity to relationship issues, reflect traditional feminine traits, while problem-solving skills emphasize traditional masculine traits. In PREP we emphasize that both partners should use both types of skills. Further, our emphasis on perceptual and behavioral degrees of freedom is consistent with the notion of flexibility, which is a major component of current conceptions of sharing masculine and feminine roles (e.g., Olds & Shaver, 1980).

Unfortunately, space limitations prohibit a full discussion of the issues raised by considering changing sex roles in intervention programs. Additionally, basic research on the influence of sex roles in relationships would clearly be useful in helping program developers make decisions regarding this important issue.

Retention and Overload Problems

In any skill-training program such as ours, the retention of information is an important issue. Unfortunately, there are few discussions of the related issues of information overload and retention of information. In this section we briefly address this potential problem.

While teaching skills to couples involves providing information, we have not found that couples suffer from information overload. This may be due to the multiple methods used to present information and the ample opportunities (during the sessions and at home) to assimilate and practice the new skills. Nevertheless, the question of how couples best learn and then make use of the information we provide must be addressed. We consider the learning of skills and retention of information to be two of the immediate goals of the intervention program. The more long-term goals are to enhance current and future relationship functioning.

For example, consider the sexual enrichment session, which is loaded with information content. The specific, immediate goals of the sessions are threefold: (1) to enhance positivity of attitudes toward sex, (2) to provide information and dispel myths, and (3) to improve sexual communication. Preliminary evaluations of Goals 1 and 2 suggest that PREP couples are learning the information provided in the sessions (Markman, Jamieson, & Floyd, 1983). In addition to learning a set of principles about human sexuality and sensual/sexual communication, couples (we hope) acquire a cognitive set that asking questions and getting information about human sexuality is important and that they can do this together. Developing this cognitive set may be more important to future relationship satisfaction than the specific principles, which may be forgotten over time. Thus, we may be teaching couples to "learn how to learn" about human sexuality. These are empirical questions that we hope will be answered as we progress with our research.

To summarize, the issues of information overload and retention directly relate to the need to identify the effective ingredients of PREP. The basic question here is how the immediate and longer-term goals are related. Although this question should be addressed by all intervention programs, most remain silent on the issue. We hope that this situation will improve as we conduct long-term evalutions of our programs.

Ethical Issues

One of the most important ethical issues that needs consideration involves the imposition onto couples of our values (and perhaps evidence) concerning what makes a good relationship. There is clearly a value structure inherent in our thinking about the program. Our major values include: communication is good; both people need to share in the communication process; and behavioral and perceptual flexibility are good. These values have clearly guided the selection and presentation of program components.

In general, we strive to make our values (and data base) as clear as possible to couples and to respect couples' values. However, there are times when we may want to alter a couple's attitudes and/or values as part of the objectives of the intervention. For example, earlier we discussed the issue of how traditional sex roles might be related to future unhappiness, particularly for women. When we work with couples who enter our program with rigid gender roles already established, we may want to help the couple assess the functional value of these roles. We recognize that the program will implicitly challenge some of the assumptions underlying such a couple's patterns (e.g., men should not need to express their feelings). A basic issue, of course, is how satisfied the couple is with their choice of roles, or for that matter, any aspect of their relationship. Some couples with whom we have worked have had very traditional sex roles and have been very satisfied with them. For example, several Mormon couples clearly had adopted a church norm that men make the final decisions in the family. Thus, our basic values – (1) use research findings as a basis for our program and (2) respect couples' values – are sometimes put in conflict. In some instances, the couples' values are in transition and we can help them "refreeze" at a different level. In general, we emphasize that a couple can consider what we have to offer and can select aspects to integrate into their relationship.

Our prevention situation is different from a treatment situation. When the couple is seeking out a therapist, the therapist would be remiss if he/she did not attempt to alter inappropriate cognitions and values. However, the situation is not as clear in a prevention situation, where we are seeking out couples who are satisfied with their relationship. Unfortunately, space limitations preclude a more detailed discussion of these and other issues.

Future Directions

Before considering what the future holds, let us briefly review what we are able to offer Harvey and Susan, our hypothetical couple planning marriage. The basic contribution of BMT to prevention is a set of techniques and assessment and evaluation methods, grounded in a conceptual model of marriage and based on some empirical findings. However, the lack of research on both the short- and long-term effects of premarital intervention does not allow us to make more than very preliminary statements about the possibilities of preventing marital distress. Further, there remains the difficult question of what we are trying to prevent (or enhance). Since how we define a problem determines how we attempt to prevent it from developing (Qualls, 1978), the question of how we define a dysfunctional (or functional) marriage is clearly very relevant. The PREP program has been influenced by a cognitive-behavioral perspective on the etiology and treatment of marital distress. Thus, our primary hypotheses are that good use of communication skills and the ability to develop and maintain positive interactions are related to the maintenance of happy relationships and have a preventive effect on the development of both marital and family distress.

Future progress will rest on increased knowledge of the determinants of marital and family distress. Further, we need to evaluate whether intervention strategies that modify interaction and relationship components are linked to future outcomes. Perhaps most important is the need for feedback on our current preventative efforts, so that we can modify our approaches to better achieve the goals of primary prevention of marital and family distress.

Finally, there remain numerous unsolved conceptual, methodological, and ethical issues concerning the enterprise of primary prevention with couples. Some of these have been discussed earlier, but raising the issues does not mean that they are solved.

There is clearly a lot of work to be done.

ACKNOWLEDGMENTS

This research was partially supported by National Institute of Mental Health Grant No. MH35525-01 and by a Faculty Research Grant from Bowling Green State University.

REFERENCES

Bandura, A. Self-efficacy: Toward a unifying theory of behavioral change. *Psychological Review,* 1977, *84,* 191–215.

Baucom, D. *Cognitive-behavioral strategies in the treatment of marital discord.* Paper presented at the meeting of the Association for Advancement of Behavior Therapy, Toronto, 1981.

Birchler, G. R., Weiss, R. L., & Vincent, J. P. Multimethod analysis of social reinforcement exchange between maritally distressed and nondistressed spouse and stranger dyads. *Journal of Personality and Social Psychology*, 1975, *31*, 349-360.

Blanck, G., & Blanck, R. *Marriage and personal development*. New York: Columbia University Press, 1968.

Blechman, E., & Rabin, C. *Concepts and methods of explicit marital negotiation training with the Marriage Contract Game*. Unpublished manuscript, Wesleyan University, 1981.

Blew, A., & Trapold, M. *Fixing what isn't broken: Methodological and ethical considerations in premarital interventions*. Paper presented at the meeting of the Association for Advancement of Behavior Therapy, Los Angeles, 1982.

Braiker, H. B., & Kelley, H. H. Conflict in the development of close relationships. In R. L. Burgess & T. L. Huston (Eds.), *Social exchange in developing relationships*. New York: Academic Press, 1979.

Bruner, J. On perceptual readiness. *Psychological Review*, 1957, *64*, 123-152.

Burgess, R., & Huston, T. *Social exchange in developing relationships*. New York: Academic Press, 1979.

Burgess, E., & Wallin, P. *Engagement and marriage*. Philadelphia: J. B. Lippincott, 1953.

Christensen, A. *Perceptual biases in couples' reports of their own interaction*. Paper presented at the annual meeting of the Association for Advancement of Behavior Therapy, Toronto, 1981.

Cohen, R., & Christensen, A. Further examination of demand characteristics in marital interaction. *Journal of Consulting and Clinical Psychology*, 1980, *48*, 121-123.

Curran, J. Social skills: Methodological issues and future directions. In A. Bellack & M. Hersen (Eds.), *Research and practices in social skill training*. New York: Plenum Press, 1979.

Druckman, J. M., Fournier, D. M., Robinson, B., & Olson, D. H. *Effectiveness of five types of premarital preparation programs*. Final Report. Grand Rapids, MI: Education for Marriage, 1980.

Edelson, R., & Epstein, N. *Cognition and marital maladjustment: Development of a measure of unrealistic relationship beliefs*. Paper presented at the meeting of the Association for Advancement of Behavior Therapy, Toronto, 1981.

Evans, R., Henderson, A., Hill, P., & Raines, B. Current psychological, social and educational programs in the control and prevention of smoking: A critical methodological review. In A. Gotto & R. Paolelli (Eds.), *Atherosclerosis review* (Vol. 6). New York: Raven Press, 1979.

Farrell, J., & Markman, H. Individual and interpersonal factors in the etiology of marital distress: The example of remarital couples. In B. Gilmour & S. Duck (Eds.), *Personal relationships*. Hillsdale, NJ: Erlbaum, in press.

Floyd, F., & Markman, H. Observational biases in spouse interaction: Toward a cognitive/behavioral model of marriage. *Journal of Consulting and Clinical Psychology*, 1983, *51*, 450-457.

Glick, P., & Norton, G. Marrying, divorcing and living together in the U.S. today. *Population Bulletin*, 1977, *32*, 5.

Gottman, J. M. *Marital interaction: Empirical investigations*. New York: Academic Press, 1979.

Gottman, J. M., Markman, H. J., & Notarius, C. I. The topography of marital conflict: A sequential analysis of verbal and nonverbal behavior. *Journal of Marriage and the Family*, 1977, *39*, 461-478.

Gottman, J. M., Notarius, C., Gonso, J., & Markman, H. J. *A couple's guide to communication*. Champaign, IL: Research Press, 1976.

Gurman, A. Behavioral marriage therapy in the 1980's: The challenge of integration. *American Journal of Family Therapy*, 1980, *89*, 86-96.

Heiman, J., LoPiccolo, L. T., LoPiccolo, J. *Becoming orgasmic: A sexual growth program for women*. Englewood Cliffs, NJ: Prentice-Hall, 1976.

Jacobson, N. S. Problem-solving and contingency contracting in the treatment of marital discord. *Journal of Consulting and Clinical Psychology*, 1977, *45*, 52–60.

Jacobson, N. S. Personal communication, July 1981.

Jacobson, N. S., Elwood, R. W., & Dallas, M. Assessment of marital dysfunction. In D. H. Barlow (Ed.), *Behavioral assessment of adult disorders*. New York: Guilford Press, 1981.

Jacobson, N. S., McDonald, D., & Follette, W. *Attributional differences between distressed and nondistressed married couples.* Paper presented to annual meeting of the Association for Advancement of Behavior Therapy, Toronto, 1981.

Jacobson, N. S., & Margolin, G. *Marital therapy: Strategies based on social learning and behavior exchange principles.* New York: Brunner/Mazel, 1979.

Jamieson, K. *A competency-based communication model for predicting the relationship satisfaction of couples planning marriage.* Unpublished manuscript, University of Denver, 1981.

Kaplan, H. S. *The new sex therapy.* New York: Brunner/Mazel, 1974.

Kaplan, H. S. *Disorders of sexual desire.* New York: Brunner/Mazel, 1979.

Kegel, A. Sexual functioning of the pubococcygeus muscle. *Western Journal of Surgery*, 1952, *60*, 521–524.

Kelley, H., & Thibaut, J. *Interpersonal relations: A theory of interdependence.* New York: Wiley, 1978.

Kelly, G. *The psychology of personal constructs* (Vol. 1). New York: Norton, 1955.

LoPiccolo, J., & Lobitz, C. The role of masturbation in the treatment of sexual dysfunction. *Archives of Sexual Behavior*, 1972, *2*, 163–171.

LoPiccolo, J., & Miller, V. A program for enhancing the sexual relationship of normal couples. *Counseling Psychologist*, 1975, *5*, 41–45.

Markman, H. J. The application of a behavioral model of marriage in predicting relationship satisfaction of couples planning marriage. *Journal of Consulting and Clinical Psychology*, 1979, *4*, 743–749.

Markman, H. The prediction of marital distress: A five year follow-up. *Journal of Consulting and Clinical Psychology*, 1981, *49*, 760–762.

Markman, H. J., & Floyd, F. Possibilities for the prevention of marital discord: A behavioral perspective. *American Journal of Family Therapy*, 1980, *8*, 29–48.

Markman, H. J., Floyd, F., & Dickson-Markman, F. Toward a model for the prediction and prevention of marital and family distress and dissolution. In S. Duck (Ed.), *Personal relationships 4: Dissolving personal relationships.* London: Academic Press, 1982.

Markman, H., Floyd, F., Stanley, S., & Stephen, T. *Baby steps toward the primary prevention of marital distress.* Unpublished manuscript, 1983.

Markman, H. J., Jamieson, K., & Floyd, F. The assessment and modification of premarital relationships: Preliminary findings on the etiology and prevention of marital and family distress. In J. Vincent (Ed.), *Advances in family interventions, assessment and theory* (Vol. 3). Greenwich, CT: JAI Press, 1983.

Markman, H. J., Notarius, C., Stephen, T., & Smith, R. Behavioral observation systems for couples: The current status. In E. Filsinger & R. Lewis (Eds.), *Observing marriage: New behavioral approaches.* Beverly Hills, CA: Sage, 1981.

Masters, W., & Johnson, V. *Human sexual inadequacy.* Boston: Little, Brown, 1970.

Meadows, M. E., & Taplin, J. F. Premarital counseling with college students: A promising triad. *Journal of Counseling Psychology*, 1970, *17*, 516–518.

Olds, D., & Shaver, P. Masculinity, femininity, academic performance and health: Further evidence concerning the androgen controversy. *Journal of Personality*, 1980, *48*, 323–341.

Qualls, C. The prevention of sexual disorders: An overview. In C. Qualls, J. Wincze, & D. Barlow, (Eds.), *The prevention of sexual disorders: Issues and approaches.* New York: Plenum Press, 1978.

Rabin, C., Blechman, E. A., & Milton, M. C. *A multiple-baseline study of the Marriage Con-

tract Game's effects on problem-solving and affective behavior. Unpublished manuscript, Wesleyan University, 1981.

Sager, C. *Marriage contracts and couples therapy.* New York: Brunner/Mazel, 1976.

Satir, V. *Conjoint family therapy.* Palo Alto, CA: Science and Behavior Books, 1967.

Sullivan, M., & Markman, H. *Coercive interaction in distressed and nondistressed marriages.* Paper presented at the meetings of the Midwestern Psychological Association, Minneapolis, May 1982.

Trower, P. Fundamentals of interpersonal behavior: A social-psychological perspective. In A. Bellack & M. Hersen (Eds.), *Research and practices in social skills training.* New York: Plenum Press, 1979.

Vincent, J. P., Friedman, L., Nugent, J., & Messerly, L. Demand characteristics in observations of marital interaction. *Journal of Consulting and Clinical Psychology,* 1979, *47,* 557-566.

Waller, W., & Hill, R. *The family.* New York: Dryden Press, 1951.

Weiss, R. Strategic behavioral marital therapy: Toward a model for assessment and intervention. In J. Vincent (Ed.), *Advances in family intervention, assessment and theory* (Vol. 1). Greenwich, CT: JAI Press, 1980.

Weiss, R. Personal communication, July 1981.

Wheeler, L., Reis, H., & Nezlek, J. Loneliness, sex roles, and social interaction. *Journal of Social and Personality Psychology,* 1983, *45,* 943-953.

Author Index

Subject Index

Ability versus performance, 398
Acceptance, 8, 134, 135, 167, 168, 174, 175, 186, 192, 194, 196, 329
  feeling accepted, 201, 217, 219
  of imperfection, 124
Accommodation, 46–48, 408
Accuracy, 256, 257, 262, 265
Advice in therapy, 56
Affect, 134–137, 148, 152–153, 334
  simultaneity of, 150
Affection, 17–18, 41, 42
Affective-emotional relationship quality, 21
Affective role areas, 383
Affiliation, 358, 363
Age effect in treatment effectiveness, 21, 74, 81–82, 85–86
Aggression, 327, 358
Agreement, 76, 94, 110, 123, 134, 141, 148, 187, 192, 194, 196, 237, 241
  agreement-disagreement ratios, 141–142
Alliance building, 402
Alternate life-styles. *See* "Natural groups"
Alternative frameworks, 296–297
Alternative treatment, behavioral marital therapy comparison with, 118–121
Ambiguity, 232
Ambivalence, 394
Analysis
  of interpersonal communication, 182–198
  of outcome data, 114
  statistical, of marital conflict, 159–181
  time series, of outcome, 199–231
Analysis of Relational Communication, 142
Analytic skills in therapy, 292
Anger, 303–304, 313, 328, 403, 405, 412
Antecedents, 315
  of attributions, 339, 344
  and consequences in interaction, 219, 224
  impact of, 169–170, 174
Anticipation, 404
Anxiety, 110, 293, 327, 393, 394, 416
Appeals, 136
Apprehension, 328
Approval, 76, 94, 134, 141, 148

Areas of Change Questionnaire, 76, 94, 100
Arousal, 333
Arrangement in sexual dysfunction, 394
Artifact model of sex differences in psychiatric illness, 375–376
Assent, 94, 134, 135, 141, 148, 165, 187
Assertiveness, 42, 135
  assertiveness training, 360
Assessment
  of clinically distressed couples, 37–38
  phase of therapy, 345–349
  strategies, 313–315
  of therapist intervention approaches, 61–71
Assessment Task, 141–142
Assortative mating, psychiatric symptoms and, 378–379
At-risk couples, 273–274, 421
Attacks. *See* Personal attacks
Attend, 183, 185
Attention, 94, 134, 141, 161–166
Attentiveness, 201, 224
Attitudes, 297–298, 314, 315, 320, 346, 401, 414, 424
  on sexual interaction, 387, 391
Attraction, 159, 174, 178, 326
Attribution, 288, 293, 296–297, 338–342, 408
  of distress in therapy, 325–336
  in perceptions of interaction, 270–271
  reattribution, 325–326
  in sexual dysfunction, 392–393
Authority, 56
Autocorrelation in time series analysis, 208, 222, 224, 226, 230
Automaticity, 312
  automatic transactions, 343
Autonomy, 27, 47
  see also Equality; Independence
Autoregression in time series analysis, 209–210
Aversion, 159, 170
  aversiveness-positiveness, 134
  aversive stimuli, 310–311
Avoidance, 56, 123
Awareness, 42, 412, 418

436